# The Language of EU and Polish Judges

STUDIES IN LANGUAGE, CULTURE AND SOCIETY

Edited by Łucja Biel, Andrzej Kątny and Piotr Ruszkiewicz

VOLUME 16

PETER LANG

Dariusz Koźbiał

# The Language of EU and Polish Judges

## Investigating Textual Fit Through Corpus Methods

PETER LANG

**Bibliographic Information published by the Deutsche Nationalbibliothek**
The Deutsche Nationalbibliothek lists this publication in the Deutsche Nationalbibliografie; detailed bibliographic data is available online at http://dnb.d-nb.de.

**Library of Congress Cataloging-in-Publication Data**
A CIP catalog record for this book has been applied for at the Library of Congress.

This publication was financially supported by the National Science Centre NCN (grant 2014/14/E/HS2/00782) and the Faculty of Applied Linguistics of the University of Warsaw

This work has been peer reviewed by: Stanisław Goźdź-Roszkowski (University of Łódź) and Łukasz Grabowski (University of Opole)

ISSN 2195-7479
ISBN 978-3-631-82226-5 (Print)
E-ISBN 978-3-631-83893-8 (E-Book)
E-ISBN 978-3-631-83894-5 (EPDF)
E-ISBN 978-3-631-83895-2 (MOBI)
DOI 10.3726/b17734



Peter Lang – Berlin · Bern · Bruxelles · New York · Oxford · Warszawa · Wien



www.peterlang.com

# Table of contents


**List of tables** ..... 13

**List of figures** ..... 19

**Abbreviations and acronyms** ..... 21

**Glossing abbreviations** ..... 21

**Acknowledgments** ..... 25

**Introduction** ..... 27

**Part I. Theoretical background**

**Chapter 1. Multilingualism and translation at the Court of Justice of the European Union** ..... 33

1.1 Context of production of CJEU judgments: policy of multilingualism ..... 33

1.2 The translation process ..... 37

1.3 The translator profile: lawyer-linguists ..... 41

**Chapter 2. Approach to genre analysis** ..... 47

2.1 Genre, register, style, discourse (community), legal language – setting the scene for the analysis of judgments ..... 47

2.2 A mixed genre-register approach to the linguistic profiling of judgments ..... 56

**Chapter 3. Corpus-linguistic methodology and the operationalization of textual fit** ..... 61
3.1 Corpus Linguistics as a methodology ..... 61
3.1.1 Corpus-based and corpus-driven approaches to the study of language ..... 62
3.1.2 Advantages and disadvantages of corpus methodology ..... 64
3.2 Multi-perspective framework for analysis of judicial language ..... 65
3.3 The relation of textual fit and its operationalization ..... 68

**Part II. Empirical study**

**Chapter 4. Design of the JURIDIC corpus** ..... 77
4.1 Corpus design ..... 77
4.2 Structure of the individual sub-corpora ..... 79
4.2.1 CJEU corpus ..... 79
4.2.2 SN corpus ..... 83
4.2.3 The National Corpus of Polish (NKJP) ..... 86
4.3 Representativeness, balance and comparability of the sub-corpora .. 86
4.4 Software ..... 89
4.5 Normalization of corpus data and statistical measures ..... 89

**Part II.A Macro level**

**Chapter 5. Contextual and macrostructural analysis of CJEU and SN judgments** ..... 93
5.1 Contextual analysis of CJEU and SN judgments ..... 93
5.1.1 Situational characteristics ..... 94
5.1.2 Discourse participants ..... 95
5.1.3 Communicative purposes ..... 96
5.1.4 Communicative conventions ..... 97

5.2 Macrostructural analysis of CJEU and SN judgments ... 99
5.2.1 Macro- and microstructure of CJEU judgments ... 106
5.2.2 Macro- and microstructure of SN judgments ... 127
5.3 Conclusions ... 134

**Part II.B. Micro level: Pillar I – Lexico-grammatical patterns**

**Chapter 6. Analysis of chosen lexico-grammatical patterns** ... 137
6.1 Global comparison of corpora ... 138
6.2 Analysis of keyword lists: identification of lexico-grammatical categories for further analysis ... 141
6.3 Phraseological framing with prepositions ... 149
6.3.1 Prepositions as a word class ... 150
6.3.2 Distribution of simple prepositions ... 150
6.3.3 Distribution of top 50 compound and secondary prepositions 154
6.3.4 Grammaticalized discourse functions of compound and secondary prepositions ... 165
6.3.4.1 Time ... 170
6.3.4.2 Cause-effect, result, contravention and condition ... 170
6.3.4.3 Reference ... 174
6.4.4.4 Intra- and inter-textual reference ... 180
6.3.4.5 Participation ... 180
6.3.4.6 Modality ... 180
6.3.4.7 Apposition ... 184
6.3.4.8 Manner and instrumental relations ... 184
6.3.4.9 Adversariality ... 187
6.3.4.10 Measure ... 187
6.3.4.11 Inclusivity/exclusivity ... 191
6.3.4.12 Commutative relations ... 191
6.3.4.13 Purpose ... 194
6.3.4.14 Distribution ... 194

6.3.4.15 Comparison ..... 194
6.3.4.16 Space relations ..... 198
6.3.4.17 Partitive relations ..... 198
6.3.4.18 Active relations ..... 198
6.3.5 Prepositions in judgments – summary ..... 202
6.4 Structurization of judicial arguments ..... 205
6.4.1 Parataxis ..... 205
6.4.2 Hypotaxis ..... 209
6.5 Deixis ..... 212
6.6 Depersonalization ..... 218
6.6.1 Auxiliary verbs ..... 219
6.6.2 Passive voice ..... 219
6.6.3 The *się* impersonal pattern ..... 224
6.6.4 The –*no/to* impersonal pattern ..... 226
6.7 Legal reasoning and argumentation ..... 229
6.7.1 Verdictive, exercitive (argumentative) and reporting verbs ..... 229
6.7.2 Causal patterns ..... 236
6.7.3 If-then conditionals and related patterns ..... 240
6.7.4 Patterns of purpose ..... 246
6.8 Framing with adverbials and participles ..... 249
6.8.1 Adverbials ..... 250
6.8.2 Participles ..... 260

**Part II.C. Micro level: Pillar II – Formulaicity**

**Chapter 7. Lexical bundles** ..... 273
7.1. Lexical bundles in the frequency-based (distributional) approach to phraseology ..... 274
7.2. Related studies and research questions ..... 277
7.3. Research material and methodology ..... 285

7.4. Overall distribution of 2–8-grams in judicial language .................... 287

7.5. Refinement of 3–4-grams .................... 295

7.5.1 Thematic classification into content and non-content bundles 296

7.5.2 Overlap of 3- and 4-grams in the translation and non-translation corpora .................... 300

7.6. Functional classification of lexical bundles .................... 310

7.6.1 Referential bundles .................... 316

7.6.1.1 Agents/institutions .................... 320

7.6.1.2 Bundles denoting abstract concepts .................... 322

7.6.1.3 Bundles denoting documents .................... 324

7.6.1.4 Legal procedure bundles .................... 326

7.6.1.5 Dates .................... 328

7.6.1.6 Places .................... 330

7.6.2 Discourse-organizing bundles .................... 330

7.6.2.1 Intra-/Intertextual bundles .................... 337

7.6.2.2 Causative-resultative and inferential bundles .................... 339

7.6.2.3 Focus bundles .................... 341

7.6.2.4 Framing bundles .................... 343

7.6.2.5 Topic elaboration/clarification bundles .................... 345

7.6.2.6 Transition bundles .................... 345

7.6.2.7 Purpose bundles .................... 348

7.6.2.8 Conditional bundles .................... 350

7.6.3 Stance bundles .................... 352

7.6.3.1 Evaluative bundles .................... 355

7.6.3.2 Epistemic stance bundles .................... 357

7.7 Conclusions and implications for the future .................... 357

**Chapter 8. Binomials** .................... 363

8.1 Research material and methodology .................... 368

8.2 Binomials and multinomials .................... 372

8.2.1 Distribution of non-extended binomials .................... 374

8.2.2 Structural and semantic qualities of non-extended binomials . 375
8.2.3 Distribution of extended binomials ............ 389
8.2.4 Structural and semantic qualities of extended binomials ......... 390
8.2.5 Distribution and structural qualities of multinomials ............... 408
8.2.6 Functional typology of binomials ............ 411
8.3 Conclusions ............ 417

**Part II.D. Micro level: Pillar III –Terminology**

**Chapter 9. Terms in the common conceptual base of EU and national judgments** ............ 421
9.1 Key (EU and national) terminology-related terms ............ 421
9.2 Methodological approach and research material ............ 430
9.3 Global distribution and overlap of simple terms and complex terms ............ 435
9.4 Top 30 simple terms and top 15 complex terms ............ 441
9.5 Conceptual classification of node terms ............ 445
9.5.1 Agentive and institutional node terms and their environment ............ 451
9.5.2 Node terms related to substantive law and case-law and their environment ............ 465
9.5.3 Legal procedure node terms and their environment ............ 483
9.6 Conclusions ............ 490

**Chapter 10. Latinisms** ............ 495
10.1 Research material and methodology ............ 498
10.2 Distribution of Latinisms in the corpora ............ 499
10.3 Overlap of Latinisms between the corpora ............ 512
10.4 Repertoire of key Latinisms in the genre of judgments ............ 516

10.5 Degrees of textual integration and discourse functions of Latinisms ........ 538
10.6 Conclusions ........ 540

**Chapter 11. Synthesis and conclusions** ........ 543

11.1 Divergence of translated EU judgments from non-translated Polish judgments, internal variation within the Eurolect, and judicial Polish against general Polish ........ 543
11.1.1 Pillar I – Divergence at the lexico-grammatical level: CJ and GC vs SN_2011–2015, CJ vs GC, SN_2011–2015 vs NKJP ........ 543
11.1.2 Pillar II – Divergence at the phraseological level: CJ and GC vs SN_2011–2015, CJ vs GC ........ 559
11.1.3 Pillar III – Divergence at the terminological level: CJ and GC vs SN_2011–2015, CJ vs GC ........ 565
11.1.4 Possible causes of divergence and acceptability of translated language ........ 568
11.2 The limited impact of translated EU judgments on national judgments (microdiachronic language change) – 1999 vs 2011–2015 ........ 571
11.2.1 Pillar I – Microdiachronic change at the level of chosen lexico-grammatical features ........ 572
11.2.2 Pillar II – Microdiachronic change at the phraseological level ........ 577
11.2.3 Pillar III – Microdiachronic change at the terminological level ........ 579
11.3 Limitations of the study and suggestions for further research ........ 581
11.4 Practical applications of the study ........ 583

**Bibliography** ........ 585

**Index** ........ 619

# List of tables


Table 2.1. GENTT genre characterization template (adapted from Borja Albi *et al.* 2009: 65; cf. Peruzzo 2019: 56) .......... 57
Table 3.1. Research model for the analysis of the relation of textual fit within the genre of judgments (adapted from Biel 2014a: 287–289) .......... 71
Table 4.1. Polish language versions of Court of Justice of the EU judgments (Court of Justice and General Court) .......... 80
Table 4.2. Corpora of Polish language versions of CJ and GC judgments (2011–2015) broken down according to the year of publication .......... 81
Table 4.3. Corpora of Polish language versions of CJEU judgments (CJ and GC) broken down according to the language of procedure (time period: 2011–2015) .......... 82
Table 4.4. SN corpus – judgments of the Civil Chamber of the Supreme Court of the Republic of Poland .......... 84
Table 4.5. Corpora of non-translated SN judgments (1999, 2011–2015) broken down according to the year of publication .......... 85
Table 5.1. Macrostructure of CJ (columns I – III, and V) and GC judgments (column IV) .......... 104
Table 5.2. Macrostructure of SN judgments .......... 106
Table 6.1. Global statistics for the unsampled and sampled corpora of EU and national judgments .......... 139
Table 6.2. Occurrences of 1–45–letter words in the corpora .......... 142
Table 6.3. Lexico-grammatical categories for identified with the 500-word CJEU and SN keyword lists (positions of individual keywords on the respective keyword lists are shown in square brackets) .......... 147
Table 6.4. Distribution of simple prepositions in the corpora (ordered according to their NF in the corpora) .......... 151
Table 6.5. Distribution of top 50 compound and secondary prepositions in CJEU judgments .......... 156
Table 6.6. Number of types of compound and secondary prepositions shared between the individual corpora (from among the top 50 list) .......... 164
Table 6.7. Number of types of compound and secondary prepositions shared between the individual corpora (from among the refined list, RF>1, NF>0) .......... 165
Table 6.8. Number of types of compound and secondary prepositions with NF greater than or equal to 5 fulfilling 18 functions and the number of tokens in the functional categories .......... 167

Table 6.9. Distribution of compound and secondary prepositions expressing time relations ..... 171
Table 6.10. Distribution of compound and secondary prepositions expressing cause-effect, permission and condition relations ..... 175
Table 6.11. Distribution of secondary prepositions expressing reference ..... 178
Table 6.12. Distribution of compound and secondary prepositions expressing intra- and inter-textual relations ..... 181
Table 6.13. Distribution of compound and secondary prepositions expressing participation relations ..... 183
Table 6.14. Distribution of compound and secondary prepositions expressing modality relations ..... 185
Table 6.15. Distribution of compound and secondary prepositions expressing apposition relations ..... 186
Table 6.16. Distribution of compound and secondary prepositions expressing manner and instrumental relations ..... 188
Table 6.17. Distribution of compound and secondary prepositions expressing adversariality relations ..... 189
Table 6.18. Distribution of compound and secondary prepositions expressing measure relations ..... 190
Table 6.19. Distribution of compound and secondary prepositions expressing inclusivity/exclusivity relations ..... 192
Table 6.20. Distribution of compound and secondary prepositions expressing commutative relations ..... 193
Table 6.21. Distribution of compound and secondary prepositions expressing purpose relations ..... 195
Table 6.22. Distribution of compound prepositions expressing distribution relations ..... 196
Table 6.23. Distribution of compound and secondary prepositions expressing comparison relations ..... 197
Table 6.24. Distribution of compound and secondary prepositions expressing space relations ..... 199
Table 6.25. Distribution of compound prepositions expressing partitive relations ..... 200
Table 6.26. Secondary prepositions expressing active relations ..... 201
Table 6.27. Aggregate quantitative data on the distribution of compound and secondary prepositions conveying various discourse functions (semantic relations) ..... 203
Table 6.28. Distribution of paratactic markers ..... 206
Table 6.29. Distribution of hypotactic markers ..... 210
Table 6.30. Personal, possessive, demonstrative, indefinite pronouns and quantifiers ..... 214
Table 6.31. Adjectival deictic expressions ..... 217
Table 6.32. Distribution of the auxiliary verbs *być* [to be] and *zostać* [to become] ..... 220

Table 6.33. Passive voice – auxiliary verbs *być* [to be] and *zostać* [to become] ... 222
Table 6.34. Top L1 collocations of *się* [-self REFL] ... 225
Table 6.35. The *-no/to* impersonal pattern and the top types ... 227
Table 6.36. Distribution of verdictive, exercitive (argumentative) and reporting verbs ... 231
Table 6.37. Causal markers expressing justification ... 237
Table 6.38. Causal markers expressing inference ... 239
Table 6.39. Prototypical if-then conditional markers (conjunctions) ... 242
Table 6.40. Other conditional markers related to the prototypical *jeżeli* [if-FORM] and *jeśli* [if-NEUT] conjunctions ... 244
Table 6.41. Patterns of purpose ... 248
Table 6.42. Distribution of adverbials expressing addition, exemplification and particularization, and enumeration ... 251
Table 6.43. Distribution of adverbials expressing stance ... 256
Table 6.44. Distribution of adverbials expressing contrast and exclusion ... 259
Table 6.45. Distribution of active adjectival participles identified as keywords ... 262
Table 6.46. Distribution of passive adjectival participles identified as keywords ... 263
Table 6.47. Distribution of present adverbial participles ... 265
Table 6.48. Distribution of perfective adverbial participles ... 268
Table 7.1. Tested frequency and dispersion variables ... 286
Table 7.2. Frequency and distribution threshold values for each of the corpora ... 286
Table 7.3. Global distribution of 2–8–grams in the EU corpora and the PL corpus ... 288
Table 7.4. Global distribution of 2–8–grams in the EU corpora and the PL corpora ... 289
Table 7.5. Distribution of 2–8–grams in the translation and reference corpora (NF), frequency threshold — <40, dispersion threshold — <5 ... 293
Table 7.6. Refinement of 3–4–grams (occurrences – NF) ... 295
Table 7.7. Top ten 3–grams in the corpora after refinement ... 297
Table 7.8. Top 10 4–grams in the corpora after refinement ... 299
Table 7.9. Content and non-content 3–4–grams in the corpora (after refinement) ... 301
Table 7.10. Overlap of 2–8–grams in the translation and non-translation corpora (before refinement) ... 302
Table 7.11. Overlap of 3–4–grams in the translation and non-translation corpora (after refinement) ... 303
Table 7.12. Discourse functions of lexical bundles (based on Biber *et al.* 2004: 384–388, Goźdź-Roszkowski 2011: 109–143, and Jablonkai 2009: 6, 2010: 262) ... 311

Table 7.13. Quantitative data on the distribution of lexical bundles acting as stance, discourse-organizing and referential expressions (bundle types are listed according to the number of types in the corpus of post-accession SN judgments) .................................. 315
Table 7.14. Distribution of 3–4–word referential bundles in the corpora and their classification into individual functional sub-categories (ordered according to the normalized frequency of occurrence in the individual corpora) ............................................ 317
Table 7.15. Distribution of 3–4–word bundles denoting agents/institutions . 321
Table 7.16. Distribution of 3–4–word bundles denoting abstract concepts .... 323
Table 7.17. Distribution of 3–4–word bundles denoting documents .............. 325
Table 7.18. Distribution of 3–4–word legal procedure bundles ........................ 327
Table 7.19. Distribution of 3–4–word bundles denoting dates ......................... 329
Table 7.20. Distribution of 3–4–word bundles denoting places ....................... 331
Table 7.21. Distribution of 3–4–word discourse-organizing bundles and their classification into individual functional sub-categories (ordered according to the normalized frequency of occurrence in the individual corpora) ............................................ 333
Table 7.22. Distribution of 3–4–word intra-/intertextual bundles ................... 338
Table 7.23. Distribution of 3–4–word causative-resultative and inferential bundles ......................................................................... 340
Table 7.24. Distribution of 3–4–word focus bundles ........................................ 342
Table 7.25. Distribution of 3–4–word framing bundles .................................... 344
Table 7.26. Distribution of 3–4–word topic elaboration/clarification bundles ..................................................................................... 346
Table 7.27. Distribution of 3–4–word transition bundles ................................. 347
Table 7.28. Distribution of 3–4–word purpose bundles .................................... 349
Table 7.29. Distribution of 3–4–word conditional bundles .............................. 351
Table 7.30. Quantitative data concerning the distribution of 3–4–word lexical bundles and their classification into individual functional sub-categories (ordered according to the normalized frequency of occurrence in the individual corpora) .. 353
Table 7.31. Distribution of 3–4–word evaluative bundles ................................ 356
Table 7.32. Distribution of 3–4–word bundles expressing intensification ...... 358
Table 8.1. Corpus design (analysis of binomials) ............................................ 369
Table 8.2. Total number of clusters structured around *i* [and], *lub* [or], and *albo* [or] in the corpora prior to the extraction of bi- and multinomials proper ...................................................................... 370
Table 8.3. Distribution of non-extended binomials in the corpora ................ 373
Table 8.4. Total number of non-extended binomial structures and distribution of individual structural types built around *i* [and] and *lub* [or] in the EU corpora ......................................................... 377

Table 8.5. Total number of non-extended binomial structures and distribution of individual structural types built around *i* [and] and *lub* [or] in the SN corpora ........ 379
Table 8.6. Full list of types of non-extended binomials in the EU corpora ... 382
Table 8.7. Full list of types of non-extended binomials in the SN corpora ... 385
Table 8.8. Total number of extended binomials in the corpora ........ 391
Table 8.9. Total number of basic extended binomial structures and distribution of individual structural types based around *i* [and] and *lub* [or] in the EU corpora ........ 394
Table 8.10. Total number of basic extended binomial structures and distribution of individual structural types based around *i* [and] and *lub* [or] in the SN corpora ........ 397
Table 8.11. Extended binomials in the EU corpora ........ 398
Table 8.12. Extended binomials in the SN corpora ........ 402
Table 8.13. Total number of multinomials in the corpora ........ 409
Table 8.14. Multinomials across the corpora ........ 410
Table 8.15. Examples of binomials fulfilling various discourse functions ...... 412
Table 8.16. Total number of binomials conveying referential functions ......... 414
Table 8.17. Total number of binomials conveying discourse-organizing functions ........ 416
Table 9.1. Corpus design (analysis of terminological items) ........ 433
Table 9.2. Total number of types of simple and complex terms in the EU and SN corpora following refinement ........ 436
Table 9.3. Degree of terminological overlap between the EU and SN corpora (overlapping types) ........ 437
Table 9.4. Top 30 simple terms in the sampled corpora (frequencies normalized to 1 million) ........ 442
Table 9.5. Top 15 complex terms in the corpora ........ 446
Table 9.6. Node terms belonging to the semantic fields (ordered according to the frequency of occurrence in the SN_2011–2015 corpus) ........ 450
Table 9.7. Agentive and institutional complex terms with the head term *sąd* [court] ........ 455
Table 9.8. Agentive and institutional complex terms with the head term *strona* [party] ........ 459
Table 9.9. Agentive and institutional complex terms structured around the node term *spółka* [company] ........ 462
Table 9.10. Agentive and institutional complex terms with the head term *państwo* [state] ........ 464
Table 9.11. Complex terms related to substantive law and case-law structured around the term node *wyrok* [judgment] ........ 467
Table 9.12. Complex terms related to substantive law and case-law with the head term *prawo* [law] ........ 472

Table 9.13. Complex terms related to substantive law and case-law with the head term *decyzja* [decision] ..... 478
Table 9.14. Complex terms related to substantive law and case-law with the head term *wniosek* [application] ..... 482
Table 9.15. Legal procedure complex terms with the head term *postępowanie* [proceedings] in the corpora ..... 485
Table 9.16. Legal procedure complex terms with the head term *koszty* [costs] ..... 489
Table 10.1. Distribution of Latin phrases and maxims in the corpora ..... 501
Table 10.2. Latinisms in the EU corpora (idiosyncratic types with 0 NF are not shown) ..... 502
Table 10.3. Latinisms in the SN corpora (idiosyncratic types with 0 NF are not shown) ..... 505
Table 10.4. Overlap between the translation and non-translation corpora (types) ..... 512
Table 10.5. Latinisms shared by both EU corpora and the SN_2011–2015 corpus ordered according to the aggregate NF in both CJ and GC ..... 514
Table 10.6. Latinisms shared by the SN_2011–2015 corpus and both EU corpora ordered according to the NF in the SN_2011–2015 corpus ..... 515
Table 11.1. Pillar I – Divergence of translated CJEU judgments from non-translated SN_2011–2015 judgments at the level of chosen lexico-grammatical features ..... 544
Table 11.2. Pillar I – Non-translated judicial Polish against general Polish (NKJP) ..... 557
Table 11.3. Pillar II – Divergence of translated CJEU judgments from non-translated SN_2011–2015 judgments at the phraseological level ..... 560
Table 11.4. Pillar III – Divergence of translated CJEU judgments from non-translated SN_2011–2015 judgments at the terminological level ..... 566
Table 11.5. Pillar I – Microdiachronic change at the level of chosen lexico-grammatical features in non-translated national judgments: SN_1999 vs SN_2011–2015 ..... 573
Table 11.6. Pillar II – Microdiachronic change at the phraseological level in non-translated national judgments: SN_1999 vs SN_2011–2015 ..... 578
Table 11.7. Pillar III – Microdiachronic change at the terminological level in non-translated SN judgments: SN_1999 vs SN_2011–2015 ..... 580

# List of figures


Figure 1.1. The pivot translation system at the CJEU in the preliminary ruling procedure (adapted from McAuliffe 2008: 815, 2012: 440) .... 41
Figure 2.1. Bhatia's classification of the language of the law (adapted from Bhatia 1987: 227) .... 54
Figure 2.2. Zieliński's categorization of the language of the law and legal language (adapted from Zieliński 1999) .... 55
Figure 2.3. Dontcheva-Navratilova's model for contextual genre analysis (adapted from Dontcheva-Navratilova 2009: 15; adapted by Szczyrbak 2014: 118–124) .... 58
Figure 3.1. Multi-perspective framework for researching the judicial variety of translated legal language .... 66
Figure 3.2. Micro-level operationalization of the relation of textual fit of translated CJEU judgments to non-translated SN judgments .... 73
Figure 4.1. JURIDIC corpus design – monolingual comparable corpus of translated CJEU judgments and non-translated SN judgments .... 79
Figure 4.2. Pre-accession and post-accession sub-corpora of non-translated SN .... 86
Figure 6.1. Tokens (running words) in text .... 140
Figure 6.2. Types (distinct words) .... 140
Figure 6.3. Mean word and sentence length in non-lemmatized corpora .... 141
Figure 6.4. Occurrences of 1–20–letter words .... 145
Figure 6.5. Total distribution of paratactic markers .... 208
Figure 6.6. Total distribution of hypotactic markers .... 213
Figure 6.7. Global distribution of deictic devices .... 218
Figure 6.8. Distribution of the auxiliary verb *być* [to be] .... 221
Figure 6.9. Distribution of the auxiliary verb *zostać* [to become] .... 221
Figure 6.10. Distribution of *być*-passives .... 223
Figure 6.11. Distribution of *zostać*-passives .... 223
Figure 6.12. Distribution of past passives and *-no/to* impersonal patterns .... 229
Figure 6.13. Total distribution of the epistemic exercitive (argumentative) modal verb *należy* [(it/one) must/should be, #7, PRES/PAST] .... 235
Figure 6.14. Distribution of prototypical causal markers expressing justification .... 238
Figure 6.15. Total distribution of causal markers expressing justification and inference .... 240
Figure 6.16. Distribution of *jeżeli* [if-FORM] and *jeśli* [if-NEUT] .... 243
Figure 6.17. Distribution of implicit conditional markers .... 246
Figure 6.18. Total distribution of prototypical and implicit markers of conditional relations .... 247

Figure 6.19. Distribution of addition, enumeration and exemplification and particularization adverbials ... 254
Figure 6.20. Distribution of adverbials expressing stance ... 258
Figure 6.21. Distribution of contrast and exclusion adverbials ... 260
Figure 6.22. Total distribution of active and passive adjectival participles ... 264
Figure 6.23. Total distribution of present and perfective adverbial participles (based on the distribution of listed participles) ... 269
Figure 7.1. All 135 3–grams shared by the CJ and GC corpora (ordered alphabetically, after refinement) ... 304
Figure 7.2. All 52 3–grams shared by the CJ and SN_2011–2015 corpora (ordered alphabetically, after refinement) ... 305
Figure 7.3. All 44 3–grams shared by the GC and SN_2011–2015 corpora (ordered alphabetically, after refinement) ... 305
Figure 7.4. All 158 3–grams shared by the *SN_2011–2015* corpus and the *SN_1999* corpus (ordered alphabetically, after refinement) ... 306
Figure 7.5. All 38 4–grams shared by the Polish Eurolect corpora (CJ and GC) (ordered alphabetically) (after refinement) ... 307
Figure 7.6. All 9 4–grams shared by the CJ corpus and the SN_2011–2015 corpus (ordered alphabetically) (after refinement) ... 308
Figure 7.7. All 10 4–grams shared by the GC corpus and the SN_2011–2015 corpus (ordered alphabetically) (after refinement) ... 308
Figure 7.8. All 10 4–grams shared by the SN_2011–2015 corpus and the SN_1999 corpus (ordered alphabetically) (after refinement) ... 309
Figure 8.1. Total number of non-extended binomials in the corpora ... 374
Figure 8.2. Distribution of structural types of non-extended binomials across the corpora ... 381
Figure 8.3. Total number of extended binomials in the corpora ... 392
Figure 8.4. Structural distribution of extended binomials across the EU corpora and the national corpus ... 396
Figure 8.5. Total distribution of binomials structured around *i* [and] and *lub* [or] ... 417
Figure 9.1. Common conceptual base of supranational and national judgments and its further specialization at the level of complex terms ... 491
Figure 10.1. Distribution of Latinisms in the corpora (RF≥1) ... 510
Figure 11.1. Scale for the assessment of the degree of divergence ... 549

# Abbreviations and acronyms

| | |
|---|---|
| A | argumentative |
| AntPConc | freeware parallel corpus concordancing tool |
| BIC | Bayes Factor |
| BNC | British National Corpus |
| BT | backtranslation |
| CAT | Computer-assisted Translation |
| CBOS | Centre for Public Opinion Research |
| CC | Polish Civil Code |
| CCP | Polish Code of Civil Procedure |
| CJ | Court of Justice |
| CJEU | Court of Justice of the European Union |
| CL | Corpus Linguistics |
| CLARIN-PL | Common Language Resources and Technology Infrastructure |
| CuriaTerm | terminology database of the Court of Justice of the European Union |
| DGC | Directorate-General for Communication |
| DGT | Directorate-General for Translation |
| DGTrad | Translation Directorate General at the CJEU |
| ECHR | European Court of Human Rights |
| EEUD | Jablonkai's English EU Discourse Corpus |
| EMT | European Master's in Translation |
| EPSO | European Personnel Selection Office |
| EU | European Union |
| EUR-Lex | official website enabling access to European Union law and other documents |
| GC | General Court |
| GENTT | Textual Genres for Translation |
| I | informative |
| IATE | Interactive Terminology for Europe |
| InfoCuria | official website of the Court of Justice of the European Union |
| ISO | International Organization for Standardization |
| JURIDIC | monolingual comparable corpus used in the present study |
| LF-Aligner | corpus alignment tool |
| LL | Log Likelihood |
| LTS | Legal Translation Studies |
| NATO | North Atlantic Treaty Organization |
| NF | normalized frequency |
| NKJP | National Corpus of Polish |
| OHIM | Office for Harmonization in the Internal Market |
| OJ | Official Journal of the European Union |

| | |
|---|---|
| OR | overrepresentation |
| P | performative |
| PELCRA | Polish and English Language Corpora for Research and Applications |
| pmw | per million words |
| POS | part(s) of speech |
| RF | raw frequency |
| SJPD | Słownik języka polskiego, ed. Doroszewski |
| SL | source language |
| SN | Supreme Court of the Republic of Poland |
| ST | source text |
| STTR | standardized type/token ratio |
| TermoPL | online tool for automatic extraction of domain-related terminology |
| TEU | Treaty on European Union |
| TFEU | Treaty on the Functioning of the European Union |
| TL | target language |
| TQA | Translation Quality Assessment |
| TS | Translation Studies |
| TT | target text |
| TTR | type/token ratio |
| UN | United Nations |
| UNESCO | United Nations Educational, Scientific and Cultural Organization |
| UR | underrepresentation |
| UTF-8 | 8-bit Unicode Transformation Format |
| VJM | Comparative Multilingual Legal Vocabulary |
| WS | Wordsmith Tools 7.0 |
| WSJP | Wielki słownik języka polskiego PAN |

## Glossing abbreviations

| | |
|---|---|
| ABBRV | abbreviation |
| Adj | adjective |
| Adv | adverb |
| COM | complementation |
| CON | consequence |
| FORM | formal register |
| FUT | future tense |
| IFORM | informal register |
| IMPRS | impersonal |
| INF | infinitive |
| MID | middle voice |
| N | noun |

| | |
|---|---|
| NEUT | neutral register, neuter gender |
| NOM | nominative case |
| Num | numeral |
| OPP | opposition |
| PAST | past tense |
| PFV | perfective participle |
| POSS | possessive pronoun |
| PR | preposition |
| PRES | present tense |
| PRO | pronoun |
| REFL | reflexive |
| REL | relative pronoun |
| SEM | semantic relation |
| SUB | sub-division |
| SYN | near-synonymy |
| V | verb |

# Acknowledgments

This publication presents the outcome of the author's work package carried out within the framework of a research project financed by the Polish National Science Centre (NCN) with a SONATA BIS 4 grant no. UMO-2014/14/E/HS2/00782, "The Eurolect – An EU variant of Polish and its impact on administrative Polish." The project studied four legal and semi-legal genres (legislation, judgments, reports and websites for citizens) representative of the Polish Eurolect. The grant was awarded to dr hab. Łucja Biel, principal investigator. The author of this study was employed as an investigator/doctoral student in the project and this book is a revised version of his PhD thesis entitled "Translation of Judgments: A Corpus Study of the Textual Fit of EU to Polish Judgments" which was submitted to the Scientific Discipline Council for Linguistics of the University of Warsaw in May 2020.

I am indebted to Professor Łucja Biel for acting as my supervisor throughout the course of my PhD studies, sharing her vast knowledge and providing scientific guidance. I also wish to express my gratitude to Professor Stanisław Goźdź-Roszkowski and Professor Łukasz Grabowski for reviewing the manuscript. Any shortcomings are my own.

# Introduction

Judgments passed by the Court of Justice of the European Union (CJEU) have a very distinctive style, which highlights the nature of the supranational European legal order (McAuliffe 2013b: 878). To a certain degree, this may be advantageous, as hybrid judgments translated from French into national languages may "alert readers and those using such case-law to the fact that they are dealing not with their own national language but with a new and distinct EU legal language" (McAuliffe 2013b: 878). Based on the assumption that this phenomenon may be perceived as a *de facto* contradiction of the principles of the policy of multilingualism and a cause of the full or partial inability of many EU citizens to become familiar with EU case law, as only a small fraction of them are versed in national law, let alone EU law, the research questions of study are as follows:

1) Is the language of CJEU judgments translated into Polish different from the language of national judgments?
2) Does the translated case law of the CJEU influence the language of national judgments?

I assume that the audience of translated EU judgments develops certain expectancy norms (cf. Biel 2020, *forthcoming*) concerning the readability (naturalness) of supranational judgments through exposure to national judgments, which are the primary point of contact with judicial decisions for most Polish citizens. Therefore, I posit that translated CJEU judgments should exhibit close (convergent) fit to comparable, non-translated national judgments, in order to allow EU citizens to have true equal access to justice and jurisprudence at the EU level (cf. Wright 2016: 161). On the other hand, I will use distortions exhibited by unnatural language patterns and dissimilar distributional patterns to determine the divergent textual fit of translated judgments.

Considering the orientation of the research questions, this publication focuses on the discourse of judges, a type of specialized discourse which is steadily attracting increasing attention from linguists and legal scholars alike. It investigates the judicial variety of the Polish Eurolect by profiling the linguistic make-up of two sub-genres of judgments – Polish language versions of judgments issued by the CJEU and non-translated judgments passed by the Supreme Court of the Republic of Poland (SN) through the prism of Corpus Translation Studies. The essence of the analysis involves: (1) the application of a translation-driven monolingual comparable corpus, which includes translated Court of Justice (CJ) judgments, translated General Court (GC) judgments, non-translated post-accession SN judgments from 2011–2015, and non-translated pre-accession SN judgments from 1999, (2) the operationalization of the intertextual relation of the textual fit (Chesterman 2004; Biel 2014) to examine over- and underrepresentation within three pillars: chosen lexico-grammatical features, formulaicity (lexical bundles, binomials) and terminology (single and complex terms, Latinisms). The research goals of the present study focus on the linguistic profiling of the judicial variety of the Polish Eurolect and its influence on comparable national judgments from the point of view of the end product of the translation process, rather than the translation process itself. As regards the second research question, I aim to compare the language of pre-accession (1999) SN judgments with post-accession (2011–2015) judgments, which will allow me to establish the occurrence of any changes in the distributional characteristics of the language of Polish judges following Poland's accession to the EU in 2004, and whether they could have been facilitated by the over- and underrepresentation of certain patterns in translated EU judgments.

The study aims to either confirm or disprove the existence of the judicial variety (sub-type) of the Polish Eurolect (cf. Biel 2014a). More specifically, a high degree of textual fit of translated EU judgments will deny the existence of such a variety of specialized Polish legal language. The overarching aims are: (1) to provide more knowledge on the language of translated texts, (2) to aid the readers in better understanding the multilingual context of production and translation of EU judgments, (3) to further popularize and explore the concept of textual fit, which lends itself to the study of final translated texts of different genres, (4) to demonstrate the applicability of corpus-linguistic methodology and the operationalized notion of textual fit to the linguistic profiling of specialized legal genres, and (5) to provide reference material for future related studies.

This book is divided in two parts – the first part succinctly presents the theoretical background, while the second part describes the results of the empirical study. Part I, which is composed of three chapters, lays the theoretical foundations for the corpus study of the textual fit (understood as the degree of naturalness or linguistic distance, cf. Chesterman 2004; Biel 2014) of translated EU judgments to non-translated national judgments by integrating the theories and methods of Corpus Linguistics and genre analysis. Chapter 1 covers the subject of multilingualism and translation at the CJEU and the SN while concentrating on the context of multilingual production of CJEU judgments, the translation process, and the translator (lawyer-linguist) profile. Chapter 2 describes the mixed genre-register approach to the linguistic analysis of judgments by conceptualizing terms such as *genre, register, discourse (community)* and *legal language*. Chapter 3 examines the role of corpus-linguistic methodology in the profiling of the two sub-genres of judgments by describing the combined corpus-based and corpus-driven approach to the study of judicial language and the advantages and disadvantages of corpus methodology. It also presents a multi-perspective framework for the analysis of judicial language and operationalizes the intertextual relation of textual fit. Part II, which comprises seven chapters, presents the results of an empirical study into the textual fit of EU judgments translated into Polish and of non-translated national judgments. Chapter 4 discusses the design of the JURIDIC corpus used in this study, touching upon issues concerning the balance, representativeness and comparability of the individual (sub-)corpora (and their sampled versions), corpus software, and the manner of the normalization of quantitative data. Chapter 5 presents the results of the macro-level contextual and structural genre analysis of EU and national judgments. Chapter 6 contains a detailed description of the textual fit at the micro-textual level by discussing the distributional characteristics of chosen lexico-grammatical patterns identified through the analysis of keyword lists. Chapter 7 measures the formulaicity of judicial language with the lexical bundle methodology. It also provides an analysis of the discourse functions of lexical bundles. Chapter 8 further examines the degree of formulaicity in judgments by focusing on non-extended and extended binomial structures. Chapter 9 studies simple and complex terms in supranational and national judgments, enabling the identification of terms creating the common conceptual base of judgments from both legal contexts, while Chapter 10 discusses Latinisms used frequently by EU and Polish judges. A synthesis of the results and their interpretation, limitations of the study, suggestions for further research as well as practical applications of the study are presented in Chapter 11.

# Part I. Theoretical background

# Chapter 1. Multilingualism and translation at the Court of Justice of the European Union

The aim of this chapter is to describe the context in which CJEU judgments are translated into official EU languages, thus accounting for the multidimensional nature (cf. Biel 2020, *forthcoming*) of legal translation at the supranational (EU) level (cf. Chapter 3, Section 3.2, Figure 3.1).[1] A multidimensional framework is applied here, as linguistic research in Legal Translation Studies (LTS) requires a hybrid (holistic) approach which evaluates the most important factors of not only the target legal texts, but also the environment in which they are drafted and translated. The contextual and situational analysis of translation at the CJEU encompasses four primary dimensions: (1) the context of production (see Section 1.1), (2) the profile of translators working for the CJEU (see Section 1.2), (3) the translation process, and its (4) reception[2] (cf. Saldanha and O'Brien 2014: 5; Biel 2017d: 81). These four dimensions are an essential part of a study focused primarily on corpus-linguistic analysis (linguistic profiling) of two sub-genres of judgments, namely CJEU judgments translated into Polish and non-translated SN judgments (cf. Chapter 2). The overarching goal of the chapter is to establish the background for the investigation of the key dimension of legal translation – the end product of translation (cf. Part II).

## 1.1 Context of production of CJEU judgments: policy of multilingualism

Multilingualism lies at the heart of the EU. Its language policy, which entails the production of multilingual language versions of legal acts, is proof that language is a very important tool for integration within the EU (Künnecke 2013: 245).

---

1 This chapter is descriptive in that it outlines the policy of multilingualism and the process of translation at the CJEU without empirical research methods, such as observational studies, interviews or questionnaires (cf. Biel 2020, *forthcoming*). It draws primarily on the review of relevant literature, as well as the knowledge obtained during my traineeship at the Polish Translation Unit of the European Parliament in 2016 (cf. Koźbiał 2016), during which I conducted an informal interview with one of the Polish lawyer-linguists working at the CJEU. More information on the topic may be found in articles authored by Karen McAuliffe (2008, 2009, 2010, 2011, 2012, 2013a,b, 2014, 2016), Michal Bobek (2015), and Susan Wright (2016, 2018).

2 See Chapter 3, Section 3.2 for information as to why reception is not investigated in this study.

Consequently, the policy of multilingualism at the CJEU is interwoven with the linguistic regime of the EU set out in Article 342 of the TFEU:

> The rules governing the languages of the institutions of the Union shall, without prejudice to the provisions contained in the Statute of the Court of Justice of the European Union, be determined by the Council, acting unanimously by means of regulations.

The Council determined the official and working languages in Regulation No 1 [1958] (OJ 17/358, as amended); however, it did so without clearly specifying the meaning of the terms *working language* and *official language* (Doczekalska 2018: 167). As of today, the total number of official languages laid out in Article 1 of that regulation is 24.[3] These are the languages designated by Member States as their official languages – languages in which acts of primary and secondary law are published, languages which can serve as the language of a case before EU courts, and languages which can be used to communicate with the EU (Derlén 2015: 54). Since certain languages, such as German, are spoken in several countries, there are fewer official languages than Member States. Further, Articles 4 and 5 of that regulation state that regulations and other documents of general application must be drafted in all official languages and be published in the Official Journal of the EU (OJ) (Sarčević and Robertson 2013: 182).[4] Due to the fact that EU law-making activity applies not only to Member States, but also to each EU citizen and legal person, EU legal texts (even if they are addressed only to Member States) should be understood by each person to whom they apply, either directly or indirectly (McAuliffe 2012: 201). For this reason, Article 55 of the TEU, Article 358 of the TFEU and Article 225 of the EURATOM Treaty provide that all language versions of primary and secondary legislation be equally authentic.[5] These articles "maintain the illusion that the treaties were simultaneously produced in all 24 official languages, thereby emphasizing their equal authority" (Derlén 2015: 54).

The practical outcome of the principle of equal authenticity of translated EU legal acts is, at least in theory, the equal status of all EU citizens (cf. Šarčević 1997: 64). Nevertheless, there are criticisms that this principle along with Institutional Multilingualism have failed in facilitating EU citizens' access to and

3 These are: Bulgarian, Croatian, Czech, Danish, Dutch, English, Estonian, Finnish, French, German, Greek, Hungarian, Irish, Italian, Latvian, Lithuanian, Maltese, Polish, Portuguese, Romanian, Slovak, Slovenian, Spanish, and Swedish (source: https://europa.eu/european-union/about-eu/eu-languages_en, accessed: August 18, 2020). This differentiates the EU from other international organizations which function with only several languages, such as the UN (Arabic, Chinese, English, French, Russian, and Spanish) or NATO (English and French) (McAuliffe 2012: 201)

4 The CJEU has held that an EU legal act is not enforceable against natural and legal persons before they have the possibility to become familiar with the authentic text of the act in their own language published in the OJ (Graziadei 2015: 22).

5 This has been confirmed by the CJEU, for instance, in Case 282/81 Srl CILFIT and Lanificio di Gavardo SpA v Ministry of Health (cf. Derlén 2009: 67–78).

understanding of EU law (cf. Baaij 2018), and that English should act as the sole authentic language of legislative (and judicial) documents and effectively become a pan-European *lingua franca*, thereby eliminating the need for translation (cf. Šarčević 2010; Felici 2015; Baaij 2018). However, such an endeavor could potentially backfire, since "EU English remains a vehicular language drafted by non-native speakers" (Bajčić 2018: 15).

With regard to the CJEU, Article 7 of Regulation No 1/1958/EEC states that the CJEU may develop autonomous rules regarding the languages to be used in judicial proceedings in its Rules of Procedure[6] (McAuliffe 2008: 807, McAuliffe 2009: 101).[7] The policy of multilingualism[8] is indeed of great importance when it comes to the interpretation of the law (cf. Derlén 2009), as EU law takes precedence over the national law of Member States (Chalmers et al. 2010: 203–205; Borchardt 2017: 46, 126) and CJEU judgments are directly binding on national courts (Sarčević and Robertson 2013: 182). If there is any doubt as to the interpretation of EU legislation, it must be resolved by the CJEU, which is the sole institution authorized to confirm the validity of the primary and secondary acts of the EU and interpret them (cf. Borchardt 2017: 80–83). Thanks to its interpretative practice, which often goes beyond what was expressly agreed on by the Member States, the CJEU may be viewed as the motor of European integration (cf. Schmidt 2018: 28) which has developed, for instance, the doctrine of direct effect and supremacy (primacy) of EU law (Borchardt 2017: 103–106, 139–141; Schmidt 2018: 8). Therefore, the extension of the policy of multilingualism to the CJEU allows EU citizens, national judges, and lawyers in particular, to become familiar with its jurisprudence, enabling equal access to justice (Wright 2016: 161). It also allows the Court itself to ensure the broad effectiveness of EU law (McAuliffe 2012: 202, 218). All of the above points to the crucial link between the law, judicial activity and language in the European context.

On its website, the CJEU introduces itself as a unique multilingual institution[9]:

> As each Member State has its own language and specific legal system, the Court of Justice of the European Union is a multilingual institution. Its language arrangements

---

6 Rules of Procedure of the Court of Justice. https://eur-lex.europa.eu/legal-content/EN/TXT/?uri=celex:32012Q0929(01) (accessed: August 18, 2020)
Rules of Procedure of the General Court. https://eur-lex.europa.eu/legal-content/EN/TXT/?uri=CELEX%3A32015Q0423 %2801 %29 (accessed: August 18, 2020)

7 The rules governing the use of languages at the CJ and the GC are set out in their Rules of Procedure – Articles 36–42 and Articles 44–49, respectively.

8 For more information on multilingualism in the wider context of the whole EU, see, for instance, Kjær (2004, 2007a), Horspool (2006: 158–163), Šarčević (2007), Felici (2010, 2015), Krzyżanowski and Wodak (2010), Biel (2014: 60–63), Derlén (2015), and Baaij (2018).

9 CJEU – General Presentation – http://curia.europa.eu/jcms/jcms/Jo2_6999/en/ (accessed: August 18, 2020).

> have no equivalent in any other court in the world, since each of the official languages of the European Union can be the language of a case. The Court is required to observe the principle of multilingualism in full, because of the need to communicate with the parties in the language of the proceedings and to ensure that its case-law is disseminated throughout the Member States.

Despite this fact, the CJEU is the only monolingual EU institution (Derlén 2015: 57–59). French is the language in which judges hold their deliberations and conduct proceedings (Derlén 2015: 57) and which effectively shapes the case law of the CJEU (McAuliffe and Trklja 2018: 433). French was chosen in the 1950s by judges from the original Member States, as it enabled successful communication among them; however, it was not the mother tongue of all the judges, which still holds true (Wright 2016: 158). In practice, the use of just one working language simplifies the proceedings and reduces costs (Derlén 2015: 57). Currently, it is generally held that changing the working language of the CJEU to English would require a large amount of work and reorganization, including adaptation of the style and vocabulary of the judgments, which makes the whole endeavor unrealistic (McAuliffe 2008: 817).

When discussing the issue of language use at the CJEU, it is important to differentiate between the internal *working language* of the CJEU (see above) and the *language of the case*[10] (the so-called procedural language), which can be any of the 24 official EU languages (Šarčević and Robertson 2013: 184; Derlén 2015: 56; McAuliffe and Trklja 2018: 433). In direct actions, the language of the case is chosen by the applicant, unless the defendant is a Member State or a natural person with the nationality of a Member State or a legal person, in which case the language of procedure is the official language of the defendant (McAuliffe and Trklja 2018: 433). In references for a preliminary ruling under Article 267 TFEU, the language of procedure is the language of the national court which submits the reference (see Figure 1.1). Member States may use their own language when submitting written statements and observations as well as in their oral submissions when they intervene in a direct action or participate in a preliminary reference procedure (McAuliffe and Trklja 2018: 434). In appeals, the language of the case is the language which was used before the General Court (McAuliffe 2012: 202).[11]

Readers of CJEU judgments are not necessarily aware of the fact that both the working language of the CJEU and the languages of the cases heard by the Court

10 Article 36 of the Rules of Procedure before the Court of Justice states that: "The language of a case shall be Bulgarian, Croatian, Czech, Danish, Dutch, English, Estonian, Finnish, French, German, Greek, Hungarian, Irish, Italian, Latvian, Lithuanian, Maltese, Polish, Portuguese, Romanian, Slovak, Slovene, Spanish or Swedish." The same is stated in Article 44 of the Rules of Procedure of the General Court.

11 For a listing of different types of documents translated in direct actions and references for a preliminary ruling, see McAuliffe (2012: 216–218).

affect the process of drafting and translating judgments and other court documents by the CJ and the GC (McAuliffe 2016: 6). Although legal translation is a topic widely covered in the relevant literature, the creation of multilingual case law at the supranational level is not (McAuliffe 2016: 24). In the next section, I aim to shed more light on the intertwined drafting and translation process at the CJEU.[12]

## 1.2 The translation process

The general process of producing and translating CJEU judgments (and Advocates General's opinions) is as follows (McAuliffe 2012; McAuliffe and Trklja 2018: 435):

1. When a case is brought before the CJEU, all applications and documents drawn up in the official EU languages received at the CJEU are translated into French (Wright 2016: 161).
2. Once an application has been translated into French, it is assigned to a reporting judge (Judge Rapporteur), who manages the case file and drafts a preliminary report (an internal document) in French with the help of their référendaires (legal assistants)[13] (McAuliffe 2012: 204). In order to enable the parties to the proceedings to prepare for the hearing (if one is to take place), the report for the hearing is translated from French into the language of the case (McAuliffe 2012: 204; Wright 2016: 162).[14]
3. The Court decides what further steps are to be taken, whether to deal with the case in a plenary session or refer it to a Chamber, and whether it is necessary to conduct an oral hearing and have an Advocate General draft their opinion (McAuliffe and Trklja 2018: 435). Opinions are typically stylized differently from judgments in that they are rather personal, which is also indicative of the fact that the authors of opinions are clearly visible, unlike the authors of collegiate judgments drafted primarily by judges' référendaires, who are constrained by the rigid style of the report for the hearing and the judgment (McAuliffe 2012: 203, 207, McAuliffe 2013b: 869; Wright 2016: 162). As opposed to judgments, opinions tend to read like academic papers (McAuliffe 2012: 207). If an Advocate General is not a native speaker of the language in which they draft an opinion, such an opinion needs to be edited by the translation service (Wright 2016: 162). If an Advocate General is to draft an opinion, the reporting

12 The major types of publicly available documents produced by the CJEU are: judgments, orders, Opinions of the Advocates General, press releases and annual reports (InfoCuria – Case-law), all of which, to a greater or lesser extent, are embedded in the Court's policy of multilingualism (Wright 2016: 157).

13 For more information on the topic of judges' and Advocates General's référendaires, see McAuliffe (2012: 203–205).

14 The CJEU's Interpretation Directorate provides interpretation during oral hearings, which ensures participation in the procedure before the Court (Wright 2016: 162).

judge and their référendaire(s) must wait to receive that opinion before beginning to draft the judgment (McAuliffe 2012: 204).

4. If an opinion is drafted by an Advocate General, it also needs to be translated into French by the French language division (McAuliffe 2016: 11), since Advocates General may use one of the 24 official languages, but typically use one of the pivot languages when writing opinions (see Figure 1.1) (Wright 2016: 162). Opinions also need to be translated into the language of the case for the parties (Wright 2016: 162). At the end of this process, they may or may not be taken into consideration by the Court.
5. The first version of the judgment is drafted in French by a référendaire. During the course of her fieldwork at the CJEU, McAuliffe (2012: 204) found that non-Francophone drafters of judgments tend to conduct their reasoning (cf. Paunio 2013: 112–119) and thinking about the case in their own mother tongue, which they later translate into French. This may also affect the outcome of the drafting stage of the French-language versions (i.e. STs) by introducing an element of translation. The reporting judge and their référendaires draft the final judgment in French, once the judges deliberating *in camera* in a given Chamber have agreed on their decision (McAuliffe and Trklja 2018: 434).[15]
6. After the drafting stage in the production of CJEU case law follows the translation stage, in which the judgment is translated into the language of the case for the day of its delivery (Wright 2016: 162) and other official languages (McAuliffe and Trklja 2018: 435). The fact that drafters of judgments at the CJEU use French as the working language does not necessarily mean that they are all Francophones, which is indeed rarely the case (McAuliffe 2012: 213). As in most cases, judges sitting in a given Chamber (typically three or five judges, Schmidt 2018: 29) who deliberate on the contents of a judgment are not Francophone. Their version of the judgment is read by a Francophone lawyer, the so-called "reader of judgments," and proofread by a Francophone proofreader to ensure that it is written in perfect legal French consistent with the conventions of previous CJEU judgments (Wright 2016: 158). Thus, their input greatly affects the terminology and language of judgments (Wright 2016: 162). This element may be perceived as a measure which ensures the overall stability of the genre (cf. Leech 2007: 143, Chapter 4, Section 4.2). Due to constraints such as the use of certain translation tools and terminological databases[16] and the need to stay true to the

15 There are no accompanying dissenting judgments (Wright 2016: 158).

16 The CJEU does not provide specific information regarding the use of translation tools and language resources. The literature contains information about software known as "Generic Text Interface" (GTI) (McAuliffe 2012: 205, 2013a: 495), which is a computer program developed by the CJEU to aid and speed up the translation process by retrieving sentences and phrases which have already been translated; however, it cannot identify context (cf. McAuliffe 2014). Lawyer-linguists working at the CJEU make extensive use of terminological databases, such as CuriaTerm

nature of CJEU case law shaped over the decades, "Court French" differs significantly from traditional French (McAuliffe 2012: 203; Wright 2016: 158), and contributes to the special character of CJEU case law (McAuliffe 2012, 2013a, 2013b) (McAuliffe and Trklja 2018: 436). "Court French" has a formulaic and overly-formal character, although it is a feature which may facilitate the translation process (Künnecke 2013: 255; McAuliffe and Trklja 2018: 436). CJEU judgments are full of routine formulae with fixed meanings and follow a predetermined structure (see Chapter 2). This formulaic and pompous style of CJEU judgments is noticed by most lawyer-linguists (see Section 1.3), référendaires and even judges (McAuliffe 2013b: 871).

If the language of procedure is French, then the final judgment drafted in French is the authentic version (the ST or the *de facto* original text, Derlén 2015: 60–61) of the judgment (McAuliffe 2013b: 865; McAuliffe and Trklja 2018: 436); however, if the language of procedure is another official language, the final judgment drafted in French is not the authentic version of the judgment (McAuliffe 2012: 209; McAuliffe and Trklja 2018: 434–435). The latter occurs most frequently, as most proceedings do not originate in France (cf. McAuliffe 2012: 214). Therefore, with French being the working language of the CJEU, authentic versions of judgments (*de jure* originals, Derlén 2015: 60–61) are in fact translations of the French language versions of those judgments (Wright 2016: 157, 162).

The status of French at the CJEU raises the issue of "vanishing sources" (Künnecke 2013). The impact of French on the traditional notions of source and target text in the translation process at the CJEU has already been observed in LTS research (cf. Künnecke 2013). According to Article 41 of the Rules of Procedure of the CJ and Article 49 of the Rules of Procedure of the GC, documents drawn up in the language of the case (or in another authorized language) are typically the authentic language versions. The immediate result is that the only authentic version of the judgment is that in the language of the case and not that drafted originally in French (Künnecke 2013: 250). For instance, if a German court submits a reference for a preliminary ruling in its own official language, the only authentic version of the judgment given in that case will be the German version, despite the French version being the true ST (cf. Künnecke 2013: 251). In such a case, the German language division starts to translate the judgment early, while, if need be, working closely with a German-speaking judge who can best understand the initial reference, in order to ascertain the proper intended meaning and avoid

(Künnecke 2013: 259–260). They also use, among other things, CAT tools (SDL Trados), alignment tools (SDL Trados WinAlign), terminology management tools (SDL Multiterm), Word, Excel, PowerPoint, and SDL Trados WinAlign (Sarčević and Robertson 2013: 196–197).

ambiguities or incorrect concepts[17] in the final judgment (cf. Künnecke 2013: 251; Wright 2016: 159). However, such a judge may not have been in the Chamber that decided a particular case and may not be aware of the deliberations that took place (McAuliffe 2012: 220). If other language divisions have doubts, they can discuss them with the German language division, and if there are any discrepancies between language versions, the version in the language of the case is the authentic one (cf. Künnecke 2013: 251). In this way, cooperation between language divisions further contributes to quality assurance.[18] The present status of French as the internal working language of the CJEU is a cause of difficulties in researching equivalence (cf. Chapter 3) based on texts produced in the CJEU environment.

McAuliffe (2018: 437) observes that 22 official EU languages (with the exception of Irish) are subordinate to French, which is the *de facto* source language of translated judgments. This creates what is called a flat hierarchy, in which the focus is French and its status as the working language of the CJEU. In addition to this hierarchy, there is also the (1) rotational flat hierarchy, which is based on the language of procedure acting as the superordinate language towards the other 22 subordinate languages, (2) the pivot translation hierarchy, in which the five pivot languages are superordinate, and (3) the temporal linguistic hierarchy, which relates to the fact that not all official languages have exerted the same influence on the case law of the CJEU because each enlargement of the EU has brought in more and more languages (McAuliffe 2018: 437–440).

The enlargement of the EU in 2004[19] (cf. McAuliffe 2008) necessitated the introduction of pivot languages and the pivot translation system (Šarčević and Robertson 2013: 184) in May 2004 (McAuliffe 2013b: 871), which are the languages of the first translation from which translations are made into "smaller" EU languages (McAuliffe 2010: 254, McAuliffe 2012: 208). This system is used by the Directorates for Legal Translation to cope with the ever-increasing workload and to reduce the total number of language combinations from 552 to roughly 39

---

17 The translation of judgments involves an exercise in comparative law, as legal concepts differ across incongruent legal systems (cf. Künnecke 2013: 246; Wright 2016: 161) and it is required to translate concepts from one legal system to another (McAuliffe 2016: 9). Translation of legal texts at the supranational level which are intended to be read primarily by the audience in national settings also involves an inter-systemic transfer of concepts, as terms and concepts stemming from the national context may not have the same meaning in EU law and vice versa; EU legal concepts may even be fully autonomous (Künnecke 2013: 248; cf. Engberg 2015).

18 For more information on the topic of TQA at the CJEU, see Koźbiał (2017).

19 Prior to the accession of ten new Member States in 2004, lawyer-linguists from each candidate country were hired as contractual agents by the legislative institutions and the European Central Bank (Šarčević and Robertson 2013: 197).

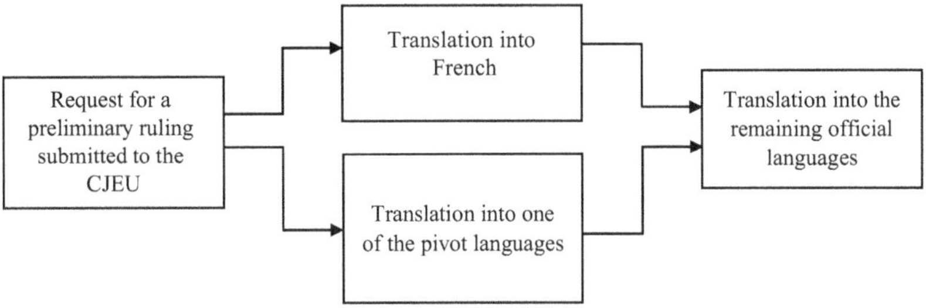


**Figure 1.1.** *The pivot translation system at the CJEU in the preliminary ruling procedure (adapted from McAuliffe 2008: 815, 2012: 440)*

(McAuliffe 2012: 439). There are currently five pivot languages used for translation purposes – English, French, German, Italian, and Spanish (Arnull 2018: 13). Figure 1.1 represents the manner in which the pivot translation system works at the CJEU based on the preliminary reference procedure.

The pivot translation system entails a great number of organizational difficulties. It requires language divisions, i.e. those which translate into the pivot languages[20] and those which translate from the pivot languages into the remaining official languages, to cooperate to produce translations within tight deadlines (McAuliffe 2008: 813–814).

To sum up the description of the translation process, the policy of multilingualism at the CJEU adds an additional layer to the concepts of legal certainty and uniform application of EU law (McAuliffe 2018: 448), which are, however, safeguarded by the preliminary reference procedure (Paunio 2013: 196–197). In the case of the CJEU, it is not enough to regard multilingualism in the traditional way; it is also necessary to take into consideration the variety of hierarchical relations between different languages, particularly that of French and the target languages. McAuliffe (2018: 448) refers to multilingualism at the CJEU as multilinguistic superdiversity and regards it as a means of enhancing our understanding of the EU legal system and CJEU case law. The custodians of this superdiversity are lawyer-linguists, who are the subject of the next section (see Section 1.3).

## 1.3 The translator profile: lawyer-linguists

Efficient translation at the CJEU is possible thanks to the highly specialized lawyer-linguists who make up the CJEU's language service[21] (Wright 2016: 159). In order

20 Lawyer-linguists from pivot language divisions also provide linguistic assistance to the Advocates General and référendaires who typically draft opinions in a language other than their mother tongue (McAuliffe 2016: 16).

21 Lawyer-linguists are also employed by other EU institutions, such as the European Commission, the Council, the European Parliament or the European Central Bank (cf. Šarčević and Robertson 2013: 185–193), which require professional legal assistance

to ensure that the translations of judgments and other procedural documents are of high quality and that their meaning is correctly understood by national judges,[22] the CJEU delegates the task of timely translation to national lawyers, who are expected to have the best possible understanding of the target national legal cultures (Łachacz and Mańko 2013: 85–86; Wright 2016: 160), being typically required to translate from a foreign language into their mother tongue (Sarčević and Robertson 2013: 184; McAuliffe 2016: 15). In order to gain a better understanding of the role of lawyer-linguists, it is necessary to fully understand the process of translation at the CJEU and its impact on the end product of translation.

Lawyer-linguists working at the CJEU need to be distinguished from regular translators working at, for instance, the European Parliament, who are mostly linguists with a degree in translation (Šarčević and Robertson 2013: 181, 194). The interdisciplinary nature (cf. Šarčević and Robertson 2013: 201) of the profession of lawyer-linguists can be inferred from Article 42 of the Rules of Procedure of the Court of Justice, which states that:

> The Court shall set up a language service staffed by experts with adequate legal training and a thorough knowledge of several official languages of the European Union.

McAuliffe (2016: 6) rightly observes that translation (along with the drafting stage of text production at the CJEU) plays a significant role in the document production process and has an impact on the texts produced (cf. Baaij 2018). Nevertheless, lawyer-linguists, despite having great influence on the end products of the translation process, remain invisible to the audience of the translated texts (McAuliffe 2016: 11–14).

The CJEU's language services are grouped together in the Directorate-General for Multilingualism,[23] which is the institution's largest service, comprising the Directorate for Interpretation and Directorates A and B for Legal Translation. The Directorates A and B for Legal Translation, both of which work for the CJ as well as the GC, are composed of lawyer-linguists organized into different language divisions for each of the official EU languages (McAuliffe 2012: 209) who have a

---

in legal-linguistic revision of legal documents throughout the legislative process (Šarčević and Robertson 2013: 181, 183). As a consequence, lawyer-linguists working for different EU institutions may have a different profile due to divergent work tasks and specific practical needs of each EU institution (cf. Šarčević and Robertson 2013: 195).

22 The CJEU interprets primary and secondary EU legislation in accordance with its aims and objectives (cf. Paunio 2016: 21), whereas national courts and national judges are required to apply national law in accordance with the EU law and its interpretation provided by the CJEU (Paunio 2007: 401–402). EU judgments, on the other hand, are directly binding on the national courts and legal systems (Šarčević and Robertson 2013: 183).

23 Directorate-General for Multilingualism – https://curia.europa.eu/jcms/jcms/Jo2_10742/ (accessed: August 18, 2020).

degree in law or an equivalent professional qualification[24] (Wright 2016: 159). There are 23 language divisions[25] (Bulgarian, Croatian, Czech, Danish, Dutch, English, Estonian, Finnish, French, German, Greek, Hungarian, Italian, Latvian, Lithuanian, Maltese, Polish, Portuguese, Romanian, Slovak, Slovenian, Spanish and Swedish).[26] Given the CJEU's language arrangements, the total number of language combinations is 552 (not taking into account the pivot translation system), whereas the output of both Directorates exceeds 1.2 million pages a year. As of December 31, 2019, the CJEU employed a total of 600 lawyer-linguists.[27] Among other things, the texts translated by lawyer-linguists include references for a preliminary ruling, written observations, reports for the hearing, opinions of the Advocates General, and, most notably, judgments (Šarčević and Robertson 2013: 184).

The recruitment of lawyer-linguists is conducted by the European Personnel Selection Office (EPSO) and depends on the actual needs of the individual language divisions. Candidates[28] for the position of lawyer-linguist need to possess a law degree from the Member State for which the recruitment is organized, a perfect command of the language of the competition (typically one's mother tongue), and a thorough knowledge of at least two other official languages (Šarčević and Robertson 2013: 194).[29] In addition, they need to have a thorough understanding of not only their own legal system but also the legal systems of other Member States and the case law of the CJEU (McAuliffe 2016: 13). A lawyer-linguist's work is demanding and requires the ability to balance a dual professional identity (that of a lawyer and a linguist) (McAuliffe 2016: 14) and to adapt to strict and changing

24 Language arrangements at the Court of Justice of the European Union – https://curia.europa.eu/jcms/jcms/Jo2_10739/regime-linguistique-de-la-cour-de-justice-du-tribunal-de-premiere-instance-et-du-tribunal-de-la-fonction-publique (accessed: August 18, 2020).

25 Source: CJEU Annual Report 2018 – The Year in Review https://curia.europa.eu/jcms/upload/docs/application/pdf/2019-05/rapport_gestion_2018_en.pdf (accessed: August 18, 2020). So far Irish has never been used in submissions before the CJEU (McAuliffe 2012: 219) and there is no Irish language division (McAuliffe 2018: 437).

26 Directorates for Legal Translation – https://curia.europa.eu/jcms/jcms/Jo2_10744/ (accessed: August 18, 2020).

27 The Court in figures – https://curia.europa.eu/jcms/jcms/P_80908/en/ (accessed: February 16, 2020).

28 To apply for a job as a lawyer-linguist, it is necessary not only to meet the admissibility criteria, but also to pass written and oral tests in a competition; the written tests involve translating legal texts from two chosen languages into the language of the competition. Successful candidates are placed on a reserve list and offered a post when one for their language becomes available.

29 How to become a lawyer-linguist at the Court of Justice? https://curia.europa.eu/jcms/jcms/Jo2_10740/recrutement-comment-devenir-juriste-linguiste-a-la-cour-de-justice (accessed: August 18, 2020).

working conditions, as well as to strive for continuous professional development (cf. McAuliffe 2010: 254).[30]

The work of lawyer-linguists is valuable because EU judges are not able to assist national judges (and other members of the audience of CJEU judgments) due to the lack of direct communication and different factual contexts (the supranational vs the national level), as well as the fact that a written judgment is necessarily the only link between EU and national judges (Łachacz and Mańko 2013: 85). Lawyer-linguists educated in Member States, who belong to the same legal cultures as national judges and thus internalize both the supranational perspective of the CJEU as well as the national perspective, are able to lay out the CJEU's argumentation in the TL and to convey essentially the same meaning (Sarčević and Robertson 2013: 201) and the same degree of persuasive value in a way that will be identical or at least close to the intention of the CJEU judges (Łachacz and Mańko 2013: 86). Their role is to ensure that the interpretation of EU judgments by national judges is uniform across Member States (Łachacz and Mańko 2013: 87; cf. Derlén 2009, 2015).

The uncommon method of case-law production at the CJEU, including the policy of multilingualism and translation, may have implications for the rule of law within the EU, in particular regarding the uniform application of that law in 24 languages across 27 legal orders, leading to distortions in the end products of the translation process. Therefore, particular attention to detail needs to be paid at the level of the pivot translation divisions (see Section 1.2), the task of which it is to ensure that their translations into the pivot languages will not create the risk of legal approximations (cf. McAuliffe 2016: 7–8), mistranslations and discrepancies[31] between language versions when other language divisions translate from the pivot languages (McAuliffe 2008: 814). It may also happen that due to time pressures imposed on the French language division, the quality of procedural documents translated into French will vary (McAuliffe 2013b: 870), notably when lawyer-linguists do not consult on problematic issues with the judges' cabinets[32] and come up with their own translation solutions, which may lead to discrepancies between language versions (McAuliffe 2013b: 873). This might, in turn, lead to misapplication of EU law at the Member State level, as national judges cannot be reasonably expected to compare so many language versions of a given CJEU judgment in order to come up with a proper interpretation, especially if only one language

30 Lawyer linguists are encouraged throughout their careers to learn additional languages by following in-house and residential courses. Source: Working as an English-language lawyer linguist at the Court of Justice of the European Union, available at: https://curia.europa.eu/jcms/upload/docs/application/pdf/2009-03/brochure_en.pdf (accessed: August 18, 2020).

31 Any legally significant changes to already delivered judgments require a formal corrigendum issued by the CJEU (Wright 2016: 160).

32 It needs to be remembered that judges are never allocated cases which concern their home country (Schmidt 2018: 30).

version is authentic (McAuliffe 2013b: 877; cf. Derlén 2009, 2015: 60–63). The CJEU emphasizes the relationship between law and language, as well as stresses the importance of multilingual law-making in the EU when, for instance, it "rules against the language version of a provision consulted by one of the litigants in favour of the other language versions, which in its opinion spell out the applicable rule" (Graziadei 2015: 21); however, it does so to emphasize the flexible nature of this relationship. In other words, the principle of equal authenticity requires, unrealistically, the consultation of all language versions (Derlén 2015: 55–56).[33]

The translation of CJEU case law may involve a number of issues concerning the relations between the STs and TTs. Although some of these issues are well-known in research on (EU) legal translation, it is worth noting that translated EU judgments (non-French language versions[34]) might, for instance, (1) exhibit unintended terminological inconsistencies with the existing case law, which may be wrongly interpreted as a (slight) change in the Court's jurisprudence (the continuity/consistency relation, cf. Chapter 3), (2) be produced by lawyer-linguists (see Section 1.3) who, while translating from French into other official languages, may be prone to unintended transfer (interference), which might disturb the concordance relation between the ST and TTs (cf. Chapter 3),[35] (3) inadvertently depart from modern legal usage in the TL[36] (Wright 2016: 162–163) (the relation of textual fit, cf. Chapter 3). It is also important to remember that, for the most part, original texts in French are drafted by non-Francophone référendaires (McAuliffe 2012: 209, McAuliffe 2013b: 871), who tend to use the same expressions repeatedly, which may obscure the meaning intended by the Court and expressed originally in French. Additionally, lawyer-linguists translating into various official languages may translate a certain ambiguity when they should not do so, which may, in turn, lead to divergences between language versions. This might be particularly harmful if the problematic translation is the authoritative version[37] of the judgment (McAuliffe 2012: 212–215, McAuliffe 2016: 17). Wright (2016: 161–162) observes

33 An in-depth discussion on the different facets of multilingual drafting of legislation and its translation can be found in Robertson (2016).

34 It might also be argued that the French language versions are also translations due to the multi-level drafting process involving not only Francophones but also non-Francophones.

35 This issue should be studied with the help of the relation of equivalence on the basis of a parallel corpus of French language versions of CJEU judgments (most favorably ones with French as the language of the case), (Wright 2016: 163) and other language versions which are the product of direct translation (not the pivot translation system).

36 This issue is related to the relation of textual fit, which is studied in-depth in Part II.

37 Derlén (2015: 68) observes that "the absence of full multilingualism for case law indicates a limited view of adjudication," which might mean that the single authoritative language version of a judgment restricts the importance of case law in the EU legal system.

that such inconsistencies and inaccuracies in translations "may go unnoticed by the non-Francophone public, which will be unaware of the Court's intention." All of these circumstances affect the final outcome of the translation process, which leads, unavoidably, to the creation of hybrid and not particularly easily readable texts (cf. McAuliffe 2014).

# Chapter 2. Approach to genre analysis

Chapter 2 lays the groundwork for the empirical part of this study (cf. Part II) by showing that both sub-genres of judgments are indeed comparable. Section 2.1 discusses, as briefly as possible considering the wealth of literature on discourse studies, genre analysis and specialized language varieties, the manner in which I operationalize the concepts of *genre*, *register* and *style*, as well as *discourse (community)* and *legal language*, so as to substantiate the adoption of the combined genre-register approach, which is presented in Section 2.2.

In a corpus study aiming to linguistically profile the genre of judgments, more specifically CJEU (CJ and GC) judgments translated into Polish and non-translated SN judgments,[38] it is essential to provide: (1) a contextual analysis of the genre, and (2) an analysis of its generic structure. This approach has been advocated by researchers working in the fields of specialized discourse analysis and domain-restricted specialized translation (cf. Biber 2009b; Biel 2007, 2014; Cao 2009; Goźdź-Roszkowski 2011). Information on the contextual and macrostructural characteristics of the sub-genres of CJEU and SN judgments will be presented in Part II.A (Chapter 5).

## 2.1 Genre, register, style, discourse (community), legal language – setting the scene for the analysis of judgments

Even though the specialized variety of language used by judges and lawyers is commonly referred to as legal language (cf. Mattila 2006), due to its polysemous nature the term *legal language* is a source of confusion. This adds to the fact that judgments, that is documents produced by judges, are difficult to categorize based on either functional, subject-matter, or structural criteria (cf. Peruzzo 2019: 54). This section aims to provide the context for the linguistic analysis of judgments by presenting the operationalized definitions of commonly confused terms: (1) *genre*, (2) *register*, (3) *style*, (4) *(legal) discourse (community)*, and (5) *legal language*, which are widely used to describe language related to law (cf., among others, Bhatia 1987; Kurzon 1997; Cao 2009; Goźdź-Roszkowski 2011; Borja Albi 2013; Biel 2014a; Peruzzo 2019). Considering that the present study does not clearly occupy a niche in either Legal Linguistics[39] or Translation Studies, but rather relates to both fields

38 In this study, CJEU and SN judgments are viewed as sub-genres of the genre of judgments [PL: *wyroki*]. This will be discussed in Section 2.1.

39 For more information on the development of legal linguistics as a discipline and connected research topics, see Matilla (2006: 6–19).

of linguistic inquiry, it is necessary to briefly examine the most relevant views on *legal language* from both of those domains,[40] and then to explore the remaining terms which are crucial to understanding my approach (see Section 2.2).

*Genre, register* and *style*

A *genre* is the main instrument with which communicative purposes are realized (Swales 1990: 58):

> A genre comprises a class of communicative events, the members of which share some set of communicative purposes. These purposes are recognized by the expert members of the parent discourse community, and thereby constitute the rationale for the genre. This rationale shapes the schematic structure of the discourse and influences and constrains choice of content and style. [...] In addition to purpose, **exemplars of a genre exhibit various patterns of similarity in terms of structure, style, content and intended audience** [emphasis added].

According to this definition, a *genre* is primarily defined on the basis of its communicative purposes which affect its internal structure. The structural characteristics of a *genre* are, in turn, formed by conventionalized rhetorical elements (moves) shaped by the members of the *discourse community* (see below), thanks to their specialized knowledge, (professional) experience or training. Therefore, any deviations from the typical use of lexico-grammatical or discursive features of a given *genre* may be perceived as divergent (cf. Martín Martín 2003: 162). It also follows from Swales' (1990: 58) definition that *genres*, as exhibits of discoursal practices within *discourse communities*, are differentiated by their communicative purposes, structure, style, content and intended audience, which accords with Bhatia's definition of the *language of the law* and its constituent *genres* (cf. Bhatia 1987: 227, see below). According to Tiersma (1999: 139 after Peruzzo 2019: 49), on the other hand, *genres* are grouped together based on their structure, level of formality and function; function allows for differentiation of operative texts (such as statutes, pleadings, contracts), explanatory texts, and persuasive texts. Tiersma (1999: 139) views judgments as expository documents in which judges not only state the law based on legal provisions, but also decide the case in an operative and persuasive manner. Wodak (2003: 136) perceives *genres* as the use of language associated with a particular activity which may have varying degrees of fixedness.

These observations further justify the comparison of contextual, structural, and linguistic (see Part II.A) characteristics of the sub-genres of CJEU and SN judgments, as a result of which it may be possible to establish whether the intended audience of judgments passed by a national supreme court might have difficulties in familiarizing itself with EU case law by reading EU judgments (in other words, not have the feeling of "being in a genre," Biel 2017b) which are drafted and delivered at the supranational level, and thus within a different discourse

40 For a more in-depth classification of *legal language* in Legal Linguistics and Translation Studies, see Peruzzo (2019: 42–54).

community. The study might also indicate whether national judges might potentially perceive EU judgments as different from national judgments and whether such perceptions might warrant creating a more convergent degree of textual fit (cf. Chapter 3) of translated EU judgments to non-translated national judgments by adapting the translation process. The choice of a specific *genre* of texts to be included in corpora is seen by Lee (2001: 37) as essential to ensuring that any generalizations made based on the results of a study are limited to a specific kind of language (cf. Chapter 4). Therefore, *genres* seem to present the most practical level of text categorization to work with and may allow for the drawing of reliable conclusions (Lee 2001: 37–38).

The organized study of *genres* is termed (applied) genre analysis. Bhatia (2002: 4) describes genre analysis as the study of situated linguistic behavior, which requires the chosen texts to reflect the complex and dynamic realities of the world of institutionalized communication and discourse in general. Bhatia emphasizes that:

> analyzing genre means investigating instances of conventionalized or **institutionalized textual artefacts in the context of specific institutional and disciplinary practices, procedures and cultures** in order to understand how members of specific discourse communities construct, interpret and use these genres to achieve their community goals and why they write them the way they do [emphasis added] (Bhatia 2002: 5).

According to Bhatia (2002: 6), an in-depth genre analysis should integrate four distinct yet complementary views on language use: purposes (institutionalized community goals and communicative purposes), products (instances of texts or genres), practices (discursive practices, procedures and processes), and players (discourse community members) (cf. Biel 2017b, Biel 2020, *forthcoming*). The problem faced by many studies on various types of discourse lies in the fact that most researchers often focus on analysis at the lexico-grammatical (or intra-textual) level and only deal with the social context in a superficial manner (Bhatia 2002: 17–18). However, it is equally important to examine the text-external factors which are located in the broadly understood socio-cognitive space, namely the tactical aspects of language use and the correlation between text-internal and text-external (i.e. contextual) factors (Bhatia 2014: 156). Bhatia's approach provides an insight into the construction of texts and the text-internal features of genre-dependent language use that they exhibit (with regard to rhetorical moves, discourse strategies, regularities of organization, intertextuality and, to some degree, interdiscursivity). Bhatia also mentions professional space and social space – professional space encompasses participant relationships and their contributions to genre construction, interpretation, use and exploitation within the context of disciplinary, professional and institutional practices, whereas social space accounts for the influence of social actions in creating and maintaining social identities, social structures and the operation of social institutions through discursive practices (Bhatia 2014: 156). When explaining the investigation into professional space, he adds that two other aspects of analysis might concern the way experts exploit and manipulate generic resources in order to devise hybrid *genres* (due to mixing, embedding and appropriating features of other *genres*), and how they use their specialist knowledge to maintain control over the genres they make use of to attain their professional goals (Bhatia 2014: 156).

Other convoluted concepts in the field of discourse studies are *register* and *style*. Biber and Conrad (2009: 15) identify three approaches to analyzing text varieties in particular situations of use – the *genre*, the *register* and the *style* approach. However, they caution that there is no general agreement as to the exact meaning of the concepts of *genre*, *register* and *style* and their use is not consistent (Biber and Conrad 2009: 21). What exacerbates this problem is Biber's somewhat arbitrary manner of using the terms *genre* and *register* in his own works (cf. Biber 1988, 1995).

According to Biber and Conrad (2009: 16), the study of *genres* differs from the study of *registers* and *styles* in terms of textual focus, since various studies concentrate on complete texts rather than text excerpts. Furthermore, with regard to linguistic characteristics, the study of *genres* focuses on specialized expressions, rhetorical organization and text structure, whereas approaches focusing on *registers* and *styles* entail the analysis of lexico-grammatical features. Furthermore, in terms of the distribution of linguistic characteristics, *genres* are perceived to display them as usually occurring once, in a particular place in the text, while *registers* and *styles* may show linguistic characteristics which are frequent and pervasive in texts from a given variety. Lastly, as regards interpretation, that is the underlying reasons for the observed linguistic patterns, frequently-occurring linguistic features serve important communicative functions from the perspective of *register*. By contrast, linguistic features from the perspective of *style* are esthetic rather than functional. In *genres*, linguistic features are conventionally associated with the *genre*, and the format (structure) is conventional (Biber and Conrad 2009: 16; cf. Goźdź-Roszkowski 2011: 20). Lee (2001: 45) suggests using the term *style* to describe the internal properties of texts or language use by individual authors; in other words, the text producer's use of language in that particular instance. It needs to be pointed out that style can vary not only between different genres, but also within the same *genre*, since the author (speaker/writer) can switch from being formal (frozen, ponderous) to informal (colloquial, intimate) (Lee 2001: 45). The category of style would be difficult to investigate using judgments which are delivered as a product of deliberations of a panel of judges passing a judgment (cf. Chapter 1), hence its exclusion from the present approach. It follows that *genres* and *styles* are better suited to qualitative analyses, whereas *registers* are more accessible through quantitative analyses.

*Discourse and discourse community*

Bhatia (2004: 3) stresses that he uses the term *discourse* mainly with reference to naturally occurring written language produced in general social contexts, but also, more importantly, in institutional and organized professional contexts (cf. Koskinen 2008; Prieto Ramos 2018). According to Bhatia (2004: 3), analysis of written discourse has been viewed according to several distinct traditions as *text, genre, professional practice*, and *social practice*. It has also progressed through three phases, in which analysis was centered around the textualization of lexico-grammar, followed by a focus on the structural organization of discourse, and finally the contextualization of discourse (Bhatia 2014). The aforementioned traditions and perspectives will be reflected in the mixed-method approach adopted in the current study (see Section 2.2), as written judicial discourse has not developed in a vacuum, but has been subject to many norms which have come about through the process of institutionalization (cf. Chapter 1).

In her seminal work titled *Tekst, dyskurs, komunikacja międzykulturowa* [*Text, Discourse, Intercultural Communication*], Duszak (1998: 19) adopts a view on *discourse* according to which *discourse* encompasses the whole act of communication, meaning both its specific verbalization (which may also take the form of a written text) and the accompanying extra-linguistic (extra-textual) factors, including a specific context of use and participants. It follows that various forms of *discourse* form one of the elements of interactive communicative competence of language users. Therefore, the degree to which language users are proficient in communicating in a given *discoursal* situation may differ depending on the context. Some instances of discourse may not be accessible to language users who are not familiar with a type of *discourse* requiring a high degree of content knowledge. This, in turn, means that the ability to construe and partake in specific acts of communication is not only dependent on membership of the wider linguistic and cultural community, but also on belonging to a specific *discourse community* (Duszak 1998).

Swales (1990: 9) perceives *discourse communities* as "socio-rhetorical networks that form in order to work towards sets of common goals." According to Swales (1990: 9), those goals are realized by means of specific types of texts (*genres*, see below), the knowledge of which has to be possessed by the members of a particular *discourse community*. Thus, it can be concluded that there are *genres* which are specific (or exclusive) to certain *discourse communities*, but not to their individual members. Duszak (1998: 254) mentions that types of texts such as articles, reviews, or monographs belong to the range of *genres* used within academic *discourse communities*. Likewise, judgments and other related text types are drafted and used primarily within *discourse communities* involved in the practice of law. Belonging to a given *discourse community* means that its members are able to comprehend the information they send or receive in specific text types, but also that they are able to produce such texts according to a set of specific contextual, structural and rhetorical criteria (cf. Rasmussen and Engberg 1999: 114; Bhatia 2014: 163; Borja Albi et al. 2009: 65). Furthermore, competence within *discourse communities* can be gradual, i.e. their members can be either experts (e.g. judges in the respective legal systems), professionals (legal representatives of the parties to the proceedings or active legal professionals), individuals with an intermediate level of knowledge, or novices lacking adequate content and cultural knowledge (cf. Dontcheva-Navratilova 2009: 37; Szczyrbak 2014: 120). It should also be noted that a lack of socio-cultural knowledge may prevent individuals from being a part of a given *discourse community*. Thus, given that CJEU judgments are passed at the supranational level, they may not be fully accessible to the audience in the Member States, including Poland, which may be accustomed (to varying degrees) solely to judgments passed in the national legal system (context). This observation warrants an inquiry into the genre- and register-based analysis of the degree of textual fit of CJEU judgments translated into Polish and non-translated SN judgments (cf. Part II).

It is now possible to establish certain defining characteristics which will allow us to identify CJEU and SN judges as prototypical members of a *discourse community* involved in communicating written authoritative decisions in the form of judgments. According to Swales (1990: 24–27), a *discourse community*:

1. has a broadly agreed set of common public goals (cf. Section 2.3.1);
2. has a mechanism of intercommunication among its members;
3. uses its participatory mechanism primarily to provide information and feedback;
4. utilizes and therefore possesses one or more *genres* in order to attain its goals;
5. in addition to possessing genres, it has acquired some specific lexical items (specialist terminology, acronyms and abbreviations) which allow for efficient communication (cf. Chapter 9);
6. has a threshold level of members with a suitable degree of relevant content and discoursal expertise (ratio between experts and novices).

As observed by Mazzi (2007: 27), CJEU judgments (and, by extension, SN judgments) belong to the *genre* of judicial legal texts, since both of the mentioned types of judgments are:

> governed by the “discourse community” (Swales 1990: 9) of judges, whose communicative purpose is to settle a dispute by presenting well-founded arguments in support of a judicial conclusion through which a number of [...] facts are interpreted within the framework of a valid legal order.

The *discourse communities* made up of CJEU and SN judges, however, cannot be narrowed down only to judges (in the narrow sense of the term) due to the fact that judges have to communicate their judgments to the parties to the proceedings and the wider public (in the wider sense of the term).

A valid account of the judicial *discourse community* is provided by Vannier (2001 after Mazzi 2007: 27). His representation is situated in the context of a democratic state and takes into account a wide range of participants: parties to the proceedings who are not satisfied with the outcome of the proceedings before lower-instance courts may apply to courts of higher instance, which make their binding judgments known to public opinion, which, in turn, may affect future actions of the legislature (cf. Section 3.1.2). Vannier’s framework is particularly important to individuals who become involved in legal proceedings and rely on the rule of law to settle their dispute. Since this representation shows an interconnected system, a court ruling given in a particular legal system, whether it be governed by common or civil law, may find its way to the Supreme Court, which has the power to reverse the decisions of lower-instance courts. The role of the general public in the above system is to express its opinion by taking part in elections, and thereby prompting the legislature to introduce new normative acts or change the already existing ones. Based on the response of public opinion, the legislator may introduce measures aimed at safeguarding the rule of law. In the case of the European Union, being perceived as an institution to which its Member States have delegated parts of their sovereignty,[41] and Poland being one of the EU Member States, the courts representing the highest tier are the CJEU and the SN, respectively. Despite the incongruity of the legal systems, that is EU law and civil law of a Member State, the functions of both courts can be compared to the role of the supreme courts in Vannier's (2001) representation of the judicial *discourse community*.

*Legal language* vs *language of the law*

*Legal language* has both its spoken and written varieties and is concerned with the domain of law (Bhatia 1987: 227). Moreover, without even delving deeper into the different categorizations of *legal language*, it is possible to observe that *legal language* (and, in turn, spoken or written texts produced in this language) is essentially bound to a specific national legal system in which it functions as a communication tool in the legal environment. The *legal language* of the EU is a special case of a specialized language variety, as it is supranational in nature and encompasses a high number of legal cultures from Member States thanks to the policy of multilingualism (see Chapter 1) and translation (cf. Salmi-Tolonen 1994: 39; Derlén 2009, 2015, 2019; Biel 2014a: 57–58) (cf. Chapter 1). Polish *legal language* is essentially confined to the boundaries of the state, as it enables written and oral legal communication within the Polish state entity (cf. Jopek-Bosiacka 2006, 2010); however, it does also exist in the supranational legal order of the EU as a tool for communicating supranational law to Polish citizens and institutions (cf. Biel 2014a).

The terms *legal language* and *language of the law* have fuzzy boundaries, and both are often used interchangeably. According to Bhatia (1987: 227), who does not differentiate between them, the term *language of the law* subsumes:

> several usefully distinguishable genres [see below] depending upon the **communicative purposes** they tend to fulfil, the settings or **contexts** in which they are used, the **communicative events** or activities they are associated with, the **social or professional relationship between the participants** taking part in such activities or events, the **background knowledge** that such participants bring to the situation in which that particular event is embedded and a number of other factors. These genre distinctions are also reflected in the lexico-grammatical, semantico-pragmatic, and discoursal resources that are typically and conventionally employed to achieve successful communication in various legal settings [emphasis added].

---

41 For more information on the topic of exclusive, shared and supportive competences, see Articles 3, 4 and 6 of the TFEU, respectively, as well as Zawidzka-Łojek (2018: 29–39) or consult https://eur-lex.europa.eu/legal-content/EN/TXT/?uri=LEGISSUM%3Aai0020 (accessed: August 18, 2020).

| LANGUAGE OF THE LAW | | | | | |
|---|---|---|---|---|---|
| **Spoken mode of communication** | | | **Written mode of communication** | | |
| Pedagogical setting (lectures, moots) | Academic setting (interaction among academics and students) | Professional setting (lawyer-client consultation, jury instructions, counsel-witness examination) | Academic setting (textbooks, journals) | Juridical setting (cases, judgments) | Legislative setting (I. frozen, e.g. contracts, insurance policies, II. formal, e.g. legislation) |

**Figure 2.1.** *Bhatia's classification of the language of the law (adapted from Bhatia 1987: 227)*

Bhatia's (1987: 227) definition enables the discernment of spoken and written varieties of the *language of the law* and their categorization into communication-enabling *genres* (or varieties of text; this term is explained later in this section) with the use of a range of criteria (communicative purpose, context of use, users and their shared knowledge, as well as lexico-grammatical characteristics) and based on various settings. In Bhatia's classification (see Figure 2.1), judgments are an instance of a written text variety composed in the juridical setting.

Although Bhatia uses the term *language of the law* as an overarching term which encompasses six different settings in which legal texts are produced, it should be stressed that this term should not be used interchangeably with the term *legal language* (cf. Kurzon 1989, 1997). The reason for this is that the former term refers to the language of normative legal acts, whereas the latter concerns the language used to discuss the law (by both professionals and non-professionals) (Kurzon 1989: 283–284). The same observation was made much earlier in the field of Polish legal theory in Bronisław Wróblewski's posthumous book (1948: 56, 136–140) in which *language of the law* [PL: *język prawny*] is the language used primarily by the legislature, whereas *legal language* [PL: *język prawniczy*] is the metalanguage of the law used by lawyers dealing with the law. In the following years, these categorizations started to become more detailed in the Polish language area. Another Polish legal scholar, Maciej Zieliński (1999: 50–72), presented a categorization of the varieties of the *language of the law* and *legal language* based on Wróblewski's (1948) and Ziembiński's (1960, 1974) dichotomous typologies:

Proposing an all-encompassing definition of the term *legal language* remains difficult due to the sheer variety of *legal languages* and the polysemy of the adjective *legal*. Mattila (2006: 4–5) confirms that *legal language* can be divided into

| LANGUAGE OF THE LAW | LEGAL LANGUAGE | | |
|---|---|---|---|
| Language of legal provisions | Language of legal practice | | Language of legal doctrine and education |
| Language of legal norms | Language of jurisprudence | Language of non-jurisprudence | |
| | I. (Quasi-) legal court proceedings | | |
| | II. Court decisions and their justifications | | |

**Figure 2.2.** *Zieliński's categorization of the language of the law and legal language (adapted from Zieliński 1999)*

"sub-genres" according to the various legal professions (e.g. legislators, judges, legal representatives, etc.) and the branches of law and their unique terminology, although he notes that a large part of legal terminology is universal.[42] However, referring to Kurzon's classification (1997: 119–123), Mattila also notes that any classifications of *legal language* are essentially in the eye of the beholder (Mattila 2006: 4). Judgments also resist a clear-cut classification based on either subject matter or function criteria (Peruzzo 2019: 54). In the following section, I will understand the term *judgment(s)* as a hyperonym, that is a term encompassing all varieties (including CJEU and SN judgments as sub-*genres*) of judgements.[43]

*Legal language* also withstands uniform categorization in Translation Studies, which study translated texts in order to understand how they function and, as a side-effect, provide translators and legal practitioners with practical tools. The most valuable classification relevant to the present discussion has been presented by Šarčević (1997: 11), who, drawing on Bocquet (1994), divides legal texts functionally into texts which are: primarily prescriptive (e.g. statutes, contracts), primarily

42 Terminological units in CJEU and SN judgments are dealt with in detail in Chapter 9.

43 A *judgment* [PL: *wyrok*] is a written procedural act consisting of a decision of a court (court ruling) regarding the rights and liabilities of parties to the proceedings before a given court. Apart from judgments, other types of court rulings are: orders [PL: *postanowienia*], orders for payment [PL: *nakazy zapłaty*] and resolutions [PL: *uchwały*] (cf. Bronny 2009: 7; Bladowski 2013: 321–325). CJEU and SN judgments are the sole subject of this study (cf. Chapter 4).

descriptive but also prescriptive (e.g. judgments, appeals), and purely descriptive (e.g. textbooks, articles). The second function-based category includes judgments and shows that they are hybrid in nature, due to the fact that they contain both descriptive and prescriptive elements (cf. Section 2.3.2).

In virtually all legal systems, law depends to a large degree on one primary legal *genre*, that is legislation (normative acts), which is distinct but dependent to a certain extent on three derived secondary genres (e.g. judgments, courtroom genres), pedagogical genres (e.g. textbooks), and target genres (e.g. contracts) (Bhatia 2006: 6–7, 2014: 175) due to their inter-generic relations (cf. Borja Albi 2013: 38; Goźdź-Roszkowski 2011: 22–23). As will be shown later in Part II.A, judgments exhibit frequent references to, for instance, legal acts, which indicates that legislation and judgments form a *system of genres* (cf. Bazerman 1994), or, in a similar vein, a *genre chain* (cf. Fairclough 2003), a *network of genres* (cf. Fairclough 2006), in which legislation occupies a prominent place (cf. Biel 2014a). The question of judgments being related to any other *genres* will not, however, be further investigated in this study, as this topic goes beyond the scope of the study.[44]

The next section will present the theoretical model for the contextual analysis of the genre of judgments.

## 2.2 A mixed genre-register approach to the linguistic profiling of judgments

Despite the fact that the methodology in this study relies heavily on quantitative analysis of corpora, it does not preclude a thorough qualitative analysis of the contexts of the sub-genres of CJEU and SN judgments. In fact, such an analysis may enrich and supplement the quantitative data discussed in Part II of this study by allowing the reader to understand certain linguistic characteristics of judgments thanks to the contextual and structural analysis (cf. Chapter 5). For this reason, my approach draws on the above considerations and stays faithful to the multidimensional GENTT genre-characterization template developed as a methodological starting point for the organization of doctoral research in specialized translation (Borja Albi *et al.* 2009: 65).

Although all of the approaches discussed in Section 2.1, the *genre*, *register* and *style* approaches, may be used to study different varieties of texts, the *genre* approach suits best the purpose of describing the contextual characteristics of complete judgments and their internal structure (cf. Chapter 5). On the other hand, the *register* perspective also seems to be useful, especially when identifying and

44 It needs to be noted that the present study is part of a larger research project (cf. Chapter 1) studying four (legal and semi-legal) genres (legislation, judgments, reports and websites for citizens) representative of the Polish Eurolect – a new hybrid, translator-mediated variety of the Polish language that has been evolving since the accession of Poland to the European Union (EU).

**Table 2.1.** *GENTT genre characterization template (adapted from Borja Albi et al. 2009: 65; cf. Peruzzo 2019: 56)*

| | |
|---|---|
| **1. GENRE** | Name of the genre |
| **2. SUBGENRE** | (if applicable) |
| **3. COMMUNICATIVE ASPECTS** | Register: socio-professional field, mode, level of formality; participants (sender(s), receiver(s)); function |
| **4. FORMAL PROFILE** | Grammatical and lexical cohesion; includes contrastive aspects. |
| **5. MACROSTRUCTURE (MOVE ANALYSIS)** | Identification of the fundamental rhetorical parts of the text (moves and steps, cf. Swales 1981, 1990) |
| **6. RELATION TO OTHER GENRES** | *Systems of genres* (Bazerman 1994), *genre chains* (Fairclough 2003), *networks of genres* (Fairclough 2006) |
| **7. MISCELLANEOUS** | Bibliographical references, etc. |

analyzing frequent and pervasive "formal" lexico-grammatical features of the language (e.g. nominal constructions, prepositions, modal verbs, etc.) prevalent in the stated text type with corpus software (Section 4 of the GENTT template, see Table 2.1). For this reason, the present study focuses on linguistic analysis of the *genre* of judgments and follows the approach adopted in Goźdź-Roszkowski's (2011: 20–23) corpus-based study of seven major genres representing American legal English[45] by using a **combined genre-register approach** supplemented with corpus methodology (cf. Chapter 3).[46]

The research goals connected with investigating the communicative aspects of judgments (Section 3 of the GENTT template, see Table 2.1) will be realized using Dontcheva-Navratilova's (2009: 15) model for contextual genre analysis (later adapted in Szczyrbak 2014) (see Figure 2.3).

45 These genres included: academic journals, briefs, contracts, opinions, professional articles, legislation, and textbooks (Goźdź-Roszkowski 2011: 20–23).

46 In his corpus-based study of linguistic variation in American legal English, Goźdź-Roszkowski (2011: 20) perceives *genre* and *register* as "different *approaches* or *perspectives* for analyzing legal texts rather than different kinds of *texts* or different *varieties*" and uses both of them in a complementary manner by studying complete texts representative of American legal English, as a result of which he identifies important lexico-grammatical features based on their intra-textual frequency of occurrence and analyzes their immediate co-text against the overall macrostructure of a *genre* (Goźdź-Roszkowski 2011: 21–22).

| | |
|---|---|
| **1. Situational characteristics** | 1) Spatio-temporal setting<br>2) Scene<br>3) Subject area |
| **2. Discourse participants** | 1) Identity of the participants (sender(s), addressee(s))<br>2) Social role of the participants<br>3) Extent of shared knowledge<br>a) Shared professional knowledge, including content and terminology<br>b) Shared knowledge of institutional/professional communicative conventions and discoursal expertise<br>c) Shared cultural knowledge |
| **3. Communicative purposes** | 1) Speech acts<br>a) Participation<br>b) Type of speech act<br>c) Directness (direct/indirect)<br>2) Participants' attitude towards the discourse and the message |
| **4. Communicative conventions** | 1) Medium and channel<br>2) Level of interactiveness<br>3) Simple or complex discourse type<br>4) Institutional/professional norms of interaction and interpretation, conventions of discourse production, processing mechanism and circumstances, based on prior experience with specimens of the genre |

**Figure 2.3.** *Dontcheva-Navratilova's model for contextual genre analysis (adapted from Dontcheva-Navratilova 2009: 15; adapted by Szczyrbak 2014: 118–124)*

Figure 2.3 outlines a model for contextual analysis of a genre proposed by Dontcheva-Navratilova (2009: 15). In her work titled *Analysing Genre: The Colony Text of UNESCO Resolutions* (2009), Dontcheva-Navratilova (2009) sets out to establish whether and how the situational context of an international governmental organization and the pragmatic goals involved in cross-cultural interaction influence the linguistic means and the structure of the genre of resolutions and how the language and generic structure influence the process of shaping social relations in this type of discourse. She pays attention to the typical style markers in this language variety, as well as their variation. Dontcheva-Navratilova, using the above framework, observes that UNESCO resolutions developed towards a systematized and codified genre over the decades. Her method of conducting genre analysis is based on the premise that contextually-motivated intentions and expectations of the discourse participants involved in the act of communication shape their linguistic choices. Her theoretical framework builds upon a range of approaches to analyzing discourse, including views on genre analysis introduced by Bhatia (1987, 2002, 2004) and Swales (1981, 1990, 2004). Her model encompasses four levels – situational characteristics, discourse participants, communicative purposes, communicative conventions – each of which encompasses a set of more detailed values.

The macrostructure of CJEU and SN judgments will be analyzed using the analytical-structural approach, consisting of a rhetorical move analysis (cf. Swales 1990, 2004; Bhatia 1993, Duszak 1998: 286; Rasmussen and Engberg 1999; Mazzi 2007a,b; Szczyrbak 2014). The results of the analysis will be presented in Part II.A (Chapter 5), thereby making it possible to establish whether they are conventionalized in terms of variation of generic structure components.

# Chapter 3. Corpus-linguistic methodology and the operationalization of textual fit

This chapter outlines the methodological framework adopted in the present study. First, it briefly describes Corpus Linguistics as a methodology (see Section 3.1), the main approaches to doing corpus research (see Section 3.1.1), and the advantages and disadvantages of corpus methods (see Section 3.1.2). The methodology of the study draws on the design of the Polish Eurolect research project (cf. Introduction), since one of its objectives was to gather data on judgments as one of the four institutional genres representative of EU and Polish administrative discourse. Following Borja *et al.* (2009), in order to account for the multifaceted character of my study (see Section 3.2), I propose the concept of genre as its main organizing principle (cf. Chapter 2). The study applies Biel's (2017 and 2020, *forthcoming*) multi-perspective research framework for the study of legal translation and focuses on translated CJEU judgments, which are the end product of the translation process, and their linguistic distance to non-translated SN judgments (cf. Biel 2014a). To achieve this aim, the chapter re-introduces the concept of textual fit, adapting it for micro-level linguistic analysis of the register of translated CJEU judgments and non-translated SN judgments (see Section 3.3).

## 3.1 Corpus Linguistics as a methodology

Corpus Linguistics (CL) is commonly regarded as a methodology (Lewandowska-Tomaszczyk 2005a,b; Gries 2009: 1; Biel 2010, Biel 2014a: 87–92; Biel and Giczela-Pastwa 2016: 140) which is widely applied in many types of linguistics-oriented studies, Translation Studies (TS) being one such research field (Olohan 2004: 9). Among other research areas applying Corpus Linguistics are Lexicography, Terminology, Discourse Analysis, Computational Linguistics, Sociolinguistics, Forensic Linguistics, the study of language change, and language teaching (Tognini-Bonelli 2001: 1; McEnery *et al.* 2006b: 33; Biel and Giczela-Pastwa 2016: 140–141). It should be noted, however, that there is no general agreement as to the status of Corpus Linguistics in contemporary linguistic research, since some perceive it to be a discipline of its own, not merely a methodology.[47] At the time when CL started to gain popularity thanks to the more widespread use of computers, the development of specialized software enabling the analysis of electronic corpora, and growing public access to institutional documents (cf. Biel 2020), Leech (1992: 106)

47 See Taylor (2008) for a more in-depth investigation.

stated that the use of computers and corpora in linguistic research "defines not just a newly emerging methodology for studying language, but a new research enterprise." Stubbs (1993: 23–24) added that "a corpus is not merely a tool of linguistic analysis but an important concept in linguistic theory" which effectively allows researchers to perceive previously imperceptible phenomena (1996: 231–232). CL is also regarded as a discipline by, among others, Aarts (2002) and Teubert (2005), who posit that CL is a theoretical approach to the analysis of language, and McEnery and Hardie (2012: 1), who describe it as "an area which focuses upon a set of procedures, or methods, for studying language." On the other hand, many researchers, including Thompson and Hunston (2006: 8), and McEnery and Gabrielotos (2006a: 44),[48] view Corpus Linguistics solely as a methodology.

In this study, I regard Corpus Linguistics as an empirical, data-driven, quantitative, descriptive and inductive approach to the study of language use and language varieties (specialized genres) (cf. Chapter 2), which enables observation and analysis of (large) sets of authentic data (with or without prior assumptions) and makes it possible to draw generalizable conclusions (cf. Baker 1995; Stubbs 1996, 2004; Taylor 2008; Gries 2010; Laviosa 2010). In other words, I perceive it as a methodology enabling linguistic research, not a discipline in itself.

### 3.1.1 Corpus-based and corpus-driven approaches to the study of language

The lack of general agreement on the status of Corpus Linguistics as either a fully-fledged theory or a methodological approach does not, however, detract from its usefulness. CL allows for the investigation of naturally-occurring language and its varieties by enabling analyses of vast, balanced and representative collections of electronic texts (corpora), thus greatly increasing the potential of empirical linguistic research on translations and the generalization of research results (cf. Gries 2006: 192; Hu 2016: 3). The extensive application of corpus-linguistic methods in descriptive studies on translations[49] (cf. Toury 1995) focusing primarily on TTs has given rise to the research area called Corpus-based Translation Studies (Laviosa 2002: 5; Biel 2014a: 95). The rise of this new hybrid field of research can be attributed largely to Mona Baker, who laid the groundwork for using corpus methods in comparing translations to non-translations of literary texts (Baker 1993) and predicted that the creation of various types of corpora (including parallel, comparable and

---

48 For more insights into the nature and scope of Corpus Linguistics and corpus-linguistic approaches, see McEnery (2006), Lüdeling (2008, 2009) and O'Keeffe (2010). For a comprehensive overview of corpus studies on EU legal translation, see Biel (2020).

49 On the other hand, corpus-based applied studies focus, among other things, on the development of tools and resources for translators (Biel 2014a: 95).

multilingual corpora[50]) and the application of Corpus Linguistics methodology would facilitate research into the linguistic features of translations and what are known as 'translation universals'[51] (Baker 1995, 1996, 1999) (cf. Tymoczko 1998; Mauranen 2006).

When discussing Corpus Linguistics, one should also not overlook the two seemingly similar but dichotomous approaches to doing research in this area which are often mixed up, namely the corpus-based and corpus-driven approaches[52] (Tognini-Bonelli 2001: 65–100; Biel 2020). In general, the former uses data obtained with the help of corpora to either validate or refute pre-determined hypotheses, whereas the latter uses corpora themselves as sources of hypotheses about language (McEnery and Hardie 2012: 5–6). Corpus-based research takes a given theoretical standpoint as a starting point (Tognini-Bonelli 2001: 65). In the corpus-driven approach, which is inductive and based primarily on unannotated corpora (McEnery *et al.* 2006b: 36), theoretical statements reflect directly the (contextual) evidence provided by the corpus, which makes it possible to determine recurrent patterns and frequency distributions (Tognini-Bonelli 2001: 84, 87). Therefore, corpus-driven research takes practice as the starting point and then moves on to formulating theories. According to Biber and Conrad (2009: 2), in the corpus-driven approach to Corpus Linguistics one assumes only the existence of words and the co-occurrence of patterns among words (as well as quantitative data on their distribution), which are discovered by means of corpus analysis and form the basis for further linguistic descriptions, including qualitative interpretations (cf. Goźdź-Roszkowski 2011: 45).[53]

Although the corpus-based and corpus-driven approaches seem to be quite distinct, in reality they are not as distinct as they might appear at first (Aarts 2002: 121 after McEnery *et al.* 2006b: 35; Pontrandolfo 2019: 16). Both involve articulation of theories at various stages of research, distorting the dichotomous distinction between theory and practice, as it is not possible to approach either corpora or data obtained with their help without any preconceived assumptions (Biel 2017d: 82). This study aims to adopt a mixed version of both approaches to corpus analysis, as will be shown in Section 3.3. For this reason, the present study treats Corpus Linguistics holistically as a comprehensive set of methodological

---

50 For a detailed description of various types of corpora, see Zanettin (2012), Hu (2016: 35–44).

51 See Biel (2014: 96–110) for further discussion (cf. Section 3.3).

52 Other less often discussed approaches involve the corpus-assisted and corpus-informed approach. The former synergizes corpus-linguistic methods with methods from other linguistic and non-linguistic sub-disciplines, e.g. corpus-assisted discourse analysis, whereas the latter involves the consultation of corpora which act as references, e.g. by translators (cf. McEnery *et al.* 2006b).

53 For a more detailed discussion on the two approaches, see Biber (2012). Generally, this distinction is exaggerated, as most contemporary studies combine both approaches (cf. McEnery *et al.* 2006b: 6; Biel 2020).

tools for the linguistic profiling of a specialized language variety (or genre) and leaves the discussion on their nature to theorists (cf., among others, Tognini-Bonelli 2001; Laviosa 2002; McEnery *et al.* 2006b; Gries 2009; Hardie and McEnery 2010). I describe it intentionally as a corpus study, without the qualifications -based or -driven. In a nutshell, the study provides a ready corpus-research model for analysis of the relation of textual fit that can be replicated to investigate other related legal genres (see Section 3.3).

### 3.1.2 Advantages and disadvantages of corpus methodology

The use of corpus methodology in linguistic studies is becoming increasingly popular. The present study continues this tendency by studying comparable corpora of EU and national judgments (cf. Chapter 4). Before I turn to presenting the framework for the analysis of judicial language and the research model, I would like to discuss the advantages and disadvantages of using corpus methods in linguistic analyses of electronic collections of texts, in order to briefly assess the usefulness of corpus methods and, therefore, the framework of the present study in an objective manner.

The use of corpora and corpus-linguistic methodology has many advantages. It is generally held that it expands "methodological horizons and enable[s] researchers to scrutinize translations from a new angle, breaking away from conventional methods and foci" (Biel 2014a: 95). With appropriate software, researchers are able to use corpus methods to swiftly identify patterns of language use, be this at phrase, clause, text or genre level (Biel 2014a: 90) in either small or large collections of texts, and to obtain objective quantitative data on the distribution of lexico-grammatical patterns to methodically verify research hypotheses as well as statistical data on, for instance, the total number of words (tokens) in a corpus, type to token ratio (TTR), the mean word or sentence length, or the average text length. These patterns of language use make it possible to discover certain tendencies (regularities), possibly linking them to cognitive salience (Stubbs 2004: 117). By adopting certain (oftentimes rather subjective) frequency thresholds, which allow for replication, researchers are able to determine what may be considered important and what may be viewed as rather marginal (cf. Gries 2006: 191; Biber and Jones 2009). In general, corpora are either large or small – if the texts in a small specialized corpus are homogenous, the corpus itself does not need to include many texts to be representative of a given language variety (Lee 2010: 114). Generally, it is held that the more specialized the genre, the smaller the corpus can be (Handford 2010: 258). Genre-based corpora have a great potential for identifying recurrent linguistic qualities of various types of texts (Biel 2014a: 94). Lastly, despite focusing on the quantitative characterization of language use, quantitative corpus methods may be supplemented by qualitative methods (methodological triangulation, cf. Zanettin 2012: 12, 28), which is particularly beneficial in Legal Translation Studies (LTS) (Biel 2014a: 95).

Despite its many advantages, the use of corpus methods also has its downsides. The most striking seem to be the problems connected with the creation of representative, balanced and, if applicable, comparable corpora (Biel 2014a: 89; cf. Biber 1993; Wynne 2005; Corpas Pastor 2010). Tymoczko questions the objectivity of corpus-based research by stressing that corpora are "products of human sensibility, connected with human interests and self-interests" (1998: 655), which means that corpus research may be destined to fail if the first stages involving corpus creation are based on false premises and the corpora themselves do not meet the above criteria. The issue of representativeness affects the research questions that can be addressed using a given corpus and the generalizability of research results (Goźdź-Roszkowski 2011: 28). According to Biel (2014: 89), any claims and generalizations made about language are representative of the language sample researched, not of the entire language. The fact that working with corpora allows for the generation of solely quantitative data is also a negative side of corpus methods. In fact, when dealing with large corpora, sometimes "the sheer volume of data for high-frequency items may become unmanageable and result in analysts having to work with a smaller sub-sample" (Koester 2010: 66).[54] This is particularly true when having to analyze dozens or hundreds of concordances, as corpus software requires the vertical reading of texts in the search for recurrence and tendencies, in contrast to traditional horizontal reading practices (Tognini-Bonelli 2001: 3), which, however, may be alleviated by working with annotated corpora. Using unannotated corpora, it is difficult to study certain grammatical patterns and textual phenomena, which may be very time-consuming for inflectional and less used and rarely researched languages, such as Polish, for which there is a low availability of corpora, in particular parallel corpora (Biel 2014a: 90). Furthermore, while it is easy to study patterns, other aspects of discourse, such as communicative and cognitive aspects, or interdiscursivity typical of hybrid genres (cf. Duszak 2006: 49–50), pose technical and methodological problems (Biel 2014a: 90).

My observations concerning the application of the chosen corpus methods and the research model, as well as their limitations, will follow in Chapter 11, which concludes the study and synthesizes the results.

## 3.2 Multi-perspective framework for analysis of judicial language

Linguistic research on translated legal texts conducted in the area of LTS requires a hybrid approach which takes into consideration the most important factors concerning such texts and their environment using both quantitative and qualitative methods (cf. Lewandowska-Tomaszczyk 2012b; Biel 2014a: 95). Biel's

54 This issue will be raised in Chapters analyzing bi- and multinomial structures, terminology (cf. Part II.C, Chapter 8 and Part II.D, Chapter 9).

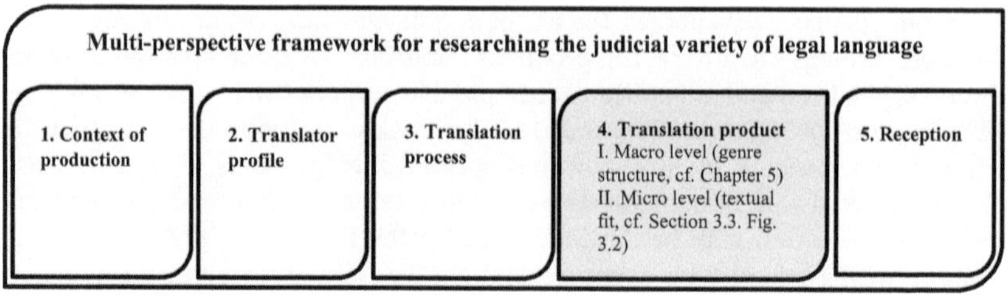


**Figure 3.1.** *Multi-perspective framework for researching the judicial variety of translated legal language (adapted from Biel 2017 and 2020, forthcoming, Saldanha and O'Brien 2014).*

multi-perspective and mixed-method framework for the analysis of legal translation[55] meets these criteria, as it goes beyond the textual level and addresses the context of translated texts (Biel 2020, *forthcoming*). Despite the fact that Biel (2014, 2017) studies predominantly the language of legislative acts – a primary legal genre – court judgments as a secondary legal genre, and written exhibits of the judicial variety of legal language (cf. Chapter 2) also lend themselves to a holistic, multi-dimensional analysis following five key dimensions of translation: (1) the context of production, (2) the translator profile, (3) the translation process, (4) the end product of translation, i.e. the translated texts, and (5) reception (Biel 2020, *forthcoming*, adapted from Biel 2017d: 80–82).

Corpus Linguistics provides possibly the best set of tools for conducting large-scale quantitative investigations into the nature of translated legal (and judicial) texts. It allows for gathering large collections of texts, analyzing them at a speed which would not be possible if we were to rely exclusively on manual analysis, and enables generalizations. Qualitative research, on the other hand, focuses on smaller-scale, manual, descriptive analyses and involves (critical) discourse analysis or sociology of translation (Biel 2017d: 79). Until recently, LTS-based research has been mostly qualitative, which means that corpus methods were not widely used to provide generalizations based on large collections of texts (Biel 2017d: 79; Biel *et al.* 2013: 2), and only rarely accounted for the multidimensional character of legal translations. The first notable forays into this territory were made by several researchers, such as Mazzi (2007a,b), Goźdź-Roszkowski (2011), Borja Albi (2013), Biel (2014), Szczyrbak (2014), Koźbiał (2018), Nikitina (2018), and Biel *et al.* (2019), who primarily employed quantitative methods to empirically study specialized-genre corpora.

Since legal translation is multidimensional, it is no wonder that investigations into the nature of any given legal genre should necessarily take into account the

55 Biel (2017 and 2020, *forthcoming*) adopted this framework from Saldanha and O'Brien (2014).

five main dimensions posited by Biel (2017: 80–82) and triangulate both qualitative and quantitative research methods. Biel (2017: 80) also encourages researchers to provide for the bi-directionality of legal translations in the planning stage of research. According to her, translated legal texts can be characterized by two types of relations: (1) equivalence and (2) textual fit. The former is the relation between STs and TTs, whereas the latter is the relation of TTs to non-translated texts belonging to a comparable (sub-)genre (cf. Chesterman 2004, 2010; Biel 2014a).

Biel (2017: 84) notes that faithfully following her multi-perspective and mixed-method framework for the analysis of legal translation might be difficult in a single study. Therefore, in the present study, the framework dimensions for the analysis of legal translation: (1) the context of production, (2) the translator profile, (3) the translation process, and (4) reception,[56] are studied somewhat perfunctorily in Chapters 1 and 5. Chapter 1 addresses the CJEU's policy of multilingualism, which affects the production and reception of EU judgments, and the translation process, which is facilitated by lawyer-linguists. Chapter 5, on the other hand, uses the methods of genre analysis and describes the profile of translated EU and non-translated SN judgments by examining their contextual (discourse community, communicative purpose and conventions), structural (macro- and micro-structure), and rhetorical characteristics. Biel's (2017: 80) framework resembles the genre-description model in the research area of genre analysis which is presented in Chapter 2, namely the GENTT genre characterization template (Borja Albi *et al.* 2009: 65); however, the latter does not give enough prominence to the role of contextual characteristics involving the production and reception of specialized texts and the specific research methods.

The penultimate dimension in Biel's (2017: 80–82) framework concerns the product itself, which is translated texts. Translated CJEU judgments are the principal focus of this study; they are analyzed comprehensively in relation to comparable non-translated texts in Part II. The present study uses corpus-linguistic methodology (both corpus-based and corpus-driven) to study, that is describe in an organized and quantitative manner, the relation of textual fit of translated CJEU judgments to non-translated SN judgments. By doing so, this study is limited to the investigation of a single specialized genre using the monolingual comparable corpus of translated CJEU judgments and non-translated SN judgments, which is discussed in more detail in Chapter 4. This corpus is well-adapted to investigating

56 Due to the complexity of analyzing reception, I do not empirically explore the topic of TT recipients' expectancy norms and tolerance of the foreign, that is the Polish Eurolect. Any strictly qualitative investigations into the nature of reception should encompass, among others, application and interpretation of translations by recipients and courts, recipients' expectancy norms, legal consequences of TTs and errors, and intralingual translation necessitated by transposition of supranational legal acts into national law (cf. Biel 2020, *forthcoming*).

the degree of naturalness (acceptability) of translations of EU judgments relative to non-translated texts belonging to a comparable (sub-)genre.

The quantitative data obtained in the analysis serve not only to paint a large-scale (macro) picture of the two sub-genres of judgments, allowing for generalizations, but are also used to identify linguistic units for further qualitative analyses, thus shifting to the micro perspective (Biel 2017d: 84).

## 3.3 The relation of textual fit and its operationalization

EU legal translations can be characterized with regard to three dimensions of intertextual relations – concordance, continuity and fit (Biel 2019: 32–35). Although the last type of relation is treated in this study with great detail, it is still necessary to describe the first two types of intertextual relations in which translated CJEU judgments are embedded, so as to provide the context for this study and to indicate issues for further research.

The concordance relation, also referred to as multilingual concordance (TT's appropriacy vis-à-vis the ST; Toury 1995: 70), refers to the horizontal dimension (Robertson 2015: 44) of relations between the translation, all language versions of the same document, and the ST (equivalence between the ST and the TTs). In the context of EU legal genres, the concordance relates primarily to legislative acts, as all language versions are presumed to carry the same meaning in the EU context (Biel 2019: 32). The concordance (equivalence) does not apply directly to CJEU judgments, as "the only authentic version of the judgment handed down by either the Court of Justice or the General Court is that which appears in the language of the case," which can be any of the 24 official EU languages.[57] This means that concordance can be established only between the French language versions of judgments (STs) and other language versions which are the product of direct translation from French (cf. Chapter 1).[58]

The continuity relation also refers to the equivalence between the ST and the TT(s); however, it refers to the vertical dimension within a single language (Biel 2019: 33). Biel (2019: 33–34) modifies Robertson's (2015: 40–42) vertical dimension by dividing it into two sub-dimensions, the relation of continuity and the relation of (textual) fit, to reflect both the supranational and the national context, respectively.

---

57 Source: https://curia.europa.eu/jcms/jcms/Jo2_10739/regime-linguistique-de-la-cour-de-justice-du-tribunal-de-premiere-instance-et-du-tribunal-de-la-fonction-publique (accessed: August 18, 2020).

58 Official EU languages belong to several language families. For instance, both French and Polish belong to the Indo-European family, although the former is a part of the Romance group, while the latter is a part of the Balto-Slavic group as a highly inflectional language with flexible word order. The side-effects of the wide distance between languages might comprise translation difficulties and discrepancies between language versions (cf. Biel 2020).

Continuity is also referred to as consistency (Biel 2019: 33), as it requires translated texts to be in line with the earlier text (especially higher-ranking texts, such as primary EU legislation), mostly in regard to the applied terminology (Prieto Ramos 2014; Stefaniak 2017). Investigation of this type of relation also goes beyond the scope of the present study.

Lastly, the relation of the fit does not describe the equivalence between the ST and the TT(s), but rather the scalar degree of linguistic convergence (or divergence) between the TT(s) (in the case of this study – translated CJEU judgments) and comparable texts[59] in the TL which act as a point of reference (linguistic distance) (Biel 2019: 34–35). Nevertheless, it also refers to the vertical relation within a single language, focusing rather on the supranational context and its relation to the national context (Biel 2014a: 118; Biel 2019: 34–35). The textual fit is also described as naturalness, acceptability or target text family fit (TT vis-à-vis the TL and the target culture, Toury 1995: 70; Chesterman 2004: 6–7), as TL texts are expected over time to create certain expectancy norms among the audience of TTs, determining either a positive or negative reception of translated EU texts in national contexts (Biel 2019: 34, 2020, *forthcoming*). This issue relates to the question of intra-generic variation of EU and national judgments.

It needs to be noted that Toury (1995: 70–74) proposes that the relation of textual fit be studied first, to determine the degree of general acceptability among the audience of TTs, while the relation of equivalence should be investigated afterwards, to establish non-conformities between the STs and TTs. However, both textual fit and equivalence are generally perceived as critical for the quality of translated texts (Biel 2014a: 297). Obviously, prioritizing the relation of textual fit (T-universal) means that the relation of equivalence (S-universal) needs to be abandoned altogether and left for further research. Nevertheless, my preoccupation with textual fit might yield results which could potentially be generalizable to a higher degree than results obtained in a study focused solely on the equivalence relation.

Biel (2014a) popularized the relation of textual fit in her book on the fit of EU legislation translated into Polish to non-translated Polish legislative acts and showed that this relation presents a meaningful parameter for describing translations (Biel 2014a: 287). Her inspiration for the corpus-based study is indebted to, among others, Newmark's principle of equivalent frequency of usage of lexico-grammatical patterns in STs and TTs (1981, 1988 after Biel 2014a: 106), Toury's (1995: 70) call for empirical descriptive studies on translations, Baker's (1995, 1996) proposal to study translated texts against non-translated texts, and Chesterman's (2004: 6–8) approach to the study of translation universals and the differences between translated and non-translated texts which can be brought to attention by means of studying the relations of equivalence and textual fit (see above). Focusing only

59 The equivalence relation is studied with the help of parallel corpora, whereas the textual fit is analyzed with comparable corpora.

on the end product of the translation process, the design of Biel's corpus study did not allow for investigation into the variables which affect the translation process and those which do not. In fact, she postulates that the features of translated texts cannot be attributed only to the translation process and perceives translation universals to be affected by a host of variables (cf. Figure 3.1, Section 3.2), including the wider context of text production and reception or the sub-genre. In her study, Biel (2014: 119) adopted a data-driven approach and took quantitative data on over- and under-representation (cf. Tirkkonen-Condit 2004) obtained with the help of corpora as a starting point for the analysis of textual fit. She did not begin her analysis proper with any of the translation universals (cf. Mauranen and Kujamäki 2004; Mauranen 2006, 2007; Malmkjær 2011).

Biel (2014a: 287–289) presented a model for the description of translated texts and comparable non-translated texts which extends the relation of textual fit beyond translation universals (Biel 2014a: 118–119).[60] Biel operationalized the textual fit by atypical (divergent) frequency (over- or under-representation) of lexico-grammatical (more particularly, textual, grammatical, lexical), phraseological and terminological patterns and their atypical form, focusing on key generic (and salient) features of legislative acts (Biel 2014a: 118). Bearing in mind that the present study is conducted within the framework of the Polish Eurolect project (Biel 2016a), which is a continuation of Biel's (2014) earlier research project limited to the study of the primary EU legal genre, i.e. legislation, I intend to replicate this approach and adapt it to the study of another important EU legal genre – CJEU judgments, since the textual fit hypotheses have not yet been extensively tested on translated court judgments. Despite the fact that Biel conducted a study on the fit of translated EU legislation to national (Polish) legislation, little is known about the extent to which translated judgments differ from TL non-translations.

Below, I present my adaptation of Biel's model (2014: 287–289) which will be used in the study on EU judgments and their fit to non-translated national judgments (see Table 3.1).

The textual fit at the macro (global) level, that is the overall distance of TTs to TL non-translations in terms of their genre macro- and micro-structure is investigated in Part II.A (Chapter 5), partly with the use of corpus methods and manual discourse analysis. Parts II.B-D account for the multi-dimensional nature of the distance of TTs to TL non-translations at the micro (local) level (cf. Goźdź-Roszkowski 2011: 44–51; Biel 2014a: 137–138) by analyzing multiple parameters of variation grouped into three pillars: (I) chosen lexico-grammatical patterns, (II) formulaicity, and (III) terminology. Figure 3.2 outlines the core structure of Part II of the present study.

Pillar I was identified during the literature review. In the analysis of this Pillar, I adopt the same data-driven approach as the one developed by Biel (2014: 119, 137),

60 So far, Biel's model has been replicated by Nikitina (2018: 106–108) in a small-scale study on written pleadings before the European Court of Human Rights.

**Table 3.1.** *Research model for the analysis of the relation of textual fit within the genre of judgments (adapted from Biel 2014a: 287–289)*

| | |
|---|---|
| 1. | **Textual fit** is the degree of linguistic distance between translated and non-translated texts belonging to a comparable (sub-)genre within the vertical dimension of a single language. It may also be referred to as naturalness or acceptability of translations. |
| 2. | Textual fit is scalar and ranges between two extremes – divergence and convergence:<br>• **divergent textual fit** is determined if TTs have a low degree of similarity with TL non-translated texts, whereas<br>• **convergent textual fit** is a result of a high degree of similarity between TTs and TL non-translated texts. |
| 3. | Textual fit is investigated at two levels:<br>• **macro (global) level** – the overall distance of TTs to TL non-translations in terms of their generic macro- and micro-structure (moves and steps),[a]<br>• **micro (local) level** – the distance of TTs to TL non-translations at the (1) lexico-grammatical, (2) phraseological and (3) terminological level (see Figure 3.2). |
| 4. | The measurement of the degree of textual fit is conducted with the help of atypical frequencies[b] and forms of linguistic units:<br>• **overrepresentation** relates to the higher frequency of occurrence of a unit in TTs as compared to TL non-translations, while<br>• **underrepresentation** concerns the lower frequency of occurrence of a unit in TTs relative to TL non-translations. |
| 5. | The study employs several benchmarks in the form of reference corpora to analyze the distribution of linguistic units[c]:<br>• **corresponding TT (sub-)genre** – the reference corpus of translated judgments passed by the General Court (GC) to determine any intra-generic variation or divergence from judgments passed by the Court of Justice (CJ),<br>• **corresponding TL (sub-)genre** – the reference corpus of non-translated judgments passed by the Polish Supreme Court (Civil Chamber) (SN),<br>• **sample of general TL** – the reference corpus of a representative and balanced sample of TL in the form of the National Corpus of Polish (NKJP) as a means of verifying the acceptability (naturalness) of TTs and the degree of divergence from the conventions of general TL.[d]<br>To be more precise, the present study follows three major trajectories of research (Biel 2010, Biel 2014a: 93), aiming to investigate: (1) external variation, i.e. how judicial language (EU and Polish judges' language) differs from general Polish, (2) internal variation, i.e. how judicial sub-genres within the Eurolect differ from each other, and (3) microdiachronic language change (Europeanization), that is how post-accession judicial Polish differs from its pre-accession predecessor. |

(*continued on next page*)

**Table 3.1.** *Continued*

| | |
|---|---|
| 6. | The study employs several key variables apart from the variable of translation product (TT) (see Figure 3.1):<br>• the **context of text production**, the **translator profile**, and **institutional linguistic policy**. |
| 7. | Linguistic units discovered at the micro (local) level (see Point 3 above) are tested for the status of key genre (register) markers based on their distribution in the corpora of judgments relative to general Polish, with the threshold values varying between lexico-grammatical categories[e]:<br>• **positive (salient) markers** have a noticeably higher distribution in both EU and national judgments,<br>• **negative (non-salient) markers** are relatively infrequent in both EU and national judgments as compared to general Polish. |

[a] Although the contextual characteristics (cf. Chapter 5) of the sub-genres of CJ, GC, and SN judgments affect their composition, they are not perceived to form a part of the final linguistic profile of the texts per se. The so-called move analysis, that is the analysis of rhetorical moves and steps, aims to analyze the discourse structure of texts belonging to a given genre (cf. Swales 1981, 1990).
[b] Section 4.5 in Chapter 4 describes the normalization of quantitative data. Normalization is at best a necessary evil, but it enables comparisons of data obtained with the help of corpora with dissimilar sizes.
[c] For a discussion on the design of the corpora used in this study, see Chapter 4.
[d] In the case of, for instance, the analysis of lexical bundles, it is not possible to efficiently investigate the distribution of bundles in the reference corpus of general Polish with the help of an on-line search engine (cf. Chapter 4).
[e] Due to the fact that certain language units, such as conjunctions, have a very high distribution, it is not possible to establish a single threshold value allowing for the differentiation between positive (salient) and negative (non-salient) markers among units belonging to different grammatical categories.

taking into account that it takes translations as the starting point of the analysis. The selection of linguistic features of lexis and grammar in Pillar I was motivated primarily by previous corpus research into the primary legal genre of EU legislative acts (Biel 2014a: 137–222). Other key linguistic units and patterns (demonstrating either over- or under-representation) of the register of judgments to be examined (as potential indicators of translationese, cf. Tirkkonen-Condit 2002; Biel 2014a: 141) were identified with the help of the corpora of judgments by analyzing wordlists and keyword lists generated in Wordsmith Tools 7.0 (WS) (cf. Chapter 4); they were later supplemented with domain-specific patterns identified in the literature review as typical of legal language (cf., among others, Biber 1991; Coulthard and Johnson 2010: 10; Góźdź-Roszkowski 2011; Biel 2014a; Nikitina 2018). These patterns were then analyzed as underlying dimensions of intra-linguistic variation between translated CJEU judgments and non-translated SN judgments (cf.

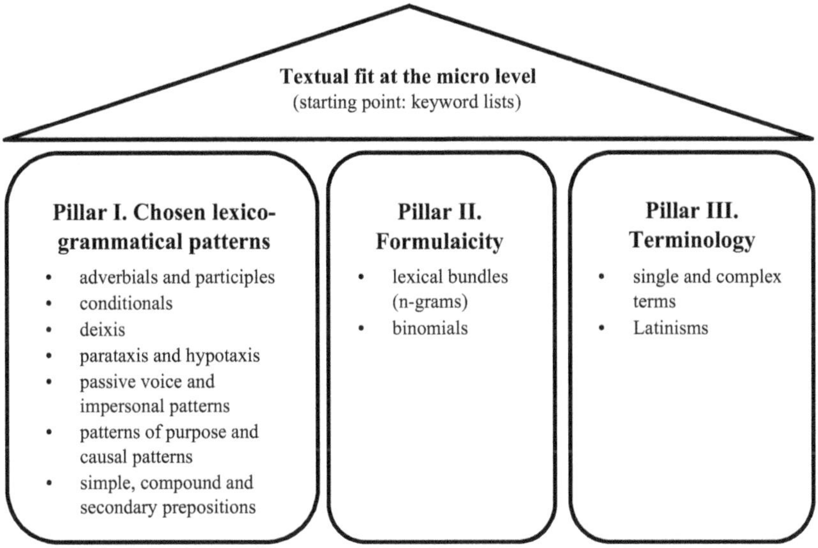


**Figure 3.2.** *Micro-level operationalization of the relation of textual fit of translated CJEU judgments to non-translated SN judgments*

Goźdź-Roszkowski 2011: 45). None of the translation universals served as a sole starting point for the analysis.

Later, upon completion of analysis into the features of language comprising Pillar I and inspired by other studies into the formulaic profile of specialized genres and their terminology (cf., among others, Goźdź-Roszkowski 2011; Biel *et al.* 2018b; Nikitina 2018; Peruzzo 2019), I decided to extend the operationalized model for the analysis of the degree of textual fit of judgments at the micro (local) level by adding two supplementary pillars, i.e. formulaicity (Pillar II) and terminology (Pillar III), in order to more fully profile the genre of judgments. The analysis of the formulaic profile of judgments with the lexical bundles approach is the focus of Pillar II, while the analysis of bi- and multinomials is an exploratory analysis which aims to discover whether bi- and multinomial constructions, which are a salient feature of legal English, are also a characteristic feature of judicial Polish.

Although, from the linguistic point of view, it might seem that Pillar III should be included in the first one, as terms form the larger lexicon of any language, the special position occupied by terminology and terminology work in the EU (cf. Koźbiał 2017; Stefaniak 2017) calls for particular attention to be paid to this topic. The inclusion of Latinisms in this pillar is due to the important role they play in judicial (and overall in legal) language. Another argument in favor of studying term-related units separately from lexis contained in Pillar I is that terms and

Latinisms represent a major focus of the study due to the nature of the genre of judgments.

The methodological approaches adopted in each of the three pillars will be discussed at the beginning of the respective chapters in Part II. Any aspects of linguistic analysis accounting not only for the relation of textual fit but also the relation of equivalence not undertaken in my study will be identified in the synthesis (see Chapter 11).

# Part II. Empirical study

# Chapter 4. Design of the JURIDIC corpus

This chapter describes the design of the monolingual, genre-restricted comparable corpus used in this study. The overarching purpose of the corpus of EU and national judgments is to allow and facilitate an extensive genre-register analysis of the degree of textual fit of CJEU judgments translated into Polish and non-translated SN judgments, which are representative of judicial language (see Section 4.1). A well-thought-out corpus structure (see Section 4.2) is crucial in a study which aims to uncover the characteristics of translated and non-translated language at the macro- and micro-level for the generalization of quantitative results. The chapter aims to demonstrate that both corpora used in the present study can be analyzed using corpus-linguistic methodology (see Chapter 3) within the wider research area of Translation Studies (cf. Biel 2010, 2014, 2016; Biel *et al.* 2019). The applicability of the said corpora will be evaluated based on three basic criteria – representativeness, balance and comparability (see Section 4.3). These (somewhat subjective) criteria are widely used to evaluate large (electronic) corpora in terms of their suitability for corpus studies and their specific research goals (cf. Biber 1993; McEnery and Wilson 2001; McEnery *et al.* 2006b; Biel 2010; Tognini-Bonelli 2011; Zanettin 2011, 2012). Section 4.4. discusses the software used in the study, while Section 4.5 discusses the normalization procedure and statistical measures.

## 4.1 Corpus design

McEnery and Wilson's (2001: 24) definition of a corpus states that a corpus is "a finite-sized body of machine-readable texts sampled in order to be maximally representative of the language variety under consideration." Since corpora made up of texts belonging to one specific genre enable research into patterns of linguistic variation within the realm of legal language studies (cf., among others, Goźdź-Roszkowski 2011; Trklja and McAuliffe 2019; Peruzzo 2019; Prieto Ramos *et al.* 2019), as well as research into the differences between translations and non-translations (cf. Biel 2014a; Biel *et al.* 2019; Nikitina 2018), I believe that the creation of a genre-restricted corpus of judgments will allow research into the characteristic features of the language of CJEU and Polish judges. Consequently, both corpora created for the purpose of this study comprise solely judgments passed by the Court of Justice of the European Union (CJEU), more specifically the Court of Justice (CJ) and the General Court (GC) judgments, and judgments delivered by the Civil Chamber of the Supreme Court of the Republic of Poland (SN).[61] These two sub-genres of CJEU judgments translated into Polish and

61 The question of comparability of CJEU and SN as regards their contextual characteristics will be addressed in Chapter 5.

non-translated SN judgments constitute one of the four prototypical genres of EU communication studied within the Polish Eurolect project. My involvement in the Polish Eurolect project necessitated the adoption of basic characteristics of corpus design set by the principal investigator, such as: the language of non- and translated texts, the number of sub-corpora, the time frames of the pre- and post-accession corpora, the inclusion of only full-length texts (cf. Goźdź-Roszkowski 2011: 28), the application of the NKJP reference corpus, or the unified base value for the normalization of quantitative results (cf. Biel 2016a). The adoption of the same key criteria of corpus design was motivated by the need to provide data that could be related to other genre-restricted corpora within the Polish Eurolect,[62] thus making it possible to gain insights, among others, into the inter-generic variation within the Eurolect.

The EU corpus, that is the genre-restricted CJEU monolingual corpus comprising Polish language versions of CJ and GC judgments (see Section 4.2.1), will be used to conduct a quantitative corpus analysis of the register of translated EU judgments in terms of their formal characteristics (typical features of translations). The results will be juxtaposed with the data gathered from the comparable national corpus of SN judgments (see Section 4.2.2), thanks to which it will be possible to determine the degree of textual fit of translated EU judgments to non-translated national judgments, in an effort to determine the overall linguistic profile of the two sub-genres of judgments. This preliminary description demonstrates that this study makes use of a translation-driven monolingual comparable corpus (Baker 1995: 234–238; Biel 2010: 3).[63] Such a corpus contains translated texts and non-translated texts in a single language, Polish, and allows investigations into the textual fit of the former to the latter (Biel 2010: 3). A comparable corpus should allow me to capture and compare both global (e.g. average text, sentence and word length, type-token ratio, lexical density) and local lexico-grammatical, formulaic and terminological patterns (see Figure 3.2, Chapter 3) which are either restricted to translated judgments or

62 The Polish Eurolect project investigated four genres representative of EU administrative discourse, that is legislation, judgments, reports and official websites for EU citizens, and juxtaposed the texts belonging to these genres with non-translated, comparable Polish texts (cf. Biel 2016a: 202).

63 CJEU judgments are generally drafted in French (unless the language of procedure is English, in which case judges may resort to English to draft a given judgment), which means that a parallel corpus of English and Polish language versions of CJEU judgments would not be methodologically adequate to study the relation of equivalence (Biel 2010: 8, 2014). This type of relation is studied on the basis of the other genres in the Polish Eurolect Project. For this reason, the present study focuses on the relation of textual fit (lexical variety/density, under- and over-representation of lexico-grammatical items), by analyzing all CJEU judgments (with the following languages of the case: English, French, German and Polish), and the issue of Europeanization (cf. Chapter 3).

| | | |
|---|---|---|
| Polish language versions of CJEU judgments | Non-translated SN judgments | NKJP – Reference corpus of general Polish |

**Figure 4.1.** *JURIDIC corpus design – monolingual comparable corpus of translated CJEU judgments and non-translated SN judgments*

which occur with a significantly higher or lower frequency in translations relative to comparable non-translated judgments.

The structure of the JURIDIC corpus, a translation-driven **monolingual comparable corpus** used in the present study,[64] is shown in Figure 4.1.

The application of the National Corpus of Polish (NKJP) reference corpus (see Section 4.2.3) will make it possible to compare the data obtained from the genre-restricted corpora against general Polish.

The next section will describe the structure of the sub-corpora comprising the JURIDIC corpus. In addition, it will provide information on the source of texts incorporated into the corpora, the criteria according to which they were selected, and their format.

## 4.2 Structure of the individual sub-corpora

This section provides an account of the structure and characteristics of both corpora containing EU and national judgments, including the criteria adopted to compile the individual sub-corpora.

### 4.2.1 CJEU corpus

The CJEU corpus is a monolingual corpus of two sub-genres of judgments — CJ and GC judgments translated into Polish. Table 4.1 shows the number of texts included in the individual sub-corpora of CJ and GC judgments, the total number of tokens (running words) in each corpus and the number of types (different words).

The full texts of CJ and GC judgments included in the corpus of CJEU judgments were downloaded at the beginning of 2016 from the InfoCuria portal, which stores the case-law of the CJEU.[65] The main sub-corpora of the CJEU corpus are the sub-corpora of CJ and GC judgments, all of which encompass the same five-year period 2011–2015.

64 For replication purposes, the JURIDIC corpus is available at https://eurolekt.ils.uw.edu.pl/pl-eurolect-corpus/ (accessed: August 18, 2020).

65 The InfoCuria portal is available at http://curia.europa.eu/juris/recherche.jsf?language=en (accessed: August 18, 2020).

**Table 4.1.** *Polish language versions of Court of Justice of the EU judgments (Court of Justice and General Court)*

| Sub-corpus | Texts | Time depth | Tokens | Types |
|---|---|---|---|---|
| CJ | 897 | 2011–2015 | 4,693,968 | 72,310 |
| GC | 384 | 2011–2015 | 4,515,866 | 65,318 |
| **Total** | **1281** | **2011–2015** | **9,209,834** | **97,335** |

In the process of compiling the CJEU corpus, I also decided to collect more detailed statistical data, which are organized: (1) according to the year of publication of CJ and GC judgments (see Table 4.2), and (2) according to the language of procedure[66] (see Table 4.3).

Table 4.2 shows that there are certain differences not only between the CJ and GC sub-corpora, but also internal differences in each of them. The differences in statistical measures between parts of the sub-corpora containing judgments delivered in each year of the five-year time frame can be attributed to differing volumes of case-work carried out by the CJ and the GC.[67] On the whole, small discrepancies notwithstanding, both sub-corpora are comparable. Furthermore, the sub-genres of CJ and GC judgments are perceived to remain at the same stage of their evolution (cf. Leech 2007: 143).

The homogeneity of the CJEU corpus can also be observed if it gets broken down according to the language of procedure (see Table 4.3). This breakdown shows that the low number of judgments with Polish as the language of procedure (the language in which a case before the Court is initiated) may affect the overall statistical characteristics of a corpus. Nevertheless, since the CJEU corpus contains all CJ and GC judgments passed in the 2011–2015 period with four different languages of procedure, this does not in any way affect the overall usefulness of the corpus. In other words, the sub-corpora are analyzed as a whole, as it is not the goal of this study to investigate the influence of the language of the case on translated judicial language.

All CJEU judgments were downloaded according to the following criteria:

- Case status: cases closed,
- Court: either the Court of Justice (CJ) or the General Court (GC),
- Documents: Documents published in the ECR (judgments),
- Period or date: Date of delivery (1 January 2011 – 31 December 2015).

66 The texts included in the CJEU sub-corpora are judgments with four languages of procedure – English, German, French, and Polish.

67 Judicial activity of the CJEU in the form of the statistics concerning the number of new cases, completed cases, and cases pending can be verified in annual reports available at the website of the CJEU – https://curia.europa.eu/jcms/jcms/Jo2_7000/en/ (accessed: August 18, 2020).

**Table 4.2.** *Corpora of Polish language versions of CJ and GC judgments (2011–2015) broken down according to the year of publication*

| Sub-corpus | Texts | Tokens | Types | Average text length (tokens) | TTR | STTR | STTR SD | Mean sentence length (words) | SD | Mean word length (letters) | Word length SD |
|---|---|---|---|---|---|---|---|---|---|---|---|
| CJ 2011 | 176 | 1,024,741 | 34,945 | 5,371 | 3,70 | 43,35 | 56,39 | 27,00 | 25,08 | 5,91 | 3,77 |
| CJ 2012 | 172 | 901,115 | 32,520 | 4,836 | 3,91 | 43,04 | 56,81 | 26,94 | 24,75 | 5,91 | 3,77 |
| CJ 2013 | 193 | 1,002,880 | 33,994 | 4,800 | 3,67 | 43,46 | 56,33 | 26,99 | 24,46 | 5,91 | 3,78 |
| CJ 2014 | 173 | 857,409 | 31,980 | 4,572 | 4,04 | 42,94 | 57,04 | 28,17 | 25,43 | 5,93 | 3,78 |
| CJ 2015 | 183 | 907,823 | 33,699 | 4,556 | 4,04 | 42,84 | 56,78 | 28,11 | 25,08 | 5,93 | 3,80 |
| GC 2011 | 97 | 1,283,136 | 32,933 | 12,260 | 2,77 | 42,49 | 57,65 | 27,94 | 22,47 | 5,85 | 3,70 |
| GC 2012 | 59 | 685,510 | 26,231 | 10,753 | 4,13 | 43,55 | 55,73 | 27,96 | 21,45 | 5,86 | 3,71 |
| GC 2013 | 56 | 659,259 | 25,450 | 10,880 | 4,18 | 43,02 | 57,22 | 28,79 | 23,12 | 5,91 | 3,74 |
| GC 2014 | 75 | 842,166 | 30,030 | 10,353 | 3,87 | 43,26 | 56,61 | 27,13 | 21,85 | 5,88 | 3,72 |
| GC 2015 | 97 | 1,045,795 | 34,975 | 9,921 | 3,63 | 42,59 | 57,33 | 27,67 | 22,85 | 5,85 | 3,73 |

**Table 4.3.** *Corpora of Polish language versions of CJEU judgments (CJ and GC) broken down according to the language of procedure (time period: 2011–2015)*

| Language of procedure | Texts | Tokens | Types | Average text length (tokens) | TTR | STTR | STTR SD | Mean sentence length (words) | SD | Mean word length (letters) | Word length SD |
|---|---|---|---|---|---|---|---|---|---|---|---|
| English | 430 | 3,773,571 | 62,438 | 8,119 | 1,79 | 43,02 | 42,02 | 27,89 | 23,33 | 5,89 | 3,73 |
| French | 312 | 2,283,868 | 48,651 | 6,753 | 2,31 | 43,01 | 56,85 | 27,47 | 23,82 | 5,87 | 3,73 |
| German | 488 | 2,897,898 | 58,699 | 5,469 | 2,20 | 43,04 | 56,84 | 27,46 | 24,21 | 5,92 | 3,79 |
| Polish | 51 | 254,497 | 15,020 | 4,569 | 6,45 | 42,73 | 56,56 | 26,89 | 23,39 | 5,91 | 3,78 |

The texts were downloaded manually and saved as individual files in TXT format, in order to ensure compatibility with the corpus analysis software WS (see Section 4.4). Prior to analysis in WS, the encoding of the files was changed to UTF-16 with the help of the *Text converter* utility in WS.

The individual files were named according to the following conventions:

- the first character stands for the type of a court judgment — it is the letter "W" in the case of all CJEU judgments,
- the next four characters indicate the year in which a given judgment was delivered, ranging from 2011 to 2015,
- the next character ("C" – Court of Justice, or "T" – General Court) along with the following number (in some cases also with the letter "P" indicating an appeal) form the case signature,
- letters "T" and "S" stand for judgments passed by the CJ and the GC, respectively,
- the last two characters stand for the language of the judgment ("PL" – Polish).

Here are some exemplary names of files comprising the CJEU corpus:

1. W2011T809SPL – Judgment of the General Court delivered in 2011 (case no. T-8/09),
2. W2015C2013TPL – Judgment of the Court of Justice delivered in 2015 (case no. C-20/13).

### 4.2.2 SN corpus

The SN corpus is also a monolingual reference corpus. It serves as a benchmark for comparing the data obtained with the help of the CJEU corpus. As opposed to the CJEU corpus, it contains only one sub-genre of judgments, that is judgments passed by the Civil Chamber of the Supreme Court of the Republic of Poland (SN). I decided not to include judgments passed by other chambers of the SN, since this would lead to further inflation of the already high total number of texts in this corpus. Table 4.4 below contains data regarding the number of texts included in individual corpora of judgments, number of tokens (running words) and number of types (different words). All judgments included in the post-accession corpus (SN_2011–2015) were delivered in the period 2011–2015 and downloaded from the Court's online repository of judgments,[68] whereas the pre-accession corpus (SN_1999) contains all judgments which could be retrieved from Wolter Kluwer's LEX database, a portal for practicing lawyers.[69]

---

68 It is available at http://www.sn.pl/orzecznictwo/SitePages/Baza_orzeczen.aspx (accessed: August 18, 2020).

69 Wolter Kluwer's LEX requires a subscription fee and is available at https://borg.wolterskluwer.pl/ (accessed: August 18, 2020). The official SN repository does not enable access to judgments delivered as early as 1999.

**Table 4.4.** *SN corpus – judgments of the Civil Chamber of the Supreme Court of the Republic of Poland*

| Sub-corpus | Texts | Time depth | Tokens | Types |
|---|---|---|---|---|
| SN_2011–2015 | 2,564 | 2011–2015 | 6,833,997 | 76,783 |
| SN_1999 | 401 | 1999 | 504,605 | 24,336 |

All texts comprising the SN sub-corpus were downloaded at the beginning of 2016. Table 4.5 contains detailed data (average text/sentence/word length, TTR, STTR, among other things) on the composition of the SN sub-corpora broken down according to the year of publication.

The distributional characteristics of the sub-corpora making up the larger SN_2011–2015 corpus are indicative of its uniform composition. The purpose of the pre-accession SN corpus is to study the influence (Europeanization) of CJEU case-law on the language of national judgments. The size of this corpus is about 85 % smaller than the SN_2011–2015 corpus and includes 401 judgments passed by the same chamber of the SN in 1999. Although it could be assumed that for this research purpose the pre-accession corpus should be compared with a post-accession corpus of a more comparable size, I discovered that it was not necessary to create a separate post-accession corpus to establish the degree of Europeanization of national judgments, since the present post-accession corpus produces almost identical results as a corpus comprising only judgments delivered in, say, 2015.[70] The decision not to create such a corpus will allow me to present less cluttered tables containing quantitative data in the later chapters (see Part II). Overall, SN judgments are also perceived to remain at the same stage of their evolution (cf. Leech 2007: 143).

The manner of text selection applied in the creation of the pre-accession corpus guarantees the possibility of relating the pre-accession data to the post-accession period, the only difference being that the texts included in the former were downloaded from a different source (see above). Following the requirements set out by the Polish Eurolect project, I chose the year 1999 as a cut-off date to ensure that the EU's influence on national judgments would still be non-existent, or at best minimal, prior to Poland's accession to the EU in 2004. Of course, this solution does not take into consideration such non-textual (or rather non-systemic) factors as the wider geo-political context.

---

70 During the analysis of empirical data, I found out that both the 2011–2015 and the 2015 post-accession corpora produce nearly identical normalized results (see Section 4.5). Nevertheless, this finding did not alter the fact that the 2011–2015 needed to remain the main post-accession corpus, which was necessitated by the framework of the Eurolect project.

**Table 4.5.** *Corpora of non-translated SN judgments (1999, 2011–2015) broken down according to the year of publication*

| Sub-corpus | Texts | Tokens | Types | Average text length (tokens) | TTR | STTR | STTR SD | Mean sentence length (words) | SD | Mean word length (letters) | Word length SD |
|---|---|---|---|---|---|---|---|---|---|---|---|
| SN 1999 | 401 | 504,605 | 24,336 | 1,176 | 5,16 | 45,09 | 54,57 | 21,44 | 17,28 | 5,67 | 3,68 |
| SN 2011 | 507 | 1,272,006 | 36,679 | 2,317 | 3,12 | 43,78 | 56,14 | 23,66 | 19,55 | 5,64 | 3,76 |
| SN 2012 | 531 | 1,426,861 | 39,510 | 2,485 | 2,99 | 44,04 | 55,93 | 23,48 | 19,75 | 5,66 | 3,76 |
| SN 2013 | 478 | 1,324,443 | 39,679 | 2,566 | 3,24 | 44,10 | 55,99 | 23,95 | 20,96 | 5,67 | 3,77 |
| SN 2014 | 495 | 1,330,725 | 40,173 | 2,487 | 3,26 | 44,56 | 55,39 | 23,89 | 20,63 | 5,66 | 3,76 |
| SN 2015 | 553 | 1,479,103 | 40,397 | 2,470 | 2,96 | 43,97 | 55,79 | 23,33 | 19,66 | 5,63 | 3,77 |

| | |
|---|---|
| SN_1999 | SN_2011-2015 |

**Figure 4.2.** *Pre-accession and post-accession sub-corpora of non-translated SN*

All SN judgments were downloaded according to the following criteria:

- Form of judicial decision (PL – *Forma orzeczenia*) → Polish Supreme Court judgments (PL – *wyroki SN*);
- Issue date (PL – *Data wydania*) → from... to... → 1 January 2011 – 31 December 2015;
- Chamber (PL – *Izba*) → Civil Chamber (PL – *Izba Cywilna*).

The naming conventions of files contained in the pre- and post-accession SN sub-corpora are less complicated than in the case of files in the CJEU corpus. The name of each file in this corpus contains only the case signature of a judgment. Here are two exemplary names of files from the SN corpus:

1. i cnp 1–11[71] (case no. I CNP 1/11),
2. v csk 379–11 (case no. V CSK 379/11).

### 4.2.3 The National Corpus of Polish (NKJP)

Since the SN corpus is used as a benchmark corpus of specialized judicial language against which the data collected with the help of the CJEU corpus are compared, in the study, I decided to include another reference corpus, the National Corpus of Polish (NKJP), as a representative sample of general (as opposed to specialized) Polish language (Przepiórkowski *et al.* 2012). This will allow me to provide a background for the interpretation of data gathered with the (sub-)genre-specific corpora. The balanced version of the corpus contains about 240.2 million words and is composed of: books (29 %), press articles (50 %), other written texts (administrative texts, letters) (4 %), Internet sources (7 %) and spoken texts (10 %). I searched the balanced version of the NKJP corpus using PELCRA (cf. Pęzik 2012).

## 4.3 Representativeness, balance and comparability of the sub-corpora

In order to create a corpus suitable for its intended purpose, the corpus linguist needs to ensure that it meets three criteria: representativeness, balance, and comparability (cf. Rieger 1979; Biber 1990, 1993; Wynne 2005; Leech 2007;

71 The last two digits in the names of files from the SN corpus do not necessarily indicate the actual year in which a judgment was delivered.

Biel 2010; Corpas Pastor and Seghiri Domínguez 2010; Goźdź-Roszkowski 2011; Prieto Ramos *et al.* 2019). The corpus compiled for the purpose of this study follows the genre-based framework of the Polish Eurolect corpus built within the framework of the Polish Eurolect research project (cf. Biel 2016a).[72] To a certain degree, this constitutes a limitation imposed on this study, since its general framework must comply with that of the research project in order to provide comparable quantitative data which allow for determination of the inter-generic variation in EU discourse, its textual fit to non-translated Polish administrative discourse, and the degree of Europeanization of Polish administrative discourse. In light of the above, it was essential that the sub-corpora of CJEU and SN judgments compiled for the purpose of this study also be comparable, balanced and representative, in order to conform to the requirements posed by the larger research project.

The question of delineating the scope of texts to be included in corpora (population) is crucial in studies conducted with the help of corpus-linguistic methodology. In practice, corpus design may limit the researcher as to the scope of studies carried out on a given corpus (cf. Sinclair 1991). According to Biber (1993: 243), before attempting to define the sampling procedures for the corpora, it is necessary to define as clearly as possible the limits of the population. In the case of corpora used in this study, the strict boundaries are perceived as the post-accession period of 2011 to 2015, as well as the pre-accession period marked by the year 1999. There was no need to establish any complex sampling method, since all sub-corpora were to include every single judgment passed by the CJ, GC and the Civil Chamber of the SN within the stated period, thus avoiding additional problems connected with representativeness. Sampled versions of the post-accession corpora have only been used to conduct several analyses for the purposes of this study, in order to limit the total number of concordances requiring manual verification and to make their analysis more feasible (cf. Chapters 8 and 9). As regards the accessibility of texts included in the corpora, they are available in the public domain in electronic form and have no copyright restrictions (cf. Sinclair 1991: 14–15).

The first key issue related to designing corpora is their representativeness. Since corpora are designed to represent certain language varieties, findings based on them can be generalized only to the given language variety (Leech 1991: 27). Biber claims that representativeness relates to the question of whether a corpus represents the range of text types in a given population, which, in turn, may guarantee the representativeness of the range of linguistic distributions in a given language variety (Biber 1993: 243). In other words, "representativeness refers to the extent to which a sample includes the full range of variability in a population"

72 The Eurolect: An EU variant of Polish and its impact on administrative Polish, NCN grant (the Polish National Science Centre) no. 2014/14/E/HS2/00782, Sonata BIS, 2015–2020.

(Biber 1993: 243). In my opinion, all individual sub-corpora described in Section 4.2 meet this requirement, since all are large[73] and contain only judgments which are clearly representative of the judicial variety of legal language. The fact that both corpora comprise all the texts published in the post-accession period of 2011–2015 and the pre-accession period of 1999 is a guarantee of their (subjective) representativeness. Thus, it will be possible to generalize the results of this study to the whole population under analysis. The results will be generalizable to the totality of texts belonging to the same sub-genres only to a limited degree (cf. McEnery and Wilson 2001: 77). Based on the compiled corpora, I will be able to draw tentative conclusions as to whether the linguistic patterns present in translated and non-translated texts are also characteristic of other texts which make up the same textual universe but remain outside the sampling frame of the created corpora (Zanettin 2011: 15).

Appropriate balance presents the second important issue concerning compilation of corpora for specific purposes. However, it refers to corpora which are to comprise texts belonging to more than one genre. Sinclair (2005) refers to balance as a rather vague notion and claims that a balanced corpus relies on the researcher's intuition and estimates, which reveals that there is possibly no objective way of balancing a corpus. Gries claims that:

> ideally not only should all parts of which a variety consists be sampled into the corpus but also that the proportion with which a particular part is represented in a corpus should reflect the proportion the part makes up in this variety and/or the importance of the part in this variety (Gries 2009: 7).

An appropriate balance would become an issue if I were to include other types of texts produced by the respective courts, such as orders, summaries or press releases. Such a decision would necessitate assessing a significantly larger amount of quantitative data. This means that balance is not a *sine qua non* of this study, as the embeddedness of this study in the Polish Eurolect project has pre-determined the composition of genre-restricted corpora of judgments, which required the inclusion of all texts published in a given period. Therefore, the only sub-genres included here are CJEU and SN judgments, which eliminated the need for balancing the corpora.

The last issue connected with the design of the sub-corpora used in this study relates to their comparability, which depends to a great degree on representativeness (Leech 2007: 142). This criterion will be touched upon in the description of the contextual, macro-textual and rhetorical characteristics of CJEU and SN judgments (see Chapter 5). Both CJEU judgments representing the supranational context and SN judgments representing the national context belong to the same

73 Goźdź-Roszkowski (2011: 28) recommends specialized corpora representing a given general category of specialized language to ideally include full-texts totaling over one million words.

genre of judicial texts, namely the genre of judgments. For this reason, they are perceived here as two separate but (to a limited extent) comparable sub-genres owing to the totality of their textual and extratextual qualities and despite the distinct jurisdictions of both types of courts, which are those of the CJEU and the SN. This means that they can be subjected to a synchronic and diachronic comparative (contrastive) linguistic analysis.

## 4.4 Software

The corpora were analyzed primarily with Wordsmith Tools 7.0 developed by Mike Scott[74] (Scott 2017). Due to the large size of both corpora, the time-consuming nature of the process of analysis and the lack of reliable resources facilitating its automation, I decided not to lemmatize[75] and annotate the texts included in the corpus. The bulk of the analysis of quantitative data obtained with WS was carried out in Microsoft Excel.

To a limited degree, I also used several online tools, including Sketchengine[76] (Kilgariff *et al.* 2014) and TermoPL,[77] an online tool equipped with a POS-tagger for automatic extraction of domain-related terminology (see Chapter 9). I also used AntPConc,[78] a freeware parallel corpus concordancing tool, and LF-Aligner 4.1[79] to automatically align a small sample of English and Polish language versions of CJEU judgments, in order to swiftly obtain corresponding excerpts containing chosen lexico-grammatical patterns from the English language versions of CJEU judgments.

## 4.5 Normalization of corpus data and statistical measures

Due to the dissimilar sizes of both the CJEU sub-corpora and the SN sub-corpora in terms of the total number of tokens, the observed raw frequencies of occurrence

---

74 Wordsmith Tools 7.0 is available at https://www.lexically.net/wordsmith/downloads (accessed: August 18, 2020).

75 At the initial stage of my work in the research project, I attempted to lemmatize my corpora with LEM, an online tool available within the CLARIN-PL network (https://ws.clarin-pl.eu/lem.shtml), which makes it possible to derive base forms of inflected words in Polish. Upon a closer examination of the lemmatized corpora, I decided not to use them in my study due to numerous errors.

76 Sketchengine is available at: https://www.sketchengine.eu (accessed: August 18, 2020).

77 TermoPL is available at: http://ws.clarin-pl.eu/termopl.shtml# (accessed: August 18, 2020).

78 AntPConc is available at: https://www.laurenceanthony.net/software/antpconc (accessed: August 18, 2020).

79 LF Aligner is available at: https://sourceforge.net/projects/aligner (accessed: August 18, 2020).

(RF) obtained in WS based on the corpora in whole (that is not based on single texts) need to be normalized. Goźdź-Roszkowski rightly observes that normalization of data in quantitative research is necessary to compare the distribution of various linguistic features across corpora varying in sizes (2011: 31); however, he does not employ a single base of 1,000,000 words (he uses it only to compare the distribution of lexical bundles), but also uses a second base of 1,000 words to compare the distribution of linguistic features such as pronouns, nouns or prepositions. Since, as has already been stated, this study forms a part of research conducted within the Eurolect project, it also needs to use the same or similar methodological approach, in order to allow for comparability of quantitative data (cf. Biel 2014a; Biel *et al.* 2018b, 2019). For this reason, I decided to use a single common base of 1,000,000 words for normalization of my data in all empirical chapters. The normalized frequencies (NF) were obtained by multiplying the raw frequency by 1 million[80] and dividing the result by the total number of tokens in a given corpus. Excel spreadsheets were used to normalize RF values (cf. Goźdź-Roszkowski 2011: 31; Biel 2014a: 135–136).

In order to compare quantitative data from any two given corpora, I use the effect size metric, %DIFF, which effectively measures the size of the difference between two normalized frequencies in a pair of corpora. This metric does not provide any measures of statistical significance[81] (cf. Taylor and Marchi 2018: 236).

The corpora used in Chapters 8 and 9 to analyze binomials and terminological units are sampled versions of the corpora described in this chapter. Since these corpora are sampled and do not contain all the texts published in the post-accession period, I decided to provide two statistical measures next to the quantitative data, namely Log Likelihood (LL) and Bayes Factor (BIC), which were calculated with the downloadable spreadsheet available at http://ucrel.lancs.ac.uk/llwizard.htm. LL and BIC measures are not provided in the remaining empirical chapters because of the assumption that unsampled corpora containing the whole population of texts from a given time frame allow for sufficient generalization of the quantitative results and do not necessarily require tests of statistical significance (cf. Section 4.3).

80 I decided to choose 1 million as a base value, in order to allow for a certain degree of comparability of the results with similar studies on specialized language varieties. It should be noted, however, that some studies on varieties of legal language set the base value at 100,000 words (cf. Goźdź-Roszkowski 2011). It is standard procedure to normalize data to the closest round number relative to the total number of tokens in a corpus.

81 For more information, see http://ucrel.lancs.ac.uk/ll/DIFF_FAQ.pdf (accessed: August 18, 2020).

# Part II.A Macro level

# Chapter 5. Contextual and macrostructural analysis of CJEU and SN judgments

This chapter describes the contextual and macrostructural characteristics of the sub-genres of supranational CJEU judgments and national SN judgments included in the JURIDIC corpus (see Chapter 4) and aims to provide information as to their overall comparability at the macro (global) level. The goal of the analysis at this level is to gauge the overall distance of TTs to TL non-translations in terms of their generic macro- and micro-structure (moves and steps, respectively).

## 5.1 Contextual analysis of CJEU and SN judgments

A contextual analysis of judgments passed by both courts, that is judgments of the CJEU translated into Polish and non-translated SN judgments, and their text-external features is necessary to demonstrate the comparability of the wider contexts in which they are drafted and made known to their audience. Such an analysis will make it possible to assess the comparability of the texts themselves.[82] This approach follows Bhatia's view that genres can be analyzed in terms of their: (1) communicative purpose and (2) intra-textual structural qualities (cf. Bhatia [2013]1993, 2002). The first element of the analysis, the communicative purpose of the genre (cf. Chapter 2), is analyzed using the comprehensive framework for contextual genre analysis introduced by Dontcheva-Navratilova (2009: 15) (see Section 2.2, Figure 2.3). Her model was later adapted by Szczyrbak in the contextual analysis of judgments drafted by two different judicial discourse communities – the CJEU and the Polish Constitutional Tribunal (Szczyrbak 2014: 93–96, 118–124).[83]

---

82 Such an analysis is required by the framework of my corpus study (cf. Chapter 3), which aims to describe the degree of textual fit of supranational EU judgments to national judgments (intra-generic and inter-systemic linguistic variation), as it makes it possible to establish their overall comparability, and by extension the representativeness of the results.

83 A similar approach was recently adapted by Goźdź-Roszkowski who presented a move analysis of legal justifications in judgments of the Polish Constitutional Tribunal (Goźdź-Roszkowski 2020).

### 5.1.1 Situational characteristics

*Spatio-temporal setting*
CJEU and SN judgments represent public discourse in the socio-professional field of law (cf. Borja Albi *et al.* 2009: 70). Norms contained in justifications of CJEU judgments are generally binding and some of them have become general principles of EU law by referring to the constitutional traditions of EU Member States and international agreements signed by them (Zawidzka-Łojek and Łazowski 2018: 104–108). By contrast, SN judgments are binding in the territory of Poland.

In general, the sender (the judges' cabinet) and addressees of the communicative act share the same non-immediate context but are spatially and temporally remote, since judgments are not perceived and interpreted at the same time and in the same place as they are produced. At the moment of the pronouncement of EU and national judgments, the deictic center (i.e. the fact of being present at a particular time and place, cf. Dontcheva-Navratilova 2009: 27) is shared by discourse participants present at the hearing (judges, the parties to the proceedings and their representatives); however, following the pronouncement and the inclusion of the judgments in the court repositories, the deictic center is no longer shared by the discourse participants.

*Scene*
EU judgments are an instance of cross-cultural judicial communication spanning the EU legal system and the national legal systems of Member States, and various official EU languages. On the other hand, decisions contained in SN judgments, which are binding only in the territory of Poland, do not span borders and are issued exclusively in Polish (cf. Article 27 of the Polish Constitution). Both CJEU and SN judgments confer rights and impose obligations on the immediate audience of the judgments (parties to the proceedings), while at the same time exerting influence on the judiciary of lower ranks, the legal doctrine, and, to a lesser extent, the legislature, thanks to the institutional authority of the courts (cf. Vannier 2001).

CJEU and SN judgments indicate their institutional and cultural background in their introductory moves (cf. Sections 5.2.1, 5.2.2) by stating the name of the institution issuing the judgment, which implies shared institutional and cultural knowledge and has a positive bearing on the non-negotiable and authoritative nature of the judicial decisions provided (cf. Paunio 2013: 160).

*Subject area*
The CJEU gives judgments on a range of subjects provided for by the sources of primary and secondary EU law, including competition, the environment, fundamental rights, social security, state aid, and transport.[84] The Civil Chamber of the SN hands out judgments in areas provided for by Article 23 of the Act of 8 December 2017

84 See Section 5.2 for information on the different types of procedure used to pass CJEU judgments in the period 2011–2015. The type of procedure in which a judgment is given has been found to affect the structural characteristics of CJ judgments.

on the Supreme Court (Journal of Laws of 2019, item 825) in the fields of civil, commercial, family and guardianship law, as well as matters relating to the registration of entrepreneurs and registration of pledges. SN judgments included in the JURIDIC corpus were issued solely by the Civil Chamber of the SN.

### 5.1.2 Discourse participants

*Senders*
Both the CJEU (cf. Bobek 2015) and the SN (Civil Chamber) are examples of institutional senders. The CJEU acts simultaneously as a supreme (by providing answers to references for a preliminary ruling sent by the Member States, cf. Chalmers *et al.* 2019[2010]: 166–167), constitutional (by solving disputes between EU institutions and between EU institutions and Member States, deciding on the legality of EU legal acts), and administrative (by controlling the legality of non-legislative action on the part of the EU institutions) court of the EU (Borchardt 2017: 81; Zawidzka-Łojek and Łazowski 2018: 89–90; Kellerbauer *et al.* 2019: 175). Its two organs, the Court of Justice (CJ) and the General Court (GC), are functionally separate but institutionally linked (Borchardt 2017: 82; Zawidzka-Łojek and Łazowski 2018: 90). It should be observed, however, that the communication of EU judges is subject to multilingual mediation due to the nature of the EU environment. The translation of judgments is carried out by lawyer-linguists (cf. Koźbiał 2017: 162–165; McAuliffe 2008, 2009, 2011). The SN is the supreme judicial authority, which exercises judicial supervision over the activities of common and military courts (cf. Article 183 of the Polish Constitution).

*Addressees*
Judgments issued by the CJEU and the SN have multiple (in)direct as well as collective and individual (primarily expert, cf. Biel *et al.* 2019: 69) addressees. The CJEU audience is "significantly wider and more diverse compared to that of national courts in Member States," which "operate within a linguistically and culturally more homogenous community" (Paunio 2013: 167). CJEU judgments are addressed to the EU legal community (Paunio 2013: 164), and, more specifically, the parties to the proceedings and their representatives (primary audience, Paunio 2013: 136), EU Member States and national courts, EU institutions, EU citizens, including legal practitioners and scholars, and the general public (secondary audience, cf. Paunio 2013: 140; Rzucidło-Grochowska 2019: 477–479). Likewise, SN judgments are directed to the national legal community – the parties to the proceedings and their representatives (primary audience), national institutions representing the legislature, executive and the judiciary (courts of lower instance), Polish citizens interested in the outcome of the proceedings, including legal practitioners and scholars, and the general public (secondary audience).

*Social role of the participants*
Both judicial institutions have an asymmetrical relationship with the audience of their judgments (Szczyrbak 2014: 120). The status and role of the CJEU in the EU is particularly important with regard to the preliminary reference procedure which

ensures the consistent application of EU law by national courts in the Member States (Paunio 2013: 144, 147, 160–163) and which situates the CJEU above national courts in matters of interpretation of EU law. In the EU legal system, national courts, including the SN, are also perceived as EU courts due to the fact that they have to apply EU law in Member States[85] (cf. Chalmers *et al.* 2019[2010]).

*Extent of shared knowledge*
The level of professional knowledge and familiarity with communicative or institutional conventions among the discourse participants (audience) depends on whether the participants are professionally involved in the legal procedure on a regular basis. In general, judges in the CJEU and SN are nominated from among candidates with the highest level of professional knowledge and unquestionable moral integrity (cf. Article 2 of the Statute of the CJEU, Article 30 of the Act on the Polish Supreme Court,[86] respectively). Legal representatives of the parties, judges of lower instance courts, legal practitioners and legal scholars are also bound to have a high level of domain-specific knowledge (including the knowledge of substantive and procedural law). In the Polish context, knowledge about the EU legal system on the part of legal practitioners may vary due to the fact that Poland is a relatively new Member State and it may depend to a certain degree on whether EU law is a legal practitioner's field of expertise. The parties to the proceedings (except for Member States when they are represented by state-appointed legal professionals) and the general public possess a rather low level of professional knowledge, be it EU or national law, as well as knowledge about communicative or institutional conventions. Owing to the fact that most proceedings before the CJEU span various cultures, the level of cultural knowledge among the discourse participants may vary despite the foundations of the continental tradition of Member States being rooted in the same Roman legal tradition (cf. Wołodkiewicz and Zabłocka 2014: 331–380; Bunikowski 2016). On the other hand, the level of cultural knowledge is expected to be higher in the context of national proceedings before the SN.

### 5.1.3 Communicative purposes

*Communicative purposes*
Both the CJEU and SN issue judgments to communicate the conferral of rights and imposition of obligations, aiming to regulate the future behavior of the addressees and to establish, maintain or change legal relations (cf. Szczyrbak 2014: 121, 124).

---

85 The CJEU has its own definition of a *national court*, which has a bearing on the admissibility of references for a preliminary ruling. For more information on the definition of a court within the meaning of Article 267 of the Treaty on the Function of the European Union, see Zawidzka-Łojek and Łazowski (2018: 197–200).

86 Ustawa z dnia 8 grudnia 2017 r. o Sądzie Najwyższym (Dz.U.2019.825 t.j. z dnia 2019.05.06) [Act on the Polish Supreme Court of 8 December 2017]

The CJEU reviews the legality of the acts of EU institutions, annuls EU legal acts (actions for annulment), ensures that Member States comply with obligations under the Treaties by enforcing the law (infringement proceedings), ensures that EU institutions take action (actions for failure to act) and sanctions them if their inaction causes harm to natural or legal persons claiming compensation (actions for damages), and interprets EU law at the request of the national courts and tribunals (references for a preliminary ruling) (Borchardt 2017: 80–83; Zawidzka-Łojek and Łazowski 2018: 88–90). The CJ deals primarily with requests for preliminary rulings from national courts, which enable a dialectical relationship between them and the CJ (Paunio 2013: 109), certain actions for annulment and appeals (cf. Section 2.3.2) (Borchardt 2017: 80–81), while the GC rules on actions for annulment and actions for failure to act brought by Member States, natural and legal persons against EU institutions, dealing mainly with, among others, competition law, state aid, trade, agriculture, trademarks (cf. Section 2.3.2) (Borchardt 2017: 82–83). The SN administers justice by ensuring the legality and uniformity of case law of common courts and military courts, as well as recognizing appeal measures and adopting resolutions for resolving legal issues (cf. Article 1 of the Act on the Supreme Court of 8 December, 2017[87]). The overarching goal of both courts is to present coherent argumentation, in order to persuade the audience of judgments about the impartial and non-negotiable interpretation of the law by the judges (cf. Salmi-Tolonen 2005).

*Speech acts*
Both CJEU and SN judgments represent group speech acts due to the participation of several types of discourse participants in the communicative act. Both courts pass judgments collectively, in the name of the respective court, employing performatives, directives, declarations, and expressives in the form of direct speech acts (cf. Szczyrbak 2014: 121).

*Participant attitude towards the discourse and the message*
Judgments passed by the courts are expected to be based on facts and provisions of the law. However, discourse participants, that is the general public, tend to have limited trust towards both the CJEU (cf. DGC 2016: 25) and the SN (cf. CBOS 2016: 7) as judicial institutions, despite their being vested with high authority by the law, which serves as a means of legitimation (cf. van Leuween 2007; Paunio 2013: 167).

### 5.1.4 Communicative conventions

*Medium and channel*
Both CJEU and SN judgments are written documents. According to Article 88 of the Rules of Procedure of the CJ, CJ judgments are delivered orally in open court

87 Ibid.

(cf. Article 118 of the Rules of Procedure of the GC). They are also stored in electronic format. CJ and GC judgments can be retrieved from the InfoCuria database[88] and the EUR-Lex portal.[89] The SN, as a rule, reads out judgments at the last hearing in open court (cf. Article 326 of the CCP[90]). According to Article 8 of the Act on the Supreme Court of 8 December 2017,[91] SN is obligated to publish its judgments in the public information bulletin available on its website.[92] Pursuant to Article 9 of the same act, the SN may also publish court reports titled "Orzecznictwo Sądu Najwyższego" [Case law of the Supreme Court].

*Level of interactiveness*
There is no immediate interaction among the plurality of discourse participants in the process of pronouncing judgments by the CJEU or the SN. A certain form of dialogical relationship between the CJEU and national courts may be observed in the preliminary ruling procedure (cf. Tridimas 2015).

*Simple or complex discourse type*
Judicial discourse as exemplified by the judgments is highly specialized due to the usage of domain-specific terminology, high intertextuality and interdiscursivity, among other things (interactions with EU and national legislative acts, international agreements, already existing judgments, etc.) (cf. Fairclough 2003; Asensio 2007; Goźdź-Roszkowski 2011: 22; Bhatia 2014[2004]: 58).

*Institutional/professional norms of interaction and interpretation, conventions of discourse production, processing mechanism and circumstances, based on prior experience with specimens of the genre*
The norms and conventions of the EU and Polish judicial discourse communities apply to CJEU and SN judgments, respectively. Knowledge of the content and contextual characteristics of judgments is crucial in fully understanding the specificity of the genre (cf. Swales 1990; Borja Albi *et al.* 2009: 68; Bhatia [2013]1993; Biel 2017b, 2020, *forthcoming*). This can be achieved by means of genre analysis, which in conjunction with contrastive corpus studies allows for a better understanding of the principles of specialized genres (cf. Rasmussen and Engberg 1999: 131). With

88 http://curia.europa.eu/juris/recherche.jsf?language=en (accessed: August 18, 2020)
89 https://eur-lex.europa.eu/collection/eu-law/eu-case-law.html (accessed: August 18, 2020)
90 Ustawa z dnia 17 listopada 1964 r. – Kodeks postępowania cywilnego [Act of November 17, 1964 – Code of Civil Procedure] http://prawo.sejm.gov.pl/isap.nsf/download.xsp/WDU19640430296/U/D19640296Lj.pdf (accessed: August 18, 2020)
91 Ustawa z dnia 8 grudnia 2017 r. o Sądzie Najwyższym [Act on the Polish Supreme Court of 8 December 2017] Dz.U.2019.825 (consolidated text) of May 5, 2019
92 http://www.sn.pl/orzecznictwo/SitePages/Baza_orzeczen.aspx (accessed: August 18, 2020)

regard to specialized translation, Alcaraz Varó and Hughes (2002: 103) believe that the study of genres allows translators to focus on the functions of the original text and its wider context. In addition, given the fact that this study concerns CJEU judgments translated into Polish and non-translated SN judgments, the characteristics of the latter may serve as a point of reference for translators aiming to produce translations with a relatively high degree of textual fit (naturalness) (cf. Borja Albi *et al.* 2009: 66; Biel 2014a).

The next section presents the analysis of the macro- and micro-structure of the sub-genres of CJEU and SN judgments, the point of which is to demonstrate that judgments issued by both courts are comparable in terms of not only their text-external characteristics, but also their internal generic structure, thus ensuring the viability of my mixed genre-register approach (cf. Chapter 3).

## 5.2 Macrostructural analysis of CJEU and SN judgments

Judgments as well as other related legal genres exhibit a distinctive genre structure. According to Bhatia (1993: 230), legal cases,[93] not unlike any other genre, display a distinct structure, which can be analyzed in terms of *moves* (cf. Duszak 1998: 286; Hyland 2002: 15–18, Hyland 2004; Swales 2004: 106). Bhatia used an exemplary common law case, Roles v. Nathan [1963], to outline the typical linear four-move structure of judgments delivered in common law jurisdictions:

(1) identifying the case,
(2) establishing the facts of the case,
(3) arguing the case:
  (a) stating the history of the case,
  (b) presenting arguments,
  (c) delivering *ratio decidendi*,
(4) pronouncing judgment (Bhatia [2013]1993: 135–136).

Move 1 contains a standardized, formulaic expression which presents the names of the parties followed by information on the type of case, the court it was tried in and the year it was decided or reported, while Move 2 lists in a detailed manner the circumstances which gave rise to the dispute (Bhatia [2013]1993: 135–136). The purpose of a detailed account of circumstances is to allow judges, who might be deciding similar cases in the future, to extract all relevant facts from the case.[94]

93 Legal cases need to be differentiated from judgments due to different discourse organization and the fact that they act as case descriptions, playing an important role in law students' education in the area of common law (Bhatia 1987: 230, 2014: 56).

94 Mazzi (2007: 25) rightly points out that the most pronounced feature of the common law system is that cases in which legally material facts are the same must be decided in the same way.

Bhatia (1993: 233) perceives Move 3 as the most important argumentative section of a legal case and divides it into further sub-moves (or *steps*) which vary depending on the nature of the case. Step (a) serves the purpose of discussing the previous stages of the proceedings; in Step (b) the judge presents their argumentation based on the law and any viable precedents; whereas in Step (c) the judge derives the rule of law (*ratio decidendi*) which they would like to establish for both the present question and any similar cases which might appear before the court in the future (Bhatia [2013]1993: 233). Move 4 contains information regarding the binding settlement of the dispute and is usually indicated by the verdictive verb "held," as in: "The Court of Appeal has held that [...]" (Bhatia [2013]1993: 233).

An initial, cursory analysis of judgments comprising the JURIDIC corpus allowed me to establish that CJEU judgments, apart from having substantially different text lengths, also vary in terms of the sequence of sections, in contrast with the results of previous research (cf., among others, Mazzi 2007a, Mazzi 2007b; Vázquez-Orta 2010; Szczyrbak 2014: 125–127). Upon closer examination, I observed that CJEU judgments differ in terms of their internal sub-genre structure, depending on the type of procedure in which they are passed.

I decided to use corpus methods to manually analyze all texts included in the corpora of CJ and GC judgments, in order to determine what types of procedure they were passed in. The results of this stage of the analysis show that CJ judgments included in the post-accession corpus (cf. Chapter 4) are primarily: actions for annulment, actions for failure to fulfil obligations, appeals, applications, references and requests for a preliminary ruling, or reviews of judgments, thus relating in total to 15 different types of procedure[95]:

1. Action brought on 22 December 2009 under Article 26 of the Convention defining the Statute of the European Schools (only C-545/09),[96]
2. Actions for annulment under Article 263 TFEU (e.g. C-490/10, C-111/10, C-117/10, C-81/13, C-114/12),
3. Action for annulment under Articles 263 TFEU and 106a(1) EA (only C-48/14),
4. Action under Article 88(2) EC for failure to fulfil obligations (only C-331/09),
5. Actions under Article 108(2) TFEU for failure to fulfil obligations (e.g. C-527/12, C-63/14),

95 The appendix containing the list of all CJ, GC, and SN judgments included in the JURIDIC corpus can be found at the website of the Polish Eurolect research project available at: https://eurolekt.ils.uw.edu.pl/publications-and-materials/additional-materials (accessed: August 18, 2020).

96 Letter C indicates that the judgment is from the Court of Justice (C-73/08); letter T indicates that the judgment is from the General Court (T-545/11). The numbers after forwardslash '/' indicate the year in which the case was registered before the Court (2008; 2011). The numbers before forward-slash '/' indicate the numeric order of the case registered during that specific year. Sometimes cases are joined together, especially if their facts are similar (e.g. Joined Cases C-585/08 and C-144/09).

6. Actions under Article 226 EC for failure to fulfil obligations (e.g. C-28/09, C-47/08, C-50/08, C-50/09, C-51/08),
7. Actions under Article 258 TFEU for failure to fulfil obligations (e.g. C-539/09, C-150/11, C-281/11, C-383/10, C-525/12),
8. Actions under Article 260 TFEU for failure to fulfil obligations (e.g. C-533/11),
9. Appeals under Article 56 of the Statute of the Court of Justice (e.g. C-96/09 P, C-106/09 P and C-107/09 P, C-249/10 P, C-335/09 P, C-404/10 P, C-501/11 P, C-601/11 P, C-247/11 P and C-253/11 P, C-382/12 P, C-293/13 P and C-294/13 P),
10. Applications for annulment under the first paragraph of Article 230 EC (e.g. C-176/09),
11. References for a preliminary ruling under Article 234 EC (e.g. C-372/09 and C-373/09, C-347/09, C-323/09, C-288/09 and C-289/09, C-235/09),
12. References for a preliminary ruling under Article 267 TFEU (e.g. C-366/10, C-583/10, C-338/13, C-549/13, C-589/13),
13. References for a preliminary ruling under Articles 234 EC and 267 TFEU (e.g. C-446/09 and C-495/09),
14. Request for a preliminary ruling pursuant to the First Protocol of 19 December 1988 on the interpretation by the Court of Justice of the European Communities of the Convention on the Law applicable to Contractual Obligations (only C-305/13),
15. Reviews, under the second subparagraph of Article 256(2) of the TFEU, of judgments of the General Court of the European Union (only C-334/12 RX-II, C-579/12 RX-II).

GC judgments, on the other hand, are: actions, appeals, applications for (full or partial) annulment, applications for compensation, applications for interpretation, and applications for reimbursement, totaling 29 different types of procedure:

1. Actions brought against the decision of the Boards of Appeal of OHIM of (DATE) (e.g. T-50/09, T-108/08, T-267/11, T-396/11, T-10/09 RENV, T-247/12, T-278/10 RENV),
2. Action for annulment of the Eurosystem Oversight Policy Framework published by the ECB on 5 July 2011 (only T-496/11),
3. Action for damages in respect of the harm allegedly suffered by the applicant as a result of the failure of the European Union Delegation in Cairo (only T-138/14),
4. Action for the partial annulment of the decision of the ECHA (only T-96/10),
5. Appeal against the judgment of the European Union Civil Service Tribunal (only T-347/12 P),
6. Application for annulment of EASA's decision of (only T-102/13),
7. Application for annulment in part of Council Implementing Regulation (only T-169/12),
8. Application for a declaration that the Commission has failed to act (only T-423/07),

9. Applications for annulment and variation of Commission Decisions (e.g. T-372/10, T-418/10),
10. Applications for annulment of Article XXX of Commission Decisions (e.g. T-406/09, T-250/12, T-421/07 RENV),
11. Applications for annulment of Commission Decisions (e.g. T-138/07, T-587/08, T-90/11, T-242/12, T-655/11),
12. Applications for annulment of Commission Implementing Decisions (e.g. T-301/12),
13. Applications for annulment of Council Regulation (e.g. T-304/11, T-290/14),
14. Application for annulment of debit note No 3241011712, issued by the Commission on 4 November 2010 (only T-29/11),
15. Application for annulment of the decision of the European Anti-Fraud Office (OLAF) (only T-447/11),
16. Application for annulment of the decision of the Secretary General of the Commission (only T-250/08),
17. Application for annulment of the EMA's decision (e.g. T-140/12),
18. Application for annulment of the oral decision allegedly taken by the President of the Commission (only T-562/12),
19. Application for compensation based on the combined provisions of Article 268 TFEU and the second paragraph of Article 340 TFEU (only T-309/10),
20. Application for compensation for the damage allegedly suffered by the applicants following the adoption of Commission Regulation (only T-168/12),
21. Application for interpretation of the judgment (only T-1/08 INTP),
22. Applications for partial annulment of Commission Decision (e.g. T-192/08, T-370/09, T-564/12),
23. Applications for the full or partial annulment of Commission Decision (e.g. T-486/11),
24. Applications for the partial annulment of Council Implementing Regulation (e.g. T-412/13),
25. Applications for, principally, annulment of Commission Decision (e.g. T-299/08, T-217/06),
26. Applications to annul the Parliament's decision (e.g. T-48/12),
27. Application, in the first place, for the partial annulment of Commission Decision and, in the alternative, for a reduction in the amount of fine imposed on the applicant (only T-110/07),
28. Applications, primarily, for annulment in part of Commission Decision and, in the alternative, for a reduction in the amount of the fine imposed on the applicant (e.g. T-566/08, T-541/08),
29. Application for reimbursement of the principal sum of EUR XXX paid by the Commission in respect of the guarantee it provided in connection with financing granted to SEMEA (T-168/10 and T-572/10).

Owing to the high total number of texts, it was not practicable to analyze all of the judgments in a qualitative manner to determine their macrostructure. Therefore,

I decided to choose random judgments from each of the three post-accession corpora of CJ, GC and SN judgments, providing that the chosen judgments would reflect: (1) every major type of procedure before each of the courts,[97] and (2) the overall length of texts from the corpora, in that the chosen sample of judgments should contain similar proportions of short, medium and long texts.[98]

The mixed qualitative and quantitative analysis[99] of the internal structure of 10 CJ and 10 GC judgments passed in the four principal types of procedure allowed me to establish their total number of rhetorical moves (and steps within some of the main moves) (see Table 5.1) and the estimated proportion of text occupied by each of the moves (see columns I, II, III, IV, and V in Table 5.1). The structure of CJ judgments concerning references for a preliminary ruling diverges from the structure of both CJ and GC judgments passed in other types of procedure, which is why it is presented in the second part of Table 5.1 (column V). The structure of GC judgments is presented in a single column (see column IV, Table 5.1) due to the fact that all of the judgments chosen for this analysis were actions/applications for annulment. The table also provides information on the main discourse functions of each move and step. The case numbers of judgments subjected to the qualitative analysis are included in Table 5.1.

10 SN judgments were subjected to an identical analysis to that of CJEU judgments. This shows that national judgments exhibit a conventionalized structure similar to that of CJEU judgments, which, however, is remarkably more standardized and straightforward (see Table 5.2).

Sections 5.2.1 and 5.2.2 present the results of a contrastive rhetorical move analysis of CJEU (CJ and GC) and SN judgments, respectively. The analysis draws on findings presented earlier by Mazzi (2007a: 26, 2007b) and Szczyrbak (2014: 125–127). All of the researchers made claims as regards the highly standardized nature of the generic structure of EU judgments, without taking into consideration the fact that judgments drafted in a given legal system might also exhibit internal differentiation due to the different types of procedures that can be initiated before the CJEU (see above). The description of individual moves is carried out primarily in a qualitative manner. Despite this fact, the macrostructural qualities of EU and national judgments presented here are not deemed to be wholly representative of

97 In the case of CJ judgments, these were: two actions/applications for annulment, two actions for failure to fulfil obligations, three appeals, and three references for a preliminary ruling (see Table 5.1).

98 This sample was not meant to be fully representative. In order to choose a representative sample, I should have chosen a higher number of texts for the analysis. However, this would, in turn, significantly extend the time required for manual analysis.

99 I proceeded to analyze the texts using a close-reading technique, as part of which I copied the texts to Microsoft Excel and then highlighted Moves and Steps in the individual judgments. Afterwards, I summed up the total number of words forming each of the Moves and Steps by copying fragments of text to Microsoft Word; this allowed me to calculate the proportions occupied by the rhetorical segments.

**Table 5.1.** *Macrostructure of CJ (columns I – III, and V) and GC judgments (column IV)*

| **I – CJ – Actions/applications for annulment (C-117/10; C-490/10)**<br>**II – CJ –Actions for failure to fulfil obligations (C-281/11; C-47/08)**<br>**III – CJ –Appeals (C-249/10 P; C-404/10 P; C-382/12 P)**<br>**IV – GC –Actions/applications for annulment (T-90/11; T-138/07; T-304/11; T-372/10; T-192/08; T-169/12; T-290/14; T-655/11; T-55/14; T-660/11)**<br>* – tentative value due to the fact that not all reviewed judgments contain this step<br>Discourse functions of moves/steps: I – informative, A – argumentative, P – performative | I | II | III | IV |
|---|---|---|---|---|
| Move 1 – Identifying the case (I) | 3 % | 2 % | 2,3 % | 3,0 % |
| Move 2 – Identifying the scope of proceedings before the Court (I) | 1 % | 1 % | 1,3 % | 1,8 %* |
| Move 3 – Retrieving relevant Community and/or (inter)national law (I) | 17 % | 23 % | 8,3*% | 0,5 %* |
| Step 1 – retrieving relevant EU legislation (I) | 17 % | 8 % | 8,3*% | 0,5 %* |
| Step 2 – retrieving relevant national legislation (I) | --- | 15 % | --- | --- |
| Move 4 – Stating background to the dispute and/or stating the pre-litigation procedure and/or the forms of order sought by the parties (I) | 5 % | 2 % | 30 % | 11,4 % |
| Step 1 – Stating background to the dispute (I) | 5 % | --- | 50 % | --- |
| Step 2 – Stating the pre-litigation procedure (I) | --- | 2 % | 12 % | 2,8 % |
| Step 3 – Stating the forms of order sought by the parties (I) | 0,5 % | --- | 1,5 % | 0,7 % |
| **Move 5 – Arguing the case (A)** | **72,5 %** | **70 %** | **53,7 %** | **80,9 %** |
| Step 1 – Arguments of the parties (A) | 22 % | 23,5 % | 18,7 % | 2,7 %* |
| Step 2 – Findings of the Court (A) | 51 % | 46,5 % | 38,7 % | 78,2 % |
| Move 6 – Settling costs (P) | 1 % | 1,5 % | 1,3 % | 0,7 % |
| Move 7 – Pronouncing judgment (P) | 0,5 % | 2 % | 1,3 % | 0,7 % |
| Move 8 – Signatures (P) | 0 % | 0 % | 0 % | 0 % |
| **V – CJ – References for a preliminary ruling (C-366/10; C-347/09; C-589/13)**<br>* – tentative value due to the fact that not all reviewed judgments contain this step | | | | **V** |
| Move 1 – Identifying the case (I) | | | | 3,3 % |

Table 5.1. *Continued*

| I – CJ – Actions/applications for annulment (C-117/10; C-490/10)<br>II – CJ –Actions for failure to fulfil obligations (C-281/11; C-47/08)<br>III – CJ –Appeals (C-249/10 P; C-404/10 P; C-382/12 P)<br>IV – GC –Actions/applications for annulment (T-90/11; T-138/07; T-304/11; T-372/10; T-192/08; T-169/12; T-290/14; T-655/11; T-55/14; T-660/11)<br>* – tentative value due to the fact that not all reviewed judgments contain this step<br>Discourse functions of moves/steps: I – informative, A – argumentative, P – performative | I | II | III | IV |
|---|---|---|---|---|
| Move 2 – Identifying the scope of proceedings before the Court (I) | | | | 1 % |
| Move 3 – Retrieving relevant Community and/or (inter)national law (I) | | | | 20,6 % |
| Step 1 – Retrieving relevant provisions of international law (I) | | | | 5,6 %* |
| Step 2 – Retrieving relevant EU legislation (I) | | | | 6 %* |
| Step 3 – Retrieving relevant national legislation (I) | | | | 9 % |
| Move 4 – Stating history of the dispute in the main proceedings before the national court and the questions referred for a preliminary ruling (I) | | | | 13 % |
| Step 1 – Stating history of the dispute in the main proceedings before the national court and its facts (I) | | | | 8,7 % |
| Step 2 – Stating questions referred for a preliminary ruling (I) | | | | 4,3 % |
| **Move 5 – Consideration of the questions referred (A)** | | | | **58,7 %** |
| Move 6 – Settling costs (P) | | | | 0,7 % |
| Move 7 – Pronouncing judgment (P) | | | | 2,3 % |
| Move 8 – Signatures (P) | | | | 0 % |

all three sub-genres of judgments due to the small sample of texts chosen for the analysis. Nevertheless, the current description presents an improvement over past research in that it takes into consideration possible internal (intra-generic) differentiation within each of the sub-genres.[100] The following analysis of individual moves contained in CJ and GC judgments will be carried out in parallel due to their embeddedness in the same legal system,[101] whereas the analysis of SN judgments will be presented subsequently. The description of each move will contain excerpts

100 This finding pertains solely to CJ judgments which exhibit a high degree of internal variation of rhetorical moves and steps (see Table 5.1).

101 However, most attention will be paid to CJ judgments due to space constraints.

**Table 5.2.** *Macrostructure of SN judgments*

| | |
|---|---|
| **I – SN – Cassation appeals (I CSK 201/14; IV CSK 665/10; IV CSK 142/13; III CSK 294/12; V CSK 414/10; I CSK 292/12; V CSK 371/11; I CSK 392/13; V CSK 528/14; V CSK 254/14)**<br>Discourse functions of moves/steps: I – informative, A – argumentative, P – performative | |
| Move 1 – Identifying the case (I) | 2,2 % |
| Move 2 – Pronouncing the judgment (P) | 0,5 % |
| **Move 3 – Providing justification (A)** | **96,6 %** |
| Step 1 – Reporting procedural history and background of the case (A) | 44,5 % |
| Step 2 – Findings of the court (A) | 52 % |
| Move 4 – Restating the judgment or settling costs (P) | 0,6 % |

from all three types of judgments (with corresponding text from the English-language versions of CJEU judgments), in order to contrast their realization across translated EU judgments and non-translated Polish judgments.

The present approach enables the study of distinguishing, repetitive structural and lexico-grammatical elements of court judgments. It is assumed that being familiar with the structural conventions of this legal genre may facilitate text processing, which seems to be of particular importance to the non-legal audience as well as to translators (cf. Biel 2017b).

### 5.2.1 Macro- and microstructure of CJEU judgments

The obligatory elements of CJ judgments are laid out in Article 87 of the Rules of Procedure of the Court of Justice of September 25, 2012:

(a) a statement that it is the judgment of the Court;
(b) an indication as to the formation of the Court;
(c) the date of delivery;
(d) the names of the President and of the Judges who took part in the deliberations, with an indication as to the name of the Judge Rapporteur;
(e) the name of the Advocate General;
(f) the name of the Registrar;
(g) a description of the parties or of the interested persons referred to in Article 23 of the Statute who participated in the proceedings;
(h) the names of their representatives;
(i) in the case of direct actions and appeals, a statement of the forms of order sought by the parties;
(j) where applicable, the date of the hearing;
(k) a statement that the Advocate General has been heard and, where applicable, the date of his Opinion;

(l) a summary of the facts;
(m) the grounds for the decision;
(n) the operative part of the judgment, including, where appropriate, the decision as to costs.

On the other hand, Article 117 of the Rules of Procedure of the General Court of March 4, 2015 specifies the de rigueur elements of GC judgments:

(a) a statement that it is the judgment of the General Court;
(b) an indication as to the formation of the Court;
(c) the date of delivery;
(d) the names of the President and of the Judges who took part in the deliberations, with an indication as to the name of the Judge-Rapporteur;
(e) the name of the Advocate General, if designated;
(f) the name of the Registrar;
(g) a description of the parties;
(h) the names of their representatives;
(i) a statement of the forms of order sought by the parties;
(j) where applicable, the date of the hearing;
(k) a statement, where appropriate, that the Advocate General has been heard and, where applicable, the date of his Opinion;
(l) a summary of the facts;
(m) the grounds for the decision;
(n) the operative part of the judgment, including the decision as to costs.

Since the above specification of mandatory information required in every CJ or GC judgment provides only cursory information, it is necessary to look into the contents of each of the rhetorical moves (and steps within some of the main moves) to gain insight as to how judges frame the history of each case, as well as their argumentation. It should be observed that the aforementioned statutory provisions constitute *text-external factors* affecting the overall profile of the sub-genre of CJEU judgments, forming a de facto meta-genre which determines the structure of another genre (cf. Giltrow 2001). In addition, the organization of this genre is also affected by other factors, such as contextual (institutional tradition) and communicative (imposed by the discourse community of judges and the wider context of a democratic supranational organization or state, cf. Vannier 2001), which affect the overall stability of the genre (Leech 2007: 143). Thus, it needs to be borne in mind that the subject of my analysis are judicial texts, which are the end product of a complicated drafting process affected by a number of different factors, of which multilingualism and translation in the case of CJEU judgments are just one example (cf. Chapter 1).

The following move analysis pertains to 10 judgments passed by the CJ and 10 judgments passed by the GC (see Table 5.1). Since CJ judgments are passed by the Court within a number of different types of procedure (cf. Section 2.3.2), I decided to analyze three references for a preliminary ruling, three appeals under Article 56 of the Statute of the Court of Justice, two actions under Article 258 TFEU for failure to fulfil obligations, and two applications for annulment,[102] in order to account in some measure for the internal differences in the rhetorical structure of judgments passed by that court. GC judgments, on the other hand, were predominantly applications for annulment; therefore, I chose eight applications for (partial) annulment of, for instance, Commission or Council regulations or decisions, and two actions brought against the decisions of the First Board of Appeal of OHIM.[103] The excerpts were taken from the Polish-language (left-hand columns) and English-language (right-hand columns) versions of the judgment with case no. C-249/10 P (see Table 5.1). Excerpts from another judgment were taken in the case of steps not realized in the judgment in the said case no.

**Move 1 – Identifying the case**

The informative function of the opening move of both CJ and GC judgments consists of identifying the case. It allows the judges to inform the audience about the details of each case in a standardized and fixed order:

a) a statement that it is the judgment of either the CJ or the GC and an indication as to the formation of the Court:

| | |
|---|---|
| WYROK TRYBUNAŁU (trzecia izba) | JUDGMENT OF THE COURT (Third Chamber) |

b) the date of delivery and the language of the case:

| | |
|---|---|
| z dnia 2 lutego 2012 r. (*) | 1 February 2012 (*) |

c) concise listing of types of subject matter evoked by the judgment:

| | |
|---|---|
| Odwołanie – Dumping – Rozporządzenie (WE) nr 1472/2006 – Przywóz niektórych rodzajów obuwia ze skórzanymi cholewkami pochodzącego z Chińskiej Republiki Ludowej i Wietnamu – Rozporządzenie (WE) nr 384/96 – Artykuł 2 ust. 7, art. 9 ust. 5 i art. 17 ust. 3 – Status przedsiębiorstwa działającego w warunkach gospodarki rynkowej – Indywidualna procedura – Kontrola wyrywkowa | (Appeal — Dumping — Regulation (EC) No 1472/2006 — Imports of certain footwear with uppers of leather originating in China and Vietnam — Regulation (EC) No 384/96 — Articles 2(7), 9(5) and 17(3) — Market economy treatment — Individual treatment — Sampling) |

102 This choice corresponds roughly to the total number of CJ judgments passed in each of the four stated types of procedure.
103 This selection corresponds roughly to the total number of GC judgments passed in each of the two respective types of procedure.

d) case number:

| | |
|---|---|
| W sprawie C-249/10 P | In Case C-249/10 P, |

e) type of procedure:

| | |
|---|---|
| mającej za przedmiot odwołanie w trybie art. 56 statutu Trybunału Sprawiedliwości Unii Europejskiej, wniesione w dniu 18 maja 2010 r., | APPEAL under Article 56 of the Statute of the Court of Justice of the European Union, brought on 18 May 2010, |

f) a listing of the parties (in bold) or the interested persons referred to in Article 23 of the Statute who participated in the proceedings, and their representatives (e.g. appellants, defendants, interveners):

| | |
|---|---|
| **Brosmann Footwear (HK) Ltd**, z siedzibą w Kowloon (Chiny),<br>**Seasonable Footwear (Zhongshan) Ltd**, z siedzibą w Zhongshan (Chiny),<br>**Lung Pao Footwear (Guangzhou) Ltd**, z siedzibą w Guangzhou (Chiny),<br>**Risen Footwear (HK) Co. Ltd**, z siedzibą w Kowloon,<br>reprezentowane przez adwokatów L. Ruessmanna, A. Willemsa, S. De Knopa i C. Dackö,<br>wnoszące odwołanie,<br>w której drugą stroną są:<br>**Rada Unii Europejskiej**, reprezentowana przez J.P. Hixa oraz R. Szostaka, działających w charakterze pełnomocników, wspieranych przez G. Berrischa, Rechtsanwalt, oraz N. Chesaites, barrister,<br>strona pozwana w pierwszej instancji,<br>**Komisja Europejska**, reprezentowana przez T. Scharfa oraz H. van Vlieta, działających w charakterze pełnomocników,<br>**Confédération européenne de l'industrie de la chaussure (CEC)**,<br>interwenienci w pierwszej instancji, | **Brosmann Footwear (HK) Ltd**, established in Kowloon (China),<br>**Seasonable Footwear (Zhongshan) Ltd**, established in Zhongshan (China),<br>**Lung Pao Footwear (Guangzhou) Ltd**, established in Guangzhou (China),<br>**Risen Footwear (HK) Co. Ltd**, established in Kowloon,<br>represented by L. Ruessmann, A. Willems, S. De Knop and C. Dackö, avocats,<br>appellants,<br>the other parties to the proceedings being:<br>**Council of the European Union**, represented by J.-P. Hix and R. Szostak, acting as Agents, and by G. Berrisch, Rechtsanwalt, and N. Chesaites, Barrister,<br>defendant at first instance,<br>**European Commission**, represented by T. Scharf and H. van Vliet, acting as Agents,<br>**Confédération européenne de l'industrie de la chaussure (CEC)**,<br>interveners at first instance, |

g) composition of the court (the names of the President and of the Judges who took part in the deliberations, with an indication as to the names of the Judge Rapporteur, the Advocate General and Registrar:

| | |
|---|---|
| w składzie: K. Lenaerts, prezes izby, J. Malenovský, R. Silva de Lapuerta, G. Arestis (sprawozdawca) i D. Šváby, sędziowie,<br>rzecznik generalny: P. Mengozzi,<br>sekretarz: C. Strömholm, administrator, | composed of K. Lenaerts, President of the Chamber, J. Malenovský, R. Silva de Lapuerta, G. Arestis (Rapporteur) and D. Šváby, Judges,<br>Advocate General: P. Mengozzi,<br>Registrar: C. Strömholm, Administrator, |

h) a statement that a written procedure and hearing have taken place, the Advocate General has been heard, and, where applicable, information about the date of their Opinion:

| | |
|---|---|
| uwzględniając procedurę pisemną i po przeprowadzeniu rozprawy w dniu 25 maja 2011 r.,<br>po zapoznaniu się z opinią rzecznika generalnego na posiedzeniu w dniu 6 września 2011 r., | having regard to the written procedure and further to the hearing on 25 May 2011,<br>after hearing the Opinion of the Advocate General at the sitting on 6 September 2011, |

At the end of Move 1 there is a short performative phrase:

| | |
|---|---|
| wydaje następujący<br>**Wyrok** | gives the following<br>**Judgment** |

Move 1 is realized essentially in the same manner in all 10 CJ and 10 GC judgments analyzed, differing only with regard to the particulars of each case. This move is of great practical importance to the functioning of the courts, as it allows for the quick identification and retrieval of judgments.[104]

**Move 2 – Identifying the scope of proceedings before the Court**

The purpose of the second move in CJEU judgments is to inform the audience about the scope of proceedings before the Court. It is realized very briefly, usually in one to three paragraphs. Move 2 seems to be mandatory in the case of CJ

104 The on-line portal InfoCuria available at http://curia.europa.eu/juris/recherche.jsf?language=en allows for the retrieval of CJEU case-law according to a number of search criteria (such as: case status, case number, names of the parties, date, subject matter, type of procedure, etc.).

judgments; however, in the case of GC judgments, it appears in only two of the 10 judgments. The following excerpt shows how this move is realized in Case C-249/10 P.

| **Ramy prawne** | **Legal framework** |
|---|---|
| 1 W odwołaniu Brosmann Footwear (HK) Ltd (zwana dalej "Brosmann"), Seasonable Footwear (Zhongshan) Ltd, Lung Pao Footwear (Guangzhou) Ltd (zwana dalej "Lung Pao") i Risen Footwear (HK) Co. Ltd **wnoszą** do Trybunału **o uchylenie wyroku** Sądu Unii Europejskiej z dnia 4 marca 2010 r. w sprawie T-401/06 Brosmann Footwear (HK) i in. przeciwko Radzie, Zb.Orz. s II-671 (zwanego dalej "zaskarżonym wyrokiem"), w którym Sąd oddalił ich skargę o stwierdzenie częściowej nieważności rozporządzenia Rady (WE) nr 1472/2006 z dnia 5 października 2006 r. nakładającego ostateczne cła antydumpingowe oraz stanowiącego o ostatecznym pobraniu cła tymczasowego nałożonego na przywóz niektórych rodzajów obuwia ze skórzanymi cholewkami pochodząc[ego] z Chińskiej Republiki Ludowej i Wietnamu (Dz.U. L 275, s. 1, zwanego dalej "spornym rozporządzeniem"). | 1 By their appeal, Brosmann Footwear (HK) Ltd ('Brosmann'), Seasonable Footwear (Zhongshan) Ltd, Lung Pao Footwear (Guangzhou) Ltd ('Lung Pao') and Risen Footwear (HK) Co. Ltd **claim that** the Court **should set aside the judgment** of the General Court of the European Union of 4 March 2010 in Case T-401/06 Brosmann Footwear (HK) and Others v Council [2010] ECR II-671, ('the judgment under appeal'), by which that court dismissed their action for the partial annulment of Council Regulation (EC) No 1472/2006 of 5 October 2006 imposing a definitive anti-dumping duty and collecting definitely the provisional duty imposed on imports of certain footwear with uppers of leather originating in the People's Republic of China and Vietnam (OJ 2006 L 275, p. 1, 'the contested regulation'). |

In references for a preliminary ruling, the CJ uses this move to state what provision of EU law a given reference relates to:

| | |
|---|---|
| 1 Wniosek o wydanie orzeczenia w trybie prejudycjalnym **dotyczy** wykładni art. 43 WE i 49 WE. | 1 This reference for a preliminary ruling **concerns** the interpretation of Articles 43 EC and 49 EC. |
| 2 Wniosek ten **został złożony** w związku z postępowaniem karnym przeciwko J. Dickingcrowi i F. Ömcrowi w przedmiocie naruszenia przez spółkę prawa austriackiego bet-at-home.com Entertainment GmbH (zwaną dalej "bet-at-home.com Entertainment"), którą zarządzają, ustawodawstwa austriackiego w zakresie prowadzenia działalności w zakresie gier losowych, a dokładniej oferty udziału za pośrednictwem Internetu w grach rozgrywanych w kasynach. | 2 The reference **was made** in the course of criminal proceedings brought against Mr Dickinger and Mr Ömer alleging failure by bet-at-home.com Entertainment GmbH ('bet-at-home.com Entertainment'), a company incorporated under Austrian law of which they are the directors, to comply with the Austrian legislation on the operation of games of chance, more precisely the offering of casino games over the internet. |
| (C-347/09) | (C-347/09) |

In general, this move contains a brief, matter-of-fact presentation of the subject matter of a dispute or reference for a preliminary ruling, which includes narrative verbs in the past tense (bolded) (cf. Mazzi 2007: 126) and no evaluative markers.

**Move 3 – Retrieving relevant Community and/or (inter)national law**

Move 3 states the pertinent legal framework, that is the law that relates to the questions raised in a case. Typically, this move outlines provisions of EU law (primary or secondary legislation) and national law. However, it may also include international law (e.g. international Treaties that the EU is a party to; cf. Klabbers 2015) (cf. Rzucidło-Grochowska 2019: 469). Move 3 is usually sub-divided into a maximum of three informative steps (cf. Table 5.1).

- **Step 1 – retrieving relevant provisions of international law**

Step 1 is used to retrieve the provisions of international law (international agreements) necessary to provide a national court with a preliminary ruling. It has been found only in Case C-366/10 (reference for a preliminary ruling) (cf. Table 5.1):

| I – Ramy prawne | I – Legal context |
|---|---|
| *A – Prawo międzynarodowe* | *A – International law* |
| Konwencja chicagowska | The Chicago Convention |
| Konwencja o międzynarodowym lotnictwie cywilnym, podpisana w Chicago (Stany Zjednoczone) dnia 7 grudnia 1944 r. (zwana dalej "konwencją chicagowską"), została ratyfikowana przez wszystkie państwa członkowskie Unii Europejskiej, przy czym sama Unia nie jest stroną tej konwencji. Ową konwencją ustanowiono Organizację Międzynarodowego Lotnictwa Cywilnego (International Civil Aviation Organisation, ICAO), której celem – zgodnie z art. 44 tejże konwencji – jest rozwijanie zasad i techniki międzynarodowej żeglugi powietrznej oraz popieranie stworzenia międzynarodowych przewozów lotniczych i stymulowanie ich rozwoju. | The Convention on International Civil Aviation, signed in Chicago (United States) on 7 December 1944 ('the Chicago Convention'), has been ratified by all the Member States of the European Union, but the European Union is not itself a party to it. The Chicago Convention established the International Civil Aviation Organisation (ICAO), which, as provided in Article 44, has the objective of developing the principles and techniques of international air navigation and of fostering the establishment and stimulating the development of international air transport. |

The contents of Step 1 in Case C-366/10 are rather lengthy due to the fact that the CJ cites all relevant provisions, using their exact wording without paraphrasing. It takes up around 17 % of the text of the preliminary ruling. What is more, the CJ provides no evaluation of these provisions in this move.

- **Step 2 – retrieving relevant EU legislation**

Step 2 is realized in the same manner as Step 1. However, its function consists of stating relevant provisions of EU law as opposed to international law:

| Ramy prawne | Legal framework |
|---|---|
| 2 Przepisy regulujące stosowanie przez Unię Europejską środków antydumpingowych zawarte zostały w rozporządzeniu Rady (WE) nr 384/96 z dnia 22 grudnia 1995 r. w sprawie ochrony przed dumpingowym przywozem z krajów niebędących członkami Wspólnoty Europejskiej (Dz.U. 1996, L 56, s. 1), zmienionym rozporządzeniem Rady (WE) nr 461/2004 z dnia 8 marca 2004 r. (Dz.U. L 77, s. 12) (zwanym dalej "rozporządzeniem podstawowym"). | 2 The provisions governing the application of anti-dumping measures by the European Union ('EU') are set out in Council Regulation (EC) No 384/96 of 22 December 1995 on protection against dumped imports from countries not members of the European Community (OJ 1996 L 56, p. 1), as amended by Council Regulation (EC) No 461/2004 of 8 March 2004 (OJ 2004 L 77, p. 12, 'the basic regulation'). |

| | |
|---|---|
| 8 Artykuł 18 ust. 3 i 4 rozporządzenia podstawowego **ma następujące brzmienie**:<br><br>"3. W przypadku gdy zainteresowana strona przekaże informacje, które nie są idealne pod każdym względem, nie zostaną one pomimo to pominięte, pod warunkiem że braki te nie spowodują zbędnych trudności w dokonywaniu ustaleń o uzasadnionej dokładności i są one właściwe i terminowo przekazane oraz weryfikowalne, a zainteresowana strona działała, dokładając wszelkich starań. | 8 Article 18(3) and (4) of the basic regulation **is worded as follows**:<br><br>'3. Where the information submitted by an interested party is not ideal in all respects it should nevertheless not be disregarded, provided that any deficiencies are not such as to cause undue difficulty in arriving at a reasonably accurate finding and that the information is appropriately submitted in good time and is verifiable, and that the party has acted to the best of its ability. |
| *B – Prawo Unii*<br><br>24 Rada wydała decyzję 94/69/WE z dnia 15 grudnia 1993 r. dotyczącą zawarcia Ramowej konwencji Narodów Zjednoczonych w sprawie zmian klimatu (Dz.U. 1994, L 33, s. 11) oraz decyzję 2002/358/WE z dnia 25 kwietnia 2002 r. dotyczącą zatwierdzenia przez Wspólnotę Europejską Protokołu z Kioto do Ramowej konwencji Narodów Zjednoczonych w sprawie zmian klimatu i wspólnej realizacji wynikających z niego zobowiązań (Dz.U. L 130, s. 1). Zgodnie z art. 2 akapit pierwszy tej drugiej decyzji Unia i jej państwa członkowskie wypełniają wspólnie swoje zobowiązania wynikające z protokołu z Kioto. | *B – European Union law*<br><br>24 The Council has adopted Decision 94/69/EC of 15 December 1993 concerning the conclusion of the United Nations Framework Convention on Climate Change (OJ 1994 L 33, p. 1) and Decision 2002/358/EC of 25 April 2002 concerning the approval, on behalf of the European Community, of the Kyoto Protocol to the United Nations Framework Convention on Climate Change and the joint fulfilment of commitments thereunder (OJ 2002 L 130, p. 1). In accordance with the first paragraph of Article 2 of the latter decision, the European Union and its Member States are to fulfil their commitments under the Kyoto Protocol jointly. |

Overall, Step 2 is realized in seven out of 10 CJ judgments, and only one GC judgment (T-169/12), in which it appears as the sole step in Move 3 (cf. Table 5.1).

- **Step 3 – retrieving relevant national legislation**

The purpose of Step 3 is to state relevant provisions of national law:

| *C – Prawo krajowe* | *C – National law* |
|---|---|
| 41 W Zjednoczonym Królestwie dyrektywa 2008/101 została przetransponowana w drodze wydania rozporządzeń z 2009 r. w sprawie systemu handlu uprawnieniami do emisji gazów cieplarnianych (Aviation Greenhouse Gas Emissions Trading Scheme Regulations 2009, SI 2009, nr 2301) oraz innych przepisów, których wydanie było przewidziane w trakcie roku 2010. | 41 In the United Kingdom, Directive 2008/101 has been transposed by the Aviation Greenhouse Gas Emissions Trading Scheme Regulations 2009 (SI 2009 No 2301), and by other provisions envisaged to be adopted in 2010. |
| (C-366/10) | (C-366/10) |

This step is realized in five CJ judgments (two actions for failure to fulfil obligations: C-281/11, C-47/08, and all three references for a preliminary ruling: C-366/10, C-347/09, and C-589/13); it is not realized in any of the 10 GC judgments.

**Move 4:**

- **Stating background to the dispute and/or stating the pre-litigation procedure and/or the forms of order sought by the parties, or:**
- **Stating history of the dispute in the main proceedings before the national court and the questions referred for a preliminary ruling**

Move 4 serves a strictly informative function and is devoid of judicial evaluation. It takes two structural forms, depending on whether a given judgment concerns: (1) an action or application for annulment, an action for failure to fulfil obligations, an appeal, or (2) a reference for a preliminary ruling. Judgments passed in the first three types of procedure contain three steps within Move 4, whereas preliminary rulings involve two steps within this move. First, I will present the basic structure of steps contained in the former types of judgments. The steps (sub-moves) of Move 4 are easy to identify using the in-text headings (see the excerpts below).

**Move 4 in actions or applications for annulment, actions for failure to fulfil obligations, and appeals:**

- **Step 1 – Stating background to the dispute**

Step 1 aims to state the background to the dispute. It aids the audience in understanding why the legal proceedings before the CJ or the GC were initiated, which is evidenced by the predominance of past tense verbs reporting on past states or actions (bolded):

| Okoliczności powstania sporu | Background to the dispute |
|---|---|
| 9 Okoliczności powstania sporu **zostały przedstawione** przez Sąd w pkt 10–42 zaskarżonego wyroku w następujący sposób:<br><br>"10 Skarżące [...] są spółkami produkującymi i eksportującymi obuwie, posiadającymi siedziby w Chinach.<br><br>11 Przywóz obuwia z Chin klasyfikowanego w pewnych klasach Nomenklatury scalonej **był objęty** reżimem kontyngentów ilościowych, który wygasł w dniu 1 stycznia 2005 r.<br><br>12 W następstwie skargi złożonej w dniu 30 maja 2005 r. przez Confédération européenne de l'industrie de la chaussure [Europejską Konfederację Producentów Obuwia, zwaną dalej »CEC«] Komisja Wspólnot Europejskich **wszczęła postępowanie antydumpingowe** w zakresie przywozu pewnych rodzajów obuwia ze skórzanymi cholewkami pochodzącego z Chin i Wietnamu. Ogłoszenie o wszczęciu tego postępowania zostało opublikowane w Dzienniku Urzędowym Unii Europejskiej z dnia 7 lipca 2005 r. (Dz.U. C 166, s. 14, zwane dalej »ogłoszeniem o wszczęciu postępowania«).<br><br>13 Wobec znacznej liczby zainteresowanych stron w pkt 5.1 lit. a) ogłoszenia o wszczęciu postępowania **przewidziano** zastosowanie kontroli wyrywkowej, na podstawie art. 17 rozporządzenia podstawowego. | 9 The facts of the dispute **were set out as** follows by the General Court in paragraphs 10 to 42 of the judgment under appeal:<br><br>'10 The applicants [Brosmann, Seasonable Footwear (Zhongshan) Ltd, Lung Pao and Risen Footwear (HK) Co. Ltd] are footwear-producing and exporting companies established in China.<br><br>11 Imports of footwear from China falling within certain categories of the combined nomenclature **were subject to** a quantitative quota regime which lapsed on 1 January 2005.<br><br>12 Following a complaint lodged on 30 May 2005 by the Confédération européenne de l'industrie de la chaussure ("CEC"), the Commission of the European Communities (now the European Commission) initiat**ed an anti-dumping proceeding** concerning imports of certain footwear with uppers of leather originating in China and Vietnam. The notice of initiation of that proceeding was published in the Official Journal of the European Union of 7 July 2005 (OJ 2005 C 166, p. 14) ("the notice of initiation").<br><br>13 In view of the large number of parties involved, **it was envisaged**, at point 5.1(a) of the notice of initiation, to apply sampling, in accordance with Article 17 of the basic regulation. |

In this step, references are made, for instance, to the judgment under appeal, the applicants' actions, or the Commission's regulations. Step 1 of Move 4 includes an elaborate summary of the scope of proceedings before the Court identified in Move 2.

- **Step 2 – Stating the pre-litigation procedure**

Step 2 further focuses on the history of the case; it is used by the Courts to describe the immediate pre-litigation procedure. In this step, the judges may use evaluative language when referring to past actions (cf. Mazzi 2007: 134; Pontrandolfo and Goźdź-Roszkowski 2014) (e.g. *oczywiście błędna* [manifestly erroneous]):

| **Postępowanie przed Sądem i zaskarżony wyrok** | **The proceedings before the General Court and the judgment under appeal** |
|---|---|
| 10 Pismem złożonym w dniu 28 grudnia 2006 r. w sekretariacie Sądu **skarżące wniosły skargę o stwierdzenie nieważności spornego rozporządzenia**. Pismem złożonym w dniu 26 marca 2007 r. w sekretariacie Sądu Komisja wniosła o dopuszczenie jej do udziału w postępowaniu w charakterze interwenienta popierającego żądania Rady. (...) | 10 By application lodged at the General Court Registry on 28 December 2006, **the applicants brought before it an action for the annulment of the contested regulation**. By document lodged at that registry on 26 March 2007, the Commission sought leave to intervene in the case in support of the form of order sought by the Council. (...) |
| 11 Na poparcie skargi **skarżące podniosły osiem zarzutów** opartych kolejno na: | 11 In support of their action, **the applicants raised eight pleas in law**, alleging, respectively: |
| – naruszeniu art. 2 ust. 7 lit. b) i art. 9 ust. 5 rozporządzenia podstawowego oraz naruszeniu zasad równego traktowania i ochrony uzasadnionych oczekiwań; | – breach of Article 2(7)(b) and Article 9(5) of the basic regulation and breach of the principles of equal treatment and protection of legitimate expectations; |
| (...) | (...) |
| 17 Wreszcie **Sąd oddalił także ósmy zarzut podniesiony przez skarżące** na poparcie ich skargi – zgodnie z którym dokonana przez Radę w spornym rozporządzeniu ocena dotycząca poziomu, jaki powinny osiągnąć ostateczne środki antydumpingowe w celu usunięcia szkody, była **oczywiście** błędna – orzekając w pkt 208 zaskarżonego wyroku, że Rada nie dopuściła się oczywistego błędu w ocenie, opierając się na marży zysku, którą przemysł wspólnotowy uzyskał przy sprzedaży obuwia innego rodzaju niż będące przedmiotem dochodzenia, ponieważ te inne rodzaje obuwia są wystarczająco zbliżone do produktu objętego dochodzeniem. | 17 Lastly, the **General Court also rejected the eighth plea in law** relied on by the applicants in support of their action – whereby they had claimed that the Council's assessment, in the contested regulation, of the level which the definitive anti-dumping measures had to attain in order to eliminate injury was **manifestly** erroneous – holding, in paragraph 208 of the judgment under appeal, that the Council had not made a manifest error of assessment by taking into account the profit margin that the Community industry had attained for footwear other than that covered by the investigation because that other footwear is sufficiently similar to the product concerned. |

Step 2 does not appear in actions/applications for annulment (cf. C-117/10, C-490/10).

- **Step 3 – Stating the forms of order sought by the parties**

The last step of Move 4 in actions or applications for annulment, actions for failure to fulfil obligations, and appeals is a statement of the forms of order sought by the parties to the proceedings:

| | |
|---|---|
| **Żądania stron**<br>18 W odwołaniu **wnoszące odwołanie wnoszą** do Trybunału **o**:<br>– **uchylenie** zaskarżonego wyroku w zakresie, w jakim Sąd nie stwierdził nieważności spornego rozporządzenia oraz obciążył je kosztami postępowania przed Sądem,<br>– **stwierdzenie** nieważności spornego rozporządzenia, oraz<br>– **obciążenie** Rady kosztami postępowania odwoławczego i kosztami postępowania przed Sądem. | **The forms of order sought by the parties**<br>18 By their appeal, **the appellants claim that** the Court should:<br>– **set aside** the judgment under appeal, in so far as the General Court did not annul the contested regulation and in so far as it ordered them to pay the costs of the proceedings before the General Court;<br>– **annul** the contested regulation;<br>– **order** the Council to pay the costs of the appeal and of the proceedings before the General Court. |
| 19 Rada wnosi do Trybunału o:<br>– tytułem żądania głównego – **oddalenie odwołania**,<br>– tytułem żądania ewentualnego – **przekazanie sprawy** Sądowi do ponownego rozpoznania, oraz<br>– tytułem dalszego żądania ewentualnego – **oddalenie odwołania** i w każdym razie **obciążenie** wnoszących odwołanie **kosztami** postępowania odwoławczego. | 19 The Council contends that the Court should:<br>– **dismiss the appeal**;<br>– in the alternative, **refer the case back to** the General Court;<br>– in the further alternative, **dismiss the appeal** and, in any event, order the appellants to **pay the costs of** the appeal. |
| 20 Komisja wnosi o **oddalenie odwołania** i obciążenie wnoszących odwołanie poniesionymi przez nią kosztami postępowania. | 20 The Commission contends that the Court should **dismiss the appeal** and order the appellants to pay the costs incurred by the Commission. |

**Move 4 in References for a preliminary ruling:**

Move 4 has a different structure in references for a preliminary ruling.

- **Step 1 – Stating history of the dispute in the main proceedings before the national court and its facts**

Step 1 of Move 4 realized in references for a preliminary ruling is used by the CJ to state the history of the case reviewed by a national court (the referring court) of an EU Member State.

| | |
|---|---|
| **II – Okoliczności faktyczne sprawy przed sądem krajowym i pytania prejudycjalne**<br><br>42 Zgodnie z **informacjami pochodzącymi od sądu krajowego** Air Transport Association of America, podmiot niemający celu zarobkowego, jest głównym stowarzyszeniem handlu i usług rejsowego przemysłu lotniczego w Stanach Zjednoczonych. Linie lotnicze American Airlines Inc., Continental Airlines Inc. i United Airlines Inc. obsługują połączenia lotnicze w Stanach Zjednoczonych, w Europie i w pozostałej części świata. Ich administrującym państwem członkowskim w rozumieniu dyrektywy 2003/87 zmienionej dyrektywą 2008/101 jest Zjednoczone Królestwo.<br><br>43 W dniu 16 grudnia 2009 r. ATA i in. **wniosły do sądu krajowego skargę o stwierdzenie nieważności środków mających na celu transpozycję dyrektywy 2008/101** w Zjednoczonym Królestwie, które to środki należały do kompetencji Secretary of State for Energy and Climate Change. Na poparcie swojej skargi powołały się one na niezgodność z prawem tej dyrektywy w świetle międzynarodowego prawa umownego i zwyczajowego.<br><br>44 W dniu 28 maja 2010 r. **sąd krajowy dopuścił** z jednej strony International Air Transport Association (IATA) i National Airlines Council of Canada do sprawy w charakterze interwenientów popierających skargę ATA i in., zaś z drugiej strony – pięć organizacji ochrony środowiska naturalnego, to jest Aviation Environment Federation, WWF-UK, European Federation for Transport and Environment, Environmental Defense Fund i Earthjustice w charakterze interwenientów popierających Secretary of State for Energy and Climate Change.<br><br>(C-366/10) | **II – The facts in the main proceedings and the questions referred for a preliminary ruling**<br><br>42 According to the **information provided by the referring court**, the Air Transport Association of America, a non-profit-making entity, is the principal trade and service association of the United States scheduled airline industry. The airlines American Airlines Inc., Continental Airlines Inc. and United Airlines Inc. operate flights in the United States, Europe and the rest of the world. The United Kingdom is their administering Member State within the meaning of Directive 2003/87, as amended by Directive 2008/101.<br><br>43 On 16 December 2009, ATA and others **brought judicial review proceedings asking the referring court to quash the measures implementing Directive 2008/101** in the United Kingdom, which fall within the competence of the Secretary of State for Energy and Climate Change. In support of their action, they pleaded that that directive was unlawful in the light of international treaty law and customary international law.<br><br>44 On 28 May 2010, **the referring court granted** the International Air Transport Association (IATA) and the National Airlines Council of Canada permission to intervene in support of ATA and others, and granted five environmental organisations, namely the Aviation Environment Federation, WWF-UK, the European Federation for Transport and Environment, Environmental Defense Fund and Earthjustice, permission to intervene in support of the Secretary of State for Energy and Climate Change.<br><br>(C-366/10) |

By stating the history of the case before the national court, the CJ uses numerous verbs to report the actions of the parties to the proceedings and the referring court.

- **Step 2 – Stating questions referred for a preliminary ruling**

Step 2 of Move 4 in preliminary rulings serves to provide a listing of questions of the national court referred for a preliminary ruling. When a national court decides to submit a reference for a preliminary ruling to the CJ, it stays the proceedings and awaits an answer from the CJ.

| | |
|---|---|
| 45 W takich okolicznościach High Court of Justice (England and Wales), Queen's Bench Division (Administrative Court) **postanowił zawiesić postępowanie i zwrócić się do Trybunału z następującymi pytaniami prejudycjalnymi**:<br><br>"1) Czy jedna lub więcej z wymienionych poniżej norm prawa międzynarodowego może służyć jako podstawa dla zakwestionowania ważności dyrektywy 2003/87/WE zmienionej dyrektywą 2008/101/WE, w celu uwzględnienia działalności lotniczej w ramach unijnego systemu handlu uprawnieniami do emisji [...]:<br><br>a) zasada międzynarodowego prawa zwyczajowego, zgodnie z którą każde państwo posiada całkowitą i wyłączną suwerenność w przestrzeni powietrznej nad swoim terytorium;<br><br>(C-366/10) | 45 It is in those circumstances that the High Court of Justice of England and Wales, Queen's Bench Division (Administrative Court), **decided to stay the proceedings and to refer the following questions to the Court for a preliminary ruling**:<br><br>'(1) Are any or all of the following rules of international law capable of being relied upon in this case to challenge the validity of Directive 2003/87/EC as amended by Directive 2008/101/EC so as to include aviation activities within the EU Emissions Trading Scheme ...:<br><br>(a) the principle of customary international law that each State has complete and exclusive sovereignty over its airspace;<br><br>(C-366/10) |

In judgments C-366/10 and C-347/09, the referring court poses a long list of interrelated questions, whereas in judgment C-589/13 the referring court poses a single question framed in one long sentence.

## Move 5 in actions or applications for annulment, actions for failure to fulfil obligations, and appeals – Arguing the case

The argumentative Move 5 in actions or applications for annulment, actions for failure to fulfil obligations, and appeals is sub-divided into two steps:

- **Step 1 – Arguments of the parties**

Step 1 of Move 5 contains the reported arguments submitted by the parties to the proceedings:

| **Argumentacja stron** | **Arguments of the parties** |
|---|---|
| 23 W ramach zarzutu pierwszego **wnoszące odwołanie utrzymują, że** Sąd naruszył prawo w zakresie stosowania art. 2 ust. 7 lit. c) i art. 9 ust. 5 rozporządzenia podstawowego, orzekając, że instytucje nie były zobowiązane do zbadania wniosków o przyznanie MET lub IT złożonych przez skarżące ani do wzięcia ich w jakikolwiek sposób pod uwagę. **Zdaniem wnoszących** odwołanie, gdyby chińscy producenci eksportujący byli w stanie wykazać, że spełniają przesłanki ustanowione w tych przepisach, powinni być traktowani tak, jak gdyby mieli siedzibę w innym państwie niż państwo producentów, którzy nie spełniają wspomnianych przesłanek, to jest państwo, w którym nie istnieje gospodarka rynkowa. Wspomniane przepisy z definicji mogą być stosowane wyłącznie w sposób indywidualny dla każdego przypadku, gdyż wymagają scharakteryzowania warunków gospodarczych, w jakich działa każda spółka analizowana oddzielnie. **Wnoszące odwołanie twierdzą, że** Sąd dopuścił się naruszenia prawa, kiedy ograniczył ich wniosek o przyznanie MET lub IT do wniosku o uzyskanie indywidualnego marginesu dumpingu w rozumieniu art. 17 rozporządzenia podstawowego. W każdym razie wnoszące odwołanie żądały uznania faktu, że prowadzą działalność "w Chinach posiadających gospodarkę rynkową," dlatego też powinna im zostać przyznana stawka średniego ważonego cła dla producentów działających w warunkach gospodarki rynkowej. Ponadto **w opinii wnoszących** odwołanie Sąd naruszył prawo, przyjmując, że instytucje mogły słusznie powołać się na okoliczność, iż liczba wniosków o przyznanie MET lub IT była tak duża, że ich analiza uniemożliwiłaby instytucjom zakończenie dochodzenia w odpowiednim czasie.<br>(...) | 23 By their first ground of appeal, the **appellants submit that** the General Court erred in law concerning the application of Articles 2(7)(c) and 9(5) of the basic regulation, by holding that the institutions were not required to examine or in any manner take account of the appellants' MET/IT claims. **The appellants submit that** if the Chinese exporting producers were able to show that they meet the conditions laid down by those provisions, they should have been treated as though they were established in a country different from that of producers that do not meet those conditions, that is, a non-market economy country. By definition, Article 2(7)(c) and Article 9(5) may be applied only on an individual basis, as they require a characterisation of the economic conditions under which each individual company operates. **The appellants state that** the General Court erred in law when it reduced their MET/IT claim to a claim for an individual margin of dumping within the meaning of Article 17 of the basic regulation. In any event, they requested recognition of the fact that they operate in 'market economy China,' and that they should therefore be granted the weighted average duty rate applicable to producers operating under those conditions. In addition, **in the appellants' view**, the General Court also erred in law in finding that the institutions could validly argue that the number of MET/IT claims was so large that examining them would have prevented them from completing the investigation in good time.<br>(...) |

Again, Step 1 contains many reporting verbs which advance the appellants' views. It should be noted, however, that this step is absent in GC judgments in which the parties' arguments are indirectly presented in Move 4.

- **Step 2 – Findings of the Court**

Article 36 of the Statute of the Court of Justice of the European Union states that "Judgments shall state the reasons on which they are based [...]." Step 2 of Move 5 contains the core argumentation of the Court. In this step, the Court reformulates a national court's questions (if the procedure concerns a preliminary ruling), relies on the Advocate General's Opinion (if one was supposed to be drawn up) and existing CJEU case law, identifies legal facts, cites and interprets the law, and applies legal rules.

| **Ocena Trybunału** | **Findings of the Court** |
|---|---|
| 30 Tytułem wstępu **należy** zauważyć, że zgodnie z art. 2 ust. 7 lit. a) rozporządzenia podstawowego w przypadku przywozu z państw nieposiadających gospodarki rynkowej, w drodze wyjątku od zasad określonych w art. 2 ust. 1–6, normalną wartość określa się co do zasady w oparciu o cenę lub wartość skonstruowaną w warunkach gospodarki rynkowej państwa trzeciego. | 30 It **should** be noted, first of all, that Article 2(7)(a) of the basic regulation provides that in the case of imports from non-market economy countries, in derogation from the rules set out in paragraphs 1 to 6 of that provision, normal value must, as a rule, be determined on the basis of the price or constructed value in a market economy third country. |
| 31 Niemniej na mocy art. 2 ust. 7 lit. b) w postępowaniach antydumpingowych dotyczących przywozu między innymi z Chin normalną wartość ustala się zgodnie z art. 2 ust. 1–6 rozporządzenia podstawowego, jeżeli zostanie wykazane, na podstawie właściwie uzasadnionych wniosków producenta lub producentów, w stosunku do których toczy się postępowanie, oraz zgodnie z kryteriami i procedurami określonymi w art. 2 ust. 7 lit. c), że warunki gospodarki rynkowej przeważają w przypadku tego producenta lub tych producentów w odniesieniu do produkcji oraz sprzedaży rozpatrywanego produktu podobnego. | 31 However, under Article 2(7)(b), in anti-dumping investigations concerning imports from, inter alia, China, normal value is to be determined in accordance with Article 2(1) to (6) of the basic regulation, if it is shown, on the basis of properly substantiated claims by one or more producers subject to the investigation and in accordance with the criteria and procedures set out in Article 2(7)(c), that market economy conditions prevail for that producer or producers in respect of the manufacture and sale of the like product concerned. |
| 43 Wobec powyższego **należy** stwierdzić nieważność spornego rozporządzenia w zakresie dotyczącym wnoszących odwołanie. | 43 In those circumstances, the contested regulation **must** be annulled in so far as it relates to the appellants. |

By doing so, the judges frequently use the modal verb *należy* [one should/must], which bolsters the non-negotiability of their findings (cf. Chapter 6, Section 6.8.1). To some degree, it may be concluded that the use of this modal verb shows that the judges' reasoning is not dependent on their personal understanding of the law, but is rather derived directly from the law itself. In this process, judges are only the mediators of the law, without whom (or with another composition of the panel of judges) the presented interpretation would, at least in an ideal world, be exactly the same.

## Move 5 in references for a preliminary ruling – Consideration of the questions referred

In preliminary rulings, Move 5 is not sub-divided into steps. In this move, the CJ provides answers to the preliminary question. In doing so, it reformulates them when necessary and relies on the factual and legal findings provided in the previous moves.

| **A – W przedmiocie pytania pierwszego** | **A – Question 1** |
|---|---|
| 46 W pytaniu pierwszym **sąd krajowy zmierza zasadniczo do ustalenia, czy** w ramach omawianego tu wniosku o wydanie orzeczenia w trybie prejudycjalnym można się powołać na wymienione przez niego zasady i normy prawa międzynarodowego w celu dokonania oceny ważności dyrektywy 2008/101 w zakresie, w jakim uwzględnia ona lotnictwo w systemie handlu uprawnieniami przewidzianym w dyrektywie 2003/87. | 46 By its first question, **the referring court asks, in essence, whether** the principles and provisions of international law which it mentions are capable of being relied upon in the context of the present reference for a preliminary ruling for the purpose of assessing the validity of Directive 2008/101 inasmuch as it includes aviation in the allowance trading scheme under Directive 2003/87. |
| 111 **Mając na uwadze** całość powyższych rozważań, na pytanie pierwsze **należy odpowiedzieć, że** w takich okolicznościach jak okoliczności sprawy przed sądem krajowym spośród zasad i norm prawa międzynarodowego wymienionych przez sąd krajowy w celu dokonania oceny ważności dyrektywy 2008/101 można się powołać jedynie na:<br>– z jednej strony, w granicach kontroli oczywistego błędu, który może zostać przypisany Unii, w ocenie jej kompetencji do wydania tej dyrektywy w świetle tych zasad:<br>– zasadę, zgodnie z którą każde państwo posiada całkowitą i wyłączną suwerenność w przestrzeni powietrznej nad swoim terytorium; | 111 **Having regard to** all the foregoing considerations, **the answer to the first question is that** the only principles and provisions of international law, from among those mentioned by the referring court, that can be relied upon, in circumstances such as those of the main proceedings and for the purpose of assessing the validity of Directive 2008/101, are:<br>– first, within the limits of review as to a manifest error of assessment attributable to the European Union regarding its competence, in the light of those principles, to adopt that directive:<br>– the principle that each State has complete and exclusive sovereignty over its airspace, |

| | |
|---|---|
| **B – W przedmiocie pytań od drugiego do czwartego**<br>113 **Mając na względzie** sformułowanie powyższych pytań i okoliczność, że skarżące przed sądem krajowym są liniami lotniczymi zarejestrowanymi w państwie trzecim, **należy** w pierwszej kolejności ustalić, czy i w jakim zakresie dyrektywa 2008/101 ma zastosowanie do części lotów międzynarodowych wykonywanych poza przestrzenią powietrzną państw członkowskich przez takie linie. W drugiej kolejności **trzeba** będzie zbadać ważność tej dyrektywy w tym kontekście. | **B – Questions 2 to 4**<br>113 **Having regard to** the wording of these questions and the fact that the claimants in the main proceedings are airlines registered in a third State, it **should** first be determined whether and to what extent Directive 2008/101 applies to those parts of international flights that are performed outside the airspace of the Member States by such airlines. Second, the directive's validity **should** be examined in that context. |
| 155 W tym względzie **należy stwierdzić** – jak wynika zresztą wyraźnie z motywu 21 dyrektywy 2008/101 – że Unia przewidziała wyraźnie jednolite zastosowanie systemu handlu uprawnieniami do wszystkich operatorów statków powietrznych wykorzystywanych w połączeniach lotniczych rozpoczynających się lub kończących się na lotnisku znajdującym się na terytorium państwa członkowskiego i że w szczególności chciała ona ściśle przestrzegać postanowień o niedyskryminacji zawartych w dwustronnych umowach o usługach lotniczych podpisanych z państwami trzecimi, na wzór tego, co zostało przewidziane w art. 2 i art. 3 ust. 4 umowy "otwartego nieba." | 155 In that regard, **it must be stated that**, as is indeed apparent from the express terms of recital 21 in the preamble to Directive 2008/101, the European Union has expressly provided for uniform application of the allowance trading scheme to all aircraft operators on routes which depart from or arrive at an aerodrome situated in the territory of a Member State and, in particular, it has sought to comply strictly with the non-discrimination provisions of bilateral air service agreements with third States, like the provisions in Articles 2 and 3(4) of the Open Skies Agreement. |
| 157 W świetle całości powyższych rozważań **należy dojść do wniosku, że** analiza dyrektywy 2008/101 nie wykazała istnienia okoliczności, które wpływałyby na jej ważność. | 157 Having regard to all of the foregoing, **it must be concluded that** examination of Directive 2008/101 has disclosed no factor of such a kind as to affect its validity. |

In Polish-language versions of Move 5, the CJ bolsters the degree of authoritativeness of its answers with frequent use of the impersonal, epistemically-modalized verb *należy* [one should/must]. Overall, Move 5 is the most extensive move in all CJ and GC judgments, including references for a preliminary ruling (cf. Table 5.1).

**Move 6 – Settling costs**

Article 38 of the Statute of the Court of Justice of the European Union states that "The Court of Justice shall adjudicate upon costs." Move 6 incorporates the settlement of the costs of the procedure. In this move, the CJ and the GC judges decide who is to bear the costs of the procedure before the Court based on the relevant provisions of the statutes of both courts.

| **W przedmiocie kosztów** | **Costs** |
|---|---|
| 44 Na mocy art. 122 akapit pierwszy regulaminu postępowania przed Trybunałem, jeśli odwołanie jest zasadne i Trybunał orzeka wyrokiem kończącym postępowanie w sprawie, Trybunał rozstrzyga o kosztach. Zgodnie z art. 69 § 2 tego regulaminu, mającym zastosowanie do postępowania odwoławczego na podstawie art. 118 regulaminu, **kosztami zostaje obciążona**, na żądanie strony przeciwnej, strona przegrywająca sprawę. Artykuł 69 § 4 akapit pierwszy regulaminu stanowi, że państwa członkowskie, które wstąpiły do sprawy w charakterze interwenienta, pokrywają własne koszty, natomiast art. 69 § 4 akapit trzeci regulaminu przewiduje, że Trybunał może postanowić, iż interwenienci niewymienieni w akapitach poprzednich pokrywają własne koszty.<br><br>45 Ponieważ odwołanie złożone przez wnoszące odwołanie zostało uwzględnione i stwierdzono nieważność spornego rozporządzenia w zakresie dotyczącym wnoszących odwołanie, **należy obciążyć Radę kosztami** poniesionymi przez wnoszące odwołanie zarówno w pierwszej instancji, jak i w ramach niniejszego postępowania, zgodnie z żądaniem wnoszących odwołanie. Ponadto Komisja i CEC **pokryją własne koszty** poniesione zarówno w pierwszej instancji, jak i w ramach niniejszego postępowania. | 44 Under the first paragraph of Article 122 of its rules of procedure, where the appeal is well founded and the Court itself gives final judgment in the case, the Court is to make a decision as to costs. Article 69 of those rules, applicable to appeal proceedings by virtue of Article 118 thereof, provides in paragraph 2 that the unsuccessful party **is to be ordered to pay the costs** if they have been applied for in the successful party's pleadings. The first subparagraph of Article 69(4) of those rules provides that institutions which intervene in the proceedings are to bear their own costs and the third subparagraph of Article 69(4) provides that the Court may order an intervener other than those expressly mentioned in the preceding subparagraphs to bear his own costs.<br><br>45 Since the appeal brought by the appellants has been allowed and the contested regulation annulled in so far as it relates to them, **the Council must be ordered to pay the costs** incurred by the appellants, both at first instance and in connection with the present proceedings, as asked for in their pleadings. In addition, the Commission and CEC **must also be ordered to bear their own costs**, both at first instance and in connection with the present proceedings. |

## Move 7 – Pronouncing judgment

In the case of all CJ and GC judgments, Move 7 includes the pronouncement of the judgment and follows immediately the move containing the settlement of costs (see Move 6 above). This performative move is realized succinctly, usually in the form of a list of binding decisions made by the Court.

| | |
|---|---|
| Z powyższych względów Trybunał (trzecia izba) **orzeka, co następuje**:<br><br>1) **Uchyla się** wyrok Sądu Unii Europejskiej z dnia 4 marca 2010 r. w sprawie T-401/06 Brosmann Footwear (HK) i in. przeciwko Radzie.<br><br>2) **Stwierdza się** nieważność rozporządzenia Rady (WE) nr 1472/2006 z dnia 5 października 2006 r. nakładającego ostateczne cła antydumpingowe oraz stanowiącego o ostatecznym pobraniu cła tymczasowego nałożonego na przywóz niektórych rodzajów obuwia ze skórzanymi cholewkami pochodząc[ego] z Chińskiej Republiki Ludowej i Wietnamu w zakresie dotyczącym Brosmann Footwear (HK) Ltd, Seasonable Footwear (Zhongshan) Ltd, Lung Pao Footwear (Guangzhou) Ltd i Risen Footwear (HK) Co.Ltd.<br><br>3) Rada Unii Europejskiej **zostaje obciążona kosztami** poniesionymi przez Brosmann Footwear (HK) Ltd, Seasonable Footwear (Zhongshan) Ltd, Lung Pao Footwear (Guangzhou) Ltd i Risen Footwear (HK) Co. Ltd zarówno w pierwszej instancji, jak i w ramach niniejszego postępowania.<br><br>4) Komisja Europejska i Confédération européenne de l'industrie de la chaussure (CEC) **pokrywają** własne koszty poniesione zarówno w pierwszej instancji, jak i w ramach niniejszego postępowania. | On those grounds, the Court (Third Chamber) **hereby**:<br><br>1. **Sets aside** the judgment of the General Court of the European Union of 4 March 2010 in Case T-401/06 Brosmann Footwear (HK) and Others v Council;<br><br>2. **Annuls** Council Regulation (EC) No 1472/2006 of 5 October 2006 imposing a definitive anti-dumping duty and collecting definitely the provisional duty imposed on imports of certain footwear with uppers of leather originating in the People's Republic of China and Vietnam in so far as it relates to Brosmann Footwear (HK) Ltd, Seasonable Footwear (Zhongshan) Ltd, Lung Pao Footwear (Guangzhou) Ltd and Risen Footwear (HK) Co.Ltd;<br><br>3. **Orders** the Council of the European Union **to pay the costs incurred by** Brosmann Footwear (HK) Ltd, Seasonable Footwear (Zhongshan) Ltd, Lung Pao Footwear (Guangzhou) Ltd and Risen Footwear (HK) Co. Ltd both at first instance and in connection with the present proceedings;<br><br>4. **Orders** the European Commission and the Confédération européenne de l'industrie de la chaussure (CEC) **to bear** their own costs, both at first instance and in connection with the present proceedings. |

What is interesting is that Polish-language versions of judgments seem to convey a higher perceived degree of impersonality than the corresponding English-language versions. This is due to the fact that Polish lawyer-linguists use the phrase *orzeka, co następuje* [hereby rules] which requires the use of impersonal verdictive verbs in the present tense, e.g. *uchyla się* [sets aside]. This translation choice seems to bolster the level of authoritativeness and non-negotiability of the judicial decisions presented in this move. This, however, does not correspond to non-translated judgments of the Polish Supreme Court, which uses a performative (or reporting, depending on the context) verb in the past tense, *orzekł* [ruled], in the same move (cf. Section 5.2.2).

**Move 8 – Signatures**

Article 37 of the Statute of the Court of Justice of the European Union states that "judgments shall be signed by the President and the Registrar. They shall be read in open court." Therefore, all CJ and GC judgments need to be signed. Article 88(2) of the Rules of Procedure of the Court of Justice of 25 September 2012 additionally states that:

> The original of the judgment, **signed** by the President, by the Judges who took part in the deliberations and by the Registrar, shall be sealed and deposited at the Registry; certified copies of the judgment shall be served on the parties and, where applicable, the referring court or tribunal, the interested persons referred to in Article 23 of the Statute and the General Court.

Article 118(2) of the Rules of Procedure of the General Court of 4 March 2015 states that:

> The original of the judgment, **signed** by the President, by the Judges who took part in the deliberations and by the Registrar, shall be sealed and deposited at the Registry. A copy of the judgment shall be served on each of the parties.

Move 8 is the last move in all EU judgments. In some of the more complicated judgments it is immediately followed by a table of contents presenting the structure of a given judgment (e.g. T-90/11, T-138/07).

### 5.2.2 Macro- and microstructure of SN judgments

The following move analysis concerns judgments passed by the SN. In general, the operative parts of these judgments (PL: *sentencje wyroków*), which do not contain the justification section (see Move 3), are composed of two main parts, namely *rubrum* and *tenor* (Bladowski 2012: 24), both of which correspond to two separate rhetorical moves (see Move 1 and Move 2, respectively).

The contents of Moves 1 and 2, that is the obligatory elements of the operative parts of judgments and their justifications, are dictated by Article 325 of the CCP,[105] according to which the operative part should contain the court's decision as to

105 Ustawa z dnia 17 listopada 1964 r. – Kodeks postępowania cywilnego [Act of November 17, 1964 – Code of Civil Procedure]. http://prawo.sejm.gov.pl/isap.nsf/download.xsp/WDU19640430296/U/D19640296Lj.pdf (accessed: 18 August, 2020)

the forms of order sought by the parties. For this reason, the justifications do not have to reiterate this decision word for word; they simply contain the paraphrased decision of the court (see Move 4 – Restating the judgment or settling costs below). What is interesting is that, according to the law, the judgment pronounced by the Court in *rubrum* overrides the contents of the justification (grounds for its judgments) (cf. SN judgment of November 20, 2002 – Case II CKN 1132/00).

**Move 1 – Identifying the case**

The opening move of judgments passed by the Civil Chamber of the SN is similar to the corresponding move in EU judgments in that it also contains standardized elements listed in a fixed order which distinguish cases from each other. Move 1 allows for an easy identification of judgments, including their retrieval from the on-line repository of judgments made available by the Court.[106] SN judgments included in the corpus are devoid of non-textual elements, such as the signatures of the judges placed at the end of judgments or the black and white coat of arms of Poland found in the top-most part of written judgments. The excerpts in Polish were taken from judgment case no. I CSK 201/14 and the backtranslations are my own.

a) Case number:

| | |
|---|---|
| Sygn. akt I CSK 201/14 | Case no. I CSK 201/14 |

The Roman numeral in the case number stands for the number of the Division of the Civil Chamber (cf. § 40(2)[107] of the Ordinance of the President of the Republic of Poland of March 29, 2018 on the Supreme Court Regulations; Bladowski 2012: 25).

b) a statement (in bold) that the judgment is passed in the name of the Republic of Poland:

| | |
|---|---|
| **WYROK W IMIENIU RZECZYPOSPOLITEJ** | **JUDGMENT IN THE NAME OF THE REPUBLIC OF POLAND** |

The obligation of the Court to pronounce judgments in the name of the Republic of Poland can be inferred from Article 174 of the Constitution. On the other hand, Article 27 of the Constitution, which states that Polish is the official language in the Republic of Poland, obligates the SN to draft and publish judgments in the Polish language (cf. Bladowski 2013: 25).

c) date of delivery of the judgment:

106 The repository of SN judgments and other court documents is available at: http://www.sn.pl/orzecznictwo/SitePages/Baza_orzeczen.aspx (accessed: August 18, 2020).

107 "Izba dzieli się na wydziały tworzone na podstawie kryteriów terytorialnych i rzeczowo-problemowych." [The Chamber is divided into Divisions created on the basis of territorial and subject-matter criteria.]

| | |
|---|---|
| Dnia 12 marca 2015 r. | 12 March 2015 |

d) composition of the court (the names of the presiding judge and of the judges who took part in the deliberations, with an indication of the judge rapporteur and the name of the registrar);

| | |
|---|---|
| SSN Antoni Górski (przewodniczący)<br>SSN Mirosław Bączyk<br>SSN Zbigniew Kwaśniewski (sprawozdawca)<br>Protokolant Justyna Kosińska | SSN Antoni Górski (presiding judge)<br>SSN Mirosław Bączyk<br>SSN Zbigniew Kwaśniewski (judge rapporteur)<br>Registrar Justyna Kosińska |

e) indication of the subject matter:

| | |
|---|---|
| o uznanie postanowienia wzorca umowy za niedozwolone, | for pronouncement that the general contract clauses are prohibited, |

f) statement that a hearing regarding the plaintiff's cassation against another court's judgment had already taken place:

| | |
|---|---|
| po rozpoznaniu na rozprawie w Izbie Cywilnej w dniu 12 marca 2015 r.,<br>skargi kasacyjnej powódki<br>od wyroku Sądu Apelacyjnego<br>z dnia 19 czerwca 2013 r., | having examined on 12 March 2015, in the Civil Chamber at a hearing,<br>the plaintiff's cassation against the judgment of the Court of Appeal<br>of 19 June 2013, |

### Move 2 – Pronouncing the judgment

In contrast to CJ and GC judgments, the move including the pronouncement of the judgment (in bold) immediately follows Move 1 (see above), together with which it forms one long, logically inter-connected sentence. The verdictive (performative) verb *uchyla* [sets aside] used in the cited excerpt indicates that the judgment is passed by means of a collective decision of the judges sitting in the panel.

| | |
|---|---|
| **uchyla zaskarżony wyrok i przekazuje sprawę Sądowi Apelacyjnemu do ponownego rozpoznania<br>i orzeczenia o kosztach postępowania kasacyjnego.** | **sets aside the judgment under appeal and refers the case to the Court of Appeal for re-examination<br>and decision on the costs of cassation proceedings.** |

This move is realized very concisely in all 10 judgments, and only rarely is it expressed in two or more points, each with its own verdictive (performative) verb, e.g. *zasądza* [awards] or *znosi (koszty postępowania kasacyjnego)* [abrogates (the costs of cassation proceedings)]. This move is rephrased in Move 4.

**Move 3 – Providing justification**

According to Article 328(2) of the CCP,[108] the justification of a judgment should include an indication of the factual basis for the decision, namely: establishment of the facts that the court has found to be proven, the evidence on which it relied, and the reasons why it refused the credibility and probative value of other evidence, as well as an explanation as to the legal basis of the judgment with references to relevant provisions of the law.

Move 3 occupies the most textual space, around 96.6 %, in every national judgment. This is not surprising considering that the Court's entire line of argumentation is unveiled in this rhetorical move. Move 3 is introduced with a bolded title:

| **UZASADNIENIE** | **JUSTIFICATION** |
|---|---|

According to § 106(3) of the Ordinance of the President of the Republic of Poland of March 29, 2018 on the Supreme Court Regulations,[109] justification of a SN judgment should be clear, as short as possible and limited to relevant matters; in addition, the judge drafting the justification should avoid foreign and uncommon expressions, and unnecessary references to legal literature. The justification should be authoritative and undebatable, and relate to the totality of the judgment pronounced in Move 2 (Bladowski 2013: 329).

Being the longest rhetorical move, Move 3 is sub-divided in every judgment into two steps, namely: Step 1 – Reporting the procedural history and background of the case (factual findings), which serves as an introduction to the proper justification of the Court contained in the following step and is drafted in view of its contents (Rzucidło-Grochowska 2017: 61), and Step 2 – Findings of the court, in which the Court justifies its reasoning based on the factual and legal basis (cf. Bladowski 2013: 329; Rzucidło-Grochowska 2017: 60). The results of the analysis of the 10 SN judgments show that the realization of Step 1 takes up around 44.5 % of textual space, whereas Step 2 takes up around 52 % (cf. Table 5.2).

108 Ustawa z dnia 17 listopada 1964 r. – Kodeks postępowania cywilnego [Act of November 17, 1964 – Code of Civil Procedure] http://prawo.sejm.gov.pl/isap.nsf/download.xsp/WDU19640430296/U/D19640296Lj.pdf (accessed: 18 August, 2020)

109 Ordinance of the President of the Republic of Poland of March 29, 2018 on the Supreme Court Regulations http://prawo.sejm.gov.pl/isap.nsf/download.xsp/WDU20180000660/O/D20180660.pdf (accessed: 18 August, 2020)

- **Step 1 – Reporting procedural history and background of the case**

The purpose of Step 1 is to recount the previous stages of proceedings in lower-instance court(s) prior to the Supreme Court's judgment, which is exemplified by numerous reporting verbs in the past tense or present tense in the Court's references to the cassation appeal (cf. Rzucidło-Grochowska 2015).

| | |
|---|---|
| Sąd pierwszej instancji **oddalił** wyrokiem powództwo skierowane przeciwko Bankowi o uznanie postanowienia wzorca umowy za niedozwolone. | The court of first instance **dismissed** the judgment against the Bank for declaring the model contract provision to be unlawful. |
| W skardze kasacyjnej opartej na obu podstawach powód w ramach pierwszej podstawy **zarzucił** naruszenie art. (...). | In the cassation appeal based on both grounds, the plaintiff **alleged** a violation of Article (...) under the first ground. |
| W części uzasadnienia skargi kasacyjnej poświęconej wykazaniu wystąpienia podstaw kasacyjnych, powódka **akcentuje** tezę, że ustalenie przez Sąd odwoławczy, iż postanowienia wzorca umowy w postaci o.w.u. są integralną częścią umowy kredytowej oferowanej przez pozwanego, nie może <u>racjonalnie</u> prowadzić do wniosku, że pozwany nie stosuje tych postanowień wzorca, a w konsekwencji, że nie ma legitymacji biernej w niniejszej sprawie. To z kolei **skutkowało** błędnym zaniechaniem dokonania oceny abuzywności spornej klauzuli (...). | In the part of the justification of the cassation appeal devoted to demonstrating the existence of cassation grounds, the plaintiff **emphasizes** the hypothesis according to which the finding by the court of appeal that the provisions of the standard contract in the form of General Terms and Conditions are an integral part of the loan agreement offered by the defendant, which cannot <u>reasonably</u> lead to the conclusion that the defendant does not apply these standard provisions and, consequently, that he has no capacity to be a party in the present case. This, in turn, **resulted in** an erroneous failure to assess the abusiveness of the disputed clause (...). |
| Na rozprawie strony **podtrzymały** dotychczas reprezentowane stanowiska. | At the hearing, the parties **maintained** their positions. |

Although Step 1 focuses on the history of the case, SN judges do not refrain from evaluating the parties' actions and argumentation, as exemplified by the underlined evaluative adverb *racjonalnie* [rationally].

- **Step 2 – Findings of the court**

The most argumentative part of a judgment of the Polish Supreme Court is comprised of "Uzasadnienie," i.e. "Grounds for the judgment." It contains the factual basis for the Court's decision along with the legal basis. In all 10 judgments, Step 2 is introduced with the standardized phrase *Sąd Najwyższy zważył, co następuje*

[The Supreme Court held as follows],[110] which seems to suggest to the reader that the following deliberations are non-negotiable, categorical and final (cf. Bladowski 2013: 329; Rzucidło-Grochowska 2017).[111]

| | |
|---|---|
| Sąd Najwyższy z mocy art. 398 § 1 k.p.c. rozpoznaje skargę kasacyjną w granicach zaskarżenia oraz w granicach podstaw, biorąc z urzędu pod rozwagę nieważność postępowania. | Pursuant to Article 398 § 1 of the Code of Civil Procedure the Supreme Court hears the cassation appeal within the limits of the appeal and within the limits of grounds, taking ex officio into consideration the invalidity of the proceedings. |
| **W piśmiennictwie stwierdzono, że** legitymacja bierna przysługuje w omawianym postępowaniu przedsiębiorcy, który [...]. | It has been found in the literature that the capacity to be a party in a given case is, in the present proceedings, a prerogative of an entrepreneur in question, who [...]. |
| **Zasadnie** zarzuciła skarżąca naruszenie art. (...). | The applicant **legitimately** alleged infringement of Article (...). |
| **Chybiony** okazał się natomiast zarzut naruszenia art. (...). | On the other hand, the allegation of violation of Article (...) turned out to be **misconceived**. |

The excerpts above show that SN judges rely on the provisions of the law (see excerpt 1), as well as the legal doctrine (see excerpt 2), when justifying their judgments, which bolsters the legitimacy and authoritativeness of their decisions. In addition, similar to Step 1, they also frequently resort to evaluative adverbs (*zasadnie* [legitimately], see excerpt 3) and adjectives (*chybiony* [misconceived], see excerpt 3) to assess the parties' claims and arguments. In this step, judges also use many reporting verbs in the past tense (see excerpts 3 and 4). Having discussed all relevant matters in Step 2, in Move 4 the judges restate the judgment pronounced earlier in Move 2 (see Move 4 below).

In Polish legal doctrine, judicial justifications are of paramount importance in the process of implementing the law, as judgments serve a number of functions which enable the whole legal system to be held together. First of all,

110 In several judgments included in the SN corpus this phrase does not contain a comma: *Sąd Najwyższy zważył co następuje* [The Supreme Court held as follows], which is a punctuation error. The exercitive (argumentative) verb *zważyć* [pay attention to something] relates to the sphere of human intellectual activities [WSJP] and stresses that the judges' cabinet in passing the judgment has officially weighed up all arguments presented in the justification, while being aware of the consequences of its decision.

111 For a discussion on the rhetorical strategies used by Polish judges in justifications of judgments, see Rzucidło-Grochowska (2013, 2017), Rzucidło (2020) and Łętowska *et al.* (2015). For a discussion on the nature of justifications of CJEU judgments, see Mikłaszewicz (2015) and Rzucidło-Grochowska (2019).

they provide an opportunity for the judges to frame the motives (*imperio rationis*) for their decision in writing, which acts as a separate, formal form of expression (Rzucidło 2011: 53). Justifications are descriptive in that they allow judges to determinately describe their manner of reasoning strictly relevant to the implementation of the law in a given case, which provides a chance to rationalize the whole legal system in the context of applying abstract and general legal norms in an individual decision (Rzucidło 2011: 53–55). As such, a justification of a judgment (particularly of a higher-instance court owing to its institutional authority) manifests itself as a persuasive and pedagogic tool which legitimizes (cf. van Leuween 2007) the court's decision in the eyes of the direct recipients and the general public, thus affecting the whole legal culture and doctrine (Rzucidło 2011: 53–57; Rzucidło-Grochowska 2013: 68). Justifications of judgments issued by the SN play an essential role in shaping and preserving the uniform character of national jurisprudence, thus providing a certain degree of guidance to lower-instance courts adjudicating in similar matters (Rzucidło-Grochowska 2013: 62, 70). Court judgments (and their justifications) may be also viewed as a form of dialog between judges, as well as between the judiciary and the legislature (cf. Cheng and King 2008: 268).

**Move 4 – Restating the judgment or settling costs**

Move 4 includes a paraphrase of the judgment pronounced in Move 2, although the Court uses it to cite the legal basis for its decision, that is Article 398[15] § 1 of the CCP,[112] which concerns the effects of considering a cassation appeal to be made by the Court:

> § 1. Sąd Najwyższy w razie uwzględnienia skargi kasacyjnej uchyla zaskarżone orzeczenie w całości lub w części i przekazuje sprawę do ponownego rozpoznania sądowi, który wydał orzeczenie, lub innemu sądowi równorzędnemu; Sąd Najwyższy może uchylić także w całości lub w części orzeczenie sądu pierwszej instancji i przekazać sprawę do ponownego rozpoznania sądowi temu samemu lub równorzędnemu. Przy ponownym rozpoznaniu sprawy przepis art. 415 stosuje się odpowiednio.
>
> [§ 1. If the Supreme Court accepts the cassation appeal, it shall quash the contested decision in whole or in part and refer the case back to the court that issued the decision or another equivalent court; The Supreme Court may also set aside in whole or in part the decision of the court of first instance and refer the case back to the same or an equivalent court. When the case is reconsidered, the provision of 415 shall apply accordingly.]

Move 4 is used by the Court to firmly emphasize that only the justification presented in the preceding move has been relied upon by the Court to pass the judgment. In

112 Ustawa z dnia 17 listopada 1964 r. – Kodeks postępowania cywilnego [Act of November 17, 1964 – Code of Civil Procedure]. http://prawo.sejm.gov.pl/isap.nsf/download.xsp/WDU19640430296/U/D19640296Lj.pdf (accessed: 18 August, 2020)

this move, the Court uses a verdictive (performative) verb in the past tense, *orzekł* [ruled], which evidences the fact that the actual judgment is passed in Move 2:

| | |
|---|---|
| W tym stanie rzeczy Sąd Najwyższy **orzekł** jak w sentencji na podstawie art. 398[15] § 1 k.p.c., a **o kosztach postępowania kasacyjnego** orzeczono na podstawie art. 108 § 2 k.p.c. | In this state of affairs, the Supreme Court **ruled** as in the operative part pursuant to Article 398[15] § 1 of the Code of Civil Procedure, and **the costs of cassation proceedings** were adjudicated on the basis of Article 108 § 2 of the Code of Civil Procedure. |

In addition, albeit rarely, the court may incorporate into this move the settlement of costs of the procedure.

## 5.3 Conclusions

The contrastive manual analysis of the genre structure of CJEU and SN judgments has demonstrated, based on a rather small sample, that both sub-genres are highly conventionalized. Despite the fact that the results are not perfectly conclusive, it can be established that judgments passed by both judicial institutions exhibit an intuitive linear move-structure. In order to be complete, CJEU judgments need to realize all eight moves; however, the realization of steps contained within some of the moves varies depending on the type of judgment and the type of legal procedure, which is indicative of intra-generic variation. On the other hand, the macrostructure of SN judgments is much simpler, as they contain only four moves. The contextual characteristics of CJEU and SN judgments do not completely converge, mainly due to the general characteristics of the supranational and national legal systems. Despite this fact, both CJEU and SN judgments are deemed to be comparable, as their most extensive parts contain judicial argumentation (see Tables 5.1 and 5.2). In addition, both CJEU and SN judges tend to utilize similar rhetorical strategies in the justification of their judgments.

Overall, this chapter has shown that translated CJEU and non-translated SN judgments lend themselves to a comparative corpus study of the formal linguistic issues at the micro (local) level thanks to their partly coinciding contextual and structural characteristics. The results of the analysis presented in Parts II.B-D will concern the distance of TTs to TL non-translations at the (1) lexico-grammatical, (2) phraseological and (3) terminological level (see Chapter 3, Figure 3.2).

# Part II.B. Micro level: Pillar I – Lexico-grammatical patterns

# Chapter 6. Analysis of chosen lexico-grammatical patterns

This chapter focuses on the first pillar of the micro-level analysis of the textual fit of translated CJUE judgments to non-translated SN judgments (cf. Chapter 3, Section 3.3). The overall objective is to draw conclusions as regards the intra-generic degree of linguistic variation and characteristic features (key salient genre/register markers) of EU judicial Polish, which constitutes a crucial part of the Eurolect. The chapter adapts the analytical framework presented in Chapter 5 of Biel's (2014a) study, *Lost in the Eurofog: The Textual Fit of Translated Law*, which analyzes the textual fit of translated EU legislation to non-translated national legislation in order to identify its key genre features by investigating grammatical and text-structuring patterns. The rationale is that conceptual replication[113] will allow for the comparison of quantitative data at the inter-generic level within the Eurolect by identifying features typical of a secondary legal genre – judgments, and its two sub-genres, namely EU and national judgments.

Mindful that the research material in Biel's (2014a: 137–222) study comprises texts of a different genre, legislation (a primary legal genre), it was necessary to confirm whether the key linguistic patterns she analyzed should also be regarded as key in the genre of judgments. For this reason, I used a corpus-driven method and examined the keyword lists (see Section 6.2) generated using WS in order to identify the key genre patterns applicable to EU and national judgments – categories of lexico-grammatical units with irregular frequencies of occurrence supplemented with patterns and markers identified as typical of legal and judicial language in the relevant literature:

- Divergence
  - ➢ *overrepresentation* relates to the higher frequency of occurrence of a unit in TTs as compared to TL non-translations
  - ➢ *underrepresentation* concerns the lower frequency of occurrence of a unit in TTs relative to TL non-translations
- Convergence
  - ➢ equal or similar frequency of occurrence of a unit in TTs and TL non-translations

Prior to discussing the identified patterns, I will present global statistics on the corpora used in this study. The data presented in this chapter will be synthesized in Chapter 11.

---

113 The present analysis, being a conceptual replication (cf. Earp and Trafimow 2015: 5), aims to test Biel's (2014a) hypotheses on judgments as a genre related to legislative texts.

## 6.1 Global comparison of corpora

The basic corpora used in this study are the non-lemmatized unsampled and sampled corpora. Unsampled corpora are used to conduct almost all analyses within Pillars I-III (see Chapter 3) except for the investigations into the nature of binomial structures (see Chapter 8) and terminological units (see Chapter 9), which utilize sampled corpora. Table 6.1 presents global statistics generated with WS for the corpora of EU and national judgments.

Since unsampled corpora are the main corpora used in this study, the following description applies only to them. The CJ and GC corpora contain an overall lower number of both tokens (see Figure 6.1) and types (see Figure 6.2) than the post-accession SN corpus, which can be explained by the higher number of tokens in the latter. Consequently, the EU corpora have a higher type-to-token ratio (TTR). Thus, it may be assumed that translated judgments are less lexically varied than their national counterparts. This finding seems to be in line with the normalization hypothesis, that is the tendency of TTs to exaggerate typical TL features (cf. Baker 1996: 180–185). It should be remembered, however, that although both EU and national corpora contain exclusively Polish-language texts, they also contain foreign elements, such as the names of various courts or companies, which additionally raise the total type count.

The data on standard deviation (SD) for the TTR, mean word length and mean sentence length (see Figure 6.3) do not provide unequivocal evidence as regards the levelling out hypothesis, that is the assumed tendency of translations to be more alike than non-translations (Baker 1996: 180–185). The SD data indicate not only observable inter-generic variation, but also intra-generic variation within the Eurolect, that is CJ and GC judgments. SD data on the TTR and mean sentence length are higher in both EU corpora – the only exception is the SD value concerning the mean word length in GC judgments, which is lower than in both CJ and post-accession SN judgments, although it is markedly higher than in pre-accession SN judgments.

Figure 6.3 shows that EU judgments contain both longer words and sentences than national judgments. Sentences are about 16 % (27.43 words) and 18 % (27.86 words) longer in CJ and GC judgments than in post-accession SN judgments (23.66 words), respectively, while words are about 5 % (5.92 letters) and 4 % (5.87 letters) longer than in post-accession SN judgments (5.65 letters). It remains to be verified in reception-oriented research whether such differences are perceptible by the audience of judgments. The long sentences in judgments may translate into the higher complexity of the genre compared to contemporary Polish, in which the average sentence length is about 11.22 words – sentences in popular science texts have about 17.94 words, small press pieces about 17.5 words, and prose about 11.9 words (Malinowski 2006: 203). For comparison, the average sentence length in Polish-language versions of EU regulations is 22.71 words (Biel 2014a: 139).

WS helped to calculate the total number of occurrences of words of different lengths (in characters) in the corpora (see Table 6.2).

Single-letter words are the most widely distributed words in all corpora, in particular in SN_2011–2015 corpus. This is partly due to the high distribution of simple

**Table 6.1.** *Global statistics for the unsampled and sampled corpora of EU and national judgments*

| | Unsampled corpora | | | | Sampled corpora | | |
|---|---|---|---|---|---|---|---|
| | EU corpora | | PL corpora | | EU corpora | | PL corpus |
| | CJ | GC | SN_2011–2015 | SN_1999 | CJ_100 | GC_50 | SN_2011–2015_200 |
| Texts | 897 | 384 | 2,564 | 401 | 100 | 50 | 200 |
| Tokens (running words) | 4,693,968 | 4,515,866 | 6,833,997 | 504,605 | 512,427 | 489,931 | 508,584 |
| Types (distinct words) | 72,310 | 65,318 | 76,783 | 24,336 | 24,552 | 21,786 | 24,511 |
| Type/token ratio (TTR) | 1,67 | 1,57 | 1,22 | 5,16 | 5,20 | 4,82 | 5,22 |
| Standardized TTR | 43,14 | 42,89 | 44,09 | 45,09 | 43,48 | 42,63 | 43,69 |
| STTR std. dev. | 56,68 | 57,27 | 56,03 | 54,57 | 55,61 | 57,05 | 56,21 |
| Mean word length (in characters) | 5,92 | 5,87 | 5,65 | 5,67 | 5,94 | 5,83 | 5,65 |
| Word length standard deviation | 3,78 | 3,72 | 3,76 | 3,68 | 3,79 | 3,71 | 3,78 |
| Number of sentences | 157,821 | 149,761 | 267,074 | 21,993 | 17,524 | 16,454 | 20,200 |
| Mean sentence length (in words) | 27,43 | 27,86 | 23,66 | 21,44 | 26,96 | 27,47 | 23,23 |
| Standard deviation | 26,54 | 22,47 | 20,20 | 17,28 | 24,34 | 21,48 | 19,50 |
| Mean text length (in words) | 4,825 | 10,864 | 2,464 | 1,176 | 4,724 | 9,040 | 2,346 |
| Standard deviation | 2343,95 | 8284,36 | 1257,61 | 496,23 | 1894,70 | 6943,65 | 1043,65 |

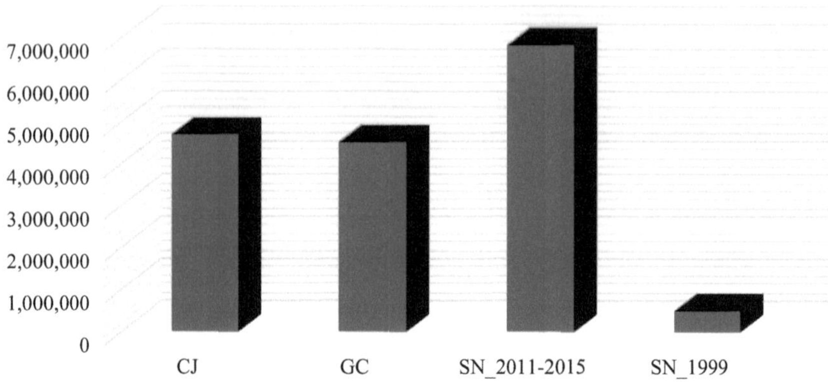


**Figure 6.1.** *Tokens (running words) in text*

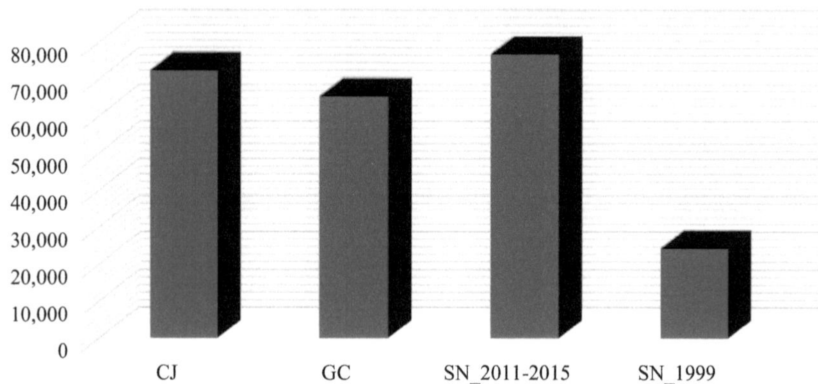


**Figure 6.2.** *Types (distinct words)*

prepositions such as: *w* [in/into], *z* [with/from/out of], or *o* [about/at/by]. The longest words in the corpora are not Polish words; for instance, in the CJ corpus the longest words are of German origin: *Mineralölsteuer-Durchführungsverordnung* [Petroleum Tax Implementing Regulation] (39 characters). In the post-accession SN corpus, the longest words are compound adjectives, such as: *usługowo-produkcyjno-handlowo-wdrożeniowe* (41 characters) [service-production-commercial-implementation]. Since Table 6.3 contains a substantial amount of quantitative data, it will be easier to discern the trends concerning the usage of different-length words in the corpora using Figure 6.4.

Figure 6.4 shows that in all post-accession corpora there are similar trends concerning the use of words of different lengths, the main difference being that

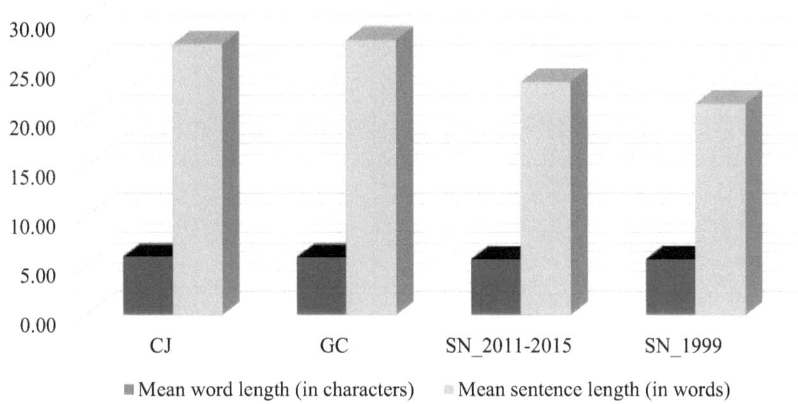


**Figure 6.3.** *Mean word and sentence length in non-lemmatized corpora*

the Eurolect corpora contain fewer words, which explains the generally lesser distribution of words of all lengths in the CJ and GC corpora compared to the post-accession SN corpus. In addition, it can be observed that the genre places particular emphasis on 7–letter words, as they are more frequent than 4–6–letter words or words of 8 or more letters. It is generally assumed that the longer the words in texts, the more difficult their reception may be. In the case of the genre of judgments, both mean sentence length and word length undoubtedly contribute to a certain degree to the overall complexity of the genre.

## 6.2 Analysis of keyword lists: identification of lexico-grammatical categories for further analysis

In order to identify the key generic patterns applicable to translated EU and non-translated national judgments, that is categories of lexico-grammatical units with irregular frequencies of occurrence, I compared the wordlist generated for the combined corpora of CJ and GC judgments with the non-lemmatized wordlist generated for the post-accession SN corpus, and vice versa, using the KeyWords feature in WS. Keywords are words with an unusually high (statistically significant) frequency of occurrence in comparison with some norm (reference corpus)[114] (Scott 2010, 2017). As a result, I was able to pinpoint salient lexico-grammatical features which are overrepresented in translations. By examining the keywords list generated with the SN wordlist set against the combined CJ and GC wordlist, I identified lexemes underrepresented in translated judgments (or overrepresented

114 The choice of a reference corpus may greatly affect the outcome of the analysis of keywords (cf. Goźdź-Roszkowski 2011: 36). Goźdź-Roszkowski (2011: 36) makes

**Table 6.2.** *Occurrences of 1–45–letter words in the corpora*

| # | Translated EU case law | | | | | | | Non-translated PL case law | | | | |
|---|---|---|---|---|---|---|---|---|---|---|---|---|
| | CJ | | CJ vs GC (%DIFF) | CJ vs SN_2011–2015 (%DIFF) | GC | | GC vs SN_2011–2015 | SN_2011–2015 | | SN_2011–2015 vs SN_1999 (%DIFF) | SN_1999 | |
| | RF | NF | % | % | RF | NF | % | RF | NF | % | RF | NF |
| 1 | 639,098 | 136,153 | +4 % | −22 % | 591,353 | 130,950 | −25 % | 1,197,093 | 175,167 | +7 % | 82,746 | 163,982 |
| 2 | 521,033 | 111,001 | −1 % | +15 % | 508,312 | 112,561 | 17 % | 659,746 | 96,539 | +2 % | 47,759 | 94,646 |
| 3 | 452,662 | 96,435 | −3 % | −1 % | 450,307 | 99,717 | +3 % | 663,192 | 97,043 | −4 % | 51,017 | 101,103 |
| 4 | 352,413 | 75,078 | −5 % | −4 % | 357,173 | 79,093 | +2 % | 532,007 | 77,847 | 0 % | 39,353 | 77,988 |
| 5 | 331,367 | 70,594 | 0 % | −2 % | 317,338 | 70,272 | −3 % | 493,910 | 72,272 | −4 % | 37,825 | 74,960 |
| 6 | 373,868 | 79,649 | +1 % | +2 % | 354,571 | 78,517 | 0 % | 535,485 | 78,356 | −3 % | 40,583 | 80,425 |
| 7 | 459,485 | 97,888 | −7 % | 13 % | 474,359 | 105,043 | +22 % | 589,570 | 86,270 | −6 % | 46,447 | 92,046 |
| 8 | 311,792 | 66,424 | −3 % | −1 % | 310,631 | 68,787 | +3 % | 456,961 | 66,866 | +1 % | 33,263 | 65,919 |
| 9 | 344,104 | 73,308 | +8 % | +1 % | 305,291 | 67,604 | −7 % | 496,882 | 72,707 | −9 % | 40,448 | 80,158 |
| 10 | 271,605 | 57,863 | −4 % | +4 % | 271,610 | 60,146 | +8 % | 381,047 | 55,758 | −2 % | 28,765 | 57,005 |
| 11 | 210,420 | 44,828 | −3 % | +5 % | 208,208 | 46,106 | +8 % | 292,767 | 42,840 | +9 % | 19,843 | 39,324 |
| 12 | 193,095 | 41,137 | +11 % | +14 % | 167,915 | 37,183 | +3 % | 245,774 | 35,963 | +1 % | 17,908 | 35,489 |
| 13 | 101,166 | 21,552 | +22 % | +7 % | 79,570 | 17,620 | −12 % | 137,247 | 20,083 | +10 % | 9,188 | 18,208 |
| 14 | 71,916 | 15,321 | +15 % | +54 % | 59,910 | 13,267 | +33 % | 68,133 | 9,970 | +24 % | 4,060 | 8,046 |
| 15 | 31,432 | 6,696 | +11 % | +13 % | 27,281 | 6,041 | +2 % | 40,673 | 5,952 | +10 % | 2,719 | 5,388 |
| 16 | 14,985 | 3,192 | −23 % | −16 % | 18,782 | 4,159 | +10 % | 25,821 | 3,778 | +37 % | 1,395 | 2,765 |

| | | | | | | | | | | | | |
|---|---|---|---|---|---|---|---|---|---|---|---|---|
| **17** | 7,187 | 1,531 | −7 % | −7 % | 7,450 | 1,650 | 0 % | 11,281 | 1,651 | +21 % | 686 | 1,359 |
| **18** | 3,261 | 695 | −14 % | +24 % | 3,634 | 805 | +44 % | 3,824 | 560 | −15 % | 334 | 662 |
| **19** | 1,289 | 275 | −14 % | +63 % | 1,438 | 318 | +89 % | 1,150 | 168 | −27 % | 117 | 232 |
| **20** | 492 | 105 | +66 % | +51 % | 286 | 63 | −9 % | 475 | 70 | −24 % | 46 | 91 |
| **21** | 302 | 64 | +68 % | +42 % | 173 | 38 | −15 % | 309 | 45 | −15 % | 27 | 54 |
| **22** | 348 | 74 | +260 % | +141 % | 93 | 21 | −33 % | 210 | 31 | −60 % | 39 | 77 |
| **23** | 124 | 26 | +109 % | +49 % | 57 | 13 | −29 % | 121 | 18 | −26 % | 12 | 24 |
| **24** | 208 | 44 | +300 % | +345 % | 50 | 11 | +11 % | 68 | 10 | −44 % | 9 | 18 |
| **25** | 99 | 21 | +132 % | +115 % | 41 | 9 | −7 % | 67 | 10 | +65 % | 3 | 6 |
| **26** | 52 | 11 | +901 % | +76 % | 5 | 1 | −82 % | 43 | 6 | +59 % | 2 | 4 |
| **27** | 59 | 13 | +1319 % | +53 % | 4 | 1 | −89 % | 56 | 8 | −17 % | 5 | 10 |
| **28** | 35 | 7 | +381 % | +363 % | 7 | 2 | −4 % | 11 | 2 | −19 % | 1 | 2 |
| **29** | 21 | 4 | +189 % | 104 % | 7 | 2 | −29 % | 15 | 2 | −45 % | 2 | 4 |
| **30** | 11 | 2 | +253 % | −38 % | 3 | 1 | −83 % | 26 | 4 | +92 % | 1 | 2 |
| **31** | 8 | 2 | | −42 % | | | | 20 | 3 | −26 % | 2 | 4 |
| **32** | 3 | 1 | | −27 % | | | | 6 | 1 | | | |
| **33** | 7 | 1 | | +155 % | | | | 4 | 1 | | | |
| **34** | 2 | 0 | | +191 % | | | | 1 | 0 | | | |
| **35** | 8 | 2 | +285 % | | 2 | 0 | | | | | | |
| **36** | 5 | 1 | +381 % | | 1 | 0 | | | | | | |
| **37** | 2 | 0 | −4 % | | 2 | 0 | | | | | | |

(*continued on next page*)

**Table 6.2.** *Continued*

| | | | | | | | | | | | | |
|---|---|---|---|---|---|---|---|---|---|---|---|---|
| **38** | 1 | 0 | | | | | | | | | | |
| **39** | 3 | 1 | | | | | | | | | | |
| **40** | | | | | | | | | | | | |
| **41** | | | | | | | | 1 | 0 | | | |
| **42** | | | | | | | | 1 | 0 | | | |
| **43** | | | | | | | | | | | | |
| **44** | | | | | | | | | | | | |
| **45** | | | | | 2 | 0 | | | | | | |

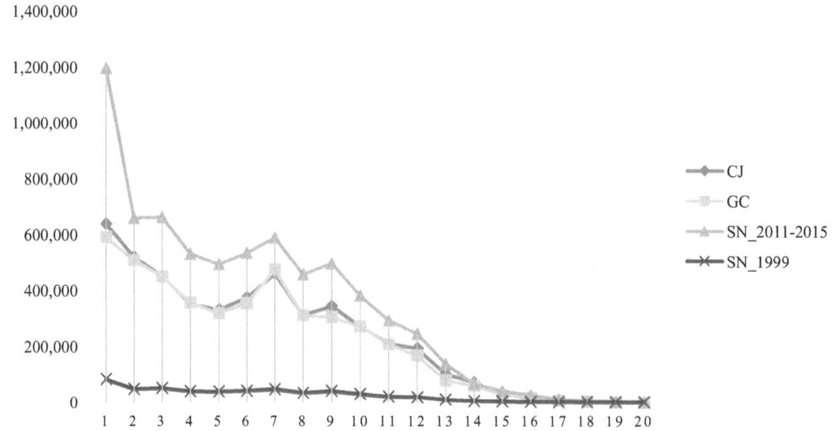


**Figure 6.4.** *Occurrences of 1–20–letter words*

in non-translated national judgments). Using the above procedure, WS generated two keyword lists with 500 lexemes with the exclusion of negative keywords,[115] both of which were analyzed manually. Some of the lexemes were extracted and manually categorized into 15 functional categories (see Table 6.3).

Keywords have the potential of revealing the "aboutness" of a particular collection of texts (Scott and Tribble 2006: 55; Goźdź-Roszkowski 2011: 35). This means that they may be categorized functionally. In his study, Goźdź-Roszkowski (2011: 96–102) proposes an extensive categorization of keywords found in American legal genres; in the case of judicial opinions, these are: keywords marking judicial stance, personal pronouns as keywords, legal terms as keywords, and keywords used to identify and interpret legal issues.[116] On examining the keyword lists generated for the corpora in three different combinations, CJ vs SN_2011–2015, GC vs SN_2011–2015, and SN_2011–2015 vs CJ, I singled out the following categories of (partly) genre-specific keywords in EU and national judgments:

---

the valid observation that "comparing a range of specialized genres from the same domain against a general reference corpus would inevitably lead to obtaining findings which may be highly homogeneous and probably valid for legal language in general, but they would not help identify features unique to a particular genre."

115 WS was instructed to limit the search for keywords to those occurring in at least 5 % of texts in a corpus. The eventual minimum dispersion of keywords generated using the combined CJ and GC wordlists set against the SN wordlist was 68 texts, and in the case of the keywords generated using the SN wordlist set against the combined CJ and GC wordlists – 128 texts. The probability value was set at 0.000001 and log likelihood chosen as the statistical significance test as opposed to chi-square.

116 Other types of keywords identified by Goźdź-Roszkowski (2011: 64–108) based on other genres include: citation keywords, keywords used to illustrate and

(1) legal terms as keywords, e.g. CJ vs SN: *podatku* [tax], *VAT* [VAT], *grzywny* [fine]; GC vs SN: *rynku* [market]; SN vs CJ: *roszczenia* [claim], *wierzytelności* [liabilities];
(2) keywords containing names of institutions, e.g. CJ vs SN: *Komisja* [Commision], *Trybunał* [Court], *krajowy* [national]; GC vs SN: *OHIM* [OHIM], *Rada* [Council]; SN vs CJ: *Najwyższy* [Supreme], *Apelacyjny* [Appellate], *Skarbu* [Treasury];
(3) keywords marking participation: GC vs SN: *skarżąca* [claimant]; SN vs CJ: *powód* [plaintiff], *pozwany* [defendant];
(4) keywords used to identify and interpret legal issues, e.g. CJ vs SN: *przedmiocie* [question], *pytania* [questions]; GC vs SN: *motyw* [motive]; SN vs CJ: *rozpoznaniu* [examination];
(5) communication/procedural keywords, e.g. CJ vs SN: *interpretować* [interpret]; GC vs SN: *przypomnieć* [remind]; SN vs CJ: *zważył* [held], *oddalił* [dismissed];
(6) judicial stance keywords, e.g. CJ vs SN: *należy* [(it/one) must/should be]; GC vs SN: *należy* [[(it/one) must/should be];
(7) text deixis keywords, e.g. CJ vs SN: *zob.* [see], *podobnie* [similarly], *ww.* [above-named-ABBRV], *Traktatu* [Treaty], *przytoczone* [referred], *pkt.* [item], *lit.* [letter], *artykuł* [article]; GC vs SN: *rozporządzenia* [regulation], *decyzji* [decision]; SN vs CJ: *umowy* [agreement], *apelacji* [appeal], *por.* [cf.];
(8) time and place keywords, e.g. CJ vs SN: *terytorium* [territory];

The identified keywords point to thematic differences between the corpora, as EU and national corpora tend to focus on different concepts. Thus, they also accentuate to a certain degree the terminological content of judgments (cf. Chapter 9). What can be observed at this point is that the identified keywords do not necessarily form part of the lexicon of one specific subject field (cf. Goźdź-Roszkowski 2011: 107).

Table 6.3 presents 15 functional categories identified upon the extraction of the function and content keywords in CJEU and SN judgments. The most salient keywords in translations are simple present and past tense verbs, infinitives, deverbal nouns, and stance adverbials, whereas the most salient keywords in non-translated judgments are deverbal nouns and past tense verbs. Overall, the similar number of grammatical keywords in EU and PL judgments suggests a similarity of linguistic patterns, despite certain quantitative differences. Nevertheless, the keywords overrepresented in translations suggest that translated judgments have slightly more varied patterns which are dissimilar to those found in national judgments. This may be due to the impact of the translation process or the result of sub-genre conventions.

---

support legal reasoning, keywords marking internal organization of a legislative text, keywords denoting legal instruments, keywords marking time/place/text deixis, keywords used to modify legislative provisions, institutional keywords, academic keywords, keywords related to crime and incarceration, evaluation keywords, keywords referring to public interest, keywords marking participation, function keywords, and general language keywords.

**Table 6.3.** *Lexico-grammatical categories for identified with the 500–word CJEU and SN keyword lists (positions of individual keywords on the respective keyword lists are shown in square brackets)*

| | CJ and GC vs SN_2011–2015 (keywords overrepresented in translations) | SN_2011–2015 vs CJ and GC (keywords underrepresented in translations) |
|---|---|---|
| **1. Prepositions** | *powyżej* [#20], *podczas* [#221] | *wyżej* [#265], *wskutek* [#311] |
| **2. Paratactic and hypotactic markers** | N/A | *tj.* [i.e.-ABBRV] [#71] |
| **3. Deictic markers** | *ww.* [#10], *niniejszego* [#57], *przytoczone* [#61], *tam* [#66], *niniejszym* [#96], *wspomnianego* [#154], *następujący* [#189], *każdym* [#242], *niniejsze* [#260], *rzeczonego* [#269], *wspomniane* [#335], *następujące* [#367], *rzeczonej* [#444], *wspomnianych* [#451], *wspomnianej* [#466], *rzeczone* [#468] | *pozostałej* [#215] |
| **4. Pronouns** | *ona* [#101], *one* [#113] | N/A |
| **5. Passive voice and auxiliary verbs** | *zostać* [#52], *zostaje* [#193] | N/A |
| **6. Impersonal patterns** | N/A | *orzeczono* [#372] |
| **7. Verbs in indicative mode (mood) – verdictive, exercitive (argumentative) and reporting verbs in the active voice** | | |
| **Present tense verbs** | *należy* [#7], *podnosi* [#70], *twierdzi* [#95], *uważa* [#138], *wnosi* [#167], *wydaje* [#168], *podnoszą* [#214], *twierdzą* [#234], *przewiduje* [#238], *utrzymuje* [#278], *orzeka* [#346], *dodaje* [#435], *przypomina* [#469] | *uchyla* [#162], *oddala* [#167], *zasądza* [#208], *przekazuje* [#219], *przesądza* [#436] |
| **Past tense verbs** | *uznała* [#116], *stwierdziła* [#152], *naruszyła* [#303], *popełniła* [#309], *postanowił* [#320], *uwzględniła* [#385], *wskazała* [#433], *uczestniczyła* [#456], *przyjęła* [#473] | *oddalił* [#60], *zważył* [#64], *uznał* [#78], *zasądził* [#103], *ustalił* [#107], *podzielił* [#116], *wskazał* [#129], *zarzucił* [#160], *zmienił* [#179], *wniósł* [#228], *ocenił* [#234], *podkreślił* [#261], *uchylił* [#270], *nastąpiło* [#273], *wyraził* [#336], *należało* [#350], *okazał* [#366], *zobowiązał* [#367], *ustaliły* [#391], *wykazał* [#405], *zawarły* [#457], *dokonał* [#489] |

(*continued on next page*)

**Table 6.3.** *Continued*

| | CJ and GC vs SN_2011–2015 (keywords overrepresented in translations) | SN_2011–2015 vs CJ and GC (keywords underrepresented in translations) |
|---|---|---|
| **8. Infinitives** | *przypomnieć* [#50], *stwierdzić* [#59], *oddalić* [#76], *interpretować* [#83], *zaznaczyć* [#296], *odpowiedzieć* [#325], *zauważyć* [#330], *zawiesić* [#336], *odrzucić* [#431] | *podzielić* [#291], *nastąpić* [#463] |
| **9. Causal markers** | *analogicznie* [#294] | *więc* [#145] |
| **10. Conditionals** | *jeśli* [#67] | *skoro* [#128] |
| **11. Purpose markers** | *celu* [#26], *celów* [#55], *by* [#163] | N/A |
| **12. Addition adverbials** | *ponadto* [#72] | *nadto* [#213] |
| **13. Participles** | | |
| **Adjectival participles** | *działających* [#94], *zatytułowany* [#173], *rozpatrywanych* [#246], *utrwalonym* [#281], *dotyczący* [#329], *dotyczącym* [#389], *zwanym* [#405], *mających* [#471], *zwany* [#457], *pochodzących* [#499] | *zaskarżony* [#96], *obowiązującym* [#384] |
| **Adverbial participles** | *rozważywszy* [#368] | *podzielając* [#388], *zarzucając* [#396] |
| **14. Stance adverbials** | *słusznie* [#360] | *trafnie* [#138], *niewątpliwie* [#254] |
| **15. Deverbal nouns** | *odwołanie* [#64], *poparcie* [#151], *obciążenie* [#286], *zapewnienia* [#304], *zatrudnienia* [#357], *przedstawieniem* [#394], *ujawnienie* [#428], *spotkanie* [#458], *przedstawienie* [#491] | *roszczenie* [#49], *zasądzenie* [#123], *uchylenie* [#136], *przedawnienia* [#137], *użytkowanie* [#177], *niezastosowanie* [#202], *przekazanie* [#227], *wykonanie* [#272], *zadośćuczynienie* [#304], *uznanie* [#319], *zobowiązanie* [#331], *oświadczenie* [#335], *odszkodowanie* [#355], *zaniechanie* [#385], *uwzględnienie* [#398] |

In Sections 6.3–6.8, I will analyze the following dimensions of textual variation in translated EU judgments and non-translated SN judgments:

1. Phraseological framing with prepositions (and their discourse functions):
   - simple prepositions,
   - compound prepositions,
   - secondary prepositions,

2. Structurization of judicial arguments:
   - parataxis,
   - hypotaxis,
3. Deixis:
   - personal, possessive, demonstrative, indefinite pronouns and quantifiers,
   - adjectival deictic expressions,
4. Depersonalization – passive voice and impersonal patterns:
   - auxiliary verbs *być* [to be] and *zostać* [to become],
   - passive voice,
   - the *się* impersonal pattern,
   - the *-no/to* impersonal pattern,
5. Legal reasoning:
   - verdictive, exercitive (argumentative) and reporting verbs,
   - causal patterns,
   - if-then conditionals and related patterns,
   - patterns of purpose,
6. Framing with adverbials and participles:
   - adverbials: addition, enumeration, exemplification and particularization, stance, contrast and exclusion,
   - participles: adjectival and adverbial participles.

I will discuss extensively only the use of prepositions and their discourse functions, since they have the greatest distribution among all identified categories. In the discussion on the remaining categories, I will focus on the distributional characteristics of various lexico-grammatical exponents which were supplemented using relevant literature (cf. Biel 2014a).

## 6.3 Phraseological framing with prepositions

Polish prepositions have been widely discussed in the literature by Milewska (2003a,b), Lesz-Duk (1993, 2007, 2011), Łapa (2006a,b, 2013), and Nowak (2008), among others. They have also been the focus of investigations into various specialized genres, such as EU and domestic legislative documents (Biel 2016b) and EU and domestic reports (Wasilewska 2018). Prepositions in EU and post-accession domestic (SN) judgments were analyzed in my earlier exploratory paper (see Koźbiał 2018b).

The results presented in this chapter build upon my previous work on prepositions by including a more exhaustive list of simple prepositions and a full account of discourse functions fulfilled by compound and secondary prepositions in judicial language, as well as by providing quantitative data on the distribution of prepositions in the pre-accession corpus of SN judgments passed in 1999 (cf. Koźbiał 2018b[117]). Prepositions have been identified as yet another potential indicator of

117 In that article (Koźbiał 2018b), I discussed only the following seven discourse functions of compound and secondary prepositions in EU and national judgments: time;

lexico-grammatical variation in translated EU judgments and non-translated Polish judgments (cf. Table 6.3), with *podczas* [during] being overrepresented in the former and *wskutek* [as a consequence of] being underrepresented in the latter. This chapter aims to examine not only the distribution of simple, compound and secondary prepositions in CJEU judgments and (pre- and post-accession) SN judgments against general Polish (based on a balanced version of the NKJP), but also to analyze the discourse functions of compound and secondary prepositions.

### 6.3.1 Prepositions as a word class

Prepositions are non-inflectional linking words which cannot be used on their own, as they require a subordinate noun (Bąk 1984: 183; Milewska 2003a: 38). They occur together with nouns in different cases (except nominative and vocative), e.g. *w celu* [for the purpose of] (*w* [in/into] + noun in the genitive case), while some prepositions can take different cases depending on meaning, e.g. *na podstawie* [on the basis of] (*na* [on] + noun in the Locative), *na rzecz* [for; in favor of] (*na* [on] + noun in the Accusative) (case government). Prepositions include not only individual words, that is **simple prepositions**, e.g. *w* [in/into], *z* [with/from/out of], *na* [on/onto], *przed* [before/in front of] (Łapa 2013: 78) and **compound prepositions** formed with two simple prepositions, e.g. *poprzez* [by], *poza* [beyond]. They also include noun phrases with simple prepositions – **secondary prepositions**, e.g. *na podstawie* [on the basis of], *w odniesieniu do* [with reference to], as well as lexicalized forms of other POS (nouns, adverbs) fulfilling functions performed by prepositions, e.g. *celem* [in order to], *powyżej* [above/over] or *tytułem* [under].

### 6.3.2 Distribution of simple prepositions

As expected, simple prepositions have been found to have the highest frequency of occurrence among the categories of prepositions, as well as lexicalized forms of other POS which act as prepositions. Simple prepositions, like *w* [in/into], may also form secondary prepositions, such as *w świetle* [in light of] and *w rozumieniu* [within the understanding of]. Due to their exceptionally high distribution in all of the corpora, it was not possible to establish their exact distribution with the exclusion of occurrences of simple prepositions within secondary prepositions by manually analyzing the concordances. Therefore, the results presented below show the aggregate distribution of simple prepositions in the corpora of CJEU judgments, pre- and post-accession SN judgments and general Polish (balanced version of the NKJP corpus). The collected data may be assumed to paint a clear picture of the overall distribution of simple prepositions in the corpora, despite the aforementioned limitation. Table 6.4 shows quantitative data concerning the distribution of simple prepositions.

---

cause-effect, permission and condition; reference; intra- and inter-textual reference; participation; modality; manner and instrumental relations. The present analysis encompasses all 18 discourse functions and presents all types of compound and secondary prepositions expressing them.

**Table 6.4.** *Distribution of simple prepositions in the corpora (ordered according to their NF in the corpora)*

| Translated EU case law | | | | | | |
|---|---|---|---|---|---|---|
| **CJ** | **NF** | **CJ vs GC (%DIFF)** | **CJ vs SN_2011–2015 (%DIFF)** | **GC** | **NF** | **vs SN_2011–2015 (%DIFF)** |
| *w* [in/into] | 48,757 | −4 % | +16 % | *w* [in/into] | 50,872 | +21 % |
| *z* [with/from/out of] | 19,119 | −3 % | −29 % | *z* [with/from/out of] | 19,660 | −27 % |
| *do* [(in)to] | 14,734 | +4 % | +15 % | *na* [on/onto] | 14,895 | +8 % |
| *na* [on/onto] | 14,267 | −4 % | +4 % | *do* [(in)to] | 14,223 | +11 % |
| *przez* [by/through] | 7,352 | +5 % | −14 % | *przez* [by/through] | 7,027 | −17 % |
| *o* [about/at/by] | 6,294 | +8 % | −37 % | *o* [about/at/by] | 5,838 | −41 % |
| *od* [from] | 3,098 | +14 % | −37 % | *po* [after] | 3,389 | +45 % |
| *za* [behind] | 2,545 | +9 % | −32 % | *od* [from] | 2,722 | −45 % |
| *dla* [for] | 2,466 | +23 % | +61 % | *za* [behind] | 2,340 | −37 % |
| *po* [after] | 2,309 | −32 % | −1 % | *ze* [with] | 2,186 | +21 % |
| *przed* [before/in front of] | 1,951 | +80 % | +101 % | *dla* [for] | 2,004 | +31 % |
| *ze* [with] | 1,855 | −15 % | +3 % | *między* [between] | 1,099 | +75 % |
| *przy* [at/next to] | 947 | −7 % | −37 % | *przed* [before/in front of] | 1,081 | +11 % |
| *między* [between] | 926 | −16 % | +47 % | *przy* [at/next to] | 1,016 | −33 % |
| *pod* [under] | 861 | −8 % | +35 % | *pod* [under] | 940 | +47 % |
| *bez* [without] | 742 | +22 % | +5 % | *bez* [without] | 609 | −14 % |
| *we* [in] | 466 | −5 % | +31 % | *we* [in] | 489 | +38 % |
| *u* [with/at] | 187 | −7 % | +5 % | *u* [with/at] | 202 | +13 % |

(*continued on next page*)

**Table 6.4.** *Continued*

| Translated EU case law | | | | | | |
|---|---|---|---|---|---|---|
| *nad* [over/above] | 156 | +3 % | +39 % | *mimo* [despite] | 165 | −51 % |
| *mimo* [despite] | 129 | −22 % | −62 % | *nad* [over/above] | 152 | +36 % |
| *ku* [unto] | 11 | +57 % | −48 % | *ku* [unto] | 7 | −67 % |
| *temu* [ago/back] | 0 | −100 % | −100 % | *temu* [ago/back] | 2 | 0 % |
| **Total** | **129,170** | **−1 %** | **−3 %** | **Total** | **130,917** | **−2 %** |
| **Non-translated PL case law** | | | | | **General Polish** | |
| **SN_2011–2015** | **NF** | **SN_2011–2015 vs SN_1999 (%DIFF)** | **SN_1999** | **NF** | **NKJP** | **NF** |
| *w* [in/into] | 41,925 | +10 % | *w* [in/into] | 38,063 | *w* [in/into] | 13,544 |
| *z* [with/from/out of] | 26,975 | +6 % | *z* [with/from/out of] | 25,341 | *z* [with/from/out of] | 10,950 |
| *na* [on/onto] | 13,782 | −5 % | *na* [on/onto] | 14,491 | *na* [on/onto] | 9,651 |
| *do* [(in)to] | 12,784 | +15 % | *do* [(in)to] | 11,137 | *do* [(in)to] | 7,483 |
| *o* [about/at/by] | 9,964 | +3 % | *o* [about/at/by] | 9,711 | *o* [about/at/by] | 4,985 |
| *przez* [by/through] | 8,507 | +3 % | *przez* [by/through] | 8,254 | *po* [after] | 3,125 |
| *od* [from] | 4,955 | −7 % | *od* [from] | 5,301 | *od* [from] | 2,969 |
| *za* [behind] | 3,718 | −1 % | *za* [behind] | 3,757 | *za* [behind] | 2,799 |
| *po* [after] | 2,334 | −18 % | *po* [after] | 2,830 | *przez* [by/through] | 2,505 |
| *ze* [with] | 1,804 | +48 % | *przy* [at/next to] | 1,708 | *dla* [for] | 2,213 |
| *dla* [for] | 1,530 | +10 % | *dla* [for] | 1,385 | *ze* [with] | 1,569 |

| | | | | | | |
|---|---|---|---|---|---|---|
| *przy* [at/next to] | 1,510 | −12 % | *ze* [with] | 1,215 | *przed* [before/ in front of] | 1,342 |
| *przed* [before/in front of] | 970 | 0 % | *przed* [before/in front of] | 971 | *przy* [at/next to] | 1,213 |
| *bez* [without] | 707 | −7 % | *między* [between] | 820 | *pod* [under] | 1,095 |
| *pod* [under] | 640 | +9 % | *bez* [without] | 761 | *bez* [without] | 815 |
| *między* [between] | 629 | −23 % | *pod* [under] | 585 | *nad* [over/ above] | 733 |
| *we* [in] | 355 | +14 % | *mimo* [despite] | 386 | *u* [with/at] | 603 |
| *mimo* [despite] | 339 | −12 % | *u* [with/at] | 323 | *we* [in] | 523 |
| *u* [with/at] | 178 | −45 % | *we* [in] | 311 | *między* [between] | 439 |
| *nad* [over/above] | 112 | −24 % | *nad* [over/above] | 147 | *mimo* [despite] | 288 |
| *ku* [unto] | 21 | +50 % | *ku* [unto] | 14 | *temu* [ago/ back] | 184 |
| *temu* [ago/back] | 2 | --- | *temu* [ago/back] | 0 | *ku* [unto] | 120 |
| **Total** | **133,744** | **+5 %** | **Total** | **127,740** | **Total** | **69,162** |

The above quantitative data clearly show that simple prepositions play a crucial role in judicial language, as proven by their very high normalized frequency of occurrence relative to general Polish. They are two times more frequent in the CJEU and SN corpora of judgments than in the balanced version of the NKJP corpus.

Overall, simple prepositions are only slightly underrepresented in translated CJ and GC judgments compared to non-translated SN judgments, by 3 % and 2 %, respectively. The distribution of simple prepositions in the post-accession SN corpus is about 5 % higher than in the pre-accession corpus. It may be assumed, however, that their distribution is rather even across EU and national judgments. This is confirmed by the analysis of keyword lists (see Section 6.2), as simple prepositions have not been found on any of the lists of keywords, meaning that simple prepositions do not have an untypically high or low distribution in either the EU corpora or the national corpora, and vice versa. The high occurrence frequency of simple prepositions in both EU corpora and the national corpus suggests that prepositions play an important role in the language of judgments, and that, at this stage of the analysis, the high reliance on simple prepositions may be tentatively perceived as a genre marker (cf. Biel 2016b; Koźbiał 2018b), although it should be noted that the above data do not exclude occurrences of simple prepositions within secondary prepositions. Consequently, the distribution of simple prepositions should be contrasted with the distribution of compound and secondary prepositions.

### 6.3.3 Distribution of top 50 compound and secondary prepositions

The existence of the word class of secondary prepositions is the result of language users' efforts to render communication more precise. The development of secondary prepositions, which has mainly taken place in recent decades (Milewska 2003b: 7), is a result of the grammaticalization of simple prepositions which leads to the generalization and intensification of their functions (Jadacka 2005: 213–214; Łapa 2006a: 358–359). Examples of secondary prepositions include *na podstawie* [on the basis of] or *w rozumieniu* [within the understanding of]. Secondary prepositions also include words which were not formed by means of coupling with simple prepositions. At first sight, they look like declension nouns, e.g. *tytułem* [under], *zdaniem* [according to], *drogą* [by way of], being generally more difficult to extract from corpora. For this reason, the examination of every single concordance is required in order to eliminate words acting as declension nouns without any prepositional functions, e.g.:

(1) SN (II CSK 196/11): *Po otwarciu hipermarketu podstawową *<u>drogą</u> dojazdową była droga przez działkę 7/16.*
[After the opening of the hypermarket, the basic access road was via plot of land number 7/16.]

(2) SN (III CSK 73/12): *W październiku 2008 r. strony prowadziły ze sobą korespondencję drogą elektroniczną.*
[In October 2008, the parties exchanged correspondence electronically.]

The class of secondary prepositions is not clearly delineated, as simple prepositions are still subject to an ongoing process of grammaticalization and lexicalization (Milewska 2003b: 39). Therefore, there is no exhaustive account of secondary prepositions in the Polish language (cf. Milewska 2003a,b), which may potentially impede corpus-based research into prepositions in specialized genres (cf. Biel 2016b; Koźbiał 2018b; Wasilewska 2018). For the purposes of this study, I created a list of all possible secondary prepositions using the relevant literature (cf. Milewska 2003a, 2003b; Łapa 2006a, 2013; Lesz-Duk 2007, 2011; Nowak 2008) and supplemented it with prepositions identified in similar studies on other specialized genres, including EU and domestic legislative acts and reports (cf. Biel 2016b; Koźbiał 2018b; Wasilewska 2018).

Apart from the distribution of secondary prepositions, this section also examines the distribution of compound prepositions, such as *poza* [beyond], *pomiędzy* [between], and *poprzez* [by]. Compound prepositions are formed by combining two simple prepositions, which allows language users to express more complicated and precise meanings. In this section, since compound prepositions occur less frequently than secondary prepositions, the former are considered together with the latter (see Table 6.5).

The distribution of the top 50 compound and secondary prepositions in the corpora of EU and national judgments and the corpus of general Polish (NKJP) shows that these prepositions are very salient in the language of judgments, since their distribution in general Polish is markedly lower compared to the specialized corpora. When it comes to the total number of tokens of the top 50 compound and secondary prepositions, the post-accession corpora of judgments exhibit ca. 4.1, 4.6, and 3.9 times more occurrences of such prepositions, respectively. Such degree of overrepresentation of compound and secondary prepositions in the corpora of EU and national judgments demonstrates that the genre of judgments requires high precision in conveying information. It also seems that CJ and GC judgments require an even greater degree of precision than post-accession SN judgments, as the total number of occurrences of compound and secondary prepositions is 7 % and 18 % higher in the EU corpora, respectively. The post-accession corpus of SN judgments contains about 12 % more tokens than the pre-accession corpus, which may be indicative of a growing need for preciseness, which, in turn, results in a higher number of analytical structures. This tendency may be correlated with the overrepresentation of compound and secondary prepositions in EU judgments relative to the pre-accession SN corpus.

It should be noted that numerous secondary prepositions include simple prepositions, such as *w sprawie* [in the matter of] or *na podstawie* [on the basis of],

**Table 6.5.** *Distribution of top 50 compound and secondary prepositions in CJEU judgments*

| Translated EU case law | | | | | | |
|---|---|---|---|---|---|---|
| **CJ** | **NF** | **CJ vs GC (%DIFF)** | **vs SN_2011–2015 (%DIFF)** | **GC** | **NF** | **GC vs SN_2011–2015 (%DIFF)** |
| *w sprawie* [in the matter of] | 3,694 | −14 % | +129 % | *w sprawie* [in the matter of] | 4,284 | +165 % |
| *z dnia* [of] | 3,361 | −18 % | −50 % | *z dnia* [of] | 4,110 | −38 % |
| *zgodnie z* [according to] | 2,631 | +16 % | +170 % | *przeciwko* [against] | 2,338 | +168 % |
| *na podstawie* [on the basis of] | 1,727 | +17 % | −11 % | *zgodnie z* [according to] | 2,273 | +133 % |
| *w dniu/dniach* [on] | 1,401 | −25 % | −19 % | *w dniu/dniach* [on] | 1,874 | +9 % |
| *w ramach* [within the framework of] | 1,359 | −19 % | +130 % | *w przedmiocie* [on] | 1,817 | --- |
| *jako* [as/in the capacity of] (excl. *jako że*) | 1,324 | −16 % | −33 % | *w ramach* [within the framework] | 1,673 | +184 % |
| *w przedmiocie* [on] | 1,268 | −30 % | --- | *jako* [as/in the capacity of] | 1,583 | −20 % |
| *w celu* [for the purpose of] | 1,209 | +47 % | +330 % | *powyżej* [above] | 1,573 | --- |
| *przeciwko* [against] | 1,189 | −49 % | +36 % | *na podstawie* [on the basis of] | 1,471 | −24 % |
| *w odniesieniu do* [with reference to] | 1,156 | −18 % | +244 % | *w odniesieniu do* [with reference to] | 1,402 | +317 % |
| *w rozumieniu* [within the understanding of] | 1,035 | +79 % | +163 % | *w zakresie* [in respect of] | 1,160 | +62 % |
| *w zakresie* [in respect of] | 1,016 | −12 % | 42 % | *w przypadku* [in the case of] | 833 | +219 % |
| *w przypadku* [in the case of] | 959 | +15 % | +267 % | *w celu* [for the purpose of] | 823 | +193 % |
| *w imieniu* [on behalf of] | 824 | --- | +79 % | *wobec* [towards] | 789 | −20 % |

| | | | | | | |
|---|---|---|---|---|---|---|
| *w charakterze* [acting as/represented by] | 810 | +192 % | --- | *co do* [as to] | 757 | −20 % |
| *w związku z* [it follows from] | 806 | +20 % | −35 % | *ze względu na* [in respect of] | 685 | +115 % |
| *ze względu na* [in respect of] | 654 | −5 % | +105 % | *w związku z* [it follows from] | 670 | −46 % |
| *co do* [as to] | 592 | −22 % | −38 % | *w świetle* [in light of] | 587 | +107 % |
| *na mocy* [pursuant to/BT: by power of article] | 564 | +83 % | --- | *w rozumieniu* [within the understanding | 579 | +47 % |
| *poprzez* [by] | 546 | +41 % | +17 % | *podczas* [during] | 572 | --- |
| *w świetle* [in light of] | 534 | −9 % | +88 % | *zdaniem* [according to] | 569 | +39 % |
| *wobec* [towards] | 504 | −36 % | −49 % | *w konsekwencji* [as a result] | 489 | +53 % |
| *na terytorium* [in the territory of] | 479 | --- | --- | *pomiędzy* [between] | 415 | +19 % |
| *zdaniem* [according to] | 441 | −22 % | +8 % | *poza* [beyond] | 386 | +59 % |
| *pomiędzy* [between] | 433 | +4 % | +24 % | *poprzez* [by] | 386 | −18 % |
| *w trybie* [under] | 416 | --- | --- | *od dnia* [from] | 367 | −33 % |
| na rzecz [for; in favour of] | 371 | +48 % | −69 % | *do dnia* [by] | 343 | −3 % |
| *w konsekwencji* [as a result] | 354 | −28 % | +11 % | *według* [according to] | 328 | −46 % |
| *z tytułu* [under the title of] | 347 | +91 % | −43 % | *w okresie* [within the period of] | 327 | +14 % |
| *do celów* [for the purposes of] | 337 | --- | --- | *w ocenie* [in the opinion of] | 326 | +7 % |
| *podczas* [during] | 329 | −42 % | --- | *na mocy* [pursuant to] | 309 | --- |
| poza [beyond] | 305 | −21 % | +26 % | *na temat* (without: nt.) [on the subject of] | 299 | --- |

(*continued on next page*)

**Table 6.5.** *Continued*

| Translated EU case law | | | | | | |
|---|---|---|---|---|---|---|
| **CJ** | **NF** | **CJ vs GC (%DIFF)** | **vs SN_2011–2015 (%DIFF)** | **GC** | **NF** | **GC vs SN_2011–2015 (%DIFF)** |
| *według* [according to] | 291 | −11 % | −52 % | *w trakcie* [during the course of] | 282 | --- |
| w dziedzinie [in the area of] | 264 | +31 % | --- | *w charakterze* [acting as/ represented by] | 277 | --- |
| *w drodze* [by way of] | 262 | +70 % | +28 % | *na rzecz* [for; in favour of] | 251 | −79 % |
| *od dnia* [from] | 250 | −32 % | −30 % | *wbrew* [contrary to] | 250 | +1 % |
| *w stosunku do* [in relation to] | 224 | −7 % | −33 % | *w odpowiedzi na* [in response to] | 248 | --- |
| *z uwagi na* [in view of] | 217 | −8 % | −30 % | *w stosunku do* [in relation to] | 242 | −27 % |
| *niezależnie od* [irrespective of] | 192 | --- | --- | *z uwagi na* [in view of] | 236 | −24 % |
| *w okresie* [within the period of] | 189 | −42 % | −34 % | *w toku* [in the course of] | 230 | −13 % |
| *w wypadku* [in the event of] | 183 | --- | --- | *w wysokości* [in the amount of] | 211 | −27 % |
| *ds.* [in charge of-ABBRV] | 167 | --- | --- | *względem* [in regard of] | 210 | --- |
| *względem* [in regard of] | 164 | --- | --- | *w dziedzinie* [in the area of] | 201 | --- |
| *w trakcie* [during the course of] | 163 | −42 % | --- | *tytułem* [under] | 200 | −60 % |
| *w chwili* [at the time of] | 160 | --- | −36 % | *z tytułu* [under the title of] | 182 | −70 % |
| *do dnia* [by] | 159 | −54 % | −55 % | *w dniach* [on … and …] | 178 | --- |
| *tytułem* [under] | 156 | −22 % | −69 % | *z powodu* [for a reason of] | 157 | --- |

| | | | | | | |
|---|---|---|---|---|---|---|
| *w razie* [in the case of] | 148 | --- | −54 % | *w drodze* [by way of] | 154 | −25 % |
| *w wyniku* [as a result of] | 146 | --- | −58 % | *w następstwie* [following] | 153 | --- |
| ***Total*** | **36,312** | **−9 %** | **+7 %** | ***Total*** | **40,059** | **+18 %** |
| **Non-translated PL case law** | | | | | **General Polish** | |
| **SN_2011–2015** | **NF** | **SN_2011–2015 vs SN_1999 (%DIFF)** | **SN_1999** | **NF** | **NKJP** | **NF** |
| *z dnia* [of] | 6,675 | +16 % | *z dnia [of]* | 5,757 | *około* [about] | 437 |
| *jako* [as/in the capacity of] | 1,990 | +6 % | *w dniu/dniach* [on] | 1,948 | *podczas* [during] | 414 |
| *na podstawie* [on the basis of] | 1,938 | +34 % | *jako* [as/in the capacity of] | 1,883 | dnia [of] | 359 |
| *w dniu/dniach* [on] | 1,721 | −12 % | *na podstawie* [on the basis of] | 1,449 | *dzięki* [as a result of/pursuant to] | 331 |
| *w sprawie* [in the matter of] | 1,614 | +23 % | *przeciwko* [against] | 1,344 | *według* [according to] | 309 |
| *w związku z* [it follows from] | 1,232 | +47 % | *w sprawie* [in the matter of] | 1,312 | *wśród* [among] | 307 |
| *na rzecz* [for; in favour of] | 1,196 | +23 % | *na skutek* [as a result of] | 1,163 | *jako* [as/in the capacity of] | 288 |
| *wobec* [towards] | 986 | +3 % | *co do* [as to] | 1,036 | *wobec [towards]* | 273 |
| *zgodnie z* [according to] | 974 | +72 % | *na rzecz* [for; in favour of] | 975 | *zdaniem [according to]* | 235 |
| *co do* [as to] | 951 | −8 % | *wobec* [towards] | 953 | *w sprawie* [in the matter of] | 214 |

(*continued on next page*)

**Table 6.5.** *Continued*

| Non-translated PL case law | | | | | General Polish | |
|---|---|---|---|---|---|---|
| **SN_2011–2015** | **NF** | **SN_2011–2015 vs SN_1999 (%DIFF)** | **SN_1999** | **NF** | **NKJP** | **NF** |
| *przeciwko* [against] | 874 | −35 % | *w związku z* [it follows from] | 840 | *w przypadku* [in the case of] | 213 |
| *w zakresie* [in respect of] | 717 | +47 % | *zdaniem* [according to] | 648 | *zgodnie z* [according to] | 204 |
| *według* [according to] | 612 | −4 % | *według* [according to] | 640 | *w czasie* [at the time of] | 202 |
| *z tytułu* [under the title of] | 609 | +41 % | *zgodnie z* [according to] | 565 | *poza* [beyond] | 201 |
| *dnia* [on] | 602 | +119 % | *w zakresie* [in respect of] | 489 | *ok.* [ca.] | 188 |
| *w ramach* [within the framework of] | 590 | --- | *od daty* [within] | 456 | *obok* [beside] | 182 |
| *od dnia* [from] | 548 | +73 % | *z tytułu* [under the title of] | 432 | *w związku z* [it follows from] | 182 |
| *tytułem* [under] | 497 | +16 % | *tytułem* [under] | 428 | *w ciągu* [in the course of] | 180 |
| *poprzez* [by] | 468 | +60 % | *wbrew* [contrary to] | 396 | *wraz z* [together with] | 177 |
| *w imieniu* [on behalf of] | 461 | --- | *w świetle* [in light of] | 375 | *do końca* [until the end of] | 172 |
| *zdaniem* [according to] | 409 | −37 % | *poza* [beyond] | 355 | *na temat* [on the subject of] | 170 |

| | | | | | | |
|---|---|---|---|---|---|---|
| *w postaci* [in the form of] | 396 | +78 % | stosownie do [in conformity with] | 353 | *przeciw* [against] | 169 |
| *w rozumieniu* [within the understanding of] | 394 | +28 % | *od dnia* [from] | 317 | *w końcu* [finally/ in the end] | 166 |
| *do dnia* [by] | 355 | --- | *w rozumieniu* [within the understanding of] | 309 | *w ramach* [within the framework of] | 159 |
| *pomiędzy* [between] | 350 | +46 % | *w stosunku do* [in relation to] | 309 | *oprócz* [in addition to] | 150 |
| *w wyniku* [as a result of] | 344 | +14 % | z mocy [under; BT by power of] | 303 | *zamiast* [instead of] | 140 |
| *na skutek* [as a result of] | 337 | −71 % | w wyniku [as a result of] | 301 | *poprzez* [by] | 140 |
| *w odniesieniu do* [with reference to] | 336 | +41 % | *poprzez* [by] | 293 | *na podstawie* [on the basis of] | 138 |
| *w stosunku do* [in relation to] | 333 | +8 % | *w ocenie* [in the opinion of] | 293 | *co do* [as to] | 135 |
| *w razie* [in the case of] | 325 | +17 % | *w kwocie* [in the amount of] | 283 | *w latach* [between] | 134 |
| *w konsekwencji* [as a result] | 319 | +21 % | *w razie* [in the case of] | 277 | *na początku* [at the beginning of] | 131 |
| *ze względu na* [in respect of] | 319 | +79 % | *dnia* [on] | 275 | *pomiędzy* [between] | 130 |

(*continued on next page*)

**Table 6.5.** *Continued*

| Non-translated PL case law | | | | | General Polish | |
|---|---|---|---|---|---|---|
| **SN_2011–2015** | **NF** | **SN_2011–2015 vs SN_1999 (%DIFF)** | **SN_1999** | **NF** | **NKJP** | **NF** |
| *z uwagi na* [in view of] | 309 | +42 % | *w konsekwencji* [as a result] | 264 | *prócz* [apart from] | 129 |
| *w ocenie* [in the opinion of] | 305 | +4 % | w czasie [at the time of] | 244 | *przeciwko* [against] | 127 |
| *wraz z* [together with] | 293 | +80 % | *pomiędzy* [between] | 240 | *do spraw* (excl. *ds.*) [in charge of] | 125 |
| *w wysokości* [in the amount of] | 291 | +28 % | w odniesieniu do [with reference to] | 238 | *wokół* [around] | 121 |
| *w okresie* [within the period of] | 286 | +29 % | *wskutek* [as a consequence of] | 238 | *w zakresie* [in respect of] | 118 |
| *w świetle* [in light of] | 284 | −24 % | *w wysokości* [in the amount of] | 228 | *na terenie* [in the territory of] | 117 |
| *w celu* [for the purpose of] | 281 | +46 % | *w toku* [in the course of] | 226 | *ze względu na* [in respect of] | 117 |
| *w kwocie* [in the amount of] | 264 | −7 % | *w okresie* [within the period of] | 222 | *w trakcie* [during the course of] | 113 |
| *w toku* [in the course of] | 264 | +17 % | *w postaci* [in the form of] | 222 | *w dniu/dniach* [on] | 105 |
| *w przypadku* [in the case of] | 261 | --- | *z uwagi na* [in view of] | 218 | *na terenach* [in the territory of] | 104 |
| *w chwili* [at the time of] | 251 | +62 % | *w następstwie* [following] | 196 | *na wzór* [similar to/following] | 104 |

| | | | | | | |
|---|---|---|---|---|---|---|
| *wbrew* [contrary to] | 247 | −38 % | *w celu* [for the purpose of] | 192 | *z powodu* [for a reason of] | 102 |
| *poza* [beyond] | 243 | −32 % | *na mocy* [pursuant to/BT: by power of article] | 180 | *na rzecz* [for; in favour of] | 96 |
| *wskutek* [as a consequence of] | 233 | −2 % | *ze względu na* [in respect of] | 178 | *celem [in order to]* | 94 |
| *w oparciu o* [on the basis of] | 209 | +24 % | *w drodze* [by way of] | 170 | *koło [about]* | 93 |
| *w drodze* [by way of] | 204 | +20 % | *w oparciu o* [on the basis of] | 168 | *w okresie* [within the period of] | 91 |
| *z naruszeniem* [in breach of] | 201 | --- | *wraz z* [together with] | 163 | *w celu* [for the purpose of] | 84 |
| *w terminie* [within the time limit] | 191 | --- | *w chwili* [at the time of] | 155 | *w wyniku* [as a result of] | 82 |
| ***Total*** | **34,091** | **+12 %** | ***Total*** | **30,501** | ***Total*** | **8,754** |

which confirms the previous observation regarding the inflated number of simple prepositions, such as *w* [in/into] or *na* [on/onto] (cf. Biel 2016b: 13). Even if the number of occurrences of simple prepositions within secondary prepositions were deducted, I would still be unable to determine the exact total number of occurrences of simple prepositions in the corpora, as the catalog of secondary prepositions is an open one and it is not feasible to account for them all.

In general, compound and secondary prepositions display a greater degree of variation than simple prepositions. Table 6.6 shows that there is a greater degree of overlap among the top 50 compound and secondary prepositions in the corpora of EU and post-accession SN judgments as well as post- and pre-accession SN judgments, whereas in the case of the corpora of judgments and the corpus of general Polish (NKJP) there is a substantially lower degree of overlap.

Taking into consideration all types of compound and secondary prepositions extracted from the corpora which have at least one occurrence, the degree of overlap is quite different (see Table 6.7). In this case, the overlap tends to be slightly higher between the individual corpora of judgments and the NKJP corpus.

The high distribution, and thus salience, of compound and secondary prepositions in both EU and national judgments may suggest that the frequent use of various types of prepositions may be regarded as a generic feature of judgments. This finding warrants an in-depth investigation into the discourse functions of compound and secondary prepositions in judicial language.

**Table 6.6.** *Number of types of compound and secondary prepositions shared between the individual corpora (from among the top 50 list)*

| | **CJ vs GC** | **CJ vs SN_2011–2015** | **GC vs SN_2011–2015** | **SN_2011–2015 vs SN_1999** |
|---|---|---|---|---|
| **Shared compound and secondary prepositions within the genre (types)** | **39** (out of: 50) (78 %) | **37** (out of: 50) (74 %) | **37** (out of: 50) (74 %) | **44** (out of: 50) (88 %) |
| | **CJ vs NKJP** | **GC vs NKJP** | **SN_2011–2015 vs NKJP** | **SN_1999 vs NKJP** |
| **Shared compound and secondary prepositions – judgments vs NKJP (types)** | **24** (out of: 50) (48 %) | **26** (out of: 50) (46 %) | **24** (out of: 50) (48 %) | **23** (out of: 50) (46 %) |

**Table 6.7.** *Number of types of compound and secondary prepositions shared between the individual corpora (from among the refined list, RF>1, NF>0)*

| | CJ vs GC | CJ vs SN_2011–2015 | GC vs SN_2011–2015 | SN_2011–2015 vs SN_1999 |
|---|---|---|---|---|
| **Shared compound and secondary prepositions within the genre (types)** | **253** (out of: 259 vs 265) (91 % vs 95 %) | **246** (out of: 259 vs 262) (95 % vs 94 %) | **255** (out of: 265 vs 262) (96 % vs 96 %) | **218** (out of: 262 vs 220) (84 % vs 99 %) |
| | **CJ vs NKJP** | **GC vs NKJP** | **SN_2011–2015 vs NKJP** | **SN_1999 vs NKJP** |
| **Shared compound and secondary prepositions – judgments vs NKJP (types)** | **258** (out of: 259 vs 277) (93 % vs 93 %) | **265** (out of: 265 vs 277) (100 % vs 96 %) | **262** (out of: 262 vs 277) (100 % vs 95 %) | **219** (out of: 220 vs 277) (99 % vs 79 %) |

## 6.3.4 Grammaticalized discourse functions of compound and secondary prepositions

The present chapter aims to provide an overview of all discourse functions of compound and secondary prepositions in the language of EU and Polish judges. The polyfunctional nature of prepositions is an impediment to a large-scale corpus study, as extensive research material encompassing hundreds of texts and, in turn, thousands of concordances does not facilitate the examination of every single context of occurrence of individual prepositions (cf. Biel 2016b). The functional taxonomy of compound and secondary prepositions presented in this analysis is based on the semantic taxonomy presented by Milewska (2003a: 98–153), which was later modified by Biel (2016a) to describe the discourse functions of compound and secondary prepositions in EU and Polish legislative documents. Milewska (2003a: 98–153) differentiates 23 semantic functions (relations) fulfilled by secondary prepositions. However, not all functions performed by prepositions are realized in a given genre (cf. Biel 2016b; Wasilewska 2018). In addition, the realization of various functions in specialized genres may depart from what is typical in general language, be it Polish or English (cf. Koźbiał 2018a,b). The following 18 discourse functions of compound and secondary prepositions have been observed in the genre of judgments: time; cause-effect, permission and condition; space; reference; measure; manner and instrumental relations; intra- and inter-textual reference; inclusivity/exclusivity; comparison; participation; modality; commutative relations; purpose; apposition; distribution; partitive relations; adversariality; and active relations.

Table 6.8 presents the total number of types and tokens of compound and secondary prepositions fulfilling 18 discourse functions. The data confirm the significance of these prepositions in the judicial genre. The classification including 193 types[118] of compound and secondary prepositions with an NF greater than or equal to 5 and occurring in at least two corpora of judgments shows that they are about two times more frequent in both EU and national judgments compared to general Polish. When it comes to differences between the EU corpora and the post-accession SN corpus, compound and secondary prepositions have a higher distribution in EU judgments by 4 % and 16 %, respectively, as compared to national judgments. There are also clear differences in the concentration of prepositions in the individual functional categories. What is visible at first sight is that in both EU corpora the first four discourse functions, (1) reference, (2) time, (3) intra- and inter-textual reference, (4) cause-effect, permission and condition, are similarly distributed across the texts. Taking into consideration the top four semantic functions and the corresponding top functions in the post-accession SN corpus, it can be observed that compound and secondary prepositions fulfill different major functions, namely (1) time, (2) cause-effect, permission and condition, (3) reference, and (4) intra- and inter-textual reference. It is surprising that, despite the striking difference in the frequency of prepositions in the post-accession SN corpus and the corpus of general Polish (NKJP), the top three discourse functions fulfilled by compound and secondary prepositions are essentially the same in these two corpora (i.e. time, cause-effect, permission and condition, and reference). In relation to the pre-accession corpus, the post-accession SN corpus has about 10 % more tokens and a divergent functional profile.

This analysis extends the results presented in Koźbiał (2018b) by discussing all 18 discourse functions identified as relevant to the genre. In the following, I will present only those prepositions with an NF greater than or equal to 5, and occurring in at least two corpora of judgments, be it two corpora of EU judgments or one corpus of EU judgments and the post-accession SN corpus. Functional categories are discussed according to the frequency of their exponents (types) in the national corpus. For want of space, the distributional differences between the individual corpora will not be discussed in detail.

118 The total number of types identified using relevant literature amounted to 277, which suggests that many have a very low distribution (≤4NF).

**Table 6.8.** *Number of types of compound and secondary prepositions with NF greater than or equal to 5 fulfilling 18 functions and the number of tokens in the functional categories*

| Number of types within the functional categories | | Translated EU case law | | | | | | |
|---|---|---|---|---|---|---|---|---|
| | | CJ | NF | CJ vs GC (%DIFF) | CJ vs SN_2011–2015 (%DIFF) | GC | NF | GC vs SN_2011–2015 (%DIFF) |
| time | 47 | reference | 10,493 | −17 % | +102 % | reference | 12,701 | +144 % |
| cause-effect, result, contravention and condition | 30 | intra- and inter-textual reference | 7,246 | 0 % | +55 % | time | 9,422 | −22 % |
| reference | 21 | time | 7,234 | −23 % | −40 % | intra– and inter–textual reference | 7,244 | +55 % |
| intra- and inter-textual reference | 15 | cause-effect, permission and condition | 5,273 | +2 % | −16 % | cause–effect, permission and condition | 5,174 | −17 % |
| manner and instrumental relations | 13 | manner and instrumental relations | 1,708 | +74 % | +45 % | adversariality | 2,386 | +167 % |
| inclusivity/ exclusivity | 11 | purpose | 1,699 | +56 % | +365 % | purpose | 1,088 | +198 % |
| space relations | 10 | apposition | 1,412 | +43 % | +20 % | participation | 1,061 | −52 % |
| measure | 9 | adversariality | 1,229 | −48 % | +37 % | modality | 1,018 | −28 % |
| comparison | 7 | participation | 907 | −15 % | −59 % | apposition | 988 | −16 % |
| commutative relations | 5 | commutative relations | 904 | +647 % | +45 % | manner and instrumental relations | 981 | −17 % |

(*continued on next page*)

**Table 6.8.** *Continued*

| Number of types within the functional categories | | Translated EU case law | | | | | | |
|---|---|---|---|---|---|---|---|---|
| | | CJ | NF | CJ vs GC (%DIFF) | CJ vs SN_2011–2015 (%DIFF) | GC | NF | GC vs SN_2011–2015 (%DIFF) |
| purpose | 5 | modality | 840 | −17 % | −41 % | inclusivity/ exclusivity | 658 | −15 % |
| participation | 4 | inclusivity/ exclusivity | 734 | +12 % | −5 % | measure | 601 | −25 % |
| modality | 4 | space relations | 622 | +240 % | +242 % | distribution | 415 | +19 % |
| apposition | 4 | distribution | 433 | +4 % | +24 % | comparison | 320 | +48 % |
| partitive relations | 3 | measure | 358 | −40 % | −55 % | space relations | 183 | +1 % |
| adversariality | 3 | comparison | 252 | −21 % | +17 % | partitive relations | 157 | +180 % |
| distribution | 1 | partitive relations | 115 | −27 % | +105 % | commutative relations | 121 | −81 % |
| active relations | 1 | active relations | 65 | −32 % | +51 % | active relations | 95 | +121 % |
| **Total** | **193** | --- | **41,524** | **−10 %** | **+4 %** | --- | **44,613** | **+16 %** |

| Non-translated PL case law | | | | | General Polish | |
|---|---|---|---|---|---|---|
| **SN_2011–2015** | **NF** | **SN_2011–2015 vs SN_1999 (%DIFF)** | **SN_1999** | **NF** | **NKJP** | **NF** |
| time | 12,136 | +9 % | time | 11,091 | time | 2,928 |
| cause-effect, permission and condition | 6,270 | +29 % | cause–effect, permission and condition | 4,859 | cause–effect, permission and condition | 1,514 |

| | | | | | | |
|---|---|---|---|---|---|---|
| reference | 5,201 | +34 % | intra– and inter–textual reference | 4,155 | reference | 1,312 |
| intra- and inter-textual reference | 4,678 | +13 % | reference | 3,868 | inclusivity/ exclusivity | 891 |
| participation | 2,209 | +13 % | apposition | 2,186 | measure | 848 |
| modality | 1,421 | −16 % | participation | 1,960 | modality | 592 |
| apposition | 1,179 | −46 % | modality | 1,682 | manner and instrumental relations | 576 |
| manner and instrumental relations | 1,177 | +8 % | adversariality | 1,376 | intra– and inter–textual reference | 545 |
| adversariality | 894 | −35 % | manner and instrumental relations | 1,094 | space relations | 526 |
| measure | 801 | +15 % | inclusivity/exclusivity | 731 | adversariality | 443 |
| inclusivity/exclusivity | 774 | +6 % | measure | 699 | apposition | 396 |
| commutative relations | 624 | +110 % | comparison | 312 | partitive relations | 388 |
| purpose | 365 | +17 % | purpose | 311 | participation | 380 |
| distribution | 350 | +46 % | commutative relations | 297 | commutative relations | 267 |
| comparison | 216 | −31 % | distribution | 240 | purpose | 265 |
| space relations | 182 | +54 % | space relations | 118 | comparison | 175 |
| partitive relations | 56 | −50 % | partitive relations | 111 | distribution | 130 |
| active relations | 43 | −36 % | active relations | 67 | active relations | 76 |
| --- | **38,576** | **+10 %** | --- | **35,157** | --- | **12,440** |

#### 6.3.4.1 Time

59 types of compound and secondary prepositions have been found to express time relations (see Table 6.9). Exponents of this functional category are used to describe time and duration of events, as well as deadlines (Milewska 2003a: 113).

Prepositions expressing time relations constitute the most widely represented discourse-functional category in the SN corpus – in the EU corpora they are underrepresented by about 40 % and 22 %. Examples of markedly underrepresented types include: *z dniem* [with effect from], *z chwilą* [upon], *na dzień* [at the date of], *dnia* [of], *od początku* [at the outset of]. Examples of types overrepresented in translated judgments include: *w momencie* [at the time of], *przez okres* [for a period of], *od momentu* [from], *do momentu* [until], *w miarę* [as], *na lata* [for the period ... to ...]. Despite the underrepresentation of time-related prepositions in EU judgments, it may still be claimed that the genre as a whole requires frequent and repeated time specification compared to general Polish, which does not make such a heavy use of prepositions expressing time relations. Furthermore, the national corpora show that post-accession SN judgments contain about 9 % more tokens of time-related compound and secondary prepositions. Overall, the high number of tokens in the SN corpora is due to the high distribution of the secondary preposition *z dnia* [of], which is used mostly in Move 1 of SN judgments to point to judgments against which cassation had been lodged, e.g. o*d wyroku Sądu Apelacyjnego* ***z dnia*** *19 czerwca 2013 r.* [against the judgment of the Court of Appeal **of** 19 June 2013], as well as to provide inter-textual references to judgments passed by the SN and lower-instance courts.

#### 6.3.4.2 Cause-effect, result, contravention and condition

The second major group of compound and secondary prepositions includes cause-effect, contravention (permission) and condition prepositions. The reason for grouping these three seemingly different functional categories together is that they are closely related (cf. Milewska 2003a: 129–138). Prepositions expressing cause relations comprise prepositions which relate to factors inducing certain phenomena. Due to the fact that cause relations partly coincide with other more complicated types of relations (e.g. intention, motivation, premise) which are difficult to clearly differentiate (Milewska 2003a: 129), all of the said relations are termed as cause relations (for instance, *ze względu na* [in the light of], *z uwagi na* [in view of]). Prepositions expressing the effect relation, which is linked to the cause relation, point to the resultative, post-factum content, and are clearly differentiated from purpose prepositions which relate to the future (for instance, *wskutek* [as a consequence of], *w następstwie* [following]) (cf. Section 6.4.5.13). Contravention prepositions indicate the type of cause allowing for an opposite effect (for instance, *niezależnie od* [irrespective of], *pomimo* [despite]) (Milewska 2003a: 134). Lastly, condition-related prepositions, such as *w wypadku* [in the event of] and *na wypadek* [in case of], refer to two possible events in a cause-effect

**Table 6.9.** *Distribution of compound and secondary prepositions expressing time relations*

| | Translated EU case law | | | | | Non-translated PL case law | | | General Polish |
|---|---|---|---|---|---|---|---|---|---|
| | **CJ** | **CJ vs GC (%DIFF)** | **CJ vs SN_2011–2015 (%DIFF)** | **GC** | **GC vs SN_2011–2015 (%DIFF)** | **SN_2011–2015** | **SN_2011–2015 vs SN_1999 (%DIFF)** | **SN_1999** | **NKJP** |
| *z dnia* [of] | 3,361 | −18 % | −50 % | 4,110 | −38 % | **6,675** | +16 % | 5757 | 79 |
| *w dniu* [on] | 1,404 | −25 % | −18 % | 1,874 | +9 % | **1,721** | −12 % | 1948 | 105 |
| *od dnia* [from] | 250 | −32 % | −54 % | 367 | −33 % | **548** | +73 % | 317 | 34 |
| *do dnia* [by] | 159 | −54 % | −55 % | 343 | −3 % | **355** | +163 % | 135 | 22 |
| *w okresie* [during the ... period] | 189 | −42 % | −34 % | 327 | +14 % | **286** | +29 % | 222 | 91 |
| *w toku* [during] | 73 | −68 % | −72 % | 230 | −13 % | **264** | +17 % | 226 | 26 |
| *w chwili* [at the time of] | 160 | +32 % | −36 % | 121 | −52 % | **251** | +62 % | 155 | 35 |
| *w terminie* [within the time limit] | 107 | +20 % | −44 % | 89 | −53 % | **191** | +50 % | 127 | 35 |
| *z dniem* [with effect from] | 32 | +28 % | −81 % | 25 | −85 % | **165** | +57 % | 105 | 19 |
| *w czasie* [at the time of] | 114 | +1 % | −21 % | 113 | −22 % | **145** | −41 % | 244 | 202 |
| *z chwilą* [upon] | 33 | +57 % | −75 % | 21 | −84 % | **132** | +52 % | 87 | 12 |
| *na dzień* [at the date of] | 31 | −26 % | −76 % | 42 | −67 % | **129** | +48 % | 87 | 34 |
| *za okres* [for the period for (which)] | 20 | −26 % | −82 % | 27 | −76 % | **114** | −9 % | 125 | 6 |
| *przed dniem* [by] | 59 | +11 % | −42 % | 53 | −48 % | **101** | +140 % | 42 | 7 |
| *do czasu* [until] | 55 | +17 % | −36 % | 47 | −45 % | **86** | +105 % | 42 | 53 |

(*continued on next page*)

**Table 6.9.** *Continued*

| | Translated EU case law | | | | | Non-translated PL case law | | | General Polish |
|---|---|---|---|---|---|---|---|---|---|
| | **CJ** | **CJ vs GC (%DIFF)** | **CJ vs SN_2011–2015 (%DIFF)** | **GC** | **GC vs SN_2011–2015 (%DIFF)** | **SN_2011–2015** | **SN_2011–2015 vs SN_1999 (%DIFF)** | **SN_1999** | **NKJP** |
| *po upływie* [after the expiry of] | 80 | +129 % | −7 % | 35 | −59 % | **86** | −25 % | 115 | 16 |
| *od daty* [within] | 40 | +18 % | −45 % | 34 | −53 % | **73** | −84 % | 456 | 7 |
| *w trakcie* [during the course of] | 163 | −42 % | +140 % | 282 | +315 % | **68** | +36 % | 50 | 113 |
| *w latach* [between] | 70 | −15 % | +6 % | 82 | +24 % | **66** | +57 % | 42 | 134 |
| *dnia* [of] | 11 | 0 % | −82 % | 11 | −82 % | **62** | −77 % | 275 | 359 |
| *podczas* [during] | 156 | −59 % | +152 % | 380 | +513 % | **62** | −15 % | 73 | 414 |
| *przed upływem* [prior to] | 27 | +145 % | −50 % | 11 | −80 % | **54** | +50 % | 36 | 6 |
| *w ciągu* [within] | 64 | +25 % | +31 % | 51 | +4 % | **49** | −2 % | 50 | 180 |
| *po dniu* [after] | 38 | −3 % | −22 % | 39 | −20 % | **49** | +250 % | 14 | 6 |
| *od chwili* [from] | 31 | +121 % | −34 % | 14 | −70 % | **47** | +135 % | 20 | 11 |
| *do chwili* [prior to] | 17 | +21 % | −60 % | 14 | −67 % | **43** | +2 % | 42 | 8 |
| *w dniach* [on … and …] | 55 | −69 % | +34 % | 178 | +334 % | **41** | +14 % | 36 | 21 |
| *na okres* [for the period] | 42 | +100 % | +2 % | 21 | −49 % | **41** | +14 % | 36 | 15 |
| *w momencie* [at the time of] | 83 | −30 % | +207 % | 118 | +337 % | **27** | +238 % | 8 | 38 |
| *do końca* [until the end of] | 10 | −38 % | −62 % | 16 | −38 % | **26** | −7 % | 28 | 172 |
| *od początku* [at the outset of] | 7 | −53 % | −73 % | 15 | −42 % | **26** | +44 % | 18 | 73 |
| *począwszy od* [from the date of] | 48 | −36 % | +100 % | 75 | +213 % | **24** | +9 % | 22 | 15 |

| | | | | | | | | | |
|---|---|---|---|---|---|---|---|---|---|
| *przez okres* [for a period of] | 68 | +172 % | +240 % | 25 | +25 % | **20** | 0 % | 20 | 7 |
| *na koniec* [for a period of] | 10 | −47 % | −38 % | 19 | +19 % | **16** | −27 % | 22 | 61 |
| *za lata* [for the years] | 15 | +50 % | +25 % | 10 | −17 % | **12** | 0 % | 12 | 2 |
| *na początku* [at the beginning of] | 13 | −66 % | +18 % | 38 | +245 % | **11** | +83 % | 6 | 131 |
| *w końcu* [finally/in the end] | 15 | −29 % | +36 % | 21 | +91 % | **11** | −50 % | 22 | 166 |
| *pod koniec* [at the end] | 6 | −77 % | −33 % | 26 | +189 % | **9** | −44 % | 16 | 77 |
| *od momentu* [from] | 24 | +200 % | +200 % | 8 | 0 % | **8** | 0 % | 8 | 13 |
| *od czasu* [since] | 12 | −33 % | +71 % | 18 | +157 % | **7** | −30 % | 10 | 42 |
| *przy okazji* [by the way] | 17 | −50 % | +143 % | 34 | +386 % | **7** | +40 % | 5 | 58 |
| *do momentu* [until] | 20 | −13 % | +186 % | 23 | +229 % | **7** | +17 % | 6 | 11 |
| *z końcem* [as the end of] | 6 | +200 % | 0 % | 2 | −67 % | **6** | 0 % | 6 | 9 |
| *w miarę* [as] | 20 | +33 % | +233 % | 15 | +150 % | **6** | −25 % | 8 | 45 |
| *w okresach* [during the periods] | 5 | −29 % | +25 % | 7 | +75 % | **4** | 0 % | 4 | 3 |
| *na lata* [for the period ... to ...] | 9 | +80 % | +200 % | 5 | +67 % | **3** | --- | 0 | 10 |
| *na zakończenie* [at the end of the] | 5 | −17 % | +150 % | 6 | +200 % | **2** | −67 % | 6 | 22 |
| **Total** | **7,234** | **−23 %** | **−40 %** | **9,422** | **−22 %** | **12,136** | **+9 %** | **11,091** | **2,928** |

relation, where the occurrence of one of them leads to a result, that is the second event (Milewska 2003a: 135).

In this broad functional group, there are three categories of prepositions which are underrepresented in translated EU judgments, namely: cause-effect (by 26 %), result (by 41 % and 31 %, respectively), and contravention prepositions (by 32 % and 18 %, respectively). Condition-related prepositions are markedly overrepresented in EU judgments relative to national judgments as the only sub-group (by 82 % and 41 %, respectively) (see Table 6.10).

Prepositions belonging to this group are crucial to judicial argumentation. They allow judges to structure their arguments by linking causes to effects, as well as introduce results. They are also used to point out contraventions of the law and to present various conditions. Relative to the national corpus, the following types are particularly overrepresented in translations: *ze względu na* [in the light of], *dzięki* [as a result of/pursuant to], *w przypadku* [in the case of], *w zależności od* [depending on], *w obliczu* [in the face of]. Examples of markedly underrepresented types include: *tytułem* [under], *na skutek* [as a result of], *wskutek* [as a consequence of], *pomimo* [despite], and *w razie* [in the case of]. Apart from the divergences between the EU corpora and the post-accession SN corpus, there are also internal divergences in the Eurolect. In addition, the post-accession SN corpus has a remarkably higher distribution of prepositions belonging to this category (mostly cause-effect and condition-related prepositions) than the pre-accession corpus, which may be attributed to a rising level of complexity of matters brought before the SN following Poland's accession to the EU.

### *6.3.4.3 Reference*

Compound and secondary prepositions which express the reference relation refer not only to concrete objects but also specify what the sender had in mind and how they interpret processes and assess situations (Lesz-Duk 2011: 47). Prepositions fulfilling reference relations are very often used to specify the scope of proceedings as well as various other matters brought up before the courts.

Reference prepositions are markedly overrepresented in translated EU judgments, by roughly 2 and 2.4 times, compared to non-translated SN judgments (see Table 6.11). The following prepositions are particularly overrepresented in translated EU judgments: *w odniesieniu do* [with reference to], *w przedmiocie* [on], *pod względem* [in terms of], *w dziedzinie* [in the area of], *ds.* [in charge of –ABBRV], and *w sektorze* [in the sector]. Only several types are markedly underrepresented in translations: *co do* [as to], *w stosunku do* [in relation to], *na gruncie* [in the context of], *pod kątem* [in terms of]. Out of 21 types, 15 are overrepresented in translations, e.g. *w sprawie* [in the matter of], *w ramach* [within the framework of], *w odniesieniu do* [with reference to]. It should be noted that there is a high level of inter-generic variation between CJ and GC judgments. Moreover, these prepositions are overrepresented in the corpus of pre-accession SN judgments relative to the pre-accession corpus, similar to prepositions belonging to the two previous functional categories.

**Table 6.10.** *Distribution of compound and secondary prepositions expressing cause-effect, permission and condition relations*

| | Translated EU case law | | | | | Non-translated PL case law | | | General Polish |
|---|---|---|---|---|---|---|---|---|---|
| | CJ | CJ vs GC (%DIFF) | CJ vs SN_2011–2015 (%DIFF) | GC | GC vs SN_2011–2015 (%DIFF) | SN_2011–2015 | SN_2011–2015 vs SN_1999 (%DIFF) | SN_1999 | NKJP |
| **Cause-effect** | | | | | | | | | |
| *w związku z* [it follows from] | 806 | +20 % | –35 % | 670 | –46 % | **1,232** | +47 % | 840 | 182 |
| *z tytułu* [by way of] | 347 | +91 % | –43 % | 182 | –70 % | **609** | +41 % | 432 | 60 |
| *tytułem* [under] | 156 | –22 % | –69 % | 200 | –60 % | **497** | +16 % | 428 | 24 |
| *ze względu na* [in the light of] | 654 | –5 % | +105 % | 685 | +115 % | **319** | +79 % | 178 | 117 |
| *z uwagi na* [in view of] | 217 | –8 % | –30 % | 236 | –24 % | **309** | +42 % | 218 | 26 |
| *z powodu* [owing to/ due to] | 140 | –11 % | –18 % | 157 | –8 % | **171** | +63 % | 105 | 102 |
| *w odpowiedzi na* [in response to] | 55 | –78 % | –41 % | 248 | +164 % | **94** | +49 % | 63 | 10 |
| *w związku ze* [it follows from] | 24 | +4 % | –48 % | 23 | –50 % | **46** | +130 % | 20 | 9 |
| *pod rygorem* [subject to] | 15 | +67 % | –63 % | 9 | –78 % | **41** | +105 % | 20 | 2 |
| *z racji* [because of] | 17 | +13 % | –29 % | 15 | –38 % | **24** | –14 % | 28 | 17 |

(*continued on next page*)

**Table 6.10.** *Continued*

| | Translated EU case law | | | | | Non-translated PL case law | | | General Polish |
|---|---|---|---|---|---|---|---|---|---|
| | **CJ** | **CJ vs GC (%DIFF)** | **CJ vs SN_2011–2015 (%DIFF)** | **GC** | **GC vs SN_2011–2015 (%DIFF)** | **SN_2011–2015** | **SN_2011–2015 vs SN_1999 (%DIFF)** | **SN_1999** | **NKJP** |
| *mocą* [by force of] | 16 | +100 % | −11 % | 8 | −56 % | **18** | −44 % | 32 | 12 |
| *dzięki* [as a result of/ pursuant to] | 40 | −29 % | +208 % | 56 | +331 % | **13** | +225 % | 4 | 331 |
| **Total** | **2,487** | **0 %** | **−26 %** | **2,489** | **−26 %** | **3,373** | **+42 %** | **2,368** | **892** |
| **Result** | | | | | | | | | |
| *w wyniku* [as a result of] | 146 | +1 % | −58 % | 145 | −58 % | **344** | +14 % | 301 | 82 |
| *na skutek* [as a result of] | 15 | −12 % | −96 % | 17 | −95 % | **337** | +42 % | 238 | 31 |
| *w konsekwencji* [as a result] | 354 | −28 % | +11 % | 489 | +53 % | **319** | +21 % | 264 | 21 |
| *wskutek* [as a consequence of] | 69 | +33 % | −70 % | 52 | −78 % | **233** | −2 % | 238 | 29 |
| *w następstwie* [following] | 128 | −16 % | +24 % | 153 | +49 % | **103** | −47 % | 196 | 5 |
| *w rezultacie* [in consequence] | 119 | −3 % | +53 % | 123 | +58 % | **78** | +16 % | 67 | 20 |
| *w efekcie* [as a result] | 14 | 0 % | −7 % | 14 | −7 % | **15** | +25 % | 12 | 32 |
| **Total** | **845** | **−15 %** | **−41 %** | **993** | **−31 %** | **1429** | **+9 %** | **1,316** | **220** |

| | | | | | | | | | |
|---|---|---|---|---|---|---|---|---|---|
| **Contravention** | | | | | | | | | |
| *wbrew* [contrary to] | 120 | −52 % | −51 % | 250 | +1 % | **247** | −38 % | 396 | 55 |
| *niezależnie od* [irrespective of] | 192 | +39 % | +11 % | 138 | −20 % | **173** | +82 % | 95 | 49 |
| *pomimo* [despite] | 64 | −29 % | −62 % | 90 | −46 % | **168** | +57 % | 107 | 52 |
| *bez względu na* [regardless of] | 63 | +37 % | +21 % | 46 | −12 % | **52** | 0 % | 52 | 32 |
| **Total** | **439** | **−16 %** | **−32 %** | **524** | **−18 %** | **641** | **−1 %** | **650** | **188** |
| **Condition** | | | | | | | | | |
| *w razie* [in the case of] | 148 | +78 % | −54 % | 83 | −74 % | **325** | +17 % | 277 | 61 |
| *w przypadku* [in the case of] | 959 | +15 % | +267 % | 833 | +219 % | **261** | +268 % | 71 | 213 |
| *w wypadku* [in the event of] | 183 | +69 % | +24 % | 108 | −27 % | **147** | +28 % | 115 | 30 |
| *na wypadek* [in case of] | 42 | +147 % | −13 % | 17 | −65 % | **48** | +118 % | 22 | 14 |
| *w zależności od* [depending on] | 130 | +23 % | +381 % | 106 | +293 % | **27** | +93 % | 14 | 43 |
| *pod warunkiem* [provided that] | 29 | +142 % | +61 % | 12 | −33 % | **18** | −31 % | 26 | 26 |
| *w obliczu* [in the face of] | 11 | +22 % | +1000 % | 9 | +800 % | **1** | --- | 0 | 15 |
| **Total** | **1,502** | **+29 %** | **+82 %** | **1,168** | **+41 %** | **827** | **+58 %** | **525** | **402** |
| **Grand total** | **5,273** | **+2 %** | **−16 %** | **5,174** | **−17 %** | **6,270** | **+29 %** | **4,859** | **1,702** |

**Table 6.11.** *Distribution of secondary prepositions expressing reference*

| | **Translated EU case law** | | | | | **Non-translated PL case law** | | | **General Polish** |
|---|---|---|---|---|---|---|---|---|---|
| | **CJ** | **CJ vs GC (%DIFF)** | **CJ vs SN_2011–2015 (%DIFF)** | **GC** | **GC vs SN_2011–2015 (%DIFF)** | **SN_2011–2015** | **SN_2011–2015 vs SN_1999 (%DIFF)** | **SN_1999** | **NKJP** |
| *w sprawie* [in the matter of] | 3,694 | −14 % | +129 % | 4,284 | +165 % | **1,614** | +23 % | 1,312 | 214 |
| *co do* [as to] | 592 | −22 % | −38 % | 757 | −20 % | **951** | −8 % | 1,036 | 135 |
| *w zakresie* [in terms of] | 1,016 | −12 % | +42 % | 1,160 | +62 % | **717** | +47 % | 489 | 118 |
| *w ramach* [within the framework of] | 1,359 | −19 % | +130 % | 1,673 | +184 % | **590** | --- | 0 | 159 |
| *w odniesieniu do* [with reference to] | 1,156 | −18 % | +244 % | 1,402 | +317 % | **336** | +41 % | 238 | 33 |
| *w stosunku do* [in relation to] | 224 | −7 % | −33 % | 242 | −27 % | **333** | +8 % | 309 | 82 |
| *na gruncie* [in the context of] | 22 | +38 % | −84 % | 16 | −89 % | **140** | +122 % | 63 | 7 |
| *w przedmiocie* [on] | 1,268 | −30 % | +1096 % | 1,817 | +1614 % | **106** | +16 % | 91 | 3 |
| *odnośnie do* [with regard to] | 78 | −31 % | −6 % | 113 | +36 % | **83** | +36 % | 61 | 9 |
| *z zakresu* [in the scope of] | 134 | +58 % | +89 % | 85 | +20 % | **71** | +109 % | 34 | 30 |

| | | | | | | | | | |
|---|---|---|---|---|---|---|---|---|---|
| *w kontekście* [in the context of] | 98 | −23 % | +75 % | 128 | +129 % | **56** | +47 % | 38 | 21 |
| *w sferze* [in the field of] | 3 | −63 % | −93 % | 8 | −80 % | **40** | +67 % | 24 | 20 |
| *na temat* (excl. nt.–ABBRV) [on the subject of] | 79 | −74 % | +132 % | 299 | +779 % | **34** | +143 % | 14 | 170 |
| *pod kątem* [in respect of] | 19 | −24 % | −39 % | 25 | −19 % | **31** | +19 % | 26 | 13 |
| *w kwestii* [relating to] | 77 | −17 % | +166 % | 93 | +221 % | **29** | −47 % | 55 | 17 |
| *pod względem* [in terms of] | 112 | −10 % | +331 % | 124 | +377 % | **26** | −13 % | 30 | 45 |
| *do spraw* (excl. *ds.*-ABBRV) [in charge of] | 43 | +48 % | +126 % | 29 | +53 % | **19** | −44 % | 34 | 125 |
| *w dziedzinie* [in the area of] | 264 | +31 % | +2540 % | 201 | +1910 % | **10** | +400 % | 2 | 31 |
| *ds.* [in charge of –ABBRV] | 167 | +44 % | +1756 % | 116 | +1189 % | **9** | −10 % | 10 | 56 |
| *w obszarze/obszarach* [on] | 17 | +143 % | +240 % | 7 | +40 % | **5** | --- | 0 | 12 |
| *w sektorze* [in the sector] | 71 | −42 % | +7000 % | 122 | +12100 % | **1** | −50 % | 2 | 12 |
| **Total** | **10,493** | **−17 %** | **+102 %** | **12,701** | **+144 %** | **5,201** | **+34 %** | **3,868** | **1,312** |

### 6.4.4.4 Intra- and inter-textual reference

Intra- and intertextual reference prepositions fulfil the role of text deixis by indicating information located in the same text, e.g. ***w świetle*** *(powyższego)* [in light of (the above)], or other texts, e.g. ***na podstawie*** *art. 424 § 1 k.p.c.* [under Art. 424 § 1 of the Code of Civil Procedure]. Prepositions of this type are markedly overrepresented in translated EU judgments (by about 55 % in both EU corpora) (see Table 6.12). The following prepositions are strongly overrepresented in translated EU judgments: *bez uszczerbku dla* [without prejudice to], *na mocy* [pursuant to/ BT: by power of article], *z zastrzeżeniem* [subject to], and *powyżej* [above], while significant underrepresentation pertains to: *z naruszeniem* [in breach of], *stosownie do* [in conformity with], *z mocy* [under; BT by power of], *niezgodnie z* [contrary to]. This is the next group of prepositions which are substantially overrepresented in all corpora of judgments compared to general Polish (NKJP). Prepositions from this group are also overrepresented in post-accession SN judgments relative to pre-accession judgments (by 13 %).

The analysis of the research material shows that text-deictic compound and secondary prepositions refer in most cases to (fragments of) texts other than the judgments themselves, which is proven by numerous references to editing units, such as articles (Art.) or paragraphs (§).

### 6.3.4.5 Participation

The group of prepositions which communicate the participation relation, despite not being very numerous, is very important, as it allows the judges to provide information that certain actions were or are conducted either "for someone's benefit" or "for someone's loss" (cf. Lesz-Duk 2011: 107).

Participation prepositions are noticeably underrepresented in translated EU judgments, by 59 % and 52 % times, respectively; these include: *na rzecz* [for; in favor of], *wobec* [towards], *na szkodę* [to the detriment of]). The only preposition overrepresented in EU judgments is *przy udziale* [in cooperation with] (see Table 6.13). Participation prepositions refer predominantly to the parties to the proceedings; however, they also refer to third parties. The secondary preposition, *na rzecz* [for; in favor of], which has a very high distribution in national judgments, is used by judges to either award financial costs to the plaintiffs (which are to be covered by the defendants) or to report that such costs had been awarded earlier by lower-instance courts. Prepositions belonging to this group are overrepresented in post-accession SN judgments as compared to pre-accession judgments (by 13 %).

### 6.3.4.6 Modality

Modal prepositions relate the propositions to their author and express modal relations (Milewska 2003a: 152). Łapa (2006b: 10) observes that prepositions may be regarded as conveying modal relations; however, their ability to express modal values depends on the intentional character of the context in which they occur. The

**Table 6.12.** *Distribution of compound and secondary prepositions expressing intra- and inter-textual relations*

| | Translated EU case law | | | | | Non-translated PL case law | | | General Polish |
|---|---|---|---|---|---|---|---|---|---|
| | CJ | CJ vs GC (%DIFF) | CJ vs SN_2011–2015 (%DIFF) | GC | GC vs SN_2011–2015 (%DIFF) | SN_2011–2015 | SN_2011–2015 vs SN_1999 (%DIFF) | SN_1999 | NKJP |
| *na podstawie* [on the basis of] | 1,727 | +17 % | −11 % | 1,471 | −24 % | **1,938** | +34 % | 1,449 | 138 |
| *zgodnie z* [according to] | 2,631 | +16 % | +170 % | 2,273 | +133 % | **974** | +72 % | 565 | 204 |
| *w rozumieniu* [within the understanding of] | 1,035 | +79 % | +163 % | 579 | +47 % | **394** | +28 % | 309 | 17 |
| w *świetle* [in light of] | 534 | -9 % | +88 % | 587 | +107 % | **284** | −24 % | 375 | 26 |
| *w oparciu o* [on the basis of] | 133 | +4 % | −36 % | 128 | −39 % | **209** | +24 % | 168 | 27 |
| *z naruszeniem* [in breach of] | 73 | 0 % | −64 % | 73 | −64 % | **201** | +43 % | 141 | 4 |
| *stosownie do* [in conformity with] | 48 | +78 % | −71 % | 27 | −84 % | **167** | −53 % | 353 | 6 |
| *z mocy* [under; BT by power of] | 26 | +1200 % | −83 % | 2 | −99 % | **151** | −50 % | 303 | 8 |
| *z uwzględnieniem* [in consideration of] | 82 | +21 % | −23 % | 68 | −36 % | **107** | +18 % | 91 | 12 |

(*continued on next page*)

**Table 6.12.** *Continued*

| | Translated EU case law | | | | | Non-translated PL case law | | | General Polish |
|---|---|---|---|---|---|---|---|---|---|
| | **CJ** | **CJ vs GC (%DIFF)** | **CJ vs SN_2011–2015 (%DIFF)** | **GC** | **GC vs SN_2011–2015 (%DIFF)** | **SN_2011–2015** | **SN_2011–2015 vs SN_1999 (%DIFF)** | **SN_1999** | **NKJP** |
| *na mocy* [pursuant to/BT: by power of article] | 564 | +83 % | +662 % | 309 | +318 % | **74** | −59 % | 180 | 17 |
| *w myśl* [with regard to] | 56 | −21 % | −20 % | 71 | 1 % | **70** | −48 % | 135 | 17 |
| *niezgodnie z* [contrary to] | 12 | 0 % | −72 % | 12 | −72 % | **43** | +79 % | 24 | 6 |
| *z zastrzeżeniem* [subject to; BT with reservations as to] | 144 | +182 % | +311 % | 51 | +46 % | **35** | +17 % | 30 | 12 |
| *powyżej* [above] | 97 | −94 % | +246 % | 1,573 | +5518 % | **28** | 0 % | 28 | 51 |
| *bez uszczerbku dla* [without prejudice to] | 84 | +320 % | +4100 % | 20 | +900 % | **2** | −50 % | 4 | 0 |
| **Total** | **7,246** | **0 %** | **+55 %** | **7,244** | **+55 %** | **4,678** | **+13 %** | **4,155** | **545** |

**Table 6.13.** *Distribution of compound and secondary prepositions expressing participation relations*

| | Translated EU case law | | | | | Non-translated PL case law | | | General Polish |
|---|---|---|---|---|---|---|---|---|---|
| | **CJ** | **CJ vs GC (%DIFF)** | **CJ vs SN_2011–2015 (%DIFF)** | **GC** | **GC vs SN_2011–2015 (%DIFF)** | **SN_2011–2015** | **SN_2011–2015 vs SN_1999 (%DIFF)** | **SN_1999** | **NKJP** |
| *na rzecz* [for; in favour of] | 371 | +48 % | −69 % | 251 | −79 % | **1,196** | +23 % | 975 | 96 |
| *wobec* [towards] | 504 | −36 % | −49 % | 789 | −20 % | **986** | +3 % | 953 | 273 |
| *na szkodę* [to the detriment of] | 14 | 0 % | −33 % | 14 | −33 % | **21** | +17 % | 18 | 7 |
| *przy udziale* [in cooperation with] | 18 | +157 % | +200 % | 7 | +17 % | **6** | −57 % | 14 | 4 |
| **Total** | **907** | **−15 %** | **−59 %** | **1,061** | **−52 %** | **2,209** | **+13 %** | **1,960** | **380** |

type of modality conveyed by modal prepositions refers to the actual sender of a statement (the judges and the courts) who may not warrant the authenticity of conveyed information and may want to distance themselves from it with prepositions such as *według* [according to] or *zdaniem* [according to]. The responsibility for the consequences of assuming the authenticity of the statement is thus shifted to the original author of a statement (Łapa 2006b: 10).

The data show that modal prepositions are significantly underrepresented in translated judgments, by about 41 % and 28 %, respectively (see Table 6.14), especially *według* [according to] and *w ocenie* [in the opinion of]. The only overrepresented preposition is *zdaniem* [according to], which is used to relate to the views held by, *inter alia*, the parties to the proceedings. The distribution of modal prepositions is lower in post-accession SN judgments relative to pre-accession judgments (by 16 %).

### *6.3.4.7 Apposition*

The meaning of prepositions expressing the apposition relation is close to adverbials of manner expressing the sense of "as" or "in the capacity of," such as *w postaci* [in the form of] or *w charakterze* [acting as/represented by] (Milewska 2003a: 144–145). These prepositions define the nature of the relationship between the activity and its object by indicating the role, function, manner of existence or specific character (Milewska 2003a: 144).

Secondary prepositions expressing the relation of apposition are markedly overrepresented in CJ judgments by about 43 %, whereas they are underrepresented in GC judgments by about 16 %. Prepositions belonging to this category further differentiate the language of judgments from general Polish (cf. Table 6.15). In this functional category, the biggest problem was posed by the preposition *jako* [as/in the capacity of], as it can also function as a conjunction.[119] Surprisingly, apposition prepositions are clearly underrepresented in post-accession SN judgments relative to pre-accession judgments (by 46 %).

### *6.3.4.8 Manner and instrumental relations*

Although Milewska (2003a: 143–144, 149–150) describes manner and instrumental prepositions separately, I examine them jointly, as both of these relations are

---

119 Due to the fact that a simple query including the preposition *jako* [as/in the capacity of] returned thousands of concordance lines containing not only the prepositional meaning, but also the conjunctive meaning, the search was narrowed down to the query encompassing only the most common combinations of the preposition *jako* and chosen suffixes: *jako *el/jako *ik/jako *nt/jako *ta/jako *kt/jako *ne/jako *ny/ jako *na/jako *nu/jako *nie/ jako *ło/jako *aw/jako *wa/jako *wa/jako *dy/jako *ek/ jako zbyt/jako *ba/jako *an/jako *óz/jako *sce/jako *two/jako *or/jako *ent/jako *cja/ jako *ca.* This allowed for a rough estimate of the frequency of this preposition.

**Table 6.14.** *Distribution of compound and secondary prepositions expressing modality relations*

| | Translated EU case law | | | | | Non-translated PL case law | | | General Polish |
|---|---|---|---|---|---|---|---|---|---|
| | **CJ** | **CJ vs GC (%DIFF)** | **CJ vs SN_2011–2015 (%DIFF)** | **GC** | **GC vs SN_2011–2015 (%DIFF)** | **SN_2011–2015** | **SN_2011–2015 vs SN_1999 (%DIFF)** | **SN_1999** | **NKJP** |
| *według* [according to][a] | *291* | −11 % | −52 % | *328* | −46 % | **612** | −4 % | 640 | 309 |
| *zdaniem* [according to] | <u>441</u> | −22 % | 8 % | <u>569</u> | 39 % | **409** | −37 % | 648 | 235 |
| *w ocenie* [in the opinion of] | *26* | −33 % | −91 % | *39* | −87 % | **305** | 4 % | 293 | 11 |
| *z punktu widzenia* [from the point of view of] | *82* | 0 % | −14 % | *82* | −14 % | **95** | −6 % | 101 | 37 |
| **Total** | **840** | **−17 %** | **−41 %** | **1,018** | **−28 %** | **1,421** | **−16 %** | **1,682** | **592** |

[a] The preposition *według* [according to] has been classified as expressing mainly modal relations; however, there are cases in which it expresses reference relations, as in *według art. 398 § 3 k.p.c.* [pursuant to Art. 398 § 3 of the Code of Civil Procedure], albeit these are not as frequent (cf. Section 6.3.4.3).

**Table 6.15.** *Distribution of compound and secondary prepositions expressing apposition relations*

| | Translated EU case law | | | | | Non-translated PL case law | | | General Polish |
|---|---|---|---|---|---|---|---|---|---|
| | CJ | CJ vs GC (%DIFF) | CJ vs SN_2011–2015 (%DIFF) | GC | GC vs SN_2011–2015 (%DIFF) | SN_2011–2015 | SN_2011–2015 vs SN_1999 (%DIFF) | SN_1999 | NKJP |
| *jako* [as/in the capacity of] | 490 | −12 % | −31 % | 558 | −21 % | **708** | −62 % | 1,883 | 288 |
| *w postaci* [in the form of] | 100 | −27 % | −75 % | 137 | −65 % | **396** | +78 % | 222 | 67 |
| *w charakterze* [acting as/ represented by] | 810 | +192 % | +1488 % | 277 | +443 % | **51** | −30 % | 73 | 11 |
| *pod nazwą* [known as] | 12 | −25 % | −50 % | 16 | −33 % | 24 | +200 % | 8 | 30 |
| **Total** | **1,412** | **+43 %** | **+20 %** | **988** | **−16 %** | **1,179** | **−46 %** | **2,186** | **396** |

similar in terms of their discourse functions. Prepositions belonging to this broad category are used to (1) characterize actions or their realization (manner relation), such as *na zasadzie* [on the principle], as well as to (2) refer to the tools required to perform a certain action (instrumental relation), such as *przy użyciu* [with the use of] (Milewska 2003a: 143, 149) (see Table 6.16).

These prepositions are not clearly overrepresented in EU judgments, as their overrepresentation can be observed only in CJ judgments (by 45 %), especially in the case of *w trybie* [under], *drogą* [by way of], and *na drodze* [towards]. GC judgments, on the other hand, have about 17 % fewer occurrences of manner and instrumental prepositions than SN judgments. Despite the questionable status of manner and instrumental prepositions as regards their overrepresentation in the Eurolect, on the whole they are still markedly more frequent in both EU and national judgments compared to general Polish (by about 3, 1.7, and 2 times), thus continuing the trend of high usefulness and salience of compound and secondary prepositions in judicial language. Post-accession SN judgments also contain more tokens than pre-accession judgments (about 8 %).

### *6.3.4.9 Adversariality*

According to Milewska (2003a: 121), the adversariality relation expresses hostility and contradictory actions, and is exemplified by *przeciwko* [against]. Prepositions expressing this relation may be easily confused with prepositions conveying spatial relations; therefore, it is necessary to examine the context of occurrence of all candidate prepositions in order to eliminate those which act as prepositions of spatial relations. The distribution of adversarial prepositions is particularly high in GC judgments, in which they are about 167 % more frequent than in post-accession SN judgments (see Table 6.21). In the CJ corpus, they are about 48 % less frequent than in non-translations. This type of preposition is also generally overrepresented in judgments compared to general Polish (NKJP).

Adversarial prepositions are employed mainly to present the antagonistic nature of the relationship between the parties to the proceedings, either in proceedings pending before the court or in other matters already settled by an EU or national court.

### *6.3.4.10 Measure*

The tenth functional category includes prepositions expressing measure relations, such as *w wysokości* [in the amount of]. Despite the fact that Milewska (2003a: 98–157) does not list this category in her work, it is very similar to the approximation relation (Milewska 2003a: 127–128), which is used to express approximated numerical values (e.g. *około* [about]).

Measure prepositions are underrepresented in translations relative to non-translated judgments (by about 55 % and 25 %, respectively), in particular: *w kwocie* [in the amount of], *na kwotę* [in the amount of], *do poziomu* [up to] (see Table 6.18). Markedly overrepresented types include *na poziomie* [at] and *poniżej* [below].

**Table 6.16.** *Distribution of compound and secondary prepositions expressing manner and instrumental relations*

| | Translated EU case law | | | | | Non-translated PL case law | | | General Polish |
|---|---|---|---|---|---|---|---|---|---|
| | **CJ** | **CJ vs GC (%DIFF)** | **CJ vs SN_2011–2015 (%DIFF)** | **GC** | **GC vs SN_2011–2015 (%DIFF)** | **SN_2011–2015** | **SN_2011–2015 vs SN_1999 (%DIFF)** | **SN_1999** | **NKJP** |
| *poprzez* [by] | 546 | +41 % | +17 % | 386 | −18 % | **468** | +60 % | 293 | 140 |
| *w drodze* [by way of] | 262 | +70 % | +28 % | 154 | −25 % | **204** | +20 % | 170 | 65 |
| *w formie* [in the form of] | 98 | +14 % | −37 % | 86 | −45 % | **155** | +40 % | 111 | 50 |
| *w trybie* [under] | 416 | +1500 % | +259 % | 26 | −78 % | **116** | −21 % | 147 | 30 |
| *za pomocą* [with the help of] | 140 | +36 % | +218 % | 103 | +134 % | **44** | +38 % | 32 | 79 |
| *na zasadzie* [on the principle] | 56 | +40 % | +37 % | 40 | −2 % | **41** | −57 % | 95 | 20 |
| *drogą* [by way of] | 35 | +169 % | +21 % | 13 | −55 % | **29** | +190 % | 10 | 64 |
| *na drodze* [towards] | 13 | +550 % | −55 % | 2 | −93 % | **29** | −83 % | 170 | 39 |
| *z zachowaniem* [subject to] | 14 | 0 % | −52 % | 14 | −52 % | **29** | +81 % | 16 | 6 |
| *za pośrednictwem* [via/through] | 73 | −26 % | +152 % | 98 | +238 % | **29** | +107 % | 14 | 36 |
| *przy pomocy* [with the aid of] | 9 | −25 % | −47 % | 12 | −29 % | **17** | −35 % | 26 | 23 |
| *przy użyciu* [with the use of] | 32 | +33 % | +256 % | 24 | +167 % | **9** | +50 % | 6 | 13 |
| *na bazie* [on the basis of] | 14 | −39 % | +100 % | 23 | +229 % | **7** | +75 % | 4 | 11 |
| **Total** | **1,708** | **+74 %** | **+45 %** | **981** | **−17 %** | **1,177** | **+8 %** | **1,094** | **576** |

**Table 6.17.** *Distribution of compound and secondary prepositions expressing adversariality relations*

| | Translated EU case law | | | | | Non-translated PL case law | | | General Polish |
|---|---|---|---|---|---|---|---|---|---|
| | **CJ** | **CJ vs GC (%DIFF)** | **CJ vs SN_2011–2015 (%DIFF)** | **GC** | **GC vs SN_2011–2015 (%DIFF)** | **SN_2011–2015** | **SN_2011–2015 vs SN_1999 (%DIFF)** | **SN_1999** | **NKJP** |
| *przeciwko* [against] | 1,189 | −49 % | 36 % | 2,338 | +168 % | **874** | −35 % | 1,344 | 127 |
| *przeciw* [against] | 9 | −10 % | −18 % | 10 | −9 % | **11** | −8 % | 12 | 295 |
| *w przeciwieństwie do* [contrary to] | 31 | −18 % | +244 % | 38 | +322 % | **9** | −55 % | 20 | 21 |
| **Total** | **1,229** | **−48 %** | **+37 %** | **2,386** | **+167 %** | **894** | **−35 %** | **1,376** | **443** |

**Table 6.18.** *Distribution of compound and secondary prepositions expressing measure relations*

| | Translated EU case law | | | | | Non-translated PL case law | | | General Polish |
|---|---|---|---|---|---|---|---|---|---|
| | CJ | CJ vs GC (%DIFF) | CJ vs SN_2011–2015 (%DIFF) | GC | GC vs SN_2011–2015 (%DIFF) | SN_2011–2015 | SN_2011–2015 vs SN_1999 (%DIFF) | SN_1999 | NKJP |
| *w wysokości* [in the amount of] | 136 | −36 % | −53 % | 211 | −27 % | **291** | +28 % | 228 | 66 |
| *w kwocie* [in the amount of] | 27 | −27 % | −90 % | 37 | −86 % | **264** | −7 % | 283 | 9 |
| *na kwotę* [in the amount of] | 22 | +5 % | −83 % | 21 | −84 % | **130** | +13 % | 115 | 7 |
| *około* (without: ok.) [about] | 35 | −54 % | −29 % | 76 | +55 % | **49** | −14 % | 57 | 437 |
| *na poziomie* [at] | 74 | −30 % | +222 % | 106 | +361 % | **23** | --- | 0 | 48 |
| *ok.* [ca.] | 2 | −75 % | −88 % | 8 | −53 % | **17** | +70 % | 10 | 188 |
| *poniżej* [below] | 49 | −59 % | +206 % | 120 | +650 % | **16** | +700 % | 2 | 53 |
| *w skali* [in the scale of] | 8 | 0 % | +14 % | 8 | +14 % | **7** | +75 % | 4 | 29 |
| *do poziomu* [up to] | 5 | −64 % | +25 % | 14 | +250 % | **4** | --- | 0 | 11 |
| **Total** | **358** | **−40 %** | **−55 %** | **601** | **−25 %** | **801** | **+15 %** | **699** | **848** |

### 6.3.4.11 *Inclusivity/exclusivity*

Inclusivity and exclusivity relations describe the reality by including items, persons, and events to a common set, or excluding them from it (Milewska 2003a: 123–125). Prepositional exponents expressing this type of relation are underrepresented in all corpora of judgments relative to the corpus of general Polish (NKJP); however, this finding has to be taken with caution, since it was not feasible to examine all concordances including *obok* [beside] with the PELCRA search engine (Pęzik 2012) (see Table 6.19). The corpus of CJ judgments has about 5 % fewer tokens, while the corpus of GC judgments has about 17 % fewer tokens than the post-accession SN corpus. On the whole, the corpora of judgments have fewer tokens of inclusive and exclusive prepositions than the NKJP, which means that it is the second relation type after the measure relation (see above) which is underrepresented in both EU and national judgments. As regards the over- and underrepresentation of individual prepositions in EU and national corpora, the following prepositions are clearly overrepresented in EU judgments: *z wyłączeniem* [with the exclusion of], *z wyjątkiem* [with the exception of], *z wykorzystaniem* [with the use of], whereas *wraz z* [together with] and *z udziałem* [with the participation of] are markedly underrepresented. The post-accession SN corpus also has about 6 % more tokens than the pre-accession corpus.

Secondary prepositions *wraz z* [together with], *poza* [beyond], *z udziałem* [with the participation of], *łącznie z* [inclusive of], *z wykorzystaniem* [with the use of], *razem z* [together with], *włącznie z* [including] are considered to express only the relation of inclusion. Prepositions *obok* [beside] and *oprócz* [in addition to] may convey either inclusivity or exclusivity relations, depending on the context (cf. Milewska 2003a: 125). Prepositions *z wyłączeniem* [with the exclusion of] and *z wyjątkiem* [with the exception of] express exclusively the relation of exclusion (Milewska 2003a: 125).

### 6.3.4.12 *Commutative relations*

Commutative relations are divided into two sub-types – exchange and substitution relations (Milewska 2003a: 126–127). Prepositions conveying the former include *zamiast* [instead of] and *w miejsce* [in place of], whereas examples of the latter are, for instance, *w imieniu* [on behalf of] and *kosztem* [at the expense of]. In general, secondary prepositions expressing commutative relations are not equally overrepresented in EU judgments due to the fact that they have very high distribution in CJ judgments (overrepresented by 45 %) and very low distribution in GC judgments (underrepresented by 81 %), indicating internal variation in the Eurolect (see Table 6.20). *W imieniu* [on behalf of] is also highly distributed in post-accession SN judgments, where it signals that certain actions had been performed on behalf of either the plaintiffs or the defendants. Post-accession SN judgments exhibit marked overrepresentation relative to pre-accession judgments, which is mainly due to the distribution of *w imieniu* [on behalf of]. Commutative prepositions are generally overrepresented in judicial language relative to general Polish (NKJP).

**Table 6.19.** *Distribution of compound and secondary prepositions expressing inclusivity/exclusivity relations*

| | Translated EU case law | | | | | Non-translated PL case law | | | General Polish |
|---|---|---|---|---|---|---|---|---|---|
| | CJ | CJ vs GC (%DIFF) | CJ vs SN_2011–2015 (%DIFF) | GC | GC vs SN_2011–2015 (%DIFF) | SN_2011–2015 | SN_2011–2015 vs SN_1999 (%DIFF) | SN_1999 | NKJP |
| *wraz z* [together with] | 96 | –8 % | –67 % | 104 | –65 % | **293** | +80 % | 163 | 177 |
| *poza* [beyond] | 305 | +7 % | +26 % | 284 | +17 % | **243** | –32 % | 355 | 201 |
| *z udziałem* [with the participation of] | 15 | –57 % | –80 % | 35 | –54 % | **76** | +153 % | 30 | 36 |
| *obok* [beside] | 17 | +42 % | –64 % | 12 | –74 % | **47** | –18 % | 57 | *182 |
| *z wyłączeniem* [with the exclusion of] | 38 | +90 % | +41 % | 20 | –26 % | **27** | +13 % | 24 | 7 |
| *oprócz* [in addition to] | 46 | –27 % | +70 % | 63 | +133 % | **27** | +23 % | 22 | 150 |
| *z wyjątkiem* [with the exception of] | 109 | +14 % | +354 % | 96 | +300 % | **24** | –8 % | 26 | 26 |
| *łącznie z* [inclusive of] | 36 | +140 % | +71 % | 15 | –29 % | **21** | –19 % | 26 | 22 |
| *z wykorzystaniem* [with the use of] | 15 | +200 % | +67 % | 5 | –44 % | **9** | +125 % | 4 | 10 |
| *razem z* [together with] | 7 | –22 % | 0 % | 9 | +29 % | **7** | –71 % | 24 | 76 |
| *włącznie z* (excl. *ze*) | 50 | +233 % | --- | 15 | --- | **0** | --- | 0 | 4 |
| **Total** | **734** | **+12 %** | **–5 %** | **658** | **–15 %** | **774** | **+6 %** | **731** | **891** |

**Table 6.20.** *Distribution of compound and secondary prepositions expressing commutative relations*

| | **Translated EU case law** | | | | | **Non-translated PL case law** | | | **General Polish** |
|---|---|---|---|---|---|---|---|---|---|
| | **CJ** | **CJ vs GC (%DIFF)** | **CJ vs SN_2011–2015 (%DIFF)** | **GC** | **GC vs SN_2011–2015 (%DIFF)** | **SN_2011–2015** | **SN_2011–2015 vs SN_1999 (%DIFF)** | **SN_1999** | **NKJP** |
| *w imieniu* [on behalf of] | 824 | +1426 % | +79 % | 54 | −88 % | **461** | +375 % | 97 | 71 |
| *zamiast* [instead of] | 29 | −29 % | −42 % | 41 | −18 % | **50** | −25 % | 67 | 140 |
| *w miejsce* [in place of] | 9 | +50 % | −79 % | 6 | −86 % | **42** | −47 % | 79 | 12 |
| *kosztem* [at the expense of] | 7 | +17 % | −83 % | 6 | −86 % | **42** | +31 % | 32 | 25 |
| *w zamian za* [in exchange for] | 35 | +150 % | +17 % | 14 | −53 % | **30** | +36 % | 22 | 19 |
| **Total** | **904** | **+647 %** | **+45 %** | **121** | **−81 %** | **624** | **+110 %** | **297** | **267** |

The pronounced difference in the distribution of commutative prepositions in both corpora of EU judgments is due to the very high number of occurrences of the substitutive *w imieniu* [on behalf of], which occurs almost exclusively in Move 1 – Identifying the case as a means of providing information that the observations submitted on behalf of various (third) parties have been heard by the Court.

#### *6.3.4.13 Purpose*

Prepositions such as *w celu* [in order to] and *celem* [in order to], describe actions which aim at achieving a specific goal leading to a certain result (Milewska 2003a: 138–139). This functional category is not included in cause-effect relations, as purpose relations relate to the future, whereas cause relations relate mainly to the past (Milewska 2003a: 138; cf. Biel 2016b: 25–27). This functional category yet again demonstrates the importance of prepositions in judicial language, since their distribution is significantly higher in judgments compared to general Polish (cf. Table 6.21). This is mainly due to the overrepresentation of *w celu* [in order to].

Almost all of the secondary prepositions expressing purpose relations are overrepresented in EU judgments relative to post-accession judgments (by 365 % and 198 %, respectively), these being: *w celu* [in order to], *celem* [in order to], *na potrzeby* [for the purposes of], and *do celów* [for the purposes of]. Only one low-frequency preposition, *w kierunku* [towards], is slightly underrepresented in EU judgments. Furthermore, there is a substantial degree of internal variation within the Eurolect, as CJ judgments exhibit about 56 % more tokens than GC judgments.

#### *6.3.4.14 Distribution*

Distribution prepositions fulfill the sole role of distribution or allotment of, for instance, physical goods or financial burdens (cf. Milewska 2003a: 128). In the context of judicial language, the sole preposition expressing distribution relations with an NF higher than five occurrences pmw is *pomiędzy* [between]. Its distribution is markedly higher in both EU and SN judgments than in general Polish; the Eurolect is marked by overrepresentation relative to post-accession SN judgments (by 24 % and 19 %, respectively) (see Table 6.22).

*Pomiędzy* [between] is used by the courts to state that costs of proceedings are distributed among the parties or that certain obligations need to be performed by both parties to an agreement.

#### *6.3.4.15 Comparison*

Milewska describes the comparison relation as characterizing the existence of a fact against the background of another one (Milewska 2003a: 146–149), the essence of which is not based on indicating any differences or similarities. Prepositions belonging to this category are overrepresented in translated EU judgments, by 17 % and 48 %, respectively, mainly due to the overrepresentation of *względem* [in regard of]. On the whole, they are less frequent in general Polish (cf. Table 6.23). Notably, the post-accession SN corpus exhibits fewer tokens than the pre-accession corpus (by 31 %).

**Table 6.21.** *Distribution of compound and secondary prepositions expressing purpose relations*

| | Translated EU case law | | | | | Non-translated PL case law | | | General Polish |
|---|---|---|---|---|---|---|---|---|---|
| | **CJ** | **CJ vs GC (%DIFF)** | **CJ vs SN_2011–2015 (%DIFF)** | **GC** | **GC vs SN_2011–2015 (%DIFF)** | **SN_2011–2015** | **SN_2011–2015 vs SN_1999 (%DIFF)** | **SN_1999** | **NKJP** |
| *w celu* [in order to] | 1,209 | +47 % | +330 % | 823 | +193 % | **281** | +46 % | 192 | 84 |
| *celem* [in order to] | 102 | −11 % | +143 % | 114 | +171 % | **42** | −44 % | 75 | 94 |
| *na potrzeby* [for the purposes of] | 43 | +48 % | +65 % | 29 | +12 % | **26** | +44 % | 18 | 20 |
| *w kierunku* [towards] | 8 | +60 % | −20 % | 5 | −50 % | **10** | −58 % | 24 | 59 |
| *do celów* [for the purposes of] | 337 | +188 % | +5517 % | 117 | +1850 % | **6** | +200 % | 2 | 8 |
| **Total** | **1,699** | **+56 %** | **+365 %** | **1,088** | **+198 %** | **365** | **+17 %** | **311** | **265** |

**Table 6.22.** *Distribution of compound prepositions expressing distribution relations*

| | Translated EU case law | | | | | Non-translated PL case law | | | General Polish |
|---|---|---|---|---|---|---|---|---|---|
| | **CJ** | **CJ vs GC (%DIFF)** | **CJ vs SN_2011–2015 (%DIFF)** | **GC** | **GC vs SN_2011–2015 (%DIFF)** | **SN_2011–2015** | **SN_2011–2015 vs SN_1999 (%DIFF)** | **SN_1999** | **NKJP** |
| *pomiędzy* [between] | 433 | +4 % | +24 % | 415 | +19 % | 350 | +46 % | 240 | 130 |

**Table 6.23.** *Distribution of compound and secondary prepositions expressing comparison relations*

| | Translated EU case law | | | | | Non-translated PL case law | | | General Polish |
|---|---|---|---|---|---|---|---|---|---|
| | **CJ** | **CJ vs GC (%DIFF)** | **CJ vs SN_2011–2015 (%DIFF)** | **GC** | **GC vs SN_2011–2015 (%DIFF)** | **SN_2011–2015** | **SN_2011–2015 vs SN_1999 (%DIFF)** | **SN_1999** | **NKJP** |
| *względem*[a] [in regard of] | 164 | −22 % | +31 % | 210 | +68 % | **125** | +2 % | 123 | 79 |
| *na tle* [against] | 4 | −50 % | −93 % | 8 | −87 % | **60** | −56 % | 135 | 28 |
| *w porównaniu z* [in comparison to] | 33 | −30 % | +267 % | 47 | +422 % | **9** | +50 % | 6 | 35 |
| *w ślad za* [in the wake of] | 1 | −86 % | −89 % | 7 | −22 % | **9** | −72 % | 32 | 8 |
| *na równi z* [on par with] | 7 | +600 % | +17 % | 1 | −83 % | **6** | 0 % | 6 | 5 |
| *w odróżnieniu od* [in contrast to] | 35 | −3 % | +775 % | 36 | +800 % | **4** | −60 % | 10 | 11 |
| *w porównaniu do* [in comparison to] | 8 | −27 % | +167 % | 11 | +267 % | **3** | --- | 0 | 9 |
| **Total** | **252** | **−21 %** | **+17 %** | **320** | **+48 %** | **216** | **−31 %** | **312** | **175** |

[a] The results do not include occurrences of *względem* in the expression *pod względem* [in terms of], which, similarly to *w stosunku do* [in relation to], expresses reference relations.

The analysis of the textual material has shown that the main type of relation fulfilled by the preposition *w stosunku do* [in relation to] in judgments is not comparison, as claimed by Milewska (2013a: 147), but reference; therefore, it has been examined in light of reference relations (cf. Section 6.3.4.3).

### *6.3.4.16 Space relations*

Compound and secondary prepositions expressing space relations are used to describe the location of certain objects as well as their placement with respect to other objects (Milewska 2003a: 98). These prepositions describe only physical spatial relations. Milewska's (2003a: 98–112) description of this category encompasses many exponents; however, in the case of the language of judgments, space prepositions are not widely represented, not only in terms of the number of their types but also tokens (see Table 6.24). They are overrepresented mostly in CJ judgments; GC judgments exhibit almost identical overall distribution as post-accession SN judgments. The distribution in the latter is higher than in pre-accession SN judgments (by about 54 %).

If it was not for the inflated number of occurrences of the preposition *na terytorium* [in the territory of] in CJ judgments which is used mostly in reference to Member States' territories as well as other non-EU countries' territories, this category would be almost equally underrepresented in the language of judgments compared to general Polish (NKJP).

### *6.3.4.17 Partitive relations*

Prepositions conveying partitive relations are somewhat similar to prepositions expressing distribution discussed in Section 6.3.4.14. While the latter are used to signal allocation of physical goods or financial burdens (cf. Milewska 2003a: 128), the former indicate that, for instance, certain persons are isolated from a given group, in order to further elaborate on their rights and obligations (cf. Milewska 2003a: 122). The immediate conclusion that can be drawn from the quantitative data is that partitive prepositions are not a staple of judicial language, either translated or non-translated judgments, as they are more frequent in general Polish (NKJP) (see Table 6.25).

Partitive prepositions are overrepresented in both CJ and GC judgments relative to SN judgments. In addition, post-accession SN judgments show underrepresentation compared to pre-accession judgments. The examination of concordances with the preposition *wśród* [among] shows that partitive relations refer mostly to groups of individuals selected from a larger group based either on their rights and obligations (CJ judgments) or on how they were affected by one of the parties to the proceedings (GC judgments).

### *6.3.4.18 Active relations*

The purpose of prepositions expressing active relations is to point to the subject carrying out a given activity (Milewska 2003a: 151).

**Table 6.24.** *Distribution of compound and secondary prepositions expressing space relations*

| | Translated EU case law | | | | | Non-translated PL case law | | | General Polish |
|---|---|---|---|---|---|---|---|---|---|
| | CJ | CJ vs GC (%DIFF) | CJ vs SN_2011–2015 (%DIFF) | GC | GC vs SN_2011–2015 (%DIFF) | SN_2011–2015 | SN_2011–2015 vs SN_1999 (%DIFF) | SN_1999 | NKJP |
| *na terenie* [in the territory of] | 19 | +90 % | −71 % | 10 | −85 % | **66** | +74 % | 38 | 117 |
| *na obszarze* [in the area of] | 33 | +267 % | +6 % | 9 | −71 % | 31 | +41 % | 22 | 16 |
| *w obrębie* [within] | 31 | −18 % | +24 % | 38 | +52 % | 25 | +213 % | 8 | 18 |
| *na terytorium* [in the territory of] | 479 | +584 % | +3321 % | 70 | +400 % | **14** | +250 % | 4 | 14 |
| *wokół* [around] | 3 | −40 % | −79 % | 5 | −64 % | **14** | +75 % | 8 | 121 |
| *na zewnątrz* [outside] | 7 | +17 % | −22 % | 6 | −33 % | **9** | −36 % | 14 | 29 |
| *wewnątrz* [inside] | 29 | −12 % | +314 % | 33 | +371 % | 7 | −30 % | 10 | 39 |
| *w pobliżu* [near] | 9 | +350 % | +50 % | 2 | −67 % | **6** | −25 % | 8 | 49 |
| *spoza* [from the outside] | 4 | −60 % | −20 % | 10 | +100 % | 5 | +150 % | 2 | 19 |
| *na terenach* [on the territories] | 8 | --- | +60 % | 0 | −100 % | 5 | +25 % | 4 | 104 |
| **Total** | **622** | **+240 %** | **+242 %** | **183** | **+1 %** | **182** | **+54 %** | **118** | **526** |

**Table 6.25.** *Distribution of compound prepositions expressing partitive relations*

| | Translated EU case law | | | | | Non-translated PL case law | | | General Polish |
|---|---|---|---|---|---|---|---|---|---|
| | **CJ** | **CJ vs GC (%DIFF)** | **CJ vs SN_2011–2015 (%DIFF)** | **GC** | **GC vs SN_2011–2015 (%DIFF)** | **SN_2011–2015** | **SN_2011–2015 vs SN_1999 (%DIFF)** | **SN_1999** | **NKJP** |
| *wśród* [among] | 69 | −22 % | +138 % | 89 | +207 % | 29 | −34 % | 44 | 307 |
| *spośród* [from] | 37 | −34 % | +42 % | 56 | +115 % | 26 | −61 % | 67 | 60 |
| *pośród* [among] | 9 | −25 % | +350 % | 12 | +500 % | 2 | --- | 0 | 21 |
| **Total** | **115** | **−27 %** | **+105 %** | **157** | **+180 %** | **56** | **−50 %** | **111** | **388** |

**Table 6.26.** *Secondary prepositions expressing active relations*

| | **Translated EU case law** | | | | | **Non-translated PL case law** | | | **General Polish** |
|---|---|---|---|---|---|---|---|---|---|
| | **CJ** | **CJ vs GC (%DIFF)** | **CJ vs SN_2011–2015 (%DIFF)** | **GC** | **GC vs SN_2011–2015 (%DIFF)** | **SN_2011–2015** | **SN_2011–2015 vs SN_1999 (%DIFF)** | **SN_1999** | **NKJP** |
| *ze strony* [on the part of] | 65 | −32 % | +51 % | 95 | +121 % | **43** | **−36 %** | 67 | 76 |

These prepositions are overrepresented in the Eurolect; however, their distribution is not even in both of the corpora, with the corpus of GC judgments having a noticeably higher distribution of the only identified active preposition than the corpus of CJ judgments. It is surprising, however, that *ze strony* [on the part of] has a fairly high distribution in general Polish; thus, it cannot be concluded that prepositions expressing this type of relation largely affect the prepositional profile of judgments, despite the fact that GC judgments contain more occurrences of *ze strony* [on the part of] than general Polish (cf. Table 6.26).

### 6.3.5 Prepositions in judgments – summary

The results confirm the initial hypothesis that the high distribution of simple, compound and secondary prepositions in both EU and Polish judgments against a representative sample of general Polish (NKJP) constitutes a generic feature of judgments. From the perspective of post-accession SN judgments, the most important discourse-functional categories of compound and secondary prepositions include: time; cause-effect, permission and condition; reference; intra- and inter-textual reference; participation; modality; apposition, and manner and instrumental relations (see Table 6.27). In CJ and GC judgments, other important relations conveyed by compound and secondary prepositions include: adversariality and purpose relations.

The data show that the phraseological profile of CJEU judgments differs from the profile of SN judgments in terms of the distribution of types of prepositions expressing various discourse functions (semantic relations) (see Table 6.27). The Eurolect is marked by a clear overrepresentation of nine functional categories of compound and secondary prepositions: reference, intra- and inter-textual reference, adversariality, purpose, distribution, comparison, space relations, partitive relations, and active relations. There are also six categories which are underrepresented in the Eurolect: time, cause-effect, result, contravention and condition, participation, modality, measure, inclusivity/exclusivity. These differences may be due to the impact of the translation process on TTs, and the scope of jurisdiction of the EU courts and the national court, which affects the subject matter of judgments, and thus their language.

In conclusion, compound and secondary prepositions are particularly crucial to the language of judgments, which is evidenced by their high distribution relative to general Polish (NKJP). The total distribution of simple prepositions is inflated by their occurrence within secondary prepositions. Furthermore, the analysis of functional properties of prepositions has shown that thanks to this word class judges are able to express themselves with greater precision.

**Table 6.27.** *Aggregate quantitative data on the distribution of compound and secondary prepositions conveying various discourse functions (semantic relations)*

| | **Translated EU case law** | | | | | **Non-translated PL case law** | | | **General Polish** |
|---|---|---|---|---|---|---|---|---|---|
| | **CJ** | **CJ vs GC (%DIFF)** | **CJ vs SN_2011–2015 (%DIFF)** | **GC** | **GC vs SN_2011–2015 (%DIFF)** | **SN_2011–2015** | **SN_2011–2015 vs SN_1999 (%DIFF)** | **SN_1999** | **NKJP** |
| 1. Time | 7,234 | −23 % | −40 % | 9,422 | −22 % | **12,136** | +9 % | 11,091 | 2,928 |
| 2. Cause-effect, result, contravention and condition: | 5,273 | +2 % | −16 % | 5,174 | −17 % | **6,270** | +29 % | 4,859 | 1,702 |
| (1) cause-effect | 2,487 | 0 % | −26 % | 2,489 | −26 % | **3,373** | +42 % | 2,368 | 892 |
| (2) result | 845 | −15 % | −41 % | 993 | −31 % | **1,429** | +9 % | 1,316 | 220 |
| (3) contravention | 439 | −16 % | −32 % | 524 | −18 % | **641** | −1 % | 650 | 188 |
| (4) condition | 1,502 | +29 % | +82 % | 1,168 | +41 % | **827** | +58 % | 525 | 402 |
| 3. Reference | 10,493 | −17 % | +102 % | 12,701 | +144 % | **5,201** | +34 % | 3,868 | 1,312 |
| 4. Intra- and inter-textual reference | 7,246 | 0 % | +55 % | 7,244 | +55 % | **4,678** | +13 % | 4,155 | 545 |
| 5. Participation | 907 | −15 % | −59 % | 1,061 | −52 % | **2,209** | +13 % | 1,960 | 380 |
| 6. Modality | 840 | −17 % | −41 % | 1,018 | −28 % | **1,421** | −16 % | 1,682 | 592 |
| 7. Apposition | 1,412 | +43 % | +20 % | 988 | −16 % | **1,179** | −46 % | 2,186 | 396 |
| 8. Manner and instrumental relations | 1,708 | +74 % | +45 % | 981 | −17 % | **1,177** | +8 % | 1,094 | 576 |
| 9. Adversariality | 1,229 | −48 % | +37 % | 2,386 | +167 % | **894** | −35 % | 1,376 | 443 |

*(continued on next page)*

**Table 6.27.** *Continued*

| | Translated EU case law | | | | | Non-translated PL case law | | | General Polish |
|---|---|---|---|---|---|---|---|---|---|
| | **CJ** | **CJ vs GC (%DIFF)** | **CJ vs SN_2011–2015 (%DIFF)** | **GC** | **GC vs SN_2011–2015 (%DIFF)** | **SN_2011–2015** | **SN_2011–2015 vs SN_1999 (%DIFF)** | **SN_1999** | **NKJP** |
| 10. Measure | 358 | −40 % | −55 % | 601 | −25 % | **801** | +15 % | 699 | 848 |
| 11. Inclusivity/ exclusivity | 734 | +12 % | −5 % | 658 | −15 % | **774** | +6 % | 731 | 891 |
| 12. Commutative relations | 904 | +647 % | +45 % | 121 | −81 % | **624** | +110 % | 297 | 267 |
| 13. Purpose | 1,699 | +56 % | +365 % | 1,088 | +198 % | **365** | +17 % | 311 | 265 |
| 14. Distribution | 433 | +4 % | +24 % | 415 | +19 % | **350** | +46 % | 240 | 130 |
| 15. Comparison | 252 | −21 % | +17 % | 320 | +48 % | **216** | −31 % | 312 | 175 |
| 16. Space relations | 622 | +240 % | +242 % | 183 | +1 % | **182** | +54 % | 118 | 526 |
| 17. Partitive relations | 115 | −27 % | +105 % | 157 | +180 % | **56** | −50 % | 111 | 388 |
| 18. Active relations | 65 | −32 % | +51 % | 95 | +121 % | **43** | −36 % | 67 | 76 |
| **Total** | **41,524** | **−7 %** | **+8 %** | **44,613** | **+16 %** | **38,576** | **+10 %** | **35,157** | **12,440** |

## 6.4 Structurization of judicial arguments

In order to convey their arguments, judges use complex sentences. Table 6.3 (see Section 6.2), which presents lexico-grammatical categories identified with the keyword lists, contains only one paratactic marker which is overrepresented in SN judgments – *tj.* [i.e.-ABBRV] [#71]. Despite this fact, following Biel's (2014a: 181–199) study, I will focus in this section on the linguistic markers of two types of relations, paratactic and hypotactic relations, which take the form of coordinate and subordinate clauses and help to structure both the judges' and reported arguments (cf. Nagórko 2010: 301–313).

### 6.4.1 Parataxis

Paratactic relations encompass coordinate clauses of five types: (1) additive, (2) alternative, (3) adversative, (4) resultative, and (5) inclusive (Grzegorczykowa 2004[1988]: 99–105; Nagórko 2010: 301–304). Due to the fact that coordinating conjunctions (coordinators) may link not only clauses but also individual words or phrases (for instance, binomials, see Chapter 8), the distribution of paratactic markers presented in Table 6.28 does not fully represent the total number of occurrences of paratactic clauses.

Additive coordinating conjunctions are used to correlate facts (Grzegorczykowa 2004[1988]: 102) and have a surprisingly equal distribution in the post-accession corpora of judgments; only the pre-accession SN corpus has about 8 % fewer tokens than the post-accession SN corpus. Compared to general Polish (NKJP) these conjunctions may be perceived as a characteristic feature of judicial language. The conjunction characterized by the highest salience is *i* [and] (cf. Chapter 8), which is also the prototypical additive marker. *Oraz* [and-FORM] is a more formal variant of *i* [and] and has a similar level of distribution in CJEU and SN judgments, with only GC judgments showing an underrepresentation of about 15 %. The distribution of both *i* [and] and *oraz* [and-FORM] shows that lawyer-linguists imitate the conventions of both general (NKJP) and judicial (SN) Polish without overly relying on either the former conjunction or the latter. The conjunction *, *a* [*, and] has an even lower number of tokens than *oraz* [and-FORM] and it is underrepresented in both CJ and GC judgments (by 53 % and 35 %, respectively). It needs to be remembered, however, that it may connect clauses by either providing new information or providing contrast and showing result or inference (Biel 2014a: 186). The analysis of concordances shows that it is mostly used for the former, which is why it is included in this category. Other additive coordinating conjunctions are not particularly salient in either CJEU or SN judgments due to their low total distribution. Overall, these conjunctions are definitely a characteristic feature of judicial language.

The aggregate number of occurrences of alternative coordinating conjunctions, adversative coordinating conjunctions, and inclusive coordinating conjunctions does not exceed that of the conjunctions discussed above. These three groups of paratactic markers do not show similar tendencies. Only the total number of tokens of alternative coordinating conjunctions is overrepresented in the Eurolect

**Table 6.28.** *Distribution of paratactic markers*

| | Translated EU case law | | | | | Non-translated PL case law | | | General Polish |
|---|---|---|---|---|---|---|---|---|---|
| | CJ | CJ vs GC (%DIFF) | CJ vs SN_2011–2015 (%DIFF) | GC | GC vs SN_2011–2015 (%DIFF) | SN_2011–2015 | SN_2011–2015 vs SN_1999 (%DIFF) | SN_1999 | NKJP |
| **I. Additive coordinating conjunctions** | | | | | | | | | |
| *i* [and] | 17,869 | +0 % | +10 % | 17,944 | +10 % | 16,298 | +12 % | 14,510 | 10,753 |
| *oraz* [and-FORM] | 3,470 | +14 % | −3 % | 3,045 | −15 % | 3,596 | +22 % | 2,959 | 1,422 |
| *, *a* (excl. *a także*) [*, and] | 1,610 | −27 % | −53 % | 2,217 | −35 % | 3,434 | −10 % | 3,809 | 572 |
| *ani* [and/neither ... nor...] | 622 | −19 % | +45 % | 766 | +79 % | 428 | −24 % | 561 | 321 |
| *zarówno... (jak i)* [both... (and)] | 311 | +15 % | −4 % | 271 | −16 % | 324 | −14 % | 379 | 203 |
| *a także* [and also] | 681 | +85 % | +129 % | 367 | +24 % | 297 | −15 % | 351 | 244 |
| *przy tym* [while] | 40 | +9 % | −76 % | 37 | −78 % | 170 | −31 % | 248 | 73 |
| *przy czym* [while] | 136 | −16 % | −17 % | 162 | −2 % | 165 | +1 % | 163 | 35 |
| *jak również* [as well as] | 203 | −15 % | +69 % | 240 | +99 % | 120 | +79 % | 67 | 39 |
| **TOTAL** | **24,944** | **0 %** | **0 %** | **25,049** | **+1 %** | **24,833** | **+8 %** | **23,046** | **13,661** |
| **II. Alternative coordinating conjunctions** | | | | | | | | | |
| *lub* [or – inclusive disjunction] | 5,669 | +72 % | +232 % | 3,299 | +93 % | 1,709 | +37 % | 1,244 | 955 |
| *albo* [or – exclusive disjunction] | 361 | +59 % | −2 % | 228 | −38 % | 367 | +54 % | 238 | 436 |

| | | | | | | | | | |
|---|---|---|---|---|---|---|---|---|---|
| *bądź* [either... (or...) – exclusive disjunction] | 199 | +22 % | +3 % | 163 | −16 % | 193 | −24 % | 256 | 112 |
| *i/lub* [and/or] | 25 | +238 % | +744 % | 7 | +150 % | 3 | −51 % | 6 | N/A |
| **TOTAL** | **6,254** | **+69 %** | **+175 %** | **3,697** | **+63 %** | **2,272** | **+30 %** | **1,743** | **1,503** |
| **III. Adversative coordinating conjunctions** | | | | | | | | | |
| *natomiast* [while] | 193 | −6 % | −72 % | 204 | −70 % | 690 | +6 % | 652 | 393 |
| *. *Natomiast* [while] | 60 | −33 % | −43 % | 89 | −15 % | 105 | −49 % | 206 | N/A |
| *ale* [but] | 239 | −29 % | −63 % | 336 | −48 % | 643 | +26 % | 509 | 2,976 |
| *zaś* [while] | 176 | −33 % | −59 % | 263 | −39 % | 430 | −42 % | 739 | 245 |
| *lecz* [but-FORM] | 429 | −7 % | +18 % | 461 | +27 % | 363 | −18 % | 444 | 303 |
| **TOTAL** | **1,097** | **−19 %** | **−51 %** | **1,353** | **−39 %** | **2,231** | **−12 %** | **2,550** | **3,917** |
| **IV. Resultative coordinating conjunctions (cf. Section 6.7.2)** | | | | | | | | | |
| **V. Inclusive coordinating conjunctions** | | | | | | | | | |
| *tj.* [i.e.-ABBRV] | 32 | −42 % | −94 % | 55 | −90 % | 534 | +66 % | 321 | 43 |
| *czyli* [namely/that is] | 168 | −31 % | +1 % | 243 | +47 % | 166 | +27 % | 131 | 455 |
| *, *to jest* [it means] | 73 | −28 % | −9 % | 101 | +27 % | 80 | −4 % | 83 | N/A |
| *to znaczy* [it means] | 52 | −41 % | +223 % | 87 | +447 % | 16 | +61 % | 10 | 102 |
| *tzn.* [it means (i.e.)-ABBRV] | 11 | −15 % | −21 % | 13 | −7 % | 14 | −53 % | 30 | 30 |
| **TOTAL** | **335** | **−33 %** | **−59 %** | **500** | **−38 %** | **810** | **+41 %** | **575** | **629** |
| **GRAND TOTAL** | **32,630** | **+7 %** | **+8 %** | **30,599** | **+2 %** | **30,147** | **+8 %** | **27,915** | **19,710** |

(by 175 % and 63 %, respectively). *Lub* [or], which expresses inclusive disjunction, is considerably overrepresented in CJ and moderately overrepresented in GC judgments, while *albo* [or] and *bądź* [or], which express exclusive disjunction are used sporadically compared to *lub* [or], which mimics the distribution in the post-accession SN corpus. The conjunction *i/lub* [and/or] is considered incorrect in Polish, as *i* [and] and *lub* [or], because the inclusive meaning of *i* [and] is included in *lub* [or]. Lawyer-linguists use *i/lub* [and/or] probably due to the influence of the ST. At this point, it needs to be observed that *i* [and] and *lub* [or] occur frequently in binomials, which will be analyzed in Chapter 8. All in all, alternative coordinating conjunctions are characteristic of judicial language, as they are more frequent in judgments (in particular in CJ and GC judgments) than in general Polish (NKJP).

The two remaining groups, adversative coordinating conjunctions introducing contrast and inclusive coordinating conjunctions, show marked underrepresentation relative to post-accession SN judgments – there are about 51 % and 39 % fewer tokens of adversative conjunctions and about 59 % and 38 % fewer tokens of inclusive conjunctions in the Eurolect. In the group of adversative conjunctions, only *lecz* [but-FORM], a more formal variant of *ale* [but] is overrepresented in translations (by 18 % and 27 %, respectively), while in the group of inclusive conjunctions, only *to znaczy* [it means] is characterized by marked overrepresentation. *Tj.* [i.e.-ABBRV], which has been found to be an underrepresented keyword in CJEU judgments is indeed more frequent in SN judgments. Neither adversative conjunctions nor inclusive conjunctions are unequivocally a characteristic feature of judicial language due to their low overall distribution compared to general Polish (NKJP).

Figure 6.5 presents the overall distribution of paratactic markers in the corpora of judgments and in general Polish (NKJP).

Overall, paratactic markers belonging to all four groups are considerably overrepresented compared to the balanced corpus of general Polish (NKJP). However,

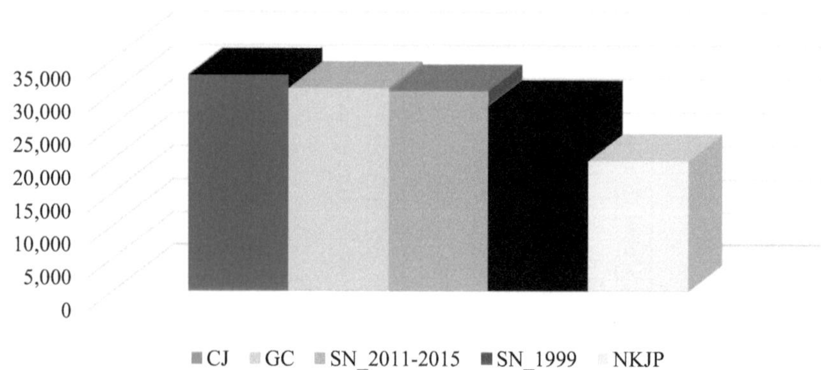


**Figure 6.5.** *Total distribution of paratactic markers*

the overrepresentation is mainly due to the high distribution of alternative and additive coordinating conjunctions. Adversative and inclusive conjunctions, on the other hand, are underrepresented in judgments, but owing to their low total distribution, they do not cause the whole category of paratactic markers to be underrepresented.

### 6.4.2 Hypotaxis

Hypotactic markers are used to create complex sentences composed of unequal clauses arranged in subordinate relationships (cf. Nagórko 2010: 304–314) in which one clause is perceived as the main (superordinate) one. Following Biel's (2014a: 191–192) study, the analysis of hypotactic structures takes into consideration relative pronouns, complementizers and concessive subordinators, in order to allow for comparability of the data with the findings concerning the genre of legislative acts. The discussion is structured around Grzegorczykowa's (2004[1988]: 97–98; cf. Biel 2014a: 191–192) typology encompassing: (1) relative clauses, (2) complement clauses, and (3) extensional clauses which include temporal, comparative and cause-effect clauses (with the latter being divided into: causal, concessive, purpose, conditional, and effect clauses). Causal, conditional, purpose and effect clauses will be described in later sections (see Sections 6.7.2, 6.7.3, and 6.7.4).

Table 6.29 presents quantitative data on the distribution of hypotactic markers in the corpora of CJEU and SN judgments, and general Polish (NKJP).

Biel (2014a: 190) notes that general Polish and the language of Polish EU and domestic legal acts use complex nominalizations rather than numerous subordinate clauses, which applied primarily to complement clauses. The same observation cannot be made with regard to the language of judgments, as complementizers, *że* [that], *iż* [that-FORM] and *czy* [if, whether] are very frequent in judicial language, with *że* [that] being about 8 times more frequent than in Polish legislation and about 4 times more frequent than in EU legislation (Biel 2014a: 192). None of the complementizers have been identified as keywords in either of the corpora of judgments, although it should be noted that *iż* [that-FORM], the more formal variant of *że* [that], is overrepresented in CJEU judgments by about 87 % and 160 %. The distribution in CJ and SN judgments is more even – marked overrepresentation is observed in the GC corpus in which translations exhibit exaggeration of features typical of non-translated Polish. It may be the case that GC judgments contain more verbs requiring complementation (cf. Biel 2014a: 197). The overall distribution of the three complementizers in the CJ corpus, with *iż* [that-FORM] being the least frequent, most closely resembles the distribution in the post-accession SN corpus; the GC corpus shows the highest degree of divergence. The post-accession SN corpus contains only about 5 % fewer tokens than the pre-accession corpus. Considering the rather low distribution of complementizers in general Polish (NKJP), it may be concluded that the use of complementizers as markers of hypotaxis is a feature of both EU and national judgments.

**Table 6.29.** *Distribution of hypotactic markers*

| | Translated EU case law | | | | | Non-translated PL case law | | | General Polish |
|---|---|---|---|---|---|---|---|---|---|
| | **CJ** | **CJ vs GC (%DIFF)** | **CJ vs SN_2011–2015 (%DIFF)** | **GC** | **GC vs SN_2011–2015 (%DIFF)** | **SN_2011–2015** | **SN_2011–2015 vs SN_1999 (%DIFF)** | **SN_1999** | **NKJP** |
| **I. Complementizers** | | | | | | | | | |
| *że* [that] | 10,771 | −27 % | +5 % | 14,726 | +44 % | 10,251 | +6 % | 9,689 | 5,653 |
| *że* (excl. complex conjunctions[a]) | 10,463 | −28 % | +4 % | 14,526 | +44 % | 10,067 | +5 % | 9,558 | 5,482 |
| *iż* [that-FORM] | 1,495 | −28 % | +87 % | 2,081 | +160 % | 801 | −64 % | 2,253 | 294 |
| *iż* (excl. complex conjunctions[b]) | 1,459 | −29 % | +86 % | 2,049 | +162 % | 783 | −65 % | 2,210 | 278 |
| *czy* [if, whether] | 2,161 | +66 % | +85 % | 1,300 | +11 % | 1,170 | +18 % | 991 | 1,971 |
| **TOTAL** | **14,427** | **−20 %** | **+18 %** | **18,108** | **+48 %** | **12,222** | **−5 %** | **12,933** | **7,918** |
| **II. Relative pronouns** | | | | | | | | | |
| *który, która…* [which] | 9,560 | +7 % | +57 % | 8,911 | +46 % | 6,093 | +16 % | 5,242 | 4,951 |
| *co, czego, czemu, czym* (excl. *wobec czego, przy czym*) [what, which] | 2,388 | −24 % | −21 % | 3,132 | +4 % | 3,011 | −16 % | 3,583 | 2,997 |
| *co następuje* [what follows] | 245 | +49 % | −34 % | 164 | −56 % | 372 | −51 % | 765 | 4 |
| *jaki, jaka…* [which] | 1,262 | −15 % | +33 % | 1,490 | +58 % | 945 | +7 % | 886 | 1,005 |
| *kiedy* [when] | 62 | −29 % | −53 % | 87 | −34 % | 133 | −12 % | 151 | 796 |

| | | | | | | | | | |
|---|---|---|---|---|---|---|---|---|---|
| *kto, kogo, komu, kim* [who, whom, whose] | 32 | +95 % | −49 % | 17 | −74 % | 64 | +69 % | 38 | 719 |
| *gdzie* [where] | 111 | +143 % | +164 % | 46 | +9 % | 42 | −41 % | 71 | 618 |
| *czyj, czyja*, czyjego… [of which, whose] | 2 | +333 % | −81 % | 0 | −96 % | 10 | +2 % | 10 | 16 |
| **TOTAL** | **13,663** | **−1 %** | **+28 %** | **13,847** | **+30 %** | **10,670** | **−1 %** | **10,745** | **11,106** |
| **III. Concessive subordinators** | | | | | | | | | |
| *mimo że/iż* [despite that] | 89 | −9 % | −14 % | 98 | −5 % | 103 | +18 % | 87 | 83 |
| *choć* [although-FORM] | 70 | −39 % | −24 % | 114 | +24 % | 92 | −35 % | 143 | 386 |
| *chociaż* [although] | 81 | −48 % | +1 % | 157 | +96 % | 80 | +31 % | 61 | 168 |
| *nawet jeśli/jeżeli/gdyby/gdy/wtedy/wówczas* [even if/when/then] | 204 | −30 % | +190 % | 291 | +313 % | 70 | +22 % | 57 | 76 |
| *choćby* [even if] | 15 | −95 % | −64 % | 296 | +604 % | 42 | −24 % | 55 | 107 |
| *pomimo, że/iż* [despite that] | 16 | +3 % | −56 % | 15 | −58 % | 36 | +157 % | 14 | 9 |
| *chociażby* [even if] | 3 | −42 % | −92 % | 4 | −86 % | 31 | +4 % | 30 | 36 |
| *aczkolwiek* [although] | 4 | −22 % | −82 % | 6 | −77 % | 25 | −27 % | 34 | 16 |
| **TOTAL** | **481** | **−51 %** | **+1 %** | **981** | **+105 %** | **479** | **−1 %** | **482** | **881** |
| **GRAND TOTAL** | **28,572** | **−13 %** | **+22 %** | **32,936** | **+41 %** | **23,371** | **−3 %** | **24,159** | **19,905** |

[a] Excluding: *chyba że, z tym że, pod warunkiem że, pod warunkiem, że, pomimo/mimo że*, which introduce causal-conditional clauses.
[b] Excluding: *chyba iż, z tym iż, pod warunkiem iż, pod warunkiem, iż, pomimo/mimo iż*, which introduce causal-conditional clauses.

Relative pronouns, which are used to form relative clauses by post-modifying the antecedent head noun (Grzegorczykowa 2004[1988]: 117–123), are slightly less frequent across all the corpora than complementizers. Their almost equal distribution in the NKJP corpus and the SN corpora, along with their overrepresentation in CJEU judgments (by 28 % and 30 %, respectively), indicates that they are only a feature of CJEU judgments. Pre- and post-accession SN judgments contain an even number of tokens of relative pronouns, which is lower than in the NKJP corpus. Relative to post-accession SN judgments, the highest degree of overrepresentation can be observed in the case of the relative pronouns *który, która...* [which], *jaki, jaka...* [which], and *gdzie* [where]. Substantial underrepresentation can be observed in the case of *kiedy* [when], and *czyj, czyja, czyjego...* [of which, whose]. Despite the overall distribution of relative pronouns in CJEU judgments, there is a certain degree of internal variation within the Eurolect as regards the distribution of individual pronouns. The pronoun *kto* [who] is used in legislation to form legal norms (cf. Biel 2014a: 194); judicial language seldom uses this pronoun, as it contains mostly interpretation of legal provisions and legal norms.

The third and last group of hypotactic markers, concessive subordinators, which are a sub-category of markers forming extensional clauses (Grzegorczykowa 2004[1988]: 98), shows very low distribution as compared to the two groups of markers discussed above (cf. Biel 2014a: 192). This is mainly due to the fact that causal, purpose, and conditional clauses are described in Sections 6.7.2, 6.7.3, and 6.7.4. Their use cannot be unequivocally described as typical of judicial language – only the GC corpus contains more tokens than general Polish (NKJP), mainly to the high distribution of *choćby* [even if] and *chociaż* [although]. In addition, concessive subordinators have an uneven distribution within the Eurolect. Pre- and post-accession SN judgments have an equal distribution of concessive subordinators.

The aggregate data on the distribution of hypotactic markers show that they may be perceived as a typical feature of judicial language, in particular of translations, owing to their lower distribution in general Polish (NKJP) (see Figure 6.6).

Unlike paratactic markers, which exhibit a more even distribution within the Eurolect, hypotactic markers in GC judgments are overrepresented relative to CJ judgments. Furthermore, the post-accession SN corpus contains a lower number of tokens than the pre-accession corpus, which also stands in contrast to the distribution of paratactic markers.

## 6.5 Deixis

The keyword lists were found to contain numerous deictic expressions (pointing devices), the vast majority of which are largely overrepresented in translated EU judgments (see Table 6.3). Examples of deictic keywords in CJ and GC judgments include: *ww.* [#10], *przytoczone* [#61], *tam* [#66], *następujący* [#189]. The only deictic keyword overrepresented in non-translations relative to CJEU judgments is *pozostałej* [#215]. Having established that the identified deictic markers have a

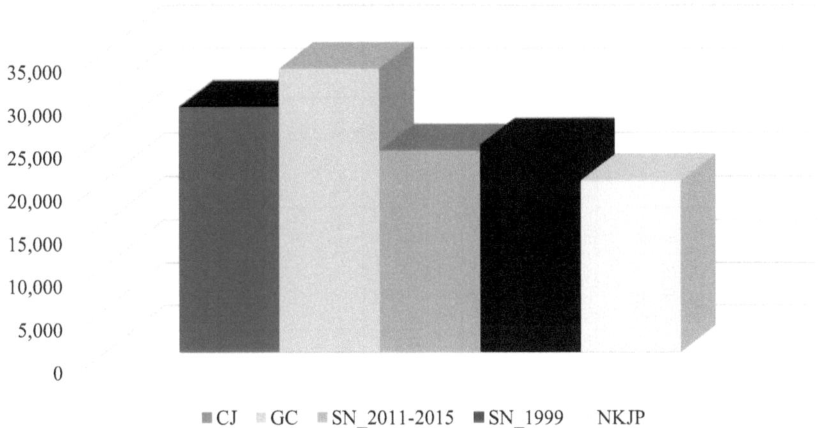


**Figure 6.6.** *Total distribution of hypotactic markers*

relatively high distribution, I decided to investigate them further by identifying their synonyms and other functional equivalents.

The distributional analysis of pointing devices encompasses personal pronouns, demonstrative pronouns, indefinite pronouns and quantifiers, as well as adjectival deictic expressions (cf. Biel 2014a: 215–222). The reflexive pronoun *się* [self-REFL] is discussed briefly in Section 6.6.3. Their distribution is presented in the following tables. Taking into consideration that judicial language is largely depersonalized (cf. Section 6.6), the analysis will start with the discussion on the distribution of personal pronouns (see Table 6.30), whose role is to indicate the participants of a communication process or other persons (or animals, etc.) (Bańko 2007: 75). The keywords identified in Table 6.3 contain two personal pronouns which are overrepresented in the language of translated judgments, *ona* [#101] and *one* [#113], both of which prompted the investigation of pronouns and pointing devices. Non-translated judgments, on the other hand, do not contain any pronouns overrepresented relative to translations.

Third-person personal pronouns in the nominative case, *on*, *ona*, *ono*, *oni/one* [he, she, it, they–PRO:NOM], are considerably overrepresented in CJEU judgments relative to SN judgments (by 116 % and 161 %, respectively). They basically do not occur in sentence-initial positions and their main role is to report on the actions of various agents and institutions, as well as to refer to various documents, abstract concepts, etc. Their overrepresentation in EU judgments may be due to the elaborate manner in which the CJ and GC discuss the history of the cases heard by them – CJEU judgments: Move 4, SN judgments: Move 3 (cf. Chapter 5). First- and second-person pronouns are virtually non–existent in the judicial corpora, which adds to its authoritativeness to some degree (cf. Section 6.6), hence they are not considered in this

**Table 6.30.** *Personal, possessive, demonstrative, indefinite pronouns and quantifiers*

| | Translated EU case law | | | | | Non-translated PL case law | | | General Polish |
|---|---|---|---|---|---|---|---|---|---|
| | **CJ** | **CJ vs GC (%DIFF)** | **CJ vs SN_2011–2015 (%DIFF)** | **GC** | **GC vs SN_2011–2015 (%DIFF)** | **SN_2011–2015** | **SN_2011–2015 vs SN_1999 (%DIFF)** | **SN_1999** | **NKJP** |
| **I. Personal pronouns** | | | | | | | | | |
| *on, ona, ono, oni/one* [he, she, it, they – PRO:NOM] | 2,539 | −17 % | +116 % | 3,065 | +161 % | 1,176 | −10 % | 1,308 | 1,527 |
| **II. Reflexive pronoun *się* [self-REFL] (cf. Section 6.6.3)** | | | | | | | | | |
| **III. Possessive pronouns** | | | | | | | | | |
| *jego, jej, ich* [his, her, its, their – PRO:POSS] | 4,411 | −16 % | −27 % | 5,237 | −14 % | 6,071 | +13 % | 5,396 | 3,404 |
| *swój, swoje, swoja, swoi, swoich, swojej, swojego, swojemu, swoim* [possessive pronouns connected with the sentence subject] | 813 | −22 % | +65 % | 1,041 | +112 % | 492 | −11 % | 553 | 1,400 |
| *swa, swego, swe, swych, swym, swej, swą, swemu* [*swój*-ARCHAIC forms] | 457 | −24 % | +164 % | 601 | +248 % | 173 | −52 % | 363 | 419 |
| **TOTAL** | **8,219** | **−17 %** | **+4 %** | **9,945** | **+26 %** | **7,912** | **+4 %** | **7,620** | **6,751** |

| | | | | | | | | | |
|---|---|---|---|---|---|---|---|---|---|
| **IV. Demonstrative pronouns** | | | | | | | | | |
| *ten, ta, to, te, ci* (+inflected variants) [this, that, these, those] | 18,277 | +9 % | +29 % | 16,764 | +18 % | 14,159 | −14 % | 16,554 | 9,921 |
| *taki, taka, takie* (+inflected variants) [such] | 3,082 | +63 % | +52 % | 1,886 | −7 % | 2,028 | +11 % | 1,819 | 2,030 |
| *tam* [there] | 441 | −22 % | +822 % | 566 | +1083 % | 48 | −29 % | 67 | 720 |
| **TOTAL** | **21,800** | **+13 %** | **+34 %** | **19,216** | **+18 %** | **16,235** | **−12 %** | **18,440** | **12,671** |
| **V. Indefinite pronouns and quantifiers** | | | | | | | | | |
| *każdy* [each, every] | 1,039 | −4 % | +130 % | 1,085 | +140 % | 452 | +27 % | 357 | 905 |
| *żaden* [none] | 597 | −39 % | +64 % | 981 | +169 % | 365 | −3 % | 375 | 494 |
| *wszystek* (*wszystko, wszystkie*, etc.) [all] | 928 | −23 % | +203 % | 1,212 | +296 % | 306 | −52 % | 644 | 1,624 |
| *niektóry* [some] | 344 | −19 % | +108 % | 422 | +156 % | 165 | +60 % | 103 | 333 |
| *wszelki* [all] | 372 | +38 % | +147 % | 269 | +79 % | 150 | +58 % | 95 | 189 |
| *jakikolwiek* [any] | 218 | +20 % | +75 % | 182 | +46 % | 124 | −17 % | 151 | 78 |
| *dowolny* [any] | 34 | +262 % | +15 % | 9 | −68 % | 29 | −49 % | 57 | 32 |
| *którykolwiek* [any] | 18 | +95 % | +15 % | 9 | −41 % | 16 | −20 % | 20 | 6 |
| *nikt* [nobody] | 7 | −37 % | −28 % | 10 | +13 % | 9 | −34 % | 14 | 293 |
| **TOTAL** | **3,556** | **−15 %** | **+120 %** | **4,180** | **+158 %** | **1,618** | **−11 %** | **1,815** | **3,952** |

analysis.[120] The overall distribution of third-person personal pronouns indicates that their use is a characteristic feature of CJEU judgments, rather than SN judgments which exhibit distribution similar to that in general Polish (NKJP), although their use may also be due to the specific sub-genre conventions.

Possessive pronouns (cf. Bańko 2007: 75) are overrepresented exclusively in GC judgments (by 26 %), which is mainly due to the overrepresentation of *swój* and its archaic form *swa*, both of which refer to objects related to the sentence subject (cf. Jadacka 2002: 54–55). The possessive pronouns *jego, jej, ich* [his, her, its, their] are underrepresented in GC judgments, which is also the case in CJ judgments, with about 17 % fewer occurrences of the three types in this category. It is surprising that translated texts exhibit higher reliance on *swój* and *swa* than non-translations, which may be attributed to higher conservatism (that is the tendency to conform to typical TL patterns to the point of exaggeration, cf. Baker 1996: 176–177). Post-accession SN judgments have been found to rely less on them than their pre-accession counterparts, although this can be regarded as a positive development. Based on the distribution of possessive pronouns in general Polish (NKJP), it can be concluded that their use in both CJEU and SN judgments is a characteristic feature of judicial language.

Demonstrative pronouns (cf. Bańko 2007: 73; Biel 2014a: 217–218), *ten, ta, to, te, ci* (and their inflected variants) [this, that, these, those], *taki, taka, takie* (and their inflected variants) [such], and *tam* [there], have an incommensurably higher distribution in all corpora of judgments compared to the distribution of personal and possessive pronouns, while being more frequent than in general Polish (NKJP). The highest distribution has been observed in the case of *ten, ta, to, te, ci* [this, that, these, those] and their inflected variants, which are considerably overrepresented in CJ and GC judgments, by 29 % and 18 %, respectively. Surprisingly, post-accession SN judgments contain about 12 % fewer tokens of demonstrative pronouns than pre-accession judgments. Considering the low distribution of demonstrative pronouns in general Polish (NKJP), the high reliance on pronouns of these types may be regarded as a genre feature which contributes to a higher degree of preciseness of information and cohesion of arguments.

The next group of pronouns contains indefinite pronouns (cf. Bańko 2007: 74) and quantifiers (cf. Biel 2014a: 217–218) (including their inflected forms). They are less frequent than possessive and demonstrative pronouns and are particularly frequent in CJEU judgments, being about 120 % and 158 % more widely distributed in CJ and GC judgments, respectively. Examples of overrepresented pronouns include: *każdy* [each, every], *niektóry* [some], and *wszelki* [all]. Like demonstrative pronouns, they are also underrepresented in post-accession SN judgments relative to pre-accession judgments (by 11 %). Considering the high distribution in general Polish (NKJP), they cannot be regarded as a characteristic feature of CJEU judgments, and in particular SN judgments.

---

120 There are almost no occurrences of 1st and 2nd person pronouns in EU corpora; in the case of the PL corpus, the scarce occurrences of the said pronouns are limited to direct quotes from the parties' statements.

**Table 6.31.** *Adjectival deictic expressions*

| | Translated EU case law | | | | | Non-translated PL case law | | | General Polish |
|---|---|---|---|---|---|---|---|---|---|
| | **CJ** | **CJ vs GC (%DIFF)** | **CJ vs SN_2011–2015 (%DIFF)** | **GC** | **GC vs SN_2011–2015 (%DIFF)** | **SN_2011–2015** | **SN_2011–2015 vs SN_1999 (%DIFF)** | **SN_1999** | **NKJP** |
| *określony* [defined] | 635 | −15 % | −8 % | 749 | +9 % | 689 | +33 % | 519 | 208 |
| *pozostały* [remaining] | 222 | −32 % | −58 % | 325 | −38 % | 524 | +1 % | 517 | 197 |
| *powyższy* [above] | 820 | −7 % | +72 % | 885 | +86 % | 476 | −28 % | 658 | 49 |
| *niniejszy* [this-FORM] | 2,063 | +15 % | +337 % | 1,799 | +281 % | 472 | +6 % | 444 | 26 |
| *wymieniony* [mentioned] (excl. *wymieniony w*) | 118 | +37 % | −36 % | 86 | −53 % | 183 | −77 % | 783 | N/A |
| *przytoczony* [cited] | 405 | −32 % | +184 % | 599 | 320 % | 143 | −71 % | 495 | 8 |
| *wspomniany* [said] | 957 | +24 % | +616 % | 772 | 478 % | 134 | +11 % | 121 | 59 |
| *następujący* [following] | 784 | +123 % | +508 % | 351 | 173 % | 129 | −48 % | 250 | 87 |
| *wyżej wymieniony/ wymieniony wyżej* [above-mentioned] (excl. *wymieniony w*) | 30 | −28 % | +8 % | 42 | 51 % | 28 | −30 % | 40 | N/A |
| *rzeczony* [said] | 492 | +61 % | +3518 % | 305 | 2141 % | 14 | +587 % | 2 | 3 |
| *odnośny* [respective] | 83 | −15 % | +789 % | 98 | 945 % | 9 | −32 % | 14 | 1 |
| *ww.* [above-named-ABBRV] | 882 | −42 % | +10480 % | 1,531 | 18251 % | 8 | −74 % | 32 | 7 |
| *poniższy* [below] | 17 | +114 % | +2229 % | 8 | 990 % | 1 | --- | 0 | 9 |
| **TOTAL** | **7,510** | **−1 %** | **+167 %** | **7,549** | **+169 %** | **2,809** | **−27 %** | **3,874** | **653** |

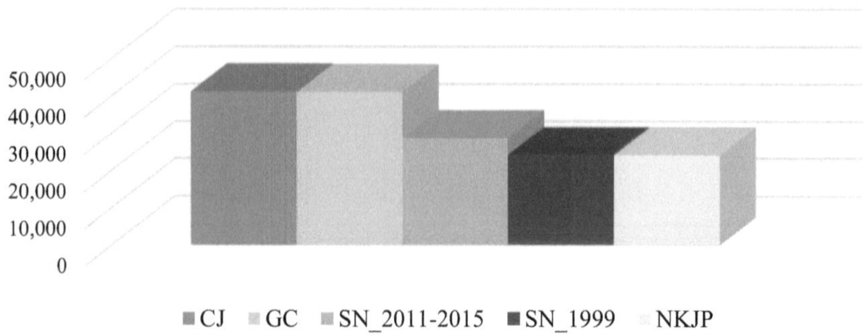


**Figure 6.7.** *Global distribution of deictic devices*

The last group of pointing devices contains adjectival deictic markers (see Table 6.31), the functions of which are mostly referential. They refer mostly to legislative documents and their parts, applications for a preliminary ruling, and the legal proceedings and arguments of the parties. CJEU judgments are characterized by an almost equal level of overrepresentation (by about 168 %) compared to post-accession SN judgments. This overrepresentation is mostly due to: *niniejszy* [this-FORM], *przytoczony* [cited], *wspomniany* [said], *rzeczony* [said], and *ww.* [above-named-ABBRV], which occur with an incommensurably higher frequency than in non-translations, acting as primarily intertextual reference devices, and in particular the last deictic expression:

(3) CJ (C-316/09): *(...) (zob.* ***ww.*** *wyrok w sprawie Damgaard, pkt 22) (...).*
[(...) (see **a.n.** Damgaard, paragraph 22) (...).]

Post-accession SN judgments, on the other hand, contain fewer tokens than pre-accession judgments. Overall, adjectival deictic markers are a feature of both translated and non-translated judgments owing to their low distribution in general Polish (NKJP).

The aggregate data on the distribution of personal, possessive, demonstrative and indefinite pronouns, along with quantifiers and adjectival deictic expressions, shows that this functional category may be regarded as a characteristic feature of judicial language (see Figure 6.7). However, it needs to be borne in mind that not all sub-categories, for instance, indefinite pronouns and quantifiers, are equally represented in both CJEU and SN judgments.

## 6.6 Depersonalization

The category of auxiliary verbs was identified owing to the presence of *zostać* [#52] and *zostaje* [#193] on the CJEU keyword list, whereas the category of *–no/to* impersonal patterns was identified owing to the SN keyword *orzeczono* [#372]. To more fully account for the nature of depersonalization in judicial language, I will also examine the passive voice and the *się* impersonal pattern (cf. Biel 2014a: 169–181).

### 6.6.1 Auxiliary verbs

The verb *być* [to be] is the most frequent verb in Polish (Bańko 2007: 103). Since none of the forms of the verb *być* [to be] were found in the keyword lists generated for the EU corpora, none of the forms of this verb are significantly overrepresented in either of the EU corpora or the SN corpus. This, however, is not the case with the auxiliary verb *zostać* [to become] [CJEU #52] (including its third person singular form – *zostaje* [becomes] [CJEU #193]), which is overrepresented in translated judgments relative to non-translations. Table 6.32 shows that the more frequently occurring auxiliary verb across all corpora is *zostać* [to become].

The data show that both auxiliaries are overrepresented in translated language. Figure 6.8 provides a more graphic representation of the total distribution of *być* forms in EU and PL corpora.

The usage of the auxiliary verb *być* [to be] is similar across the corpora of EU and national judgments. However, its distribution in the judicial corpora relative to the corpus of general Polish (NKJP) indicates that the usage of past and future forms of *być* [to be] lags behind general Polish. Overall, the distribution of this auxiliary verb is not a typical feature of judgments.

Figure 6.9 shows the distribution of the auxiliary verb *zostać* [to become]. Its usage may be described as a characteristic feature of judicial language owing to its lower distribution in general Polish (NKJP).

The data show that the most widely used forms of *być* [to be] in both EU and PL judgments are its present tense forms. The same applies to the most frequent forms of *zostać* [to become]. Their past and future forms are used only marginally.

### 6.6.2 Passive voice

The passive voice is a characteristic feature of legal acts, as it contributes to the creation of a more authoritative style (Biel 2014a: 171). In the case of the language of judgments, a genre secondary to legal acts, the passive voice may also serve to boost their authoritativeness and impersonal tone, in order to ensure greater enforceability of judicial decisions. The passive voice in Polish is created primarily with the auxiliary verbs *być* [to be] and *zostać* [to become] (cf. Bańko 2007: 100, 172; Biel 2014a: 172), which require the use of passive adjectival participles with the suffix *-ny* or *-ty* (Bańko 2007: 172).[121] Table 6.33 contains no NKJP data as the PELCRA search engine does not enable running the required queries.

121 It should be noted that the middle voice (apart from the passive and active voice) is not differentiated in contemporary Polish grammars (Bańko 2007: 99).

**Table 6.32.** *Distribution of the auxiliary verbs być [to be] and zostać [to become]*

| | Translated EU case law | | | | | Non-translated PL case law | | | General Polish |
|---|---|---|---|---|---|---|---|---|---|
| | CJ | CJ vs GC (%DIFF) | CJ vs SN_2011–2015 (%DIFF) | GC | GC vs SN_2011–2015 (%DIFF) | SN_2011–2015 | SN_2011–2015 vs SN_1999 (%DIFF) | SN_1999 | NKJP |
| **Auxiliary verbs** | | | | | | | | | |
| *być* (INF) | 1,556 | +30 % | +3 % | 1,196 | −21 % | 1,517 | +8 % | 1,403 | 1,249 |
| *jest, są* (PRES) | 7,055 | +24 % | +31 % | 5,669 | +6 % | 5,372 | −11 % | 6,058 | 6,743 |
| *był(a), były, byli* (PAST) | 1,086 | −49 % | −47 % | 2,131 | +3 % | 2,066 | +9 % | 1,891 | 4,211 |
| *będzie, będą* (FUT) | 337 | −13 % | +22 % | 387 | +40 % | 277 | +77 % | 157 | 1,946 |
| **TOTAL być** | **10,034** | **+7 %** | **+9 %** | **9,384** | **+2 %** | **9,232** | **−3 %** | **9,508** | **14,149** |
| ***zostać*** (INF) | 798 | −7 % | +438 % | 860 | +480 % | 148 | +59 % | 93 | 123 |
| *został(a), zostali* (PAST) | 1,274 | −15 % | −25 % | 1,491 | −12 % | 1,699 | −13 % | 1,950 | 1,129 |
| *zostanie, zostaną* (FUT) | 244 | −17 % | +104 % | 295 | +147 % | 120 | +255 % | 34 | 349 |
| *zostaje, zostają* (PRES) | 298 | −1 % | +689 % | 302 | +699 % | 38 | +73 % | 22 | 70 |
| **TOTAL zostać** | **2,613** | **−11 %** | **+30 %** | **2,948** | **+47 %** | **2,005** | **−4 %** | **2,099** | **1,672** |
| **TOTAL: Auxiliaries** | **12,647** | **+3 %** | **+13 %** | **12,331** | **+10 %** | **11,237** | **−3 %** | **11,607** | **15,821** |

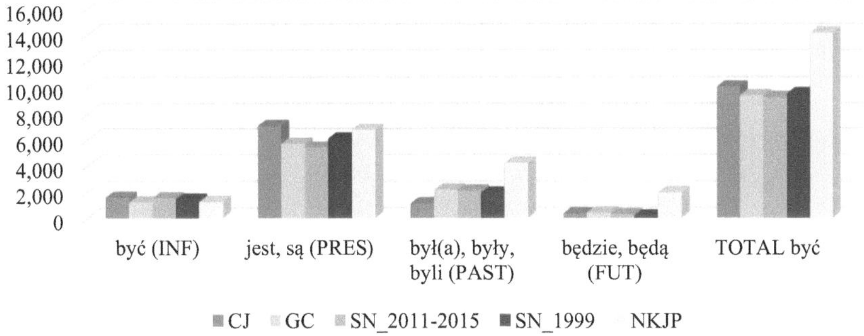


**Figure 6.8.** *Distribution of the auxiliary verb być [to be]*

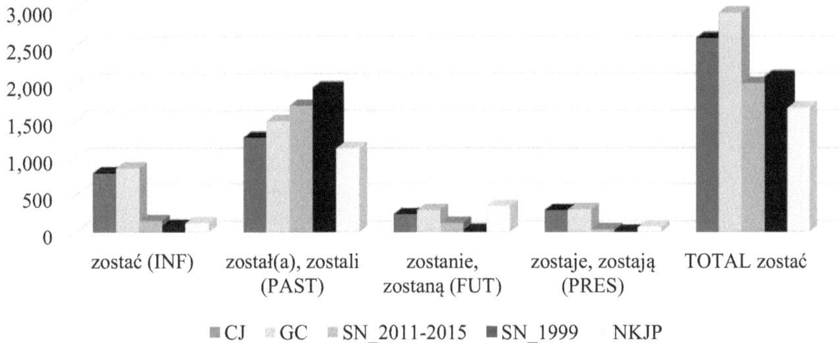


**Figure 6.9.** *Distribution of the auxiliary verb zostać [to become]*

The overall distribution of the passive voice is higher in CJEU judgments than in post-accession SN judgments. On the whole, CJ and GC judgments contain about 45 % and 42 % more passive constructions than non-translated judgments. In addition, there is a considerable degree of internal variation within the Eurolect – CJ judgments seem to favor *być*-passives, while GC judgments contain more *zostać*-passives. Post-accession SN judgments contain slightly more *być*-passives than *zostać*-passives. Compared to the pre-accession SN corpus, the data show that post-accession SN judgments contain more tokens of passives in general, which may be indicative of some influence exerted by the Eurolect.

Figure 6.10 shows that *być*-passives are considerably more frequent in the present tense in translations than in post-accession SN judgments; the latter contain almost the same number of tokens of this type as the pre-accession SN corpus. On the other hand, the CJ corpus contain fewer tokens of *być*-passives in the past

**Table 6.33.** *Passive voice – auxiliary verbs być [to be] and zostać [to become]*

| | **Translated EU case law** | | | | | **Non-translated PL case law** | | |
|---|---|---|---|---|---|---|---|---|
| | **CJ** | **CJ vs GC (%DIFF)** | **CJ vs SN_2011–2015 (%DIFF)** | **GC** | **GC vs SN_2011–2015 (%DIFF)** | **SN_2011–2015** | **SN_2011–2015 vs SN_1999 (%DIFF)** | **SN_1999** |
| **TOTAL: *być* [to be] + participle** | **3,451** | **+27 %** | **+45 %** | **2,726** | **+14 %** | **2,385** | **+11 %** | **2,148** |
| *być* (INF) + participle | 1,051 | +35 % | +16 % | 777 | −14 % | 903 | +15 % | 785 |
| *jest, są* (PRES) | 1,865 | +57 % | +142 % | 1,191 | +54 % | 772 | −1 % | 777 |
| *był(a), było, były, byli* (PAST) | 471 | −33 % | −30 % | 701 | +5 % | 669 | +20 % | 557 |
| *będzie, będą* (FUT) | 63 | +12 % | +54 % | 57 | +38 % | 41 | +38 % | 30 |
| **TOTAL: *zostać* [to become] + participle** | **3,106** | **−17 %** | **+44 %** | **3,730** | **+73 %** | **2,153** | **+23 %** | **1,754** |
| *zostać* (INF) | 736 | −9 % | +458 % | 804 | +510 % | 132 | +85 % | 71 |
| *został(a), zostali* (PAST) | 1,940 | −21 % | +2 % | 2,441 | +28 % | 1,909 | +16 % | 1,649 |
| *zostanie, zostaną* (FUT) | 180 | −19 % | +111 % | 222 | +159 % | 85 | +292 % | 22 |
| *zostaje, zostają* (PRES) | 251 | −5 % | +857 % | 263 | +904 % | 26 | +120 % | 12 |
| **TOTAL: Passives (*być* + *zostać*)** | **6,557** | **+2 %** | **+45 %** | **6,456** | **+42 %** | **4,537** | **+16 %** | **3,902** |

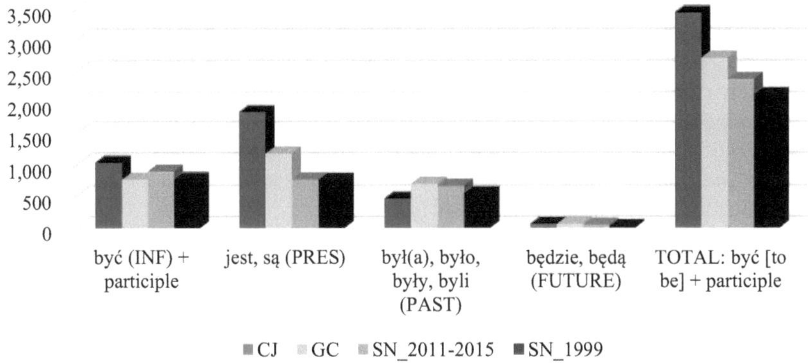


**Figure 6.10.** *Distribution of być-passives*

tense than the post-accession SN corpus, which is not the case in the GC corpus, where tokens of this type are slightly more frequent. *Być*-passives in the future tense are only marginal across all corpora, although they are slightly more frequent in the Eurolect. *Być*-passives formed with *być* in the infinitive and participles are overrepresented only in CJ judgments (by 35 %); GC judgments contain about 14 % fewer tokens of this type.

It can be observed in Figure 6.11 that *zostać* passives occur primarily in the past form. These are distributed quite evenly across the post-accession corpora, with the exception of the GC corpus, which has more tokens than the remaining corpora. *Zostać* passives formed with the infinitive and participles, as well as *zostać* passives

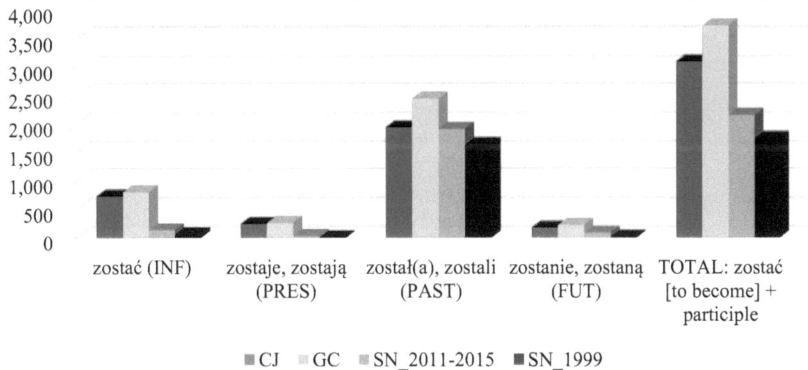


**Figure 6.11.** *Distribution of zostać-passives*

in the present form, are overrepresented in the Eurolect, which is confirmed by the keywords *zostać* [#52] and *zostaje* [#193] (see Table 6.3). *Zostać* passives in the future form are also overrepresented in translations, although their general usage remains marginal.

Overall, the use of passive constructions is a salient feature of judicial language, in particular CJ and GC judgments. However, *być* and *zostać* passives are less frequent in judicial language than in the language of translated EU legislation and non-translated Polish legal acts (Biel 2014a: 172).

### 6.6.3 The *się* impersonal pattern

The first of the two discussed impersonal patterns is formed with the reflexive pronoun *się* and a third person singular verb; this pattern does not specify the agent, being generally indefinite and including the addresser (cf. Nagórko 2010: 153–155). As in the case of the *-no/to* impersonal patterns (cf. Section 6.6.4), the *się* pattern emphasizes actions or processes. Table 6.34 presents the distribution of the reflexive pronoun *się* and its top collocates.

What is surprising is that the reflexive pronoun *się* is distributed rather evenly across all post-accession corpora. In general, it is underrepresented in both translations and non-translations compared to general Polish (NKJP), which indicates that the *się* impersonal pattern is not a typical feature of judicial language and that other means of expressing depersonalization are preferred by judges.

The reflexive pronoun *się* collocates most frequently with verbs in the present tense, which is confirmed by the distribution of the top types containing this pronoun (see Table 6.34) – for instance, *stosuje się* [(one) applies-MID], which is used to reinforce the courts' argumentation by stating the legal basis for the courts' decisions and referring to situations in which given provisions can be applied:

(4) CJ (C-596/13 P): *Należy przypomnieć, że nowy przepis* ***stosuje się*** *od wejścia w życie aktu, który go wprowadza i że choć nie* ***stosuje się*** *go do sytuacji prawnych powstałych i ostatecznie zakończonych pod rządami dawnej ustawy,* ***stosuje się*** *go do przyszłych skutków tych sytuacji oraz do nowych sytuacji prawnych.*
[A new rule of law **applies** from the entry into force of the act introducing it, and, while it does not **apply** to legal situations that have arisen and become definitive under the old law, it does **apply to** their future effects, and to new legal situations.]

Clearly, the manner of expressing depersonalization is interlocked with the category of performative, argumentative and reporting verbs (see Section 6.7.1).

**Table 6.34.** *Top L1 collocations of się [-self REFL]*

| | Translated EU case law | | | | | Non-translated PL case law | | | General Polish |
|---|---|---|---|---|---|---|---|---|---|
| | **CJ** | **CJ vs GC (%DIFF)** | **CJ vs SN_2011–2015 (%DIFF)** | **GC** | **GC vs SN_2011–2015 (%DIFF)** | **SN_2011–2015** | **SN_2011–2015 vs SN_1999 (%DIFF)** | **SN_1999** | **NKJP** |
| *się* [-self REFL] | 6,513 | −4 % | 0 % | 6,805 | −4 % | 6,509 | −11 % | 7,309 | 9,587 |
| *się* + present | 2,497 | +28 % | +30 % | 1,953 | +28 % | 1,926 | −7 % | 2,081 | N/A |
| **CJ – top types** | | | | | | | | | |
| *stosuje się* [(one) applies-MID] | 204 | +261 % | +160 % | 56 | +361 % | 78 | +52 % | 52 | 42 |
| *uznaje się* [(one) acknowledges-MID] | 54 | +222 % | +246 % | 17 | +322 % | 16 | +163 % | 6 | 5 |
| *wydaje się* [it seems] | 92 | +14 % | +630 % | 81 | +14 % | 13 | −36 % | 20 | 105 |
| **GC – top types** | | | | | | | | | |
| *stosuje się* [(one) applies-MID] | 204 | +261 % | +159 % | 56 | +361 % | 79 | +53 % | 52 | 42 |
| *wydaje się* [it seems] | 92 | +14 % | +630 % | 81 | +14 % | 13 | −36 % | 20 | 105 |
| *stwierdza się* [(one) ascertains-MID] | 12 | −73 % | +344 % | 45 | −73 % | 3 | −53 % | 6 | 3 |
| **SN_2011–2015 – top types** | | | | | | | | | |
| *przyjmuje się* [(one) assumes-MID] | 14 | +132 % | −86 % | 6 | +232 % | 97 | +144 % | 40 | 8 |
| *stosuje się* [(one) applies-MID] | 201 | +256 % | +156 % | 56 | +356 % | 78 | +52 % | 52 | 42 |
| *wskazuje się* [(one) points out-MID] | 1 | −66 % | −97 % | 3 | −66 % | 32 | −85 % | 221 | 2 |

### 6.6.4 The *–no/to* impersonal pattern

The *-no/to* pattern makes it possible to convey information about past actions in an impersonal manner without directly defining the agent (Bąk 1984: 183, 323; Bańko 2007: 168). Consequently, legal procedural actions referred to using this pattern are emphasized with an additional layer of objectivity and authoritativeness, regardless of whether they are reported actions which were performed by, for instance, the parties to the proceedings or lower instance courts, or whether they are the actions of the court itself. The only keyword expressing the impersonal *-no/-to* pattern is the SN keyword *orzeczono* [#372], which is underrepresented in translations. Table 6.35 presents quantitative data on the normalized number of occurrences of performative verbs with the suffixes *–no* and *–to*, including their three most frequent types in each of the post-accession corpora. The data contain no NKJP data as the PELCRA search engine does not enable queries with *-no/to* suffixes.

The data show that the *-no/to* pattern may be perceived as a typical feature of judicial language, in particular the usage of the *-no* pattern. In general, the markers of this pattern are extremely frequent in GC and post-accession SN judgments; CJ judgments contain about 34 % fewer tokens than the national corpus. Furthermore, it can be observed that post-accession SN judgments note an increase in the distribution of *-no/to* impersonal verbs (about 35 %). The following excerpts demonstrate that verbs with the suffix *-no* effectively raise the degree of impersonality in judicial language:

| | |
|---|---|
| (5) CJ (C-584/13): | *Tymczasem jak* ***wskazano*** *w pkt 31 niniejszego wyroku, z art. 94 regulaminu postępowania przed Trybunałem wynika, że pod nieobecność tych elementów Trybunał na argument taki nie może odpowiedzieć.* [As **one indicated** in paragraph 31 of the present judgment, it follows from Article 94 of its Rules of Procedure that, in the absence of such evidence, the Court cannot respond to such an argument.] |
| (6) SN (IV CSK 670/13): | *Jak* ***stwierdzono*** *w orzecznictwie, roszczenie to ma charakter obligacyjny i powstaje z mocy prawa (...).* [As **one found** in the jurisprudence, this claim is obligatory and arises by virtue of law (...).] |

Figure 6.12 shows that the *-no/to* patterns have a fairly high distribution. However, judges use them less frequently than past passives, which remain the primary means of depersonalizing their decisions, being about two times more frequent (cf. Figures 6.10 and 6.11).

It can be concluded that translations favor the usage of past passives, while non-translations exhibit a higher usage of the *-no/to* impersonal patterns. The frequent usage of such structures seems to raise the level of objectivity and authoritativeness

**Table 6.35.** *The -no/to impersonal pattern and the top types*

| | Translated EU case law | | | | | Non-translated PL case law | | | General Polish |
|---|---|---|---|---|---|---|---|---|---|
| | **CJ** | **CJ vs GC (%DIFF)** | **CJ vs SN_2011–2015 (%DIFF)** | **GC** | **GC vs SN_2011–2015 (%DIFF)** | **SN_2011–2015** | **SN_2011–2015 vs SN_1999 (%DIFF)** | **SN_1999** | **NKJP** |
| **I. The *-no/to* pattern** | | | | | | | | | |
| ***-no/to* pattern: TOTAL** | **1,095** | **−32 %** | **−34 %** | **1,616** | **−3 %** | **1,672** | **+35 %** | **1,243** | **N/A** |
| * ***-no*** | 1,033 | −33 % | −33 % | 1,544 | 0 % | 1,549 | +10 % | 1,405 | N/A |
| * ***-to*** | 62 | −14 % | −50 % | 72 | −42 % | 123 | −20 % | 155 | N/A |
| **CJ – top types** | | | | | | | | | |
| *wskazano* [(one) indicated-IMPRS] | 60 | −63 % | −49 % | 164 | +39 % | 118 | +36 % | 87 | 3 |
| *stwierdzono* [(one) found out-IMPRS] | 60 | −39 % | −34 % | 97 | +7 % | 91 | +63 % | 55 | 18 |
| *wniesiono* [(one) submitted that-IMPRS] | 41 | +9 % | +613 % | 37 | +552 % | 6 | −79 % | 28 | 1 |
| **GC – top types** | | | | | | | | | |
| *wskazano* [(one) indicated-IMPRS] | 60 | −63 % | −49 % | 164 | +39 % | 118 | +36 % | 87 | 3 |

(*continued on next page*)

**Table 6.35.** *Continued*

| | Translated EU case law | | | | | Non-translated PL case law | | | General Polish |
|---|---|---|---|---|---|---|---|---|---|
| | **CJ** | **CJ vs GC (%DIFF)** | **CJ vs SN_2011–2015 (%DIFF)** | **GC** | **GC vs SN_2011–2015 (%DIFF)** | **SN_2011–2015** | **SN_2011–2015 vs SN_1999 (%DIFF)** | **SN_1999** | **NKJP** |
| *stwierdzono* [(one) found out-IMPRS] | 60 | −39 % | −34 % | 97 | +7 % | 91 | +63 % | 55 | 18 |
| *ogłoszono* [(one) announced-IMPRS] | 2 | −97 % | −64 % | 81 | +1258 % | 6 | +1 % | 6 | 8 |
| **SN_2011–2015 – top types** | | | | | | | | | |
| *wskazano* [(one) indicated-IMPRS] | 60 | −63 % | −49 % | 164 | +39 % | 118 | +36 % | 87 | 3 |
| *orzeczono* [(one) adjudicated-IMPRS] | 7 | −78 % | −93 % | 31 | −70 % | 103 | −12 % | 117 | 1 |
| *stwierdzono* [(one) found out-IMPRS] | 60 | −39 % | −34 % | 97 | +7 % | 91 | +63 % | 55 | 18 |

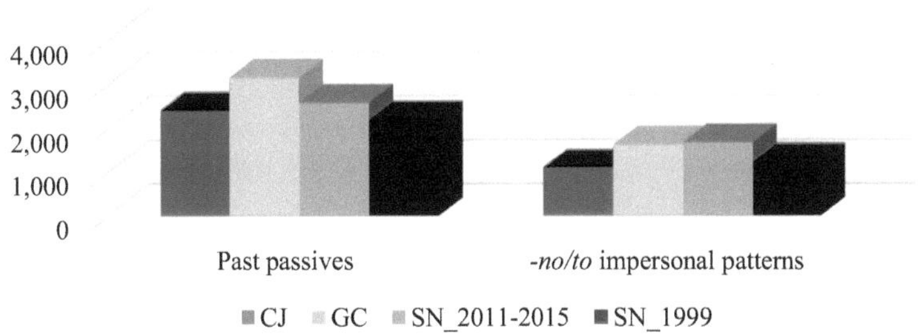


**Figure 6.12.** *Distribution of past passives and -no/to impersonal patterns*

of court rulings, the purpose of which is not only to deliver a judgment, but also to justify it and to persuade the audience about its legality and self-evident nature.

# 6.7 Legal reasoning and argumentation

## 6.7.1 Verdictive, exercitive (argumentative) and reporting verbs

The keyword lists (see Table 6.3) contain a high number of active voice, present and past tense verbs in the indicative mood, which are used to provide statements in the form of direct speech acts (Yule 1996: 54–55). Language, especially judicial language, cannot be examined independently of its uses (Trosborg 1997: 32). Therefore, it was necessary to closely examine the context of occurrence of these verbs, which led to the identification of three discourse functions:

(1) performing actions connected with the legal procedure – **CJEU judgments**: *orzeka* [rules, #346]; **SN judgments**: *uchyla* [sets aside, #162], *oddala* [dismisses, #167], *wydaje* (as in: ~ *następujący wyrok*) [gives, #168, excl. *wydaje się*], *zasądza* [adjudicates, #208], *przekazuje* [transfers, #219];
(2) presenting arguments – **CJEU judgments**: *należy* [(it/one) must/should be, #7], *wydaje* (się) [seems, #168], *przewiduje* [predicts, #238]; **SN judgments**: *zważył* [held, #64], *należało* [it must/should have been, #350], *przesądza* [decides, #436];
(3) reporting on actions events and arguments of the national and lower-instance courts, the parties to the proceedings, experts and institutions – **CJEU judgments**: *podnosi* [raises, #70], *twierdzi* [claims, #95], *uważa* [thinks, #138], *wnosi* [submits, #167], *wydaje* [issues, #168, excl. ~ *się/następujący wyrok*], *podnoszą* [raise, #214], *twierdzą* [claim, #234], *utrzymuje* [maintains, #278], *orzeka* [rules, #346], *dodaje* [adds, #435], *przypomina* [resembles, #469], *uznała* [considered, #116], *stwierdziła* [attested, #152], *naruszyła* [breached, #303], *popełniła* [committed, #309], *postanowił* [decided, #320], *uwzględniła* [allowed for, #385], *wskazała* [indicated, #433], *uczestniczyła* [participated, #456], *przyjęła* [adopted, #473]; **SN judgments**: *oddalił* [dismissed, #60], *zważył* [held, #64], *uznał* [considered, #78], *zasądził* [adjudicated, #103], *ustalił* [determined,

#107], *podzielił* [shared, #116], *wskazał* [indicated, #129], *zarzucił* [imputed, #160], *oddala* [dismisses, #167], *zmienił* [changed, #179], *przekazuje* [transfers, #219], *wniósł* [lodged, #228], *ocenił* [assessed, #234], *podkreślił* [stressed, #261], *uchylił* [set aside, #270], *nastąpiło* [ensued, #273], *wyraził* [expressed, #336], *okazał* [displayed, #366], *zobowiązał* [obliged, #367], *ustaliły* [determined, #391], *wykazał* [showed, #405], *zawarły* [concluded, #457], *dokonał* [performed, #489]).

The distribution of the above verbs is presented in Table 6.36. The keyword verb *należy* [(it/one) must/should be] (CJEU: *należy* [(it/one) must/should be, #7], SN: *należało* [it must/should have been, #350]) is a modal verb (see Figure 6.13). For this reason, its distribution cannot be examined together with the distribution of other verbs performing the three identified functions (see Table 6.36). No NKJP data are presented in this table, because the PELCRA search engine could not be used to verify the context of occurrence of the individual verbs and ensure their proper classification.

All three categories are related to the topic of speech acts in legal language owing to their ritualistic and formal components (cf. Visconti 2009). For the sake of convenience, these three categories may be labeled as verdictive, exercitive (argumentative) and reporting verbs, respectively.

The first category of verbs, such as *orzeka* [rules], *oddala* [dismisses] or *zasądza* [adjudicates], includes typical markers of performativity (understood as the signaling of the illocutionary force of an utterance, cf. Trosborg 1997: 32) in legal, and by extension, judicial language (cf. Austin 1962: 4–11). However, it should be noted that they are not used in the first person singular, but rather third person singular, which, to a certain degree, contributes to greater authoritativeness of judgments passed in the name of the respective judicial institutions and not individual judges:

| | |
|---|---|
| (7) CJEU (C-249/13): | *TRYBUNAŁ (piąta izba),*<br>*w składzie: (...)*<br>***wydaje** następujący*<br>*Wyrok*<br>[THE COURT (Fifth Chamber),<br>composed of (...)<br>**gives** the following<br>Judgment] |
| (8) CJEU (C-249/13): | *Z powyższych względów Trybunał (piąta izba)* ***orzeka**, co następuje: (...)*<br>[On those grounds, the Court (Fifth Chamber) hereby **rules**:] |
| (9) SN (II CSK 796/13): | *Sąd Najwyższy w składzie: (...)*<br>*1)* ***oddala*** *skargę kasacyjną;*<br>*2)* ***zasądza*** *na rzecz powoda od pozwanego kwotę (...)*<br>[The Supreme Court composed of: (...)<br>1) **dismisses** the cassation complaint;<br>2) **orders** the defendant to pay the plaintiff (...)] |

**Table 6.36.** *Distribution of verdictive, exercitive (argumentative) and reporting verbs*

| | **Translated EU case law** | | | | | **Non-translated PL case law** | | |
|---|---|---|---|---|---|---|---|---|
| | **CJ** | **CJ vs GC (%DIFF)** | **CJ vs SN_2011–2015 (%DIFF)** | **GC** | **GC vs SN_2011–2015 (%DIFF)** | **SN_2011–2015** | **SN_2011–2015 vs SN_1999 (%DIFF)** | **SN_1999** |
| **I. Verdictive verbs (PRES forms only, 3rd sg.)** | | | | | | | | |
| *uchyla (się)* [sets aside] | 4 | --- | −98 % | 0 | −100 % | 205 | +1377 % | 14 |
| *oddala (się)* [dismisses] | 0 | --- | −100 % | 0 | −100 % | 204 | −68 % | 640 |
| *przekazuje* [transfers] | 0 | --- | −100 % | 0 | −100 % | 185 | +15 % | 161 |
| *zasądza* [adjudicates] | 0 | −100 % | −100 % | 0 | −100 % | 127 | −21 % | 161 |
| *orzeka* [rules] | 191 | +125 % | --- | 85 | --- | 0 | --- | 0 |
| *wydaje* (następujący wyrok) [gives (the following judgment), excl. *wydaje się*] | 191 | +127 % | --- | 84 | --- | 0 | --- | 0 |
| **Total** | **386** | **+127 %** | **−46 %** | **170** | **−76 %** | **721** | **−26 %** | **975** |
| **II. Exercitive (argumentative) verbs (PRES+PAST forms, 3rd sg.)** | | | | | | | | |
| *zważył* [held, PAST] | 0 | --- | −100 % | 0 | −100 % | 373 | +15 % | 325 |
| *przewiduje* [predicts, PRES] | 601 | +128 % | +235 % | 263 | +47 % | 179 | +53 % | 117 |
| *przesądza* [decides, PRES] | 9 | +58 % | −89 % | 6 | −93 % | 79 | +29 % | 61 |
| *wydaje* się [seems, PRES/PAST] | 92 | +14 % | +630 % | 81 | +542 % | 13 | −51 % | 26 |
| **Total** | **701** | **+101 %** | **+9 %** | **349** | **−46 %** | **644** | **+22 %** | **529** |

(*continued on next page*)

**Table 6.36.** *Continued*

| | Translated EU case law | | | | | Non–translated PL case law | | |
|---|---|---|---|---|---|---|---|---|
| | **CJ** | **CJ vs GC (%DIFF)** | **CJ vs SN_2011–2015 (%DIFF)** | **GC** | **GC vs SN_2011–2015 (%DIFF)** | **SN_2011–2015** | **SN_2011–2015 vs SN_1999 (%DIFF)** | **SN_1999** |
| **III. Reporting verbs (PRES+PAST forms, 3rd sg./pl.)** | | | | | | | | |
| *uznał* [considered] | 516 | −22 % | −46 % | 665 | −30 % | 953 | −2 % | 973 |
| *wskazał* [indicated] | 412 | −50 % | −53 % | 822 | −6 % | 873 | +41 % | 620 |
| *oddala* [dismisses] | 170 | +98 % | −77 % | 86 | −88 % | 742 | −33 % | 1112 |
| *przyjęła* [adopted] | 166 | −9 % | −71 % | 182 | −68 % | 571 | −16 % | 676 |
| *stwierdziła* [attested] | 458 | −29 % | −11 % | 641 | +24 % | 515 | +10 % | 470 |
| *ustalił* [determined] | 85 | −12 % | −80 % | 97 | −78 % | 437 | −5 % | 460 |
| *zarzucił* [imputed] | 26 | −35 % | −94 % | 40 | −90 % | 417 | −6 % | 446 |
| *orzeka* [rules] | 349 | +305 % | +6 % | 86 | −74 % | 329 | −30 % | 470 |
| *podzielił* [shared] | 11 | −44 % | −97 % | 20 | −94 % | 322 | −21 % | 410 |
| *zawarły* [concluded] | 110 | −26 % | −65 % | 148 | −53 % | 314 | +4 % | 301 |
| *zmienił* [changed] | 68 | −28 % | −76 % | 94 | −67 % | 284 | −30 % | 404 |
| *zasądził* [adjudicated] | 3 | +477 % | −99 % | 0 | −100 % | 282 | −14 % | 327 |
| *nastąpiło* [ensued] | 75 | +24 % | −73 % | 60 | −78 % | 279 | −34 % | 422 |
| *dokonał* [performed] | 232 | +27 % | −14 % | 183 | −32 % | 269 | +11 % | 244 |
| *wykazał* [showed] | 128 | −55 % | −48 % | 282 | +14 % | 248 | −29 % | 349 |
| *podnosi* [raises] | 558 | −30 % | +135 % | 797 | +236 % | 237 | +13 % | 210 |
| *podkreślił* [stressed] | 169 | −22 % | −28 % | 216 | −8 % | 235 | +33 % | 176 |

| | | | | | | | | |
|---|---|---|---|---|---|---|---|---|
| *naruszyła* [breached] | 361 | −11 % | 63 % | 404 | +82 % | 222 | −18 % | 271 |
| *uwzględniła* [allowed for] | 179 | −22 % | −13 % | 230 | +12 % | 205 | −28 % | 285 |
| *wyraził* [expressed] | 56 | −13 % | −71 % | 65 | −67 % | 197 | −6 % | 210 |
| *okazał* [displayed] | 45 | −3 % | −76 % | 47 | −75 % | 190 | −18 % | 232 |
| *przewiduje* [predicts] | 601 | +128 % | +235 % | 263 | +47 % | 179 | +53 % | 117 |
| *zobowiązał* [obliged] | 76 | +24 % | −57 % | 61 | −66 % | 178 | +5 % | 168 |
| *uchyla* [sets aside] | 36 | +73 % | −79 % | 21 | −88 % | 170 | −43 % | 297 |
| *ocenił* [assessed] | 26 | −42 % | −83 % | 44 | −71 % | 151 | −15 % | 178 |
| *przekazuje* [transfers] | 66 | −46 % | −43 % | 123 | +7 % | 115 | −3 % | 119 |
| *wnosi* [submits] | 240 | −31 % | +136 % | 349 | +243 % | 102 | −29 % | 143 |
| *wydaje* [issues, excl. ~ *się/ następujący wyrok*] | 147 | −8 % | +44 % | 160 | +57 % | 102 | −5 % | 107 |
| *twierdzi* [claims] | 341 | −52 % | +583 % | 709 | +1322 % | 50 | −61 % | 129 |
| *postanowił* [decided] | 209 | +54 % | +471 % | 135 | +270 % | 37 | −16 % | 44 |
| *uważa* [thinks] | 288 | −5 % | +733 % | 303 | +777 % | 35 | −35 % | 54 |
| *uczestniczyła* [participated] | 63 | −83 % | +103 % | 366 | +1079 % | 31 | +4 % | 30 |
| *utrzymuje* [maintains] | 149 | −46 % | +469 % | 278 | +961 % | 26 | −47 % | 50 |
| *popełniła* [committed] | 53 | −73 % | +579 % | 196 | +2427 % | 8 | +291 % | 2 |
| *dodaje* [adds] | 89 | −31 % | +1070 % | 129 | +1597 % | 8 | −4 % | 8 |
| *przypomina* [resembles] | 105 | −25 % | +2458 % | 140 | +3305 % | 4 | --- | 0 |
| zważył [held, PAST] | 0 | --- | −87 % | 0 | −100 % | 2 | −100 % | 400 |
| **Total** | **6,663** | **−21 %** | **−28 %** | **8,441** | **−9 %** | **9,316** | **−15 %** | **10,913** |

These verbs have the effect of applying the law (legal provisions) in practice and committing the addressees to certain future conduct by having an effect in the law as opposed to laying down the law itself, which is related with normativity (cf. Trosborg 1997: 32; Visconti 2009: 393). Through the mere pronouncing (or rather putting the words down on paper) of the verdictive verbs by the senders (the judges, the courts), the senders create something new (new legal relationships or obligations) based on the old, that is already existing legal provisions and existing facts of the case (Austin 1962: 150–154; cf. Searle 1969, 1976). Verdictive actions are used to deliver a verdict (finding or judgment), which is based on the professional and unbiased appraisal of the law and evidence (cf. Trosborg 1997: 32). Such actions are to be distinguished from verbs indicating actions in legislative or executive acts, which are exercitives used to assert influence or exercise power (Austin 1962: 162). Verdictive actions are related to truth and falsehood, justifiability and unjustifiability, fairness and unfairness, and are performed by virtue of an official position (Austin 1962: 152–153). Verdictive verbs are more frequent in non-translated SN judgments than in translations, although their usage has decreased compared to the pre-accession period (see Table 6.36). In addition, it can be observed that both EU courts favor the verbs *orzeka* [rules] and *wydaje (następujący wyrok)* [gives (the following judgment)], and do not use any other speech act verbs from among those acting as keywords. The SN, on the other hand, uses four verdictive verbs – *uchyla (się)* [sets aside], *oddala (się)* [dismisses], *przekazuje* [transfers], and *zasądza* [adjudicates]. The verdictive verbs may also act as reporting verbs, which necessitates a close examination of the context of occurrence of such verbs.

The second category includes exercitive verbs, such as *zważył* [held], that is verbs used to perform speech acts in which it is decided that "something is to be so" and not "that something is so" (Austin 1962: 154). Exercitives are associated with giving a decision in favor of or against a certain (course of) action or line of argumentation, or simply with expressing advocacy, as in the standardized phrase in SN judgments – *Sąd Najwyższy* ***zważył****, co następuje (...)* [The Supreme Court **held** as follows]. Exercitive verbs may be regarded as laying the argumentative ground for the final verdict expressed with the verdictive verbs (see above). As opposed to verdictive verbs, these verbs may be used both in the present and past tense. CJ judgments contain about 9 % more tokens than post-accession SN judgments, while GC judgments contain about 46 % fewer tokens, which is indicative of internal variation within the Eurolect. The post-accession SN corpus shows an increase compared to the pre-accession corpus.

The third and final group of verbs includes verbs which are used in reporting on actions events and arguments of the national and lower-instance courts, the parties to the proceedings, and experts and institutions:

(10) CJ (C- 243/12 P): *Komisja* ***twierdzi****, że części pierwsza i druga omawianego zarzutu są niedopuszczalne.*
[The Commission **claims** that the first and second parts of this plea are inadmissible.]

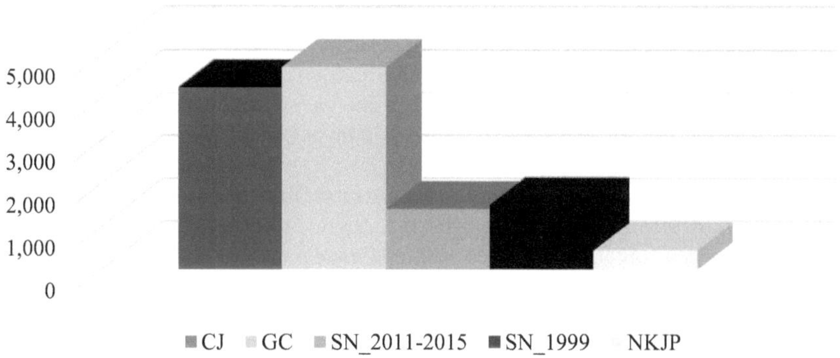


**Figure 6.13.** *Total distribution of the epistemic exercitive (argumentative) modal verb należy [(it/one) must/should be, #7, PRES/PAST]*

These verbs are not directly associated with the courts' own argumentation and speech acts. They are rather used by the courts to provide a reported perspective as opposed to their own. As such, they form the most numerous group among the verbs acting as keywords (see Table 6.3). Reporting verbs are the most widely used group among the three presented categories, which is mainly due to the frequent use of these verbs in the moves related to reporting procedural history, background of the cases, and arguments of the parties to the proceedings (cf. Chapter 5). They are underrepresented in the Eurolect (by 21 % and 9 %, respectively). The post-accession SN corpus shows a decrease in their usage relative to the pre-accession corpus.

The keyword verb *należy* [(it/one) must/should be] (*CJEU: należy* [(it/one) must/should be, #7], *SN: należało* [it must/should have been, #350]) is a (non-personal) modal verb which acts as a marker of epistemic modality (cf. Section 6.9.1) (Koźbiał, *forthcoming*). For this reason, its distribution cannot be examined together with the distribution of other verbs performing the three identified functions.

The function of the exercitive modal verb *należy* [(it/one) must/should be] is to express the courts' own, impersonal and highly authoritative opinions (cf. Koźbiał, *forthcoming*) together with the following verb in the infinitive:

(11) CJEU (C-62/14): ***Należy*** *również* <u>*zauważyć*</u>*, iż z utrwalonego orzecznictwa Trybunału wynika, że wyrok wydany przez Trybunał w trybie prejudycjalnym wiąże sąd krajowy w zakresie dotyczącym wykładni (...).*
[It **must** also <u>be noted</u> that it is settled case-law of the Court that a judgment in which the latter gives a preliminary ruling is binding on the national court, as regards the interpretation or the validity of the acts of the EU institutions in question (...).]

The WSJP describes the modal verb *należy* [(one) must/should] as conveying the sender's conviction that the action expressed by the verb in the infinitive (such as *odpowiedzieć* [to answer], cf. Table 6.3) following that modal is understandable and desirable in a given situation. The verb increases the degree of self-evident nature of the proposition expressed with it and based on the interpretation of the provisions of the law and existing case-law, thus potentially increasing the audience's willingness to accept a given proposition (Bralczyk 1978: 48; cf. Koźbiał, *forthcoming*). It also should be observed that the infinitives following the modal verb *należy* [(one) must/should], for instance *zaznaczyć* [to emphasize], are frequently followed by hypotactic markers, such as *że* [that], as in:

(12) CJ (C-421/12): *Należy* ***zaznaczyć****, że uznając zasadność zarzutu pierwszego, (...).*
[It should **be observed** that, whilst acknowledging that the first complaint is well founded (...).]

In CJEU judgments, the modal verb *należy* [(one) must/should] occurs most frequently in Move 5, containing the findings of the court or consideration of the questions referred for a preliminary ruling by a national court. In SN judgments, it occurs primarily in Move 3 Step 2 with the findings of the court (cf. Chapter 5).

The distribution of verdictive, exercitive (argumentatitve) and reporting verbs across the corpora shows that both CJEU and SN judges rely mostly on reporting verbs to convey their argumentation in the light of the background of the case and the parties' arguments. Verdictive and exercitive verbs are used to a much lesser degree, which is understandable, as the cases heard by the EU courts and the national court typically become very complex before they arrive at the respective courts.

### 6.7.2 Causal patterns

Exponents of causal patterns tend to express three types of relations in legal Polish: justification, inference, and cause-effect (cf. Biel 2014a: 154–157). This section omits the discussion on cause-effect prepositions, as they have already been discussed in Section 6.4.5.2. Causal patterns are used in events linked by a cause-effect relation; their prototypical markers are the colloquial *bo* [because], the slightly more formal *ponieważ* [because], and the formal *gdyż* [because–FORM] (Grzegorczykowa 2004[1998]: 131). In this analysis, I do not try to determine how many markers express simple causal relations and how many express logical (hypothetical) relations (cf. Grzegorczykowa 2004[1998]: 132). Due to the fact that justifications explaining the respective courts' point of view constitute a rhetorical move of CJEU and SN judgments (see Chapter 5), it is expected that their language will exhibit a great number of explanatory statements.

Table 6.37 presents the distribution of causal markers expressing justification in EU and PL judgments, as well as in general Polish (NKJP), which shows that cause-effect markers generally have a high distribution, especially when compared to conditional and purpose markers, which are discussed in Sections 6.7.3 and 6.7.4.

**Table 6.37.** *Causal markers expressing justification*

| | Translated EU case law | | | | | Non-translated PL case law | | | General Polish |
|---|---|---|---|---|---|---|---|---|---|
| | **CJ** | **CJ vs GC (%DIFF)** | **CJ vs SN_2011–2015 (%DIFF)** | **GC** | **GC vs SN_2011–2015 (%DIFF)** | **SN_2011–2015** | **SN_2011–2015 vs SN_1999 (%DIFF)** | **SN_1999** | **NKJP** |
| *bowiem* [since] | 857 | −16 % | −4 % | 1,017 | −16 % | 897 | −35 % | 1,379 | 317 |
| *gdyż* [because–FORM] | 222 | −24 % | −60 % | 293 | −24 % | 560 | −14 % | 654 | 204 |
| *ponieważ* [because] | 617 | −38 % | +70 % | 990 | −38 % | 363 | +85 % | 196 | 298 |
| *. *Ponieważ* (fronted) | 75 | −43 % | +23 % | 132 | −43 % | 61 | −56 % | 139 | N/A |
| *bo* [because] | 1 | +28 % | −99 % | 1 | +28 % | 86 | −10 % | 95 | 1,374 |
| *albowiem* [since-FORM] | 8 | −37 % | −89 % | 13 | −37 % | 75 | −37 % | 119 | 17 |
| *jako że* [inasmuch as] | 136 | +4291 % | +1623 % | 3 | −61 % | 8 | −67 % | 24 | 18 |
| **TOTAL** | **1,917** | **−22 %** | **−6 %** | **2,449** | **+20 %** | **2,049** | **−21 %** | **2,606** | **2,227** |

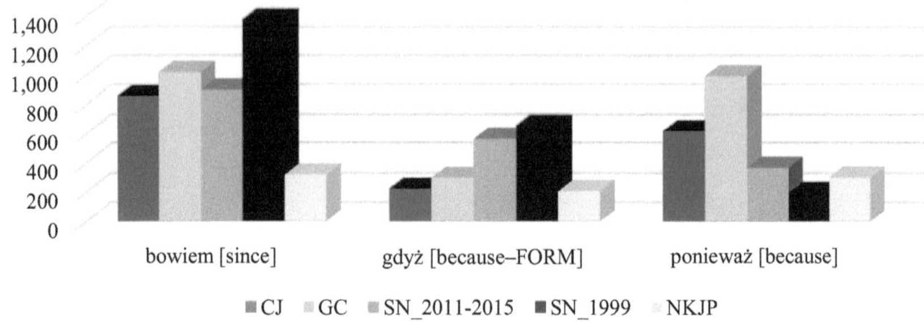


**Figure 6.14.** *Distribution of prototypical causal markers expressing justification*

It is surprising that CJEU and SN judgments, as highly argumentative subgenres, contain a similar number of justification markers to general Polish (NKJP). This is so, however, due to the unnaturally high distribution of the colloquial *bo* [because] in the NKJP corpus. Only the CJ corpus exhibits underrepresentation in relation to both SN judgments and general Polish (NKJP). The GC corpus, on the other hand, shows overrepresentation (by 20 %) relative to the post-accession SN corpus. Strangely, the post-accession SN corpus shows underrepresentation relative to the pre-accession corpus (by 21 %). It is not possible to justify this behavior based solely on quantitative data. It may be, however, that Polish judges started to justify their decisions to a lesser degree, which is reflected in the data.

The data (see Table 6.37, Figure 6.14) suggest that the use of prototypical markers of justification and their synonyms, *bowiem* [since], *albowiem* [since-FORM], *jako że* [inasmuch as], can be described as a characteristic feature of judicial language owing to their relatively high distribution relative to general Polish (NKJP). What is more, it is interesting that lawyer-linguists more often resort to *bowiem* [since] and *ponieważ* [because] at the expense of *gdyż* [because–FORM] – this tendency mirrors the distribution of these markers in general Polish (NKJP), which is probably why the former are more readily used in translations. On the other hand, Polish judges tend to use *gdyż* [because–FORM] very often, even more frequently than *ponieważ* [because].

*Analogicznie* [analogously] is keyword #294 in the Eurolect, while *więc* [so] is keyword #145 (cf. Table 6.3), and both of them are causal markers of inference. In the analysis, I have also identified a number of other markers expressing the same relation (see Table 6.38).

The data in Table 6.38 paint an inconsistent image of the Eurolect. While CJ judgments exhibit underrepresentation (by 19 %) relative to post-accession SN judgments, GC judgments exhibit overrepresentation (by 16 %). The most overrepresented are: *w związku z tym/czym/powyższym* [in connection with this, what, the foregoing], *z tego względu* [for this reason], *analogicznie* [analogously], and *ze*

**Table 6.38.** *Causal markers expressing inference*

| | Translated EU case law | | | | | Non-translated PL case law | | | General Polish |
|---|---|---|---|---|---|---|---|---|---|
| | CJ | CJ vs GC (%DIFF) | CJ vs SN_2011–2015 (%DIFF) | GC | GC vs SN_2011–2015 (%DIFF) | SN_2011–2015 | SN_2011–2015 vs SN_1999 (%DIFF) | SN_1999 | NKJP |
| *zatem* [thus] | 928 | −25 % | −4 % | 1,241 | +28 % | 969 | +1 % | 957 | 165 |
| *więc* [so] | 220 | −37 % | −74 % | 351 | −59 % | 849 | −9 % | 937 | 911 |
| *tym samym* [hence] | 283 | −20 % | +6 % | 356 | +33 % | 266 | +27 % | 210 | 136 |
| *w związku z tym/czym/powyższym* [in connection with this, what, the foregoing] | 357 | −25 % | +74 % | 479 | +134 % | 205 | +3 % | 198 | 98 |
| *dlatego* [therefore] | 62 | −58 % | −64 % | 147 | −15 % | 171 | −51 % | 349 | 479 |
| *wobec tego, czego, powyższego* [in view of this, what, the foregoing] | 137 | −46 % | −6 % | 253 | +75 % | 145 | −49 % | 283 | 32 |
| *z tego względu* [for this reason] | 118 | −10 % | +56 % | 132 | +74 % | 76 | +67 % | 46 | 8 |
| *przeto* [thus] | 0 | --- | −100 % | 0 | --- | 34 | −71 % | 115 | 8 |
| *dlatego też* [therefore] | 24 | −67 % | +21 % | 72 | +266 % | 20 | −75 % | 79 | 41 |
| *toteż* [hence] | 1 | −4 % | −87 % | 2 | −86 % | 11 | −57 % | 26 | 25 |
| *analogicznie* [analogously] | 97 | −32 % | +1563 % | 143 | --- | 6 | −51 % | 12 | 4 |
| *ze względu na fakt* [due to the fact that] | 16 | −29 % | +701 % | 23 | +1024 % | 2 | +3 % | 2 | 1 |
| **TOTAL** | **2,244** | **−30 %** | **−19 %** | **3,199** | **+16 %** | **2,754** | **−14 %** | **3,214** | **1,908** |

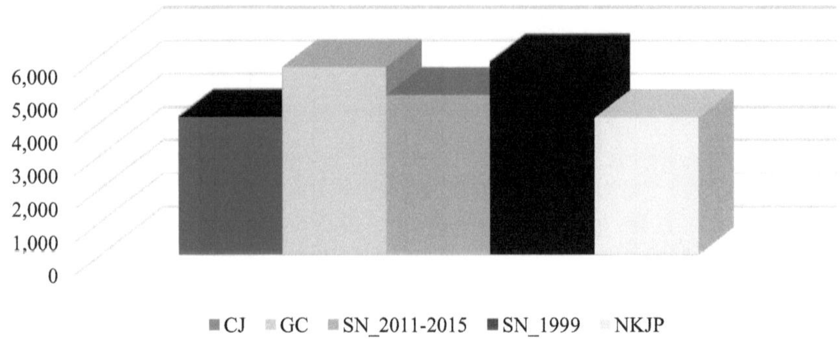


**Figure 6.15.** *Total distribution of causal markers expressing justification and inference*

*względu na fakt* [due to the fact that], while the most markedly underrepresented are: *więc* [so] and *dlatego* [therefore]. Despite their high frequency, none of the overrepresented adverbials were found on the keyword lists. It cannot be concluded decisively that judgments make greater overall use of inference markers due to internal variation in the Eurolect.

To sum up, EU judgments make greater use of *bowiem* [since] and *ponieważ* [because]; however, when it comes to other justification markers and inference markers, there is no clear difference in the distribution in translated and non-translated judgments due to internal differences in the Eurolect. Overall, causal markers are invaluable in judicial language, owing to the fact that they act as persuasive devices which legitimize the courts' arguments.

### 6.7.3 If-then conditionals and related patterns

In order to justify their decisions and make them more objective, judges need to use complex reasoning patterns to connect hypothetically possible and impossible facts (cf. Grzegorczykowa 2004[1998]: 135; Bańko 2007: 161–162) with relevant provisions of the law, and, subsequently, determine the legal consequences stemming from legal norms (cf. Malinowski 2006: 212). Such patterns are evidenced among others in conditionals and hypothetical formulations. Biel (2014a: 144) identified these language constructions as a distinctive feature of legislative language which lays out legal provisions, but these have also been found to be characteristic of judicial language, as it interprets legal provisions to determine binding legal norms – *jeśli* [if-NEUT] is a keyword in both CJ (#94) and GC (#78) judgments. Only *jeżeli* [if-FORM] is present on the non-lemmatized list of the top 100 words sorted by frequency generated for the CJ corpus.

The prototypical conditional markers in Polish are *jeżeli* [if-FORM] and *jeśli* [if-NEUT] (cf. Grzegorczykowa 2004[1998]: 135), with the latter being a less formal synonym of the former, which is proven by the higher distribution of *jeśli* [if-NEUT] in general Polish (NKJP). The data presented in Table 6.39 exclude the occurrences of *jeśli* [if-NEUT] and *jeżeli* [if-FORM] in the cohesive phrase *jeśli/jeżeli chodzi o* [BT: if it is about] (cf. Section 6.8.1), the meaning of which is similar to *as far as X is concerned* (cf. Biel 2014a: 146).

Considering the fact that judicial language is customarily formal, it is surprising to observe that *jeśli* has a rather high distribution in translated EU judgments, in particular in GC judgments in which its distribution is almost equal to that of *jeżeli* [if-FORM]. Overall, both *jeśli* and *jeżeli* are overrepresented in CJEU judgments relative to both pre- and post-accession SN judgments, by about 61 % and 20 %, respectively. Data from the NKJP corpus suggest that only the use of formal *jeżeli* [if-FORM] is a typical feature of judicial language, owing to its high salience in both EU and SN judgments as compared to general Polish (NKJP). The use of *jeśli* [if-NEUT], on the other hand, is not a typical feature, due to its low distribution, in particular in SN judgments (see Figure 6.16). This is not surprising, since judicial language is formal, which is why the more formal equivalent of *jeśli* [if-NEUT] is preferred by the judges.

*Jeżeli* [if-FORM] is the most widely used marker of conditional relations by both EU and domestic judges. The data from the pre-accession SN corpus suggest that overall the reliance on *jeśli* [if-NEUT] and *jeżeli* [if-FORM] is higher in post-accession SN judgments, mostly due to the more frequent use of the latter conditional marker.

The conditional conjunctions discussed above are not the only linguistic devices used to convey conditional relations in legal reasoning (cf. Malinowski 2006: 212–217; Biel 2014a: 146). A prime example of a related, implicit conditional marker is *skoro* [since],[122] which ranks #99 and #123 in the keyword lists generated for the wordlist of the post-accession SN corpus set against CJ and GC wordlists, respectively (cf. Table 6.3). Table 6.40 presents other conditional markers of importance to the sub-genres of CJEU and SN judgments, which were identified based on literature review and examination of concordances (cf. Grzegorczykowa 2004[1998]: 135–138; Malinowski 2006: 212–217; Biel 2014a: 146); these are: *skoro* [since], *w razie* [in the event], *w przypadku* [in the case], *w wypadku* [in the case/BT: in the accident], *o ile* [unless, if not], *chyba że* [unless], *z tym że* [however], *pod warunkiem* [on condition], *wówczas(,) gdy* [at the time when], *wtedy(,) gdy* [at the time when].

Only four markers have lower frequency in CJEU judgments than in SN judgments – *skoro* [since], *w razie* [in the event], *w wypadku* [in the case/accident], and the restrictive *z tym że* [however]. The remaining markers are overrepresented in translations relative to non-translations. Conditional markers related to the prototypical conditional conjunctions *jeśli* [if-NEUT] and *jeżeli* [if-FORM]

122 *Skoro* [since] may also act as a marker of implicit reasoning aimed at determining the cause of an event (Grzegorczykowa 2004[1998]: 133).

**Table 6.39.** *Prototypical if-then conditional markers (conjunctions)*

| | Translated EU case law | | | | | Non-translated PL case law | | | General Polish |
|---|---|---|---|---|---|---|---|---|---|
| | **CJ** | **CJ vs GC (%DIFF)** | **CJ vs SN_2011–2015 (%DIFF)** | **GC** | **GC vs SN_2011–2015 (%DIFF)** | **SN_2011–2015** | **SN_2011–2015 vs SN_1999 (%DIFF)** | **SN_1999** | **NKJP** |
| *jeżeli* (excl. *jeżeli chodzi o* [if it is about] – cohesive devise) [if-FORM] | 1,026 | +114 % | +63 % | 479 | −24 % | 628 | +34 % | 468 | 437 |
| *jeśli* (excl. *jeśli chodzi o* [if it is about] – cohesive devise) [if-NEUT] | 484 | +5 % | +219 % | 459 | +203 % | 152 | −8 % | 164 | 742 |
| **TOTAL** | **1,510** | **+61 %** | **+94 %** | **938** | **+20 %** | **780** | **+23 %** | **632** | **1,179** |

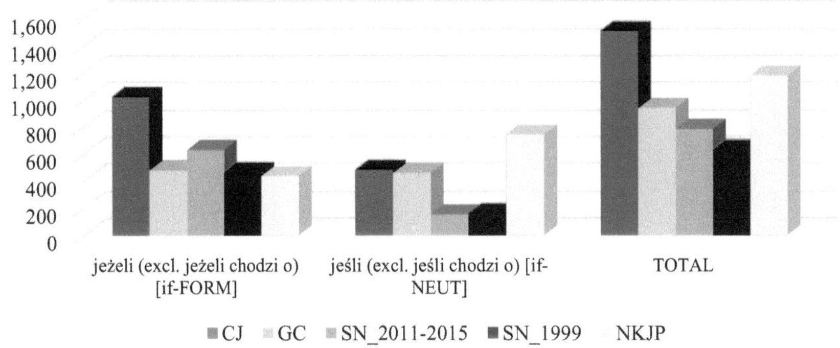


**Figure 6.16.** *Distribution of jeżeli [if-FORM] and jeśli [if-NEUT]*

are not equally distributed in the Eurolect, being overrepresented by about 23 % in CJ judgments and underrepresented by about 10 % in GC judgments. In the group of synonymous markers, *w razie* [in the event], *w przypadku* [in the case], and *w wypadku* [in the case/accident], Polish judges prefer using *w razie* [in the event] at the cost of the two other markers, while translated EU judgments exhibit overuse of the two other markers, *w przypadku* [in the case] and *w wypadku* [in the case/ accident]. Polish lawyer-linguists correctly avoid using *w wypadku* [in the case/ accident], as it has negative connotations with an accident, favoring *w przypadku* [in the case]. The pre-accession SN data show that post-accession SN judgments exhibit a higher use of all three implicit markers. They also show growing reliance on *chyba że* [unless] (cf. Malinowski 2006: 217).

The comparison of the SN corpora leads to the conclusion that the Polish judges' reliance on related conditional markers has increased substantially in the post-accession period (by 17 %), which might be indicative of the growing complexity of cases heard by the national court. Furthermore, data from the NKJP corpus suggest that the related, implicit conditional markers are indeed a characteristic feature of judicial language owing to the judges' need to connect facts with legal provisions and legal norms, which is proven by their marked overrepresentation in CJEU and SN judgments relative to general Polish (NKJP) (see Figure 6.17).

The distribution of implicit markers expressing conditional relations is not equal among the individual types, as some are clearly overrepresented in translations (for instance, *w przypadku* [in the case]) and some are underrepresented in translation (for instance, *skoro* [since]). The most frequent types include: *skoro* [since], *w razie* [in the event], *w przypadku* [in the case], and *o ile* [unless, if not]. Other types have a rather low distribution across all the corpora.

Overall, the total distribution of both prototypical and implicit markers of conditional relations shows that conditional relations are more widely relied on in translations, with the most substantial difference being between CJ and SN

**Table 6.40.** *Other conditional markers related to the prototypical jeżeli [if-FORM] and jeśli [if-NEUT] conjunctions*

| | Translated EU case law | | | | | Non-translated PL case law | | | General Polish |
|---|---|---|---|---|---|---|---|---|---|
| | CJ | CJ vs GC (%DIFF) | CJ vs SN_2011–2015 (%DIFF) | GC | GC vs SN_2011–2015 (%DIFF) | SN_2011–2015 | SN_2011–2015 vs SN_1999 (%DIFF) | SN_1999 | NKJP |
| ***skoro*** **[since]** | 95 | −9 % | −82 % | 104 | −81 % | 541 | −3 % | 559 | 137 |
| ***w razie*** **[in the event]** | 118 | +68 % | −61 % | 70 | −77 % | 299 | +16 % | 258 | 61 |
| *w razie potrzeby* [in the event of need] | 46 | +8 % | +667 % | 43 | +612 % | 6 | +51 % | 4 | 8 |
| *w razie udzielenia* [in the case of granting] | 14 | +835 % | +1880 % | 2 | +112 % | 1 | --- | 0 | 0 |
| *w razie konieczności* [in the event of a necessity] | 8 | +46 % | +403 % | 6 | +244 % | 2 | −19 % | 2 | 2 |
| *w razie stwierdzenia* [in the event of determination] | 5 | +51 % | −66 % | 3 | −78 % | 14 | +75 % | 8 | 1 |
| *w razie(,) gdy* [in the event when] | 7 | +297 % | +183 % | 2 | −29 % | 2 | +26 % | 2 | 1 |
| ***w przypadku*** **[in the case]** | 642 | 0 % | +169 % | 640 | +168 % | 239 | +234 % | 71 | 213 |
| *w przypadku(,) gdy* [in the case when] | 232 | +72 % | +2891 % | 135 | +1642 % | 8 | --- | 0 | 17 |
| *w przypadku(,) gdyby* [in the case if] | 19 | −25 % | +233 % | 25 | +342 % | 6 | --- | 0 | 2 |
| *w przypadku braku* [in the case of lack] | 22 | −14 % | +259 % | 25 | +317 % | 6 | --- | 0 | 3 |
| *w przypadku udzielenia odpowiedzi* [in the case of providing an answer] | 30 | +4390 % | --- | 1 | --- | 0 | --- | 0 | 0 |

| | | | | | | | | | |
|---|---|---|---|---|---|---|---|---|---|
| *w przypadku uchylenia* [in the case of repeal] | 7 | +646 % | 2157 % | 1 | +203 % | 0 | --- | 0 | 0 |
| *w przypadku stwierdzenia* [in the case of the determination] | 7 | −7 % | 115 % | 7 | +131 % | 3 | --- | 0 | 2 |
| ***w wypadku* [in the case/accident]** | 118 | +41 % | −16 % | 84 | −41 % | 141 | +34 % | 105 | 30 |
| *w wypadku(,) gdy* [in the case when/ BT: in the accident when] | 55 | +224 % | +1696 % | 17 | +455 % | 3 | −69 % | 10 | 1 |
| *w wypadku(,) gdyby* [in the case if/ BT: in the accident if] | 8 | +44 % | +199 % | 6 | +107 % | 3 | --- | 0 | 0 |
| ***o ile* [unless, if not]** | 285 | +54 % | +251 % | 185 | +127 % | 81 | −42 % | 141 | 71 |
| ***chyba że* [unless]** | 100 | +53 % | +64 % | 65 | +7 % | 61 | +62 % | 38 | 41 |
| ***z tym że* [however]** | 1 | −42 % | −94 % | 2 | −89 % | 21 | −13 % | 24 | 38 |
| ***pod warunkiem* [on condition]** | 29 | +139 % | +57 % | 12 | −34 % | 18 | +14 % | 16 | 26 |
| *pod warunkiem, że/iż* [on condition that] | 135 | +345 % | +1129 % | 30 | +176 % | 11 | +11 % | 10 | 19 |
| *pod warunkiem zawieszającym/ rozwiązującym* [subject to the suspensive condition/on condition subsequent] | 0 | −4 % | −96 % | 0 | −96 % | 5 | +158 % | 2 | 0 |
| ***wówczas(,) gdy* [at the time when]** | 76 | +62 % | +702 % | 47 | +394 % | 10 | +140 % | 4 | 16 |
| ***wtedy(,) gdy* [at the time when]** | 102 | +70 % | +2084 % | 60 | +1182 % | 5 | --- | 0 | 47 |
| **TOTAL** | **1,566** | **+23 %** | **+11 %** | **1,269** | **−10 %** | **1,416** | **+17 %** | **1,212** | **680** |

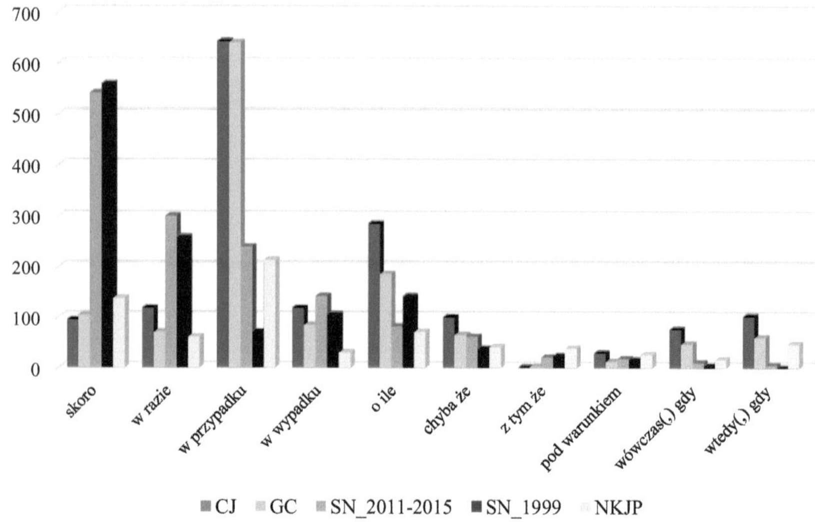


**Figure 6.17.** *Distribution of implicit conditional markers*

judgments. GC judgments have an almost equal distribution of these markers (see Figure 6.18). The most important observation concerns the higher reliance on the formal *jeżeli* [if-FORM] in judicial language, as opposed to general Polish (NKJP) which prefers *jeśli* [if-NEUT].

Due to the fact that the courts' interpretation of legal rules and existing case law is not always expressed with conditionals and related patterns, but rather with descriptive statements, the distributional analysis of prototypical and implicit conditionals needs to be supplemented with other grammatical categories.

### 6.7.4 Patterns of purpose

Patterns of purpose are an interesting area to look at more closely, since keywords such as *celów* [#55], *celu* [#26], and *by* [#163] have been found to be markedly overrepresented in translated EU judgments (see Table 6.41). Grzegorczykowa (2004[1998]: 133) treats purpose clauses as a category different from causal patterns, although it cannot be denied that purpose patterns also exhibit cause-effect relations. Purpose markers related to the aims of actions performed by various actors, such as the parties to the proceedings. The prototypical purpose marker is *żeby* [so that] (Grzegorczykowa 2004[1998]: 134). Although the two 500-word keyword lists do not point to the salience of other patterns of purpose, it is equally important to consider other expressions, such as *aby* [to] and *na celu* [with the aim of], along with prepositions expressing purpose relations *celem* [with the goal of]

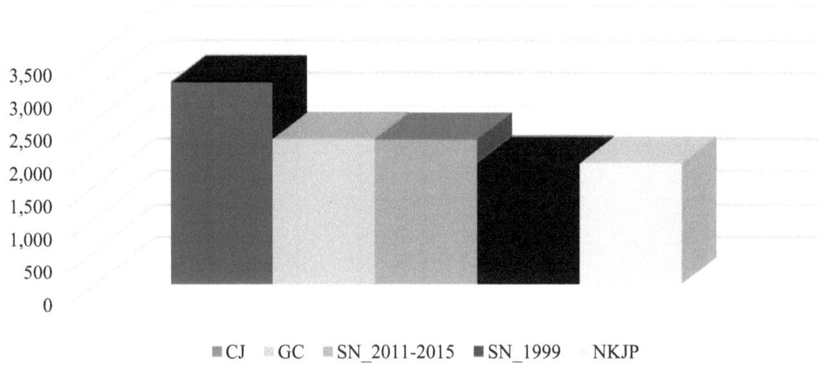


**Figure 6.18.** *Total distribution of prototypical and implicit markers of conditional relations*

(Milewska 2003a: 138–139) (cf. 6.3.4.13), in order to establish whether patterns of purpose are indeed a generic feature of judgments compared to general Polish (NKJP) (see Table 6.41).

Patterns of purpose are strongly overrepresented in CJ and GC judgments, by about 266 % and 233 %, respectively. The conjunction *żeby* [so that] has a relatively low distribution across all the corpora. Its function is performed rather by other markers, with the most clearly overrepresented ones including: *aby* [to], *w celu* [with the aim of], *celem* [with the goal of], and *by* [so that]. It is interesting that translations make greater use of purpose markers in the sentence-initial position (see excerpt below), which may be due to an overreliance on the technique of literal translation. Overall, purpose markers seem to be a characteristic feature of translated judgments, as non-translations exhibit a marked underrepresentation relative to general Polish (NKJP). Pre- and post-accession SN judgments contain a similar distribution of purpose markers.

It should be noted that *w celu* [with the aim of], *do celów* [for the purposes of] and *na celu* [with the aim of], as well as *celem* [with the goal of] contribute to greater nominalization due to the fact that they frequently trigger deverbal nouns (cf. Bańko 2007: 89–90, 107, 169):

| | |
|---|---|
| (13) CJ (C-328/12): | ***W celu*** *udzielenia odpowiedzi na to pytanie należy w pierwszej kolejności przypomnieć, że [...].*<br>[**With the aim of** providing an answer to this question, it should be noted at the outset that (...).] |
| (14) SN_2011–2015 (I CSK 272/10): | *Z okoliczności sprawy wynika, że* ***w celu*** *ustalenia odszkodowania w postępowaniu sądowym zostały przeprowadzone dowody z trzech opinii biegłych.* |

**Table 6.41.** *Patterns of purpose*

| | Translated EU case law | | | | | Non-translated PL case law | | | General Polish |
|---|---|---|---|---|---|---|---|---|---|
| | **CJ** | **CJ vs GC (%DIFF)** | **CJ vs SN_2011–2015 (%DIFF)** | **GC** | **GC vs SN_2011–2015 (%DIFF)** | **SN_2011–2015** | **SN_2011–2015 vs SN_1999 (%DIFF)** | **SN_1999** | **NKJP** |
| *aby* [to] | 842 | -4 % | +150 % | 879 | +161 % | 337 | −17 % | 408 | 658 |
| *. *Aby* (fronted) | 66 | +29 % | +834 % | 51 | +625 % | 7 | −49 % | 14 | N/A |
| *w celu* [with the aim of] | 1,099 | +6 % | +306 % | 1,040 | +284 % | 271 | +47 % | 184 | 84 |
| *. *W celu* (fronted) | 110 | +78 % | +973 % | 62 | +503 % | 10 | +29 % | 8 | N/A |
| *na celu* [with the aim of] | 421 | +13 % | +296 % | 374 | +252 % | 106 | +53 % | 69 | 49 |
| *celem* [with the goal of] | 99 | −11 % | +98 % | 112 | +124 % | 50 | +130 % | 22 | 94 |
| *. *Celem* (fronted) | 6 | +3 % | +148 % | 6 | +140 % | 2 | --- | 0 | N/A |
| *do celów* [for the purposes of] | 264 | +145 % | +4303 % | 108 | +1698 % | 6 | +203 % | 2 | 8 |
| *. *Do celów* (fronted) | 72 | +698 % | --- | 9 | --- | 0 | --- | 0 | N/A |
| *by* [so that] | 573 | 0 % | +271 % | 574 | +271 % | 155 | −40 % | 260 | 947 |
| *żeby* [so that] | 23 | −30 % | −19 % | 34 | +16 % | 29 | −36 % | 46 | 632 |
| *ażeby* [in order that] | 3 | −20 % | −5 % | 4 | +18 % | 3 | −25 % | 4 | 17 |
| TOTAL | **3,579** | **+10 %** | **+266 %** | **3,252** | **+233 %** | **977** | **−4 %** | **1,017** | **2,489** |

[It is apparent from the circumstances of the case that, **with the aim of** providing a determination of damages in court proceedings, evidence was obtained from three expert opinions.]

The considerable degree of nominalization in both CJEU and SN judgments is confirmed by the high number of deverbal nouns identified as keywords (see Table 6.3). Based on these keywords, it was possible to determine that the following deverbal nouns triggered by purpose patterns are overrepresented in the CJEU corpus – *poparcia* [support], *zapewnienia* [guarantee], *zatrudnienia* [employment], *przedstawienia* [presentation]; the post-accession SN corpus contains an overly-high representation of the following deverbal nouns relative to the CJEU corpora – *uchylenia* [abrogation], *wykonania* [performance], *uznania* [recognition], *zobowiązania* [obligation], *uwzględnienia* [inclusion].[123]

The overall overrepresentation of purposive patterns in translated judgments relative to SN judgments and general Polish (NKJP) elevates them to a generic feature.

## 6.8 Framing with adverbials and participles

The examination of the 500-word keyword lists has shown that there are several very salient types of adverbials and participles in the corpora of judgments. These include: addition adverbials (*ponadto* [CJEU: #72], *nadto* [SN: #213]), an exemplification and particularization adverbial (*chodzi* [CJEU: #140] which forms the adverbial *jeżeli/jeśli chodzi o* [if it is about]), an adverbial participle with the suffix *-wszy* (*rozważywszy* [CJEU: #368]), present adverbial participles with the suffix *-ąc* which are overrepresented only in the SN corpus (*podzielając* [#388], *zarzucając* [#396]), and epistemic stance adverbials (*słusznie* [CJEU: #360], *trafnie* [SN: #138], *niewątpliwie* [SN: #254]). Considering the salience of the mentioned keywords, the distribution of other exponents of the identified categories will be analyzed in greater detail in Sections 6.8.1 and 6.8.2. The category of exclusion and contrast adverbials is not represented in the keyword lists; however, it will be analyzed following Biel's (2014a: 206–208) study on EU and Polish legislative acts, in order to enable inter-generic comparisons between two closely related genres.

123 For want of space, I cannot fully explore the nature of nominal constructions in judgments. Chapter 8 investigates to a limited extent the phenomenon of nominalization in the corpora of judgments by studying the distribution of binomials. The analysis of binomials, however, aims to supplement the investigation into the formulaic profile by complementing the lexical bundles approach, which is why it does not enable conclusions to be drawn as regards the overall degree of nominalization in judicial language.

### 6.8.1 Adverbials

According to Biber and Barbieri (2007: 762), adverbials perform three major functions – they add circumstantial information, express the sender's stance, and link clauses (or their parts) to other units of discourse. The subject of the analysis in this section are adverbials expressing: (1) addition, (2) enumeration, (3) exemplification and particularization, (4) exclusion and contrast, and (5) stance (which is not sub-divided here into epistemic, attitude and style) (cf. Biel 2014a: 200). Circumstance adverbials including inference markers (Biber and Barbieri 2007: 763–764) are discussed in Section 6.7.2. This classification follows Biel's (2014a: 200) classification of adverbials in EU and Polish legislation and includes a number of markers specific to the genre of judgments.

**Addition, enumeration, exemplification and particularization**
The distribution of adverbials expressing addition, exemplification and enumeration is presented in Table 6.42. These categories have been identified thanks to the additive keywords *ponadto* [moreover] and *nadto* [moreover], as well as *chodzi*, which occurs in the particularizing expression *jeśli chodzi o* [if it is about], *jeżeli chodzi o* [if it is about].

The distribution of additive adverbials is the highest among the three functional groups in Table 6.42. Despite the fact that additive adverbials occur very frequently in both GC and SN judgments in relation to general Polish (NKJP), they may only be conditionally classified as a typical feature of judicial language due to their slight underrepresentation in CJ judgments and the fact that general Polish (NKJP) makes use of them to a similar degree. The CJ corpus contains about 16 % fewer tokens than the GC corpus, which indicates marked internal variation in the Eurolect, and about 14 % fewer tokens than the post-accession SN corpus. Virtually all types of additive adverbials are underrepresented in CJ judgments relative to GC judgments. Compared to the post-accession SN corpus, types such as *ponadto* [moreover], *co więcej* [what (is) more], and *oprócz tego* [except that] are considerably overrepresented in CJ judgments, while types such as *także* [also-NEUT], *też* [also-INFORM], *nadto* [moreover], *dodatkowo* [additionally] are considerably underrepresented. Both national corpora exhibit almost equal overall distribution, although there are differences in the distribution of individual types.

The group of exemplifying and particularizing adverbials contains six more types of adverbials than the first functional category and, despite this fact, it still contains slightly fewer tokens across all corpora. In this category, the total distribution in the Eurolect is about two times higher than in the SN judgments and general Polish (NKJP), which indicates that the use of exemplifying adverbials is a characteristic feature of only CJEU judgments. CJEU judgments make particularly frequent use of the following adverbials: *w szczególności* [in particular], *w pierwszej kolejności* [in the first place], *tak* jak* [such as], *na wstępie* [at the outset], *jeśli chodzi o* [if it is about], and *jeżeli chodzi o* [if it is about]. There are only three types underrepresented in CJEU judgments: ***, *w tym* [*, of which], *wraz z* [together

**Table 6.42.** *Distribution of adverbials expressing addition, exemplification and particularization, and enumeration*

| | Translated EU case law | | | | | Non-translated PL case law | | | General Polish |
|---|---|---|---|---|---|---|---|---|---|
| | **CJ** | **CJ vs GC (%DIFF)** | **CJ vs SN_2011–2015 (%DIFF)** | **GC** | **GC vs SN_2011–2015 (%DIFF)** | **SN_2011–2015** | **SN_2011–2015 vs SN_1999 (%DIFF)** | **SN_1999** | **NKJP** |
| **I. Addition** | | | | | | | | | |
| *także* [also-NEUT] | 409 | −35 % | −73 % | 625 | −59 % | 1,518 | +21 % | 1,252 | 831 |
| *a także* [and] | 681 | +85 % | +129 % | 367 | +24 % | 297 | −15 % | 351 | 244 |
| *też* [also-INFORM] | 460 | 0 % | −45 % | 459 | −45 % | 829 | −22 % | 1,062 | 1,374 |
| *również* [also-FORM] | 934 | −10 % | +20 % | 1,035 | +33 % | 779 | +15 % | 678 | 776 |
| *jak również* [as well as] | 203 | −15 % | +69 % | 240 | +99 % | 120 | +79 % | 67 | 39 |
| *ponadto* [moreover] | 841 | −37 % | +157 % | 1,332 | +307 % | 327 | +86 % | 176 | 120 |
| *jednocześnie* [simultaneously] | 97 | −6 % | −55 % | 103 | −52 % | 213 | +9 % | 196 | 172 |
| *nadto* [moreover] | 3 | −50 % | −98 % | 7 | −95 % | 148 | −67 % | 442 | 11 |
| *poza tym* [besides] | 78 | −52 % | −15 % | 162 | +76 % | 92 | +8 % | 85 | 121 |
| *dodatkowo* [additionally] | 32 | −24 % | −55 % | 43 | −41 % | 72 | +52 % | 48 | 72 |
| *a nawet* [and even] | 30 | −37 % | −16 % | 47 | +32 % | 35 | −26 % | 48 | 112 |
| *co więcej* [what (is) more] | 49 | −64 % | +144 % | 136 | +583 % | 20 | +43 % | 14 | 28 |
| *w dodatku* [in addition] | 4 | −40 % | −56 % | 6 | −26 % | 9 | +336 % | 2 | 37 |
| *oprócz tego* [except that] | 3 | −72 % | +212 % | 11 | +1003 % | 1 | −48 % | 2 | 17 |

(*continued on next page*)

**Table 6.42.** *Continued*

| | Translated EU case law | | | | | Non-translated PL case law | | | General Polish |
|---|---|---|---|---|---|---|---|---|---|
| | **CJ** | **CJ vs GC (%DIFF)** | **CJ vs SN_2011–2015 (%DIFF)** | **GC** | **GC vs SN_2011–2015 (%DIFF)** | **SN_2011–2015** | **SN_2011–2015 vs SN_1999 (%DIFF)** | **SN_1999** | **NKJP** |
| **TOTAL (14 types)** | **3,823** | **−16 %** | **−14 %** | **4,572** | **+3 %** | **4,460** | **+1 %** | **4,423** | **3,954** |
| **II. Exemplification and particularization** | | | | | | | | | |
| **, w tym* [*, of which] | 246 | +3 % | −33 % | 238 | −35 % | 367 | +95 % | 188 | N/A |
| *wraz z* [together with] | 96 | −8 % | −67 % | 104 | −65 % | 293 | +68 % | 174 | 177 |
| *w szczególności* [in particular] | 1,459 | +24 % | +456 % | 1,175 | +348 % | 262 | −44 % | 468 | 52 |
| *np.* [e.g.-ABBRV] | 17 | +67 % | −93 % | 10 | −96 % | 254 | −22 % | 327 | 341 |
| *przede wszystkim* [above all] | 136 | −44 % | −18 % | 242 | +46 % | 166 | −27 % | 228 | 272 |
| *zwłaszcza* [especially] | 102 | −38 % | −33 % | 163 | +7 % | 152 | −32 % | 224 | 207 |
| *między innymi* [among others] | 191 | +13 % | +44 % | 169 | +27 % | 133 | +12 % | 119 | 89 |
| *w pierwszej kolejności* [in the first place] | 150 | −36 % | +88 % | 233 | +192 % | 80 | −27 % | 109 | 16 |
| *tak* jak* [such as] | 867 | +126 % | +1212 % | 383 | +480 % | 66 | −5 % | 69 | 97 |
| *tym bardziej* [all the more] | 35 | −62 % | −37 % | 93 | +68 % | 55 | −24 % | 73 | 81 |
| *szczególnie* [particularly] | 85 | −41 % | +94 % | 144 | +231 % | 44 | −15 % | 52 | 188 |

| | | | | | | | | | |
|---|---|---|---|---|---|---|---|---|---|
| *na wstępie* [at the outset] | 117 | −2 % | +304 % | 120 | +313 % | 29 | −51 % | 59 | 11 |
| *najpierw* [first] | 49 | −29 % | +71 % | 69 | +142 % | 28 | +43 % | 20 | 166 |
| *łącznie z* [inclusive of] | 36 | +138 % | +75 % | 15 | −26 % | 21 | −19 % | 26 | 20 |
| *na przykład* [for example] | 53 | −40 % | +756 % | 87 | +1316 % | 6 | +55 % | 4 | 204 |
| *jeśli chodzi o* [if it is about] | 208 | −42 % | +3445 % | 355 | +5968 % | 6 | −84 % | 36 | 75 |
| *włącznie z* [inclusive of] | 50 | +240 % | +1070 % | 15 | +244 % | 4 | --- | 0 | 4 |
| *jeżeli chodzi o* [if it is about] | 136 | −15 % | +3627 % | 160 | +4270 % | 4 | −83 % | 22 | 29 |
| *w głównej mierze* [for the most part] | 3 | +92 % | +66 % | 2 | −14 % | 2 | −66 % | 6 | 3 |
| *włączając* [including] | 29 | +121 % | +2770 % | 13 | +1197 % | 1 | --- | 0 | 3 |
| **TOTAL (20 types)** | **4,065** | **+7 %** | **+106 %** | **3,790** | **+92 %** | **1,973** | **−10 %** | **2,204** | **2,035** |
| **III. Enumeration** | | | | | | | | | |
| *po pierwsze* [firstly] | 402 | −48 % | +597 % | 772 | +1239 % | 58 | −12 % | 65 | 66 |
| *po drugie* [secondly] | 393 | −48 % | +736 % | 753 | +1502 % | 47 | +58 % | 30 | 51 |
| *z jednej strony* [on the one hand] | 180 | −37 % | +534 % | 287 | +910 % | 28 | −10 % | 32 | 42 |
| *z drugiej strony* [on the other hand] | 178 | −38 % | +776 % | 287 | +1311 % | 20 | +28 % | 16 | 50 |
| *po trzecie* [thirdly] | 68 | −75 % | +331 % | 272 | +1622 % | 16 | +99 % | 8 | 16 |
| **TOTAL (5 types)** | **1,221** | **−48 %** | **+622 %** | **2,371** | **+1301 %** | **169** | **+12 %** | **151** | **224** |
| **GRAND TOTAL** | **9,109** | **−15 %** | **+38 %** | **10,733** | **+63 %** | **6,602** | **−3 %** | **6,778** | **6,116** |

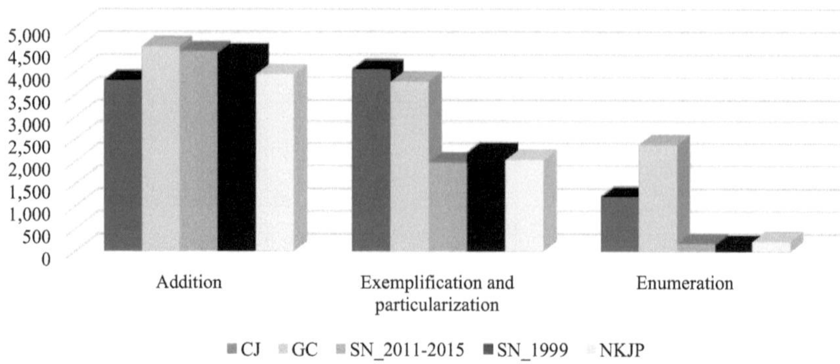


**Figure 6.19.** *Distribution of addition, enumeration and exemplification and particularization adverbials*

with], and *np.* [e.g.-ABBRV], which indicates that lawyer-linguists prefer non-abbreviated forms. This shows that CJEU judges are in greater need of providing clarification in their argumentation than SN judges. Post-accession SN judgments contain fewer tokens than the pre-accession corpus, which means that adverbials belonging to this group are not typical of non-translated judicial language.

Enumeration adverbials are the least frequent group across the corpora. Like the second group, they are also overrepresented in the Eurolect relative to both non-translated judgments and general Polish (NKJP). All five types of adverbials from this category are overrepresented in CJEU judgments. SN judges make even less use of enumerative adverbials than general Polish (NKJP).

Overall, the data show (see Figure 6.19) that only the reliance on exemplifying and particularizing together with enumerative adverbials may be identified as a feature typical of translated judgments. Additive adverbials are not such a feature, because they are underrepresented in CJ judgments.

In the case of non-translated SN judgments, the situation is reversed – only the use of additive adverbials constitutes a feature, while the adverbials in the remaining categories do not.

**Stance**

Epistemic modality serves as a means of stating judgments concerning the factual status of propositions as regards certainty, possibility or necessity (Palmer 2001; Koźbiał 2019: 43). Owing to the nature of judicial argumentation, they are very important in the language of judgments (see Table 6.43). Epistemic modality is to be differentiated from deontic modality, which is used to communicate rights, obligations and permission (Palmer 2001: 7–10; cf. Biel 2014a: 158–169). The epistemic adverbials presented here include evidential markers indicating the source of knowledge or evidence, which are perceived as a sub-class of epistemic modality (Koźbiał 2019: 44). Epistemic stance markers: (1) express the courts' attitude or stance towards the validity of the propositions as regards the degree of possibility, necessity, or certainty while relying on evidence, reasoning or beliefs or (2) identify the source of knowledge based on which the court forms a proposition (cf. Bralczyk 1978; Palmer 1979; Danielewiczowa 2002). The high salience of verbal and adverbial epistemic markers in English- and Polish-language CJ judgments and non-translated SN judgments has been reported in my earlier paper (Koźbiał 2019). In this paper, I proposed a model for categorizing epistemic markers according to their high, medium or low value (certainty-uncertainty/necessity-lack of necessity/possibility-lack of possibility continuum) and perspective (reported vs non-reported perspective), and established that the expression of epistemic modality is indispensable to judicial justification and reasoning, both across legal systems and languages (Koźbiał 2019: 65).[124] Stance adverbials are studied here, because three of them appeared in the keyword lists – *słusznie* [CJEU: #360], *trafnie* [SN: #138], and *niewątpliwie* [SN: #254]. The present analysis focuses solely on the certainty-uncertainty continuum.

Stance adverbials are the most frequent in GC judgments; CJ judgments contain about 32 % fewer tokens of the types categorized conveying a high, medium and low degree of certainty, possibility or necessity, which indicates a considerable level of internal variation in the Eurolect. Consequently, GC judgments have about 20 % more tokens than post-accession SN judgments, while CJ judgments have about 18 % fewer tokens. Post-accession SN judgments contain about 14 % fewer tokens than pre-accession judgments. Overall, there are more occurrences of stance adverbials in general Polish (NKJP) than in any of the corpora of judgments. This may suggest that stance adverbials are not a characteristic feature of judicial language; however, that is not the case, as many high-value types are very salient, e.g. *rzeczywiście* [admittedly/indeed], *słusznie* [reasonably], *w rzeczywistości* [in reality/in fact], *zasadniczo* [essentially] in CJEU judgments, or *trafnie* [pertinently], *wprawdzie* [admittedly/indeed], *niewątpliwie* [undoubtedly/surely], *w istocie* [in essence/essentially] in SN judgments. Medium-level types are not particularly salient, although the type *chyba* [maybe] occurs quite frequently in GC and SN judgments; these are very frequent in general Polish (NKJP), especially the informal *chyba* [maybe]. Adverbials classified as conveying a low level of certainty are fairly infrequent; only two types occur more than 5 times pmw, *jakoby* [allegedly] and *rzekomo* [allegedly].

Figure 6.20 better illustrates the distribution of stance adverbials in the corpora. It shows that the preponderance of adverbials can be classified as high value. While conducting the analysis, I examined the context of occurrence (concordances) of every type of adverbial, in order to provide a reliable categorization. However, this

124 More information on the nature of exponents of epistemic modality in judicial language can be found in, for instance, Cheng and Cheng (2014) or Strębska-Liszewska (2017).

**Table 6.43.** *Distribution of adverbials expressing stance*

| | Translated EU case law | | | | | Non-translated PL case law | | | General Polish |
|---|---|---|---|---|---|---|---|---|---|
| | CJ | CJ vs GC (%DIFF) | CJ vs SN_2011–2015 (%DIFF) | GC | GC vs SN_2011–2015 (%DIFF) | SN_2011–2015 | SN_2011–2015 vs SN_1999 (%DIFF) | SN_1999 | NKJP |
| **High value** | | | | | | | | | |
| *trafnie* [pertinently] | 5 | −27 % | −98 % | 6 | −97 % | 253 | −18 % | 309 | 6 |
| *wprawdzie* [admittedly/indeed] | 62 | −30 % | −69 % | 88 | −55 % | 197 | −6 % | 210 | 76 |
| *niewątpliwie* [undoubtedly/surely] | 13 | −56 % | −92 % | 29 | −83 % | 171 | +128 % | 75 | 45 |
| *w istocie* [in essence/essentially] | 211 | −18 % | +38 % | 256 | +68 % | 153 | −43 % | 266 | 27 |
| *zasadnie* [reasonably] | 15 | −47 % | −87 % | 28 | −75 % | 112 | +26 % | 89 | 1 |
| *oczywiście* [clearly/obviously] | 51 | −27 % | −51 % | 70 | −33 % | 104 | −40 % | 172 | 360 |
| *rzeczywiście* [admittedly/indeed] | 146 | −21 % | +92 % | 186 | +145 % | 76 | +32 % | 57 | 150 |
| *faktycznie* [in fact/indeed] | 75 | −15 % | +13 % | 88 | +32 % | 66 | −4 % | 69 | 46 |
| *w zasadzie* [in principle] | 20 | −20 % | −69 % | 25 | −61 % | 64 | −11 % | 71 | 43 |
| *słusznie* [reasonably] | 140 | −54 % | +133 % | 301 | +402 % | 60 | −47 % | 113 | 28 |
| *istotnie* [indeed] | 11 | −66 % | −73 % | 32 | −20 % | 40 | −37 % | 63 | 24 |
| *w rzeczywistości* [in reality/in fact] | 101 | −9 % | +251 % | 111 | +285 % | 29 | −3 % | 30 | 30 |
| *bezzasadnie* [unjustifiably] | 2 | −26 % | −91 % | 3 | −88 % | 24 | −1 % | 24 | 0 |
| *zasadniczo* [essentially] | 314 | +5 % | +1351 % | 298 | +1277 % | 22 | −1 % | 22 | 11 |
| *z pewnością* [with certainty] | 16 | −37 % | −18 % | 25 | +31 % | 19 | +61 % | 12 | 74 |
| *właściwie* [in fact/actually] | 17 | −36 % | −6 % | 27 | +48 % | 18 | −38 % | 30 | 140 |
| *na pewno* [for certain] | 1 | −65 % | −88 % | 4 | −66 % | 12 | +57 % | 8 | 215 |
| *zapewne* [probably] | 2 | −4 % | −81 % | 2 | −80 % | 11 | −29 % | 16 | 104 |
| *generalnie* [generally] | 7 | −56 % | −33 % | 16 | +51 % | 11 | +33 % | 8 | 3 |

| | | | | | | | | | |
|---|---|---|---|---|---|---|---|---|---|
| *niezasadnie* [unjustifiably] | 0 | −100 % | −100 % | 1 | −93 % | 10 | +67 % | 6 | 0 |
| *bez wątpienia* [without question] | 9 | −23 % | −4 % | 12 | +24 % | 10 | +147 % | 4 | 16 |
| *w żadnym razie* [in no case] | 16 | −51 % | +134 % | 32 | +374 % | 7 | −66 % | 20 | 3 |
| *rzecz jasna* [of course/needless to say] | 0 | --- | −100 % | 0 | −100 % | 6 | 51 % | 4 | 17 |
| *z całą pewnością* [with all certainty] | 2 | −59 % | −60 % | 6 | −2 % | 6 | --- | 0 | 14 |
| *ewidentnie* [manifestly] | 15 | −10 % | +183 % | 17 | +215 % | 5 | −67 % | 16 | 4 |
| *de facto* [de facto] | 11 | −24 % | +120 % | 15 | +190 % | 5 | −35 % | 8 | 10 |
| *najprawdopodobniej* [most likely/ probably] | 2 | −62 % | +31 % | 5 | +248 % | 1 | −63 % | 4 | 37 |
| *bezsprzecznie* [indisputably] | 3 | −65 % | +170 % | 8 | +678 % | 1 | −48 % | 2 | 2 |
| **TOTAL** | **1,267** | **−25 %** | **−15 %** | **1,691** | **+13 %** | **1,493** | **−13 %** | **1,708** | **1,486** |
| **Medium value** | | | | | | | | | |
| *chyba* [maybe] | 0 | −100 % | −100 % | 66 | −5 % | 69 | +30 % | 54 | 379 |
| *zapewne* [probably] | 2 | −4 % | −81 % | 2 | −80 % | 11 | −29 % | 16 | 104 |
| *niejako* [so to speak] | 0 | −100 % | −100 % | 0 | −98 % | 10 | −70 % | 32 | 26 |
| *prawdopodobnie* [probably] | 13 | −55 % | +158 % | 29 | +471 % | 5 | −14 % | 6 | 97 |
| *być może* [maybe] | 2 | −74 % | −59 % | 7 | +56 % | 5 | −21 % | 6 | 147 |
| *najwyraźniej* [evidently] | 5 | −7 % | +355 % | 6 | +392 % | 1 | --- | 0 | 23 |
| *podobno* [apparently] | 3 | −73 % | --- | 9 | --- | 0 | --- | 0 | 65 |
| **TOTAL** | **25** | **−79 %** | **−75 %** | **119** | **+18 %** | **101** | **−11 %** | **114** | **841** |
| **Low value** | | | | | | | | | |
| *jakoby* [allegedly] | 24 | −73 % | −33 % | 91 | +149 % | 36 | −39 % | 59 | 17 |
| *rzekomo* [allegedly] | 19 | −65 % | +170 % | 54 | +676 % | 7 | −11 % | 8 | 14 |
| **TOTAL** | **46** | **−69 %** | **+6 %** | **149** | **+243 %** | **43** | **−41 %** | **73** | **59** |
| **GRAND TOTAL** | **1,338** | **−32 %** | **−18 %** | **1,959** | **+20 %** | **1,637** | **−14 %** | **1,895** | **2,386** |

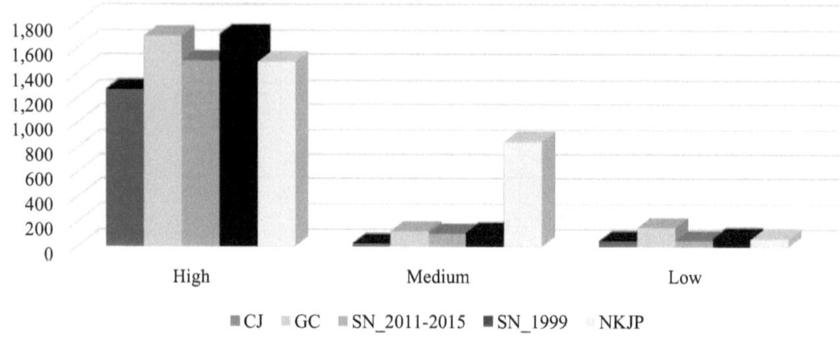


**Figure 6.20.** *Distribution of adverbials expressing stance*

procedure remains subjective to a certain degree, as the boundaries between the three categories are fuzzy, forming rather a continuum.

Medium- and low-level stance adverbials are rare in judicial language. The high salience of high-level adverbials certainly contributes to a higher level of authoritativeness of judicial decisions (cf. Koźbiał 2019: 65).

**Contrast and exclusion**

The third category of adverbials is composed of contrast and exclusion adverbials, namely exclusion and contrast, which are presented in Table 6.44 (cf. Section 6.3.4.11 on inclusive/exclusive compound and secondary prepositions).

The first category contains adverbials expressing contrast. The prototypical contrastive adverbials include *jednak* [however] and *jednakże* [however with an emphatic particle –*że*]. The difference between the two variants consists of their emphatic strength, with *jednakże* being stronger (and more formal) due to the particle –*że* (SJPD dictionary). This adverbial is underrepresented in translation; however, the number of occurrences of *jednakże* in CJ and GC judgments is higher than in non–translated judgments. What is also worth noting is that *jednakże* is used mostly in sentence-initial position in the Eurolect, which is less common in non-translated judgments. Lawyer-linguists follow the usage pattern in non-translated judgments and general Polish (NKJP), in that they rely more on the less emphatic *jednak* [however]. Other contrastive adverbials include: *mimo to/tego* [despite this/that] and *niemniej jednak* [nevertheless]. These, however, are used infrequently. The overall distribution of contrastive adverbials shows that they are underrepresented in the Eurolect relative to post-accession judgments. The latter contain about 10 % more tokens than pre-accession judgments. The overall distribution of contrastive adverbials does not lead to the conclusion that their use is a characteristic feature of either the CJEU or SN judgments, as their distribution is higher in general Polish (NKJP).

**Table 6.44.** *Distribution of adverbials expressing contrast and exclusion*

| | Translated EU case law | | | | | Non-translated PL case law | | | General Polish |
|---|---|---|---|---|---|---|---|---|---|
| | **CJ** | **CJ vs GC (%DIFF)** | **CJ vs SN_2011–2015 (%DIFF)** | **GC** | **GC vs SN_2011–2015 (%DIFF)** | **SN_2011–2015** | **SN_2011–2015 vs SN_1999 (%DIFF)** | **SN_1999** | **NKJP** |
| **I. Contrast** | | | | | | | | | |
| *jednak* [however] | 589 | −13 % | −46 % | 677 | −37 % | 1,081 | +18 % | 914 | 1,378 |
| *. *Jednak* (fronted) | 20 | −47 % | −30 % | 37 | +33 % | 28 | +1303 % | 2 | N/A |
| *jednakże* [however with an emphatic particle –*że*] | 197 | +16 % | +21 % | 169 | +4 % | 163 | −18 % | 198 | 39 |
| *. *Jednakże* (fronted) | 110 | −18 % | +64 % | 134 | +99 % | 67 | −21 % | 85 | N/A |
| *mimo to/tego* [despite this/that] | 10 | −17 % | −64 % | 12 | −56 % | 26 | −22 % | 34 | 53 |
| *niemniej jednak* [nevertheless] | 96 | −3 % | +582 % | 99 | +605 % | 14 | −45 % | 26 | 11 |
| **TOTAL** | **1,021** | **−9 %** | **−26 %** | **1,128** | **−18 %** | **1,379** | **+10 %** | **1,258** | **1,482** |
| **II. Exclusion** | | | | | | | | | |
| *z pominięciem* [with the exclusion of] | 10 | +101 % | −76 % | 5 | −88 % | 42 | +31 % | 32 | 3 |
| *z wyjątkiem* [except for] | 109 | +13 % | +347 % | 96 | +294 % | 24 | −5 % | 26 | 27 |
| *pomijając* [excluding] | 5 | −51 % | −72 % | 11 | −43 % | 19 | −56 % | 44 | 7 |
| *za wyjątkiem* [except for (incorrect)] | 1 | +92 % | −93 % | 0 | −96 % | 11 | --- | 0 | 2 |
| **TOTAL** | **125** | **+11 %** | **+30 %** | **112** | **+16 %** | **97** | **−4 %** | **101** | **39** |
| **GRAND TOTAL** | **1,268** | **−7 %** | **−15 %** | **1,365** | **−8 %** | **1,490** | **+8 %** | **1,381** | **1,671** |

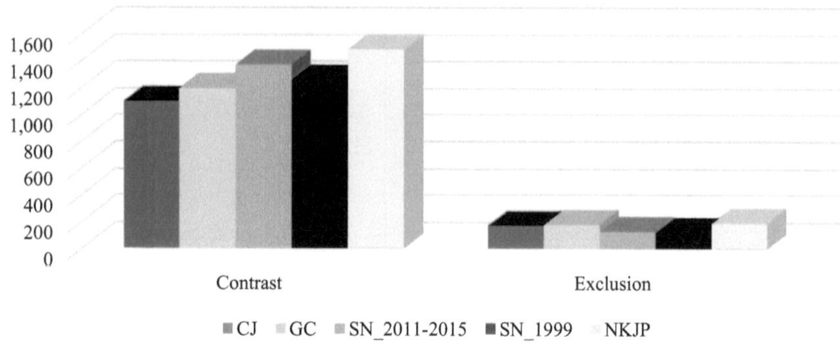


**Figure 6.21.** *Distribution of contrast and exclusion adverbials*

Adverbials expressing exclusion are used very rarely, as shown by their equally low distribution across all the corpora. In this category, there are two similar types – *z wyjątkiem* [except for] and *za wyjątkiem* [except for] – the latter is an incorrect form of the former. It is not surprising that the incorrect form is almost non-existent in translated CJEU judgments. Unexpectedly, however, it occurs, albeit rarely, in non-translated judgments, which, in theory, should act as a linguistic model for translators of similar texts into Polish. This shows that lawyer-linguists do not carelessly mimic non-translated Polish, by avoiding use of incorrect forms. The two remaining types are overrepresented in non-translated Polish – *z pominięciem* [with the exclusion of] and *pomijając* [excluding]. In general, adverbials marking exclusion are not a characteristic feature of judicial language, because it employs them less frequently than general Polish (NKJP) (see Figure 6.21).

Figure 6.21 shows that neither adverbials expressing contrast, nor adverbials expressing exclusion are a characteristic feature of judicial language.

## 6.8.2 Participles

### Adjectival participles

Adjectival participles in Polish are typically divided into active (*-ący)* and passive (*-ny/-ty*[125]) (Bąk 1984: 181; Bańko 2007: 90; Nagórko 2010: 139). They are intermediate forms between verbs and adjectives (Czachor 2019: 219). Both types were identified as keywords in the corpora of judgments. The distributional analysis of active and passive adjectival participles is narrowed down only to the keywords

125 Passive adverbial participles may also carry the suffix *-ty*; however, they are not investigated here due to the fact that no such participles were identified as keywords.

due to the high total number of different such participles across the corpora. Furthermore, it is not technically feasible to automatically find all occurrences of passive adjectival participles with the WS Concord command **ny/*na/*ne*, etc., as the queries generate overly-long lists of concordances containing a large number of adjectives; therefore, the quantitative data contain no information as regards the total number of corresponding tokens and types.

CJEU judgments rely heavily on the following active adjectival participles: *działających* [#94], *dotyczący* [#329], *dotyczącym* [#389], *mających* [#471], *pochodzących* [#499]. In the SN corpus, there is only one keyword: *obowiązującym* [#384] (see Table 6.45).

The distribution of active adjectival participles is the highest in the Eurolect, with only minor internal variation between the corpora. The CJ and GC corpora contain about 155 % and 160 % more tokens than the post-accession SN corpus. The latter, on the other hand, contains about 39 % more tokens than the pre-accession corpus. Overall, their distribution is higher in both the Eurolect and in non-translated Polish than in general Polish (NKJP), which indicates that their usage is a typical feature of judicial language.

The keyword lists contain a number of passive adjectival participles. These are – CJEU: *zatytułowany* [#173], *rozpatrywanych* [#246], *utrwalonym* [#281], *zwanym* [#405], *zwany* [#457], SN: zaskarżony [#96] (see Table 6.46).

Passive adjectival participles are used to transform active constructions into passive ones in the process of passivization (Bańko 2007: 91), which may additionally increase the degree of depersonalization and impersonality (cf. Section 6.6). Like active adjectival participles, CJEU judgments exhibit an overrepresentation of all identified passive adjectival participles. The only participle with similar distribution in CJ and post-accession judgments is *zaskarżony* [contested]; however, it is highly overrepresented in GC judgments relative to non-translations. The reliance on passive adjectival participles may also be perceived as typical of judicial language, since their usage in general Polish (NKJP) is fairly low.

The overall distribution of active and passive adjectival participles confirms that their usage is a characteristic feature of both EU and national judgments, although this applies particularly to CJEU judgments (see Figure 6.22).

The reliance on adjectival participles is perceived as a typical linguistic component of judicial language owing to the low distribution of respective types of participles in general Polish (NKJP).

**Adverbial participles**

Adverbial participles are divided into present (*-ąc*) and perfective (*-wszy* and *-łszy*) (Bąk 1984: 181–182; Bańko 2007: 90, 168–169). When it comes to present adverbial participles, two are overrepresented in non-translated Polish judgments relative to translations – *podzielając* [#388] and *zarzucając* [#396]. The role of present adverbial participles is to express actions happening simultaneously with the ones specified in the main clause. The analysis of adverbial participles is not limited to the keywords, because it is more feasible to search the corpora for all words with only

**Table 6.45.** *Distribution of active adjectival participles identified as keywords*

| | Translated EU case law | | | | | Non-translated PL case law | | | General Polish |
|---|---|---|---|---|---|---|---|---|---|
| | **CJ** | **CJ vs GC (%DIFF)** | **CJ vs SN_2011–2015 (%DIFF)** | **GC** | **GC vs SN_2011–2015 (%DIFF)** | **SN_2011–2015** | **SN_2011–2015 vs SN_1999 (%DIFF)** | **SN_1999** | **NKJP** |
| Tokens (all – **ący/ąc ego/ąca/ącej...*) | 18,837 | −83 % | −81 % | 109,283 | +12 % | 97,338 | 1275 % | 7,081 | N/A |
| *dotyczący* [concerning] | 2,277 | −32 % | +142 % | 3,362 | +257 % | 942 | +61 % | 587 | 307 |
| *obowiązujący* [binding] | 247 | +134 % | −42 % | 106 | −75 % | 424 | +81 % | 234 | 76 |
| *mający* [having] | 1,077 | +42 % | +233 % | 758 | +135 % | 323 | −17 % | 390 | 112 |
| *działający* [acting] | 817 | +248 % | +1021 % | 235 | +222 % | 73 | +41 % | 52 | 73 |
| *pochodzący* [coming (from)] | 177 | −20 % | +376 % | 222 | +496 % | 37 | +17 % | 32 | 44 |
| **TOTAL** | **4,595** | **−2 %** | **+155 %** | **4,683** | **+160 %** | **1,799** | **+39 %** | **1,294** | **613** |

**Table 6.46.** *Distribution of passive adjectival participles identified as keywords*

| | **Translated EU case law** | | | | | **Non-translated PL case law** | | | **General Polish** |
|---|---|---|---|---|---|---|---|---|---|
| | **CJ** | **CJ vs GC (%DIFF)** | **CJ vs SN_2011–2015 (%DIFF)** | **GC** | **GC vs SN_2011–2015 (%DIFF)** | **SN_2011–2015** | **SN_2011–2015 vs SN_1999 (%DIFF)** | **SN_1999** | **NKJP** |
| *zaskarżony* [contested] | 1,220 | −71 % | +15 % | 4,208 | +298 % | 1,058 | −36 % | 1,645 | 3 |
| *utrwalony* [solidified] | 259 | −10 % | +368 % | 289 | +422 % | 55 | −41 % | 93 | 5 |
| *rozpatrywany* [examined] | 534 | −10 % | +945 % | 596 | +1068 % | 51 | +134 % | 22 | 25 |
| *zwany* [called] | 948 | +41 % | +4528 % | 672 | +3179 % | 20 | +107 % | 10 | 111 |
| *zatytułowany* [entitled] | 417 | +246 % | +2810 % | 120 | +740 % | 14 | +141 % | 6 | 12 |
| **TOTAL** | **3,378** | **−43 %** | **+182 %** | **5,885** | **+391 %** | **1,199** | **−32 %** | **1,776** | **155** |

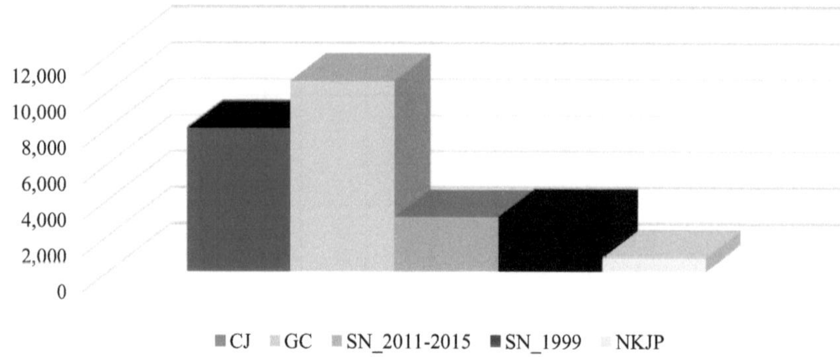


**Figure 6.22.** *Total distribution of active and passive adjectival participles*

one suffix (*-ąc*). Table 6.47 presents data on the distribution of present adverbial participles in the corpora of EU, SN judgments and general Polish (NKJP).[126]

The data show that the usage of present adverbial participles may be viewed as typical of both CJEU and SN judgments, as their distribution in general Polish (NKJP) is quite low. Nevertheless, there are noticeable differences in the distribution of individual types between the Eurolect and SN judgments, such as the marked overrepresentation of the referential participles *uwzględniając* [having regard to] and *biorąc (pod uwagę)* [taking (into consideration)] in the Eurolect. The distribution of individual types in SN judgments is more even than in CJEU judgments. Taking into consideration the collocates of the most frequent types in CJ and GC judgments, the main function of present adverbial participles is that of providing a reference, mainly to legal provisions and documents, but also to various facts of the cases heard by the courts.

The category of perfective (*-wszy* and *-łszy*) adverbial participles (Bańko 2007: 90) is investigated owing to the participle *rozważywszy* [#368], which is a keyword in CJEU judgments. The use of perfective adverbial participles, which refer to anterior actions, is on the decline in general Polish (NKJP) (Nagórko 2010: 32; Czachor 2019: 240). Table 6.48 presents quantitative data on their distribution in the corpora of judgments and general Polish (NKJP).

The data confirm that the usage of perfective adverbial participles in non-translated Polish is falling steadily, as shown by their distribution in the post-accession SN corpus relative to its pre-accession counterpart. However, they are still quite frequently used in translated CJEU judgments, which exhibit considerable overrepresentation compared to post-accession SN judgments. In general,

126 The PELCRA search engine does not enable running queries such as "*ąc."

**Table 6.47.** *Distribution of present adverbial participles*

| | Translated EU case law | | | | | Non-translated PL case law | | | General Polish |
|---|---|---|---|---|---|---|---|---|---|
| | CJ | CJ vs GC (%DIFF) | CJ vs SN_2011–2015 (%DIFF) | GC | GC vs SN_2011–2015 (%DIFF) | SN_2011–2015 | SN_2011–2015 vs SN_1999 (%DIFF) | SN_1999 | NKJP |
| **Tokens (all – *ąc)** | **2,026** | **−1 %** | **−33 %** | **2,056** | **−32 %** | **3,036** | **−19 %** | **3,730** | **N/A** |
| **Types (at least 5 occurrences)** | **46** | **−8 %** | **+4 %** | **50** | **+13 %** | **44** | **−75 %** | **178** | **N/A** |
| **Tokens (types with at least 5 occurrences)** | **1,901** | **−2 %** | **−35 %** | **1,930** | **−34 %** | **2,907** | **−18 %** | **3,535** | **N/A** |
| *wskazując* [indicating] | 25 | −43 % | −81 % | 45 | −66 % | 131 | −22 % | 168 | 12 |
| *mając* [having] | 110 | −27 % | −7 % | 151 | +29 % | 118 | −6 % | 125 | 61 |
| *uwzględniając* [having regard to] | 270 | +71 % | +137 % | 157 | +38 % | 114 | +4 % | 109 | 13 |
| *powołując (się)* [quoting] | 46 | −6 % | −58 % | 50 | −56 % | 112 | −52 % | 232 | 10 |
| *uznając* [allowing for] | 106 | +31 % | −1 % | 81 | −24 % | 107 | −38 % | 172 | 9 |
| *odnosząc (się)* [relating to] | 24 | −45 % | −75 % | 44 | −56 % | 98 | +60 % | 61 | 5 |
| *przyjmując* [assuming] | 37 | −26 % | −53 % | 50 | −37 % | 80 | −28 % | 111 | 10 |
| *dokonując* [performing] | 35 | +34 % | −54 % | 26 | −66 % | 76 | −23 % | 99 | 5 |
| *biorąc* [taking] | 100 | −17 % | +51 % | 122 | +83 % | 67 | +34 % | 50 | 43 |

(*continued on next page*)

**Table 6.47.** *Continued*

| | Translated EU case law | | | | | Non-translated PL case law | | | General Polish |
|---|---|---|---|---|---|---|---|---|---|
| | CJ | CJ vs GC (%DIFF) | CJ vs SN_2011–2015 (%DIFF) | GC | GC vs SN_2011–2015 (%DIFF) | SN_2011–2015 | SN_2011–2015 vs SN_1999 (%DIFF) | SN_1999 | NKJP |
| *zarzucając* [alleging] | 1 | +68 % | −98 % | 1 | −99 % | 64 | −61 % | 163 | 2 |
| *podzielając* [sharing] | 1 | +92 % | −99 % | 0 | −99 % | 61 | −26 % | 83 | 1 |
| *oddalając* [dismissing] | 13 | +149 % | −77 % | 5 | −91 % | 57 | −49 % | 113 | 1 |
| *oceniając* [assessing] | 7 | −25 % | −88 % | 9 | −85 % | 57 | +7 % | 54 | 5 |
| *stwierdzając* [ascertaining] | 47 | −2 % | −9 % | 48 | −6 % | 51 | 0 % | 52 | 4 |
| *rozpoznając* [hearing (the case)] | 1 | 60 % | −98 % | 1 | −99 % | 46 | −70 % | 157 | 1 |
| *opierając (się)* [basing on] | 43 | −12 % | +17 % | 49 | +33 % | 37 | −40 % | 61 | 7 |
| *twierdząc* [claiming] | 23 | −24 % | −1 % | 30 | +30 % | 23 | −68 % | 73 | 11 |
| *orzekając* [adjudicating] | 53 | +1045 % | +187 % | 5 | −75 % | 19 | −48 % | 36 | 1 |
| **TOTAL (listed -*ąc* participles)** | **943** | **+8 %** | **−28 %** | **873** | **−34 %** | **1,317** | **−31 %** | **1,918** | **200** |
| **Collocates of top participles** | | | | | | | | | |
| *powołując się na* [referring to] | 37 | −7 % | −59 % | 40 | −56 % | 91 | −53 % | 194 | 8 |
| *biorąc pod uwagę* [taking into consideration] | 82 | −14 % | +97 % | 95 | +129 % | 42 | −25 % | 55 | 22 |

| | | | | | | | | | |
|---|---|---|---|---|---|---|---|---|---|
| *mając na uwadze* [taking into consideration] | 66 | −27 % | +68 % | 91 | +131 % | 39 | −10 % | 44 | 6 |
| *mając na względzie* [taking into account] | 24 | −36 % | −1 % | 38 | +55 % | 24 | −12 % | 28 | 3 |
| *uwzględniając pisemny etap postępowania* [having regard to the written stage of the proceedings] | 114 | +370 % | --- | 24 | --- | 0 | --- | 0 | 0 |
| *uwzględniając procedurę pisemną* [having regard to the written procedure] | 72 | +89 % | --- | 38 | --- | 0 | --- | 0 | 0 |

**Table 6.48.** *Distribution of perfective adverbial participles*

| | Translated EU case law | | | | | Non-translated PL case law | | | General Polish |
|---|---|---|---|---|---|---|---|---|---|
| | **CJ** | **CJ vs GC (%DIFF)** | **CJ vs SN_2011–2015 (%DIFF)** | **GC** | **GC vs SN_2011–2015 (%DIFF)** | **SN_2011–2015** | **SN_2011–2015 vs SN_1999 (%DIFF)** | **SN_1999** | **NKJP** |
| **Tokens (all –**wszy/-łszy*)** | **415** | **+41 %** | **+451 %** | **294** | **+290 %** | **75** | **–41 %** | **127** | **N/A** |
| **Tokens (types with at least 5 occurrences)** | **394** | **–42 %** | **+470 %** | **679** | **+884 %** | **69** | **–21 %** | **87** | **N/A** |
| **Types (at least 5 occurrences)** | **4** | **+22 %** | **+592 %** | **3** | **+467 %** | **1** | **–85 %** | **4** | **N/A** |
| *zważywszy* [considering–PFV] | 91 | –39 % | +120 % | 149 | +260 % | 41 | –37 % | 65 | 9 |
| *uwzględniwszy* [allowing for–PFV] | 3 | –68 % | +82 % | 10 | +467 % | 2 | –56 % | 4 | 0 |
| *stwierdziwszy* [ascertaining–PFV] | 13 | +49 % | +1028 % | 9 | +657 % | 1 | –80 % | 6 | 1 |
| *uznawszy* [allowing for–PFV] | 18 | +247 % | +11984 % | 5 | +3381 % | 0 | --- | 0 | 0 |
| *rozważywszy* [considering–PFV] | 138 | +62145 % | --- | 0 | --- | 0 | --- | 0 | 0 |
| *podjąwszy* [taking up–PFV] | 62 | +27800 % | --- | 0 | --- | 0 | --- | 0 | 0 |
| *przypomniawszy* [reminding–PFV] | 5 | +84 % | --- | 3 | --- | 0 | --- | 0 | 1 |
| **TOTAL** | **330** | **+87 %** | **+641 %** | **176** | **+296 %** | **44** | **–41 %** | **75** | **11** |

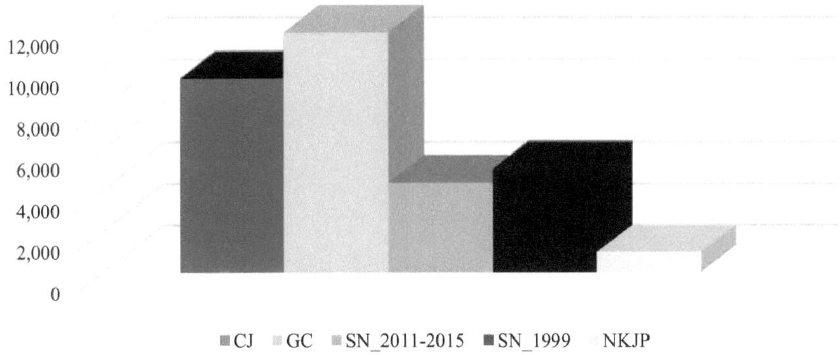


**Figure 6.23.** *Total distribution of present and perfective adverbial participles (based on the distribution of listed participles)*

the usage of perfective adverbial participles is a characteristic feature of judicial language, in CJEU judgments in particular.

Figure 6.23 shows the distribution of all types of participles discussed in this Section.

The data show that the usage of participles is a very salient feature of translated judicial language. The substantial degree of divergences between the CJEU and SN corpora translates into a low degree of textual fit in the functional category of participles.

# Part II.C. Micro level: Pillar II – Formulaicity

# Chapter 7. Lexical bundles

The aim of this chapter is to investigate the formulaic profile of EU and national judgments using lexical bundles, which are continuous sequences of two or more co-occurring words with no free slots (Granger and Paquot 2008), also known as recurrent lexical patterns, multi-word patterns, n-grams, or contiguous recurrent word combinations (cf. Wray and Perkins 2000; Biber *et al.* 2004; Schmitt 2004; Wray 2005, 2009; Grabowski 2014). The analysis adopts a frequency-based (distributional) approach to phraseology (Nesselhauf 2004, 2005: 12–18; Granger and Paquot 2008; Paquot and Granger 2012; Gablasova *et al.* 2017: 158), whose core comprises quantitative data on the distribution of lexical patterns which significantly contribute to the overall formulaicity of the genre[127] (see Section 7.1). The chapter also aims to present a functional classification of lexical bundles in EU and Polish judicial discourse. It is hypothesized that translated EU judgments, that is their Polish language versions, exhibit a dissimilar formulaic profile when compared to non-translated national judgments due to the effects that the translation process has on translations and the influence of other context-related phenomena (cf. Chapter 5). The chapter also aims to verify the findings presented by other researchers who have studied recurrent patterns of language use on other translated EU genres (cf. Jablonkai 2010; Biel 2017c, 2018; Biel *et al.* 2018b, 2019). Section 7.2 provides information on studies related to the present analysis. Section 7.3 discusses the design of the corpora and methodology used in the analysis, as well as justifying the criteria chosen for the extraction of lexical bundles (frequency/distribution and dispersion thresholds). Sections 7.4 and 7.5 present quantitative data on the overall distribution of 2–8-grams and thematic classification of lexical bundles into content and non-content bundles, which makes it possible to better understand the thematic range and to compare the corpora and data concerning the overlap of 3- and 4-grams in the translation and non-translation corpora. Section 7.6 steps away from the quantitative perspective by providing a functional classification of 3- and 4-word bundles into referential, discourse-organizing and stance bundles (including the individual sub-categories), whereas Section 7.7 presents concluding remarks and implications for future studies.

127 The concept of formulaicity is used here with reference to the frequent use of formulaic sequences of words, whose choice is dictated by a particular genre (cf. Wray 2005).

## 7.1. Lexical bundles in the frequency-based (distributional) approach to phraseology

Recurrent word combinations have served as a tool for conducting linguistic research for more than 20 years. Altenberg's studies (1993, 1998) were the first in which the author adopted a corpus-driven methodology to examine the phraseology of spoken English on the basis of recurrent word combinations (cf. Kopaczyk 2012a: 83; Cortes 2015), that is repetitive, continuous strings of words occurring more than once in identical form and automatically extracted from a corpus.[128] Biber *et al.* (1999: 988–1024) replicated Altenberg's methodology while working on his book *Longman Grammar of Spoken and Written English*, in order to study recurrent word combinations in spoken and written English as exemplified by conversation and academic prose corpora. It is very likely that a large number of studies on lexical bundles conducted in the last two decades would not have been conducted in the first place had it not been for their work. Biber *et al.* (1999: 988–1024) introduced the concept of lexical bundles, emphasizing the important distinction whereby idioms are invariable expressions with meanings not derivable from the individual constituent words, whereas lexical bundles are sequences of words commonly co-occurring in a given register which are *not salient* to language users and are not necessarily meaningful or structurally complete (Biber *et al.* 1999: 989–990; Biber and Barbieri 2007: 264). Meaning to make their investigation more manageable, Biber *et al.* (1999: 990) focused on recurring sequences of three or more words such as *it is possible, is based on, as well as*, etc. They (Biber *et al.* 1999: 990) also observed that shorter lexical bundles are incorporated into longer bundles, e.g. *should be noted* is part of *it should be noted that.* Examples of 3–4–word lexical bundles from EU case law include: *Court has held, the fact that the, on the ground that.* Later on, research methodology involving lexical bundles became an indispensable tool for corpus linguists and was fine-tuned by, among others, Biber *et al.* (2004), Biber and Barbieri (2007) and Biber (2006, 2009a,b). Since lexical bundles are combinations of words recurring in various registers, it is to be expected that they form important building blocks of specialist discourse varieties, such as legal (judicial) discourse, thus lending themselves perfectly to the analysis of phraseological profiles of law-related genres, as illustrated by studies conducted by, among others, Goźdź-Roszkowski (2006, 2011), Jablonkai (2009, 2010), Breeze (2013), Biel (2017c), and Biel *et al.* (2018b, 2019).

Regarded as an important methodological concept which enables a corpus-driven approach to the empirical study of formulaic language (Lewandowska-Tomaszczyk 2005: 133; Biber 2009a: 281), lexical bundles are identified not only on the basis of co-occurrence of contiguous words but also their high-frequency

---

128 Lexical bundles are extracted from corpora with dedicated software, e.g. Wordsmith Tools (WS) (Scott 2016), AntConc (Anthony 2014) or Sketchengine (Kilgariff *et al.* 2014).

recurrence (distribution). Therefore, frequency constitutes the main criterion which allows the identification and extraction of lexical bundles from genre-restricted corpora (Biber *et al.* 1999: 990; Biber and Barbieri 2007: 267). Researchers set frequency cut-off points (thresholds) mainly for practical reasons, such as limiting the number of extracted lexical bundles and omitting uninteresting or peculiar word combinations, thus making the empirical material more manageable (Biber *et al.* 1999: 990; Grabowski 2015b: 36). A widely utilized (conservative) frequency cut-off point (minimum recurrence in the corpus) is 40 occurrences per million words (pmw) (cf. Goźdź-Roszkowski 2006, 2011: 110; Biber and Barbieri 2007: 267). Although other thresholds, such as 20 occurrences pmw, are also used, their values are for the most part arbitrary (cf. Hyland 2008: 9). A normalized rate of bundle occurrence makes it possible to compare corpora of different sizes. The remaining key criteria used to select lexical bundles are bundle length (the number of words forming a bundle) and dispersion threshold (cf. Biber *et al.* 1999: 992–993; Biber and Barbieri 2007: 267–268).[129] The length-based criterion ensures that only bundles consisting of three or more words[130] are extracted from a corpus. The purpose of the dispersion threshold is to limit idiosyncratic occurrences of lexical bundles. According to this criterion, bundles must appear in multiple texts to be counted as a lexical bundle (Biber and Barbieri 2007: 268). In this case, researchers set various dispersion thresholds, such as a recurrent word combination, which must appear in at least 20 different texts (cf. Biber and Barbieri 2007: 26) or 5 different texts (cf. Biber *et al.* 1999: 992–993; Biber *et al.* 2003: 134; Biel 2017c: 16; Biel *et al.* 2018b, 2019) in order to be counted as a bundle. Dispersion thresholds of up to 10 % or 20 % allow for the extraction of even fewer bundles. Word combinations containing punctuation marks are typically not viewed as lexical bundles (Grabowski 2015b: 36).

So far, most of the studies on lexical bundles have been conducted on English, so it is difficult to assess what should be the threshold values for typologically different languages (cf. Gray and Biber 2015: 144). Grabowski (2014), Granger (2014) and Biel (2017: 16) explain that the criteria used to extract bundles from texts written in languages other than English should be modified with regard to typological and systemic differences (Grabowski 2015b: 60). This applies in particular to inflectional languages, including Polish. It seems that due to its many inflectional variants, a lower frequency threshold should be adopted for Polish. The length of

---

129 It should be noted that researchers studying various genres and registers often adopt varying values of the criteria to address specific research questions, which may hinder inter-generic comparisons (cf. Grabowski 2018a). Therefore, the choice of appropriate bundle length, as well as the distribution and dispersion threshold values, is crucial in ensuring at least a minimal degree of comparability with other studies.

130 Bundles consisting of three words are referred to as 3–grams, bundles consisting of four words are called 4–grams, and so on.

the examined clusters poses yet another hurdle. In the case of English, researchers focus predominantly on four-word sequences, which is dictated by practical rather than theoretical reasons, assuming that 4–grams have a more readily recognizable range of structures and discourse functions, as opposed to 3–grams, for instance (cf. Jablonkai 2010: 256; Goźdź-Roszkowski 2011: 110; Grabowski 2015b; Gray and Biber 2015: 136). When comparing clusters for the purposes of Translation Studies, it should be asked whether 4–grams indeed reflect the same level of formulaicity in different languages, and in particular, whether the English 4–grams correspond to 4–grams in Polish (Biel *et al.* 2018b), or whether they rather correspond to shorter word combinations in inflectional languages which code grammatical information morphologically through affixes, and in languages which do not mark (in)definiteness explicitly through articles, with Polish being one of such languages (Biel 2017c: 16). However, this issue remains outside the scope of the current study, as it aims to compare texts translated into Polish with non-translated Polish texts.

The categorization of lexical bundles may be conducted according to both (1) formal (bundle length, structure) and (2) functional (discourse functions) criteria. Formal criteria refer to the length (2–8–grams) as well as the grammatical structure of bundles, which varies, depending on whether a bundle contains nominal, verbal or prepositional phrases and clause fragments (cf. Jablonkai 2010; Goźdź-Roszkowski 2011; Biel 2017c). The most widely used taxonomy reflecting the structural characteristics of lexical bundles is that devised by Biber *et al.* (1999: 1001–1024). Their classification was later adopted by researchers studying different genres, including Goźdź-Roszkowski (2006, 2011: 113–117), who studied English legal texts. Currently, there is no exhaustive categorization of structural characteristics of lexical bundles extracted from either translated or non-translated texts in Polish. When it comes to the functional criterion, there are three main categories of lexical bundles which perform different discourse functions in respective genres: (1) stance, (2) discourse-organizing, and (3) reference bundles (cf. Biber and Barbieri 2007: 265; Hyland 2008: 13–19; Jablonkai 2010: 258; Goźdź-Roszkowski 2011: 117–143; Breeze 2013: 248). **Stance bundles** express personal feelings, value judgments, attitudes or assessments of certainty or probability that provide a frame for the interpretation of the following proposition (cf. Biber 2006: 139–142, Goźdź-Roszkowski 2011: 138–142). **Discourse-organizing bundles** (also known as text-oriented bundles, cf. Goźdź-Roszkowski 2011: 129–137) introduce topics and focus on them by introducing further clarification and elaboration (cf. Biber 2006: 142–145), whereas **reference bundles** identify entities, or single out their particular attributes (cf. Biber 2006: 145–146; cf. Goźdź-Roszkowski 2011: 119–129). These functions are usually identified using an inductive approach, which entails studying the context of occurrence of individual types of bundles, that is concordance lines, using suitable software tools (cf. Scott 2017). The process of assigning bundles to different functional groups is not straightforward, as many bundles serve multiple functions, e.g. *at the end of, in the middle of* (cf. Goźdź-Roszkowski 2011: 117–143). However, many are unifunctional and easily categorizable based on their discourse functions.

## 7.2. Related studies and research questions

Lexical bundles are widely used in corpus research. There are many and various fields of study concerning different genres in which lexical bundles are utilized to examine phraseology. Before I move on to review the existing influential research on lexical bundles in specialized discourse of relevance to the study of legal language, I would like to present some of the fields where lexical bundles are used extensively:

1. Development of corpus-based grammars of contemporary English (Biber *et al.* 1999),
2. Comparative analysis of spoken and written registers (Biber 1997, 2004; Biber *et al.* 2004; Biber and Barbieri 2007),
3. Identifying features characteristic of academic discourse (Cortes 2004, 2013; Pecorari 2009; Römer 2010; see e.g. Biber and Barbieri 2007; Hyland 2008 for a more detailed overview),
4. Identifying features characteristic of political discourse (Partington and Morley 2004),
5. Identifying features characteristic of English and Polish pharmaceutical discourse (Grabowski 2013, 2014, 2015a, 2015c, 2018c),
6. Extraction of lexical bundles for teaching and (machine) translation purposes (Biber *et al.* 1999; Tománková 2016; Grabowski 2018b),
7. Lexical bundles in on-line texts (Barbieri 2018; McVeigh 2018),
8. Historical and diachronic studies (Kopaczyk 2012a, 2012b; Lehto 2018),
9. Comparative analysis of legal genres and textual fit of translated texts to non-translated texts from the same genre (Jablonkai 2009, 2010; Goźdź-Roszkowski 2011; Breeze 2013; Lee 2013; Tománková 2016; Biel *et al.* 2018a,b, 2019).

Although English is the main language studied using lexical bundles, researchers also study various genres and registers in other languages using the same methodology, e.g. German (Krummes *et al.* 2011), French (Grabar and Lefer 2015), Spanish (Cortes 2008) or Korean (Lee 2013). The first studies examining the distribution and functions of lexical bundles in Polish texts concern mainly two specialized language varieties: pharmaceutical discourse (Grabowski 2014, 2018a, 2018b, 2018c) and EU legislative acts (Biel 2017c).

Throughout the last two decades, lexical bundles have been used to study mainly spoken and written varieties of English, most notably academic English (cf. Biber and Barbieri 2007). Nevertheless, recently there has also been a surge of interest in more specialized registers and genres, including legal and judicial discourse, which are of particular importance to the present study. The advent of Corpus Linguistics has entirely changed contemporary legal phraseology, resulting in an array of different approaches and perspectives (cf. Goźdź-Roszkowski and Pontrandolfo 2015: 131). The interest in phraseology has been sparked primarily by the application of corpus-linguistic methodology, specialized corpus tools and computerized text resources which allow empirical investigations into the formulaic nature of legal language. An edited volume by Goźdź-Roszkowski and Pontrandolfo (2017) presenting a comprehensive overview of the developments in the study of how phraseology is evidence of an increased interest in corpus-driven[131] linguistics phraseology[132] (or frequency-driven phraseology, cf. Goźdź-Roszkowski and Pontrandolfo 2015: 131). It is used in a wide range of legal and institutional contexts, drawing on research in legal phraseology from a variety of perspectives, including translation, comparative studies, terminology, lexicography, discourse analysis and forensic linguistics.

There are five major areas of corpus linguistic phraseological research (cf. Goźdź-Roszkowski and Pontrandolfo 2015: 133 after Pontrandolfo 2013: 151–166): (1) lexico-syntactic combinations in legal language (mainly collocations), (2) formulaic nature of legal language from the perspective of routine formulae (with increasing use of lexical bundle methodology) (cf. Goźdź-Roszkowski 2006, 2011; Jablonkai 2009, 2010; Breeze 2013; Tománková 2016; Mazzi 2017; Biel 2017c, 2018; Biel *et al.* 2018b, 2019), (3) lexicography and terminology (cf. de Groot 1999), (4) corpus-based analysis of phraseology applied to contrastive analysis of legal language (cf. Pontrandolfo 2013) and legal translation (cf. Biel 2014b), and (5) semantics of legal patterns (Mazzi 2010; Goźdź-Roszkowski and Pontrandolfo 2013; Pontrandolfo and Goźdź-Roszkowski 2014). Corpus linguistics research into the phraseology of legal and judicial discourse is subsumed under the second area.

As there are few studies examining the phraseological profile of judicial texts, I would like to mention a few works which analyze the distribution and functions of lexical bundles in not only court judgments but also other legal genres, most notably EU legislation, contracts, documents, law textbooks, professional articles, and academic journals, namely: Jablonkai (2010), Goźdź-Roszkowski (2006, 2011), Breeze (2013), Mazzi (2017), Biel (2017c, 2018), and Biel *et al.* (2018b).

Jablonkai's (2010) study of recurrent four-word combinations in English-language EU documents was based on the EEUD corpus and conducted with ESP pedagogic purposes in mind. The corpus contains 241 texts belonging to four different text categories: EU legal texts, legislative preparatory documents, EU funding-related documents, and other documents issued by EU institutions).[133] Legal texts, including case-law, constitute less than 45 % of texts in Jablokai's corpus (2010: 256). The study shows that EU administrative discourse is highly

131 The corpus-based approach to multi-word units involves pre-selecting such expressions and then analyzing the corpus to determine how they are used. The corpus-driven approach is bottom-up, inductive and more inclusive, i.e. it aims to provide a full account of possible sequences of words (Goźdź-Roszkowski and Pontrandolfo 2015).

132 A comprehensive overview of issues revolving around corpus linguistics phraseology research can be found in Grabowski (2015b, 2015c).

133 The total number of running words in the corpus is 1,174,753 tokens.

formulaic compared to the reference corpora (BNC – the three written sub-corpora of the BNC Baby: academic, fiction and news), which necessitates raising student awareness of these differences compared to general English. Jablonkai finds that the EEUD corpus contains the highest number of referential bundles (e.g. *paragraphs 1 and 2, in the absence of*), followed by subject-specific bundles (e.g. *Official Journal of the*), discourse-organizing bundles (e.g. *in addition to the*), and stance bundles (e.g. *the fact that the*) (2010: 263). Jablonkai investigates not only what types of bundles occur in English EU discourse, but also their structural and functional characteristics. The structural and functional classification of lexical bundles in the EEUD Corpus reveals some similarities with the language of textbooks and academic prose; however, on the whole, English EU administrative discourse seems to differ from other written registers as regards the structure of lexical bundles. Her findings show that EU texts make use of a higher number of bundles with verb phrases (2010: 260). In her concluding remarks, Jablonkai suggests identifying lexical bundles specific to individual EU genres (2010: 266), which is exactly what this chapter aims to do based on a corpus of EU and national judgments.

Goźdź-Roszkowski has made two major contributions to the field of distributional phraseology — the first in a paper from 2006, the later and more comprehensive contribution is his 2011 book *Patterns of Linguistic Variation in American Legal English: A Corpus-based Study*. In the former, Goźdź-Roszkowski (2006: 140–141) analyzes the distribution and functions of lexical bundles in a 500,000-token corpus of judgments delivered by the Law Lords in the House of Lords, which consists of 35 opinions delivered between 2000 and 2004. In this exploratory study, Goźdź-Roszkowski aims to look into general trends concerning the distribution of lexical bundles in judicial discourse. The frequency cut-off point is established at 15 words per half a million words and the extracted four-word lexical bundles are categorized structurally into ten major categories and functionally into three major categories (legal reference bundles, text-oriented bundles, and stance bundles). In Chapter 4 (2011: 109–143), Goźdź-Roszkowski refines the framework proposed in his earlier paper (2006) by examining multi-word patterns across a number of legal genres, including legislation, opinions, contracts, briefs, textbooks, academic journals, and professional articles. His structural categorization of lexical bundles covers nine structural types (Goźdź-Roszkowski 2011: 113). He concludes, for instance, that there is little variability across legal genres and that the high distribution of noun-phrase and prepositional-phrase bundles contributes to the perception of legal genres as highly nominal. As for the functional classification, Goźdź-Roszkowski's categorization of lexical bundles according to their discourse functions is the most original taxonomy relating to legal genres (2011: 117–142), which relies on three broad categories — bundles marking stance, legal reference, and text-oriented bundles (cf. Section 7.1) — and is divided into further subcategories. The details of his classification are important from the perspective of the present analysis.

The first category of Goźdź-Roszkowski's functional taxonomy (2011: 117–142), legal reference bundles, encompasses seven sub-categories (2011: 119–129):

a) temporal reference, e.g. *at the time of, for a period of,*
b) location, e.g. *in the district court, in United States v. Fleming,*
c) attributive, e.g. *any part of the, the nature of the, in the form of,*
d) participative, e.g. *at the request of, for the benefit of,*
e) institutional, e.g. *the Court of Appeals,*
f) terminological, e.g. *a breach of contract, right of first refusal,*
g) procedure-related, e.g. *is amending by striking, be it enacted by, shall be entitled to.*

Temporal reference bundles refer to particular points in time, location bundles provide wider institutional context by referring to institutions, attributive bundles identify attributes of the following head nouns, participative bundles signal the role performed by various participants in a legal process, institutional bundles refer to legal entities and instruments, and terminological bundles introduce domain-specific specialized vocabulary, whilst procedure-related bundles are verb-based expressions used to effect a particular legal act or describe legal procedure (Goźdź-Roszkowski 2011: 117–142).

Goźdź-Roszkowski's second broad category of lexical bundles – stance bundles – groups together bundles which are used to indicate sources of knowledge, and express emotions, attitudes, value judgments and assessments (Goźdź-Roszkowski 2011: 138–142):

a) epistemic stance bundles, e.g. *in accordance with the, the Court held that, the fact that the, pursuant to the terms, the court found that, the fact that the,*
b) attitudinal stance bundles, e.g. *it is clear that, it is difficult to see, it is easy to understand, it is necessary to consider.*

Epistemic stance bundles signal the writer's comments on the knowledge status of the information contained in the following proposition and are also used to indicate the source of knowledge or mark the (authority's) perspective from which information is given, whereas attitudinal stance bundles, which are predominantly impersonal, express attitudes towards the actions or events described in the following proposition[134] (Goźdź-Roszkowski 2011: 138–142).

The last category, text-oriented bundles, incorporates bundles which are used to signal relationships between different parts of texts (Goźdź-Roszkowski 2011: 129–137):

a) causative/resultative, e.g. *as a result of, by reason of the,*
b) condition bundles, e.g. *in the event of, in the event that,*

---

134 Bundles expressing deontic modality are classified by Goźdź-Roszkowski as procedure-related bundles (2011: 126–129).

c) clarification/topic elaboration, e.g. *at the same time, on the other hand, in the first place,*
d) focus bundles, e.g. *the purposes of this Act, at issue in this case, any of the following,*
e) framing bundles, e.g. *on the basis of the, on the ground that, in the context of, in the absence of,*
f) structuring bundles, e.g. *as described in section, contained in this Agreement,*
g) transition bundles, e.g. *in addition to the, in contrast to the, on the other hand.*

Causative/resultative bundles highlight results of an analysis, and logical links between arguments in a text in terms of cause and effect relationships; condition bundles, as the name suggests, are used to introduce conditions; clarification/topic elaboration bundles relate to the topic discussed by elaborating on it or providing further clarifications; focus bundles provide overt signals to the reader that a new issue is being introduced; framing bundles are used to define limiting conditions for making assertions, claims or arguments or providing justification; structuring bundles organize the text by providing frames for new arguments, referring to text stages, and by pointing to other parts of the texts; transition bundles mark additive or contrastive links between preceding and subsequent textual segments (Goźdź-Roszkowski 2011: 129–137).

Quantitatively, Goźdź-Roszkowski (2011) establishes that lexical bundles account for one-tenth of the total number of words in legislation and contracts, which means that these genres contain the largest proportion of formulaic expressions of all examined genres. As for his functional categorization, he finds that legislation, contracts and professional articles utilize the largest proportion of referential bundles (77 %, 78 %, 75 %, respectively), whereas academic journals and opinions contain the largest proportion of text-oriented (32 %, 29 %, respectively) and stance bundles (14 %, 12 %, respectively). He also finds that stance bundles are the smallest category in all genres (cf. Goźdź-Roszkowski 2011: 117–118). In the analysis of lexical bundles common in the discourse of EU and Polish judges, I will adapt Goźdź-Roszkowski's taxonomy of discourse functions of lexical bundles (see Section 7.6).

Breeze (2013) investigates the distribution of lexical bundles in corpora of texts from four legal genres: academic law, case law, legislation, and documents, with all the texts being related to commercial law. In the corpus of 2 million words, each of the four sub-corpora contains about 500,000 tokens. Breeze identifies not only 4–word bundles, but also 5–8–word lexical bundles in order to analyze their structural and functional characteristics. Her frequency cut-off point is established at 25 words per 500,000 words, mainly for practical reasons, to generate manageable lists of bundles. Breeze adopts an exploratory approach to the categorization of lexical bundles by proposing a mixed structural and functional classification of bundles into four groups: content-related noun and prepositional phrases, non-content noun and prepositional phrases, adjectival phrases, and bundles with a verb phrase (2013: 235). Content bundles are further divided into: agents, documents, dates, actions and abstract concepts. Bundles with a verb phrase or a part thereof are divided into: regulatives, textual navigation bundles, conditional bundles, declaratives, and other. Breeze's (2013: 248) functional categorization is based on the three main functions of lexical bundles: stance bundles (personal epistemic, impersonal deontic), text-organizing bundles (discourse organizers, textual navigation expressions, conditional expressions), and referential bundles (content reference bundles, and non-content reference bundles) (cf. Biber 2006). She establishes that case law uses noun-phrase bundles relating to agents, documents and actions, as well as many prepositional phrases acting as framing attributes, whereas legislation and documents display a high use of noun-phrase bundles and a relatively high use of verb-phrase bundles with either deontic or referential function. On the other hand, academic legal writing uses relatively little formulaic language (Breeze 2013: 250). Her findings confirm that most lexical bundles function as frames to anchor new information (Breeze 2013: 251; cf. Biber 2006: 172). Breeze's (2013) classification of bundles into content and non-content bundles will be used in my analysis to differentiate bundles referring to the thematic content of judgments (content bundles) from bundles containing function words (non-content bundles).

Davide Mazzi (2017) focuses on 3–6–word lexical bundles[135] by analyzing regularity in judicial texts on a corpus of 82 judicial opinions (742,194 tokens) delivered by the Supreme Court of Ireland between 2001 and 2014 using AntConc.[136] He analyzes the forms and functions of lexical bundles and labels them as either content or non-content bundles (cf. Breeze 2013). Lexical bundles prove to be an essential discourse element with different functions, such as defining the relationship between State and EU law (e.g. *the national law is clear*), thus bringing insights into the Court's argumentation (e.g. [observance of] *the principle of* [equivalence], [for] *the purposes of*), and identifying the core elements of the dispute before the Court from its own perspective (e.g. *seems to me*). Mazzi (2017: 195) finds that the Court attaches great importance to the framework of national legislation and that Irish justices tend to stress the need to ensure that national legislation is harmonized with and understood in the light of EU law and its principles. In his conclusions, he also puts forward an interesting suggestion, recommending that other researchers replicate his analysis of the relationship between the EU and its Member States in comparable national contexts, especially with regard to traditionally pro-EU countries (2017: 199). In his view, corpus linguistics (and thus lexical bundles) serves as a convenient methodology for verifying researchers' preliminary intuitions.

Biel's paper from 2017 examines the impact of translation on the patterning of legal language by comparing Polish language versions of EU legal acts against their English language versions with Polish national law (Biel 2017c). Biel adopts a frequency-based approach to study the distribution of 3–8–grams in three corpora, each consisting of two sub-corpora – a corpus of Polish-language versions of EU

---

135 Owing to the methodological approach adapted in his study, Mazzi (2017: 200) in fact only investigated 3–word bundles.

136 Mazzi (2017: 192) set the frequency cut-off point at 10 occurrences pmw, while the dispersion threshold was set at five texts in a corpus. His analysis was limited to the top ten most frequent lexical bundles.

regulations and directives (1,017 texts, 2,667,590 words, time frame: 2011–2015), a reference corpus of English-language versions of EU regulations and directives (1,017 texts, 3,068,479 words, time frame: 2011–2015), and a second reference corpus of Polish statutes (190 texts, 3,454,942 words, time frame: 1936–2015).[137] In her analysis, she focuses on the distribution, structure and discourse functions of 4-grams (2017: 20–23). Biel highlights the important issue of cross-linguistic comparisons of bundles; however, she leaves this question unanswered, suggesting further research into the matter (cf. Grabowski 2015b). The main conclusions from her analysis are that Polish EU translated legislation has an increased level of formulaicity, which confirms Toury's (1995) law of growing standardization and Baker's (1996) normalization hypothesis; translations exhibit their own lexical bundles prompted by STs, while at the same time failing to prime bundles typical of non-translated texts of a comparable genre (2017: 23). Another finding concerns the low overlap of lexical bundles between non-translated and translated texts, which may be due to the low thematic convergence between EU and national law. In general, the study confirms the centrality of recurrent word combinations in legal language, encouraging more in-depth studies into the nature of EU translation conducted with various types of reference corpora.

There is also one noteworthy contribution made by Biel (2018) and two made by Biel, Koźbiał and Wasilewska (Biel *et al.* 2018b, 2019). The first paper gives an overview of EU-rooted phenomena related to the Polish Eurolect. In this paper, Biel provides a brief description of the nature of 3–4–grams using three corpora (2018: 304–306): a corpus of EU directives (Enacting Terms) (658 texts, 1,245,789 words), transposition corpus (408 texts, 4,791,130 words) and a reference corpus of Polish law (755 texts, 6,842,032 words). Biel's small-scale study confirms the low overlap of bundles in the Eurolect and national law corpora, which suggests that the Eurolect makes use of its own bundles, which, in turn, may be prompted by STs, suggesting source text interference. In addition, the study also confirms the increased formulaicity of the Eurolect as compared to the Transposition corpus and the reference corpus of Polish law. The second paper, the exploratory study undertaken by Biel, Koźbiał and Wasilewska (Biel *et al.* 2018b), aims to examine the degree of formulaicity of the Polish Eurolect, that is three genres deemed representative of it, namely legislation (EU – 1,017 texts, 2,667,590 tokens, PL – 144 texts, 1,859,880 tokens), case law (EU – 1,281 texts, 9,209,834 tokens, PL – 2,564 texts, 6,833,997 tokens), and reports (EU – 498 texts, 2,329,498 tokens, PL – 110 texts, 2,556,114 tokens), against Polish administrative language.[138] The study aims to

137 Biel (2017) set the frequency cut-off point at 40 occurrences pmw without adjusting it to account for the inflectional nature of Polish, while the dispersion threshold was set at five texts in a corpus. Her analysis was limited to the top ten most frequent lexical bundles.

138 In the study, we decided to test two different threshold levels, namely 40 and 10 occurrences pmw, and two dispersion levels, namely 5 texts in a corpus and 5 % of all texts in a corpus.

examine the functional qualities of bundles according to the functional taxonomy proposed by Biber and Barbieri (2007: 265). Due to the limited number of studies investigating the nature of lexical bundles in the Polish language, the study has an exploratory character.[139] The resulting data show the highest level of formulaicity in the genre of legislation and the lowest level in reports with regard to the total distribution and concentration of the most frequent 3–grams. Legislative acts and reports show increased formulaicity in the case of TTs, which is not the case in judgments. Moreover, the study shows that the use of lexical bundles is closely connected with the genre in question, which is confirmed, among other things, by a low degree of overlap, and that methodological aspects of corpora creation (the issues of comparability of corpora, thematic convergence of corpora, and normalization of quantitative results concerning the frequency of bundle types) play a crucial role in the generalizability of the results. The third paper (Biel *et al.* 2019) explores the formulaicity of EU translations into Polish across four genres (legislation, judgments, reports, websites), aiming to show how the formulaic profile is affected by the genre variable. The study proves that there is a strong correlation between formulaicity and genre, that there are multiple facets of formulaicity (e.g. tokens and types) based on the adapted criteria of extraction of lexical bundles (distribution and dispersion thresholds), and that there is a consistently low overlap of bundles between translations and non-translations.

This Chapter aims to contribute to the existing body of research by examining the phraseological profile of a single genre, that is (EU and Polish) judgments. So far, no comprehensive lexical-bundle studies have been conducted on judicial Polish (except for Biel *et al.* 2018b). The findings presented in this Chapter will be discussed in the light of the relevant literature presented in this Section.

To sum up, this chapter aims to answer a few research questions concerning the formulaic profile of CJEU judgments and non-translated SN judgments:

1. Do 2–8–word lexical bundles influence the formulaic profile of CJEU and SN judgments?
2. Are translated EU judgments more or less formulaic than non-translated national judgments?
3. Do CJEU and SN judgments share a common set of bundle types?
4. What discourse functions are performed by lexical bundles in judgments?
5. Does the formulaic profile of post-accession SN judgments (2011–2015) differ from SN judgments from the pre-accession period (1999)?

139 The first studies examining the distribution and functions of lexical bundles in Polish texts concern pharmaceutical discourse (Grabowski 2014, 2018a,b,c).

## 7.3. Research material and methodology

The analysis, which is conducted on the unsampled CJ, GC, SN_2011–2015, and SN_1999 corpora, applies a methodology similar to that of previous studies on lexical bundles in other genres, most notably: a corpus-based analysis of lexical bundles in two EU-related registers and a corpus-driven analysis of lexical bundles in English EU documents conducted by Jablonkai (2009, 2010), a study on multi-word patterns in US legal genres (legislation, contracts, judicial opinions, briefs, textbooks, academic journals and professional articles) conducted by Goźdź-Roszkowski (2011), a study on lexical bundles in EU regulations, directives and national statutes conducted by Biel (2017), and, finally, two studies on lexical bundles undertaken by Biel, Koźbiał and Wasilewska (Biel *et al.* 2018b), which aim to examine the degree of formulaicity in four genres deemed representative of the Polish Eurolect: EU legislative acts, case law, and reports against Polish administrative language.

In the present analysis, the lists of lexical bundles were generated with WS (Scott 2017). Firstly, it was necessary to create a separate index file for each of the corpora mapping the position of each individual word in the corpus. These would later be used by the software to generate lists of n-grams from the values of frequency/distribution and dispersion criteria.

In order to create lists of clusters specific to each of the corpora, several settings in WS needed to be adjusted, including cluster size (clusters containing 2–8 words) and minimum frequency (the so-called frequency or recurrence threshold/cut-off), i.e. the value concerning the minimum frequency of occurrence of a given type of cluster in the corpus (cf. Breeze 2013: 232–233; Grabowski 2014: 26–28, 2018a: 69). In addition, the program was set to omit any clusters containing numbers and phrase frames. After a list of clusters has been generated, all the clusters which appeared in fewer than either 5 texts or 5 % of all texts had to be removed in order to exclude idiosyncratic clusters (dispersion threshold). The cut-off points relating to frequency (40 or 10 occurrences pmw) and dispersion are very important, since they can potentially significantly limit the number of bundles generated by the software, thus allowing for a more in-depth analysis; however, their values are largely arbitrary and set according to the preferences of corpus linguists (cf. Goźdź-Roszkowski 2011: 110; Biel 2017c: 16).

What needed to be determined prior to the actual analysis was the overall (aggregate) level of distribution of lexical bundles in each of the corpora. This task was conducted using four different sets of variables (frequency and distribution)[140] which were later fed into WS when generating the lists of bundles, in order to

140 In Biel, Koźbiał and Wasilewska (2018), we tested three different frequency cut-off points (40, 20 and 10 occurrences pmw) and three different dispersion cut-off points (5 texts, 5 % and 10 % of all texts). In Biel *et al.* (2019), we tested two different frequency cut-off points (40 and 20–39 occurrences pmw) and one dispersion cut-off point (5 texts). In this study, I assess the viability of two different frequency

**Table 7.1.** *Tested frequency and dispersion variables*

| # | Frequency cut-off point | Dispersion cut-off point |
|---|---|---|
| 1. | <40 occurrences pmw | <5 texts in the corpus |
| 2. | <40 occurrences pmw | <5 % of texts in the corpus |
| 3. | <10 occurrences pmw | <5 texts in the corpus |
| 4. | <10 occurrences pmw | <5 % of texts in the corpus |

**Table 7.2.** *Frequency and distribution threshold values for each of the corpora*

| Name of the corpus | Texts | Frequency threshold of 40 occurrences pmw | Frequency threshold of 10 occurrences pmw | Dispersion threshold of 5 % of all texts | Dispersion threshold 5 texts | Average text length (words) |
|---|---|---|---|---|---|---|
| **Polish Eurolect corpus: EU corpora** | | | | | | |
| CJ | 897 | 188 | 47 | 45 | 5 | 6,635 |
| GC | 384 | 181 | 45 | 19 | 5 | 4,825 |
| **Reference corpus: National corpora** | | | | | | |
| SN_2011–2015 | 2,564 | 273 | 68 | 128 | 5 | 2,464 |
| SN_1999 | 401 | 20 | 5 | 20 | 5 | 1,176 |

determine which set of variables would provide feasible sets of data by actually preventing the generation of too many lexical bundles. The sets of variables used to that end are presented in Table 7.1.

Table 7.2 presents the exact frequency and distribution cut-off points established on the basis of the total number of texts and tokens in each of the corpora.

It turned out that generating lists of lexical bundles with frequency cut-off points set at 10 occurrences pmw produced an overly-high and impractical number of bundles (cf. Tables 7.3 and 7.4), which would certainly make the task of carrying out a functional analysis of bundles across the corpora unmanageable due to its very time-consuming nature (cf. Grabowski 2018b: 193). Thanks to the methodology, the findings may be expected to be comparable with the results obtained in earlier research (cf. Goźdź-Roszkowski 2011; Biel 2017c; Biel *et al.* 2018b, 2019). Therefore, in this analysis, the frequency cut-off point was set at <40 occurrences pmw and the dispersion cut-off point was set at <5 texts in a corpus. However,

cut-off points and two different dispersion cut-off points, which was intended as a golden mean.

in this analysis, I will not only look at three- and four-word clusters (cf. Hyland 2008: 9–19; Goźdź-Roszkowski 2011: 109–143; Biel 2017c: 17–23), but also at the aggregate number of 2–8 grams, thus extending the line of current research by conducting a thorough investigation into the phraseological profile of the sub-genres of EU and national judgments.

Table 7.3 presents the quantitative data on the aggregate distribution of 2–8–grams in the EU corpora and the PL corpus. The frequencies of occurrence of 2–8–grams were normalized to one million words, whereas the bundle type values were not – the same pertains to other tables in this Chapter.

The data show that lexical bundles greatly influence the formulaicity of EU and Polish judgments, as 2–8–grams account for a substantial number of words in each of the corpora. Table 7.4 presents the distribution of 2–8–grams in the EU corpora and the PL corpus in greater detail. Its purpose is to prove that the formulaic profile is in fact multifaceted and that the choice of the bundle length, distribution and dispersion values may affect the time needed to analyze and classify extracted lexical bundles as well as the conclusions from the analysis.

The quantitative data presented above confirm the high sensitivity of formulaicity to the bundle length, frequency and dispersion criteria. The general (expected) tendency in all the corpora is that shorter bundles are more frequent than longer ones. Lexical bundles made up of 6, 7 or 8 words are relatively infrequent compared to 2–3–grams, while 4–5–grams occupy a middle ground along the distributional continuum. The two different frequency thresholds show that the cut-off value may in fact affect the overall perception of formulaicity in a genre, as a frequency threshold set at 10 occurrences pmw introduces substantially more bundle types into the analysis. Furthermore, the dispersion threshold may also affect the outcome of the analysis – the requirement that any given bundle should appear in at least 5 texts in the corpus guarantees that more bundles will be generated as opposed to the requirement that any given bundle should appear in at least 5 % of all texts in the corpus. In this analysis, I aimed to generate a high but still manageable number of lexical bundles. I decided to set the frequency threshold at <40 occurrences pmw and the dispersion cut-off point at <5 texts in the corpus, thanks to which the research data would be manageable and it would be possible to compare (at least to a limited extent) the results with similar studies (cf. Goźdź-Roszkowski 2011; Biel 2017c). The choice of a lower distribution threshold would necessitate the analysis of a much larger set of bundles.

## 7.4. Overall distribution of 2–8–grams in judicial language

The first section provides an overview of the distribution of 2–8–grams in CJEU and SN judgments. Table 7.5 shows the total number of types and occurrences of lexical bundles (NF) generated with a frequency threshold of <40 occurrences pmw and a dispersion threshold of at least 5 texts in the corpus. The columns on the right present quantitative data from the reference corpora of Polish Supreme Court judgments, which are examined along with the data from the Polish Eurolect corpus.

**Table 7.3.** *Global distribution of 2–8–grams in the EU corpora and the PL corpus*

| | Thresholds | | Translated EU case law | | | | | Non-translated PL case law | | |
|---|---|---|---|---|---|---|---|---|---|---|
| | Frequency (pmw) | Dispersion | CJ | vs GC (%DIFF) | vs SN_2011–2015 (%DIFF) | GC | vs SN_2011–2015 | SN_2011–2015 | vs SN_1999 (%DIFF) | SN_1999 |
| **Occurrences** | <40 | <5 texts | 393,364 | +12 % | 0 % | 350,147 | −11 % | 392,371 | −22 % | 503,219 |
| | <40 | <5 % | 386,215 | +11 % | +1 % | 347,569 | −9 % | 383,830 | −18 % | 470,816 |
| | <10 | <5 texts | 617,922 | +4 % | +1 % | 595,510 | −3 % | 613,970 | −24 % | 811,980 |
| | <10 | <5 % | 530,390 | −7 % | +14 % | 572,393 | +23 % | 465,771 | −1 % | 470,855 |
| **Types** | <40 | <5 texts | 3,377 | +20 % | +14 % | 2,807 | −5 % | 2,957 | −17 % | 3,573 |
| | <40 | <5 % | 3,255 | +18 % | +16 % | 2,763 | −2 % | 2,812 | −4 % | 2,938 |
| | <10 | <5 texts | 15,961 | −5 % | +2 % | 16,796 | +8 % | 15,616 | −30 % | 22,358 |
| | <10 | 5 % | 10,130 | −34 % | +67 % | 15,372 | +153 % | 6,069 | +106 % | 2,939 |

**Table 7.4.** *Global distribution of 2–8–grams in the EU corpora and the PL corpora*

| | Thresholds | | Translated EU case law | | | | | Non-translated PL case law | | |
|---|---|---|---|---|---|---|---|---|---|---|
| | Frequency (pmw) | Dispersion | CJ | CJ vs GC (%DIFF) | CJ vs SN_2011–2015 (%DIFF) | GC | GC vs SN_2011–2015 (%DIFF) | SN_2011–2015 | SN_2011–2015 vs SN_1999 | SN_1999 |
| **2–grams –** occurrences | 40 | 5 texts | 242,915 | −3 % | −5 % | 251,397 | −2 % | 255,857 | −14 % | 298,271 |
| | 40 | 5 % | 237,309 | −5 % | −5 % | 249,540 | 0 % | 250,091 | −10 % | 277,512 |
| | 10 | 5 texts | 361,397 | −4 % | −3 % | 377,123 | +2 % | 371,515 | −17 % | 447,156 |
| | 10 | 5 % | 312,387 | −14 % | +9 % | 364,103 | +28 % | 285,416 | +3 % | 277,512 |
| **2–grams –** types | 40 | 5 texts | 1,826 | 0 % | +1 % | 1,828 | +2 % | 1,800 | −12 % | 2,036 |
| | 40 | 5 % | 1,734 | −3 % | +2 % | 1,796 | +5 % | 1,704 | +4 % | 1,632 |
| | 10 | 5 texts | 8,382 | −4 % | +2 % | 8,744 | +6 % | 8,249 | −26 % | 11,078 |
| | 10 | 5 % | 5,262 | −34 % | +80 % | 7,987 | +174 % | 2,920 | +79 % | 1,632 |
| **3–grams –** occurrences | 40 | 5 texts | 73,507 | +8 % | −5 % | 68,330 | −12 % | 77,275 | −25 % | 103,542 |
| | 40 | 5 % | 72,273 | +6 % | −4 % | 67,930 | −10 % | 75,220 | −22 % | 96,390 |
| | 10 | 5 texts | 128,861 | −1 % | −1 % | 130,732 | 0 % | 130,090 | −25 % | 174,414 |
| | 10 | 5 % | 106,403 | −15 % | +16 % | 125,005 | +37 % | 91,558 | −5 % | 96,390 |
| **3–grams –** types | 40 | 5 texts | 660 | +8 % | +7 % | 611 | −1 % | 615 | −22 % | 784 |
| | 40 | 5 % | 637 | +5 % | +10 % | 604 | +4 % | 580 | −10 % | 645 |
| | 10 | 5 texts | 3,803 | −10 % | +4 % | 4,204 | +14 % | 3,674 | −27 % | 5,043 |
| | 10 | 5 % | 2,267 | −41 % | +96 % | 3,831 | +231 % | 1,157 | +79 % | 645 |

(*continued on next page*)

**Table 7.4.** *Continued*

| | Thresholds | | Translated EU case law | | | | | Non-translated PL case law | | |
|---|---|---|---|---|---|---|---|---|---|---|
| | **Frequency (pmw)** | **Dispersion** | **CJ** | **CJ vs GC (%DIFF)** | **CJ vs SN_2011–2015 (%DIFF)** | **GC** | **GC vs SN_2011–2015 (%DIFF)** | **SN_2011–2015** | **SN_2011–2015 vs SN_1999** | **SN_1999** |
| **4-grams** – occurrences | 40 | 5 texts | 30,550 | +60 % | +2 % | 19,153 | −36 % | 30,082 | −34 % | 45,753 |
| | 40 | 5 % | 30,282 | +59 % | +3 % | 19,007 | −36 % | 29,489 | −31 % | 42,671 |
| | 10 | 5 texts | 53,976 | +16 % | 0 % | 46,634 | −14 % | 54,244 | −35 % | 83,370 |
| | 10 | 5 % | 45,459 | +3 % | −9 % | 44,028 | −12 % | 50,114 | +17 % | 42,671 |
| **4-grams** – types | 40 | 5 texts | 318 | +54 % | +22 % | 207 | −21 % | 261 | −26 % | 353 |
| | 40 | 5 % | 312 | +52 % | +25 % | 205 | −18 % | 250 | −14 % | 290 |
| | 10 | 5 texts | 1,642 | −11 % | −2 % | 1,844 | +10 % | 1,680 | −36 % | 2,643 |
| | 10 | 5 % | 1,040 | −38 % | −24 % | 1,672 | +22 % | 1,365 | +371 % | 290 |
| **5-grams** – occurrences | 40 | 5 texts | 17,407 | +162 % | +21 % | 6,655 | −54 % | 14,354 | −45 % | 25,979 |
| | 40 | 5 % | 17,365 | +164 % | +22 % | 6,567 | −54 % | 14,225 | −43 % | 24,996 |
| | 10 | 5 texts | 29,745 | +49 % | +9 % | 19,982 | −27 % | 27,206 | −43 % | 47,441 |
| | 10 | 5 % | 26,149 | +38 % | +42 % | 18,905 | +2 % | 18,462 | −26 % | 24,996 |
| **5-grams** – types | 40 | 5 texts | 202 | +122 % | +52 % | 91 | −32 % | 133 | −27 % | 183 |
| | 40 | 5 % | 201 | +123 % | +55 % | 90 | −31 % | 130 | −20 % | 163 |
| | 10 | 5 texts | 888 | −2 % | −1 % | 910 | +2 % | 893 | −41 % | 1,507 |
| | 10 | 5 % | 628 | −25 % | +122 % | 837 | +196 % | 283 | +74 % | 163 |

| | | | | | | | | | | |
|---|---|---|---|---|---|---|---|---|---|---|
| **6–grams** – occurrences | 40 | 5 texts | 12,462 | +351 % | +65 % | 2,765 | −63 % | 7,536 | −52 % | 15,777 |
| | 40 | 5 % | 12,462 | +351 % | +65 % | 2,765 | −63 % | 7,536 | −51 % | 15,428 |
| | 10 | 5 texts | 19,742 | +87 % | +28 % | 10,559 | −32 % | 15,478 | −48 % | 29,788 |
| | 10 | 5 % | 17,840 | +77 % | +74 % | 10,105 | −2 % | 10,272 | −34 % | 15,468 |
| **6–grams** – types | 40 | 5 texts | 151 | +268 % | +113 % | 41 | −42 % | 71 | −34 % | 107 |
| | 40 | 5 % | 151 | +268 % | +113 % | 41 | −42 % | 71 | −29 % | 100 |
| | 10 | 5 texts | 567 | +8 % | +4 % | 525 | −3 % | 544 | −44 % | 968 |
| | 10 | 5 % | 421 | +118 % | +148 % | 193 | +14 % | 170 | +68 % | 101 |
| **7–grams** – occurrences | 40 | 5 texts | 9,196 | +651 % | +108 % | 1,225 | −72 % | 4,415 | −52 % | 9,110 |
| | 40 | 5 % | 9,196 | +708 % | +108 % | 1,138 | −74 % | 4,415 | −51 % | 9,031 |
| | 10 | 5 texts | 13,822 | +121 % | +48 % | 6,268 | −33 % | 9,317 | −50 % | 18,805 |
| | 10 | 5 % | 12,631 | +107 % | +112 % | 6,098 | +2 % | 5,967 | −34 % | 9,031 |
| **7–grams** – types | 40 | 5 texts | 120 | +532 % | +161 % | 19 | −59 % | 46 | −34 % | 70 |
| | 40 | 5 % | 120 | +606 % | +161 % | 17 | −63 % | 46 | −32 % | 68 |
| | 10 | 5 texts | 392 | +18 % | +13 % | 333 | −4 % | 346 | −49 % | 678 |
| | 10 | 5 % | 296 | −8 % | +190 % | 321 | +215 % | 102 | +50 % | 68 |
| **8–grams** – occurrences | 40 | 5 texts | 7,327 | +1078 % | +157 % | 622 | −78 % | 2,854 | −40 % | 4,788 |
| | 40 | 5 % | 7,327 | +1078 % | +157 % | 622 | −78 % | 2,854 | −40 % | 4,788 |
| | 10 | 5 texts | 10,381 | +146 % | +70 % | 4,213 | −31 % | 6,119 | −44 % | 11,007 |
| | 10 | 5 % | 9,521 | +129 % | +139 % | 4,150 | +4 % | 3,982 | −17 % | 4,788 |
| **8–grams** – types | 40 | 5 texts | 100 | +900 % | +223 % | 10 | −68 % | 31 | −23 % | 40 |
| | 40 | 5 % | 100 | +900 % | +223 % | 10 | −68 % | 31 | −23 % | 40 |
| | 10 | 5 texts | 287 | +22 % | +25 % | 236 | +3 % | 230 | −48 % | 441 |
| | 10 | 5 % | 216 | −6 % | +200 % | 231 | +221 % | 72 | +80 % | 40 |

The quantitative data show the distribution of seven types of lexical bundles, recurrent word sequences made up of 2, 3, 4, 5, 6, 7, and 8 lexical items. As is generally expected in the case of analyses involving lexical bundles, the longer the bundle, the smaller its overall distribution is. Therefore, the most frequent bundle type in each of the three corpora are 2–grams, which are on average more than three times more frequent than 3–grams. Taking into consideration the fact that most 2–grams are incomplete in terms of their meaning, in this study I will pay particular attention to 3–4–grams, which, despite generally not being salient to the audience of judgments, very often constitute units complete in terms of meaning, thus enabling functional categorizations. The distribution of 3–4–grams is similar in both the CJ and SN corpora, with the GC corpus[141] having a slightly lower number of 3–grams than the remaining corpora and a markedly lower number of 4–grams. For 5–8–grams, it can be observed that the EU corpus of CJ judgments contains a significantly higher number of such bundles than its national counterpart, whereas the corpus of GC judgments is decidedly less formulaic at the level of 5–8–grams than national judgments. The differences between the CJ and GC corpora are indicative of internal variation in the Eurolect. As for the pre-accession SN corpus, its purpose is to establish whether SN judgments have become more or less formulaic following Poland's accession to the EU. However, it is necessary to remember that the pre-accession corpus is fairly small and that the data gathered from it are normalized upwards, which might negatively affect the comparability of both SN corpora, as the post-accession corpus is significantly larger and the data gathered from it are normalized downwards to one million (see Table 7.5).

It should be remembered that the above data show the approximate total numbers of types and occurrences of n-grams and do not account for the fact that the software-generated lists of lexical bundles include overlapping bundles (cf. Grabowski 2018b: 188). The number of bundle types and the number of their occurrences provide inconclusive information on the formulaicity of the Polish Eurolect and national judgments. Therefore, refined quantitative data concerning the distribution of 3–4–grams will be presented in Section 7.5 in the hope that the formulaic profile at the level of medium-length bundles (which frequently are complete semantically) will be better suited to drawing informed conclusions.

Another peculiar finding concerns the co-relation between the total number of types and tokens in a given corpus. Although the CJ corpus seems to have a wider thematic range than the national corpus, as it has about 14 % more bundle types, the same does not hold true for the corpus of GC judgments, which has about 5 % fewer bundle types than national judgments. What still needs to be examined is the degree of thematic convergence (overlap of bundles) between the corpora, which might answer the

141 The reason for including the GC corpus in the analysis was that it is supposed to act as a corrective, meaning that any estimations and judgments made with regard to the CJ corpus should be contrasted with the data gathered from the GC corpus, suggesting potential intra-generic variation.

**Table 7.5.** *Distribution of 2–8–grams in the translation and reference corpora (NF), frequency threshold — <40, dispersion threshold — <5*

| | Translated EU case law | | | | | Non-translated PL case law | | |
|---|---|---|---|---|---|---|---|---|
| | CJ | CJ vs GC (%DIFF) | CJ vs SN_2011–2015 (%DIFF) | GC | GC vs SN_2011–2015 (%DIFF) | SN_2011–2015 | SN_2011–2015 vs SN_1999 (%DIFF) | SN_1999 |
| 2–grams – Total types | 1,826 | 0 % | +1 % | 1,828 | +2 % | 1,800 | −12 % | 2,036 |
| 2–grams – Total occurrences (NF) | 242,915 | −3 % | −5 % | 251,397 | −2 % | 255,857 | −14 % | 298,271 |
| 3–grams – Total types | 660 | +8 % | +7 % | 611 | −1 % | 615 | −22 % | 784 |
| 3–grams – Total occurrences (NF) | 73,507 | +8 % | −5 % | 68,330 | −12 % | 77,275 | −25 % | 103,542 |
| 4–grams – Total types | 318 | +54 % | +22 % | 207 | −21 % | 261 | −26 % | 353 |
| 4–grams – Total occurrences (NF) | 30,550 | +60 % | +2 % | 19,153 | −36 % | 30,082 | −34 % | 45,753 |
| 5–grams – Total types | 202 | +122 % | +52 % | 91 | −32 % | 133 | −27 % | 183 |
| 5–grams – Total occurrences (NF) | 17,407 | +162 % | +21 % | 6,655 | −54 % | 14,354 | −45 % | 25,979 |
| 6–grams – Total types | 151 | +268 % | +113 % | 41 | −42 % | 71 | −34 % | 107 |
| 6–grams – Total occurrences (NF) | 12,462 | +351 % | +65 % | 2,765 | −63 % | 7,536 | −52 % | 15,777 |

*(continued on next page)*

**Table 7.5.** *Continued*

| | Translated EU case law | | | | | Non-translated PL case law | | |
|---|---|---|---|---|---|---|---|---|
| | CJ | CJ vs GC (%DIFF) | CJ vs SN_2011–2015 (%DIFF) | GC | GC vs SN_2011–2015 (%DIFF) | SN_2011–2015 | SN_2011–2015 vs SN_1999 (%DIFF) | SN_1999 |
| 7–grams – Total types | 120 | +532 % | +161 % | 19 | –59 % | 46 | –34 % | 70 |
| 7–grams – Total occurrences (NF) | 9,196 | +651 % | +108 % | 1,225 | –72 % | 4,415 | –52 % | 9,110 |
| 8–grams – Total types | 100 | +900 % | +223 % | 10 | –68 % | 31 | –23 % | 40 |
| 8–grams – Total occurrences (NF) | 7,327 | +1078 % | +157 % | 622 | –78 % | 2,854 | –40 % | 4,788 |
| **2–8–grams – Total types** | **3,377** | **+20 %** | **+14 %** | **2,807** | **–5 %** | **2,957** | **–17 %** | **3,573** |
| **2–8–grams – Total occurrences** | **393,364** | **+12 %** | **0 %** | **350,147** | **–11 %** | **392,371** | **–22 %** | **503,219** |

question as to why EU corpora are so dissimilar from the post-accession SN corpus. Taking into consideration the observations made above, it should still be remembered that present investigations constitute only an approximation. Despite the fact that the compared texts belong to the same genre, there are no other direct links between the sub-genres of EU and national judgments (cf. Chapter 5). What can be stated for a fact is that the degree to which texts are formulaic is linked with the subgenre. In the following sections, upon the prior elimination of overlapping 3–4-grams, I will take a closer look at the functions of 3–4-grams found in the refined lists of bundles.

## 7.5. Refinement of 3–4-grams

The purpose of this section is to present refined quantitative data on the distribution of 3–4-grams across the corpora. Table 7.6 shows the distribution of 3–4-grams in each of the corpora after all overlapping bundles were removed from the lists containing all bundles. Two examples of overlapping bundles are, for instance, the two 4-grams *it should be noted* and *should be noted that* which are derived from a single 5-gram *it should be noted that*, or the two 4-grams *must be interpreted as* and *interpreted as meaning that*, which together form a 6-gram *must be interpreted as meaning that*. In the case of such overlapping 3–4-grams, only the most frequent ones were included in the final versions of 3–4-grams lists for each of the corpora. Bundles which overlapped such 3–4-grams were deleted altogether. The same method of filtering out overlapping bundles which are fragments of other longer bundles was employed by Grabowski (2018b: 188) in his study on the identification of bilingual 3–7-word lexical bundles, which aimed to improve the naturalness and textual fit of translated patient information leaflets. The overlapping n-grams could also have been combined into longer sequences; however, this would later prove unmanageable due to the high number of types of n-grams generated for each of the corpora. Moreover, there was no need for such a procedure, as I had decided that longer n-grams were also to be cleaned of any overlapping bundles.

**Table 7.6.** *Refinement of 3–4-grams (occurrences – NF)*

| | CJ | GC | SN_2011–2015 | SN_1999 |
|---|---|---|---|---|
| **3-grams before refinement (after refinement)** | | | | |
| Total – types no. of types | 660 (376) | 611 (325) | 615 (339) | 784 (436) |
| Total – occurrences | 73,507 (44,256) | 68,330 (42,727) | 77,275 (47,685) | 103,542 (62,027) |
| **4-grams before refinement (after refinement)** | | | | |
| Total – types | 318 (131) | 207 (115) | 261 (139) | 353 (162) |
| Total – occurrences | 30,550 (13,880) | 19,153 (11,779) | 30,082 (16,534) | 45,753 (20,170) |

The refined data show that the removal of overlapping 3–4–grams has not changed the overall proportions of the total number of types in the corpora, that is the range of bundles, and that almost half of all bundle types generated with WS were redundant. This refinement procedure has the potential to reveal the actual degree of formulaicity.

Table 7.7 presents the top ten 3–grams in the EU corpora and the national corpora.

Table 7.8 presents the top ten 4–grams in the EU and national corpora.

Tables 7.6, 7.7 and 7.8 show that there is a low degree of convergence between EU and national law; however, this will be verified in the following Sections (cf. Sections 7.6.1 and 7.6.2). Only in the case of 3–grams are there two bundles present both in the top ten bundles in either of the EU corpora and in the national corpus; these are *w związku z* [(read) in conjunction with] and *na podstawie art* [pursuant to Article]. In the case of the list of top ten 4–grams generated for the corpus of non-translated texts, none of the bundles overlap with any bundles from the lists representing the Polish Eurolect. The national corpora, however, contain four overlapping bundles: *w zw z art* [in accordance with article], *Sądu Najwyższego z dnia* [the supreme court of], *k p c w* [ABBRV. code of civil procedure (in)],[142] and *od wyroku Sądu Apelacyjnego* [against the ruling of the court of appeal].

### 7.5.1 Thematic classification into content and non-content bundles

For practical reasons, I will limit further examination to the refined lists of 3– and 4–word lexical bundles. This limitation is largely arbitrary; however, as shown by the relevant literature, 3–4–grams are the most widely studied types of n-grams, as they frequently constitute (almost) complete units of meaning. Bundle length is not a criterion of phraseological status, but the frequency threshold guarantees that the selected word combinations are of relevance to judicial discourse and that they may well afford insight into the nature of judicial discourse. The length restriction was adopted mainly to reduce the material to a manageable size, which still proved very extensive (cf. Grabowski 2018b: 193).

Due to the high number of 3–4–word lexical bundles generated for each of the corpora (cf. Table 7.6 – Refinement of 3–4–grams), I decided to adopt an exploratory approach to determine any general patterns. In this way, after the examination of the four extensive lists of n-grams, I established that the generated bundles belong to two overarching categories, namely content and non-content word combinations (cf. Breeze 2013: 235), with content bundles being specific to the domain of legal proceedings and law in general, e.g. *wyrok w sprawie* [judgments in case], and non-content bundles containing primarily function words not related to the

---

142 This bundle was extracted from the corpora, because WS was instructed to stop only at sentence breaks.

**Table 7.7.** *Top ten 3–grams in the corpora after refinement*

| **Translated EU case law** | | | | | |
|---|---|---|---|---|---|
| **CJ** | | | **GC** | | |
| **Bundle** | **NF** | **% of texts** | **Bundle** | **NF** | **% of texts** |
| *r w sprawie* [in case (...)] | 1,521 | 94 | *r w sprawie* [in case (...)] | 1,426 | 99 |
| *w odniesieniu do* [as regards the] | 1,156 | 93 | *w odniesieniu do* [as regards the] | 1,403 | 97 |
| *w ten sposób* [must be interpreted (as)/ by doing so] | 897 | 90 | *ww w pkt* [mentioned above in (point)] | 1,33 | 81 |
| *zgodnie z art* [under article (...)] | 831 | 90 | *w tym względzie* [in that regard] | 911 | 93 |
| *w postępowaniu głównym* [(in) the main proceedings] | 702 | 47 | *w związku z* [(read) in conjunction with] | 770 | 94 |
| *na podstawie art* [under article (...)/pursuant to article (...)] | 697 | 99 | *ze względu na* [in the light (of)/by reason of/on the ground that] | 686 | 90 |
| *w tym względzie* [in that regard] | 660 | 81 | *w niniejszej sprawie* [(in) the present case] | 686 | 89 |
| *ze względu na* [in the light (of)/by reason of/on the ground that] | 654 | 73 | *Sądu z dnia* [(judgment of) the general court] | 616 | 76 |
| *w rozumieniu art* [(for the) purposes of article/(within the) meaning of article] | 615 | 74 | *wyrok w sprawie* [case c-(...)] | 596 | 64 |
| *należy interpretować w* [must be interpreted (as)] | 545 | 63 | *w zaskarżonej decyzji* [(in) the contested decision] | 561 | 63 |
| **Non–translated PL case law** | | | | | |
| **SN_2011–2015** | | | **SN_1999** | | |
| **Bundle** | **NF** | **% of texts** | **Bundle** | **NF** | **% of texts** |
| *k p c* [code of civil procedure-ABBRV] | 3,792 | 99 | *k p c* [code of civil procedure-ABBRV] | 6,334 | 96 |
| ***w związku z* [(read) in conjunction with]** | 1,284 | 80 | *wyrok Sądu Najwyższego* [judgment of the Supreme Court] | 1,617 | 100 |

(*continued on next page*)

**Table 7.7.** *Continued*

| Non-translated PL case law | | | | | |
|---|---|---|---|---|---|
| *w zw z* [(read) in conjunction with] | 1,212 | 57 | *od wyroku sądu* [against the judgment of] | 1,090 | 99 |
| *zw z art* [in conjunction with article] | 1,157 | 57 | *wyrokiem z dnia* [by judgment of] | 959 | 74 |
| *Sądu Najwyższego z* [supreme court of] | 1,092 | 70 | *w związku z* [(read) in conjunction with] | 846 | 51 |
| ***na podstawie art* [pursuant to article]** | 1,026 | 90 | *sprawy z powództwa* [the case of] | 830 | 99 |
| *do ponownego rozpoznania* [referred back to] | 603 | 84 | *na skutek kasacji* [due to the cassation appeal] | 803 | 100 |
| *ustawy z dnia* [act of (...)] | 602 | 54 | *rozpoznaniu w dniu* [having heard (the case) on] | 791 | 100 |
| *wyrokiem z dnia* [judgment of (...)] | 597 | 81 | *na rozprawie sprawy* [at a hearing] | 785 | 99 |
| *od wyroku sądu* [(brought) against the judgment] | 595 | 98 | *Najwyższy izba cywilna* [Supreme (Court), Civil Chamber] | 769 | 97 |

proceedings and legal issues, e.g. *w związku z* [in connection with]. The following table (see Table 7.9) presents exact quantitative data concerning the classification of individual 3–4–grams to these two categories.

The data show that there is a higher number of content 3–4–grams in every single EU and national corpus. This may be due to the specialized nature of judicial discourse, which contributes to the high informational content of judgments. Furthermore, the differences also pertain to the contextual characteristics of EU and national judgments (cf. Chapter 5) and the respective legal systems in which the judgments were passed, that is the EU legal system and national legal system, since the corpus of judgments passed by the Polish Supreme Court has a considerably higher proportion of content 3–4–grams than the corpora of EU judgments. In the distribution of content 3–4–grams, there is a noticeable disparity between the two groups. Based on the presented numbers alone, 4–grams exhibit a substantially higher informational load compared to 3–grams, since they make up longer word sequences. Content 4–grams are, on average, two times less frequent than content 3–grams in each of the corpora. Table 7.9 also confirms the trend concerning post-accession SN judgments, which overall seem to exhibit lower formulaicity than their pre-accession counterparts.

**Table 7.8.** *Top 10 4-grams in the corpora after refinement*

| Translated EU case law | | | | | |
|---|---|---|---|---|---|
| CJ | | | GC | | |
| Bundle | NF | % of texts | Bundle | NF | % of texts |
| *r w sprawie C* [(year) in the case c] | 875 | 63 | *r w sprawie T* [(year) in the case t] | 574 | 67 |
| *w ten sposób że* [in such a way (that)] | 665 | 76 | *i przytoczone tam orzecznictwo* [and the case-law cited there] | 515 | 89 |
| *ww wyrok w sprawie* [above-mentioned judgment in the case] | 444 | 52 | *w zakresie w jakim* [to the extent that] | 457 | 88 |
| *działających w charakterze pełnomocników* [acting as agents] | 417 | 94 | *i in przeciwko komisji* [(and) others against the commission] | 448 | 41 |
| *i przytoczone tam orzecznictwo* [(and) the case-law cited there] | 353 | 62 | *wyrok Sądu z dnia* [judgment of the general court (of)] | 447 | 68 |
| *orzeczenia w trybie prejudycjalnym* [reference for a preliminary ruling] | 342 | 72 | *r w sprawie C* [(year) in the case c] | 402 | 65 |
| *w zakresie w jakim* [to the extent that] | 293 | 51 | *w sprawie przedstawienia zarzutów* [statement of objections] | 385 | 23 |
| *Parlamentu Europejskiego i Rady* [european parliament and council] | 268 | 48 | *wyrok Trybunału z dnia* [judgment of the court of justice of] | 354 | 65 |
| *w związku z tym* [in connection with this] | 253 | 55 | *w związku z tym* [in connection with this] | 313 | 72 |
| *o których mowa w* [referred to in] | 219 | 46 | *w tym względzie należy* [in this regard it should be] | 269 | 73 |
| **Non-translated PL case law** | | | | | |
| **SN_2011–2015** | | | **SN_1999** | | |
| **Bundle** | **NF** | **% of texts** | **Bundle** | **NF** | **% of texts** |
| *w zw z art* [in accordance with article] | 1,153 | 57 | *Sądu Najwyższego z dnia* [the Supreme Court of] | 1,157 | 100 |
| *Sądu Najwyższego z dnia* [the Supreme Court of] | 1,006 | 65 | *po rozpoznaniu w dniu* [having heard (the case) on] | 789 | 99 |

*(continued on next page)*

**Table 7.8.** *Continued*

| Non-translated PL case law | | | | | |
|---|---|---|---|---|---|
| *w związku z art* [in accordance with article] | 654 | 44 | *na rozprawie sprawy z* [during the hearing] | 781 | 98 |
| *k p c w* [code of civil procedure (in)-ABBRV] | 472 | 48 | *Sąd Najwyższy izba cywilna* [Supreme Court civil chamber] | 769 | 97 |
| *Sąd Najwyższy w składzie* [Supreme Court sitting in] | 392 | 98 | *Najwyższy zważył co następuje* [Supreme (Court) held as follows] | 711 | 89 |
| *w sprawie z powództwa* [in the action brought (by)] | 391 | 99 | *od wyroku Sądu Apelacyjnego* [against the ruling of the court of appeal] | 608 | 67 |
| *od wyroku Sądu Apelacyjnego* [against the ruling of the court of appeal] | 389 | 84 | *k p c w* [code of civil procedure (in)-ABBRV] | 428 | 38 |
| *Izbie Cywilnej w dniu* [(in) the civil chamber on] | 375 | 100 | *od wyroku sądu wojewódzkiego* [against the ruling of the provincial court] | 365 | 43 |
| *wyrok w imieniu Rzeczypospolitej* [(judgment of the court in the name) of the Republic of Poland] | 366 | 98 | *w zw z art* [in accordance with article] | 365 | 27 |
| *Sąd Najwyższy zważył co* [the Supreme Court held as follows] | 361 | 96 | *zapłatę na skutek kasacji* [payment due to the cassation appeal] | 363 | 46 |

## 7.5.2 Overlap of 3– and 4–grams in the translation and non-translation corpora

In order to establish the degree of textual fit of EU judgments translated into Polish to non-translated national judgments, it was necessary to determine the degree of overlap between the corpora of translations and non-translations. This task was carried out with Microsoft Excel 2016 and a formula for the conditional formatting of cells with repeated lexical bundles. The degree of overlap is presented in Table 7.10, which, for reference purposes, presents the number of bundles identified as overlapping in the Polish Eurolect as well as in the national judgments prior to the refinement (figures in the brackets stand for the total number of n-grams of a given length).

**Table 7.9.** *Content and non-content 3–4–grams in the corpora (after refinement)*

| | Translated EU case law | | | | | Non-translated PL case law | | |
|---|---|---|---|---|---|---|---|---|
| | CJ | | | GC | | SN_2011–2015 | | SN_1999 |
| | Types | CJ vs GC | CJ vs SN_2011–2015 (%DIFF) | Types | GC vs SN_2011–2015 (%DIFF) | Types | SN_2011–2015 vs SN_1999 (%DIFF) | Types |
| **Content 3–grams** | | | | | | | | |
| Total types | 248 | +33 % | −10 % | 187 | −32 % | 277 | −19 % | 341 |
| Total occurrences (NF) | 28,595 | +18 % | −27 % | 24,203 | −38 % | 39,018 | −26 % | 52,389 |
| **Non-content 3–grams** | | | | | | | | |
| Total types | 128 | −7 % | +106 % | 138 | +123 % | 62 | −35 % | 95 |
| Total occurrences (NF) | 15,662 | −15 % | +81 % | 18,524 | +114 % | 8,668 | −10 % | 9,638 |
| **TOTAL (3–grams):** types | **376** | **+16 %** | **+11 %** | **325** | **−4 %** | **339** | **−22 %** | **436** |
| **TOTAL (3–grams):** occurrences (NF) | **44,257** | **+4 %** | **−7 %** | **42,727** | **−10 %** | **47,686** | **−23 %** | **62,027** |
| **Content 4–grams** | | | | | | | | |
| Total types | 106 | +25 % | −17 % | 85 | −33 % | 127 | −16 % | 152 |
| Total occurrences (NF) | 10,715 | +20 % | −31 % | 8907 | −43 % | 15,632 | −19 % | 19,231 |
| **Non-content 4–grams** | | | | | | | | |
| Total types | 25 | −17 % | +108 % | 30 | +150 % | 12 | +20 % | 10 |
| Total occurrences (NF) | 3,165 | +10 % | +251 % | 2,872 | +218 % | 902 | −4 % | 939 |
| **TOTAL (4–grams):** types | **131** | **+14 %** | **−6 %** | **115** | **−17 %** | **139** | **−14 %** | **162** |
| **TOTAL (4–grams):** occurrences (NF) | **13,880** | **+18 %** | **−16 %** | **11,779** | **−29 %** | **16,534** | **−18 %** | **20,170** |

**Table 7.10.** *Overlap of 2–8–grams in the translation and non-translation corpora (before refinement)*

| N-grams | CJ vs GC | CJ vs SN_2011–2015 | GC vs SN_2011–2015 | SN_2011–2015 vs SN_1999 |
|---|---|---|---|---|
| **2–grams** | **1,013**<br>(out of: 1,826 vs 1,828)<br>(55 % vs 55 %) | **563**<br>(out of: 1,826 vs 1,800)<br>(31 % vs 31 %) | **534**<br>(out of: 1,828 vs 1,800)<br>(29 % vs 30 %) | **1,270**<br>(out of: 1,800 vs 2036)<br>(70 % vs 62 %) |
| **3–grams** | **245**<br>(out of: 660 vs 611)<br>(37 % vs 40 %) | **80**<br>(out of: 660 vs 615<br>(12 % vs 13 %) | **79**<br>(out of: 611 vs 615)<br>(13 % vs 13 %) | **347**<br>(out of: 615 vs 784)<br>(56 % vs 44 %) |
| **4–grams** | **39**<br>(out of: 318 vs 207)<br>(12 % vs 19 %) | **9**<br>(out of: 318 vs 261)<br>(3 % vs 3 %) | **10**<br>(out of: 207 vs 261)<br>(5 % vs 4 %) | **112**<br>(out of: 261 vs 353)<br>(43 % vs 32 %) |
| **5–grams** | 9<br>(out of: 202 vs 91)<br>(5 % vs 10 %) | 3<br>(out of: 202 vs 133)<br>(1 % vs 2 %) | 2<br>(out of: 91 vs 133)<br>(2 % vs 1 %) | **49**<br>(out of: 133 vs 183)<br>(37 % vs 27 %) |
| **6–grams** | **2**<br>(out of: 151 vs 41) | **0**<br>(out of: 151 vs 71) | **0**<br>(out of: 41 vs 71) | **19**<br>(out of: 71 vs 107)<br>(27 % vs 18 %) |
| **7–grams** | **0**<br>(out of: 120 vs 19) | **0**<br>(out of: 120 vs 46) | **0**<br>(out of: 19 vs 46) | 7<br>(out of: 46 vs 70)<br>(30 % vs 20 %) |
| **8–grams** | **0**<br>(out of: 100 vs 10) | **0**<br>(out of: 100 vs 31) | **0**<br>(out of: 10 vs 31) | **1**<br>(out of: 31 vs 40)<br>(3 % vs 2 %) |

The highest degree of overlap takes place, unsurprisingly, within the Polish Eurolect, followed by the corpora of translated CJ judgments and non-translated SN judgments. The degree of overlap between translated CJ judgments and non-translated SN judgments is very similar to the level of overlap between the GC and SN corpora, with the most substantial difference, although still quite negligible, observed for 2–grams. The only irregularity can be observed with the overlap of 4–grams in the CJ and the SN corpora, the degree of which is lower than in the same type of n-grams common to both the GC and SN corpora. The low overall overlap between each of the corpora representing Polish Eurolect and the corpus of post-accession SN judgments may be indicative of low thematic convergence; however, this finding needs to be verified through analysis of content and non-content

**Table 7.11.** *Overlap of 3–4–grams in the translation and non-translation corpora (after refinement)*

| N-grams | CJ vs GC | CJ vs SN_2011–2015 | GC vs SN_2011–2015 | SN_2011–2015 vs SN_1999 |
|---|---|---|---|---|
| 3–grams | **135** (out of: 376 vs 325) (36 % vs 41 %) | **52** (out of: 376 vs 339) (14 % vs 15 %) | **44** (out of: 325 vs 339) (14 % vs 13 %) | **158** (out of: 339 vs 436) (46 % vs 36 %) |
| 4–grams | **38** (out of: 131 vs 115) (29 % vs 33 %) | **9** (out of: 131 vs 139) (7 % vs 6 %) | **10** (out of: 115 vs 139) (9 % vs 7 %) | **46** (out of: 139 vs 162) (33 % vs 28 %) |

bundles among the identified bundles which are shared between the corpora. The highest degree of overlap can be determined in the case of the pre- and post-accession corpora of SN judgments, which surpasses the internal overlap between both EU corpora.

Since it would be impractical to present all 2–8–grams shared between the individual corpora which were identified prior to the refinement, I will focus only on overlapping 3–4–grams which were not removed in the refinement procedure (see Table 7.11).

The above data confirm the trends observed in unrefined data concerning the overlap between the corpora. For want of space, I will present only the types of shared bundles, without detailed quantitative data on their distribution and dispersion. General observations regarding the thematic convergence and formulaic profile of EU and national corpora established with overlapping bundles will be presented at the end of this Section.

*CJ vs GC – shared 3–grams*

The first list of shared n-grams contains 135 3–grams, from which 56 were labeled as content bundles (i.e. bundles containing at least one word related thematically to the content of the judgments, by referring to agents and institutions, abstract concepts, actions, documents, dates or places), whereas 79 bundles were labeled as non-content bundles.

The ratio of content to non-content bundles shared between the two corpora representing the Polish Eurolect shows that there is a relatively high thematic convergence, as content bundles like *zgodnie z art*, *wyrok z dnia*, *w charakterze pełnomocników*, and *w niniejszej sprawie* represent about 41 % of all shared bundles, which indicates a moderate level of thematic convergence, despite the fact that judgments in both corpora were issued by EU courts. As regards the distribution, the shared types of 3–word bundles are about 8 % more frequent in the GC corpus (25,021 occurrences pmw).

**Figure 7.1.** *All 135 3–grams shared by the CJ and GC corpora (ordered alphabetically, after refinement)*

| |
|---|
| *a po drugie; a tym samym; biorąc pod uwagę; co do istoty; co do zasady; co się tyczy; decyzją z dnia; dopuszczenie do obrotu; dostępu do dokumentów; i in przeciwko; izba w składzie; izba z dnia; jak wynika z; jeśli chodzi o; jeżeli chodzi o; komisji rec s; których mowa w; lit a rozporządzenia; lit b rozporządzenia; lit. c rozporządzenia; ma na celu; mając na uwadze; mające na celu; mającej za przedmiot; mających na celu; na mocy art; na podstawie art; na podstawie tego; na tej podstawie; na wstępie należy; należy podkreślić że; należy przypomnieć że; należy stwierdzić że; należy uznać za; należy uznać że; należy wskazać że; należy zauważyć że; nie mogą być; nie może być; nie może zostać; nie można uznać; o której mowa; o których mowa; o którym mowa; o stwierdzenie nieważności; od tego czy; odnosi się do; odnoszące się do; okoliczności powstania sporu; opiera się na; orzeka co następuje; p i c; parlamentu europejskiego i; pismem z dnia; po drugie że; po pierwsze że; po zapoznaniu się; pod warunkiem że; postanowieniem z dnia; postępowania przed sądem; powoływać się na; powyższych rozważań wynika; prawa do obrony; przeciwko komisji zb; przewidziane w art; przewidzianego w art; przez komisję w; przytoczone tam orzecznictwo; r w sprawie; Republika Federalna Niemiec; rozprawy w dniu; strona przegrywająca sprawę; towarów lub usług; w celu zapewnienia; w charakterze pełnomocników; w drugiej kolejności; w dzienniku urzędowym; w każdym razie; w niniejszej sprawie; w niniejszym przypadku; w odniesieniu do; w odpowiedzi na; w oparciu o; w pierwszej kolejności; w przedmiocie kosztów; w przedmiocie zarzutu; w ramach postępowania; w razie potrzeby; w rozumieniu art; w sprawach połączonych; w stosunku do; w sytuacji gdy; w świetle powyższych; w tej kwestii; w ten sposób; w tych okolicznościach; w tym celu; w tym kontekście; w tym samym; w tym względzie; w tym zakresie; w zakresie dotyczącym; w zależności od; w Zjednoczonym Królestwie; w żaden sposób; wątpliwości co do; wbrew temu co; wspólnotowego znaku towarowego; ww wyrok w; wydaje następujący wyrok; wyrok z dnia; z akt sprawy; z drugiej strony; z jednej strony; z powyższego wynika; z powyższych względów; z punktu widzenia; z tego powodu; z tego względu; z utrwalonego orzecznictwa; z utrwalonym orzecznictwem; z uwagi na; zakresie w jakim; zasady równego traktowania; ze wspólnym rynkiem; ze względu na; zgodnie z art; zgodnie z którą; zgodnie z którym; zgodnie z orzecznictwem; zgodnie z prawem; zgodności z prawem; zob. podobnie wyrok; że komisja nie; że w ramach* |

*CJ vs SN_2011–2015 – shared 3–grams*

The 52 types of 3–grams shared by the corpus of CJ judgments and the corpus of SN judgments are shown in Figure 7.2. Of all the identified shared bundles, 22 were labeled as content bundles, whereas 30 bundles were determined to be non-content bundles.

In the case of the list of bundles shared between the PLEU-CJ and PL-SN corpora, it can be observed that content bundles represent about 42 % of all shared bundles. Obviously, the medium level of thematic convergence coupled with the generally low number of shared bundles is connected with the fact that the CJ and the SN exercise different territorial and subject-matter jurisdiction. The shared types are about 13 % more frequent in post-accession SN judgments.

**Figure 7.2.** *All 52 3-grams shared by the CJ and SN_2011–2015 corpora (ordered alphabetically, after refinement)*

*biorąc pod uwagę; co do istoty; co do zasady; decyzją z dnia; i w konsekwencji; jak wynika z; mowa w art; na podstawie art; na tej podstawie; na to że; nie może być; niezależnie od tego; o której mowa; o których mowa; o którym mowa; odnosi się do; określonych w art; pismem z dnia; przewidziane w art; przewidzianego w art; przewidzianej w art; przewidzianych w art; sytuacji w której; tylko wtedy gdy; ustawy z dnia; w niniejszej sprawie; w odniesieniu do; w odpowiedzi na; w oparciu o; w pierwszej kolejności; w postępowaniu przed; w rozumieniu art; w stosunku do; w sytuacji, gdy; w świetle art; w ten sposób; w tym przepisie; w tym zakresie; w zaskarżonym wyroku; wątpliwości co do; wejścia w życie; wyrok z dnia; wyroki z dnia; wyrokiem z dnia; z punktu widzenia; z siedzibą w; z tego względu; z uwagi na; zakresie w jakim; ze względu na; zgodnie z art; zgodnie z którym*

*GC vs SN_2011–2015 – shared 3-grams*

The 44 types of 3-grams shared by the GC corpus and the corpus of post-accession SN judgments are presented in Figure 7.3.

From all the identified shared bundles, 15 were labeled as content bundles (i.e. bundles containing at least one word related thematically to the content of the judgments), whereas 29 bundles were identified as acting as non-content bundles, which means that only about 34 % of all shared types can be related to the content of the judgments, indicating a lower thematic convergence than in the case of CJ and SN judgments. The shared types are about 19 % more frequent in SN judgments.

*SN_2011–2015 vs SN_1999 – shared 3-grams*

The examination of 158 types of 3-grams shared by the pre- and post-accession SN corpora might provide some insight into the linguistic change that might have occurred in national judgments following Poland's accession to the EU.

**Figure 7.3.** *All 44 3-grams shared by the GC and SN_2011–2015 corpora (ordered alphabetically, after refinement)*

*zgodnie z którym; zgodnie z art; ze względu na; zakresie w jakim; z uwagi na; z tego względu; z punktu widzenia; wyrok z dnia; wątpliwości co do; w związku z; w tym zakresie; w toku postępowania; w ten sposób; w sytuacji, gdy; w stosunku do; w rozumieniu art.; w pozostałym zakresie; w pierwszej kolejności; w oparciu o; w okresie od; w odpowiedzi na; w odniesieniu do; w niniejszej sprawie; towarów i usług; przewidzianego w art; przewidziane w art; pismem z dnia; określone w art; odpowiedzi na skargę; odnosi się do; o którym mowa; o których mowa; o której mowa; niezgodności z prawem; nie może być; na tej podstawie; na rozprawie w; na podstawie art; jak wynika z; decyzją z dnia; co do zasady; co do istoty; biorąc pod uwagę; a w konsekwencji*

**Figure 7.4.** *All 158 3–grams shared by the SN_2011–2015 corpus and the SN_1999 corpus (ordered alphabetically, after refinement)*

| |
|---|
| *a w konsekwencji; bez względu na; być uznane za; co do zasady; do ponownego rozpoznania; i przekazania sprawy; jak w sentencji; jak wynika z; k c a; k c art; k c i; k c jest; k c przez; k c w; k p a; k p c; k r o; kosztów postępowania kasacyjnego; mieć wpływ na; mowa w art; na jego rzecz; na jej rzecz; na obu podstawach; na podstawie art; na podstawie przepisów; na podstawie umowy; na rzecz powoda; na rzecz powodów; na rzecz powódki; na rzecz pozwanego; na rzecz pozwanej; na rzecz strony; na wynik sprawy; naruszenia prawa materialnego; naruszenia przepisów postępowania; naruszenie prawa materialnego; naruszenie przepisów postępowania; nie może być; o kosztach postępowania; o którym mowa; o oddalenie powództwa; od Skarbu Państwa; od wyroku sądu; odnosi się do; odnosząc się do; określonych w art; orzecznictwie Sądu Najwyższego; oznacza to że; p c i; p c przez; p c w; pismem z dnia; podstaw do przyjęcia; pozwanego skarbu państwa; pozwanej od wyroku; prawa do lokalu; przeciwko Skarbowi Państwa; przewidziane w art; przewidzianego w art; przewidzianej w art; przewidzianych w art; przez błędną wykładnię; przez przyjęcie że; przez Sąd Apelacyjny; przez Sąd Najwyższy; przez sąd odwoławczy; przez stronę powodową; przez stronę pozwaną; Sąd Apelacyjny podzielił; Sąd Apelacyjny przyjął; Sąd Apelacyjny stwierdził; Sąd Apelacyjny uznał; sąd drugiej instancji; sąd i instancji; Sąd Najwyższy na; sąd pierwszej instancji; sądem pierwszej instancji; sądu drugiej instancji; sądu pierwszej instancji; składu siedmiu sędziów; treści księgi wieczystej; tytułem zwrotu kosztów; uchyla zaskarżony wyrok; ustawy z dnia; uzasadnienia zaskarżonego wyroku; w części dotyczącej; w części oddalającej; w księdze wieczystej; w niniejszej sprawie; w ocenie sądu; w odniesieniu do; w ogóle nie; w okolicznościach sprawy; w okresie od; w oparciu o; w pierwszej kolejności; w postępowaniu apelacyjnym; w postępowaniu kasacyjnym; w postępowaniu przed; w pozostałej części; w pozostałym zakresie; w ramach podstawy; w rozpoznawanej sprawie; w rozumieniu art; w skardze kasacyjnej; w sprawie o; w stosunku do; w sytuacji, gdy; w świetle art; w takiej sytuacji; w tej części; w tej sprawie; w tej sytuacji; w ten sposób; w toku postępowania; w trybie art; w tym przedmiocie; w tym przepisie; w tym stanie; w tym wypadku; w tym zakresie; w uzasadnieniu wyroku; w uzasadnieniu zaskarżonego; w w o; w zaskarżonym wyroku; w zw. z; w związku z; wątpliwości co do; wejścia w życie; wniósł o uchylenie; wpływ na wynik; wyrok Sądu Apelacyjnego; wyrok Sądu Najwyższego; wyrok z dnia; wyrokiem z dnia; z mocy prawa; z naruszeniem art; z o o; z ograniczoną odpowiedzialnością; z opinii biegłego; z punktu widzenia; z tego tytułu; z tego względu; z tej przyczyny; z tych przyczyn; z tych względów; z ustawowymi odsetkami; z uwagi na; zarzucił naruszenie art; zarzut naruszenia art; zarzutu naruszenia art.; zasadami współżycia społecznego; zdaniem Sądu Apelacyjnego; ze względu na; zgodnie z art.; zgodnie z którym; zmienił zaskarżony wyrok; że powód nie* |

3–grams shared by both SN corpora are mostly content-related. There are 117 content-related n-grams, which are almost three times more numerous than the 41 remaining non-content types. This shows that post-accession national judgments exhibit a high degree of thematic convergence with pre-accession judgments, despite the socio-political changes that have taken place in the context of Poland's

**Figure 7.5.** *All 38 4-grams shared by the Polish Eurolect corpora (CJ and GC) (ordered alphabetically) (after refinement)*

| |
|---|
| *a z drugiej strony; działających w charakterze pełnomocników; i przytoczone tam orzecznictwo; Izba orzeka co następuje; jak wynika z pkt; lit a rozporządzenia nr; lit b rozporządzenia nr; na dopuszczenie do obrotu; na żądanie strony przeciwnej; o której mowa w; o których mowa w; o którym mowa w; Parlamentu Europejskiego i Rady; po zapoznaniu się z; podobnie wyrok z dnia; powyższych rozważań wynika że; r w sprawach połączonych; r w sprawie C; r w sprawie T; r wydaje następujący wyrok; rozporządzenia Rady WE nr; w ten sposób że; w tym względzie należy; w tym względzie, że; w zakresie, w jakim; w związku z art; w związku z czym; w związku z powyższym; w związku z tym; ww wyrok w sprawie; wynika z tego że; względu na to iż; z powyższego wynika że; z tego względu że; z utrwalonego orzecznictwa wynika; ze względu na to; zgodnie z utrwalonym orzecznictwem; zob wyrok z dnia* |

accession. What should be observed, however, is that post-accession judgments contain about 11 % fewer occurrences of the shared types of 3-grams.

*CJ vs GC – shared 4-grams*
Owing to the fact that 4-grams are not as frequent in all the corpora as 3-grams, their types are less widely shared between the individual corpora. The 38 types of 4-grams shared by the corpus of CJ judgments and the corpus of GC judgments are presented in Figure 7.5. Of all shared 4-word bundles, 21 were labeled as content bundles (i.e. bundles containing at least one word related thematically to the content of the judgments), whereas 17 bundles were labeled as non-content bundles. Shared types of 4-grams occur more frequently in CJ judgments (by about 23 %).

A total of 22 bundles are labeled as content bundles which are shared between the two corpora representing the Polish Eurolect, meaning that the degree of thematic convergence stands at approximately 56 % of all shared bundles. This value is considerably higher than in the case of 3-word bundles shared by the same combination of corpora, which equaled 49 % (see above). This finding suggests that 4-grams are generally more prone to containing words connected with the thematic content of judgments, which is undoubtedly due to their length.

*CJ vs SN_2011–2015 – shared 4-grams*
There are 9 types of 4-grams shared by the corpus of CJ judgments and the corpus of post-accession SN judgments, all of which are presented in Figure 7.6. Shared 4-grams are about 45 % more frequent in CJ judgments.

Of all the identified shared bundles, only 2 were labeled as content bundles (i.e. bundles containing at least one word related thematically to the content of the judgments), whereas 7 bundles were labeled as non-content bundles, which means that only 22 % of types are content-related. This highlights the divergent thematic content of EU and national judgments.

**Figure 7.6.** *All 9 4–grams shared by the CJ corpus and the SN_2011–2015 corpus (ordered alphabetically) (after refinement)*

| |
|---|
| *w związku z tym; w związku z czym; w związku z art; w zakresie w jakim; w ten sposób że; w postępowaniu przed sądem; o którym mowa w; o których mowa w; o której mowa w* |

*GC vs SN_2011–2015 – shared 4–grams*

The 10 types of 4–grams shared by the corpus of GC judgments and the corpus of non-translated post-accession SN judgments are presented in Figure 7.7. Of all the identified shared bundles, only 3 were labeled as content bundles, whereas 7 bundles were labeled as non-content bundles. SN judgments have approximately 9 % more occurrences of shared 4–grams.

**Figure 7.7.** *All 10 4–grams shared by the GC corpus and the SN_2011–2015 corpus (ordered alphabetically) (after refinement)*

| |
|---|
| *o której mowa w; o których mowa w; o którym mowa w; w odpowiedzi na skargę; w piśmie z dnia; w ten sposób że; w zakresie w jakim; w związku z art; w związku z czym; w związku z tym* |

Compared to the distance of CJ to post-accession SN judgments at the level of 4–grams, the difference is negligible, which is in line with the previous observation. Three very commonly shared 4–grams in the Polish Eurolect (in both CJ and GC judgments) and the language of non-translated judgments are inflectional variants of the referential phrase frame *o któr* mowa w* [which is/are referred to in], which serves as an important inter- and intra-textual indicator.[143] Another shared phrase frame, which also performs essential metadiscursive functions, is the frame *w związku z ** [in accordance with/therefore], which is represented by the following bundles: *w związku z art* [in accordance with art], *w związku z czym* [therefore], and *w związku z tym* [therefore].

*SN_2011–2015 vs SN_1999 – shared 4–grams*

All 46 4–grams shared by the post-accession national corpus and the pre-accession national corpus are shown ordered alphabetically in Figure 7.8. As was to be expected after the examination of 3–grams shared by both SN corpora, shared types of 4–grams are also mostly content-related, as 89 % of all shared types relate to the thematic content. Surprisingly, however, both corpora have an almost identical distribution of shared 4–grams.

The low degree of overlap between the Polish Eurolect and the language of non-translated judgments suggests that translations exhibit the use of a quite distinct

143 The same phrase frame was also found to be shared between the corpora of Polish regulations and directives and non-translated Polish law (cf. Biel 2017c: 20–21).

**Figure 7.8.** *All 10 4-grams shared by the SN_2011–2015 corpus and the SN_1999 corpus (ordered alphabetically) (after refinement)*

| |
|---|
| *z zasadami współżycia społecznego; z odsetkami ustawowymi od; wyroku sądu pierwszej instancji; wyroku sądu apelacyjnego w; wyrok sn z dnia; wpływ na wynik sprawy; w związku z tym; w związku z czym; w związku z art; w zw z art; w wyroku z dnia; w uzasadnieniu zaskarżonego wyroku; w tym stanie rzeczy; w ten sposób że; w postępowaniu przed sądem; w orzecznictwie Sądu Najwyższego; w ocenie Sądu Apelacyjnego; sprawy do ponownego rozpoznania; spółki z o o; spółce z o o; Sądu Najwyższego z dnia; sądowi apelacyjnemu do ponownego; sąd apelacyjny wyrokiem z; r. uchyla zaskarżony wyrok; r o zmianie ustawy; przez sąd pierwszej instancji; przez sąd drugiej instancji; przed sądem pierwszej instancji; orzekł o kosztach procesu; orzekł jak w sentencji; orzeczono jak w sentencji; od wyroku sądu apelacyjnego; od pozwanego na rzecz; od powoda na rzecz; o uchylenie zaskarżonego wyroku; o kosztach postępowania kasacyjnego; k p c w; k p c przez; k p c poprzez; k p c oraz; k p c nie; k p c i; k p c a; k c i art.; i w tym zakresie; do złożenia oświadczenia woli* |

set of recurrent word sequences. Even though it might be expected that translated texts should utilize a similar set of bundle types to non-translated texts belonging to the same sub-genre, it is, in fact, quite the opposite – translations employ their own sets of bundles, prompted by the STs (i.e. judgments drafted originally in French) and their subject matter. In other words, translations of EU judgments resort to their own lexical bundles triggered by the STs and fail to prime bundles which are typical of and salient in TL texts (cf. Biel *et al.* 2019: 87). Therefore, as regards the distribution of shared 3- and 4-grams (which are expected to best reflect the formulaic profile of a genre) in translations and non-translations, EU judgments translated into Polish have a phraseological profile largely dissimilar from that of non-translated Polish judgments. It is a quite distinct formulaic profile characterized by the use of patterns not commonly used in non-translated national judgments.

As regards the degree of thematic convergence between the EU and national judgments, the identified ratios of content to non-content bundles show that the highest degree of thematic convergence is observed between the corpora representing pre- and post-accession SN judgments, despite the wider contextual factors related to Poland's accession to the EU which might have affected the formulaic profile of national judgments. The thematic convergence between the Eurolect corpora and the post-accession SN corpus remains relatively low, as most of the shared bundles do not relate to the textual content of judgments per se, but rather contain patterns made up of function words. Biel *et al.* (2019) suggest that in order to verify this finding, further studies should attempt to better control the thematic variable of corpora, which could potentially be achieved by including texts related to one specific area of law and adjudication. Analyzing texts that are similar in terms of their contents would certainly yield more reliable results on their formulaic profiles.

At this point, it should also to be stated that the identification of bundles shared by the EU corpora and the national corpus may contribute to the creation of an inventory of core lexical bundles, that is n-grams crucial to the genre as a whole, which could potentially contribute to the development of teaching materials better suited to the needs of translation students, who need to achieve a high level of generic competence.

## 7.6. Functional classification of lexical bundles

For the purposes of classifying lexical bundles occurring in EU and national judgments according to their discourse functions, I decided to apply the main tenets of the taxonomy presented in Biber *et al.* (2004: 384–388). According to their original taxonomy, recurring word combinations, depending on the functions they perform in texts, can be generally classified into three main categories: stance, discourse-organizing and referential bundles (Biber *et al.* 2004: 384–388). Stance bundles are used to express the speaker's or writer's attitudes or assessments of certainty; discourse-organizing bundles provide a scaffolding for the prior and following discourse, whereas referential bundles refer directly to physical or abstract entities (Biber *et al.* 2004: 384–388).

Owing to the nature of judicial discourse, it was necessary to modify Biber *et al.*'s (2004: 384–388) taxonomy by adapting certain elements of other taxonomies relating specifically to the administrative and judicial language varieties (cf. Goźdź-Roszkowski 2011: 109–143; Jablonkai 2009: 6, 2010: 262). This was achieved using a primarily exploratory, inductive approach, which aimed to accommodate for the specific types of discourse functions performed by lexical bundles in judicial discourse. This approach consisted of studying the textual context of the most frequent bundles in each of the corpora using the Concordance tool in WS, which made it possible to search for common traits in the functions performed by different bundle types. As a result, a modified version of the previously proposed functional taxonomies (cf. Section 7.2) was devised (see Table 7.12).

The current functional classification still revolves around the three main categories introduced by Biber *et al.* (2004: 384–388), each of which has several subcategories that serve to describe more specific discourse functions of lexical bundles occurring in the language of judgments. Table 7.12 lists only those functions which were realized in the corpora analyzed in this study, meaning that, for instance, that the sub-category of stance expressions expressing obligation or directive, identified by Goźdź-Roszkowski (2011: 138–142), is not represented.

The taxonomy presented in Table 7.12 differs from that presented in Jablonkai's analysis of lexical bundles in English-language EU documents (2010: 262) in several ways. First, the sub-category *Attitudinal/modality stance* does not contain two of the four further original sub-categories, *Desire* and *Ability* because analysis of the current material has not revealed any bundles belonging to either of these categories. Instead, they were replaced by the sub-categories *Intensification bundles* and *Evaluative bundles*, thanks to which it was possible to more precisely classify bundles expressing various types of attitudinal stance taken by the courts. In the category *Discourse-organizing*

**Table 7.12.** *Discourse functions of lexical bundles (based on Biber et al. 2004: 384–388, Goźdź-Roszkowski 2011: 109–143, and Jablonkai 2009: 6, 2010: 262)*

| Main categories | Sub-categories | Sample lexical bundles |
|---|---|---|
| **1. Stance bundles** | 1.1 Epistemic stance | *należy uznać, że* [(it) should be noted], *nie może zostać* [cannot be (transposed/upheld, etc.)], *prawdą jest, że* [it is true that], *na fakt, że* [given (that the)] |
| | 1.2 Evaluative | *sąd naruszył prawo* [erred in law]/[made an error (of law)], *rozważywszy uwagi przedstawione* [having considered the comments presented], *orzeka co następuje* [rules as follows] |
| **2. Text-oriented bundles** | 2.1 Causative-resultative expressions (and inferential) | *z tego względu* [in that regard], *związku z tym* [accordingly/consequently], *a tym samym* [and thus (make)] |
| | 2.2 Conditional expressions | *pod warunkiem że* [only if (the)] |
| | 2.3 Framing attributes | *w oparciu o* [on the basis (of)], *na podstawie tego* [on the basis (of)] |
| | 2.4 Identification/ focus | *w niniejszej sprawie* [(in) the present case], *w tej kwestii* [as regards the], *w tym zakresie* [in this regard] |
| | 2.5 Intra-/ intertextual navigation | *w świetle art* [(in) the light of], *w przedmiocie pytania* [the (first) question] |
| | 2.6 Purpose expressions | *w celu zapewnienia* [(in) order to guarantee], *w tym celu* [to that end] |
| | 2.7 Topic elaboration/ clarification | *zgodnie z orzecznictwem* [(according) to the case-law] |
| | 2.8 Transition expressions | *z jednej strony* [(it follows) first], *z drugiej strony* [(and) second (that)], *w pierwszej kolejności* [(in) the first place] |
| **3. Referential bundles** | 3.1 Abstract concepts | *zasady równego traktowania* [(principle) of equal treatment], *prawa do obrony* [rights of defence], *nieważności spornej decyzji* [(annulment of) the contested decision] |
| | 3.2 Agents/ institutions | *stron w postępowaniu* [parties to the (proceedings)], *przez państwa członkowskie* [by Member States], *przed sądem krajowym* [(in) the main proceedings] |

(*continued on next page*)

**Table 7.12.** *Continued*

| Main categories | Sub-categories | Sample lexical bundles |
|---|---|---|
| | 3.3 Dates | *rozprawy w dniu* [the hearing on], *na czas określony* [a fixed period] |
| | 3.4 Documents | *w Dzienniku Urzędowym* [(in) the Official Journal], *wniosek o udzielenie* [request to provide], *regulaminu postępowania przed* [Rules of Procedure] |
| | 3.5 Places | *na jego terytorium* [on its territory], *w państwach członkowskich* [in Member States] |
| | 3.6 Legal procedure | *w charakterze pełnomocnika* [acting as Agent], *w postępowaniu przed* [(in) the proceedings before], *po wysłuchaniu rzecznika* [after hearing the (Advocate General)], *na żądanie strony* [(applied for in the) successful party's pleadings], *na posiedzeniu w* [at the sitting (on)] |

*bundles*, the sub-category *Topic introduction bundles* was discarded, since it was established that there were not many bundles performing functions associated with it and that they could, in fact, be included in the sub-category *Topic elaboration/clarification bundles.* Based on Goźdź-Roszkowski (2011: 130) and contrary to Jablonkai (2010: 262), another sub-category added to *Discourse-organizing bundles* is *Causative-resultative bundles.* The third and last category, *Referential bundles*, also differs from that presented in Jablonkai's study (2010: 262), as it does not include the three sub-categories *Quantity specification*, *Quality specification* and *Multi-functional reference.* A new category added in this study is *Documents*, which relieves the sub-category *Intra-/inter-textual bundles* of bundles consisting solely of names of various documents (e.g. *reference for a preliminary, the Rules of Procedure*, etc.) and not pointing to specific points in other texts. A more detailed description of all the main categories and their individual sub-categories will follow later.

Owing to the high total number of 3– and 4–word lexical bundles in each of the corpora, it was not feasible to examine the co-text of each individual bundle type due to the time-consuming nature of the process. It should be borne in mind that functional classification has been conducted using the refined lists of 3– and 4–grams. Had this not been the case, the analysis would have had to encompass twice as many lexical bundles. The analysis of concordance lines was limited to lexical bundles occurring very frequently in each of the corpora and to bundles which were difficult to categorize based on their literal meaning. Considering that most, if not all, bundles form larger sequences of words prior to the refinement of lists of lexical bundles generated automatically using WS, it was not necessary to ascertain the discourse function of every single bundle type by studying its context of occurrence. Another problematic issue encountered at the first stage of the analysis concerned the fact that many lexical bundles seem to perform more than one function in the genre depending on the context in which they appear. An example of such a bundle could be *the end of the*, which might be classified as a bundle serving as either a time, place or text-deictic reference (cf. Goźdź-Roszkowski 2011: 117). The solution to this problem was to classify such bundles according to their dominant discourse functions upon prior analysis of their co-text, which eliminated the need to create an additional category containing bundles serving as multifunctional references (see above; cf. Jablonkai 2010: 262).

Table 7.13 presents quantitative data on the aggregate number of types of 3–4-grams in each of the corpora classified into the three overarching functional categories. The Table shows that 3-grams and 4-grams paint an entirely different picture of formulaicity in translated EU and non-translated Polish judgments. The analysis of the refined lists of lexical bundles (see Section 7.5 for information regarding the refinement procedure) has shown that the most frequently occurring 3-word bundles in the corpus of post-accession CJ judgments are referential bundles, followed closely by discourse-organizing bundles, with stance bundles being the least frequent. Stance bundles, as it can be observed, is the least frequently recurring category of bundles across all corpora, as regards both the total number of types and occurrences. The analysis of 4-grams from the same corpus has revealed that 4-grams are distributed in a similar manner to 3-grams when judged by the number of types in each category. The patterning of CJ and GC judgments at the level of 3-grams diverges from that of SN (both pre- and post-accession) judgments in that EU judgments prioritize discourse-organizing over referential bundles. At the level of 4-grams, CJ judgments diverge from GC judgments by prioritizing referential over discourse-organizing bundles. This is indicative of a significant degree of internal variation in the Eurolect. What can also be read from the data is that translated EU judgments markedly diverge from non-translated national judgments. The former exhibit a significantly lower number of occurrences of all types of bundles, both at the level of 3- and 4-grams. The highlighted differences indicate the divergent formulaic profile of EU judgments, which differs from national judgments. All in all, the data show that the analysis of lexical bundles should not be limited to bundles of just one length, be it 3- or 4-grams, as analyses focusing solely on bundles of a certain length may produce skewed results.

In the following, I will discuss each of the main functional categories of 3- and 4-word lexical bundles occurring in the language of EU and national judgments which were identified in the refinement procedure, as well as each of the sub-categories. In doing so, I aim to provide a detailed overview of the formulaic profile of translated EU and non-translated national judgments, in the hope that the classification of discourse functions performed by lexical bundles in judicial language could potentially be replicated by researchers studying similar judicial genres, e.g. opinions of Advocates General. The discussion of the major functional

**Table 7.13.** *Quantitative data on the distribution of lexical bundles acting as stance, discourse-organizing and referential expressions (bundle types are listed according to the number of types in the corpus of post-accession SN judgments)*

| | **Translated EU case law** | | | | | **Non-translated PL case law** | | |
|---|---|---|---|---|---|---|---|---|
| | **CJ** | | | **GC** | | **SN_2011–2015** | | **SN_1999** |
| **3-grams** | **CJ** | **CJ vs GC (%DIFF)** | **CJ vs SN_2011–2015 (%DIFF)** | **GC** | **GC vs SN_2011–2015 (%DIFF)** | **SN_2011–2015** | **SN_2011–2015 vs SN_1999 (%DIFF)** | **SN_1999** |
| **Referential bundles** | | | | | | | | |
| Total types | 160 | +28 % | −5 % | 125 | −26 % | 169 | −30 % | 240 |
| Total occurrences (NF) | 14,962 | +25 % | −25 % | 12,015 | −40 % | 20,071 | −39 % | 33,032 |
| **Discourse-organizing bundles** | | | | | | | | |
| Total types | 169 | +11 % | +30 % | 152 | +17 % | 130 | −6 % | 139 |
| Total occurrences (NF) | 24,708 | −7 % | +3 % | 26,464 | +10 % | 23,980 | +1 % | 23,704 |
| **Stance bundles** | | | | | | | | |
| Total types | 47 | −2 % | +18 % | 48 | +20 % | 40 | −30 % | 57 |
| Total occurrences (NF) | 4,587 | +8 % | +26 % | 4,248 | +17 % | 3,635 | −31 % | 5,291 |
| **TOTAL (types):** | **376** | **+16 %** | **+11 %** | **325** | **−4 %** | **339** | **−22 %** | **436** |

| | Translated EU case law | | | | | Non-translated PL case law | | |
|---|---|---|---|---|---|---|---|---|
| | CJ | | | GC | | SN_2011–2015 | | SN_1999 |
| **TOTAL (occurrences):** | **44,257** | **+4 %** | **−7 %** | **42,727** | **−10 %** | **47,686** | **−23 %** | **62,027** |
| **4-grams** | **CJ** | **CJ vs GC (%DIFF)** | **CJ vs SN_2011–2015 (%DIFF)** | **GC** | **GC vs SN_2011–2015 (%DIFF)** | **SN_2011–2015** | **SN_2011–2015 vs SN_1999 (%DIFF)** | **SN_1999** |
| **Referential bundles** | | | | | | | | |
| Total types | 70 | +63 % | −17 % | 43 | −49 % | 84 | −22 % | 108 |
| Total occurrences (NF) | 7,063 | +62 % | −26 % | 4,348 | −55 % | 9,597 | −28 % | 13,369 |
| **Discourse-organizing bundles** | | | | | | | | |
| Total types | 51 | −18 % | +28 % | 62 | +55 % | 40 | +11 % | 36 |
| Total occurrences (NF) | 5,679 | −14 % | +2 % | 6,640 | +19 % | 5,561 | +23 % | 4,526 |
| **Stance bundles** | | | | | | | | |
| Total types | 10 | 0 % | −33 % | 10 | −33 % | 15 | −17 % | 18 |
| Total occurrences (NF) | 1,138 | +44 % | −17 % | 791 | −43 % | 1,377 | −39 % | 2,275 |
| **TOTAL (types):** | **131** | **+14 %** | **−6 %** | **115** | **−17 %** | **139** | **−14 %** | **162** |
| **TOTAL (occurrences):** | **13,880** | **+18 %** | **−16 %** | **11,779** | **−29 %** | **16,534** | **−18 %** | **20,170** |

categories in Sections 7.6.1, 7.6.2 and 7.6.3 will be ordered according to the functional categorization of bundles (total number of their types) in the post-accession SN corpus, as it is the point of reference for comparing translated EU judgments to non-translated SN judgments.

## 7.6.1 Referential bundles

The analysis of referential bundles enabled the identification of a total of six sub-categories. The discourse function of referential bundles is to provide references to: (1) various entities, mainly agents and institutions, e.g. *Parlamentu Europejskiego i* [European Parliament and], *w Izbie Cywilnej* [in (the) Civil Chamber], (2) actions taken within the course of legal proceedings and their stages (e.g. *w toku postępowania* [in the course of the proceedings], *Skarżąca podnosi, że* [Applicant submits that]), (3) abstract concepts, such as terms, rights or types of obligation, e.g. *błąd w ocenie* [error of assessment], *zasady równego traktowania* [principle of equal treatment], (4) names of documents, e.g. *opinią Rzecznika Generalnego* [Advocate General's opinion], *Statutu Trybunału Sprawiedliwości* [Statute of the Court of Justice], (5) dates, e.g. *rozprawy w dniu* [the hearing on], and (6) places, e.g. *w państwie członkowskim* [in the Member State]. The classification developed in the course of the analysis of lists of 3–4–grams from the corpora of EU and national judgments is partly based on Goźdź-Roszkowski's (2011: 119–129) taxonomy, which included seven different sub-categories of referential bundles: temporal reference, location, attributive, participative, institutional, terminological, and legal procedure bundles (cf. Section 7.2). Five of these are employed in this study, albeit under different or similar names – temporal reference bundles (dates), location bundles (places), institutional bundles (agents/institutions), terminological bundles (abstract concepts) and procedure-related bundles (legal procedure bundles).

Lexical bundles classified as referential (alongside discourse-organizing bundles) constitute one of the two major functional categories across the corpora. In written genres, such as textbook and academic prose (cf. Biber *et al.* 2004; Jablonkai 2010: 263), legislation, contracts, professional articles (cf. Goźdź-Roszkowski 2011: 118), official EU documents (Commission and Council press releases, legal texts from the Official Journal of the European Union), newspaper articles dealing with EU-related issues (cf. Jablonkai 2009: 17), and EU legislative acts (regulations and directives) (Biel 2017c: 22), referential bundles have been found to constitute the largest functional group of lexical bundles, followed by discourse-organizing bundles and stance bundles. In the case of the genre of judgments, this is true only in the case of both pre- and post-accession SN judgments.

Table 7.14 presents quantitative data on the number of referential bundle types belonging to each of the sub-categories and their distribution across the corpora, as well as percentages describing the proportion of a given sub-category against the total number of bundle types in this functional category.

**Table 7.14.** *Distribution of 3–4–word referential bundles in the corpora and their classification into individual functional sub-categories (ordered according to the normalized frequency of occurrence in the individual corpora)*

| Translated EU case law | | | | | | | | | | |
|---|---|---|---|---|---|---|---|---|---|---|
| CJ | | | | | | GC | | | | |
| **3–grams** | **Types** | **% of all types** | **NF** | **CJ vs GC (%DIFF)** | **CJ vs SN_2011–2015 (%DIFF)** | **3–grams** | **Types** | **% of all types** | **NF** | **GC vs SN_2011–2015 (%DIFF)** |
| Agents/ Institutions | 64 | 40 % | 5,672 | +86 % | −29 % | Abstract concepts | 47 | 38 % | 3,737 | −37 % |
| Legal procedure | 30 | 19 % | 4,245 | +58 % | +53 % | Agents/ Institutions | 25 | 20 % | 3,056 | −62 % |
| Documents | 26 | 16 % | 2,191 | +26 % | −29 % | Legal procedure | 33 | 26 % | 2,695 | −3 % |
| Abstract concepts | 26 | 16 % | 1,575 | −58 % | −74 % | Documents | 11 | 9 % | 1,739 | −43 % |
| Places | 12 | 8 % | 1,053 | +152 % | +1925 % | Places | 4 | 3 % | 418 | +704 % |
| Dates | 2 | 1 % | 226 | −39 % | +14 % | Dates | 5 | 4 % | 368 | +86 % |
| **TOTAL:** | **160** | **100 %** | **14,962** | **+25 %** | **−25 %** | **TOTAL:** | **125** | **100 %** | **12,013** | **−40 %** |
| **4–grams** | **Types** | **% of all types** | **NF** | **CJ vs GC (%DIFF)** | **CJ vs SN_2011–2015 (%DIFF)** | **4–grams** | **Types** | **% of all types** | **NF** | **GC vs SN_2011–2015 (%DIFF)** |
| Legal procedure | 22 | 31 % | 2,231 | +207 % | +34 % | Documents | 9 | 21 | 1,812 | −16 % |
| Documents | 13 | 19 % | 1,890 | +4 % | −12 % | Legal procedure | 10 | 23 | 727 | −56 % |
| Agents/ Institutions | 16 | 23 % | 1,466 | +147 % | −61 % | Abstract concepts | 11 | 26 | 623 | −55 % |

*(continued on next page)*

**Table 7.14.** *Continued*

| Translated EU case law | | | | | | | | | | |
|---|---|---|---|---|---|---|---|---|---|---|
| Abstract concepts | 10 | 14 % | 571 | −8 % | −58 % | Agents/ Institutions | 6 | 14 | 593 | −84 % |
| Places | 6 | 9 % | 559 | +83 % | --- | Places | 2 | 5 | 305 | --- |
| Dates | 3 | 4 % | 346 | +20 % | −50 % | Dates | 5 | 12 | 288 | −58 % |
| **TOTAL:** | **70** | **100 %** | **7,063** | **+62 %** | **−26 %** | **TOTAL:** | **43** | **100** | **4,348** | **−55 %** |

| Non-translated PL case law | | | | | | | | | |
|---|---|---|---|---|---|---|---|---|---|
| **SN_2011–2015** | | | | | **SN_1999** | | | | |
| **3-grams** | **Types** | **% of all types** | **NF** | **SN_2011–2015 vs SN_1999 (%DIFF)** | **3-grams** | **Types** | **% of all types** | **NF** | |
| Agents/ Institutions | 62 | 37 % | 8,024 | −16 % | Agents/ Institutions | 74 | 31 % | 9,504 | |
| Abstract concepts | 66 | 39 % | 5,950 | −16 % | Abstract concepts | 62 | 26 % | 7,069 | |
| Documents | 21 | 12 % | 3,074 | −52 % | Documents | 37 | 15 % | 6,350 | |
| Legal procedure | 17 | 10 % | 2,772 | −66 % | Legal procedure | 58 | 24 % | 8,268 | |
| Dates | 2 | 1 % | 198 | −89 % | Dates | 9 | 4 % | 1,841 | |
| Places | 1 | 1 % | 52 | --- | Places | 0 | 0 % | 0 | |
| **TOTAL:** | **169** | **100 %** | **20,071** | **−39 %** | **TOTAL:** | **240** | **100 %** | **33,032** | |

| 4-grams | Types | % of all types | NF | SN_2011–2015 vs SN_1999 (%DIFF) | 4-grams | Types | % of all types | NF |
|---|---|---|---|---|---|---|---|---|
| Agents/ Institutions | 28 | 33 % | 3,718 | +17 % | Agents/ Institutions | 29 | 27 % | 3,181 |
| Documents | 21 | 25 % | 2,154 | −27 % | Documents | 29 | 27 % | 2,969 |
| Legal procedure | 13 | 15 % | 1,663 | −63 % | Legal procedure | 30 | 28 % | 4,556 |
| Abstract concepts | 17 | 20 % | 1,375 | +26 % | Abstract concepts | 14 | 13 % | 1,088 |
| Dates | 5 | 6 % | 686 | −55 % | Dates | 5 | 5 % | 1,508 |
| Places | 0 | 0 % | 0 | --- | Places | 0 | 0 % | 0 |
| **TOTAL:** | **84** | **100 %** | **9,596** | **−28 %** | **TOTAL:** | **107** | **100 %** | **13,302** |

As it can be observed, referential bundles are not distributed evenly across the corpora – their distribution varies depending on the length of n-grams. In the Eurolect corpora, referential bundles have a lower distribution than in national judgments, with General Court judgments exhibiting a significantly lower number of referential bundles. Referential 3–grams in non-translated SN judgments are over-represented by 25 % and 40 % respectively, whereas 4–grams are overrepresented by 26 % and 55 %. Identification of the six sub-categories of referential bundles has made it possible to conduct an in-depth distributional analysis of the specific functions of referential bundles. Upon a comparison of the distribution of 3–word bundle types in the Polish Eurolect and non-translated Polish, it is possible to observe that three out of the six sub-categories of referential bundles – agents/institutions, abstract concepts, documents, and legal procedure bundles – have accumulated the highest proportion of all types. In the case of 4–word bundles, the largest sub-categories in terms of the total number of bundle types are exactly the same, with slight variations in the total number of types belonging to each sub-category. Dates and places, the two remaining sub-categories, include a very low number of bundle types. For lack of a more suitable solution and since it serves as the main point of reference, the following description of individual sub-categories will take place according to their proportions at the level of 3–grams in the post-accession SN corpus.

### *7.6.1.1 Agents/institutions*

Lexical bundles comprising the first functional sub-category of agents/institutions are significantly underrepresented in the Polish Eurolect – in the language of CJ judgments 3–grams are 29 % less frequent and 4–grams are 61 % less frequent than in non-translated judgments, whereas in the language of GC judgments 3–grams are 62 % and 4–grams are 84 % less frequent than in national judgments (see Table 7.15). Their role consists of referring to various types of legal entities, such as institutions or parties to the proceedings before the courts.

The following sentences extracted from the corpora illustrate the use of bundles referring to agents and institutions:

(1) CJ (C-62/14): *Z powyższego wynika, że na pytania zawarte w złożonym **przez sąd odsyłający** wniosku o wydanie orzeczenia w trybie prejudycjalnym należy udzielić odpowiedzi.*
[It follows that the Court must reply to **the referring court's** request for a preliminary ruling.]

(2) SN (I CSK 148/13): *Kwestią sporną jest zaś przyjęta **przez Sąd Apelacyjny** koncepcja wymagająca na gruncie art. 448 k.c. wykazania zawinionego działania przez sprawcę szkody.*
[The controversial issue is the view adopted by the **Court of Appeal** requiring, pursuant to Article 448 of the Polish Civil Code, demonstration that the act committed by the perpetrator of the damage was culpable.]

**Table 7.15.** *Distribution of 3–4–word bundles denoting agents/institutions*

| Translated EU case law | | | | | | | | | | |
|---|---|---|---|---|---|---|---|---|---|---|
| CJ | | | | | | GC | | | | |
| **3–grams** | **Types** | **% of all types** | **NF** | **CJ vs GC** | **CJ vs SN_2011–2015** | **3–grams** | **Types** | **% of all types** | **NF** | **GC vs SN_2011–2015** |
| | 64 | 4 | 5,672 | +86 % | −29 % | | 25 | 2 | 3,056 | −62 % |
| **4–grams** | **Types** | **% of all types** | **NF** | **CJ vs GC** | **CJ vs SN_2011–2015** | **4–grams** | **Types** | **% of all types** | **NF** | **GC vs SN_2011–2015** |
| | 16 | 23 | 1,466 | +147 % | −61 % | | 6 | 14 | 593 | −84 % |
| **Non–translated PL case law** | | | | | | | | | | |
| **SN_2011–2015** | | | | | | **SN_1999** | | | | |
| **3–grams** | **Types** | **% of all types** | **NF** | **SN_2011–2015 vs SN_1999** | | **3–grams** | **Types** | **% of all types** | **NF** | |
| | 62 | 37 | 8,024 | −16 % | | | 74 | 17 % | 9,504 | |
| **4–grams** | **Types** | **% of all types** | **NF** | **SN_2011–2015 vs SN_1999** | | **4–grams** | **Types** | **% of all types** | **NF** | |
| | 28 | 33 | 3,718 | +17 % | | | 29 | 18 % | 3,181 | |

It should be noted that the frequent use of bundles referring a question for a preliminary ruling (in the case of CJ judgments) or referring to the names of the lower-instance courts which passed earlier judgments (in the case of SN judgments) significantly increases the degree of impersonality of judgments and judicial decisions. Bundles belonging to this sub-category allow the courts to employ more impersonal textual strategies, as exemplified by the first excerpt. Referential bundles found in the EU corpora refer not only to EU agents and institutions but also to agents and institutions from EU Member States, like national courts, suggesting that they are not as institutionally constrained and culture-bound as national judgments, which tend to refer almost exclusively to domestic agents and institutions.

### *7.6.1.2 Bundles denoting abstract concepts*

Bundles referring to abstract concepts contain various legal terms specific to the EU and the national legal systems. This sub-category, using Goźdź-Roszkowski's (2011: 125–126) terminology, may also be labeled as terminological bundles, as it encompasses "highly technical and specialized vocabulary," as in the following examples: *wspólnotowy znak towarowy* [Community trade mark], *zasady równego traktowania* [principle of equal treatment], *prawa do obrony* [right to defense]. Table 7.16 presents data on the distribution of 3–4–word bundles denoting abstract concepts.

Based on the data, the corpus of post-accession SN judgments contains the highest distribution of 3–4–grams referring to abstract concepts out of the 2011–2015 corpora – 3–grams are 74 % less frequent in the CJ corpus and 37 % less frequent in GC judgments, whereas 4–grams are 58 % less frequent in the CJ corpus and 55 % less frequent in GC judgments. The importance of bundles referring to abstract concepts is also reflected in the high number of their types in the post-accession SN corpus as compared to the EU corpora. What is surprising is that pre-accession SN judgments contain around 16 % fewer 3–grams and around 26 % more 4–grams than their post-accession counterparts.

The following sentences illustrate the use of bundles referring to abstract concepts:

(3) CJ (C-238/12 P): *Położenie kresu naruszeniu* ***zasady równego traktowania*** *poprzez przyznanie spółce FLSmidth takiej samej obniżki jak ta przyznana spółce Trioplast Industrier jest także zgodne ze wspomnianym podejściem.* [The remedying of the breach of the **principle of equal treatment** by granting FLSmidth the same reduction as that granted to Trioplast Industrier would also be consistent with that approach.]

(4) GC (I CSK 411/12): *W konsekwencji należy podkreślić, że przyjęcie przez sąd, iż strony zastrzegły prawo* ***odstąpienia od umowy*** *za zapłatą oznaczonej sumy (odstępne), musi znajdować wyraźną podstawę w postanowieniach umowy.*

**Table 7.16.** *Distribution of 3–4–word bundles denoting abstract concepts*

| Translated EU case law | | | | | | | | | | |
|---|---|---|---|---|---|---|---|---|---|---|
| CJ | | | | | | GC | | | | |
| 3-grams | Types | % of all types | NF | CJ vs GC | CJ vs SN_2011–2015 | 3-grams | Types | % of all types | NF | GC vs SN_2011–2015 |
| | 26 | 16 | 1,575 | −58 % | −74 % | | 47 | 38 | 3,737 | −37 % |
| 4-grams | Types | % of all types | NF | CJ vs GC | CJ vs SN_2011–2015 | 4-grams | Types | % of all types | NF | GC vs SN_2011–2015 |
| | 10 | 14 | 571 | −8 % | −58 % | | 11 | 26 | 623 | −55 % |
| Non-translated PL case law | | | | | | | | | | |
| SN_2011–2015 | | | | | | SN_1999 | | | | |
| 3-grams | Types | % of all types | NF | SN_2011–2015 vs SN_1999 | | 3-grams | Types | % of all types | NF | |
| | 66 | 39 | 5,950 | −16 % | | | 62 | 26 % | 7,069 | |
| 4-grams | Types | % of all types | NF | SN_2011–2015 vs SN_1999 | | 4-grams | Types | % of all types | NF | |
| | 17 | 2 | 1,375 | +26 % | | | 14 | 13 % | 1,088 | |

> [As a consequence, it should be emphasized that the court's acceptance of the parties' right to **withdraw from the** contract for the payment of a designated sum (compensation for termination of contract) must be clearly stated in the provisions of the contract.]

The high number of bundle types belonging to this sub-category in the SN corpora may be indicative of greater terminological content of national judgments relative to EU judgments (cf. Chapter 9).

### *7.6.1.3 Bundles denoting documents*

Bundles belonging to the sub-category of bundles referring to documents indicate various types of documents or their parts. Although it might seem that this sub-category would better fit the classification of discourse-organizing bundles, having first conducted a preliminary study, I have decided to treat them as referential bundles, in order not to inflate the category of discourse-organizing bundles. This decision stands in contrast to Goźdź-Roszkowski's study (2011: 135–136), in which he subsumed bundles referring to documents under the category of discourse-organizing bundles (text-oriented bundles, using his nomenclature). In the context of EU and national judgments, which contain numerous inter-textual navigation expressions, the decision not to classify bundles referring to documents as discourse-organizing has proven to be the correct decision, as the sub-category of discourse-organizing bundles labeled as inter- and intra-textual navigation expressions (that is bundles which point to specific points in texts) turned out to contain a very high number of types and tokens of bundles. The opposite solution would have contributed to the inflation of the discourse-organizing category and distortion of the overall picture of the formulaic profile of EU and national judgments.

Table 7.17 demonstrates that bundles referring to documents are underrepresented in the Polish Eurolect, especially in the case of 3–grams, which are 29 % and 43 % more frequent in the language of Polish judges, respectively. 4–grams are also underrepresented in the Eurolect; however, in this case the difference is not as striking.

The example sentences presented below demonstrate the context of use of bundles pointing to various types of documents.

(5) CJ (C-204/11 P): *Na poparcie skargi* ***o stwierdzenie nieważności*** *części spornej decyzji Fifa podniosła sześć zarzutów.*
[In support of its application **for partial annulment** of the contested decision, FIFA put forward six pleas in law.]

(6) SN (I CSK 98/10): *W myśl miejscowego* ***planu zagospodarowania przestrzennego*** *jest to obszar przewidziany dla zabudowy mieszkaniowej i usługowej.*
[According to the local **spatial development plan**, this is the area provided for residential and commercial development.]

**Table 7.17.** *Distribution of 3–4–word bundles denoting documents*

| Translated EU case law | | | | | | | | | | |
|---|---|---|---|---|---|---|---|---|---|---|
| CJ | | | | | | GC | | | | |
| 3–grams | Types | % of all types | NF | CJ vs GC | CJ vs SN_2011–2015 | 3–grams | Types | % of all types | NF | GC vs SN_2011–2015 |
| | 26 | 16 | 2,191 | +26 % | –29 % | | 11 | 9 | 1,739 | –43 % |
| 4–grams | Types | % of all types | NF | CJ vs GC | CJ vs SN_2011–2015 | 4–grams | Types | % of all types | NF | GC vs SN_2011–2015 |
| | 13 | 19 | 1,890 | +4 % | –12 % | | 9 | 21 | 1,812 | –16 % |
| Non–translated PL case law | | | | | | | | | | |
| SN_2011–2015 | | | | | | SN_1999 | | | | |
| 3–grams | Types | % of all types | NF | SN_2011–2015 vs SN_1999 | | 3–grams | Types | % of all types | NF | |
| | 21 | 12 | 3,074 | –52 % | | | 37 | 15 % | 6,350 | |
| 4–grams | Types | % of all types | NF | SN_2011–2015 vs SN_1999 | | 4–grams | Types | % of all types | NF | |
| | 21 | 25 | 2,154 | –27 % | | | 29 | 27 % | 2,969 | |

The decision not to treat bundles referring to documents as referential but as discourse-organizing has been mirrored in an article on lexical bundles in four EU genres (cf. Biel *et al.* 2019).

#### 7.6.1.4 Legal procedure bundles

As opposed to the findings presented by Goźdź-Roszkowski (2011: 126–129) with regard to American legal genres, according to which procedure-related bundles are particularly frequent in legislation and contracts, legal procedure bundles appearing in EU and national judgments are not solely verb-based (e.g. *które wpłynęło do* [registered with the], *został złożony w* [was filed in]); however, it still holds true that these bundles serve very important functions in judicial language by mainly referring to various aspects of legal procedure and practice (e.g. *w pierwszej instancji* [at first instance]).

Legal procedure bundles made up of three words have a higher frequency of occurrence in CJ judgments compared to national judgments (by 53 %), whereas in GC judgments they are distributed at a similar level in both the EU corpus and the national corpus, with only 3 % fewer occurrences in the GC corpus (see Table 7.18). The same tendency can be observed in the case of 4–grams, which are more frequent in CJ judgments (by 34 %) and less frequent in GC judgments (by 56 %) compared to post-accession SN judgments. Therefore, it cannot be simply concluded that legal procedure bundles are considerably over- or underrepresented in either the Polish Eurolect or national judgments, since they are overrepresented in CJ judgments but underrepresented in GC judgments. It should be noted that the underrepresentation of legal procedure bundles in the post-accession SN corpus is relative to its pre-accession counterpart – the former contain on average 65 % fewer bundles of this type.

The following examples illustrate the context of occurrence of legal procedure bundles.

(7) CJ (C-173/13): *Z wszystkich powyższych rozważań wynika, iż zarzuty podniesione przez rząd francuski muszą zostać oddalone i że wniosek o wydanie orzeczenia* ***w trybie prejudycjalnym*** *należy uznać za dopuszczalny.*
[It follows from all the foregoing that the objections put forward by the French Government must be dismissed and the request for **a preliminary ruling** must be held to be admissible.]

(8) SN (I CSK 447/12): *Powódka reprezentowana przez profesjonalnego pełnomocnika zastrzeżenia takiego nie złożyła, przez co w ocenie Sądu Apelacyjnego utraciła prawo powoływania się na nie* ***w toku postępowania*** *apelacyjnego.*
[The claimant, represented by a professional attorney, did not submit such a complaint, which, in the opinion of the Court of Appeal, caused her to lose her right to rely on it **during the appeal** proceedings.]

**Table 7.18.** *Distribution of 3–4–word legal procedure bundles*

| Translated EU case law | | | | | | | | | | |
|---|---|---|---|---|---|---|---|---|---|---|
| CJ | | | | | | GC | | | | |
| 3–grams | Types | % of all types | NF | CJ vs GC | CJ vs SN_2011–2015 | 3–grams | Types | % of all types | NF | GC vs SN_2011–2015 |
| | 30 | 19 | 4,245 | +58 % | +53 % | | 33 | 26 | 2,695 | −3 % |
| 4–grams | Types | % of all types | NF | CJ vs GC | CJ vs SN_2011–2015 | 4–grams | Types | % of all types | NF | GC vs SN_2011–2015 |
| | 22 | 31 | 2,231 | +207 % | +34 % | | 10 | 23 | 727 | −56 % |
| Non–translated PL case law | | | | | | | | | | |
| SN_2011–2015 | | | | | | SN_1999 | | | | |
| 3–grams | Types | % of all types | NF | SN_2011–2015 vs SN_1999 | | 3–grams | Types | % of all types | NF | |
| | 17 | 10 | 2,772 | −66 % | | | 58 | 13 % | 8,268 | |
| 4–grams | Types | % of all types | NF | SN_2011–2015 vs SN_1999 | | 4–grams | Types | % of all types | NF | |
| | 13 | 15 | 1,663 | −63 % | | | 30 | 19 % | 4,556 | |

None of the reviewed bundles belonging to this sub-category can be viewed as performative (cf. Goźdź-Roszkowski 2011: 127), mainly due to the fact that bundles such as *the Court has held* were classified as evaluative stance bundles (cf. Section 7.6.3).

### *7.6.1.5 Dates*

In legal language, time-deictic expressions perform a very important function by providing a temporal frame for the dates of publication of different documents, events or periods in which certain actions need to be taken. Table 7.19 shows that referential bundles are very infrequent compared to bundles expressing different functions.

Due to the overall low distribution of bundles referring to dates and low number of their types, no specific conclusions can be drawn regarding the differences between the corpora. The only peculiarity concerns the high total distribution of 4-grams in the corpus of post-accession SN judgments when compared to the EU corpora. In addition, the post-accession SN corpus exhibits a significantly lower distribution of bundles when compared to the pre-accession corpus, which may be partly due to the smaller size of the latter and the normalization procedure applied.

The following excerpts show how these bundles tend to be used in the language of judges.

(9) CJ (C-352/09 P): *Z pkt 37 i 38 zaskarżonego wyroku wynika, że podczas **rozprawy w dniu** 11 grudnia 2008 r. wysłuchano wystąpień stron i że w jej toku wnosząca odwołanie wskazała, iż odwołuje oświadczenie z dnia 23 lipca 1997 r., co zostało odnotowane w protokole z rozprawy.*
[In paragraphs 37 and 38 of the judgment under appeal, it was stated that the parties presented oral argument at **the hearing on** 11 December 2008 and that, at that hearing, the appellant stated that it revoked the statement of 23 July 1997, formal notice of the revocation being taken in the minutes of the hearing.]

(10) SN (I CSK 526/12): ***W okresie od** 1 kwietnia 2008 r. do 31 grudnia 2008 r. powód poniósł koszty związane z udzielaniem świadczeń zdrowotnych osobom nieubezpieczonym, za które to świadczenia pozwany zapłacił.*
[In **the period from** April 1, 2008 to December 31, 2008, the plaintiff incurred costs related to providing health services to uninsured persons, for which the defendant had paid.]

Overall, temporal bundles, using Goźdź-Roszkowski's terminology (2011: 120–121), fulfil a minor (considering their low distribution) but still important role in EU and Polish judgments.

**Table 7.19.** *Distribution of 3–4–word bundles denoting dates*

| Translated EU case law | | | | | | | | | | |
|---|---|---|---|---|---|---|---|---|---|---|
| CJ | | | | | | GC | | | | |
| **3–grams** | **Types** | **% of all types** | **NF** | **CJ vs GC** | **CJ vs SN_2011–2015** | **3–grams** | **Types** | **% of all types** | **NF** | **GC vs SN_2011–2015** |
| | 2 | 1 | 226 | –39 % | +14 % | | 5 | 4 | 368 | +86 % |
| **4–grams** | **Types** | **% of all types** | **NF** | **CJ vs GC** | **CJ vs SN_2011–2015** | **4–grams** | **Types** | **% of all types** | **NF** | **GC vs SN_2011–2015** |
| | 3 | 4 | 346 | +20 % | –50 % | | 5 | 12 | 288 | –58 % |
| **Non–translated PL case law** | | | | | | | | | | |
| **SN_2011–2015** | | | | | | **SN_1999** | | | | |
| **3–grams** | **Types** | **% of all types** | **NF** | **SN_2011–2015 vs SN_1999** | | **3–grams** | **Types** | **% of all types** | **NF** | |
| | 2 | 1 | 198 | –89 % | | | 9 | 5 % | 1,508 | |
| **4–grams** | **Types** | **% of all types** | **NF** | **SN_2011–2015 vs SN_1999** | | **4–grams** | **Types** | **% of all types** | **NF** | |
| | 5 | 6 | 686 | –55 % | | | 5 | 4 % | 1,841 | |

### *7.6.1.6 Places*

The last sub-category of referential bundles are bundles acting as place-deictic expressions. As can be observed in Table 7.20, bundles belonging to this category have the highest distribution in the corpus of CJ judgments, followed by the corpus of GC judgments, and lastly by the post- and pre-accession national corpora. The last corpus does not exhibit any place-deictic 3– and 4–grams; the post-accession SN corpus contains only one type of a place-deictic 3–gram: *nieruchomości położonej w* [(immovable) property located in].

The following excerpts illustrate the usage of bundles referring to places in the language of EU and Polish judges.

| | |
|---|---|
| (11) CJ (C-310/09): | *W związku z tym Accor twierdzi, że wystarczyłoby przedstawienie dowodu, że wypłacająca spółka zależna została opodatkowana podatkiem dochodowym od osób prawnych* ***w państwie członkowskim*** *jej siedziby.*<br>[Consequently, Accor considers that it is sufficient to provide evidence that the distributing subsidiary was liable to corporation tax in **the Member State** in which it was established.] |
| (12) SN (I CSK 296/12): | *W sprawie ustalone zostało między innymi, że w dniu 22 grudnia 1998 r. B. spółka z o.o. zawarła z Miejskim Przedsiębiorstwem Robot Ogrodniczych spółka z o.o. umowę dzierżawy* ***nieruchomości położonej w*** *W. przy ul. S. 33.*<br>[In the case, it was established, inter alia, that on 22 December 1998, B. spółka z o.o. has concluded with Miejskie Przedsiębiorstwo Robót Ogrodniczych spółka z o.o. a lease **contract for real** estate located in Warsaw at ul. S. 33.] |

Despite the overall low distribution, bundles classified as place reference bundles perform an important function, primarily providing information on the location of agents and institutions, thus allowing their proper identification and providing a wider background.

## 7.6.2 Discourse-organizing bundles

This section focuses on discourse-organizing bundles, which is the most widely distributed group of lexical bundles in the case of 3–grams occurring in all post-accession corpora. At the level of 4–grams, they are the most frequent only in the GC corpus, being the second most frequent group in all other corpora, including the pre-accession SN corpus. In the topic-relevant literature, discourse-organizing bundles are also referred to as discourse organizers (Biber *et al.* 2004: 386; Jablonkai 2010: 262) or text-oriented bundles (Goźdź-Roszkowski 2011: 129–137). Jablonkai

**Table 7.20.** *Distribution of 3–4-word bundles denoting places*

| Translated EU case law | | | | | | | | | | |
|---|---|---|---|---|---|---|---|---|---|---|
| | CJ | | | | | GC | | | | |
| 3-grams | Types | % of all types | NF | CJ vs GC | CJ vs SN_2011–2015 | 3-grams | Types | % of all types | NF | GC vs SN_2011–2015 |
| | 12 | 8 | 1053 | +152 % | +1925 % | | 4 | 3 | 418 | +704 % |
| 4-grams | Types | % of all types | NF | CJ vs GC | CJ vs SN_2011–2015 | 4-grams | Types | % of all types | NF | GC vs SN_2011–2015 |
| | 6 | 9 | 559 | +83 % | --- | | 2 | 5 | 305 | --- |
| **Non-translated PL case law** | | | | | | | | | | |
| | SN_2011–2015 | | | | | SN_1999 | | | | |
| 3-grams | Types | % of all types | NF | SN_2011–2015 vs SN_1999 | | 3-grams | Types | % of all types | NF | |
| | 1 | 1 | 52 | --- | | | 0 | 0 % | 0 | |
| 4-grams | Types | % of all types | NF | SN_2011–2015 vs SN_1999 | | 4-grams | Types | % of all types | NF | |
| | 0 | 0 | 0 | --- | | | 0 | 0 % | 0 | |

(2010) established that discourse organizers perform the sole function of topic elaboration and clarification, e.g. *in addition to the*, *as set out in*. This approach seems overly simplistic, as discourse-organizing bundles may also perform a number of other functions. Goźdź-Roszkowski (2011: 129–137) determined that in the language of American legal genres text-oriented bundles signal relationships between different parts of texts and perform up to seven different functions, including: causative/resultative bundles, e.g. *as a result of*, condition bundles, e.g. *in the event of*, clarification/topic elaboration, e.g. *in the same manner*, focus bundles, e.g. *at issue in this case*, framing bundles, e.g. *on the basis of the*, structuring bundles, e.g. *as provided in Section 1*, and transition bundles, e.g. *in addition to the*. Having included a wider range of possible sub-categories of text-oriented bundles, Goźdź-Roszkowski (2011: 129–137) was able to draw a more detailed picture of the nature of text-oriented bundles and their distributional patterns. Therefore, I decided to include a similar range of sub-categories in the analysis of discourse-organizing bundles, which, following a detailed analysis of the context of the occurrence of 3–4–grams, encompass eight sub-categories: (1) intra-/intertextual navigation bundles, (2) causative-resultative bundles, (3) topic elaboration/clarification, (4) identification/focus, (5) framing bundles, (6) transition expressions, (7) purpose expressions, and (8) conditional expressions. In general, the function of discourse-organizing bundles consists of providing clarification, introducing conditions and hypothetical scenarios, linking causes with ensuing results, and providing contrast.

The quantitative data concerning the distribution of individual types of 3–4–grams (following the refinement procedure) that belong to each of the functional sub-categories are presented in Tables 7.21 and 7.22.

Discourse-organizing bundles are not evenly distributed across the corpora. In fact, they are slightly overrepresented in the Eurolect. In the case of 3–grams, discourse-organizing bundles are only 3 % more frequent in CJ judgments and 10 % more frequent in GC judgments, whereas in the case of 4–grams, they are 19 % more frequent in GC judgments and 76 % less frequent in CJ judgments. Overall, in the case of 3–grams, the most frequently occurring, and thus most salient, are the following sub-categories: intra-/intertextual bundles, causative-resultative bundles, topic elaboration/clarification bundles, identification/focus bundles, framing bundles, and transition bundles. When it comes to 4–grams, the most important sub-categories are: intra-/intertextual bundles, identification/focus bundles and causative-resultative bundles. What Polish Eurolect and non-translated Polish have in common is that both lack any bundles classified as purpose and conditional bundles in the case of 4–grams. As regards the national corpora, the post-accesion SN corpus has a similar level of distribution of discourse-organizing 3–grams as the pre-accession corpus, while having about 21 % more 4–grams.

In the following, I will focus on the distribution of discourse-organizing bundles belonging to each of the sub-categories and the context of their usage.

**Table 7.21.** *Distribution of 3–4–word discourse-organizing bundles and their classification into individual functional sub-categories (ordered according to the normalized frequency of occurrence in the individual corpora)*

| Translated EU case law | | | | | | | | | | |
|---|---|---|---|---|---|---|---|---|---|---|
| CJ | | | | | | GC | | | | |
| **3–grams** | **Types** | **% of all types** | **NF** | **CJ vs GC** | **CJ vs SN_2011–2015** | **3–grams** | **Types** | **% of all types** | **NF** | **GC vs SN_2011–2015** |
| Intra-/intertextual bundles | 83 | 49 | 12,468 | 0 % | −27 % | Intra-/ intertextual bundles | 66 | 43 | 12,451 | −27 % |
| Causative-resultative and inferential bundles | 20 | 12 | 3,108 | −27 % | −27 % | Causative-resultative and inferential bundles | 21 | 14 | 4,282 | +1 % |
| Topic elaboration/ clarification bundles | 12 | 7 | 3,077 | +37 % | +1116 % | Focus bundles | 16 | 11 | 3,200 | +122 % |
| Focus bundles | 20 | 12 | 2,546 | −20 % | +76 % | Transition bundles | 15 | 10 | 2,288 | +2760 % |
| Framing bundles | 15 | 9 | 1,551 | −2 % | +64 % | Topic elaboration/ clarification bundles | 11 | 7 | 2,248 | +789 % |
| Transition bundles | 11 | 7 | 1,328 | −42 % | +1560 % | Framing bundles | 16 | 11 | 1,575 | +66 % |

*(continued on next page)*

**Table 7.21.** *Continued*

| Translated EU case law | | | | | | | | | | |
|---|---|---|---|---|---|---|---|---|---|---|
| Purpose bundles | 7 | 4 | 499 | +36 % | --- | Purpose bundles | 6 | 4 | 368 | --- |
| Conditional bundles | 1 | 1 | 131 | +152 % | --- | Conditional bundles | 1 | 1 | 52 | --- |
| **TOTAL:** | **169** | **100** | **24,708** | **−7 %** | **+3 %** | **TOTAL:** | **152** | **100** | **26,465** | **+10 %** |
| **4–grams** | **Types** | **% of all types** | **NF** | **CJ vs GC** | **CJ vs SN_2011–2015** | **4–grams** | **Types** | **% of all types** | **NF** | **GC vs SN_2011–2015** |
| Intra-/intertextual bundles | 23 | 45 | 2,625 | −29 % | −85 % | Intra-/intertextual bundles | 35 | 56 | 3,711 | −22 % |
| Causative-resultative and inferential bundles | 17 | 33 | 1,588 | +21 % | +535 % | Focus bundles | 9 | 15 | 1,319 | +181 % |
| Focus bundles | 7 | 14 | 1,225 | −7 % | +161 % | Causative-resultative and inferential bundles | 14 | 23 | 1,314 | +426 % |
| Topic elaboration/ clarification bundles | 3 | 6 | 171 | −11 % | −32 % | Topic elaboration/ clarification bundles | 3 | 5 | 193 | +264 % |
| Transition bundles | 1 | 2 | 70 | −32 % | −13 % | Transition bundles | 1 | 2 | 103 | --- |

| | | | | | | | | | | |
|---|---|---|---|---|---|---|---|---|---|---|
| Conditional bundles | **0** | 0 | **0** | --- | --- | Conditional bundles | **0** | 0 | **0** | --- |
| Framing bundles | **0** | 0 | **0** | --- | --- | Framing bundles | **0** | 0 | **0** | --- |
| Purpose bundles | **0** | 0 | **0** | --- | --- | Purpose bundles | **0** | 0 | **0** | --- |
| **TOTAL:** | **51** | **100** | **5,679** | **−14 %** | **−76 %** | **TOTAL:** | **62** | **100** | **6,640** | **+19 %** |

| **Non-translated PL case law** | | | | | | | | |
|---|---|---|---|---|---|---|---|---|
| **SN_2011–2015** | | | | | **SN_1999** | | | |
| **3-grams** | **Types** | **% of all types** | **NF** | **SN_2011–2015 vs SN_1999** | **3-grams** | **Types** | **% of all types** | **NF** |
| Intra-/intertextual bundles | 92 | 71 | 17,022 | +10 % | Intra-/intertextual bundles | 73 | 53 | 15,493 |
| Causative-resultative and inferential bundles | 16 | 12 | 4,234 | +14 % | Focus bundles | 35 | 25 | 3,252 |
| Focus bundles | 12 | 9 | 1,443 | −56 % | Causative-resultative and inferential bundles | 21 | 15 | 3,700 |
| Framing bundles | 8 | 6 | 948 | +40 % | Framing bundles | 5 | 4 | 678 |
| Topic elaboration/ clarification bundles | 1 | 1 | 253 | −46 % | Topic elaboration/ clarification bundles | 4 | 3 | 472 |
| Transition bundles | 1 | 1 | 80 | −27 % | Transition bundles | 1 | 1 | 109 |

(*continued on next page*)

**Table 7.21.** *Continued*

| Non-translated PL case law | | | | | | | | |
|---|---|---|---|---|---|---|---|---|
| Conditional bundles | **0** | 0 | **0** | --- | Conditional bundles | **0** | 0 | **0** |
| Purpose bundles | **0** | 0 | **0** | --- | Purpose bundles | **0** | 0 | **0** |
| **TOTAL:** | **130** | **100** | **23,980** | **+1 %** | **TOTAL:** | **139** | **100** | **23,704** |
| **4-grams** | **Types** | **% of all types** | **NF** | **SN_2011–2015 vs SN_1999** | **4-grams** | **Types** | **% of all types** | **NF** |
| Intra-/intertextual bundles | 30 | 75 | 4,788 | +25 % | Intra-/intertextual bundles | 27 | 73 | 3,833 |
| Focus bundles | 6 | 15 | 469 | +2 % | Focus bundles | 6 | 16 | 458 |
| Causative-resultative and inferential bundles | 3 | 8 | 250 | +6 % | Causative-resultative and inferential bundles | 3 | 8 | 236 |
| Topic elaboration/ clarification bundles | 1 | 3 | 53 | −21 % | Topic elaboration/ clarification bundles | 1 | 3 | 67 |
| Conditional bundles | **0** | 0 | **0** | --- | Conditional bundles | 0 | 0 | **0** |
| Framing bundles | **0** | 0 | **0** | --- | Framing bundles | 0 | 0 | **0** |
| Purpose bundles | **0** | 0 | **0** | --- | Purpose bundles | 0 | 0 | **0** |
| Transition bundles | **0** | 0 | **0** | --- | Transition bundles | 0 | 0 | **0** |
| **TOTAL:** | **40** | **100** | **5,561** | **+21 %** | **TOTAL:** | **37** | **100** | **4,594** |

### *7.6.2.1 Intra-/Intertextual bundles*

The most frequently occurring discourse-organizing bundles at the level of both 3– and 4–grams and across all corpora are intra- and inter-textual navigation bundles. Their function consists of signaling text deixis, that is pointing to specific points in other texts (intertextual bundles), such as *na mocy art* [pursuant to Article], or within the same text (intratextual bundles), such as *w przedmiocie zarzutu pierwszego* [the first plea], thus helping to structure the discourse within the judgments (cf. Chapter 5). The analysis of the gathered material has led me to the conclusion that it would be best to subsume both intra- and inter-textual bundles under one category. It would be unfeasible to study the context of occurrence of all bundles referring to either other texts, or parts of the same text; it is also difficult to tell the difference between intra- and inter-textual bundles without closely studying their textual context, which, in turn, might otherwise have unduly prolonged the analysis due to the high number of occurrences of such bundles. In Goźdź-Roszkowski's work (2011: 135–136) bundles which navigate the reader through a text by locating specific information in documents are termed structuring bundles. Although Goźdź-Roszkowski (2011: 135–136) did not focus on inter-textual structuring bundles, he did determine that bundles of that type are restricted to two American legal genres, namely legislation and contracts.

Table 7.22 presents data on the number of types of intra- and inter-textual bundles and their distribution.

Intra- and inter-textual navigation expressions have a very high distribution in the form of 3–grams, with 4–grams being substantially less frequent across all corpora. In the case of the former, intra- and inter-textual bundles are 27 % less frequent in the Polish Eurolect (in both EU corpora), whereas in the latter, they are 87 % and 22 % less frequent in the Eurolect, respectively. Post-accession SN judgments contain more intra- and inter-textual navigation 3– and 4–grams than pre-accession judgments (10 % and 25 %, respectively).

The following excerpts illustrate the context of occurrence of bundles belonging to this sub-category:

(13) CJ (C-404/10 P): *Co więcej, należy go analizować* ***w świetle art. 1****7 ust. 2 rozporządzenia nr139/2004, który wyklucza jedynie ujawnianie informacji »objętych ze względu na swój charakter tajemnicą zawodową«.*
[Moreover, it must be read in **the light of** Article 17(2) of Regulation No 139/2004, which prohibits the disclosure only of information "of the kind covered by the obligation of professional secrecy."]

(14) SN (I CSK 296/12): *Powód na skutek przelewu nie stał się co prawda stroną stosunku prawnego rachunku bankowego lokaty, ale,* ***zgodnie z art. 5****09 k.c. przeszedł na niego ogół uprawnień przysługujących dotychczasowemu wierzycielowi.*

**Table 7.22.** *Distribution of 3–4–word intra-/intertextual bundles*

| Translated EU case law | | | | | | | | | | |
|---|---|---|---|---|---|---|---|---|---|---|
| CJ | | | | | | GC | | | | |
| **3–grams** | **Types** | **% of all types** | **NF** | **CJ vs GC** | **CJ vs SN_2011–2015** | **3–grams** | **Types** | **% of all types** | **NF** | **GC vs SN_2011–2015** |
| | 83 | 49 | 12,468 | 0 % | −27 % | | 66 | 43 | 12,451 | −27 % |
| **4–grams** | **Types** | **% of all types** | **NF** | **CJ vs GC** | **CJ vs SN_2011–2015** | **4–grams** | **Types** | **% of all types** | **NF** | **GC vs SN_2011–2015** |
| | 23 | 45 | 2,625 | −29 % | −85 % | | 35 | 56 | 3,710 | −22 % |
| **Non–translated PL case law** | | | | | | | | | | |
| **SN_2011–2015** | | | | | | **SN_1999** | | | | |
| **3–grams** | **Types** | **% of all types** | **NF** | **SN_2011–2015 vs SN_1999** | | **3–grams** | **Types** | **% of all types** | **NF** | |
| | 92 | 71 | 17,022 | +10 % | | | 73 | 17 % | 15,493 | |
| **4–grams** | **Types** | **% of all types** | **NF** | **SN_2011–2015 vs SN_1999** | | **4–grams** | **Types** | **% of all types** | **NF** | |
| | 30 | 75 | 4,788 | +25 % | | | 27 | 17 % | 3,833 | |

[As a result of the bank transfer, the plaitiff did not become a party to the legal relation of a deposit account, but, **pursuant to Article** 509 of the Polish Civil Code, all the entitlements of the current creditor have passed on to him.]

The excerpts show that judges use intertextual navigation bundles to refer to existing case-law, as well as legislative provisions, which naturally bolsters their argumentation by lending it more persuasive power.

### *7.6.2.2 Causative-resultative and inferential bundles*

The next category of discourse-organizing bundles comprises causative-resultative and inferential bundles, such as *z powyższego wynika* [it follows that], *wynika stąd, że* [it follows that], which, like the previous sub-category of lexical bundles, are crucial to court legal argumentation, since they reveal cause and effect relationships between arguments (cf. Goźdź-Roszkowski 2011: 130–131). The reason for linking causative-resultative and inferential bundles is that both types of bundles perform similar functions, which can be discerned only after analysis of the textual context of occurrence of a given bundle, which would be impractical due to the sheer number of occurrences of such bundles. Table 7.23 shows the number of types and the distribution of tokens of bundles belonging to the sub-category of causative-resultative and inferential bundles.

As shown in Table 7.23, causative-resultative and inferential 3-grams have an equal level of distribution in GC judgments and in post-accession SN judgments, with the exception of the corpus of CJ judgments, which has around 27 % fewer tokens than the national corpus. On the other hand, 4-grams are largely overrepresented in the Polish Eurolect corpus, by around 5 and 4 times. Furthermore, the post-accession SN corpus has a slightly higher distribution of both 3- and 4-grams than the pre-accession corpus.

The following excerpts from the corpora demonstrate the context of use of bundles belonging to this sub-category.

(15) CJ (C-350/12 P): *Z całości **powyższych rozważań wynika**, że zarzut drugi również winien zostać oddalony, tak że odwołanie należy oddalić w całości.*
[It follows from all of **the foregoing considerations** that the second plea must also be rejected; accordingly, the appeal must be dismissed in its entirety.]

(16) SN (I CSK 86/13): ***Z tych względów** na podstawie art. 398 § 1 oraz art. 108 § 2 w zw. z art. 391 § 1 i art. 398 k.p.c. orzeczono, jak w sentencji.*
[**For these reasons**, pursuant to Article 398 § 1 and Article 108 § 2 in conjunction with Article 391 § 1 and Article 398 of the Polish Code of Civil Procedure it was pronounced as in the operative part of the judgment.]

**Table 7.23.** *Distribution of 3–4–word causative-resultative and inferential bundles*

| Translated EU case law | | | | | | | | | | |
|---|---|---|---|---|---|---|---|---|---|---|
| CJ | | | | | | GC | | | | |
| **3–grams** | **Types** | **% of all types** | **NF** | **CJ vs GC** | **CJ vs SN_2011–2015** | **3–grams** | **Types** | **% of all types** | **NF** | **GC vs SN_2011–2015** |
| | 20 | 12 | 3,108 | −27 % | −27 % | | 21 | 14 | 4,282 | +1 % |
| **4–grams** | **Types** | **% of all types** | **NF** | **CJ vs GC** | **CJ vs SN_2011–2015** | **4–grams** | **Types** | **% of all types** | **NF** | **GC vs SN_2011–2015** |
| | 17 | 33 | 1,588 | +21 % | +535 % | | 14 | 23 | 1,314 | +426 % |
| **Non–translated PL case law** | | | | | | | | | | |
| **SN_2011–2015** | | | | | | **SN_1999** | | | | |
| **3–grams** | **Types** | **% of all types** | **NF** | **SN_2011–2015 vs SN_1999** | | **3–grams** | **Types** | **% of all types** | **NF** | |
| | 16 | 12 | 4,234 | +14 % | | | 21 | 5 % | 3,700 | |
| **4–grams** | **Types** | **% of all types** | **NF** | **SN_2011–2015 vs SN_1999** | | **4–grams** | **Types** | **% of all types** | **NF** | |
| | 3 | 8 | 250 | +6 % | | | 3 | 2 % | 236 | |

It is important to emphasize that the post-accession SN corpus does not exhibit the same level of differentiation when it comes to signaling causative-resultative and inferential links, as the number of types of 3–4-grams in non-translated judgments is lower than in the EU corpora, especially in the case of 4-grams. The same pertains to the pre-accession SN corpus, although it has a higher number of types of 3-grams.

### *7.6.2.3 Focus bundles*

Bundles comprising the sub-category of focus bundles are used to emphasize various issues, including entities and documents, which are particularly relevant to the legal proceedings. The sub-category of focus bundles was introduced by Biber (2006: 142–143) to describe bundles that signal the introduction of a new topic, and by Goźdź-Roszkowski (2011: 133) to refer to bundles indicating the purposes of a legal instrument (e.g. *the purposes of this (Act)*). Jablokai (2010: 264) also employed the sub-category of focus bundles, describing them as bundles identifying "sub-groups of people or countries that are in focus." In this study, focus bundles are perceived as a slightly wider category. They are viewed as bundles with which judges place additional emphasis, e.g. *w tej kwestii* [in this regard], *w niniejszej sprawie* [in the present case]. The distribution of bundles for this sub-category is presented in Table 7.24.

The Polish Eurolect contains both more types of focus bundles and more tokens (particularly 3-grams), indicating their significant overrepresentation in translated judgments. Overall, in the case of the Polish Eurolect, there are around 76 % and 122 % more occurrences of 3-grams and around 161 % and 281 % more 4-grams, respectively, than in post-accession SN judgments. The Polish Eurolect also exhibits a higher number of types of both 3- and 4-grams, although the differences are not very pronounced in the case of 4-grams. Post-accession SN judgments contain around 56 % fewer 3-grams than pre-accession judgments, while the distribution of 4-grams is similar in both national corpora.

The following excerpts exemplify the usage context of bundles from this sub-category.

(17) CJ (C-51/08):

WYROK TRYBUNAŁU (wielka izba)
[...]
*W sprawie C-51/08*
***mającej za przedmiot** skargę o stwierdzenie, na podstawie art. 226 WE, uchybienia zobowiązaniom państwa członkowskiego, wniesioną w dniu 12 lutego 2008 r.*
[JUDGMENT OF THE COURT (Grand Chamber)
[...]
In Case C-51/08, **ACTION under** Article 226 EC for failure to fulfil obligations, brought on 12 February 2008,]

**Table 7.24.** *Distribution of 3–4–word focus bundles*

| Translated EU case law | | | | | | | | | | |
|---|---|---|---|---|---|---|---|---|---|---|
| CJ | | | | | | GC | | | | |
| 3–grams | Types | % of all types | NF | CJ vs GC | CJ vs SN_2011–2015 | 3–grams | Types | % of all types | NF | GC vs SN_2011–2015 |
| | 20 | 12 | 2,546 | –20 % | +76 % | | 16 | 11 | 3,200 | +122 % |
| 4–grams | Types | % of all types | NF | CJ vs GC | CJ vs SN_2011–2015 | 4–grams | Types | % of all types | NF | GC vs SN_2011–2015 |
| | 7 | 14 | 1,225 | –7 % | +161 % | | 9 | 15 | 1,319 | +281 % |
| Non–translated PL case law | | | | | | | | | | |
| SN_2011–2015 | | | | | | SN_1999 | | | | |
| 3–grams | Types | % of all types | NF | SN_2011–2015 vs SN_1999 | | 3–grams | Types | % of all types | NF | |
| | 12 | 9 | 1,443 | –56 % | | | 35 | 8 % | 3,252 | |
| 4–grams | Types | % of all types | NF | SN_2011–2015 vs SN_1999 | | 4–grams | Types | % of all types | NF | |
| | 6 | 15 | 469 | +2 % | | | 6 | 4 % | 458 | |

(18) SN (I CSK 67/11): ***W niniejszej sprawie**, mimo że doszło do zmiany rozstrzygnięcia sądu pierwszej instancji, zabrakło jednak nawet tego stwierdzenia.*
[**In the present case**, although there was a change in the decision of the court of first instance, even that finding was lacking.]

The marked overrepresentation of focus bundles in the Polish Eurolect suggests that European judges signal emphasis more frequently. This might be a side effect of the extremely high number of inter-textual navigation expressions which trigger the use of focus bundles, thanks to which judges are able to direct the reader's attention to the matters at issue in the legal proceedings.

### *7.6.2.4 Framing bundles*

The sub-category of framing attributes can be best compared to the sub-categories of intangible and tangible framing bundles introduced by Jablonkai (2010: 264), and framing signals introduced by Goźdź-Roszkowski (2011: 134–135). In Jablokai's article (2010: 264), intangible framing bundles provide abstract frames for propositions and are used to establish logical relationships, e.g. *in the absence of.* On the other hand, Goźdź-Roszkowski's (2011: 134–135) tangible framing bundles are used to describe concrete size and form, e.g. *in the form of.* According to Goźdź-Roszkowski (2011: 134–135), framing signals are used to "specify limiting conditions for making assertions, claims or arguments or providing explanation or rationale." In this study, framing bundles include both intangible and tangible framing bundles, and their functions are in line with Jablonkai's (2010) and Goźdź-Roszkowski's (2011) descriptions, e.g. *w stosunku do* [in relation to], *w zależności od* [depending on the].

Overall, 3-word framing bundles are markedly overrepresented in the Polish Eurolect compared to non-translated national judgments (see Table 7.25).

What is particularly peculiar is the absence of 4-word framing attributes in all of the corpora. In the case of 3-grams, framing attributes are 64 % and 66 % more frequent in EU judgments, respectively.

The usage context of bundles from this sub-category is as follows:

(19) CJ (C-548/09 P): *Rada mogła więc przyjąć zaskarżony akt jedynie **w oparciu o** kompetencje przyznane jej traktatem WE, czyli w niniejszej sprawie na podstawie art. 60 WE i 301 WE.*
[The Council could, therefore, adopt a Community measure only **on the basis** of the powers conferred on it by the EC Treaty, in this case Articles 60 EC and 301 EC.]

(20) SN (I CSK 124/13): *Strona pozwana **w odpowiedzi na** skargę kasacyjną wniosła o jej oddalenie i zasądzenie kosztów postępowania kasacyjnego.*
[The defendant **in response to** the cassation asked for it to be dismissed and for the costs of the cassation proceedings to be awarded.]

**Table 7.25.** *Distribution of 3–4–word framing bundles*

| Translated EU case law | | | | | | | | | | |
|---|---|---|---|---|---|---|---|---|---|---|
| CJ | | | | | | GC | | | | |
| 3–grams | Types | % of all types | NF | CJ vs GC | CJ vs SN_2011–2015 | 3–grams | Types | % of all types | NF | GC vs SN_2011–2015 |
| | 15 | 9 | 1,551 | –2 % | +64 % | | 16 | 11 | 1,575 | +66 % |
| 4–grams | Types | % of all types | NF | CJ vs GC | CJ vs SN_2011–2015 | 4–grams | Types | % of all types | NF | GC vs SN_2011–2015 |
| | **0** | 0 | **0** | --- | --- | | **0** | 0 | **0** | --- |
| **Non–translated PL case law** | | | | | | | | | | |
| SN_2011–2015 | | | | | | SN_1999 | | | | |
| 3–grams | Types | % of all types | NF | SN_2011–2015 vs SN_1999 | | 3–grams | Types | % of all types | NF | |
| | 8 | 6 | 948 | +40 % | | | 5 | 1 % | 678 | |
| 4–grams | Types | % of all types | NF | SN_2011–2015 vs SN_1999 | | 4–grams | Types | % of all types | NF | |
| | **0** | 0 | **0** | --- | | | 0 | **0** | **0** | |

The decision to include both intangible and tangible framing bundles in the same sub-category of discourse-organizing bundles was motivated by the need to avoid studying every single context of occurrence of bundle types from this sub-category and to classify them either to a sub-category of intangible or tangible framing attributes, which bolstered the analysis to a certain degree.

### *7.6.2.5 Topic elaboration/clarification bundles*

Topic elaboration/clarification bundles are employed to further elaborate on the discussed topic or to clarify it (cf. Goźdź-Roszkowski 2011: 132). Examples of such bundles include *a w szczególności* [and in particular] and *w żaden sposób* [in no manner]. In general, topic elaboration/clarification bundles are one of the least often occurring sub-categories, followed by transition, purpose and conditional bundles (see Table 7.26).

Topic elaboration/clarification bundles are significantly overrepresented in the Polish Eurolect, particularly in the case of 3–word bundles. When it comes to 4–word bundles, they are also overrepresented in the Polish Eurolect; however, the difference is not as striking.

The following excerpts from the corpora of EU and national judgments illustrate the use of bundles belonging to this sub-category.

(21) CJ (C-324/09): *Owe nakazy muszą być skuteczne, proporcjonalne i odstraszające, a ponadto nie mogą tworzyć ograniczeń w handlu prowadzonym* ***zgodnie z prawem****.*
[Those injunctions must be effective, proportionate, dissuasive and must not create barriers **to legitimate trade**.]

(22) SN (I CSK 52/11): ***W ten sposób*** *pozwany naruszył dobra osobiste powoda, co uzasadnia udzielenie mu odpowiedniej ochrony na podstawie art. 24 k.c.*
[**In this way**, the defendant infringed the right to protection of personality of the plaintiff, which justifies granting him adequate protection under Article 24 of the Polish Civil Code.]

The quantitative data suggest that EU courts make more use of elaboration and clarification bundles to legitimize their argumentation than the Polish Supreme Court.

### *7.6.2.6 Transition bundles*

Transition bundles serve to establish additive links and introduce contrasting arguments, e.g. *z jednej strony* [on the one hand], *w drugiej kolejności* [in the second place]. This sub-category was also introduced by Goźdź-Roszkowski (2011: 137–138). Table 7.27 shows the data on the distribution of transition bundles in the corpora.

**Table 7.26.** *Distribution of 3–4–word topic elaboration/clarification bundles*

| Translated EU case law | | | | | | | | | | |
|---|---|---|---|---|---|---|---|---|---|---|
| CJ | | | | | | GC | | | | |
| 3–grams | Types | % of all types | NF | CJ vs GC | CJ vs SN_2011–2015 | 3–grams | Types | % of all types | NF | GC vs SN_2011–2015 |
| | 12 | 7 | 3,077 | +37 % | +1116 % | | 11 | 7 | 2,248 | +789 % |
| 4–grams | Types | % of all types | NF | CJ vs GC | CJ vs SN_2011–2015 | 4–grams | Types | % of all types | NF | GC vs SN_2011–2015 |
| | 3 | 6 | 171 | −11 % | −32 % | | 3 | 5 | 193 | +264 % |
| **Non–translated PL case law** | | | | | | | | | | |
| SN_2011–2015 | | | | | | SN_1999 | | | | |
| 3–grams | Types | % of all types | NF | SN_2011–2015 vs SN_1999 | | 3–grams | Types | % of all types | NF | |
| | 1 | 1 | 253 | −46 % | | | 4 | 1 % | 472 | |
| 4–grams | Types | % of all types | NF | SN_2011–2015 vs SN_1999 | | 4–grams | Types | % of all types | NF | |
| | 1 | 3 | 53 | −21 % | | | 1 | 1 % | 67 | |

**Table 7.27.** *Distribution of 3–4-word transition bundles*

| | | | | | | | | | | |
|---|---|---|---|---|---|---|---|---|---|---|
| **Translated EU case law** | | | | | | | | | | |
| **CJ** | | | | | | **GC** | | | | |
| **3-grams** | **Types** | **% of all types** | **NF** | **CJ vs GC** | **CJ vs SN_2011–2015** | **3-grams** | **Types** | **% of all types** | **NF** | **GC vs SN_2011–2015** |
| | 11 | 7 | 1,328 | −42 % | +1560 % | | 15 | 10 | 2,288 | +2760 % |
| **4-grams** | **Types** | **% of all types** | **NF** | **CJ vs GC** | **CJ vs SN_2011–2015** | **4-grams** | **Types** | **% of all types** | **NF** | **GC vs SN_2011–2015** |
| | 1 | 2 | 70 | −32 % | --- | | 1 | 2 | 103 | --- |
| **Non-translated PL case law** | | | | | | | | | | |
| **SN_2011–2015** | | | | | | **SN_1999** | | | | |
| **3-grams** | **Types** | **% of all types** | **NF** | **SN_2011–2015 vs SN_1999** | | **3-grams** | **Types** | **% of all types** | **NF** | |
| | 1 | 1 | 80 | −27 % | | | 1 | 1 | 109 | |
| **4-grams** | **Types** | **% of all types** | **NF** | **SN_2011–2015 vs SN_1999** | | **4-grams** | **Types** | **% of all types** | **NF** | |
| | 0 | 0 | 0 | --- | | | 0 | 0 | 0 | |

Transition bundles, both 3– and 4–grams, are overrepresented in the Polish Eurolect, especially 3–word bundles. Both pre- and post-accession SN judgments contain only a single type of transition bundle — *w pierwszej kolejności* [firstly]. In the case of 4–grams, non-translated judgments contain no transition bundles.

The followings excerpts demonstrate the context of usage of transition bundles:

(23) CJ (C-106/09 P & C-107/09 P): ***W drugiej kolejności*** *należy oddalić podniesione przez Government of Gibraltar zastrzeżenie, zgodnie z którym Komisja w spornej decyzji ustanowiła odstępstwo od własnej praktyki decyzyjnej.*
[**Secondly**, the Government of Gibraltar's complaint that, in the contested decision, the Commission departed from its decision-making practice must be rejected.]

(24) SN (I CSK 86/13): *Z tej przyczyny* ***w pierwszej kolejności*** *należy dążyć do ustalenia rzeczywistego znaczenia użytych w czynności prawnej sformułowań, jakie nadały mu obie strony czynności prawnej (tzw. subiektywna metoda wykładni).*
[For this reason, **first of all**, one should strive to establish the real meaning of the wording used in the legal act, which was ascribed to it by both parties to the legal transaction (the so-called subjective method of interpretation).]

Transition bundles allow the judges to structure their argumentation, thus allowing the audience to easily identify the courts' arguments.

### *7.6.2.7 Purpose bundles*

The sub-category of purpose expressions is a new category, as it was not previously introduced either by Jablonkai (2010) or Goźdź-Roszkowski (2011). The primary function of purpose bundles consists of specifying the aims of legal instruments, e.g. *mające na celu* [the objective of which]; they are also used to define prerequisites for actions performed by entities other than the courts, e.g. *w celu zapewnienia* [in order to]. The distribution of purpose bundles is as follows (see Table 7.28):

EU judgments exhibit a rather high number of purpose bundles; however, no conclusions can be drawn regarding the possible over- or underrepresentation compared to the corpus of national judgments, as there are no occurrences of purpose bundles in the national corpora.

The context of use of purpose bundles in EU judgments is as follows:

(25) CJ (C-370/12): *Trzeba zaś przypomnieć, że traktat EMS* ***ma na celu*** *zapewnienie stabilności finansowej strefy euro w całości.*
[It must be recalled that **the objective of** the ESM Treaty is to ensure the financial stability of the euro area as a whole.]

**Table 7.28.** *Distribution of 3–4–word purpose bundles*

| Translated EU case law | | | | | | | | | | |
|---|---|---|---|---|---|---|---|---|---|---|
| CJ | | | | | | GC | | | | |
| 3–grams | Types | % of all types | NF | CJ vs GC | CJ vs SN_2011–2015 | 3–grams | Types | % of all types | NF | GC vs SN_2011–2015 |
| | 7 | 4 | 499 | +36 % | --- | | 6 | 4 | 368 | --- |
| 4–grams | Types | % of all types | NF | CJ vs GC | CJ vs SN_2011–2015 | 4–grams | Types | % of all types | NF | GC vs SN_2011–2015 |
| | **0** | 0 | **0** | --- | --- | | **0** | 0 | **0** | --- |
| **Non–translated PL case law** | | | | | | | | | | |
| SN_2011–2015 | | | | | | SN_1999 | | | | |
| 3–grams | Types | % of all types | NF | SN_2011–2015 vs SN_1999 | | 3–grams | Types | % of all types | NF | |
| | **0** | 0 | **0** | --- | | | **0** | 0 | **0** | |
| 4–grams | Types | % of all types | NF | SN_2011–2015 vs SN_1999 | | 4–grams | Types | % of all types | NF | |
| | **0** | 0 | **0** | --- | | | 0 | **0** | **0** | |

(26) GC (T-541/08): *Ponadto* ***w celu ustalenia*** *grzywien takich jak te w niniejszej sprawie Komisja musi przestrzegać ogólnych zasad prawa, a przede wszystkim zasad równego traktowania i proporcjonalności, tak jak zostały one rozwinięte w orzecznictwie Sądu i Trybunału.*
[Furthermore, **in setting a** fine such as that in question in the present case, the Commission was required to comply with the general principles of law, in particular the principles of equal treatment and proportionality, as developed by the case-law of the Court of Justice and the General Court.]

The reason why purpose bundles appear quite often in the EU corpora may be that EU courts refer very often in their argumentation to different documents and treaties (cf. intra-/intertextual bundles, Section 7.6.2.1), thus necessitating the need to describe their aims, which stands in contrast to national judgments.

### *7.6.2.8 Conditional bundles*

The sub-category of conditional expressions is employed to specify conditions in the courts' legal argumentation, e.g. *pod warunkiem że* [under the condition that]. Bundles belonging to this category are not present in non-translated Polish judgments, as shown in Table 7.29.

In the Polish Eurolect, there is only one type of strictly conditional 3–word bundle:

(27) CJ (C-204/11 P): *W niniejszej sprawie należy w pierwszej kolejności zaznaczyć, że aby Komisja mogła wykonać swe uprawnienia kontrolne, uzasadnienie, które skłoniło państwo członkowskie do uznania danego wydarzenia za wydarzenie o doniosłym znaczeniu, może być zwięzłe,* ***pod warunkiem że*** *jest ono adekwatne.*
[In the present case, it should be noted, first of all, that, for the Commission to be able to exercise its power of review, the statement of reasons which led a Member State to designate an event as being of major importance may be succinct, **so long as** it is appropriate.]

(28) GC (T-137/10): *Upoważnienie może także obejmować akty umowne,* ***pod warunkiem że*** *pochodzą one od władzy publicznej i są wiążące.*
[The mandate may also encompass contractual acts, **provided that** they emanate from the public authority and are binding.]

It is difficult to draw any conclusions as regards the overrepresentation of conditional bundles in the Polish Eurolect compared to non-translated Polish judgments, as there is only one bundle type classified as conditional with a low distribution in both EU corpora. Goźdź-Roszkowski (2011: 131–132) observed that conditional bundles have a low distribution in American judicial opinions, adding

**Table 7.29.** *Distribution of 3–4–word conditional bundles*

| Translated EU case law | | | | | | | | | | |
|---|---|---|---|---|---|---|---|---|---|---|
| CJ | | | | | | GC | | | | |
| 3-grams | Types | % of all types | NF | CJ vs GC | CJ vs SN_2011–2015 | 3-grams | Types | % of all types | NF | GC vs SN_2011–2015 |
| | 1 | 1 | 131 | +152 % | --- | | 1 | 1 | 52 | --- |
| 4-grams | Types | % of all types | NF | CJ vs GC | CJ vs SN_2011–2015 | 4-grams | Types | % of all types | NF | GC vs SN_2011–2015 |
| | **0** | 0 | **0** | --- | --- | | **0** | 0 | **0** | --- |
| Non-translated PL case law | | | | | | | | | | |
| SN_2011–2015 | | | | | | SN_1999 | | | | |
| 3-grams | Types | % of all types | NF | SN_2011–2015 vs SN_1999 | | 3-grams | Types | % of all types | NF | |
| | **0** | 0 | **0** | --- | | | **0** | 0 | **0** | |
| 4-grams | Types | % of all types | NF | SN_2011–2015 vs SN_1999 | | 4-grams | Types | % of all types | NF | |
| | **0** | 0 | **0** | --- | | | 0 | **0** | **0** | |

that conditional bundles tend to be characteristic of other genres, namely those containing contractual provisions, such as contracts, textbooks and professional articles, as well as EU legislation (cf. Biel 2014a: 144–152).

### 7.6.3 Stance bundles

The main function of stance bundles consists of providing a frame for the interpretation of the following proposition and conveying the degree of certainty, attitudes and evaluations of the writer (cf. Biber *et al.* 2004: 389; Hyland 2008: 14). In the following sections, I intend to briefly discuss the functions of individual types of stance bundles of import to this study and present some examples from the corpora. However, before I proceed to examine the distribution and functions of stance bundles in EU and domestic judicial discourse, it is important to introduce the classifications of stance bundles presented in earlier, similar studies.

In his explorative study, Goźdź-Roszkowski (2006) identified two rather broad categories of stance bundles: epistemic, e.g. *it is possible to, there is no doubt*, and attitudinal, e.g. *I agree with, appeal should be allowed.* In his later study, Goźdź-Roszkowski (2011) developed his earlier classification of lexical bundles (cf. Goźdź-Roszkowski 2006) by introducing epistemic stance bundles, bundles that indicate a source of knowledge or perspective from which information is given, e.g. *in accordance with the, the Court held that, the fact that the*, bundles expressing attitude/evaluation, bundles expressing ease/difficulty, and obligation/directive bundles, e.g. *it is clear that, it is difficult to see, it is necessary to consider* (Goźdź-Roszkowski 2011: 138–142).

Jablonkai (2010), based on Biber *et al.*'s classification of bundles (2004), found that there are two main categories of stance bundles in English EU discourse (cf. Section 7.2): epistemic stance, e.g. *the fact that the* and attitudinal/modality stance, with the second category having two sub-categories of attitudinal/modality stance bundles: obligation/directive bundles, e.g. *it is important to*, and ability bundles, e.g. *it is possible to* (Jablonkai 2010: 258, 262–263). In her study, Jablonkai did not classify any of the stance bundles as desire (e.g. *what do you want*) or intention/prediction (e.g. *it's going to be*) bundles, the types of bundles listed in Biber *et al.*'s classification (2004). It should be borne in mind that Jablonkai's multi-genre EU corpus contained only two CJEU judgments; therefore, its results are not immediately generalizable to the genre of judgments.

Drawing on these earlier studies, the present study divides stance bundles into two main categories expressing different meanings: (1) epistemic stance bundles and (2) evaluative bundles. Bundles belonging to these categories have been found to contain no personal pronouns, showing that EU and domestic judges express stance in an exclusively impersonal manner. In the process of classifying individual 3- and 4-grams, I have not encountered any bundles expressing deontic meanings, for which reason they are omitted from the final classification. Furthermore, I have found no attitudinal bundles expressing ease/difficulty and obligation/directive (cf. Goźdź-Roszkowski 2011: 138–142). Table 7.30 presents quantitative data on the distribution of bundles in the individual categories of stance bundles occurring in the EU and national judgments.

**Table 7.30.** *Quantitative data concerning the distribution of 3–4–word lexical bundles and their classification into individual functional sub-categories (ordered according to the normalized frequency of occurrence in the individual corpora)*

| Translated EU case law | | | | | | | | | | |
|---|---|---|---|---|---|---|---|---|---|---|
| **CJ** | | | | | | **GC** | | | | |
| **3–grams** | **Types** | **% of all types** | **NF** | **CJ vs GC** | **CJ vs SN_2011–2015** | **3–grams** | **Types** | **% of all types** | **NF** | **GC vs SN_2011–2015** |
| Evaluative | 31 | 66 % | 2,519 | +20 % | −31 % | Evaluative | 30 | 62 % | 2,106 | −42 % |
| Epistemic stance | 16 | 34 % | 2,067 | −4 % | --- | Epistemic stance | 18 | 38 % | 2,144 | --- |
| **TOTAL:** | **47** | **100 %** | **4,587** | **+8 %** | **+26 %** | **TOTAL:** | **48** | **100 %** | **4,250** | **+17 %** |
| **4–grams** | **Types** | **% of all types** | **NF** | **CJ vs GC** | **CJ vs SN_2011–2015** | **4–grams** | **Types** | **% of all types** | **NF** | **GC vs SN_2011–2015** |
| Evaluative | 7 | 70 % | 811 | +51 % | −41 % | Evaluative | 6 | 60 % | 536 | −61 % |
| Epistemic stance | 3 | 30 % | 326 | +28 % | --- | Epistemic stance | 4 | 40 % | 255 | --- |
| **TOTAL:** | **10** | **100 %** | **1,138** | **+44 %** | **−17 %** | **TOTAL:** | **10** | **100 %** | **791** | **−43 %** |
| **Non–translated PL case law** | | | | | | | | | | |
| **SN_2011–2015** | | | | | | **SN_1999** | | | | |
| **3–grams** | **Types** | **% of all types** | **NF** | **SN_2011–2015 vs SN_1999** | | **3–grams** | **Types** | **% of all types** | **NF** | |
| Evaluative | 40 | 100 % | 3,635 | −30 % | | Evaluative | 54 | 95 % | 5,164 | |
| Epistemic stance | **0** | 0 % | **0** | −100 % | | Epistemic stance | 3 | 5 % | 127 | |
| **TOTAL:** | **40** | **100 %** | **3,635** | **−31 %** | | **TOTAL:** | **57** | **100 %** | **5,291** | |

(*continued on next page*)

**Table 7.30.** *Continued*

| Non -translated PL case law | | | | | | | | |
|---|---|---|---|---|---|---|---|---|
| **4-grams** | **Types** | **% of all types** | **NF** | **SN_2011–2015 vs SN_1999** | **4-grams** | **Types** | **% of all types** | **NF** |
| Evaluative | 15 | 100 % | 1,377 | −39 % | Evaluative | 18 | 100 % | 2,275 |
| Epistemic stance | **0** | 0 % | **0** | --- | Epistemic stance | **0** | 0 % | **0** |
| **TOTAL:** | **15** | **100 %** | **1,377** | **−39 %** | **TOTAL:** | **18** | **100 %** | **2,275** |

What can be gathered from the above data is that, first of all, stance bundles occur very rarely in the language of both EU and Polish judges, being the least frequent type of lexical bundles described in Section 7.6. What stands out is the almost total non-existence of bundles expressing epistemic stance – the only corpus in which there are examples of stance-related 3-grams is the corpus of GC judgments, which includes *prawdą jest, że* [it is true that] and *na fakt, że* [the fact that]. This a very surprising observation, as judgments have been observed to contain a high number of epistemically modalized expressions (cf. Chapter 6, Section 6.8.1). With the low presence or virtual non-existence of bundles oriented towards expressing epistemic stance, any comparisons between the corpora need to be made with respect to the distribution of lexical bundles expressing attitudinal stance. In general, in the case of both 3- and 4-grams, these are markedly less frequent in non-translated SN judgments. Furthermore, in all corpora, 3-4-word bundles belonging to the sub-category of evaluative bundles are more frequent than bundles expressing intensification. In the post-accession SN corpus, all 3-4-word bundles act exclusively as evaluative expressions, as it contains no bundles expressing intensification; in the pre-accession SN corpus, there are only several types of intensification bundles.

### *7.6.3.1 Evaluative bundles*

The main sub-category of attitudinal stance bundles consists of evaluative bundles. Evaluative 3- and 4-grams are underrepresented in both EU corpora relative to the post-accession SN corpus. They are also underrepresented in the post-accession SN corpus compared to the pre-accession corpus by 30 % and 39 %, respectively (see Table 7.31).

Evaluative bundles express the writer's evaluation in a strictly impersonal manner, as in:

| | |
|---|---|
| (29) CJ (C-191/09 P & C-200/09 P): | *Z powyższych względów Trybunał (trzecia izba)* ***orzeka, co następuje***:<br>*1) Odwołanie zostaje oddalone. [...]*<br>[On those grounds, the Court (Third Chamber) **hereby**:<br>1. Dismisses the main appeal of the Council of the European Union;] |
| (30) SN (I CSK 87/13): | *W ustalonym orzecznictwie Sądu Najwyższego* ***przyjmuje się, że*** *art. 120 k.c. nie uzasadnia odpowiedzialności pracodawcy, gdy szkoda wynikła tylko przy okazji wykonywania obowiązków pracowniczych (...).*<br>[In the established case law of the Supreme Court, it **is assumed that** Article 120 of the Polish Civil Code does not justify the employer's liability when the damage resulted only from the performance of employee duties (...).] |

**Table 7.31.** *Distribution of 3–4–word evaluative bundles*

| Translated EU case law | | | | | | | | | | |
|---|---|---|---|---|---|---|---|---|---|---|
| CJ | | | | | | GC | | | | |
| 3–grams | Types | % of all types | NF | CJ vs GC | CJ vs SN_2011–2015 | 3–grams | Types | % of all types | NF | GC vs SN_2011–2015 |
| | 31 | 66 | 2,519 | +26 % | −31 % | | 28 | 58 | 1,998 | −45 % |
| 4–grams | Types | % of all types | NF | CJ vs GC | CJ vs SN_2011–2015 | 4–grams | Types | % of all types | NF | GC vs SN_2011–2015 |
| | 7 | 70 | 811 | +51 % | −41 % | | 6 | 60 | 536 | −61 % |
| Non–translated PL case law | | | | | | | | | | |
| SN_2011–2015 | | | | | | SN_1999 | | | | |
| 3–grams | Types | % of all types | NF | SN_2011–2015 vs SN_1999 | | 3–grams | Types | % of all types | NF | |
| | 40 | 100 | 3,635 | −30 % | | | 54 | 12 % | 5,164 | |
| 4–grams | Types | % of all types | NF | SN_2011–2015 vs SN_1999 | | 4–grams | Types | % of all types | NF | |
| | 15 | 100 | 1,377 | −39 % | | | 18 | 11 % | 2,275 | |

The findings regarding the distribution of 3–4–grams expressing evaluation stand in contrast to Goźdź-Roszkowski's (2011: 140–141) findings, according to which attitudinal/evaluative lexical bundles (e.g. *it is clear* that) are not present in US court opinions. In the case of EU and national judgments, evaluative bundles have been observed to perform a crucial role, as they contribute significantly to the impersonal tone of judicial language (as demonstrated in the above examples).

### *7.6.3.2 Epistemic stance bundles*

The second sub-category of stance bundles is composed of bundles expressing intensification and epistemicity. In the EU corpora, these bundles are slightly less frequent than evaluative bundles and are non-existent in the corpora of non-translated judgments (see Table 7.32).

Their role consists of intensifying the proposition (cf. Jablonkai 2010: 263), as shown in the following examples:

(31) CJ (C-281/11): ***Należy stwierdzić, że*** *argumenty te opierają się na błędnej interpretacji rozpatrywanych przepisów prawa Unii.*
[**It should be** noted that those arguments are based on a misinterpretation of the relevant provisions of European Union law.]

(32) GC (T-541/08): *Ten argument* ***nie może zostać*** *uwzględniony.*
[That argument **cannot succeed**.]

It is remarkable that bundles expressing epistemic stance have not been found in the post-accession SN corpus, especially considering that the word *należy* [one needs to] occupies 88th position in the top 100 words in this corpus. Although *należy* [one needs to] has been found to function as an important exponent of epistemic modality (cf. Koźbiał 2019, *forthcoming*), it could be assumed to be the focal point of a number of different bundles expressing epistemic values due to the combinations of *należy* with various verbs, i.e. *stwierdzić* [to note], *podkreślić* [to point out/emphasize].

## 7.7 Conclusions and implications for the future

The analysis presented in this Chapter falls within the scope of the frequency-based (distributional) approach to phraseology. The present approach uses quantitative data of the distribution of lexical bundles (n-grams, clusters) to investigate the formulaic profile (cf. Wray 2005, 2009) of CJEU and SN judgments. The overall aim of the analysis was to draw conclusions regarding the textual fit (linguistic distance) of translations to non-translations at the phraseological level, without examining the syntactic relationships between words.

Grabowski (2018b: 193) rightly observes that the biggest drawback of analyses taking advantage of the concept of lexical bundles is their time-consuming

**Table 7.32.** *Distribution of 3–4–word bundles expressing intensification*

| Translated EU case law | | | | | | | | | | |
|---|---|---|---|---|---|---|---|---|---|---|
| CJ | | | | | | GC | | | | |
| 3–grams | Types | % of all types | NF | CJ vs GC | CJ vs SN_2011–2015 | 3–grams | Types | % of all types | NF | GC vs SN_2011–2015 |
| | 16 | 34 | 2,067 | –4 % | --- | | 18 | 38 | 2,144 | --- |
| 4–grams | Types | % of all types | NF | CJ vs GC | CJ vs SN_2011–2015 | 4–grams | Types | % of all types | NF | GC vs SN_2011–2015 |
| | 3 | 30 | 326 | +28 % | --- | | 4 | 40 | 255 | --- |
| Non–translated PL case law | | | | | | | | | | |
| SN_2011–2015 | | | | | | SN_1999 | | | | |
| 3–grams | Types | % of all types | NF | SN_2011–2015 vs SN_1999 | | 3–grams | Types | % of all types | NF | |
| | 0 | 0 | 0 | –100 % | | | 3 | 1 % | 127 | |
| 4–grams | Types | % of all types | NF | SN_2011–2015 vs SN_1999 | | 4–grams | Types | % of all types | NF | |
| | 0 | 0 | 0 | --- | | | 0 | 0 | 0 | |

and labor-intensive nature, which was also the case in this analysis. However, the results are very reassuring as regards the usefulness of the methodology in studying the formulaicity of the judicial genre. The highly inflectional morphology of the Polish language may be the reason for the inflated number of lexical bundles occurring in each of the corpora, in particular 2–grams, (cf. Grabowski 2018b: 188), which is why it still needs to be adjusted.

The findings show that the high distribution of 2–8–word lexical bundles greatly influences the formulaicity of both EU and Polish judgments. Although much depends on the frequency/distribution and dispersion thresholds adopted at the outset of the analysis, based on the aggregate number of occurrences of 3–4–grams belonging to the three functional categories (cf. Table 7.13, Section 7.6), it can be tentatively concluded that translated EU judgments are slightly less formulaic than their non-translated national counterparts.

When it comes to the functional classification of 3–4–grams, the results show that stance bundles are the least common among the three major categories of lexical bundles. This is in contrast to the overall perception of the genre, according to which judgments seem to be very persuasive and highly argumentative (cf. Salmi-Tolonen 2015), which should therefore entail many stance-related expressions. Both of the two remaining categories, that is discourse-organizing expressions and referential bundles, have a very high distribution in EU and national judgments. Overall, referential bundles are underrepresented in the Eurolect, whereas discourse-organizing bundles are overrepresented relative to post-accession SN judgments. In addition, there are also considerable internal divergences within the Eurolect, as well as underrepresentation in almost all categories at the level of both 3– and 4–grams in the post-accession SN corpus compared to the pre-accession corpus. The total frequency of occurrence of either discourse-organizing or referential bundles differs depending on the length of n-grams subjected to analysis. For instance, in the corpus of post-accession SN judgments, most occurrences of 3–grams are categorized as discourse-organizing, whereas most occurrences of 4–grams are classified as referential. This observation confirms the need to examine the formulaicity of a given genre with more than one type of recurrent word combination (bundles of varying length); for instance, using 3–grams as well as 4–grams, and potentially even longer-n-grams, to avoid skewed results. Furthermore, this confirms that the formulaicity of a given genre is multifaceted.

There is a rather low degree of overlap between translations and non-translations (cf. Section 7.5.2). The low proportion of overlapping bundles (in the case of both EU corpora) is due to the incomplete thematic convergence between EU corpora and national corpora, due partially to different ranges of subject-matter, and the territorial and functional jurisdiction of the CJEU and the SN. Moreover, translated EU judgments employ their own lexical bundles, which are triggered by STs drafted in French and fail to prime bundles which are typical of and salient in TL genres (cf. Biel *et al.* 2019).

The findings do not unequivocally confirm Toury's law of growing standardization and Baker's normalization hypothesis, as the number of tokens of 2–8-grams (cf. Table 7.6, Section 7.5) in the CJ corpus is only slightly higher than in the corpus of SN judgments, whereas in the GC corpus the total number of tokens is about 11 % lower than in national judgments. A similar conclusion can be drawn with regard to Mauranen's hypothesis, according to which translations use more varied patterns, as only CJ judgments have a broader range of bundle types than SN judgments (by 14 %), while GC judgments have about 5 % fewer bundle types (cf. Table 7.5, Section 7.4) (cf. Biel *et al.* 2019). It is difficult to provide a tentative explanation to this behavior in translated texts without investigating the ST-TT (concordance) relationship (cf. Chapter 3); however, it may be presumed that a great degree of influence on the TTs is exerted by lawyer-linguists.

All in all, considering the overall high formulaicity of both EU and national judgments, it should be noted that the language of judges is highly formulaic. This may be due to the formal and informal pressures of the legal system, which necessitates the use of certain word combinations for judgments to take effect. Kjaer (1990: 26, 28) observes that prefabricated word combinations are defined by the direct influence of the law on the lawyer's choice of words and are subject to the highest possible degree of conditioning. Failure to employ these word combinations in accordance with the form prescribed by the law leads to the invalidation of the whole text. Judgments, on the whole, do not seem to allow judges a great deal of leeway when drawing up their contents. Due to the highly recurrent nature of many types of lexical bundles, they may be perceived as such prefabricated combinations of co-occurrent words.

The findings presented in this analysis could serve to improve the degree of naturalness of translated EU judgments as compared to non-translated Polish judgments. Naturalness is perceived here as language users' preferences for the use of certain linguistic items in a particular context, which contributes to greater readability and less processing effort on the part of readers (cf. Lewandowska-Tomaszczyk 2012a: 34; Biel 2015: 159). A higher level of textual fit of translations to non-translations could potentially allow native speakers of Polish who need to familiarize themselves with the contents of EU judgments to better comprehend them, assuming that they are already familiar (to a certain degree) with national law and associated legal texts. It would not, however, be of much import to laypersons.

Moreover, the development of an inventory of core lexical bundles in judgments (bundles shared by both EU and national judgments) may contribute to developing teaching materials better suited to the needs of translation students and professional translators, who need to have a high generic competence, allowing them to improve their awareness of inter-generic differences in the formulaic profiles of judgments.

Further research is still required to examine the influence of the selection criteria of lexical bundles on the quantitative data. In order to be able to draw comparisons between genres comprising texts of only one type, the research field needs a comprehensive set of criteria, such as frequency and dispersions thresholds. Further studies should also focus on the ST-TT (concordance) relationship in translated EU judgments. Lastly, it could be useful to account for the organizational structure of the genre of judgments and to examine, for instance, only the rhetorical move containing judicial justifications (cf. Chapter 5).

# Chapter 8. Binomials

In this chapter, I further investigate the formulaic profile of EU and national judgments by studying binomials, which, according to Gustaffson (1984), Johnson and Coulthard (2010: 10), Kopaczyk (2017a: 160), and Basaneže (2017, 2018), are a typical feature of English legal language (see Mellinkoff 1963; Gustafsson 1984; Hiltunen 1990; Bhatia 1994; Kopaczyk 2009, 2013, 2017; Kopaczyk and Sauer 2017a; Basaneže 2018; Nikitina 2018). I hypothesize that binomials are also a linguistic feature of Polish judicial language as exemplified by the sub-genres of CJEU judgments translated into Polish and non-translated SN judgments. In the following, I will describe the nature of essential and redundant binomial constructions (their structural and semantic characteristics) and compare them with Polish pleonasms and tautologies, which are described as primarily redundant word combinations (cf. Jadacka 2002: 100–101).

The Polish literature stresses that texts for specific purposes (as opposed to literary texts) should be characterized by economy (Jadacka 2002: 100–101). According to Jadacka (2002: 100–101), Polish language users often create sentences with excess semantic knowledge, such as: **Należy wykorzystać wszystkie* ***potencjalne możliwości*** [Advantage must be taken of all **potential opportunities**], in which it is unnecessary to stress that opportunities are potential (possible), because that is what lies in their nature. Such superfluous semantic information is called a pleonasm. Jadacka believes that pleonasms hinder the audience's understanding of the message (Jadacka 2002: 100), adding that tautologies are another type of language construction which degrades linguistic economy to an even greater extent by including words with identical meaning, as in: ****źródła pochodzenia*** *kapitałów spółki* [**sources of origin** of the company's capital] (Jadacka 2002: 101). In order to correct a pleonasm, it is necessary to remove the word whose meaning is included in the semantic content of the other word, whereas in order to correct a tautology, eliminating either of the two words is required (or more if the tautology involves more words) (Jadacka 2002: 101). Bąk (2018: 10–11) uses the term "semantic reduplication" to stress that both pleonasms and tautologies are synonymous with redundancy.[144] Pleonasms and tautologies resemble the English concept of a binomial, both the former and the latter introduce redundant wordiness, but not every binomial is redundant.

144 The topic of semantic redundancy in Polish has been described extensively by, for instance, Buttler (1971) and Małocha-Krupa (2003). Kłodawski (2012, 2017) deals with the topic of redundancy in Polish legal texts.

English binomials are described as relatively stable word combinations which consist of two words belonging to the same word class (grammatical category)[145] (typically N–N, Adj–Adj, Adv–Adv, or V–V), both of which show a certain degree of semantic relation and are joined by the syntactic devices (conjunctions) *and* or *or* (Bhatia 2013[1993]: 108; Kopaczyk 2017b: 2–3), e.g. *examine and inspect* or *act or omission* (cf. Gustafsson 1984: 135–136). Over time, researchers have developed several classifications of binomials. According to Malkiel (1959: 126–129), they can be sub-divided into five categories expressing different semantic relations between constituent words:

(1) near-synonymy, e.g. *checks and balances, null and void,*
(2) complementation, e.g. *assault and battery, full and equal,*
(3) opposition, e.g. *assets and liabilities, true or false,*
(4) sub-division, e.g. *dollars and cents, months and years,*
(5) consequence (mainly in the case of verbal binomials), e.g. *to shoot and kill.*

Mellinkoff (1963) divides binomials simply into those introducing: (1) useful doubling, e.g. *full faith and credit,* and (2) useless (redundant) doubling, e.g. *force and effect.* The former type contributes to a higher degree of legal certainty, whereas the latter does not and instead introduces more redundant verbosity. Gustaffson, according to whom "binomials are definitely an essential stylistic feature in law language" (1984: 134), introduces only three categories of binomials, which are: (1) synonymous binomials, e.g. *last will and testament,* (2) antonymous binomials, e.g. *in person or by proxy,* and (3) complementary binomials, e.g. *shoot and kill* (the first two examples are extended binomials, see below). Kopaczyk's (2017: 160–164) more recent contribution to the study of English binomials focuses on classifying binomials occurring in English and Scottish legislative acts into semantic fields in order to determine which semantic areas are most prone to generating binomials. Most importantly, Kopaczyk (2017: 167) also investigates the semantic motivations behind coining binomials and differentiates between binomials expressing:

(1) complementation (the primary meanings of both words contribute in equal measure to the overall meaning of the pair, while retaining individual meanings, e.g. *time and place, television and radio, powers and duties*),
(2) contiguity (the meaning of one word extends or overlaps with the meaning of the other one, e.g. *knowledge and experience, management and control, powers and privileges*),

---

145 Norrick (1988: 73–74 after Malkiel 1959: 139) rightly observes that English binomials may also contain words belonging to different word classes, e.g. *by and large* (PR–ADJ). Such binomials are not investigated in this chapter.

(3) cause and effect (often with a temporal dimension, e.g. *search and seizure, investigation and report, offences and proceedings*),
(4) hyponymy (the overarching meaning of one word subsumes the meaning of the other one, e.g. *education and training, care and support, words and expressions*),
(5) antonymy (the words have opposite meanings while sharing common semantic ground, e.g. *landlord and tenant, rights and obligations, births and deaths*).

Lastly, she distinguishes so-called (6) binomials proper, which display semantic repetition (doubling) and are most often accused of introducing redundant wordiness due to almost absolute synonymy[146] between the constituent words, e.g. *terms and conditions, practice and procedure, profits and gains.*

Kopaczyk's (2017) classification of semantic motivations for binomials[147] overlaps largely with Malkiel's typology (1959: 126–129, see above). The more recent classification adds the category of contiguity, which is missing in Malkiel's typology – it might not necessarily be regarded as a useful contribution, as contiguity is difficult to tell apart from hyponymy and complementation. Therefore, in the empirical part of this chapter, I will use Malkiel's (1959: 126–129) typology to classify the semantic motivations for binomials occurring in CJEU and SN judgments, as his categories allow for a sufficient level of granularity without making the categorization overly detailed.[148] At this point, it also should be observed that only binomials motivated by absolute or near synonymy (binomials proper) are indicative of redundancy. Such binomials may be juxtaposed with Polish pleonasms and tautologies. Binomials with other types of semantic motivations will be perceived here as introducing the so-called useful doubling, which contributes to raising the degree of legal certainty.

The catalog of binomial expressions is an open one, which means that certain word combinations become binomial (are solidified) with time and that frequency-based corpus linguistics makes it possible to identify such units and to determine

---

146 It needs to be noted, however, that "it is extremely rare for words to be totally interchangeable" (Goźdź-Roszkowski 2013: 96).

147 Kopaczyk (2017: 164–165) also investigated the semantic fields referred to by binomials in English and Scottish legislative acts using an automatic semantic tagger (UCREL Semantic Analysis System. http://ucrel.lancs.ac.uk/usas/ (accessed: August 18, 2020), which allowed her to determine which of the 21 major semantic fields (discourse fields) are most prone to generating binomials. Since there is no semantic tagger for Polish, it was not possible to classify binomials according to the semantic fields. Instead, I will determine the major discourse functions of binomials found in CJEU and SN judgments (see Section 8.2.6).

148 I modify his category of near synonymy to include any possible absolute synonyms, while noting that absolute synonymy is generally a rare phenomenon.

their degree of fixedness based on the distribution of the typical linking words across corpora, namely *i* [and], *lub* [or] or *albo* [or] (cf. Mollin 2014: 21; Kopaczyk and Sauer 2017b: 3). In order for a given word combination to be described as a binomial, it is necessary to evaluate its degree of fixedness, which creates a rather conventionalized new semantic unit. For instance, the common word combination *shoulders and head* cannot necessarily be classified as a binomial, whereas when inverted, *head and shoulders* is a binomial expression. Two examples of Polish binomials based around the conjunctions *i* [and] and *lub* [or] include: *prawa i obowiązki* [rights and obligations] (N–N) and *rzeczywisty lub potencjalny* [actual or probable] (Adj–Adj), because they are fixed co-ordinated pairs which form unique semantic units. It follows that apart from being fixed, that is having a high distribution, constituent elements of binomials may also be irreversible if the word pair is to retain its idiomatic meaning (cf. Malkiel 1959; Bukovčan 2009; Mollin 2014; Kopaczyk and Sauer 2017b: 3).

In legal language, binomials are used widely by lawyers as a means of ascertaining that, for example, contractual provisions are all-inclusive (Basaneže 2018: 227) and can be applied to the widest possible set of factual circumstances, thus guaranteeing higher legal certainty, which, however, may invoke the opposite effect (cf. *synonymical chains*, Chromá 2011: 42–45). They also appear in codified legal provisions (cf. Bhatia 2013[1993]). Nevertheless, the structural qualities of binomials may, in turn, lead to undue wordiness resulting from the overuse of redundant synonymous binomials (binomials proper, see above), which translators often try to eliminate by using just one word, in order to make the TTs more easily comprehensible. Therefore, TTs may have a lower distribution of binomials than non-translated texts owing to the decisions of translators. On the other hand, the wording of legal texts (particularly legal acts) may be expected to be constructed in a way that lends meaning to every (content-related) word, which might mean that the lack of a certain word in the TT, or even a superfluous word for that matter, might have grave consequences and lead to a legal dispute, which is why binomials are problematic from the point of view of legal translators. In addition, binomials are rarely present in legal dictionaries, which requires translators to have knowledge of cultural conventions governing the language of STs as well as TTs, as binomials reflect the legal cultures in which they are created (Mellinkoff 1963: 363 after Basaneže 2018: 227).

For present purposes, binomials are operationalized as fixed word combinations which consist of two words belonging to the same word class (N–N, Adj–Adj, Adv–Adv or V–V), both of which are joined by the syntactic devices *i* [and], *lub* [or] or *albo* [or]; they are labeled as non-extended binomials. In general, binomials do not solely encompass sequences of words belonging exclusively to one class and forming enumerations, but also "parallel phrases as well as words or word tokens along with the link" (Norrick 1988: 73–74). Such binomials are referred to as extended binomials. Examples of extended Polish binomials extracted from the corpora of CJEU and SN judgments include: *osoba fizyczna lub prawna* [natural or legal person], and *czynność odnosząca się do dochodzenia lub postępowania* [act relating to investigation or proceedings]. Surprisingly, apart from enumeration, another function of binomials is the reduction of text length, as exemplified by *bezpośredni i szczególny udział* [direct and specific connection], which is only possible if there is case agreement between the constituent words and which allows for not duplicating the same noun (e.g. **bezpośredni udział i szczególny udział* [direct connection and specific connection]).[149] The present analysis would not, however, be complete without taking into account a separate category of binomials, which is binomials extended by adding more than two co-ordinated elements, e.g. *give, devise, and bequeath* (Crystal 2005: 152) or *frameworks, guidelines, communications and notices* (Basaneže 2018: 246), which are classified here as multinomials (also referred to as trinomials) (Crystal 2005: 152; Kopaczyk and Sauer 2017b: 3). Multinomials may also be extended by adding words to the main constituent elements.

It seems to be a justified endeavor to identify potential binomials in the translated case-law of the CJEU and non-translated case-law of the SN, especially since there is a dearth of empirical studies on binomials in legal Polish, and previous studies on related specialized genres analyze English texts, such as EU legislative texts (Basaneže 2018), English and Scottish legislative acts (Kopaczyk 2017) and written pleadings before the ECHR (Nikitina 2018). Moreover, research into bi- and multinomial expressions has the potential for supplementing corpus-driven research involving lexical bundles (cf. Chapter 7) and thus may provide a better understanding of the nature of formulaicity in judgments, as bi- and multinomials provide information on patterns which are idiosyncratic and do not recur typically in texts as often as other types of "fossilized" word sequences.

The present chapter aims to compare the language of translated CJEU judgments and non-translated SN judgments as regards the distribution of bi- and multinomial structures. It aims to answer the following questions:

(1) What are the semantic motivations behind the use of Polish bi- and multinomials (cf. Kopaczyk 2017: 166–167)?
(2) What POS are most widely used to generate bi- and multinomials?
(3) What are the discourse functions of bi- and multinomials?
(4) Are Polish bi- and multinomials prone to reversibility and what is their degree of fixedness?
(5) Do they boost the nominal style of the genre due to the hypothesized underrepresentation of bi- and multinomials based on parts of speech other than nouns?
(6) Can their frequent use be regarded as a genre feature of CJEU judgments translated into Polish and non-translated national judgments?

---

149 The analysis has shown that there is only one type of extended binomial which repeats the same noun on both sides of the linking word, namely *ośrodki pobytu dziennego i ośrodki pobytu nocnego* [day-care centres and night-care centres] which can be found in CJ judgments (see Section 8.2.4, Table 8.11).

These questions will enable me to test the hypothesis that bi- and multinomials are a feature of Polish judicial writing and, consequently, the genre of judgments. Since it is not possible to use the NKJP corpus as a reference corpus of general Polish in this part of the study, I will compare the overall distribution of bi- and multinomials with the high distribution of lexical bundles, in order to verify whether they are frequent enough to be regarded as a generic feature.

## 8.1 Research material and methodology

Table 8.1 presents information on the total number of texts and tokens in each of the corpora used in the present analysis. The corpora of CJEU and SN judgments are sampled versions of the corpora which have been used to study other linguistic phenomena in this book (except for the pre-accession SN corpus).[150] The bigger corpora used in the previous analyses were sampled in order to facilitate the semi-automatic extraction of bi- and multinomials and analysis of their context of occurrence (concordances), as an examination of the unsampled versions of the corpora would have been too unwieldy and time-consuming.

Although the corpora contain a dissimilar number of texts, they have a similar number of tokens (running words). This was deliberate, so as to ensure comparability of results normalized to 1 million words.[151] Since the main corpora used in this analysis are sampled, I decided to also provide two statistical measures next to the data (types and NF values) presented in this chapter, namely Log Likelihood (LL) and Bayes Factor (BIC), which were calculated with the downloadable spreadsheet available at http://ucrel.lancs.ac.uk/llwizard.htm. Tables with quantitative data include statistical measure values presented in round brackets (e.g. LL value; BIC value).

The method of extracting bi- and multinomial expressions involved the generation of lists of clusters based on fixed elements, that is the linking words *i* [and] and *lub* [or] or *albo* [or],[152] with the help of the Clusters functionality in the Concord tool of WS. In order to classify a given word combination as a binomial, it needed to contain two lexical elements belonging to the same word class, one located to the left and one to the right of the aforementioned conjunctions. In order to classify a given word combination as a multinomial, it needed to contain two lexical elements belonging to the same word class, one located to the left and

150 Sampled corpora are also used in Chapter 9.

151 Normalization formula: (tokens x 1,000,000)/corpus size.

152 In general Polish, the conjunction *albo* [or] is largely synonymous with *lub* [or]. However, in legal logic, *lub* [or] means "at least one of the two" (non-exclusive disjunction), whereas *albo* [or] means "exactly one of the two" (exclusive disjunction) (Lewandowski *et al.* 2017: 78–80). In general Polish, *lub* [or] is used to express not only the two aforementioned meanings, but also the meaning "at most one of the two" (Lewandowski *et al.* 2017: 78).

**Table 8.1.** *Corpus design (analysis of binomials)*

| | Texts | Tokens |
|---|---|---|
| **Polish Eurolect corpus** | | |
| Court of Justice judgments (CJ) (sampled) | 100 | 512,427 |
| General Court judgments (GC) (sampled) | 50 | 489,931 |
| **Reference corpus** | | |
| Supreme Court judgments (SN_2011–2015) (sampled) | 200 | 508,584 |
| SN judgments (SN_1999) (unsampled) | 401 | 504,605 |

one to the right of the aforementioned conjunctions, as well as accompanying words. Clusters were generated using the following settings: WS was set to search for clusters containing *i* [and], *lub* [or] and *albo* [or] within the word span of 3 to 8 words[153] and within the horizon of six words to the left and six words to the right (6L-6R). In order to limit the number of generated clusters, the frequency limit was set at ≥6 occurrences in the corpus (RF), that is ≥12 occurrences per million words (NF). The total number of clusters generated using the described method was still high (see Table 8.2); however, it would have been almost twice as high if the frequency threshold was set at min. 5 occurrences in the corpus, which, in turn, would have made the analysis impractical. The NF value set at ≥12 occurrences pmw allowed me to analyze the context of occurrence of the highest possible number of types of bi- and multinomials, whilst ensuring the analysis remained feasible. A lower NF value would necessitate the inspection of a considerably higher number of types of multi-word clusters, most of which would not contain a significant number of new types of bi- and multinomials.

During the process of extracting suitable clusters based on the number of constituent lexical elements, it turned out that the majority involved overlapping word combinations which needed to be excluded from the analysis. Only non-repeated word combinations with a clearly decipherable meaning were later classified as either bi- or multinomials. It was also observed that there were no bi- and multinomials structured around *albo* [or], as none of the generated clusters could be identified as having a clear-cut meaning. The data show that translated judgments utilize mostly the largely synonymous *lub* [or] as opposed to *albo* [or].

There are two other remarks that need to be made about the approach adapted in this analysis. The generated lists of clusters contained one problematic

153 In cases in which an 8-word cluster was a unit with incomplete meaning, an effort was made to manually supplement it with a maximum of two lexemes from a congruent cluster with the same frequency of occurrence.

**Table 8.2.** *Total number of clusters structured around i [and], lub [or], and albo [or] in the corpora prior to the extraction of bi- and multinomials proper*

| | Translated EU case law | | | | | | |
|---|---|---|---|---|---|---|---|
| | CJ | | | | GC | | |
| | **Cluster types (CJ vs GC) (CJ vs SN_2011–2015)** | **Cluster tokens (NF)** | **CJ vs GC (%DIFF)** | **CJ vs SN_2011–2015 (%DIFF)** | **Cluster types (GC vs SN_2011–2015)** | **Cluster tokens (NF)** | **GC vs SN_2011–2015 (%DIFF)** |
| *i* [and] | 3,135 (34,08; 20,26) (101,56; 87,72) | **72,030** | −6 % (75,03; 61,22) | +11 % (181,75; 167,91) | 3,461 (249,04; 235,23) | **76,750** | +18 % (482,97; 469,16) |
| *lub* [or] | 584 (3,51; −10,31) (473,41; 459,57) | **10,173** | +5 % (6,17; −7,65) | +1013 % (4616,52; 4602,68) | 622 (543,26; 529,44) | **9,677** | +959 % (4245,03; 4231,21) |
| *albo* [or] | 31 (41,60; 27,78) (5,56; −8,27) | **554** | --- (381,10; 367,28) | **193 %** (95,82; 81,99) | 0 (20,24; 6,43) | 0 | **−100 %** (129,53; 115,72) |

| | Non-translated PL case law | | | | |
|---|---|---|---|---|---|
| | SN_2011–2015 | | | SN_1999 | |
| | Cluster types (SN_2011–2015 vs SN_1999) | Cluster tokens (NF) | SN_2011–2015 vs SN_1999 (%DIFF) | Cluster types | Cluster tokens (NF) |
| *i* [and] | 2,368 (3,38; −10,45) | **65,045** | **−6 %** (62,03; 48,20) | 2,477 | **69,098** |
| *lub* [or] | 65 (0,15; −13,68) | **914** | **−28 %** (28,92; 15,09) | 69 | **1266** |
| *albo* [or] | 15 (1,05; −12,78) | **189** | **−34 %** (10,05; −3,78) | 21 | **287** |

binomial – *komórkę piwniczną i/lub boks rowerowy* (12 NF) [basement cell and/or bicycle box] found in the national corpus which is structured around a hybrid linking conjunction, *i/lub* [and/or]. This unique syntactic construction signals that both of the two conditions or elements need to take place either at the same time or alternatively. It conveys the meaning of the sole *lub* [or], that is "at least one of the two" (non-exclusive disjunction); however, it is used together with *i* [and] as a safeguard against misconstruing the provided information as meaning "exactly one of the two" (exclusive disjunction). This single type of binomial is generally regarded as a language error[154] and was not taken into consideration in the analysis due to the fact that it is not structured around a typical linking word, that is *i* [and] or *lub* [or]. Secondly, the analysis accounts for the inflectional nature of Polish. This means that occurrences of binomials such as *jednolite i ciągłe* [single and continuous] and *jednolitego i ciągłego* [single and continuous] are examined together as one type of binomial with an aggregate frequency of occurrence (cf. Section 8.2).

Following the extraction of non-extended binomials, e.g. *plany i programy* [plans and programmes], extended binomials, e.g. *dostosowanie wynagrodzeń i emerytur* [adjustment of remuneration and pensions], and non-extended multinomials, e.g. *finansowy, ekonomiczny i organizacyjny* [financial, economic and organizational] and extended multinomials, e.g. *przepisy ustawowe, wykonawcze i administracyjne* [legislative, statutory and administrative provisions], I proceeded to calculate their distribution (see Sections 8.2.1, 8.2.3 and 8.3.5, respectively) and categorize them according to the word classes of their constituent elements, e.g. Adj + *i* [and] + Adj (*bezpośredni i szczególny* [direct and specific]) (see Sections 8.2.2, 8.2.4 and 8.2.5, respectively). Afterwards, I categorized the bi- and multinomials according to their discourse functions (see Section 8.2.6).

## 8.2 Binomials and multinomials

This section discusses the nature of binomials in the genre of CJEU judgments translated into Polish and non-translated SN judgments. The goal is to describe the distributional and structural qualities of binomials, their degree of fixedness and their thematic range, in order to determine whether they can be regarded as a genre feature. Considering that binomials are not uniform as regards the number of constituent words structured around the linking words *i* [and] and *lub* [or], I will first examine non-extended binomials (see Sections 8.2.1, 8.2.2), that is binomials with just two constituent words and a linking word. Following this, I will study extended binomials (see Sections 8.2.3, 8.2.4), that is binomials with parallel phrases and words along with the linking word (cf. Norrick 1988: 73–74). Next, I will analyze the distribution and structural qualities of multinomials, that is binomials extended by adding more co-ordinated elements (cf. Crystal 2005: 152) (see Section 8.2.5). Lastly, I will list the discourse functions of bi- and multinomial expressions (see Section 8.2.6).

---

154 The correct equivalent of the phrase *i/lub* [and/or] in Polish is *lub* [or] (DGT 2016: 101).

**Table 8.3.** *Distribution of non-extended binomials in the corpora*

| | **Translated EU case law** | | | | | | |
|---|---|---|---|---|---|---|---|
| | **CJ** | | | | **GC** | | |
| | **Types (CJ vs GC) (vs SN_2011–2015)** | **NF** | **CJ vs GC (%DIFF)** | **CJ vs SN_2011–2015 (%DIFF)** | **Types (GC vs SN_2011–2015)** | **NF** | **GC vs SN_2011–2015 (%DIFF)** |
| *i* [and] | 19 (4,47; −9,35) (2,10; −11,74) | **623** | −21 % (9,51; −4,30) | +90 % (47,96; 34,12) | 33 (12,35; −1,47) | **786** | +140 % (97,87; 84,06) |
| *lub* [or] | 12 (1,78; −12,04) (7,85; −5,99) | **455** | +130 % (51,81; 38,00) | +1796 % (242,19; 228,35) | 6 (2,25; −11,57) | **198** | +725 % (78,74; 64,92) |
| **Total** | **31 (1,31; −12,51) (7,45; −6,39)** | **1,077** | **+9 % (0,30; −13,51)** | **+206 % (174,03; 160,20)** | **39 (14,59; 0,78)** | **984** | **+180 % (157,04; 143,23)** |

| | **Non-translated PL case law** | | | | |
|---|---|---|---|---|---|
| | **SN_2011–2015** | | | **SN_1999** | |
| | **Types (SN_2011–2015 vs SN_1999)** | **NF** | **SN_2011–2015 vs SN_1999 (%DIFF)** | **Types** | **NF** |
| *i* [and] | 11 (25,32; 11,49) | **328** | −69 % (186,96; 173,13) | 47 | **1,056** |
| *lub* [or] | 2 (0,21; −13,62) | **24** | −54 % (5,39; −8,44) | 3 | **52** |
| **Total** | **13 (24,42; 10,59)** | **352** | **−68 % (208,56; 194,73)** | **50** | **1,108** |

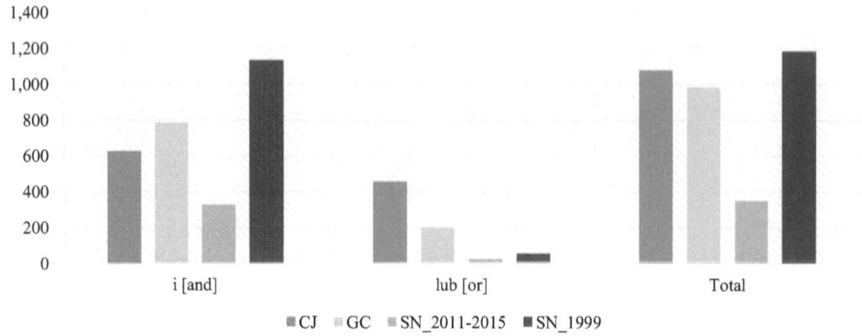


**Figure 8.1.** *Total number of non-extended binomials in the corpora*

### 8.2.1 Distribution of non-extended binomials

The quantitative data show that non-extended binomials built around *i* [and] and *lub* [or] are a characteristic feature of contemporary judicial language due to their recurrent nature. Overall, they are about three times more frequent in translated CJ and GC judgments, respectively, as compared to non-translated national judgments (see Table 8.3; LL and BIC values are presented in round brackets). In addition, EU judgments exhibit a larger variety of non-extended binomials – CJ and GC judgments have ca. 191 % and 241 %, respectively, more types of binomials structured around *i* [and] than post-accession SN judgments, and about 19 and 8 times more types of non-extended binomials structured around *lub* [or], respectively.

The data also demonstrate that apart from the differences between the Eurolect and domestic judgments, there are internal differences within the former. However, in this case the divergences are noticeably less pronounced (statistically less significant based on LL and BIC values), as GC judgments contain overall ca. 9 % fewer non-extended binomials than CJ judgments. Additionally, CJ judgments contain fewer binomials built around *i* [and] (ca. 26 %) but more than twice as many *lub* [or] binomials (ca. 29 %). Surprisingly, binomials are underrepresented in post-accession SN judgments relative to pre-accession SN judgments. Underrepresentation concerns primarily *i* [and] binomials, which are less frequent as regards both the number of types and tokens. This change cannot be attributed directly to the influence exerted by CJEU judgments, although it might be presumed that over time Polish judges began to draft in a less convoluted manner as regards the use of binomials.

Figure 8.1 more adequately depicts the distribution of non-extended binomials in the corpora.

It can be clearly seen that translated CJEU judgments contain more non-extended binomials than non-translated post-accession SN judgments, both those structured around *i* [and] and *lub* [or]. Based on the above, it may be concluded that when translating into Polish, CJEU lawyer-linguists do not perceive binomial expressions as impeding the comprehensibility of translated judgments; hence their high distribution relative to non-translated judgments. At any rate, TTs could be expected to have a similar or at best lower distribution of binomials than non-translated texts of a similar genre. It remains to be verified what proportion of binomials in EU judgments are characterized by absolute or near synonymy (binomials proper) – binomials proper are perceived to introduce redundant verbosity; thus, it may be assumed that a large proportion of such binomials should not occur in translated CJEU judgments. It may also be presumed that the EU STs contain binomials which need to be translated without omitting any of the constituent words. In other words, none of them contain superfluous meaning and are motivated semantically by, for instance, complementation or antonymy. In order to verify this, it is necessary to assess the quantitative distribution of types of binomials in non-translated and translated language as regards the semantic motivation for their creation. If all or most binomials in translated EU judgments express complementation, opposition, sub-division or consequence (cf. Malkiel 1959: 126–129), then lawyer-linguists have no other choice than to translate the binomials in full, in order not to omit any essential information. However, if a large proportion of binomials in translated judgments contains absolute or near synonyms (cf. Malkiel 1959: 126–129), then it might be presumed that the total number of binomials could be lower in lawyer-linguist-mediated texts. The same reasoning could be applied to the other two categorizations of semantic motivations for binomials presented at the beginning of this chapter. Following Mellinkoff's (1963) categorization, a high distribution of binomials could only be justified if they introduced useful doubling, whereas following Gustaffson's (1984) categorization, binomials would need to introduce antonymous or complementary relations between the constituent words in order for them to be necessary (non-redundant).

### 8.2.2 Structural and semantic qualities of non-extended binomials

The internal structure of non-extended binomials is based on four different word classes – nouns (N),[155] adjectives (Adj), adverbs (Adv), and numerals (Num), and thus four structural patterns. However, as evidenced by the quantitative data, the sole word class that occurs with both linking words, *i* [and] and *lub* [or], is nouns. Adjective-based non-extended binomials could also be regarded as widely distributed, but only in the case of the Adj + *i* [and] + Adj pattern. Adjective-based binomials structured around the *lub* [or] link appear in the CJEU corpora, but not in the SN corpora. Here are examples of structures of non-extended binomials which are based around *i* [and]:

155 The category of nouns also includes deverbal nouns, the so-called *nomina actionis*, which end with the suffixes: *-anie*, *-enie*, and *-cie* (cf. Bańko 2007: 89–90).

1. N + *i* [and] + N, e.g. *pakowanie i etykietowanie* [packaging and labelling], *prawa i obowiązki* [rights and obligations], *przebudowa i modernizacja* [reconstruction and modernisation], *zatrudnienie i wnioski* [vacancies and applications]
2. Adj + *i* [and] + Adj, e.g. *bezpośredni i szczególny* [direct and specific],
3. Adv + *i* [and] + Adv, e.g. *bezpośrednio i indywidualnie* [directly and individually].

The following examples show structures of non-extended binomials which are built around *lub* [or]:

1. N + *lub* [or] + N, e.g. *plan lub program* [plan or programme], *oferenci lub kandydaci* [tenderers or applicants],
2. Adj + *lub* [or] + Adj, e.g. *fizyczny lub prawny* [natural or legal],
3. Adv + *lub* [or] + Adv, e.g. *bezpośrednio lub pośrednio* [directly or indirectly],
4. Num + *lub* [or] + Num, e.g. *jeden lub więcej* [one or more].

The data show that not a single binomial takes two verbs (V + *i* [and] / *lub* [or] + V). This is due to the fact that grammatical case government in the Polish language hinders the construction of such verb-governed binomials (cf. Bąk 1984: 379–381). Tables 8.4 and 8.5 show more detailed information regarding the distribution of individual structural types of binomials across the corpora.

In all the corpora, non-extended binomials based around *i* [and] are much more widely distributed across all the corpora than those structured around *lub* [or], particularly in the pre- and post-accession SN corpora, in which the total number of binomials with *i* [and] is more than 13 and 21 times, respectively, higher than with the other linking word. In the GC corpus, there is a similar tendency, as binomials with *i* [and] are only 4 times more frequent than binomials with *lub* [or]. In the CJ corpus, the former are merely 37 % more frequent than the latter. The striking prevalence of noun-based binomials relative to the distribution of other structural types of non-extended binomials is more easily observable in Figure 8.2.

The data show that binomials occurring in non-translated post-accession SN judgments are not only less frequent than their counterparts in translated judgments, but also that they are less varied structurally. Polish judges favor non-extended binomials structured almost exclusively around one word class, namely nouns, since adjective-based binomials occur in non-translated judgments only sporadically and exclusively with the linking word *i* [and]. This is particularly visible in the corpus of pre-accession SN judgments, in which noun-based binomials are even more frequent than in the post-accession corpus. The reason for such overrepresentation may simply be greater reliance on nominal structures in past judgments; however, lesser reliance on noun-based binomials in post-accession judgments cannot be justified by the influence of translated CJEU judgments. What is more, EU judgments show a substantial degree of internal variation

**Table 8.4.** *Total number of non-extended binomial structures and distribution of individual structural types built around i [and] and lub [or] in the EU corpora*

| | Translated EU case law | | | | | | |
|---|---|---|---|---|---|---|---|
| | CJ | | | | GC | | |
| ***i* [and]** | **Types** | **NF** | **CJ vs GC (%DIFF)** | **CJ vs SN_2011–2015 (%DIFF)** | **Types** | **NF** | **GC vs SN_2011–2015 (%DIFF)** |
| N + *i* [and] + N | 12<br>(1,11; −12,71)<br>(0,41; −13,43) | **308** | +3 %<br>(0,01; −13,81) | +24 %<br>(3,02; −10,81) | 17<br>(2,81; −11,00) | **300** | +21 %<br>(3,22; −10,59) |
| Adj + *i* [and] + Adj | 6<br>(3,66; −10,16)<br>(2,06; −11,77) | **277** | −28 %<br>(10,62; −3,20) | +242 %<br>(56,78; 42,94) | 14<br>(10,58; −3,24) | **384** | +374 %<br>(112,10; 98,29) |
| Adv + *i* [and] + Adv | 1<br>(0,39; −13,43)<br>(1,38; −12,46) | **37** | −64 %<br>(16,89; 3,07) | ---<br>(25,51; 11,67) | 2<br>(2,85; −10,97) | **102** | ---<br>(71,91; 58,09) |
| **Total** | **19**<br>**(4,47; −9,35)**<br>**(2,10; −11,74)** | 622 | **−21 %**<br>**(12,59 −1,23)** | **+90 %**<br>**(45,15; 31,31)** | **33**<br>**(12,35; −1,47)** | 786 | **140 %**<br>**(102,93; 89,12)** |
| ***lub* [or]** | **Types** | **NF** | **CJ vs GC (%DIFF)** | **CJ vs SN_2011–2015 (%DIFF)** | **Types** | **NF** | **GC vs SN_2011–2015 (%DIFF)** |
| N + *lub* [or] + N | 7<br>(0,70; −13,12)<br>(2,90; −10,93) | **299** | +83 %<br>(17,91; 4,09) | +1146 %<br>(137,38; 123,54) | 4<br>(0,76; −13,06) | **163** | +579 %<br>(59,66; 45,84) |
| Adj + *lub* [or] + Adj | 2<br>(0,30; −13,52)<br>(1,38; −12,46) | **35** | +192 %<br>(11,47; −2,35) | ---<br>(24,13; 10,29) | 1<br>(1,42; −12,39) | **12** | ---<br>(8,46; −5,35) |

(*continued on next page*)

**Table 8.4.** *Continued*

| | Translated EU case law | | | | | | |
|---|---|---|---|---|---|---|---|
| | CJ | | | | GC | | |
| Adv + *lub* [or] + Adv | 1<br>(0,00; −13,82)<br>(1,38; −12,46) | **68** | +209 %<br>(35,56; 21,74) | ---<br>(46,88; 33,04) | 1<br>(1,42; −12,39) | **22** | ---<br>(15,51; 1,69) |
| Num + *lub* [or] + Num | 2<br>(2,68; −11,13)<br>(2,76; −11,08) | **53** | ---<br>(47,31; 33,49) | ---<br>(36,54 22,70) | 0<br>(0,00; −13,81) | **0** | ---<br>(0,00; −13,81) |
| **Total** | **12**<br>**(1,78; −12,04)**<br>**(7,85; −5,99)** | **455** | **+130 %**<br>**(7,33; -6,49)** | **+1796 %**<br>**(235,16; 221,33)** | **6**<br>**(2,25; −11,57)** | **198** | **725 %**<br>**(79,95; 66,14)** |
| ***i* [and] and *lub* [or]** | **Types** | **NF** | **CJ vs GC (%DIFF)** | **CJ vs SN_2011–2015 (%DIFF)** | **Types** | **NF** | **GC vs SN_2011–2015 (%DIFF)** |
| N + *i* [and]/*lub* [or] + N | **19**<br>(0,21; −13,61)<br>(2,10; −11,74) | **607** | +31 %<br>(6,54; −7,28) | +124 %<br>(64,70; 50,87) | 21<br>(3,56; −10,25) | **463** | +71 %<br>(27,98; 14,16) |
| Adj + *i* [and]/*lub* [or] + Adj | 8<br>(2,49; −11,33)<br>(3,81; −10,03) | **312** | −21 %<br>(1,25; −12,57) | +285 %<br>(71,60; 57,76) | 15<br>(11,74; −2,07) | **396** | +389 %<br>(117,23; 103,41) |
| Adv + *i* [and]/*lub* [or] + Adv | 2<br>(0,25; −13,57)<br>(2,76; −11,08) | **105** | −16 %<br>(1,25; −12,57) | ---<br>(72,39; 58,55) | 3<br>(4,27; −9,54) | **125** | ---<br>(88,12; 74,31) |
| Num + *lub* [or] + Num | 2<br>(2,68; −11,13)<br>(2,76; −11,08) | **53** | ---<br>(35,56; 21,74) | ---<br>(36,54; 22,70) | 0<br>(0,00; −13,81) | **0** | ---<br>(0,00; −13,81) |
| **Total** | **31**<br>**(1,31; −12,51)**<br>**(7,45; −6,39)** | **1,077** | **+9 %**<br>**(0,78; −13,03)** | **+206 %**<br>**(190,03; 176,19)** | **39**<br>**(14,59; 0,78)** | **984** | **+180 %**<br>**(163,73; 149,91)** |

**Table 8.5.** *Total number of non-extended binomial structures and distribution of individual structural types built around i [and] and lub [or] in the SN corpora*

| | **Non-translated PL case law** | | | | |
|---|---|---|---|---|---|
| | **SN_2011–2015** | | **SN_2011–2015 vs SN_1999** | **SN_1999** | |
| ***i* [and]** | **Types** | **NF** | **(%DIFF)** | **Types** | **NF** |
| N + *i* [and] + N | 9 (20,45; 6,62) | **248** | –75 % (233,91; 220,08) | **38** | **904** |
| Adj + *i* [and] + Adj | 2 (4,87; –8,96) | **80** | –48 % (11,92; –1,91) | **9** | **153** |
| Adv + *i* [and] + Adv | 0 (0,00; –13,83) | **0** | --- (0,00; –13,83) | **0** | **0** |
| **Total** | **11 (25,32; 11,49)** | **328** | **–71 % (235,59 221,77)** | **47** | **1,057** |
| ***lub* [or]** | **Types** | **NF** | **(%DIFF)** | **Types** | **NF** |
| N + *lub* [or] + N | 2 (0,21; –13,62) | **24** | –54 % (5,39; –8,44) | 3 | **52** |
| Adj + *lub* [or] + Adj | 0 (0,00; –13,83) | **0** | --- (0,00; –13,83) | **0** | **0** |
| Adv + *lub* [or] + Adv | 0 (0,00; –13,83) | **0** | --- (0,00; –13,83) | **0** | **0** |
| Num + *lub* [or] + Num | 0 (0,00; –13,83) | **0** | --- (0,00; –13,83) | **0** | **0** |
| **Total** | **2 (0,21; –13,62)** | **24** | **–54 % (5,39 -8,44)** | **3** | **52** |

(*continued on next page*)

**Table 8.5.** *Continued*

| | Non-translated PL case law | | | | |
|---|---|---|---|---|---|
| | SN_2011–2015 | | SN_2011–2015 vs SN_1999 | SN_1999 | |
| ***i* [and] and *lub* [or]** | **Types** | **NF** | **(%DIFF)** | **Types** | **NF** |
| N + *i* [and]/*lub* [or] + N | **11**<br>(19,58; 5,76) | **271** | −72 %<br>(204,52; 190,69) | **41** | **956** |
| Adj + *i* [and]/*lub* [or] + Adj | 2<br>(4,87; −8,96) | **81** | −47 %<br>(11,54; −2,29) | **9** | **153** |
| Adv + *i* [and]/*lub* [or] + Adv | 0<br>(0,00; −13,83) | **0** | ---<br>(0,00; −13,83) | **0** | **0** |
| Num + *lub* [or] + Num | 0<br>(0,00; −13,83) | **0** | ---<br>(0,00; −13,83) | **0** | **0** |
| **Total** | **13**<br>**(24,42; 10,59)** | **352** | **−68 %**<br>**(210,25; 196,42)** | **50** | **1,109** |

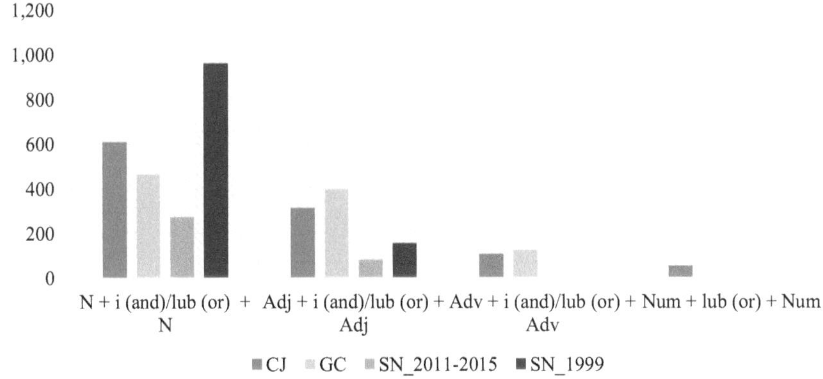


**Figure 8.2.** *Distribution of structural types of non-extended binomials across the corpora*

when it comes to the use of non-extended binomials. The most visible difference pertains to the lack of binomials following the structure Num + *lub* [or] + Num in GC judgments. Additionally, CJ judgments have fewer types of adjective-based binomials than GC judgments (see Figure 8.2).

It can be seen in Figure 8.2 that the fit of translated CJEU judgments to non-translated SN judgments is only partly convergent when it comes to the distribution of individual structural types of non-extended binomials. Despite the overall low distribution of binomials in post-accession SN judgments, it can be observed that when compared to translated judgments, national judgments contain a higher proportion of non-extended binomials involving nouns. It may be concluded that the high salience of noun-based binomials and the underrepresentation of bi- and multinomials based on parts of speech other than nouns contributes to the nominal style of both translated and non-translated judgments. In addition, none of the corpora have been found to contain verb-based binomials, which further strengthens the perceived salience of noun-based binomials.

Owing to the fact that the overall number of types of non-extended binomials extracted from the corpora is not very high, the following tables (see Tables 8.6 and 8.7) present a complete list of binomials found in EU and national judgments. The columns with the heading SEM, which stands for "semantic relation (motivation)," categorize the semantic motivations for binomials according to Malkiel's typology (1959: 126–129), which includes five categories.[156]

156 The abbreviations for the individual categories are as follows: COM – complementation, OPP – opposition (antonymy, cf. Kopaczyk 2017: 166–167), SYN – absolute or near synonymy (binomials proper, cf. Kopaczyk 2017: 166–167), SUB – sub-division (hyponymy, cf. Kopaczyk 2017: 166–167), and CON – consequence (cause and result, cf. Kopaczyk 2017: 166–167).

**Table 8.6.** *Full list of types of non-extended binomials in the EU corpora*[a]

| Translated EU case law | | | | | |
|---|---|---|---|---|---|
| **CJ** | **SEM** | **NF** | **GC** | **SEM** | **NF** |
| ***towary lub usługi* [goods or services]** | COM | 103 | *jednolite i ciągłe* [single and continuous] | COM | 139 |
| *bezpośredni i szczególny* [direct and specific] | COM | 86 | ***towary lub usługi* [goods or services]** | COM | 117 |
| *wynagrodzenia i emerytury* [remuneration and pensions] | COM | 72 | *podobnie i analogicznie* [see, to that effect] | COM | 64 |
| *bezpośrednio lub pośrednio* [directly or indirectly] | OPP | 68 | *faktyczny i prawny* [factual and legal] | COM | 44 |
| *dochodzenie lub postępowanie* [investigation or legal proceedings] | COM | 68 | *bezpośrednio i indywidualnie* [directly and individually] | COM | 40 |
| *drugi i trzeci* [second and third] | SUB | 53 | *ochrona i gwarancje* [protection and guarantees] | SYN | 36 |
| *poważny i nagły* [serious and sudden] | COM | 53 | *pierwszy i drugi* [first and second] | SUB | 32 |
| *cywilne i handlowe* [civil and commercial] | COM | 47 | *urządzenia i przyrządy* [instruments and appliances] | SYN | 30 |
| *zatrudnienie i wnioski* [vacancies and applications] | COM | 45 | *bezpośrednio lub pośrednio* [directly or indirectly] | OPP | 23 |
| *bezpośrednio i indywidualnie* [directly and individually] | COM | 37 | *substancje lub technologie* [substances or technologies] | COM | 23 |
| *akt lub umowa* [document or agreement] | COM | 33 | *procesowe i dowodowe* [procedural and evidence-gathering] | COM | 22 |
| *plan lub program* [plan or programme] | SYN | 33 | *waga i czas* [gravity and duration] | COM | 22 |
| *jednego lub kilku* [one or more] | SUB | 33 | *żądania i zarzuty* [forms of order and pleas in law] | COM | 22 |
| *przestępstwa lub wykroczenia* [crimes and offences] | OPP | 31 | *towary i usługi* [goods and services] | COM | 20 |

| | | | | | |
|---|---|---|---|---|---|
| *wjazd i pobyt* [entry and stay] | COM | 27 | *niezależny i bezstronny* [independent and impartial] | SYN | 18 |
| *miejsca i regiony* [localities and regions] | SUB | 25 | *drugi i trzeci* [second and third] | SUB | 18 |
| *plany i programy* [plans and programmes] | COM | 25 | *ogólny i abstrakcyjny* [general and abstract] | SYN | 18 |
| ***prawa i obowiązki* [rights and obligations]** | COM | 23 | *Komisja i interwenient* [Commission and the intervener] | SUB | 18 |
| *pakowanie i etykietowanie* [packaging and labelling] | COM | 21 | *substancje i mieszaniny* [substances and mixtures] | SYN | 18 |
| *rzeczywisty lub potencjalny* [actual or probable] | OPP | 20 | *organizacyjne i prawne* [organisational and legal] | COM | 16 |
| *jeden lub więcej* [one or more] | SUB | 20 | *produkcja i sprzedaż* [production and sale] | COM | 16 |
| *techniczny i naukowy* [technical and scientific] | COM | 20 | *eksporter i importer* [exporter and the importer] | OPP | 16 |
| *wykonawcze i administracyjne* [regulations and administrative (provisions)]* | COM | 20 | *bankowość i finanse* [banking and finance] | COM | 16 |
| *bezpośredni lub pośredni* [direct or indirect] | OPP | 16 | *żywieniowe i zdrowotne* [nutrition and health] | COM | 14 |
| *emerytury lub renty* [pensions or pensions (for incapacity for work)] | SUB | 16 | *bezpośredni i konkretny* [direct and specific] | COM | 14 |
| *substancje i mieszaniny* [substances and mixtures] | SYN | 16 | *uzupełniające lub zmieniające* [supplementing or amending] | COM | 12 |
| *czynności i formalności* [acts and formalities] | SYN | 16 | *identyczność lub podobieństwo* [identity or similarity] | OPP | 12 |
| *sekcje lub działy* [sections or chapters] | COM | 14 | *oferenci lub kandydaci* [tenderers or applicants] | SYN | 12 |
| *organizowanie i prowadzenie* [arranging and conducting] | COM | 14 | *odpowiednie i konieczne* [appropriate and necessary] | COM | 12 |

(*continued on next page*)

**Table 8.6.** *Continued*

| | | | | | |
|---|---|---|---|---|---|
| *obraz i dźwięk* [image and sound] | COM | 12 | *zmieniające i uchylające* [amending and repealing] | COM | 12 |
| *zobowiązania i płatności* [obligations and payments] | COM | 12 | *techniczna i ekonomiczna* [technical and economic] | COM | 12 |
| | | | *naukowy i techniczny* [scientific and technical] | COM | 12 |
| | | | *zarzuty i argumenty* [pleas and arguments] | COM | 12 |
| | | | *fundusze i zasoby* [funds and economic resources] | SYN | 12 |
| | | | *spotkania i kontakty* [meetings and consultations] | COM | 12 |
| | | | *ludzie i zwierzęta* [humans and animals] | SUB | 12 |
| | | | *dostępność i wykonalność* [availability and feasibility] | COM | 12 |
| | | | *zdrowie i uroda* [health and beauty] | COM | 12 |
| | | | *funkcjonalność i praktyczność* [functionality and practicality] | **SYN** | 12 |
| **Total (31 types)** | **COM: 19** | **1,077** | **Total (39 types)** | **COM: 24** | **984** |
| | **SYN: 3** | | | **SYN: 8** | |
| | **SUB: 5** | | | **SUB: 4** | |
| | **OPP: 4** | | | **OPP: 3** | |
| | **CON: 0** | | | **CON: 0** | |

[a] Translations of binomials extracted from the EU corpora were adapted from a parallel corpus of English and Polish language versions of CJEU judgments available at: https://old.sketchengine.co.uk/corpus/corp_info?corpname=preloaded/judgments_eurlex_pol&struct_attr_stats=1&subcorpora=1 (accessed: August 18, 2020).

**Table 8.7.** *Full list of types of non-extended binomials in the SN corpora*

| Non-translated PL case law | | | | | |
|---|---|---|---|---|---|
| **SN_2011–2015** | **SEM** | **NF** | **SN_1999** | **SEM** | **NF** |
| ***prawa i obowiązki* [rights and obligations]** | COM | 78 | *wyrok i sprawę* [judgment and case] | COM | 81 |
| *geodezyjny i kartograficzny* [geodetic and cartographic] | COM | 64 | *uchylenie i przekazanie* [repeal and referral] | COM | 59 |
| *konkurencja i konsumenci* [competition and consumers] | SUB | 34 | *wiarygodności i mocy* [reliability and power] | COM | 57 |
| ***towary lub usługi* [goods or services]** | COM | 27 | *kasacji i zasądzenie* [cassation and adjudication] | COM | 57 |
| *akcje i udziały* [shares and financial holdings] | COM | 25 | *wyroku i oddalenie* [judgment and dismissal] | COM | 55 |
| *przebudowa i modernizacja* [reconstruction and modernisation] | SYN | 24 | *rozpoznania i rozstrzygnięcia* [consideration and settlement] | COM | 46 |
| *apelacyjny i kasacyjny* [appellate and cassation] | COM | 16 | *rozpoznania i orzeczenia* [consideration and judgment] | COM | 36 |
| *doktryna i orzecznictwo* [doctrine and case-law] | COM | 16 | *ustalenia i wnioski* [findings and conclusions] | COM | 36 |
| *staranność i rzetelność* [diligence and reliability] | **SYN** | 16 | *odsetkami i kosztami* [interest and costs] | COM | 34 |
| *działanie lub zaniechanie* [act or omission] | OPP | 14 | *trwały i zupełny* [durable and complete] | COM | 32 |
| *ustalenia i wnioski* [findings and conclusions] | COM | 14 | *utrzymania i wychowania* [maintenance and upbringing] | COM | 28 |
| *powstanie lub zwiększenie* [causation or aggravation] | COM | 12 | *treści lub znaczenia* [content or meaning] | COM | 26 |

(*continued on next page*)

**Table 8.7.** *Continued*

| Non–translated PL case law | | | | | |
|---|---|---|---|---|---|
| *zabudowa i zagospodarowanie* [housing and development] | COM | 12 | *pierwszej i drugiej* [first and second] | COM | 26 |
| | | | *zupełny i trwały* [complete and durable] | COM | 20 |
| | | | *lokali i dodatkach* [premises and additions] | COM | 20 |
| | | | *towarów i usług* [goods and services] | COM | 20 |
| | | | *praw i obowiązków* [rights and obligations] | COM | 18 |
| | | | *fakty i dowody* [facts and evidence] | COM | 18 |
| | | | *ustaleniach i wnioskach* [findings and conclusions] | COM | 18 |
| | | | *kluczyków i dokumentów* [keys and documents] | COM | 18 |
| | | | *podstawy i wnioski* [grounds and conclusions] | COM | 18 |
| | | | *rozbiórce i naprawie* [demolition and repair] | COM | 16 |
| | | | *powoda i pozwanego* [plaintiff and defendant] | COM | 16 |
| | | | *pracy i ubezpieczeń* [work and insurance] | COM | 16 |
| | | | *wiarygodność i moc* [credibility and power] | COM | 16 |
| | | | *czystości i porządku* [cleanliness and order] | COM | 16 |
| | | | *adwokata lub radcy* [lawyer or adviser] | COM | 14 |
| | | | *cywilnej i administracyjnej* [civil and administrative] | COM | 14 |
| | | | *rolnych i leśnych* [agricultural and forestal] | COM | 14 |
| | | | *zdrowia i opieki* [health and care] | COM | 14 |
| | | | *wiedzą i zgodą* [knowledge and consent] | COM | 14 |
| | | | *wodociągów i kanalizacji* [waterworks and sewerage] | COM | 14 |

| | | | | | |
|---|---|---|---|---|---|
| | | | *faktów i dowodów* [facts and evidence] | COM | 14 |
| | | | *miasta i gminy* [cities and municipalities] | SUB | 14 |
| | | | *logiki i doświadczenia* [logic and experience] | COM | 14 |
| | | | *podstaw i wniosków* [grounds and conclusions] | COM | 14 |
| | | | *postępowanie i orzeczenie* [proceedings and judgment] | COM | 14 |
| | | | *istnienia lub nieistnienia* [existence or non-existence] | OPP | 12 |
| | | | *życiową i materialną* [vital and material] | COM | 12 |
| | | | *zniszczonych i uszkodzonych* [damaged and corrupt] | COM | 12 |
| | | | *rodzinnego i opiekuńczego* [family and guardianship] | COM | 12 |
| | | | *geologicznego i górniczego* [geological and mining] | COM | 12 |
| | | | *odszkodowanie i rentę* [compensation and pension] | COM | 12 |
| | | | *ubezpieczeń i reasekuracji* [insurance and reinsurance] | COM | 12 |
| | | | *kredytu i odsetek* [credit and interest] | COM | 12 |
| | | | *mocy i wiarygodności* [power and reliability] | COM | 12 |
| | | | *męża i ojca* [husband and father] | COM | 12 |
| | | | *dowodów i ustaleń* [evidence and findings] | COM | 12 |
| | | | *geodezji i gospodarki* [geodesy and economy] | COM | 12 |
| | | | *doktrynie i orzecznictwie* [doctrine and case-law] | COM | 12 |
| **Total (13 types)** | **COM: 9** | **352** | **Total (50 types)** | **COM: 48** | **1,109** |
| | **SYN: 2** | | | **SYN: 0** | |
| | **SUB: 1** | | | **SUB: 1** | |
| | **OPP: 1** | | | **OPP: 1** | |
| | **CON: 0** | | | **CON: 0** | |

Across the corpora there are several types of binomials with more than one declension variant, e.g. *jednolity i ciągły* [single and continuous] (*jednolite i ciągłe, jednolitego i ciągłego, jednolitym i ciągłym*) or *geodezyjny i kartograficzny* [geodetic and cartographic] (*geodezyjnego i kartograficznego, geodezyjne i kartograficzne, geodezyjnej i kartograficznej*). Listing such inflected binomials as separate types would artificially raise their total number, which is indicative of the manner in which Polish declension affects formulaicity of both translations and non-translations. Considering that this phenomenon occurs in every corpus, I decided to subsume the variants under individual entries with the basic declension form. Therefore, all of the binomials in Tables 8.6 and 8.7 are presented in the nominative case (either masculine or feminine, and either in the singular or plural).

Tables 8.6 and 8.7 demonstrate the degree of overlap between the corpora – only two non-extended types of binomials are shared between the CJEU corpora and the post-accession SN corpus, CJ and GC judgments together with post-accession SN judgments share the binomial *towary lub usługi* [goods or services], while CJ and post-accession SN judgments share the binomial *prawa i obowiązki* [rights and obligations] (bolded and underlined). This level of overlap is very low, which further confirms the finding concerning the low thematic convergence of translated EU and non-translated national judgments made in the chapter on lexical bundles (cf. Chapter 7). As for binomials overlapping within the Eurolect, there are only five: *towary lub usługi* [goods or services], *bezpośrednio lub pośrednio* [directly or indirectly], *drugi i trzeci* [second and third], *substancje i mieszaniny* [substances and mixtures], and *bezpośrednio i indywidualnie* [directly and individually] (underlined). The type-based analysis of binomials extracted from the corpora shows that binomials relate largely to the thematic content of judgments and that there is little thematic overlap between EU and national judgments.

In order to answer the research question concerning semantic motivations behind the use of Polish binomials, I decided to first analyze the semantic relations between the constituent elements of non-extended binomials. For this purpose, I employed Malkiel's (1959: 126–129) detailed categorization of binomial components based on five different semantic relations: absolute or near-synonymy (SYN), complementation (COM), opposition (OPP), sub-division (SUB), and consequence (CON). The analysis shows that a striking majority of constituents of non-extended binomials express complementary semantic relations, e.g. *towary lub usługi* [goods or services], *jednolite i ciągłe* [single and continuous].[157] This type of relation between words constituting binomials justifies their high distribution in translated judgments. In addition, binomials expressing complementation are indispensable to the genre on account of their equally high representation in non-translated national judgments, as well as the useful doubling (cf. Gustaffson

157 In order to gain a better view of the distribution of non-extended binomials expressing different semantic relations, it is necessary to consider not only the number of types of binomials but also their normalized frequency of occurrence across the corpora.

1984) they introduce, which may guarantee a greater degree of legal certainty. The second most salient semantic category is absolute near-synonymy (SYN),[158] e.g. *staranność i rzetelność* [diligence and reliability]. Binomials expressing this semantic category are regarded as introducing redundancy, which means that the doubling they introduce does not necessarily contribute to raising the informational value of the propositions. Instead, it leads to undue verbosity and impedes readers' understanding of the texts; it can therefore be presumed that the binomials motivated by either absolute or near-synonymy (binomials proper) could easily be omitted in TTs (cf. Kopaczyk 2017: 167). The reason for their high representation in TTs may be that they are prompted by the STs and that lawyer-linguists approach them conservatively by reproducing them faithfully in translations, even though these binomials convey no more meaning than one well-chosen word possibly could. With the three remaining semantic categories, it should be noted that the relation of consequence is not represented in binomials, as it is mainly associated with verbs, which, as already shown, do not form non-extended binomials (cf. Section 8.3.4). The two other relations, namely sub-division (SUB), e.g. *miejsca i regiony* [localities and regions] and opposition (antonymy) (OPP), e.g. *bezpośredni lub pośredni* [direct or indirect], are the least widely represented across the corpora, particularly in the national corpus. All semantic motivations for the use of binomials except for absolute and near-synonymy are regarded as introducing redundancy.

Based on the above presentation and description of non-extended binomials, it is also possible to conclude that non-extended binomials are not prone to reversibility (see Tables 8.6 and 8.7). This is evidenced by the fact that none of the binomials in the individual corpora appear in a reversed order. Therefore, they are characterized by a high degree of fixedness, which is only superficially alleviated by the Polish declension system.

### 8.2.3 Distribution of extended binomials

Extended binomials are similar to non-extended binomials in that they are also structured around the linking words *i* [and] or *lub* [or] and not around the linking word *albo* [or]. However, the difference between them is that the former involve more than just two words belonging to the same word class apart from the linking word; for instance, the extended binomial *reguły procesowe i dowodowe* [procedural and evidence-gathering rules] forms the pattern: [N + Adj] + *i* [and] + Adj. Extended binomials also differ from multinomials which involve more than two, typically three co-ordinated elements, e.g. *finansowy, ekonomiczny i organizacyjny* [financial, economic and organizational], which forms the pattern Adj, Adj + *i* [and] + Adj (see Section 8.2.5).

158 I modified the relation of near-synonymy (SYN) to also include any possible cases of almost absolute synonymy. For the purposes of this analysis, I did not differentiate between the two types of synonymy, judging that binomials expressing both of these types introduce redundant wordiness.

In the case of extended binomials, GC judgments have practically the same level of distribution as post-accession SN judgments, the only difference being the difference in the total number of types of binomials based around *i* [and] and *lub* [or] – GC judgments have a lower number of types structured around *i* [and] and a higher number of types based around *lub* [or] than SN judgments. As for CJ judgments, they display a much wider range of extended binomial types than the SN corpus, mostly thanks to the comparatively high level of types based around *lub* [or]. They also contain around 24 % more occurrences of extended binomials than the national corpus. On the whole, it should be noted that the total distribution of extended binomials differs significantly from that of non-extended binomials (cf. Section 8.2.1). Extended binomials exhibit a much more convergent distribution across all the corpora, which is quite surprising considering the fact that the frequency of occurrence of non-extended binomials is about three times lower in post-accession national judgments compared to the EU judgments. What is also surprising is the fairly even distribution of both tokens and types in the pre- and post-accession SN corpora, which stands in contrast to the distribution of non-extended binomials.

Table 8.8 shows that there are also noticeable differences within the Eurolect itself. According to the data, CJ judgments contain about 24 % more occurrences of extended binomials than GC judgments. The discrepancies also pertain to the total number of types of both binomials based around *i* [and] and, even more so, *lub* [or]. Figure 8.3 more adequately visualizes the distribution of extended binomials across the corpora.

Overall, non-extended binomials (see Figure 8.1, Section 8.2.1) do not exhibit such a convergent distribution across the corpora as extended binomials (see Figure 8.3). This might mean that translated and non-translated judgments are relatively convergent at the level of longer binomial structures, but largely divergent at the level of short, non-extended binomials. Leaving out the differences between the corpora regarding the distributional differences, it should be noted that extended binomials based around *lub* [or] are less frequent than those based around *i* [and], a tendency which is also reflected by non-extended binomials.

### 8.2.4 Structural and semantic qualities of extended binomials

The internal structure of non-extended binomials has been established to be based around four word classes – nouns, adjectives, adverbs, and numerals. This gives seven structural patterns, that is three patterns of binomials structured around *i* [and] and four structured around *lub* [or] (see Tables 8.4 and 8.5, Section 8.2.2). Non-extended binomials have also been determined not to contain any verbs. Additionally, the only word classes that occur with both linking words across all the corpora are nouns and adjectives.

Extended binomials, on the other hand, exhibit much more varied structures, as they occur in a total of 75 structural patterns. Owing to the fact that *i* [and] is the more frequently occurring linking word, there are more extended binomial structures based around it, that is a total of 54 different structural patterns. On the other hand, the total number of patterns with *lub* [or] amounts to 21 (see Tables 8.9

**Table 8.8.** *Total number of extended binomials in the corpora*

| | Translated EU case law | | | | | | |
|---|---|---|---|---|---|---|---|
| | CJ | | | | GC | | |
| | Types (vs GC) (vs SN_2011–2015) | NF | CJ vs GC | CJ vs SN_2011–2015 | Types (GC vs SN_2011–2015) | NF | GC vs SN_2011–2015 |
| *i* [and] | 23 (0,22; −13,59) (0,10; −13,74) | **837** | +92 % (63,96; 50,15) | +106 % (0,75; −13,09) | 19 (0,61; −13,20) | **437** | **−45 %** (51,00; 37,18) |
| *lub* [or] | 12 (1,78; −12,04) (4,13; −9,71) | **209** | −49 % (32,38; 18,56) | +312 % (39,15; 25,31) | 6 (0,48; −13,33) | **406** | **506 %** (135,60; 121,78) |
| **Total** | **35 (1,26; -12,56) (0,52 -13,32)** | **1,046** | **+24 % (10,94; −2,87)** | **+122 % (9,78; −4,06)** | **25 (0,17; −13,65)** | **843** | **−1 % (0,04; −13,77)** |

| | Non-translated PL case law | | | | |
|---|---|---|---|---|---|
| | SN_2011–2015 | | SN_2011–2015 vs SN_1999 | SN_1999 | |
| | Types (SN_2011–2015 vs SN_1999) | NF | | Types | NF |
| *i* [and] | 25 (0,33; −13,50) | **788** | −5 % (0,60; −13,23) | **29** | **831** |
| *lub* [or] | 4 (0,42; −13,41) | **67** | −36 % (3,94; −9,89) | **6** | **104** |
| **Total** | **29 (0,61; −13,22)** | **855** | **−9 % (1,81; −12,01)** | **35** | **935** |

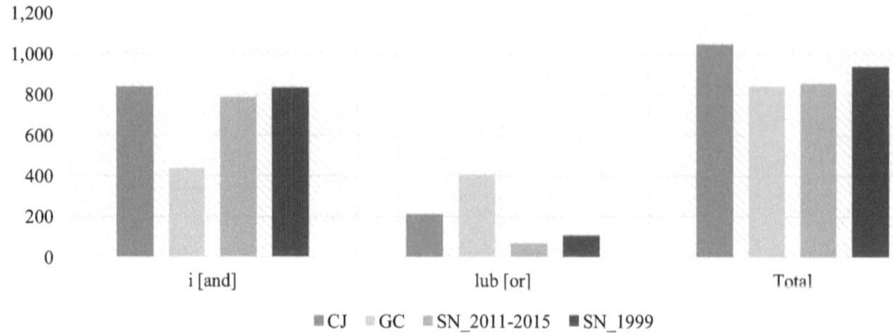


**Figure 8.3.** *Total number of extended binomials in the corpora*

and 8.10). What is more, a certain proportion of extended binomials is structured around verbs, which might to some degree alleviate the influence of a large number of noun-based non-extended binomials and tone down the resulting nominal style. In the following, I will present the structural patterns most frequently occurring across the post-accession corpora along with examples.

The examples below show structures of the top three extended binomials based around *i* [and] which occur most frequently in the CJ corpus (examples 1–3) and the GC corpus (examples 4–6):

(1) [N + Adj] + *i* [and] + N, e.g. *Parlament Europejski i Rada* [(of) the European Parliament and (of) the Council],
(2) [V + N] + *i* [and] + [V + Pr + N], e.g. *zawiesić postępowanie i zwrócić się do Trybunału* [to stay the proceedings and to refer the following question to the Court of Justice],
(3) [N + Adj] + *i* [and] + [N + Adj], e.g. *postępowanie główne i pytania prejudycjalne* [the dispute in the main proceedings and the questions referred for a preliminary ruling],
(4) [N + N] + *i* [and] + [N + N], e.g. *przebieg postępowania i żądania stron* [course of proceedings and requests of the parties],
(5) [N + Adj] + *i* [and] + Adj, e.g. *okoliczności faktyczne i prawne* [factual and legal circumstances],
(6) [N + N + Adj] + *i* [and] + N, e.g. *ochrona zdrowia ludzkiego i środowiska* [protection of human health and the environment].

The following examples show structures of the top three extended binomials based around *lub* [or] which occur most frequently in the CJ corpus (examples 7–9) and the GC corpus (examples 10–12):

(7) [N + Adj] + *lub* [or] + Adj, e.g. *cele przemysłowe lub handlowe* [industrial or commercial purposes],
(8) [N + N] + *lub* [or] + N, e.g. *właściwości towarów lub usług* [characteristics of the goods or services],
(9) [N + N] + *lub* [or] + [N + N], e.g. *produkcja towaru lub świadczenie usługi* [production of the goods or of rendering of the service],

(10) [N + Adj] + *lub* [or] + Adj, e.g. *osoba fizyczna lub prawna* [natural or legal person],
(11) [N + Pr + N] + *lub* [or] + N, e.g. *gumy do żucia lub pastylki* [chewing gums or pastilles],
(12) Adj + *lub* [or] + [Adj + N], e.g. *potencjalne lub rzeczywiste skutki* [potential or actual effects].

Examples 13 to 18 present the top three extended binomial structures based around *i* [and] (13–15) and *lub* [or] (16–18) which occur most frequently solely in the post-accession SN corpus:

(13) [N + Pr + N] + *i* [and] + N, e.g. *podatek od towarów i usług* [tax on goods and services],
(14) [V + Adj + N] + *i* [and] + [V + N + N + Adj], e.g. *uchyla zaskarżony wyrok i przekazuje sprawę (sądowi apelacyjnemu)* [sets aside the judgment under appeal and refers the case to (the appellate court)],
(15) [Adj + N] + *i* [and] + [N + Pr + N +N], e.g. *ponowne rozpoznanie i rozstrzygnięcie o kosztach postępowania* [handing over the case for reconsideration and decision regarding the costs of the proceedings],
(16) [Adj + N] + *lub* [or] + [Pr + N], e.g. *byli właściciele lub ich spadkobiercy* [former owners or their heirs],
(17) N + *lub* [or] + [N + Pr + N], e.g. *nieważność lub wydanie z naruszeniem (art.)* [invalidity or issue in violation of (art.)],
(18) [Adj + N] + *lub* [or] + [Adj + N], e.g. *błędna wykładnia lub niewłaściwe zastosowanie* [wrong interpretation or improper application].

Examples 19 to 21 present the top three extended binomial structures based around *i* [and] (19–21) and *lub* [or] (22–24) which occur most frequently solely in the pre-accession SN corpus:

(19) [N + Adj + N] + *i* [and] + [N + N], e.g. *uchylenie zaskarżonego wyroku i przekazanie sprawy* [setting aside of the judgment under appeal and referral of the case]
(20) [V + N] + *i* [and] + V, e.g. *oddala kasację i zasądza* [dismiss the cassation appeal and award]
(21) [N + N] + *i* [and] + N, e.g. *oddalenie kasacji i zasądzenie* [dismissal of the cassation and award]
(22) N + *lub* [or] + [Adj + N], e.g. *wykładnię lub niewłaściwe zastosowanie* [interpretation or misapplication]
(23) [Pr + N] + *lub* [or] + [Pr + N], e.g. *w całości lub w części* [in whole or in part]
(24) N + *lub* [or] + [N + N + Adj], e.g. *treści lub znaczenia normy prawnej* [content or meaning of a legal norm]

Since quantitative data concerning the total number of extended binomial structures and distribution of individual structural types based around *i* [and] and *lub* [or] across the corpora presented in a detailed manner would hinder generalizations, I decided to reduce the list structural types to only a handful of types based around the node constituents of extended binomials belonging to the same word class, as I did with the analysis of non-extended binomial structures (cf. Table 8.8 and Figure 8.2, Section 8.2.2). The following tables (see Table 8.9 and 8.10) show the distribution of individual basic structural types of extended binomials across the corpora.

**Table 8.9.** *Total number of basic extended binomial structures and distribution of individual structural types based around i [and] and lub [or] in the EU corpora*

| | Translated EU case law | | | | | | |
|---|---|---|---|---|---|---|---|
| | CJ | | | | GC | | |
| ***i* [and]** | **Types (CJ vs GC) (CJ vs SN_2011–2015)** | **NF** | **CJ vs GC** | **CJ vs SN_2011–2015** | **Types (GC vs SN_2011–2015)** | **NF** | **GC vs SN_2011–2015** |
| N + *i* [and] + N | 19 (0,55; −13,27) (0,55; −13,27) | **683** | +110 % (63,52; 49,70) | +23 % (6,79; −7,05) | 14 (0,01; −13,80) | **326** | −41 % (29,29; 15,48) |
| V + *i* [and] + V | 1 (1,34; −12,48) (1,14; −12,68) | **103** | --- (70,52; 56,70) | −36 % (6,65; −7,19) | 0 (4,05; −9,77) | **0** | −100 % (110,40; 96,58) |
| Adj + *i* [and] + Adj | 3 (0,00; −13,81) (0,16; −13,66) | **53** | −50 % (9,45; -4,37) | −27 % (1,59; −12,24) | 3 (0,24; −13,57) | **107** | +47 % (3,35; −10,47) |
| **Total** | **23** (0,65; −13,16) (0,22; −13,59) | **839** | **+92 %** (63,30; 49,48) | **+6 %** (0,88; −12,96) | **17** (0,05; −13,77) | **437** | **−45 %** (49,37; 35,55) |
| ***lub* [or]** | **Types (CJ vs GC) (CJ vs SN_2011–2015)** | **NF** | **CJ vs GC** | **CJ vs SN_2011–2015** | **Types (GC vs SN_2011–2015)** | **NF** | **GC vs SN_2011–2015** |
| N + *lub* [or] + N | 7 (0,70; −13,12) (0,70; −13,12) | **120** | +140 % (14,64; 0,82) | +76 % (7,46; −6,37) | 4 (0,00; −13,81) | **50** | −26 % (1,30; −12,51) |

| | Translated EU case law | | | | | | |
|---|---|---|---|---|---|---|---|
| | CJ | | | | GC | | |
| Adj + *lub* [or] + Adj | 5<br>(1,20; −12,62)<br>(6,71; −7,11) | **90** | −75 %<br>(85,40; 71,58) | ---<br>(63,31; 49,48) | 2<br>(2,85; −10,97) | **355** | ---<br>(247,81; 233,99) |
| **Total** | **12**<br>(1,78; −12,04)<br>**(3,83; −9,98)** | **210** | **−48 %**<br>**(32,00; 18,18)** | **209 %**<br>**(38,77; 24,93)** | **6**<br>**(0,48; −13,33)** | **405** | **+496 %**<br>**(134,22; 120,41)** |
| ***i* [and] and *lub* [or]** | **Types (CJ vs GC) (CJ vs SN_2011–2015)** | **NF** | **CJ vs GC** | **CJ vs SN_2011–2015** | **Types (GC vs SN_2011–2015)** | **NF** | **GC vs SN_2011–2015** |
| N + *i* [and]/*lub* [or] + N | 26<br>(1,13; −12,69)<br>(1,13; −12,69) | **803** | +114 %<br>(77,88; 64,06) | +29 %<br>(11,67; −2,17) | 18<br>(0,01; −13,80) | **376** | −29 %<br>(29,96; 16,15) |
| V + *i* [and] + V | 1<br>(1,34; −12,48)<br>(1,14; −12,68) | **103** | ---<br>(70,52; 56,70) | −36 %<br>(6,65; −7,19) | 0<br>(4,05; −9,77) | **0** | −100 %<br>(110,40; 96,58) |
| Adj + *i* [and]/*lub* [or] + Adj | 8<br>(0,57; −13,25)<br>(3,59; −0,23) | **143** | −69 %<br>(89,62; 75,80) | +96 %<br>(11,81; −2,02) | 5<br>(1,44; −12,37) | **462** | +533 %<br>(158,95; 145,14) |
| **Total** | **35**<br>(1,99; −11,83)<br>**(1,99; −11,83)** | **1,049** | **+25 %**<br>**(11,30; −2,52)** | **+22 %**<br>**(9,87; −3,96)** | **23**<br>**(0,02; −13,80)** | **838** | **−2 %**<br>**(0,06; −13,75)** |

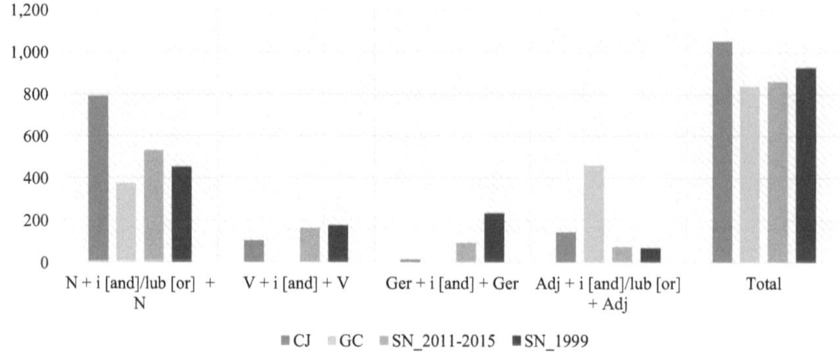


**Figure 8.4.** *Structural distribution of extended binomials across the EU corpora and the national corpus*

Thanks to the reduction of all identified structural types to types based around the node constituents, it is now possible to observe that the vast majority of extended binomials is noun-based (N + *i* [and] + N), thus further contributing to the nominal style of judgments. Furthermore, among extended binomials, there are types of a structure involving verbs, V + *i* [and] + V, particularly in the national corpora, but also in the CJ corpus. All in all, verb-based extended binomials form only a fraction of all binomials, which is not enough to compensate for the highly nominal nature of both translated and non-translated judgments. One other word class forming extended binomials in the corpora is adjectives. What is also easily observable is that extended binomials based around *lub* [or] are underrepresented in the national corpora. However, in general, the total distribution of extended binomials is quite similar across the corpora, with slight overrepresentation in the CJ corpus (about 23 %). As regards the language change in national judgments, the data show that extended binomials, similar to non-extended binomials, are less frequent in post-accession SN judgments as compared to pre-accession judgments, although overall the use of extended binomials has not changed as drastically as the use of non-extended binomials.

The strikingly pervasive nature of noun-based binomials relative to the distribution of other structural types of extended binomials is more visible in Figure 8.4.

Both translated and non-translated judgments can be distinguished by their highly nominal style due to the underrepresentation of binomials based on parts of speech other than nouns (cf. Tables 8.4 and 8.5 and Figure 8.2, Section 8.2.2). The following tables (see Tables 8.11 and 8.12) present an exhaustive list of binomials found in EU and national judgments. All of the binomials are presented in the nominative case (either masculine or feminine, and either in the singular or plural).[159]

159 Bolded and underlined binomials are shared between both EU corpora and the post-accession national corpus; underlined binomials are shared between the EU corpora.

**Table 8.10.** *Total number of basic extended binomial structures and distribution of individual structural types based around i [and] and lub [or] in the SN corpora*

| | **Non-translated PL case law** | | | | |
|---|---|---|---|---|---|
| | **SN_2011-2015** | | | **SN_1999** | |
| ***i* [and]** | **Types** | **NF** | **SN_2011-2015 vs SN_1999** | **Types** | **NF** |
| N + *i* [and] + N | 14 (0,15; −13,68) | **556** | −6 % (0,69; −13,14) | **16** | **591** |
| V + *i* [and] + V | 3 (0,19; −13,64) | **162** | −7 % (0,27; −13,56) | **2** | **174** |
| Adj + *i* [and] + Adj | 2 (0,21; −13,62) | **73** | +11 % (0,15; −13,68) | **3** | **66** |
| **Total** | **19 (0,12; −13,71)** | **788** | **−5 % (0,76; −13,07)** | **21** | **831** |
| ***lub* [or]** | **Types** | **NF** | **SN_2011-2015 vs SN_1999** | **Types** | **NF** |
| N + *lub* [or] + N | 4 (0,42; −13,41) | **68** | −26 % (1,92; −11,91) | **6** | **92** |
| Adj + *lub* [or] + Adj | 0 (0,00; −13,83) | **0** | --- (0,00; −13,83) | **0** | **0** |
| **Total** | **4 (0,42; −13,41)** | **68** | **−26 % (1,92; −11,91)** | **6** | **92** |
| ***i* [and] and *lub* [or]** | **Types** | **NF** | **SN_2011-2015 vs SN_1999** | **Types** | **NF** |
| N + *i* [and]/*lub* [or] + N | 18 (0,43; −13,40) | **624** | +38 % (13,44; −0,38) | **22** | **451** |
| V + *i* [and] + V | 3 (0,19; −13,64) | **162** | −7 % (0,27; −13,56) | **2** | **174** |
| Adj + *i* [and]/*lub* [or] + Adj | 2 (0,21; −13,62) | **73** | +11 % (0,15; −13,68) | **3** | **66** |
| **Total** | **23 (0,35; −13,48)** | **859** | **−7 % (1,43; −12,40)** | **27** | **923** |

**Table 8.11.** *Extended binomials in the EU corpora*

| Translated EU case law | | | | | |
|---|---|---|---|---|---|
| **CJ** | **SEM** | **NF** | **GC** | **SEM** | **NF** |
| ***Parlament Europejski i Rada*** [the European Parliament and the Council] | SUB | 210 | *osoba fizyczna lub prawna* [natural or legal person] | COM | 341 |
| *zawiesić postępowanie i zwrócić się do Trybunału* [to stay the proceedings and to refer the following question to the Court of Justice] | CON | 102 | *przebieg postępowania i żądania stron* [course of proceedings and requests of the parties] | COM | 84 |
| *postępowanie główne i pytania prejudycjalne* [the dispute in the main proceedings and the questions referred for a preliminary ruling] | COM | 70 | *ochrona zdrowia ludzkiego i środowiska* [protection of human health and the environment] | COM | 43 |
| *Zjednoczone Królestwo Wielkiej Brytanii i Irlandii Północnej* [the United Kingdom of Great Britain and Northern Ireland] | SUB | 60 | ***Parlament Europejski i Rada*** [the European Parliament and the Council] | SUB | 35 |
| *oferty zatrudnienia i wnioski o zatrudnienie* [vacancies and applications for employment] | COM | 43 | *okoliczności faktyczne i prawne* [factual and legal circumstances] | COM | 31 |
| *produkty energetyczne i energia elektryczna* [energy products and electricity] | COM | 31 | *ekonomiczny i techniczny punkt widzenia* [economical and technical point of view] | COM | 22 |
| *tkanki i komórki ludzkie* [human tissues and cells] | COM | 29 | *reguły procesowe i dowodowe* [procedural and evidence-gathering rules] | COM | 22 |
| *właściwości towarów lub usług* [characteristics of the goods or services] | COM | 27 | *nowość i indywidualny charakter* [novelty and individual character] | COM | 20 |
| *postępowanie przed sądem krajowym i pytania prejudycjalne* [the dispute in the main proceedings and the questions referred for a preliminary ruling] | COM | 27 | *kasety audio i wideo* [audio and video tapes] | COM | 18 |

| Translated EU case law | | | | | |
|---|---|---|---|---|---|
| *cele przemysłowe lub handlowe* [industrial or commercial purposes] | COM | 25 | *wystąpienia stron i ich odpowiedzi na pytania sądu* [the parties' oral arguments and replies to the questions of the (General) Court] | COM | 18 |
| *dostosowanie wynagrodzeń i emerytur* [adjustment of remuneration and pensions] | COM | 25 | *poprawa konkurencyjności i innowacyjności* [improvement of competitiveness and innovation] | COM | 18 |
| *pracodawcy i pracownicy najemni* [employers and employees] | COM | 25 | ***Konwencja o ochronie praw człowieka i podstawowych wolności*** [European Convention for the Protection of Human Rights and Fundamental Freedoms] | SYN | 18 |
| *ośrodki pobytu dziennego i ośrodki pobytu nocnego* [day-care centres and night-care centres] | COM | 23 | *spółka dominująca i jej spółka zależna* [parent company and its subsidiary] | COM | 16 |
| *produkcja towaru lub świadczenia usługi* [production of the goods or of rendering of the service] | COM | 21 | *gumy do żucia lub pastylki* [chewing gums or pastilles] | COM | 14 |
| *pierwotne lub wtórne prawo Unii Europejskiej* [primary or secondary law of the European Union] | COM | 21 | *potencjalne lub rzeczywiste skutki* [potential or actual effects] | OPP | 14 |
| *nomenklatura taryfowa i statystyczna* [tariff and statistical nomenclature] | COM | 21 | *prawo do obrony i prawo do skutecznej ochrony sądowej* [rights of the defence and of the right to effective judicial protection] | SYN | 14 |
| *ten akt lub ta umowa* [the document or agreement] | SYN | 20 | *w sposób jasny i jednoznaczny* [in a clear and unequivocal manner] | SYN | 14 |
| *w stanie niezmontowanym lub rozmontowanym* [in an unassembled or disassembled state] | OPP | 20 | *rozporządzenie lub każda przyszła decyzja* [regulation or any future decision] | COM | 12 |

(*continued on next page*)

**Table 8.11.** *Continued*

| Translated EU case law | | | | | |
|---|---|---|---|---|---|
| *postęp techniczny i naukowy* [technical and scientific progress] | COM | 20 | *organy lub jednostki organizacyjne Unii* [offices or agencies of the European Union] | SYN | 12 |
| *Unia Europejska i jej państwa członkowskie* [European Union and its Member States] | SUB | 18 | *importer lub strona trzecia* [importer or a third party] | COM | 12 |
| *prawa obywateli Unii i członków ich rodzin* [right of citizens of the Union and their family members] | SUB | 18 | *wspólna polityka zagraniczna i bezpieczeństwa* [common foreign and security policy] | COM | 12 |
| ***Konwencja o ochronie praw człowieka i podstawowych wolności*** [European Convention for the Protection of Human Rights and Fundamental Freedoms] | SYN | 18 | *ustalanie cen i podział rynku* [price-fixing and market-sharing] | COM | 12 |
| *zasoby genetyczne roślin dla wyżywienia i rolnictwa* [plant genetic resources for food and agriculture] | COM | 16 | *zasady dobrej administracji i ochrony* [principles of good administration and protection] | COM | 12 |
| *emerytury urzędników i innych pracowników* [pensions of officials and other servants] | COM | 16 | *ochrona zdrowia ludzkiego i bezpieczeństwa w miejscu pracy* [protection of human health and safety at the workplace] | COM | 12 |
| *paliwo do ogrzewania lub paliwo silnikowe* [heating fuel or motor fuel] | OPP | 14 | *charakter i stopień surowości* [nature and degree of severity] | **SYN** | 12 |
| *z tytułu wypadku przy pracy lub z tytułu choroby* [an accident at work or occupational disease] | COM | 14 | | | |
| *pakowanie i etykietowanie substancji niebezpiecznych* [classification of packaging and labeling of dangerous substances] | COM | 14 | | | |

| | | | | | |
|---|---|---|---|---|---|
| *żądania stron i postępowanie przed Trybunałem* [forms of order sought and procedure before the Court] | COM | 14 | | | |
| *osoba fizyczna lub prawna* [natural or legal person] | COM | 12 | | | |
| *wyrób kompletny lub gotowy* [complete or finished article] | SYN | 12 | | | |
| *wspólność majątkowa lub współwłasność* [joint ownership or co-ownership] | OPP | 12 | | | |
| *współmałżonek lub partner cywilny* [spouse or civil partner] | OPP | 12 | | | |
| *sytuacja gospodarcza i społeczna* [economic and social situation] | COM | 12 | | | |
| *okoliczności powstania sporu i sporna decyzja* [background to the dispute and the contested decision] | COM | 12 | | | |
| *wynagrodzenia i zabezpieczenie emerytalnego urzędników* [Remuneration and Pensions of Civil Servants] | COM | 12 | | | |
| **Totals (35 types)** | **COM: 23** | **1,046** | **Totals (25 types)** | **COM: 18** | **843** |
| | **OPP: 4** | | | **SYN: 5** | |
| | **SUB: 4** | | | **OPP: 1** | |
| | **SYN: 3** | | | **SUB: 1** | |
| | **CON: 1** | | | **CON: 0** | |

**Table 8.12.** *Extended binomials in the SN corpora*

| Non–translated PL case law | | | | | |
|---|---|---|---|---|---|
| **SN_2011–2015** | **SEM** | **NF** | **SN_1999** | **Semantic relation** | **NF** |
| *uchyla zaskarżony wyrok i przekazuje sprawę (sądowi apelacyjnemu/sądowi okręgowemu)* [sets aside the judgment under appeal and refers the case to (the appellate court/district court)] | CON | 125 | *uchylenie zaskarżonego wyroku i przekazanie sprawy* [setting aside of the judgment under appeal and referral of the case] | CON | 127 |
| *podatek od towarów i usług* [tax on goods and services] | COM | 119 | *oddala kasację i zasądza* [dissmisses the casssation and orders] | CON | 119 |
| *ponowne rozpoznanie i rozstrzygnięcie o kosztach postępowania* [handing over the case for reconsideration and decision regarding the costs of the proceedings] | COM | 99 | *oddalenie kasacji i zasądzenie* [dismissal of the cassation and the order (of)] | CON | 55 |
| *błędna wykładnia i niewłaściwe zastosowanie* [wrong interpretation and improper application] | COM | 78 | *uchyla zaskarżony wyrok i przekazuje sprawę (sądowi apelacyjnemu/sądowi okręgowemu)* [sets aside the judgment under appeal and refers the case to (the appellate court/district court)] | CON | 55 |
| *uchylenie zaskarżonego wyroku i przekazanie sprawy do ponownego rozpoznania* [setting aside the contested judgment and referring the case back to] | CON | 34 | *ponownego rozpoznania i rozstrzygnięcia o kosztach* [for re-consideration and decision on the costs of cassation proceedings] | COM | 38 |

| | | | | | |
|---|---|---|---|---|---|
| ***<u>Konwencja o ochronie praw człowieka i podstawowych wolności</u>*** [European Convention for the Protection of Human Rights and Fundamental Freedoms] | SYN | 27 | *uchylenie i przekazanie sprawy do ponownego rozpoznania* [setting aside of the judgment and referral of the case for re-consideration] | CON | 38 |
| *tereny w miastach i osiedlach* [areas in cities and housing estates] | SUB | 27 | *przez błędną wykładnię i niewłaściwe zastosowanie* [due to misinterpretation and misapplication] | COM | 36 |
| *uchyla zaskarżony wyrok i* ***sprawę*** *przekazuje sądowi apelacyjnemu* [sets aside the judgment under appeal and refers the case to the appellate court] | CON | 24 | *ponownego rozpoznania i orzeczenia o kosztach* [for re-consideration and decision on the costs of cassation proceedings] | COM | 34 |
| *byli właściciele lub ich spadkobiercy* [former owners or their heirs] | SUB | 22 | *wykładnię lub niewłaściwe zastosowanie* [interpretation or misapplication] | COM | 32 |
| *zasób geodezyjny i kartograficzny* [geodetic and cartographic resource] | COM | 22 | *z odsetkami i kosztami* [including interest and costs] | COM | 30 |
| *Agencja Restrukturyzacji i Modernizacji Rolnictwa* [Agency for the Restructuring and Modernisation of Agriculture] | SYN | 20 | *wiarygodności i mocy dowodów* [reliability and power of evidence] | COM | 28 |
| *sposób i tryb finansowania z budżetu państwa* [manner and mode of financing from the state budget] | COM | 20 | *pierwszej i drugiej instancji* [first and second instance] | COM | 26 |
| *nieważność lub wydanie z naruszeniem (art.)* [invalidity of issue in violation of (art.)] | COM | 18 | *w całości lub w części* [in whole or in part] | SUB | 18 |

*(continued on next page)*

**Table 8.12.** *Continued*

| | | | | | |
|---|---|---|---|---|---|
| *prawo geodezyjne i kartograficzne* [surveying and cartographic law] | COM | 18 | *na następujących ustaleniach i wnioskach* [on the following findings and conclusions] | COM | 18 |
| *zbieranie i wykorzystanie materiałów prasowych* [collecting and using press materials] | COM | 16 | *treści lub znaczenia normy prawnej* [content or meaning of a legal norm] | COM | 16 |
| *błędna wykładnia lub niewłaściwe zastosowanie* [wrong interpretation or improper application] | COM | 14 | *zaskarżonego wyroku i poprzedzającego go wyroku* [of the judgment under appeal and the preceding judgment] | COM | 16 |
| *niewykonanie lub nienależyte wykonanie zobowiązania* [failure to perform or improper performance of an obligation] | COM | 14 | *trwały i zupełny rozkład pożycia małżeńskiego* [durable and complete breakdown of marriage] | COM | 16 |
| *uchylenie zaskarżonego wyroku i przekazanie sprawy sądowi apelacyjnemu do ponownego rozpoznania* [setting aside the judgment under appeal and referring the case to the appellate court] | CON | 14 | *rozbiórce i naprawie budynków* [demolition and repair of buildings] | COM | 16 |
| *produkty lecznicze i wyroby medyczne* [medicinal products and medical devices] | SYN | 14 | *kluczyków i dokumentów pojazdu* [keys and vehicle documents] | COM | 16 |
| *Monitor Sądowy i Gospodarczy* [Court and Commercial Gazette] | COM | 14 | *adwokata lub radcy prawnego* [lawyer or legal adviser] | COM | 14 |
| *Kodeks rodzinny i opiekuńczy* [Family and guardianship code] | COM | 14 | *kosztów utrzymania i wychowania* [costs of maintenance and upbringing] | COM | 14 |

| | | | | | |
|---|---|---|---|---|---|
| *regulamin rachunków oszczędnościowo-rozliczeniowych, oszczędnościowych i terminowych lokat oszczędnościowych* [regulations of savings and billing, savings and savings term deposit accounts] | COM | 14 | *ustawy o najmie lokali mieszkalnych i dodatkach mieszkaniowych* [Act on the rental of residential premises and housing allowances] | COM | 14 |
| *fundusz restrukturyzacji i oddłużenia rolnictwa* [restructuring and debt repayment fund] | COM | 14 | *podatku od towarów i usług* [tax on goods and services] | COM | 14 |
| *planowanie i zagospodarowanie przestrzenne* [planning and spatial development] | COM | 14 | *pracy i ubezpieczeń społecznych* [work and social security] | COM | 14 |
| *cierpienia fizyczne i psychiczne* [physical and mental distress] | COM | 12 | *sądowi apelacyjnemu lub sądowi wojewódzkiemu* [appellate court or voivodship court] | COM | 12 |
| ***Parlament Europejski i Rada*** [the European Parliament and the Council] | SUB | 12 | *stosunku prawnego lub prawa* [legal relationship or right] | COM | 12 |
| *fundusz gospodarki zasobem geodezyjnym i kartograficznym* [fund for geodetic and cartographic resource management] | COM | 12 | *nowe fakty i dowody* [new facts and evidence] | COM | 12 |
| *gospodarka gruntami i wywłaszczanie nieruchomości* [land management and expropriation of real estate] | COM | 12 | *zmianę zaskarżonego wyroku i uwzględnienie powództwa* [change of the judgment under appeal and allowance of the claim] | COM | 12 |
| *oddala skargę kasacyjną i zasądza* [dismisses the cassation appeal and orders] | CON | 12 | *Kodeksu rodzinnego i opiekuńczego* [Family and Guardianship Code] | COM | 12 |
| | | | *prawa geologicznego i górniczego* [geological and mining law] | COM | 12 |
| | | | *ministra zdrowia i opieki społecznej* [Minister of Health and Social Welfare] | COM | 12 |

(*continued on next page*)

**Table 8.12.** *Continued*

| | | | | | |
|---|---|---|---|---|---|
| | | | *za wiedzą i zgodą* [with knowledge and consent] | COM | 12 |
| | | | *w doktrynie i orzecznictwie* [in doctrine and case law] | COM | 12 |
| | | | *odmówił wiarygodności i mocy* [refused credibility and power] | COM | 12 |
| | | | *geodezji i gospodarki gruntami* [geodesy and land management] | COM | 12 |
| **Total (29 types)** | **COM: 18** | **855** | **Total (35 types)** | **COM: 30** | **936** |
| | **CON: 5** | | | **CON: 4** | |
| | **SYN: 3** | | | **SYN: 0** | |
| | **SUB: 3** | | | **SUB: 1** | |
| | **OPP: 0** | | | **OPP: 0** | |

The overall degree of overlap between the corpora is very low, as it is limited to only a handful of extended binomials. Bolded and underlined binomials are shared between both EU corpora and the national corpus; these are: *Konwencja o ochronie praw człowieka i podstawowych wolności* [European Convention for the Protection of Human Rights and Fundamental Freedoms] and *Parlament Europejski i Rada* [the European Parliament and the Council]. The only binomial shared by both EU corpora is *osoba fizyczna lub prawna* [natural or legal person]. What is more, the analysis of concordances has demonstrated that virtually all extended binomials refer strictly to the thematic content of both EU and national judgments, with the exception of one binomial found in GC judgments: *(w) sposób jasny i jednoznaczny* [(in) a clear and unequivocal manner]. This further confirms the indispensable nature of extended legal binomials used frequently in judicial language.

For the semantic relations between the constituent elements of extended binomials, the most frequently occurring type of semantic relation across all the corpora is complementation (COM) (cf. Malkiel 1959: 126–129). Examples of extended binomials expressing complementary relations between their constituent elements include *błędna wykładnia i niewłaściwe zastosowanie* [wrong interpretation and improper application] and *oferty zatrudnienia i wnioski o zatrudnienie* [vacancies and applications for employment]. The second most frequently occurring semantic relation differs across the corpora – for CJ judgments it is opposition (antonymy) (OPP), for GC judgments it is absolute or near-synonymy (SYN), and for SN judgments it is consequence (CON). All three types of semantic relations are noticeably less frequent than the relation of complementation (COM). Binomials expressing opposition (OPP) are characterized by antonymy of their constituent elements, for instance, *potencjalne lub rzeczywiste skutki* [potential or actual effects] and *w stanie niezmontowanym lub rozmontowanym* [in an unassembled or disassembled state]. Absolute or near-synonymous binomials (SYN), such as *organy lub jednostki organizacyjne Unii* [offices or agencies of the European Union] and *wyrób kompletny lub gotowy* [complete or finished article] introduce redundancy, as both of the core (that is belonging to the same word class) constituent elements could readily be replaced by each other or a (near) synonym, so as to reduce wordiness which might impede the reception of the judgments. The relation of consequence (CON) is exclusive to extended binomials, as it is not present in non-extended binomials (see Section 8.2.2) and appears in only one type of extended binomial in CJ judgments, *zawiesić postępowanie i zwrócić się do Trybunału* [to stay the proceedings and to refer the following question to the Court of Justice], but not in GC judgments. It is much more frequent in national judgments, as in *uchylenie zaskarżonego wyroku i przekazanie sprawy do ponownego rozpoznania* [setting aside the contested judgment and referring the case back for review]. Examples of binomials expressing the last semantic relation, sub-division (SUB), include *Unia Europejska i jej państwa członkowskie* [European Union and its Member States] and *prawa obywateli Unii i członków ich rodzin* [rights of citizens of the Union and their family members].

Extended binomials in translated and non-translated judgments are characterized by a high degree of irreversibility, and thus fixedness. This is evidenced by the fact that virtually all types of binomials found across the corpora do not have any structural variants created through inversion. The sole exception to this observation seems to be the binomial *uchyla zaskarżony wyrok i przekazuje sprawę sądowi (apelacyjnemu/okręgowemu)* [sets aside the judgment under appeal and refers the case to (the appellate/district court)], which has another variant – *uchyla zaskarżony wyrok i sprawę przekazuje sądowi apelacyjnemu* [sets aside the judgment under appeal and refers the case to the appellate court]. However, this is only a case of permutation, different placement of emphasis in the sentence, as shown in the following examples taken from the post-accession national corpus:

SN (I CSK 237/14): *Sąd Najwyższy w składzie: (...) uchyla zaskarżony wyrok i przekazuje sprawę Sądowi Apelacyjnemu do ponownego rozpoznania i rozstrzygnięcia o kosztach postępowania kasacyjnego.*

SN (I CSK 245/14): *Sąd Najwyższy w składzie: (...) uchyla zaskarżony wyrok i sprawę przekazuje Sądowi Apelacyjnemu do ponownego rozpoznania i orzeczenia o kosztach postępowania kasacyjnego.* [The Supreme Court in a panel consisting of: (...) sets aside the judgment under appeal and refers the case to the appellate court for re-consideration and decision on the costs of cassation proceedings].

No extended binomials with similar syntactic behavior have been observed in translated EU judgments, which is presumably thanks to the wide use of CAT tools and translation memories by lawyer-linguists and the influence of the source language of TTs.

### 8.2.5 Distribution and structural qualities of multinomials

The quantitative data show that these formulaic word combinations are drastically underrepresented as compared to non- and extended binomials. There is only a total of five different types of multinomials in the EU corpora, whereas the national corpus has none (see Table 8.13).

All multinomials extracted from the corpora relate directly to the thematic content of judgments, and for this reason they were classified as content-related (see Table 8.14).

As regards the semantic relations between the core constituent elements of multinomials, all multinomials in the CJ corpus express the relation of complementation. In the GC corpus, the only multinomial, *Republika Włoska, Irlandia i Republika Francuska* [The Italian Republic, Ireland and The French Republic], expresses the relation of sub-division, as it contains the names of three EU Member

**Table 8.13.** *Total number of multinomials in the corpora*

| | Translated EU case law | | | | | | | Non-translated PL case law | | | | |
|---|---|---|---|---|---|---|---|---|---|---|---|---|
| | CJ | | | | GC | | | SN_2011–2015 | | SN_2011–2015 vs SN_1999 | SN_1999 | |
| | **Types (vs GC)** | **NF** | **CJ vs GC** | **CJ vs SN** | **Types** | **NF** | **GC vs SN** | **Types** | **NF** | % | **Types** | **NF** |
| *i* [and] | 2 (0,30; −13,52) | **32** | +129 % (3,23; −10,59) | --- | 1 | **14** | --- (9,97; −3,85) | 0 | **0** | --- | **0** | **0** |
| *lub* [or] | 2 (2,68; −11,13) | **35** | --- (24,15; 10,34) | --- | 0 | **0** | --- (0,00; −13,81) | 0 | **0** | --- | **0** | **0** |
| **Total** | **4 (1,80; −12,02)** | **67** | **+379 % (89,91; 76,09)** | --- | **1** | **14** | **--- (0,00; −13,81)** | **0** | **0** | --- | **0** | **0** |

**Table 8.14.** *Multinomials across the corpora*

| CJ | SEM | NF | GC | SEM | NF | SN_2011–2015 | NF | SN_199 | NF |
|---|---|---|---|---|---|---|---|---|---|
| **i [and]** | | | | | | | | | |
| *przepisy ustawowe, wykonawcze i administracyjne* [legislative, statutory and administrative provisions] | COM | 20 | *Republika Włoska, Irlandia i Republika Francuska* [The Italian Republic, Ireland And The French Republic] | SUB | 14 | --- | --- | --- | --- |
| *finansowy, ekonomiczny i organizacyjny* [financial, economic and organizational] | COM | 12 | | | | | | | |
| **lub [or]** | | | | | | | | | |
| *dokument urzędowy, akt lub umowa* [official document, act or agreement] | COM | 23 | | | | | | | |
| *zapobieżenie, ograniczenie lub zakłócenie konkurencji* [prevention, restriction or distortion of competition] | COM | 12 | | | | --- | --- | | |
| **Totals** | **COM: 4** | **67** | | **SUB: 1** | **14** | --- | --- | | |

States. All multinomials present in the EU corpora are irreversible, as the order of their constituent elements remains fixed.

Overall, the data show that the judicial language of judgments is based primarily on non-extended and extended binomials, and that multinomials, such as *zapobieżenie, ograniczenie lub zakłócenie konkurencji* [prevention, restriction or distortion of competition], are used only marginally and cannot be regarded as a genre feature. For this reason, I have omitted a detailed analysis of structural and discourse-functional qualities of multinomials.

### 8.2.6 Functional typology of binomials

In order to present a classification of discourse functions of binomials, I decided to employ the taxonomy used to classify lexical bundles (cf. Chapter 7). This taxonomy is based on three overarching discourse-functional categories – discourse organization, referencing and stance (cf. Biber *et al.* 2004: 384–388; Jablonkai 2009: 6, 2010: 262; Goźdź-Roszkowski 2011: 109–143). The analysis has shown that binomials present in translated and non-translated judgments convey only the first two discourse functions. For want of space, this section does not aim to provide a detailed description of the two discourse-functional categories and their sub-categories, as well as examples of binomials occurring in the wider context of judgments. The goal is rather to list the types of discourse functions performed by binomials, including the functional sub-categories, and to provide quantitative data on the total number of structures conveying each of the discourse functions (see Table 8.15).

Table 8.16 provides an overview of exemplary binomials expressing mainly referential functions, as well as and to a much lesser extent, discourse-organizing functions. The number of examples included in each of the discourse-functional sub-categories gives an idea of how many types of bi- and multinomials belong to it. Quantitative data on the distribution of binomials in each of the sub-categories are presented in Tables 8.16 and 8.17.

The data show that non-extended and extended binomials have a much narrower range of discourse functions than lexical bundles, which complements to a certain degree the results on the discoursal nature of recurrent word combinations obtained with the corpus-driven methodology involving lexical bundles. It also allows the two methodologies to be compared for their applicability in genre analysis. Recurrent word combinations analyzed in this chapter perform primarily referential functions across all three corpora, which is reflected in the total number of binomials referring to abstract concepts, elements of legal procedure, agents and institutions, documents, and places. Although referencing is the main functional category, each corpus has a different profile within this category. However, what is true for both EU corpora and the national corpus is that providing reference to abstract concepts occurs most frequently in each of them, while providing reference to places occurs least frequently. In addition, it can be observed that bi- and multinomials also perform, to a very limited extent, discourse-organizing

**Table 8.15.** *Examples of binomials fulfilling various discourse functions*

| Main discourse-functional categories | Sub-categories | Sample binomials |
|---|---|---|
| | 1.1 abstract concepts | • *akcje i udziały* [shares and financial holdings] (SN_2011–2015: 25 NF),<br>• *cierpienia fizyczne i psychiczne* [physical and mental distress] (SN_2011–2015: 12 NF),<br>• *nomenklatura taryfowa i statystyczna* [tariff and statistical nomenclature] (CJ: 21 NF),<br>• *ochrona konkurencji i konsumentów* [competition and consumer protection] (SN_2011–2015: 35 NF),<br>• *ochrona zdrowia ludzkiego i środowiska* [protection of human health and the environment] (GC: 42 NF),<br>• *osoba fizyczna lub prawna* [natural or legal person] (GC: 340 NF),<br>• *towary lub usługi* [goods or services] (CJ: 102 NF, GC: 117 NF),<br>• *wynagrodzenia i emerytury* [remuneration and pensions] (CJ: 71 NF). |
| | 1.2 agents/ institutions | • *importer lub strona trzecia* [the importer or a third party] (GC: 12 NF)<br>• *oferenci lub kandydaci* [tenderers or applicants] (GC: 12 NF),<br>• *organy lub jednostki organizacyjne Unii* [offices or agencies of the European Union] (GC: 12 NF),<br>• *Parlament Europejski i Rada* [European Parliament and of the Council] (CJ: 211, GC: 35, SN_2011–2015: 12 NF). |
| **1. Reference** | 1.3 legal procedure | • *bezpośredni i szczególny udział* [direct and specific connection] (CJ: 85 NF)<br>• *błędna wykładnia i niewłaściwe zastosowanie (art.)* [by wrong interpretation and improper application of Art.] (SN_2011–2015: 78 NF),<br>• *procesowe i dowodowe* [procedural and evidence-gathering] (GC: 22 NF),<br>• *przebieg postępowania i żądania stron* [course of proceedings and requests of the parties] (GC: 84 NF), |

| | | |
|---|---|---|
| | | • *przekazanie sprawy do ponownego rozpoznania i rozstrzygnięcie o kosztach postępowania* [handing over the case for reconsideration and decision regarding the costs of the proceedings] (SN_2011–2015: 99 NF),<br>• *uwzględniając pisemny etap postępowania i po przeprowadzeniu rozprawy* [having regard to the written procedure and further to the hearing] (CJ: 78, GC: 27 NF),<br>• *zawiesić postępowanie i zwrócić się do Trybunału* [to stay the proceedings and to refer (the following questions) to the Court] (CJ: 102 NF). |
| | 1.4 documents | • *dyrektywy Parlamentu Europejskiego i Rady* [Directive (...) of the European Parliament and of the Council] (CJ: 23 NF),<br>• *Konwencja o Ochronie Praw Człowieka i Podstawowych Wolności* [European Convention for the Protection of Human Rights and Fundamental Freedoms] (CJ, GC: 18 NF),<br>• *orzeczenia sądowe w sprawach cywilnych i handlowych* [judgments in civil and commercial matters] (CJ: 12 NF),<br>• *przepisy ustawowe, wykonawcze i administracyjne* [legislative, statutory and administrative provisions] (CJ: 20 NF),<br>• *w doktrynie i orzecznictwie* [in doctrine and case-law] (SN_2011–2015: 16 NF). |
| | 1.5 places | • *tereny w miastach i osiedlach* [areas in cities and housing estates] (SN_2011–2015: 27 NF),<br>• *w poszczególnych miejscach i regionach* [in individual places and regions] (CJ: 25 NF). |
| **2. Discourse-organization** | 2.1 intra-/intertextual navigation | • *podobnie i analogicznie* [to that effect and by analogy] (GC: 64 NF),<br>• *ten akt lub ta umowa* [a document or agreement] (CJ: 20 NF). |

**Table 8.16.** *Total number of binomials conveying referential functions*

| Referential binomials | | | | | | | | |
|---|---|---|---|---|---|---|---|---|
| Translated EU case law | | | | | | | | |
| CJ | | | | | GC | | | |
| **Categories** | **Types (CJ vs GC) (CJ vs SN_2011–2015)** | **NF** | **CJ vs GC (%DIFF)** | **CJ vs SN (%DIFF)** | **Categories** | **Types (GC vs SN_2011–2015)** | **NF** | **GC vs SN (%DIFF)** |
| Abstract concepts | 41 (0,24; −13,57) (9,04 -4,80) | 1,134 | 51 % (38,67; 24,85) | 115 % (46,63; 32,79) | Abstract concepts | 35 (6,20; −7,61) | 753 | 43 % (0,30; −13,52) |
| Procedure-related | 10 (0,28; −13,53) (0,70 -13,14) | 402 | −16 % (0,09; −13,73) | −19 % (5,00; −8,84) | Agents/ institutions | 9 (3,37; −10,45) | 476 | −4 % (194,83; 181,02) |
| Agents/ institutions | 7 (0,35; −13,47) (1,62 -12,22) | 359 | −13 % (8,18; −5,64) | 239 % (129,92; 116,08) | Procedure-related | 12 (0,09; −13,73) | 412 | 289 % (3,64; −10,18) |
| Documents | 6 (0,05; −13,77) (0,00 -13,84) | 183 | 151 % (23,58; 9,77) | 245 % (10,80; −3,04) | Documents | 5 (0,06; −13,76) | 73 | 38 % (2,66; −11,15) |
| Places | 1 (1,34; −12,48) (0,00 -13,84) | 25 | --- (17,44 3,63) | −11 % (0,04; −13,79) | Places | 0 (1,35; −12,46) | 0 | −100 % (18,89; 5,08) |
| **TOTAL:** | **65 (0,01; −13,81) (4,81 -9,03)** | **2,103** | **23 % (19,89; 6,07)** | **74 % (124,79; 110,95)** | **TOTAL:** | **61 (4,27; −9,54)** | **1,715** | **42 % (43,85; 30,03)** |

| Referential binomials | | | | | | |
|---|---|---|---|---|---|---|
| **Non-translated PL case law** | | | | | | |
| **SN_2011–2015** | | | | **SN_1999** | | |
| **Categories** | **Types (SN_2011–2015 vs SN_1999)** | **NF** | **SN_2011–2015 vs SN_1999 (%DIFF)** | **Categories** | **Types** | **NF** |
| Abstract concepts | 18 (15,92; 2,09) | 527 | −40 % (44,96; 31,13) | Procedure-related | 19 | 888 |
| Procedure-related | 14 (0,80; −13,03) | 495 | −44 % (57,84; 44,01) | Abstract concepts | 49 | 877 |
| Documents | 6 (1,00; −12,83) | 106 | 179 % (16,45; 2,62) | Documents | 3 | 38 |
| Agents/institutions | 3 (0,52; −13,31) | 53 | −22 % (0,86; −12,97) | Agents/institutions | 5 | 68 |
| Places | 1 (1,38; −12,45) | 28 | --- (19,30; 5,47) | Places | 0 | 0 |
| **TOTAL:** | **42 (0,00; −13,83)** | **1,209** | **−35 % (74,28; 60,45)** | **TOTAL:** | **77** | **1,871** |

**Table 8.17.** *Total number of binomials conveying discourse-organizing functions*

| Discourse-organizing binomials | | | | | | | | |
|---|---|---|---|---|---|---|---|---|
| Translated EU case law | | | | | | | | |
| CJ | | | | | GC | | | |
| **Categories** | **Types (CJ vs GC) (CJ vs SN_2011–2015)** | **NF** | **CJ vs GC (%DIFF)** | **CJ vs SN (%DIFF)** | **Categories** | **Types (GC vs SN_2011–2015)** | **NF** | **GC vs SN (%DIFF)** |
| Intra-/ intertextual navigation | 1 (1,14; −12,68) (1,38; −12,46) | 20 | −82 % (36,35; 22,53) | --- (13,79; −0,05) | Intra-/intertextual navigation | 3 (4,27; −9,54) | 112 | --- |
| **TOTAL:** | **1 (1,14; −12,68) (1,38; −12,46)** | **20** | **−82 % (36,35; 22,53)** | **--- (13,79; −0,05)** | **TOTAL:** | **3 (4,27; −9,54)** | **112** | **---** |
| Non–translated PL case law | | | | | | | | |
| SN_2011–2015 | | | | SN_1999 | | | | |
| **Categories** | **Types (SN_2011–2015 vs SN_1999)** | **NF** | **SN_2011–2015 vs SN_1999 (%DIFF)** | **Categories** | **Types** | **NF** | | |
| Intra-/ intertextual navigation | **0** (12,55; −1,28) | 0 | 0 % (6,97; −6,86) | Intra-/intertextual navigation | 9 | 171 | | |

functions, as they may also act as inter- and intratextual references. On the other hand, they do not express any stance.

## 8.3 Conclusions

This chapter serves as a response to the call for analysis of binomials in CJEU case-law (Basaneže 2018: 242). It compares the data concerning the distributional and structural qualities of binomials occurring in translated CJEU case-law with those occurring in judgments of the Polish Supreme Court. In addition, it presents a catalog of the discourse functions of binomials. In the following, I will focus mostly on non-extended and extended binomials, as multinomials are only marginally relevant due to their very low distribution across the corpora.

Translated judgments contain more non-extended and extended binomials than non-translated judgments, both those structured around *i* [and] and *lub* [or]. The differences in the distribution of *lub* [or] binomials between the EU corpora and the national corpus are much more defined than in the case of *i* [and] binomials (see Figure 8.5).

As regards the structural variety of binomials, non-extended binomials are based mostly around nouns (N), followed by adjectives (ADJ), adverbs (ADV), and numerals (NUM) (see Section 8.2.2), whereas extended binomials are based predominantly around nouns (N), but also verbs (V) and adjectives (ADJ) (see Section 8.2.4). The striking prevalence of noun-based binomials relative to the distribution of other structural types of non-extended binomials contributes to the highly nominal style of the genre. In addition, their structural types indicate little potential for reversibility (except for the example presented in Section 8.2.4), meaning that Polish binomials in judicial language are highly fixed and irreversible constructions.

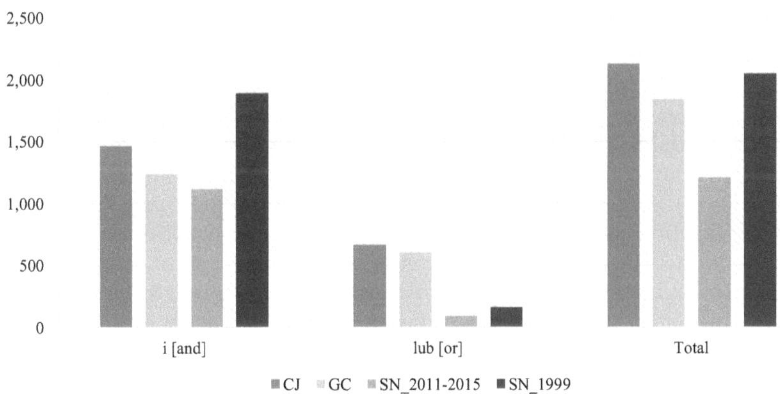


**Figure 8.5.** *Total distribution of binomials structured around i [and] and lub [or]*

Binomials conveying the relation of absolute or near-synonymy (SYN) have been found to introduce redundancy similar to that introduced by Polish pleonasms and tautologies. Such binomials could potentially be replaced with one suitable word. Non-extended and extended binomials convey primarily semantic relations other than absolute or near-synonymy (SYN), namely complementation (COM), opposition (antonymy) (OPP), and sub-division (SUB). The relation of consequence (CON) is conveyed exclusively by extended binomials, as it is expressed with verbs which do not form non-extended binomials at all. Even if lawyer-linguists were to eliminate near-synonymous binomials exhibiting redundancy, the total number of binomials would still be very high, owing to the fact that binomials expressing this type of semantic relation play only a marginal role in binomial constructions (as opposed to binomials motivated semantically by complementation). The few multinomials were also found to express mostly complementation. The semantic motivation of complementation (cf. Kopaczyk 2017: 166–167) contributes to legal certainty and the all-inclusiveness of judicial justifications.

The thematic overlap of (non-)extended binomials found in the EU corpora and the national corpus is very low. Only a few binomials occur both in the Eurolect and national judgments. The analysis of concordances of binomials has shown that a striking majority of binomials indicate the thematic content of judgments across all the corpora. All in all, they are strongly embedded in the respective legal cultures and are used to structure judicial reasoning in a manner specific to the territorial and functional jurisdictions of the respective courts. The discourse functions of bi- and multinomials have been found to convey primarily referential functions by providing references to: abstract concepts, agents/institutions, legal procedure, documents, and places (see Section 8.2.6). Only a fraction of bi- and multinomials acts as discourse-organizing expressions and, unlike lexical bundles, bi- and multinomials do not convey any stance-related functions (cf. Chapter 7, Section 7.6).

To conclude, binomials play a minor role in the phraseological structuring of judicial discourse from the point of view of distribution. They are very infrequent, compared to lexical bundles, for instance, which occur with an incommensurately higher frequency in all the corpora. Being mostly built around nouns, binomials contribute significantly to the nominal style of judgments. Non-extended and extended binomials point to the thematic content of judgments, are highly embedded in the respective legal cultures, and are highly irreversible. To a certain degree, they contribute to legal certainty and the all-inclusivity of judicial justifications, owing to the semantic motivations behind their use. Their main discourse function consists of providing reference. The results of the analysis do not confirm that the general low recurrence of binomials (and to a significantly lesser extent multinomials) can be regarded as an obvious stylistic feature of translated EU judgments and non-translated Polish judgments. It might even be argued that they are not recurrent enough to label them a genre feature. Future research should aim to determine to what degree judicial binomials are acquired from the language of legal acts, as well as whether TTs include more or less binomials than original CJEU judgments drafted in French.

# Part II.D. Micro level: Pillar III – Terminology

# Chapter 9. Terms in the common conceptual base of EU and national judgments

Lawyer-linguists working at the CJEU (cf. Koźbiał 2017) are an example of a professional discourse community involved in specialized communication which recognizes the need for terminological consistency, accuracy and clarity (cf. Stefaniak 2017; Prieto Ramos and Guzmán 2018) in translated court documents. Their goal is to enable communication on three inter-related levels: within the CJEU as an EU institution, between the CJEU and other EU institutions, and, finally, among EU citizens (Fischer 2010: 22). The present chapter deals with the nature of the most salient terms and their underlying concepts in CJEU and SN judgments, a topic which by itself requires terminological consistency. Therefore, in the following, I will establish a common framework of reference for the description of terminology-related terms, such as *term*, *concept* and *conceptual system*. The most authoritative framework of this kind is the international terminology standard ISO 1087:2019, whose goal is to provide a systematic explanation of the concepts in the field of terminology and describe the use of field-related terms. I will make use of relevant literature to substantiate the definitions provided by the ISO standard.

## 9.1 Key (EU and national) terminology-related terms

*Terminology*

According to the ISO 1087:2019 standard, terminology[160] is a set of designations[161] and *concepts*[162] belonging to one domain or subject (ISO 1087:2019: 2). Apart from this definition, the older, withdrawn version of this ISO standard, ISO 1087–1:2000, proposed that *terminology* is also the study of the structure, formation, development, usage and management of terminologies in various subject fields (ISO 1087–1:2000: 10), that is fields of special knowledge defined from a purpose-related point of view (cf. ISO 1087:2019: 2). Legal language (cf. Chapter 2, Section 2.1), as

160 Terminology is to be differentiated from terminography which is a related discipline concerned with the development of terminographic dictionaries and databases (Bajčić 2017: 13; ISO 1087:2019: 10).

161 A designation is a "representation of a concept by a sign which denotes it in a domain or subject"; there are three types of designations: symbols, appellations and **terms** (ISO 1087:2019: 7). Designation may also be understood as the process of naming objects and *concepts* (De Bessé *et al.* 1997: 129).

162 (Legal) concepts are discussed in more depth later in this Section.

a specialized language variety, has its own *terminology*, that is the vocabulary of the subject field (cf. De Bessé *et al.* 1997: 154) of law (and, consequently, adjudication), which is prototypically used among legal experts (cf. Bajčić and Martinović 2018: 209), thus validating research into its characteristics.

*Terminology work and terminological databases in the EU*

*Terminology work* is an indispensable element of multilingual institutions. It is "work concerned with the systematic collection, description, processing and presentation of concepts (...)" (ISO 1087:2019: 13). *Terminology work* is prioritized in the EU institutions with their own translation service,[163] since it helps to achieve high-quality, terminologically consistent translations. Within the EU, terminology coordination units cooperate with each other at the inter-institutional level dealing primarily with multilingual projects, whereas language departments at the individual institutions work on bilingual projects (Stefaniak 2017: 110).

Aware of terminology-related issues, CJEU lawyer-linguists have made available online a collection of multilingual terminological data (in 24 official EU languages encompassing 30 EU legal systems), resulting from their comprehensive research work on comparative law at the Translation Directorate General (DGTrad) of the CJEU, called Comparative Multilingual Legal Vocabulary (VJM)[164] (Vocabulaire juridique multilingue comparé[165]). VJM contains about 646 legal concepts: 242 in the domain of immigration law, and 404 in family law. In addition to the terminological data records, a concept tree is available for each domain.[166] This vocabulary can be useful to both legal experts and non-professionals (legal professionals, students, linguists, terminologists, translators, and members of the general public) as a source of information or terminological support. The VJM's terminological data records have very detailed information, such as definitions[167] (adapted to the

163 For detailed information on the terminology work in the Polish Language Department of the Directorate General for Translation of the European Commission, see Stefaniak (2017: 109–121).

164 https://termcoord.eu/comparative-multilingual-legal-vocabulary-vjm (accessed: May 9, 2020)

165 https://curia.europa.eu/trad/Affiche%20VJM_en.pdf (accessed: May 9, 2020)

166 The concept trees (conceptual structures), representations of the concepts which belong to each domain allowing quick reference to the semantic relationships between them, are available at: https://termcoord.eu/comparative-multilingual-legal-vocabulary-vjm (accessed: May 9, 2020)

167 A definition is a "representation of a concept by an expression that describes it and differentiates it from related concepts" (ISO 1087:2019: 6). An example of a statutory legal definition can be found, for instance, in Article 10 § 1 of the Polish Civil Code – "Pełnoletnim jest, kto ukończył lat osiemnaście" [An adult is any individual who has attained the age of eighteen years]. This classical definition is made up of a *definiendum*, that is the term that is being defined – *pełnoletni* [adult], *connecting phrase – (jest) to* [(it) is], and a *definiens*, that is the explanation or description of a *concept – kto ukończył lat osiemnaście* [who has attained the age of eighteen years]

national legal systems), notes on comparative law, legal references (legislation, case law, doctrine of national, EU and international legal systems), the different designations of a *concept* (in the same language and sometimes different languages according to the legal system), a clear indication of the origin of a *term* (functional equivalent or formulation – paraphrase), warnings concerning usage (false legal friends, risk of confusion, obsolete terms). The VJM term database is available within a larger database of EU-related terminology – IATE.[168]

Interactive Terminology for Europe (IATE) is a terminology database (term bank) (cf. ISO 1087:2019: 15; De Bessé *et al.* 1997: 153) which contains EU-related terminological data and is administered by a number of EU institutions.[169] It has been the primary source of terminology for all EU institutions and agencies since 2004. As of May 9, 2020, IATE includes 7,972,914 terms of varying reliability distributed across 970,706 entries related to individual concepts in 24 official EU languages (as well as in Latin).[170] The CJEU has its own internal multilingual database of legal terms – CuriaTerm (Koźbiał 2017: 169), which migrated into IATE in December 2019. The migration encompassed approximately 4,000 concepts and 60,000 terms from CuriaTerm.[171] This means that a large part of the original CuriaTerm database is now available for internal and external users (external translators, for example), including the national courts.

Although terminological databases serve the purpose of raising the quality of translations and facilitating translators' work, they do not eliminate the need to gain relevant background domain (subject field) knowledge in order to fully comprehend the *concepts* which are to be rendered into the target language (Bajčić 2017: 15). As noted by Gibbons (2006: 286), "the law and its

---

(Lewandowski *et al.* 2017: 62). The main function of legal definitions seems to consist of enabling successful communication between the legislator and persons and bodies governed by law by providing the meaning of *legal terms* which on their own would otherwise be quite vague. However, many citizens not versed in law are not aware of the fact that *legal terms* are conventional names for various *concepts*, whose meaning (not all) is laid out in their definitions. The lack of familiarity with legal definitions, in turn, inhibits proper understanding of legal texts – this pertains to "pure" legal terms (e.g. *pytanie prejudycjalne* [preliminary ruling]) as well as semi-legal terms used commonly in general language (e.g. *sąd apelacyjny* [appellate court]).

168 IATE website is available at https://iate.europa.eu/home (accessed: May 9, 2020)

169 These include: the European Parliament, the Council of the European Union, the European Commission, the Court of Justice of the EU, the European Central Bank, the European Court of Auditors, the European Economic and Social Committee, the European Committee of the Regions, the European Investment Bank, and the Translation Centre for the Bodies of the European Union. Source: https://iate.europa.eu/about (accessed: May 9, 2020)

170 https://iate.europa.eu/info/statistics/global (accessed: May 9, 2020)

171 Migration of CuriaTerm into IATE. https://cdt.europa.eu/en/news/migration-curiaterm-iate (accessed: May 9, 2020)

practitioners have developed a range of unique legal concepts, and these can be expressed efficiently only by using legal jargon." The permeation of legal texts by *terms* contributes to the perception of legal language as highly specialized, whereby non-expert citizens need ordinary, non-technical terms which are easy to understand (Fischer 2010: 29). Intersystemic translation of legal texts stemming from different legal systems and cultures or containing autonomous *concepts* (cf. Šarčević 2013: 10; Engberg 2015) exacerbates this issue. Therefore, familiarity with the basics of *terminology work* and *terminological databases*, as well as the technicality of specialized domains of knowledge, is essential for translators working in multilingual settings, because terminological know-how enables them to become more proficient in the legal practice (Husinec 2011; Bajčić 2017: 24).

*Terminology work* is also critical at the EU and national level; it is manifested by, among others, the EU institutions consulting national experts in various fields of specialized knowledge (cf. Fischer 2010: 24; Robinson 2014: 206). At the CJEU, the Projects and Terminological Co-ordination Unit is responsible for managing comparative multilingual legal terminology; it defines and co-ordinates the terminological projects which contribute to the overall quality of the final TTs, and carries out the terminological and legal pre-processing of the documents to be translated.[172] Terminological consistency in translated CJEU judgments is crucial, as judgments are hybrid descriptive-prescriptive legal texts, secondary relative to normative texts (legislative acts), which are a source of legal terminology (cf. Šarčević 1997: 11–12). This means that any inconsistencies in language versions[173] of normative acts as well as CJEU judgments may have far-reaching consequences for the whole supranational legal system.

*(Legal) terms*

*Terms* are "designations that represent general concepts by linguistic means" – they may contain symbols and have variants, such as different forms of spelling (ISO 1087:2019: 7). According to the ISO standard (ISO 1087–1:2000: 8–9), there are several basic types of *terms*: (1) *simple (single-word) terms*, which contain only one word or lexical unit (root) (e.g. *court, translation*), (2) *compound terms*, which are single-word terms that can be split morphologically into separate components, e.g. *keyboard*, (3) *complex (multi-word) terms*, which consist of more than one word or lexical unit (e.g. *bijural translation, multilingual legal terminology*), (4) *borrowed terms*, which are terms taken from another language or from another domain or subject, and (5) *neoterms* (terminological neologisms), which are new terms coined

172 https://curia.europa.eu/jcms/jcms/p1_641406/en/ (accessed: March 27, 2019)

173 Between 1960 and 2010, the CJEU acknowledged discrepancies between language versions of EU legislation in about 170 judgments (Baaij 2012 after Robinson 2014: 209).

for a given concept.[174] *Terms* are linguistic representations of *concepts* which act as depositories of knowledge with specific reference (Sager 1990: 57). Faber (2012: 11) posits that *terms* are linguistic units which convey conceptual meaning within specialized texts. *Terms* "refer to discrete conceptual entities, properties, activities or relations which constitute the knowledge space of a particular subject field" (Sager 1990: 261). In other words, *terms* are not semantically isolated units (Cabré Castellví 1999: 42). An important distinction is to be made between *terms* and *words*. Sager *et al.* (1980: 75) explain that *terms* are lexical items with special reference within a specialized subject field, whereas *words* have general reference in a variety of codes. In general, *terms* are the subject matter of terminology, whereas *words* are studied within the discipline of lexicography.

According to Jopek-Bosiacka (2019: 58), *legal terms* are linguistic realizations of *concepts* from the domain of law. *Legal terms* are no different from general terms as regards their close relation to concepts and semantic representations (Bajčić 2017: 79). More specifically, *legal terms* are perceived as points of access to concepts, which allow for the activation of relevant background knowledge (Biel 2008: 23). They effectively act as "signposts" enabling the identification of *legal concepts* (Bajčić and Martinović 2018: 210). There are two essential characteristics of *legal terms* (and terms in general), namely the continuity (consistency) relation and the concordance relation (cf. Vigier and Sánchez Ramos 2017; Biel and Doczekalska 2020b, *forthcoming*; Biel and Koźbiał 2020a, *forthcoming*). The continuity relation relates to (1) the internal consistency of terminology in a given text and (2) the external consistency with preceding legal texts in the same domain and higher-ranking texts (e.g. legislation) (cf. Stefaniak 2017: 114–116; Prieto Ramos 2014: 314; Robertson 2015: 42). The concordance relation relates the requirement imposed on terms according to which they need to trigger the same concept in all language versions of a legal act (Biel and Koźbiał 2020a, *forthcoming*).

In layman's terms, *legal terms* tend to be described as "technical" (Chromá 2011: 36), although the actual classification of legal vocabulary is much more complex. The perceived technicality (cf. Chromá 2011: 36) of legal language and *legal terms* stems from the fact that legal terms express definite *concepts* and institutions which (to a certain extent) do not exist outside the sphere of law (Jopek-Bosiacka 2011: 13). Nevertheless, the language of law and, by extension, judicial language consist of technical (legal) terms as well as non-technical, generic terms from ordinary language, such as *thing*, *property* (Jopek-Bosiacka 2011: 10). However, these non-technical, generic terms, despite deriving their general meaning from ordinary language, may be assigned a unique legal meaning by any legal system. According to Riley (1995: 73–79), there exist three groups of *legal terms*:

174 In the present analysis, due to space constraints, I will focus exclusively on simple and complex (phrasal) terms, leaving aside any investigations into compound terms, borrowed terms and neoterms (cf. Temmerman 2018) for further studies.

1. **“pure” legal terms** which are used solely in the branch of law and encapsulate concepts of substantive or procedural law generally inaccessible to a non-expert audience, e.g. estoppel or various Latinisms, such as *ratio decidendi* (cf. Chapter 10);
2. **legal terms also found in everyday speech** with legal meanings related to, but more specialized than, their meanings in general language, e.g. *assault, land, negligence*, or legal meanings completely different from their meanings in general language, e.g. *consideration, summary, title*; terms belonging to this group may cause misunderstanding due to their special legal connotations on the part of the non-expert audience and also being falsely familiar, e.g. *party, law, negligence*; legal terms in this category may also have more than one legal meaning (e.g. *decision, judgment*); Hughes and Alcaraz (2002: 16–18; cf. Goźdź-Roszkowski 2011: 57) call terms belonging to this group semi-technical or mixed terms;
3. **everyday words with special connotations in a given legal context** acquired through legal definitions, by virtue of the law, which may expand or narrow their original meaning, e.g. *racial hatred*.[175]

This manner of categorizing terms seems only to take into account the process of semantic transformation that occurs when everyday words enter the legal vocabulary. However, when studying *legal terms*, it is equally important to consider the *concepts* that underlie them.

*(Legal) concepts*

*Concepts*, which are also at the core of *terminology work* (see above, ISO 1087:2019: 3, 13), tend to be confused with *terms*. As a discipline, *terminology* defines and delineates *concepts* from other related concepts, and classifies and structures *conceptual systems* (or fields, see below), which means that *concepts* and not *terms* are crucial to this discipline (Bajčić and Martinović 2018: 209). The ISO standard (ISO 1087:2019: 3) states that *concepts* are abstract units “of knowledge created by a unique combination of characteristics”; *characteristics* are abstractions of (sets of) objects’ properties (ISO 1087:2019: 3). In other words, *concepts* are mental representations of concrete or abstract objects (De Bessé *et al.* 1997: 124) which are linked to both *terms* and their semantic representations. Characteristics of those objects are selected according to specific conventional or scientific criteria

175 Malinowski claims that common words from everyday language which did not undergo a change in meaning in order to be used in a legislative act (that is not a judgment) are not *legal terms*, even if their meaning is recreated in a legal definition (Malinowski 2006: 154). Using the frequency-based corpus approach which takes into account empirical data, it can be determined that the sole fact that a certain word, such as *sąd* [court] or *koszt* [cost], appears disproportionately more frequently in judgments points to its legal nature, and, consequently, its terminologicality (cf. Shelov 1982 after Thelen 2002: 196; cf. Section 9.6).

appropriate for a given subject field (domain, area of knowledge) (De Bessé *et al.* 1997: 124). According to Sager (1990: 22), *concepts* are constructs of human cognition processes which assist in the classification of concrete or abstract objects by way of systematic or arbitrary abstraction.

Different theoretical schools have diverse definitions of *concepts*, meaning there is no unanimous agreement on their nature (Picht and Draskau 1985: 36). A certain degree of unification in this regard is provided by the ISO standard, which also notes that concepts are not necessarily bound to particular languages, but are influenced by the social or cultural background. What is important from the point of view of the methodological approach in this study (see Section 9.2) is that *concepts* are either general (ISO 1087:2019: 4; Picht and Draskau 1985: 38), referring to a class of objects (e.g. *supreme courts*), or individual (ISO 1087:2019: 3; Picht and Draskau 1985: 38), having a single reference (e.g. *Supreme Court of the Republic of Poland*).

*EU legal concepts* may be regarded through the lens of multilingualism and conceptual autonomy, which is a main characteristic of EU law and its *concepts* (Bajčić 2017: 89). Bajčić (2017: 80; cf. Biel 2008: 23) claims that "from the perspective of cognitive linguistics, a concept can be regarded as autonomous if it activates its own knowledge elements at the supranational EU level, as opposed to the national levels of the Member States." Thanks to *EU legal concepts,* the CJEU is able to circumvent "the burden of comparing and translating between legal languages and cultures" (Bajčić 2017: 89). In the context of EU law, *legal concepts* have been described as unstable, fuzzy and vague (Kjær 2007: 81). The creation of the autonomous nature of EU law and its *concepts* is attributable to CJEU case law, which applies the teleological method of interpretation, thus enabling uniform application of EU law and its interpretation irrespective of differences at the level of Member States and their national laws (Bajčić 2017: 80; cf. Bajčić and Martinović 2018). In turn, interpretation independent of the laws of Member States strengthens autonomous *concepts* of EU law (Kjær 2010: 312; cf. Biel and Doczekalska 2020b, *forthcoming*). The stage involving the CJEU's interpretation of concepts, possibly following interpretation by national courts, is the last stage in the life path of a *supranational term* and its underlying *concept* which follows its entry into the national legal system through the transposition of EU legal acts (Biel 2014a: 59; Biel and Doczekalska 2020b, *forthcoming*). Despite the fact that supranational concepts (and terms) are created at the supranational level, they are applied in national legal systems (Kjær 2007: 79) and later shaped by means of interpretation, both at the national and supranational levels, and in particular when national courts refer questions for a preliminary ruling to the CJEU (Biel and Doczekalska 2020b, *forthcoming*). Bajčić (2017: 89) argues that the autonomous nature of EU law should be regarded "as both semantic and *de jure* independence." This further justifies examining the degree of convergence (**fit**) between *terms* (and related *concepts*) in translated EU judgments and non-translated national judgments, which may make it possible to determine (at least in part) whether and to what degree EU *terms* and *concepts* are indeed "sovereign" and free from national influence. And vice versa, it may make it possible to determine whether EU *terms* and *concepts* influence the national terminological and conceptual base.

Robinson (2014: 202) presents a four-level classification of legal terms encountered in EU legislation which refer to both the EU context and the national legal contexts:

1. specifically EU concepts, e.g. *Advocate General, Directive, subsidiarity,*
2. generic concepts, e.g. *lawyer, penalties,*
3. specifically national concepts, e.g. *avocat, Rechtsanwalt, solicitor,*
4. terms which may have a specific meaning in national legal systems, but, according to CJEU case-law, must be interpreted as having an EU meaning, e.g. *force majeure.*

Robinson's classification confirms that there is an interplay between the supranational and the national contexts (cf. Biel and Doczekalska 2020b, *forthcoming*).

*Conceptual systems*

Terms display various types of ontological or logical associations – these types of relationships are called *conceptual relationships* (De Bessé *et al.* 1997: 125). Conceptual relationships between *concepts* of a given domain build structured systems called *conceptual systems* (or knowledge structures), in which every *concept* occupies a certain position (De Bessé *et al.* 1997: 125). *Concepts* may also be grouped in *conceptual fields*, groups which are semantically linked and grouped around a keyword, e.g. the conceptual field of *seat* also covers *chair, bench, stool,* etc. (De Bessé *et al.* 1997: 125; Bajčić 2011: 89).

*Conceptual properties* are used to describe and classify *concepts* (Bowker 1995: 12). The totality of properties characterizing a concept is called its *intension*, while the range of things to which a concept refers to is called its *extension* (Sager 1990: 24). Wide intension entails narrow extension, and vice versa. Conceptual properties enable the determination of concepts' *intension*, the structuring of *concepts* into *conceptual systems* (see below), defining *concepts*, and accounting for the conceptual equivalence of terms in different languages, or verifying the synonymy between *terms* in the same language (Picht and Draskau 1985: 48). In order to distinguish a given concept from another closely related concept, one needs to know the properties which reflect the essence of a *concept* (Bowker 1995: 14, 28).

Owing to the fact that legal terms are products of different national legal systems and cultures governed by different realia, the legal terminology of different legal systems is mostly incongruent as regards the applied *conceptual systems* (Šarčević 1989: 277–278; Šarčević 1997: 232). In the EU legal context, as has been noted in the Judgment of the Court of 6 October 1982 Srl CILFIT and Lanificio di Gavardo SpA v Ministry of Health (cf. Case 283/81):

> [...] even where the different language versions are entirely in accord with one another, [...] **Community law uses terminology which is peculiar to it**. Furthermore, it must be emphasized that **legal concepts do not necessarily have the same**

**meaning in Community law and in the law of the various Member States.** (own emphasis) (C-283/81)

The Court states that the *legal terms* used within the European legal context may have a different meaning than within a national legal context and the discourse of national courts, which is (partly) due to the supranational and autonomous nature of the *EU conceptual system* (see Fischer 2010: 27). This is legitimized by the need to apply the EU law in a uniform manner across all EU Member States, and this fact must be reflected in the translated texts, be it legislative acts or court judgments. EU judges play a very important role in developing the specific character of the European law and its *concepts.* Although the judges come from various Member States, where they have obtained their legal education and become embedded, in a sense, in the legal culture of their country of origin, in their work at the CJEU, they use French as the procedural language (cf. Chapter 1). They establish the correct interpretation of EU law, while maintaining a safe distance from their national legal cultural backgrounds and the meaning of legal terms in their national contexts.

Biel (2008: 22) rightly observes that, contrary to other types of translation involving specialized languages, legal translation involves more culture-bound terms than universal terms (Šarčević 2013: 10; Biel 2019: 29). This culture- and system-bound nature (and related intersystemic non-congruence, non-equivalence) is an integral quality of many *legal terms* (Šarčević 1997: 232), and without information on their origin (a given national legal system) terms lose their meaning, unlike terms belonging to fields of knowledge which are known across more than one society, such as certain technical, geographic or medical terms (Kierzkowska 2008: 22). Conceptual incongruence may occur to a particularly high degree in the context of the EU and its Member States, as EU law combines different legal systems and, in turn, *conceptual systems* (Jopek-Bosiacka 2011: 26). The EU legal system is a legal system of its own, which is superimposed onto those of Member States. Since EU law represents an independent legal order with an autonomous *conceptual system* (see below), *EU legal terms* may derive their meaning from a common *conceptual system* at the EU level (Šarčević 2010: 27; Bajčić 2017: 153), as well as from the national *conceptual systems.* Fischer (2010: 27) notes that, in reality, "both terms belonging to the EU and terms belonging to the national conceptual systems may occur in the same EU text" (cf. Kjær 2007).

Within each official EU language, a constant interaction occurs between the national *conceptual systems* and the *EU conceptual system,* due to double supranational-national coding of legal terminology (Biel 2019: 29; cf. Biel and Sosoni 2019: 216).[176] EU terms have been observed to "travel" through supranational and national contexts (Biel and Doczekalska 2020b, *forthcoming*). Although EU law, which may be regarded as a primary source of legal terminology which is

176 This is due to the fact that EU translation is largely intersystemic rather than intrasystemic (Šarčević 2013: 10).

subsequently used in judgments, is drafted at the supranational level, it is derived from and forms an integral part of the Member States' national legal systems where it is applied (Doczekalska 2018: 175). For instance, EU supranational terms related to consumer protection have been observed to "travel" into the national legal systems of three English-language jurisdictions (the UK, Ireland and Malta) during the transposition of EU directives, that is the process of incorporating EU directives into national law and transferring (adapting) supranational terms into national legal systems (Biel and Doczekalska 2020b, *forthcoming*).

Prieto Ramos observes that genres related to adjudication and monitoring have more "references to national legal realities" than legislation (Prieto Ramos 2014: 319), which suggests that EU genres, including judgments, vary in the degree of saturation with autonomous concepts and national terms (Biel and Koźbiał 2020a, *forthcoming*). This means that the *EU conceptual system* cannot be considered completely separately from the *national conceptual systems*, since its official languages belong to and form the *national conceptual systems* (Fischer 2010: 28). Furthermore, the interaction of *conceptual systems* and languages at EU-level may lead to the formal and conceptual instability of terms, whereby instability means that either one concept has more designations (terms) (formal instability) or one designation (term) that refers to more concepts (conceptual instability) (Fischer 2010: 30). The need to avoid *legal terms* in their national legal meaning (and the associated standardization of terminology) is particularly emphasized at the level of the creation of EU legislation due to the institutional nature of EU translation. The Joint Practical Guide of the European Parliament, the Council and the Commission for persons involved in the drafting of European Union legislation (2015: 18, point 5.3.2), states: "As regards legal terminology, terms which are too closely linked to a particular national legal system should be avoided" (cf. Prieto Ramos 2014: 318).

## 9.2 Methodological approach and research material

Before the 20th century, it was mainly scientists and technologists who took an interest in the nature of concepts and terms. Technologists were particularly involved in the naming of new concepts by labeling them with terms due to the rapid development of technology across all the specialized fields of human activity (Sageder 2010: 124). Today, terminology is not only associated with developing practical tools used by, among others, translators or technologists. Considering the volume of research into terminological units and concepts, it has already become a true discipline (see, among others, Wüster 1979; Cabré Castellví 1999; Temmerman 2000; Bajčić 2017). The greatest development in the field of terminology has taken place in recent decades, although it first began to materialize in the 1930s (Cabré Castellví 1999). It has evolved from a prescriptive to descriptive theory with an increased focus on the cognitive understanding of meaning (Bajčić 2017: 24). Nevertheless, terminology is still not a homogenous field of study, as evidenced by the range of approaches to the theory of terminology (Sageder 2010: 123–124) and the fact that there is no universal theory of terminology applicable to all specialized domains of knowledge (Bajčić 2017: 23). Furthermore, the application of terminology studies to the field of law and legal translation still lags behind, although it could certainly contribute to the study of legal concepts, legal interpretation and translation, as well as the development of mono- and bilingual dictionaries (Bajčić 2017: 11). In this small-scale exploratory analysis, I adapt certain elements from the following theoretical approaches to the study of terminology: the Communicative Theory of Terminology, Frame-based Terminology, and the Textual Approach to Terminology.[177]

According to the **Communicative Theory of Terminology** (cf. Cabré Castellví 2000, 2003), terminology is "a set of needs, a set of practices to resolve these needs and a unified field of knowledge" which operates with multifaceted terminological units within specialized discourse and which are simultaneously: (1) units of knowledge, (2) units of language, and (3) units of communication (Cabré Castellví 2003: 182–183). The description of these "terminological units" should cover three components: (1) the cognitive component (*concept*), (2) linguistic component (*term*), and (3) communicative component (*situation*) (Cabré Castellví 2003: 183–184). This is what differentiates these terminological units from other units of language with the same structural features, i.e. words, and from the units that also express specialized knowledge, namely specialized, morphological and phraseological units. What is most important in this theory from the perspective of the present analysis is that **terms may be regarded as linguistic manifestations of concepts belonging to four broad semantic categories: entities (concrete or abstract), activities/events, properties (attributes) or relations (cf. Bowker 1995: 8)** which serve to facilitate specialized communication.

**Frame-based Terminology** (cf. Faber *et al.* 2005; Faber *et al.* 2006; Faber *et al.* 2007; Faber 2009) shares many assertions made by the Communicative Theory of Terminology and Sociocognitive Terminology and focuses on: (1) conceptual organization, (2) the multidimensional nature of terminological units, and (3) the extraction of semantic and syntactic information with multilingual corpora (Faber 2009: 123). Frame-based Terminology advocates "organization of specialized fields in which a dynamic, process-oriented event frame provides the conceptual underpinnings for the location of sub-hierarchies of concepts within a specialized domain event" (Faber *et al.* 2006: 189). This approach maintains that trying to find a distinction between terms and words is not practicable and that it is most efficient to study specialized knowledge units in their textual context (Faber 2009: 109). These units are mostly represented by compound nominal forms, have

177 Other major theories of Terminology include: the General Theory of Terminology (cf. Wüster 1974, 1979; Temmerman 2000: 222–228; Cabré Castellví 2003; Sageder 2010; Campo 2012), the Extended Theory of Terminology (cf. Myking 2001; Cabré Castellví 2003; Campo 2012), and the Sociocognitive Theory of Terminology (cf. Temmerman 1998, 2000).

meanings specific of a given field, and are used within a scientific or technical field (Faber 2009: 109). The high occurrence frequency of such language units in texts entails the activation of domain-specific knowledge. Therefore, understanding a text with a high concentration of topic-specific terminology requires knowledge of the domain, the concepts, and relations between them within the domain (Faber 2009: 121). **Thanks to the principles of this theory, it is possible to determine the underpinning conceptual system of a specialized domain by means of a bottom-up approach which consists of extracting information from corpora of texts representing specialized domains (Faber 2009: 124), including the domain of adjudication.**

The **Textual Approach to Terminology** (cf. Campo 2012: 168–175) is yet another theory advocating the use of corpora to extract terminological units and describe their distribution in a given field of knowledge. This approach capitalizes on the recent developments in corpus and computational linguistics by proposing **a descriptive working method used to explore and describe specialized knowledge units in context based on a predetermined set of texts in electronic form** (Campo 2012: 168).

In this study, terminological units are examined from the perspective of a bottom-up, distributional (frequency-based) corpus approach. Following Cabré Castellví (2003: 182–183) terms are viewed as units of language (linguistic manifestations of concepts) which are used to communicate and structure knowledge and which belong to four broad semantic categories: abstract or concrete entities, activities/events, properties, or relations (cf. Bowker 1995: 8). The present study combines chosen principles of the three discussed theoretical approaches to the study of terminology. The notion of **semantic fields** (cf. Felber 2001: 58–59) will be used to categorize the most salient simple terms extracted from the corpora and to outline the common conceptual base of the sub-genres of CJEU and SN judgments. The analysis combines a quantitative, frequency-based approach of corpus linguistics with a qualitative analysis of selected (key) terms and associated complex terms which use them as head terms.

The chapter aims to draw a comparison between the terminological content of translated EU judgments and non-translated Polish judgments by answering the following research questions:

(1) What is the distribution of simple[178] and complex terms in the corpora of CJEU and SN judgments and what are the most salient terms?
(2) What is the level of terminological overlap between the CJEU corpora and the post-accession SN corpus?

178 For the sake of simplicity, no distinction is made between simple and compound terms (see Section 9.2).

**Table 9.1.** *Corpus design (analysis of terminological items)*

| | Texts | Time period | Tokens |
|---|---|---|---|
| **Polish Eurolect corpus** | | | |
| Court of Justice judgments (CJ) (sampled) | 100 | 2011–2015 | 512,427 |
| General Court judgments (GC) (sampled) | 50 | 2011–2015 | 489,931 |
| **Reference corpora** | | | |
| SN judgments (SN_2011–2015) (sampled) | 200 | 2011–2015 | 508,584 |
| SN judgments (SN_1999) (unsampled) | 401 | 1999 | 504,605 |

(3) What simple terms may be perceived as key to the genre of judgments passed in both legal systems? In other words, what terms evoke the common conceptual base of the EU and national judgments (cf. Šarčević 2010: 27; Bajčić 2011: 85)?
(4) Are the key simple terms conceptualized in the same manner in the supranational and national legal system at the level of complex terms which use them as head terms?

In order to provide an in-depth overview of terminological items in CJEU and SN judgments, it was necessary to sample the primary corpora, so that the material for analysis would be of manageable size. To this end, I apply the same sampled corpora which were used to analyze binomials in Chapter 8. The present analysis investigates the terminological profile of a specialized language variety; therefore, it does not encompass the reference corpus of general Polish (NKJP). The advantage of using comparable corpora in the present approach is that they make it possible to fully enjoy the benefits of the quantitative approach; parallel corpora, on the other hand, would entail "time-consuming small-scale manual analyses" which do not fit the overall aim of the present study involving the analysis of textual fit (cf. Biel and Koźbiał 2020a, forthcoming; cf. Chapter 3).

In order to extract candidate simple and complex terms (cf. Daille 2017: 177), I employed TermoPL, which is an online tool[179] for extracting terminological units from domain-restricted corpora of Polish texts. It is available through the CLARIN-PL website (Common Language Resources and Technology Infrastructure) (cf. TermoPL 3.1.2 user manual).[180] TermoPL operates on simplified base forms of

179 TermoPL is available at: http://ws.clarin-pl.eu/termopl.shtml# (accessed: August 18, 2020).

180 The tool is also available as a stand-alone program; however, at the time of writing this chapter, I ran into technical problems connected with the Java Runtime Environment 8 and libraries of the morphological analysis tool Morfeusz 2.0 used by TermoPL to generate base forms of candidate terms (Morfeusz 2.0 is available at

words, which allows it to unify morphological variants of terms, recognize their context, and extract candidate terms in the form of noun phrases based on word-connection strength (C-value). The tool requires morphologically annotated (POS-tagged) texts in UTF-8 format, which can be uploaded in the form of individual TXT files or files bundled into a ZIP archive. The on-line version of TermoPL is capable of automatic POS annotation of the texts it is fed with, whereas the stand-alone version requires the user to provide already annotated texts. At the outset, TermoPL was instructed to eliminate stop words along with simple and compound prepositions. Subsequently, upon the transfer of four sets of texts comprising the sampled CJ and GC corpora and the pre- and post-accession SN corpora (see Table 9.1), it generated four separate lists of candidate simple and complex terms, each for every corpus of EU and national judgments.

The lists obtained with TermoPL contained a total of 901 candidate simple and complex terms, which needed to be refined, in order to eliminate occasional occurrences of wrongly extracted candidate terms, e.g. **prywatny wierzyciela* [private creditor] or **prawomocen wyrok* [final judgment]. The lists obtained in this manner provided a global overview of the terminological content in each of the corpora. In addition, phrases containing occasional adjectives signifying direct reference (e.g. *niniejszy* [present], *wspomniany* [said], *dany* [given], etc.) were also removed from the lists. By default, TermoPL omits items containing conjunctions, pronouns, names of months and numbers. Following the refinement stage, the final lists containing both candidate simple and complex terms were separated into two types of lists (two for each of the four corpora), a list of simple terms and a list of complex terms. Afterwards, a Microsoft Excel formula[181] was used to establish the degree of terminological overlap between the Eurolect and the national corpus (see Section 9.3, Table 9.3). Subsequently, the top 30 simple terms and the top 15 complex terms were categorized according to their semantic characteristics (see Section 9.4). The proposed semantic categories are similar to the categories described in the chapter on lexical bundles (see Chapter 7). At the final stage, 10 simple terms from the list of the top 30 simple terms present in the EU corpora and the national corpus were classified as node terms of paramount importance to the genre as a whole owing to their frequent occurrence in both EU and post-accession SN judgments and their propensity to form (as head terms) a number of complex terms (see Section 9.5). The degree of overlap provides important insights into the common, intersystemic points of reference of the supranational legal system of the EU and the legal system of Poland as an

http://morfeusz.sgjp.pl/download/, accessed: August 18, 2020) on the Windows 10 operating system, which effectively precluded me from using the off-line version of TermoPL. It is worth noting that TermoPL, as a stand-alone program, offers an attractive and functional graphical interface and makes it possible to develop own stop lists or to compare two candidate term lists obtained from two different corpora.

181 The form of the Excel formula is as follows: =IF(OR(C1=C2;C2=C3);"X";"").

EU Member State – their **common conceptual base**. The analysis also makes use of the Collocates function of WS to examine the collocational environment (cf. Daille 2017: 70) of the node terms, in order to identify complex and phrasal terms not extracted by TermoPL. Additionally, in order to take advantage of the data gathered for the purposes of the analysis presented in Chapter 7, I searched the refined lists of 4–grams, because they (n-grams in general) may contain terms and their collocations (Biel and Doczekalska 2020b, *forthcoming*), the reason for searching the lists of n-grams was to determine whether the key (node) terms also occur in longer word sequences and whether these sequences are multi-word terms (complex or phrasal terms) or not.

This approach will be helpful in determining the degree of **fit** between *terms* and *concepts* in translated EU judgments and non-translated national judgments, which may make it possible to determine whether and to what degree EU *terms* and *concepts* in adjudicative documents are indeed "sovereign" and free from national influence and vice versa, as well as whether more terms "travel" from the supranational conceptual system to the national conceptual system or the other way round. It will also be used to establish whether the concepts underlying the most salient simple terms become specialized when they are used as head terms in complex terms.

The remaining part of this chapter proceeds to describe the distributional qualities of simple and complex terms (see Sections 9.3, 9.4). The classification of key (node) terms forming three broad semantic fields of EU and national judgments and the description of their collocational environment constitutes the focal point of the chapter (see Section 9.5) – these terms are perceived to be of paramount importance to the genre of judgments as a whole.

## 9.3 Global distribution and overlap of simple terms and complex terms

Based on the lists of candidate simple and complex terms generated jointly with TermoPL, each of which contained a total 901 candidate (simple and complex) terms, it was possible to gain an overall impression of the terminological content of EU and SN judgments and answer the first two research questions. As previously mentioned in Section 9.2, the lists required manual refinement to remove wrongly extracted candidate terms. This refinement led to the elimination of approximately 21 %, 25 %, 12 %, and 42 % of all candidate terms in the corpora of CJ, GC, post-accession SN judgments, and pre-accession SN judgments, respectively.

From a global perspective, SN judgments seem to have the highest terminological content, as CJ judgments were found to contain 10 % fewer types of simple and complex terms than post-accession SN judgments, whereas GC judgments contain 15 % fewer terms. When it comes to the distribution of simple and complex terms, they are the least frequent in GC judgments, thus revealing minor internal variations within the Eurolect. The differences concerning the underrepresentation

**Table 9.2.** *Total number of types of simple and complex terms in the EU and SN corpora following refinement*

| | Translated EU case law | | | | | Non-translated PL case law | | |
|---|---|---|---|---|---|---|---|---|
| | **CJ** | **CJ vs GC (%DIFF) (LL/BIC value)** | **CJ vs SN_2011–2015 (%DIFF) (LL/BIC value)** | **GC** | **GC vs SN_2011–2015 (%DIFF) (LL/BIC value)** | **SN_2011–2015** | **SN_2011–2015 vs SN_1999 (%DIFF) (LL/BIC value)** | **SN_1999** |
| simple terms (types) | 164 | +15 % (0,75; −13,07) | −14 % (2,26; −11,57) | 142 | −26 % (5,52; −8,29) | 191 | +35 % (6,86; −6,97) | 142 |
| complex terms (types) | 548 | +4 % (0,02; −13,79) | -9 % (2,86; −10,98) | 529 | −12 % (2,29; −11,52) | 601 | +57 % (47,00; 33,17) | 383 |
| **Total** | **712** | **+6 % (0,07; −13,75)** | **−10 % (4,88; −8,96)** | **671** | **−15 % (6,01; −7,81)** | **792** | **+51 % (52,43; 38,60)** | **525** |

**Table 9.3.** *Degree of terminological overlap between the EU and SN corpora (overlapping types)*

| | Translated EU case law | | | Non-translated PL case law |
|---|---|---|---|---|
| | CJ vs GC | CJ vs SN_2011–2015 | GC vs SN_2011–2015 | SN_2011–2015 vs SN_1999 |
| simple terms | **90** (out of: 164 vs 142) | **75** (out of: 164 vs 191) | **72** (out of: 142 vs 191) | **121** (out of: 191 vs 142) |
| complex terms | **127** (out of: 548 vs 529) | **52** (out of: 548 vs 601) | **49** (out of: 529 vs 601) | **201** (out of: 601 vs 383) |
| **Total** | **217 (out of: 712 vs 671)** | **127 (out of: 712 vs 792)** | **121 (out of: 671 vs 792)** | **322 (out of: 792 vs 525)** |

of terms in the Eurolect may be regarded as negligible, providing weak evidence against the null hypothesis (see LL and BIC values). The comparison of the total number of types of both simple and complex terms in post-accession SN judgments and pre-accession SN judgments leads to the conclusion that national judgments have acquired substantially more terminological content over time; the differences between both corpora are statistically significant exclusively as regards the distribution of complex terms and the total number ofterms.

The total number of types of simple and complex terms obtained after the refinement stage indicated the quantitative divergence between the Eurolect and post-accession SN judgments. Nevertheless, there are also similarities between the corpora which can be observed at the level of terminological overlap between the individual corpora (see Table 9.3).

The comparison of the degree of overlap between both EU corpora and between the EU corpora and the post-accession SN corpus shows that EU judgments have a largely dissimilar terminological range compared to SN judgments – only approx. 17 % of all simple and complex terms overlap between the CJ and SN_2011–2015 corpus as well as the GC and SN_2011–2015 corpus. At the level of simple terms, the overlap between the Eurolect corpora and the post-accession SN corpus is much higher, at 42–43 %, whereas at the level of complex terms it is considerably lower, at only 9–10 %. This finding suggests that the Eurolect and national judgments share a **common conceptual base** (especially in relation to simple terms) which consists of concepts typically evoked at both the supranational and national level. The lower overlap at the level of complex terms indicates that the shared concepts evoked with simple terms are subject to far-reaching specialization, which may be the reason for fewer shared complex terms. These general findings need to be confirmed using a qualitative approach (see Section 9.5). On the other hand, the overlap within the Eurolect, as expected, is much higher. It amounts to about 31 %

of all terminological units in both EU corpora – 58 % at the level of simple terms and 24 % at the level of complex terms. This indicates, quite understandably, that the Eurolect also shares certain core concepts which are expressed with simple terms, while at the same time demonstrating a quite high degree of specialization of these concepts at the level of complex terms. The highest degree of overlap can be observed in the case of both national corpora – about 49 % of all simple and complex terms are shared by both the pre- and post-accession SN corpora (72 % at the level of simple terms and 41 % at the level of complex terms). What is most important from the perspective of this analysis is the overlap of terms and their underlying concepts in both supranational and national judgments.

The total number of simple and complex (including phrasal) terms occurring in both the CJ and GC corpora and the post-accession SN corpus amounts to 85 terms. These are (in alphabetical order)[182]:

1. **akta* [case],
2. *akta sprawy* [case file],
3. *cena* [price],
4. *członek* [member],
5. *decyzja* [decision],
6. **dokonanie* [performance],
7. **dokument* [document],
8. *dowód* [evidence],
9. **druga strona* [other party],
10. **działalność* [activity],
11. **działalność gospodarcza* [economic activity],
12. **działanie* [action],
13. *fakt* [fact],
14. *interes* [interest],
15. *interes prawny* [legal interest],
16. *izba* [chamber],
17. *konsekwencja* [consequence],
18. **kontrola* [control],
19. *koszt* [cost],
20. **koszty postępowania* [costs of proceedings],
21. *kwota* [amount],
22. *naruszenie* [infringement],
23. *naruszenie prawa* [infringement of a right],
24. *nieważność* [invalidity],
25. *obowiązek* [obligation],

182 Terms marked with an asterisk do not occur in the pre-accession SN corpus (they only occur in the post-accession SN corpus and the Eurolect corpora), while unmarked terms occur in both pre- and post-accession SN corpora.

26. **obrót* [trade],
27. **ochrona* [protection],
28. **ochrona praw człowieka* [protection of human rights],
29. *ogólna zasada* [general principle],
30. *okoliczność* [circumstance],
31. *okoliczność faktyczna* [factual circumstance],
32. *organ* [body],
33. **orzecznictwo* [case-law],
34. *osoba* [person],
35. *osoba fizyczna* [natural person],
36. *osoba prawna* [legal person],
37. *osoba trzecia* [third party],
38. *państwo* [state],
39. **podmiot* [entity],
40. *podstawa prawna* [legal basis],
41. *postanowienie* [order],
42. *postępowanie* [proceedings],
43. **postępowanie administracyjne* [administrative procedure],
44. *prawo* [law],
45. **prawo autorskie* [copyright],
46. **prowadzenie działalności gospodarczej* [business activity],
47. *przedsiębiorstwo* [company],
48. *przepis* [provision],
49. **przepis prawa* [legal provision],
50. *przesłanka* [premise],
51. *rozporządzenie* [regulation],
52. *sąd* [court],
53. **skarga* [complaint],
54. *skład* [composition],
55. *skutek prawny* [legal effect],
56. *spółka* [complany],
57. *sprzedaż* [sales],
58. *stan faktyczny* [factual state],
59. *stanowisko* [position],
60. *strona* [party],
61. **strona internetowa* [website],
62. *strona pozwana* [defendant],
63. **strona skarżąca* [applicant],
64. **stwierdzenie* [determination],
65. *stwierdzenie nieważności* [annulment],
66. *stwierdzenie nieważności decyzji* [annulment of a decision],
67. *termin* [deadline],
68. *towar* [good],
69. *udział* [participation],

70. *umowa* [agreement],
71. *uprawnienie* [entitlement],
72. **usługa* [service],
73. **ustalenie* [finding],
74. *wartość* [value],
75. **warunki* [conditions],
76. **władza publiczna* [public authority],
77. *wniosek* [application],
78. **wspólnotowy znak towarowy* [Community trade mark],
79. *wydanie* [adoption],
80. **wydanie decyzji* [adoption of a decision],
81. *wykładnia* [interpretation],
82. *wyrok* [judgment],
83. *zarzut* [plea],
84. **znak towarowy* [trade mark],
85. *zwrot* [recovery].

Out of the 85 terms shared by the Eurolect corpora and the post-accession SN corpus, 16 simple terms and 15 complex terms have been determined not to be on the list of terms generated for the pre-accesison SN corpus (these are marked with an asterisk). This means that 41 simple terms and 13 complex terms are shared by the post-accession corpora. Out of the group of 31 simple and complex terms which were not extracted from the pre-accession corpus, there are only two complex terms, which may indicate a very limited degree of Europeanization of terminology in national judgments – *wspólnotowy znak towarowy* [Community trade mark], which refers to a "trade mark afforded protection specific to the European Union, in accordance with Regulation (EU) 2015/2424" (IATE ID: 773104). The occurrence of this term in post-accession SN judgments suggests that issues connected with the registration of EU trade marks by national (or foreign) businesses seeking protection are brought up in proceedings before national courts. The other term which may be indicative of Europeanization is *ochrona praw człowieka* [protection of human rights]. Following the accession of Poland to the EU, the country became bound by the provisions of the treaties (and the EU Charter of Fundamental Rights) to respect and protect human rights, which may be the reason why this term became more salient in post-accession national judgments. Other than these two terms, none of the listed terms which were not extracted from the pre-accession SN corpus are indicative of Europeanization.

The above 85 terminological units may be considered to form the core of the conceptual systems of two separate legal systems interacting with each other (Biel 2019: 29; cf. Biel and Sosoni 2019: 216) owing to the largely intersystemic nature of EU translation (Šarčević 2013: 10) – the Polish legal system and the supranational legal system of the EU. In the following, considering the high total number of simple terms and complex terms identified with TermoPL, I will examine only the most salient simple and complex terms from the perspective of their distributional characteristics and underlying concepts. This will enable me to determine whether EU judgments have "references to national legal realities" (Prieto Ramos 2014: 319), whether they contain more autonomous concepts expressed with complex terms, and whether national judgments refer to the supranational legal context by evoking EU-related complex terms and concepts.

## 9.4 Top 30 simple terms and top 15 complex terms

This section examines the distribution of the most frequent simple and complex terms extracted from the corpora. For want of space, the analysis is limited to the top 30 simple terms (see Table 9.4) and top 15 complex terms (see Table 9.5).

Simple terms are exclusively nouns and, as such, point to concepts central to the genre of judgments, thus indicating their thematic content. Overall, simple terms are contained within three broad semantic fields[183] based on the ontological and logical associations (conceptual relationships) between the terms:

(1) agents and institutions (category A), e.g. *państwo* [state], *sąd* [court], *spółka* [company],
(2) substantive law and case-law, that is concepts of substantive law/case-law, etc. (category S), e.g. *dyrektywa* [directive], *wyrok* [judgment], *podatek* [tax],
(3) procedural law (category P), e.g. *postępowanie* [proceedings], *okoliczność* [circumstance].

The analysis of the most frequent simple terms proves that EU and national judgments do indeed differ in terms of the most frequently evoked legal concepts. In Table 9.4, bolded terms are those which appear in both CJ, GC and post-accession SN judgments; underlining is used to mark terms which occur in both pre- and post-accession SN judgments.

The quantitative data show that top 30 simple terms exhibit a more dense distribution in GC judgments than in CJ judgments. Furthermore, it can be observed that post-accession SN judgments have about 14 % more occurrences of top 30 simple terms than CJ judgments and about 3.5 % more tokens compared to GC judgments. It may be concluded that EU judgments do not completely converge with national judgments, not only in terms of the thematic content, as indicated by the types of simple terms (e.g. *rozporządzenie* [regulation], *Komisja* [Commission], *Trybunał* [Court (of Justice)], *Rada* [council]), but also the total distribution of these types. There are also noticeable differences in the number of simple term types belonging to each of the thematic categories – CJ judgments have the highest number of agentive and institutional simple terms (12), and GC judgments have the highest number of terms relating to legal procedure (11), whereas post-accession SN (domestic) judgments have the most simple terms relating to substantive law and case-law (15). This might be indicative of the fact that supranational and national judgments emphasize different aspects of adjudication. Nevertheless, certain terms appear across all post-accession corpora and may be perceived to be

183 The same classification has been used to classify the node terms (see Table 9.6).

**Table 9.4.** *Top 30 simple terms in the sampled corpora (frequencies normalized to 1 million)*

| Translated EU case law | | | | | | Non-translated PL case law | | | | | |
|---|---|---|---|---|---|---|---|---|---|---|---|
| CJ | | | GC | | | SN_2011–2015 | | | SN_1999 | | |
| Simple term | Cat. | NF | Simple term | Cat. | NF | Simple term | Cat. | NF | Simple term | Cat. | NF |
| ***państwo*** **[state]** | A | 5,681 | *Komisja* [Commission] | A | 9,914 | ***sąd*** **[court]** | A | 13,024 | *sąd* [court] | A | 19,974 |
| *dyrektywa* [directive] | S | 5,472 | ***decyzja*** **[decision]** | S | 7,971 | ***wyrok*** **[judgment]** | S | 5,869 | *wyrok* [judgment] | S | 8,634 |
| ***sąd*** **[court]** | A | 4,676 | *rozporządzenie* [regulation] | S | 5,493 | *powód* [claimant] | A | 5,561 | *powód* [claimant] | A | 6,946 |
| *rozporządzenie* [regulation] | S | 4,369 | ***sąd*** **[court]** | A | 3,882 | *umowa* [agreement] | S | 5,016 | *kasacja* [cassation] | S | 6,581 |
| *Komisja* [Commission] | A | 4,354 | *naruszenie* [infringement] | P | 3,543 | ***prawo*** **[law]** | S | 4,642 | *przepis* [provision] | S | 4,881 |
| ***wyrok*** **[judgment]** | S | 4,348 | ***wyrok*** **[judgment]** | S | 3,474 | ***strona*** **[party]** | A | 3,466 | *sprawa* [case] | P | 4,514 |
| ***prawo*** **[law]** | S | 4,084 | ***postępowanie*** **[proceedings]** | P | 3,088 | *przepis* [provision] | S | 2,975 | *prawo* [law] | S | 4,189 |
| ***postępowanie*** **[proceedings]** | P | 3,491 | ***prawo*** **[law]** | S | 3,007 | ***postępowanie*** **[proceedings]** | P | 2,847 | *umowa* [agreement] | S | 4,047 |
| *przepis* [provision] | S | 3,087 | ***spółka*** **[company]** | A | 2,817 | *ustawa* [act] | S | 2,621 | *uzasadnienie* [justification] | P | 3,868 |
| *Trybunał* [Court (of Justice)] | A | 2,875 | *zarzut* [plea] | P | 2,807 | *sprawa* [case] | P | 2,615 | *zarzut* [plea] | P | 3,638 |

| | | | | | | | | | | | |
|---|---|---|---|---|---|---|---|---|---|---|---|
| ***decyzja* [decision]** | S | 2,623 | *sprawa* [case] | P | 2,776 | *kwota* [amount] | P | 2,599 | *strona* [party] | A | 3,551 |
| *Unia* [Union] | A | 2,262 | *Rada* [Council] | A | 2,486 | *naruszenie* [infringement] | P | 2,595 | *instancja* [instance] | P | 3,363 |
| ***spółka* [company]** | A | 2,229 | *izba* [chamber] | A | 2,204 | *powódka* [claimant] | A | 2,491 | *postępowanie* [proceedings] | P | 3,193 |
| *Rada* [council] | A | 2,065 | *okoliczność* [circumstance] | P | 2,111 | *nieruchomość* [real estate] | S | 2,436 | *powódka* [claimant] | A | 3,125 |
| *osoba* [person] | A | 2,053 | *znak* [mark] | S | 2,051 | *roszczenie* [claim] | S | 2,393 | *powództwo* [action] | P | 2,975 |
| *artykuł* [article] | S | 1,786 | ***strona* [party]** | A | 2,039 | *skarga* [action] | P | 2,379 | *naruszenie* [infringement] | P | 2,699 |
| ***wniosek* [application]** | S | 1,770 | *grzywna* [fine] | P | 1,966 | *zarzut* [plea] | P | 2,320 | *kwota* [amount] | P | 2,206 |
| ***strona* [party]** | A | 1,665 | *substancja* [substance] | S | 1,962 | ***decyzja* [decision]** | S | 1,943 | *dowód* [evidence] | P | 2,134 |
| *pytanie* [question] | P | 1,610 | *środek* [procedure] | P | 1,835 | *powództwo* [action] | P | 1,860 | *pozwany* [defendant] | A | 2,017 |
| *okoliczność* [circumstance] | P | 1,598 | *wniosek* [application] | S | 1,833 | ***spółka* [company]** | S | 1,813 | *ustalenie* [finding] | P | 1,950 |
| *usługa* [service] | S | 1,374 | *skarżąca* [applicant] | A | 1,808 | ***koszt* [cost]** | S | 1,789 | *apelacja* [appeal] | S | 1,776 |
| *umowa* [agreement] | S | 1,313 | *pismo* [letter] | S | 1,790 | *pozwany* [defendant] | A | 1,726 | *koszt* [cost] | P | 1,774 |

*(continued on next page)*

**Table 9.4.** *Continued*

| | | | | | | | | | | | |
|---|---|---|---|---|---|---|---|---|---|---|---|
| *notariusz* [notary] | A | 1,286 | *przedsiębiorstwo* [undertaking] | A | 1,788 | ***wniosek*** **[application]** | S | 1,636 | *sędzia* [judge] | A | 1,746 |
| *republika* [republic] | A | 1,280 | *zasada* [principle] | S | 1,737 | *osoba* [person] | A | 1,593 | *ustawa* [act] | S | 1,673 |
| *odwołanie* [appeal] | S | 1,268 | *skarga* [action] | P | 1,708 | *świadczenie* [obligation] | S | 1,577 | *rozpoznanie* [examination] | P | 1,621 |
| *podatek* [tax] | S | 1,255 | *rynek* [market] | S | 1,692 | *instancja* [instance] | P | 1,551 | *stan* [status] | S | 1,609 |
| ***koszt*** **[cost]** | P | 1,249 | ***kwota*** **[amount]** | P | 1,688 | *postanowienie* [order] | S | 1,536 | *orzeczenie* [judgment] | S | 1,577 |
| *akt* [act] | S | 1,226 | ***państwo*** **[state]** | A | 1,604 | ***państwo*** **[state]** | A | 1,488 | *okoliczność* [circumstance] | P | 1,520 |
| *obowiązek* [obligation] | S | 1,218 | *motyw* [recital] | S | 1,568 | *obowiązek* [obligation] | S | 1,386 | *lokal* [dwelling] | S | 1,403 |
| *obywatel* [citizen] | A | 1,206 | ***koszt*** **[cost]** | P | 1,506 | *uzasadnienie* [justification] | S | 1,353 | *spółka* [company] | A | 1,330 |
| ***Total*** | **A12 P4 S14** | **74,773** | ***Total*** | **A9 P10 S11** | **84,148** | ***Total*** | **A7 P8 S15** | **87,100** | ***Total*** | **A7 P13 S10** | **110,516** |

of particular importance to the genre as a whole. More attention will be paid to them in Section 9.5.

Table 9.5 presents the distribution and categorization of the top 15 complex terms. They exhibit a higher degree of specialization compared to simple terms (cf. Table 9.4). This means that complex terms evoke very specific concepts which could hardly be expressed with simple terms.

The distributional pattern of complex terms diverges from that of simple terms. CJ judgments have a higher concentration of complex terms than GC judgments (by 22 %). In total, there are four terms which appear in both CJ and GC judgments (in bold): *państwo członkowskie* [Member State], *znak towarowy* [trade mark], *Unia Europejska* [European Union], and *stwierdzenie nieważności* [annulment]. Moreover, EU judgments are characterized by a marked underrepresentation of tokens of the top 15 complex terms relative to post-accession SN judgments (about 39 % and 50 %, respectively).

As regards the degree of Europeanization of national judgments, based on the presented data, it cannot be reasonably maintained that the co-existence of the European legal order and the national legal system of Poland have affected the terminological content of post-accession SN judgments. Post-accession domestic judgments, largely similarly to pre-accession judgments, do not contain any terms which could be inextricably linked to the EU legal system. The quantitative discrepancy between the pre- and post-accession national corpora is, however, not to be regarded as definite; it is highly probable that the upwards normalization of quantitative data from the pre-accession SN corpus inflated the results in the case of both simple and complex terms. In addition, it could be the case that complex terms with a lower distribution than those in Table 9.5 do show signs of the EU's influence; however, in order to determine that, it would be necessary to peruse the unabridged lists of complex terms extracted from the corpora,[184] which remains outside the scope of the present analysis.

## 9.5 Conceptual classification of node terms

The aim of this section is to establish what terms form the **common conceptual base** of the EU and national judgments (cf. Šarčević 2010: 27; Bajčić 2011: 85). The starting point of the present investigation are simple terms (see Table 9.4), which in the language of adjudication have been observed to convey unambiguous and not particularly highly specialized concepts (the exact status of which depends on the type of legal or non-legal audience) related to, for instance, institutions (e.g. *sąd* [court]) or legal procedure (e.g. *postępowanie* [proceedings]). At this point, no distinction is made between simple terms (and underlying concepts, cf. Bajčić 2017: 79) also

184 The complete, refined lists of terms extracted from the corpora can be found on the PL Eurolect's website at: https://eurolekt.ils.uw.edu.pl/publications-and-materials/additional-materials/ (accessed: August 18, 2020).

**Table 9.5.** *Top 15 complex terms in the corpora*

| Translated EU case law | | | | | |
|---|---|---|---|---|---|
| CJ | | | GC | | |
| **Complex term** | **Cat.** | **NF** | **Complex term** | **Cat.** | **NF** |
| ***państwo członkowskie* [member state]** | A | 3,981 | ***znak towarowy* [trade mark]** | S | 1,753 |
| *sąd krajowy* [national court] | A | 1,019 | ***stwierdzenie nieważności* [annulment]** | P | 947 |
| *postępowanie główne* [main proceedings] | P | 945 | *wyrok Sądu* [judgment of the General Court] | S | 769 |
| *prawo Unii* [Union law] | S | 572 | *Izba Odwoławcza* [Board of Appeal] | A | 755 |
| *rzecznik generalny* [Advocate General] | A | 531 | *spółka zależna* [subsidiary] | A | 708 |
| *władza publiczna* [public authority] | A | 470 | ***państwo członkowskie* [Member State]** | A | 708 |
| ***znak towarowy* [trade mark]** | S | 459 | *wyrok Trybunału* [judgment of the Court (of Justice)] | S | 572 |
| *państwo trzecie* [third country] | A | 455 | *rozporządzenie podstawowe* [basic regulation] | S | 512 |
| ***Unia Europejska* [European Union]** | A | 451 | *kwota grzywny* [amount of the fine] | P | 476 |
| *Parlament Europejski* [European Parliament] | A | 433 | *pomoc państwa* [state aid] | S | 341 |
| *pytanie prejudycjalne* [question referred for a preliminary ruling] | S | 392 | *koszty postępowania* [costs of proceedings] | P | 337 |
| ***stwierdzenie nieważności* [annulment]** | P | 369 | *wspólnotowy znak towarowy* [Community trade mark] | S | 316 |
| *Republika Austrii* [Republic of Austria] | A | 349 | *regulamin postępowania* [rules of procedure] | S | 314 |

**Table 9.5.** *Continued*

| | | | | | |
|---|---|---|---|---|---|
| *prawo krajowe* [national law] | S | 342 | ***Unia Europejska* [European Union]** | A | 304 |
| **Translated EU case law** | | | | | |
| *tryb prejudycjalny* [preliminary ruling] | P | 334 | *przedstawienie zarzutów* [statement of objections] | P | 290 |
| **Total** | **A=8, P=3, S=4** | **11,100** | **Total** | **A=4, P=4, S=7** | **9,103** |
| **Non-translated PL case law** | | | | | |
| **SN_2011–2015** | | | **SN_1999** | | |
| **Complex term** | **Cat.** | **NF** | **Complex term** | **Cat.** | **NF** |
| *Sąd Apelacyjny* [Court of Appeal] | A | 3,537 | *Sąd Najwyższy* [Supreme Court] | A | 5,024 |
| *Sąd Najwyższy* [Supreme Court] | A | 3,124 | *Sąd Apelacyjny* [Court of Appeal] | A | 3,710 |
| *Sąd Okręgowy* [Regional Court] | A | 2,067 | *Sąd Wojewódzki* [Provincial Court] | A | 3,167 |
| *skarga kasacyjna* [cassation appeal] | S | 1,823 | *wyrok Sądu Najwyższego* [judgment of the Supreme Court] | S | 1,643 |
| *Skarb Państwa* [State Treasury] | A | 1,256 | *prawo materialne* [substantive law] | S | 1,225 |
| *koszty postępowania* [costs of court proceedings] | P | 816 | *zarzut naruszenia* [plea in law] | P | 1,011 |
| *zarzut naruszenia* [plea in law] | P | 759 | *Sąd Rejonowy* [District Court] | A | 969 |
| *użytkowanie wieczyste* [perpetual usufruct] | S | 714 | *druga instancja* [second instance] | P | 904 |
| *wyrok Sądu Apelacyjnego* [judgment of the Court of Appeal] | S | 655 | *pierwsza instancja* [first instance] | P | 880 |
| *strona pozwana* [defendant] | A | 635 | *Izba Cywilna* [Civil Chamber] | A | 818 |
| *pierwsza instancja* [first instance] | P | 613 | *Skarb Państwa* [State Treasury] | A | 813 |

(*continued on next page*)

**Table 9.5.** *Continued*

| Non -translated PL case law | | | | | |
|---|---|---|---|---|---|
| *wyrok Sądu Najwyższego* [judgment of the Supreme Court] | S | 606 | *wyrok Sądu Apelacyjnego* [judgment of the Court of Appeal] | S | 809 |
| *druga instancja* [second instance] | P | 556 | *uzasadnienie faktyczne* [factual justification] | S | 789 |
| *strona powodowa* [plaintiff] | A | 549 | *sąd drugiej instancji* [court of second instance] | A | 765 |
| *sąd pierwszej instancji* [court of first instance] | A | 495 | *uzasadnienie prawne* [legal justification] | S | 753 |
| **Total** | **A=7, P=4, S=4** | **18,205** | **Total** | **A=7, P=3, S=5** | **23,278** |

found in everyday speech and everyday words with special connotations in a given legal context (cf. Riley 1995: 73–79; Jopek-Bosiacka 2011: 10), as well as between terms and concepts specific to either the EU or national context (Robinson 2014: 202) and interdisciplinary concepts, that is concepts used in more than one field of law (Bajčić 2011: 81). These simple terms will be perceived as genre markers (cf. Nikitina 2018: 186–203) and hence key to the genre of judgments at both the supranational and national level, as they act as points of access to crucial legal concepts which allow for the **activation of relevant background knowledge** (Biel 2008: 23), being key in the transfer of specialized knowledge. Based on the examination of the top 30 simple terms and the top 15 complex terms, it is assumed that simple terms undergo a process of further terminologization (or, using different terminology, conceptualization encompassing complicated mental processes), which lends them more specialized meanings. In this process, simple terms act as head terms and are used to form complex terms of varying degrees of terminologicality in both national and supranational judgments (cf. Biel 2014a: 36; Biel 2014b: 180).

The comparison of the lists of the top 30 most frequent simple terms in both the EU corpora and the post-accession SN corpus (see Table 9.4, Section 9.5) identified simple terms which occur in all post-accession corpora. A closer examination made it possible to group them into **three broad semantic fields** based on the properties characterizing the underlying concepts (their *intension*, cf. Sager 1990: 24). These semantic fields, which group terms in close relationships with one another (Daille 2017: 67), are understood to form the foundations of the conceptual (knowledge) system of judgments:

1) agentive and institutional node terms (A): *sąd* [court], *strona* [party], *spółka* [company], *państwo* [state],
2) node terms related to substantive law and case-law (including documents/dates/places/subject-matter, etc.) (S): *wyrok* [judgment], *prawo* [law], *decyzja* [decision], *wniosek* [application],
3) legal procedure node terms (concepts of procedural law) (P): *postępowanie* [proceedings], *koszt* [cost].

The identification of these terms, which are perceived to convey the most important concepts in adjudication, leads to the last research question: Are the key simple terms conceptualized in the same manner in the supranational and national legal system at the level of complex terms which use them as head terms? A cursory analysis of the list of the top 30 complex terms indicates that the identified node terms serve as the foundation for complex terms. For instance, the simple term *sąd* [court] serves as a head term in complex terms, such as: ***sąd** krajowy* [national court], ***Sąd** Najwyższy* [Supreme Court], and ***sąd** pierwszej instancji* [court of first instance]. It remains to be verified to what degree terms found in judgments, particularly complex terms which specialize the meaning of simple terms, **fit** the distributional features of national judgments (cf. Biel and Koźbiał 2020a, *forthcoming*).

The above terms demonstrate that the core of legal knowledge conveyed by judges is expressed not with "pure" legal terms (cf. Riley 1995: 73–79), but rather with generic terms, e.g. *koszt* [cost], *wniosek* [application], and underlying concepts, which seem to be accessible to a non-expert audience, owing to the fact that these are terms found in everyday speech, but which might cause misunderstandings. The identification of the above node terms specific to the two sub-genres of judgments as a whole contributes to the line of current research into the "core" legal vocabulary (cf. Pieńkos 1999; Goźdź-Roszkowski 2011).

Although certain complex terms formed with the node terms may be categorized into more than one category, e.g. *uchylenie zaskarżonego wyroku* [annulment of the contested decision] (legal framework or legal procedure, cf. Sections 9.5.2, 9.5.3), I tried to classify the node terms to only one main semantic field. Terminological units are referential by nature (they refer to concrete or abstract concepts); consequently, the introduced fields[185] constitute an attempt to encompass all six types of referential lexical bundles presented in Chapter 7. Table 9.6 presents quantitative data on normalized frequencies of distribution of all ten node terms, as well as data on how their distribution compares to the distribution in the pre- and post-accession national corpora.

---

185 The semantic fields partly follow the categorization introduced by Nikitina (2018: 186–188), in which she differentiated institutional and procedural nodes, agentive nodes and legal framework nodes. In my opinion, it is more suitable to group institutional and agentive nodes together, as both of the said node types refer to various entities, and to introduce legal procedure nodes as a separate field.

**Table 9.6.** *Node terms belonging to the semantic fields (ordered according to the frequency of occurrence in the SN_2011–2015 corpus)*

| | Translated EU case law | | | | | Non-translated PL case law | | |
|---|---|---|---|---|---|---|---|---|
| | CJ | CJ vs GC (%DIFF) | CJ vs SN (%DIFF) | GC | GC vs SN (%DIFF) | SN_2011–2015 | SN_2011–2015 vs SN_1999 (%DIFF) | SN_1999 |
| **1. Agents and institutions** | | | | | | | | |
| *sąd* [court] | 4,676 | +20 % | −64 % | 3,882 | −70 % | 13,024 | −35 % | 19,974 |
| *strona* [party] | 1,665 | −18 % | −52 % | 2,039 | −41 % | 3,466 | −2 % | 3,551 |
| *spółka* [company] | 2,229 | −21 % | +23 % | 2,817 | +55 % | 1,813 | +36 % | 1,330 |
| *państwo* [state] | 5,681 | +254 % | +282 % | 1,604 | +8 % | 1,488 | +65 % | 900 |
| **Total** | **14,251** | **+38 %** | **−28 %** | **10,342** | **−48 %** | **19,791** | **−23 %** | **25,755** |
| **2. Substantive law and case-law** | | | | | | | | |
| *wyrok* [judgment] | 4,348 | +25 % | −26 % | 3,474 | −41 % | 5,869 | −32 % | 8,634 |
| *prawo* [law] | 4,084 | +36 % | −12 % | 3,007 | −35 % | 4,642 | +11 % | 4,189 |
| *decyzja* [decision] | 2,623 | −67 % | +35 % | 7,971 | +310 % | 1,943 | +296 % | 491 |
| *wniosek* [application] | 1,770 | −3 % | +8 % | 1,833 | +12 % | 1,636 | +34 % | 1,225 |
| **Total** | **12,825** | **−21 %** | **−9 %** | **16,285** | **+16 %** | **14,090** | **−3 %** | **14,539** |
| **3. Legal procedure** | | | | | | | | |
| *postępowanie* [proceedings] | 3,491 | +13 % | +23 % | 3,088 | +8 % | 2,847 | −11 % | 3,193 |
| *koszt* [cost] | 1,249 | −17 % | −30 % | 1,506 | −16 % | 1,789 | +1 % | 1,774 |
| **Total** | **4,740** | +3 % | +2 % | **4,594** | −1 % | **4,636** | −7 % | **4,967** |
| **Total (all three categories)** | **31,816** | **+2 %** | **−17 %** | **31,221** | **−19 %** | **38,517** | **−15 %** | **45,261** |

Out of the three above semantic fields (see Table 9.6), only the field containing legal procedure node terms shows an almost equal level of distribution among the corpora. Terms in the first field, that is agentive and institutional node terms, are markedly underrepresented in the translation corpora relative to the post-accession SN corpus (by 28 % and 48 %, respectively). This is mostly due to the exceptionally high distribution of the node term *sąd* [court] in non-translations. The category of node terms related to substantive law and case-law, on the other hand, shows varied distribution – node terms belonging to this field are underrepresented in CJ judgments (by 21 %) and overrepresented in GC judgments (by 16 %), showing a considerable internal variation within the Eurolect, particularly when it comes to the distribution of the node *decyzja* [decision].

The high frequency of the node terms is indicative of their high cognitive salience. Therefore, as already noted, they may be regarded as key concepts forming the conceptual foundations and "aboutness" of the genre of judgments (Biel *et al.* 2018a: 261). Their combinatory potential evidences a special property of legal language, whereby many simple terms combine with other lexical units (collocates) to form more specific terminological units, i.e. complex (and phrasal) terms, which in turn develop their own collocations (Biel *et al.* 2018a: 262). The method of establishing this potential involved searching the refined lists of candidate complex terms produced with TermoPL for complex terms built around the node terms (without applying any cut-off value). WS was used to analyze the collocational range of the node terms using the same corpora. In addition, the refined lists of 4-grams (cf. Chapter 7) were searched for complex and phrasal terms containing the node terms. This approach makes it possible to ascertain what types of terminological units can be retrieved from the corpora by using a term as the search node (cf. Pearson 1998: 191–203). In order to limit the number of collocates of node terms obtained in this manner, I decided to use a frequency cut-off point of 10 occurrences in the corpus (NF).

The node terms in the three conceptual categories (see Sections 9.5.1, 9.5.2, 9.5.3) are presented in order of frequency of occurrence in the post-accession SN corpus (see Table 9.6). The description of the node terms includes information on the normalized distribution of the complex terms with the nodes as head terms from the refined lists generated with the candidate term-extraction tool TermoPL, and their collocational environment (collocates and other complex terms) established using the Collocates functionality in WS and the refined lists of 4-grams. The collocational environment does not contain complex terms related exclusively to each of the three semantic fields, in order to account for the true nature of the environment of the node terms and the possible system-bound nature of certain terms. The data also show the degree of overlap between the EU corpora and the pre- and post-accession national corpora. In the case of overlapping units, the distributional difference is expressed in percentages.

### 9.5.1 Agentive and institutional node terms and their environment

Agentive and institutional terms are nodes which refer to various agents – parties to the proceedings (*strona pozwana* [defendant]), Member States (*państwo członkowskie* [Member State]), judicial institutions (*sąd Unii Europejskiej* [Court of the European Union]), and national courts (*sąd rejonowy* [district court]). This category involves four key node terms: *sąd* [court], *strona* [party], *spółka* [company], and *państwo* [state].[186]

**1. *Sąd* [court] (CJ: 4,676 NF; GC: 3,882 NF; SN_2011–2015: 13,024 NF; SN_1999: 19,974 NF)**

The first node term, *sąd* [court], denotes a range of concepts related to the functioning of individuals in society and law in general, their opinions and the discipline of logic (WSJP entry – *sąd*):

1a. institution – a state institution dealing with the resolution of legal disputes and ruling on guilt or innocence in accordance with applicable law (cf. Garner 2009: 405),
1b. building – the seat of the court – a state institution dealing with dispute settlement in accordance with applicable law,
1c. judges – a team of legal professional who deal with the settlement of legal disputes on behalf of the state and in accordance with applicable law,
2. hearing – consideration of a case during court proceedings to finally deliver a verdict,
3. opinion – what someone could say on a given topic,
4. logic – the meaning of a sentence that states a certain state of affairs, or the sentence itself.

In the corpora, the most common concepts evoked by this node term are 1a. institution and 1c. judges. In the EU context, the node *sąd* [court] is the name of one of the two CJEU courts — the Court. In the national context, the node forms a part of the name of the Polish Supreme Court — *Sąd Najwyższy*. The analysis of the refined lists of 4-grams[187] (cf. Chapter 7) shows that this node is used mainly to (1) report on previous proceedings conducted either by national courts (CJ: *postępowania przed* ***sądem*** *krajowym*, SN_2011–2015: *przed* ***sądem*** *pierwszej instancji*) or an EU court, or lower-instance courts in the national legal context, and report on actions of agents and institutions (GC: *wnosi do Sądu o*), (2) to provide intertextual references to judgments or other documents (GC: *wyrok* ***Sądu*** *z dnia*, SN_2011–2015: *wyrok* ***sądu*** *pierwszej instancji, w orzecznictwie* ***Sądu*** *Najwyższego*) (3) to introduce own (GC: *z powyższych względów* ***Sąd,*** SN_2011–2015: ***Sąd*** *Najwyższy w składzie*) or reported argumentations (SN_2011–2015: ***Sąd*** *Apelacyjny stwierdził że,* ***sąd*** *ten ustalił że*).

186 In tables presented in Sections 9.5.1, 9.5.2 and 9.5.3, complex terms and term phrases occurring in both EU corpora are bolded. Complex terms (and term phrases) which appear in either of the EU corpora and the post-accession SN corpus are marked with an asterisk (*). Complex terms and term phrases which appear in both the pre- and post-accession SN corpora are underlined.

187 The bundles presented in this chapter do not account for the inflectional nature of Polish.

Based on the lists of complex terms generated with TermoPL, it has been determined that the complex terms with the node *sąd* [court] as a head term are complex terms denoting various types of courts occupying different tiers in the EU and Polish hierarchy of courts (their proper names), e.g. *Sąd Najwyższy* [Supreme Court], as well as complex terms with more broad sets of referents, e.g. *sąd pierwszej instancji* [court of first instance] (see Table 9.7). It should be noted that court names are an archetypal example of legal system-bound terms (Vigier and Sánchez Ramos 2017: 262).

Complex terms structured around the node *sąd* [court] reflect the hierarchical structure of the respective judicial systems. In this regard, the national corpora exhibit a wider range of references to specialized courts which differ in subject-matter jurisdiction, e.g. *Sąd Rejonowy* [District Court] (generally a first-instance court), *Sąd Okręgowy* [Regional Court] (the appeal or first-instance court in certain cases), *Sąd Najwyższy* [Supreme Court] (the highest judicial authority), *Naczelny Sąd Administracyjny* [Supreme Administrative Court]. In national judgments, there are also terms of general reference to individual tiers of the judiciary, e.g. *sąd pierwszej instancji* [court of first instance], *sąd drugiej instancji* [court of second instance]. Terms with this node found in EU judgments, on the other hand, do not clearly reflect the structure of the EU judiciary (see Table 9.7). Both the CJ and the GC seem to be keen on drawing the dividing line between the EU and national legal system using complex terms such as: *sąd Unii* [Union Court], *sąd krajowy* [national court]. They very often refer to referring courts (*sąd krajowy*) in the preliminary ruling procedure using the term *national court*, thereby foregoing the need to mention them by their official names (cf. Prieto Ramos 2014: 320), as in the following excerpt:

(1) CJ (C-337/10): *W drodze pytania piątego* ***sąd krajowy*** *zmierza zasadniczo do ustalenia, czy (...).*
[By its fifth question, the **national court** asks, in essence, whether (...).]

By doing so the CJEU takes on a different perspective and asserts more dominance as a superior supranational judicial institution independent of national courts in Member States; as a consequence, its judgments may be perceived as having a greater degree of persuasive force and non-negotiability (cf. Van Dijk 2008: 37–41). On the other hand, the SN, as a superior court exercising supervision over common and military courts (cf. Article 183 of the Polish Constitution), stresses its important position in the Polish legal system with frequent self-references, as evidenced by the high distribution of *Sąd Najwyższy* [Supreme Court], as in, for instance:

(2) SN (IV CSK 225/11): ***Sąd Najwyższy*** *zważył, co następuje:* (...)
[The **Supreme Court** held as follows (...)]

This standard phrase is used by the SN to introduce its findings in the case (cf. Chapter 5). The SN also refers to itself in other standard phrases, such as restating its judgment.

**Table 9.7.** *Agentive and institutional complex terms with the head term sąd [court]*

| Translated EU case law | | | | | | |
|---|---|---|---|---|---|---|
| **CJ** | | **CJ vs GC (%DIFF)** | **CJ vs SN_2011–2015 (%DIFF)** | **GC** | | **GC vs SN_2011–2015 (%DIFF)** |
| ***sąd krajowy*** **[national court]** | 1,019 | +2988 % | - | ***sąd Unii*** **[Union Court]** | 243 | - |
| ***sąd Unii*** **[Union Court]** | 70 | −79 % | - | ***sąd krajowy*** **[national court]** | 33 | - |
| *sąd apelacyjny** [appeal court] | 49 | - | −91 % | | | |
| *sąd administracyjny* [administrative court] | 43 | - | - | | | |
| *sąd Unii Europejskiej* [Court of the European Union] | 33 | - | - | | | |
| **Total (5 types) CJ vs GC overlapping types: 3 CJ vs SN_2011–2015 overlapping types: 1** | **1,214** | **+340 %** | **−84 %** | **Total (2 types) GC vs SN_2011–2015 overlapping types: 0** | **276** | **−96 %** |

| Non-translated PL case law | | | | |
|---|---|---|---|---|
| **SN_2011–2015** | | **SN_2011–2015 vs SN_1999 (%DIFF)** | **SN_1999** | |
| *Sąd Najwyższy* [Supreme Court] | 3,124 | −38 % | *Sąd Najwyższy* [Supreme Court] | 5,024 |
| *Sąd Okręgowy* [Regional Court] | 2,067 | +1478 % | *Sąd Apelacyjny* [Court of Appeal] | 3,710 |
| *Sąd Apelacyjny** [Court of Appeal] | 537 | −86 % | *Sąd Wojewódzki* [Provincial Court] | 3,167 |
| *sąd pierwszej instancji* [court of first instance] | 495 | −26 % | *Sąd Rejonowy* [District Court] | 969 |
| *sąd drugiej instancji* [court of second instance] | 480 | −37 % | *sąd drugiej instancji* [court of second instance] | 765 |
| *Sąd Rejonowy* [District Court] | 320 | −67 % | *sąd pierwszej instancji* [court of first instance] | 672 |
| *sąd odwoławczy* [appeal court] | 236 | −19 % | *sąd I instancji* [court of I instance] | 531 |
| *sąd I instancji* [court of I instance] | 83 | −84 % | *sąd II instancji* [court of II instance] | 454 |
| *sąd powszechny* [ordinary court] | 69 | - | *sąd odwoławczy* [appeal court] | 291 |
| *sąd II instancji* [court of II instance] | 61 | −87 % | *Sąd Okręgowy* [Regional Court] | 131 |
| *Sąd Ochrony Konkurencji i Konsumentów* [court of competition and consumer protection] | 29 | - | *sąd kasacyjny* [court of cassation] | 55 |
| *Naczelny Sąd Administracyjny* [Supreme Administrative Court] | 29 | - | | |
| **Total (12 types) SN_2011–2015 vs SN_1999 overlapping types: 9** | **7,530** | **−52 %** | **Total (11 types)** | **15,769** |

(3) SN (IV CSK 206/11): *Z przedstawionych powodów* ***Sąd Najwyższy*** *orzekł, jak w sentencji wyroku.*
[In this state of affairs, the **Supreme Court** ruled as in the operative part]

Both corpora of EU judgments have very few complex terms with the node *sąd* [court] compared to domestic non-translated judgments. There is only one term type found in CJ judgments which is also found in national judgments, that is *sąd apelacyjny* [appellate court]. *Sąd*-based complex terms are, overall, considerably more frequent compared to EU judgments, and in particular GC judgments. No radical change can be observed as regards the overlap of complex terms in pre- and post-accession SN judgments. The most striking change refers to the lack of the complex term *Sąd Wojewódzki* [Provincial Court] in the post-accession national corpus, which, however, has not been caused by the influence of the EU legal system, but rather an intrasystemic change within the Polish legal system.[188] Overall, none of the complex terms shown above indicate a high level of conceptual **fit** between the supranational and the national context. Partial conceptual congruity can be observed in the case of two CJ terms: *sąd apelacyjny* [appeal court] and *sąd administracyjny* [administrative court], as both also appear in the national context, although not necessarily with the same designations. This indicates that the complex terms formed with the head term *sąd* [court] display a highly system-bound nature, being tied either to the supranational or national context. In addition, it should be noted that the national court does not mention any of the EU courts, which is indicated by the lack of complex terms denoting them.

The collocational range (other complex terms not extracted with TermoPL and phrasal terms) established with the Collocates functionality of WS is as follows[189]:

**CJ:** *sąd odsyłający* [referring court] (509), *sąd apelacyjny* [appeal court] (18), *Sąd Najwyższy* [Supreme Court] (16), *sąd gospodarczy* [commercial court] (14), *właściwy sąd* [competent court] (10), *Sąd Rejonowy* [District Court] (10), *sąd odwoławczy* [appeal court] (10) [587]

188 *Sądy Wojewódzkie* [Provincial Courts] functioned between 1950 and 1999; they were later transformed into *Sądy Okręgowe* [Regional Courts], pursuant to Article 2(1) of the Act of December 18, 1998 amending the Act – Law on the structure of common courts (Journal of Laws of 1998 No. 160, item 1064) and the Regulation of the Minister of Justice of December 30, 1998 on the establishment of courts of appeal, regional courts and district courts, as well as determining their seats and areas of jurisdiction (Journal of Laws of 1998 No. 166, item 1253, as amended).

189 The figures in round brackets indicate NF values. The figures in square brackets indicate total NF values.

**GC:** *none*
**SN_2011–2015:** *sędzia Sądu Najwyższego* [judge of the Supreme Court] (260), *sąd polubowny* [arbitration court] (20), *sąd orzekający* [adjudicating court] (14), *sąd arbitrażowy* [arbitration court] (10) [304]
**SN_1999:** *sąd odwoławczy* [appeal court] (42), *sąd gospodarczy* [commercial court] (20), *sąd rewizyjny* [Court of review] (12) [74]

For the total number of types of complex terms discovered using WS, the environment of *sąd* [court] seems to be considerably richer in EU judgments compared to national judgments, in particular in CJ judgments. Examination of the list of collocates of *sąd* [court] in WS has also led to the identification of other less salient complex terms referring to various courts (in CJ judgments, for instance, *sąd odsyłający* [referring court], *Sąd Najwyższy* [Supreme Court], *sąd apelacyjny* [appeal court], *sąd gospodarczy* [commercial court], *Sąd Rejonowy* [District Court], *sąd odwoławczy* [appeal court], whereas in post-accession SN judgments: *sąd polubowny* [arbitration court], *sąd arbitrażowy* [arbitration court]).

**2. *Strona* [party] (CJ: 1,665 NF; GC: 2,039 NF; SN_2011–2015: 3,466 NF; SN_1999: 3,551 NF)**
The node *strona* [party] denotes almost a dozen concepts in general Polish related to, among other things, physical features and properties of space, the functioning of individuals in society and principles of community life (see pts. 6–7) (WSJP entry – *strona*); however, not all of them can be encountered in judicial language:

1. content – content on one of the two surfaces of the paper,
2. page – book or magazine page,
3. website – a set of information presented in a graphic manner, which is displayed on the computer screen after starting the appropriate program and entering the internet address,
4. direction in space – direction in space marked by an object in a certain place,
5. course of action – the direction of development of activities,
6. people – a group of people representing views that are different in a given matter from another group of people,
7. in court – a natural or legal person involved in judicial or administrative proceedings,

The most frequently evoked concept by the node *strona* [party] is that which denotes persons taking part in judicial proceedings. This can be better portrayed with 4-grams such as: CJ: *stron w postępowaniu głównym*, GC: *na żądanie strony przeciwnej*, SN_2011–2015: *strony powodowej od wyroku, skargi kasacyjnej strony powodowej*. An example of a different concept evoked by this node term is the description of a course of action (or rather expressing transition) in the bundle CJ/GC: *a z drugiej strony*.

Complex terms extracted from the lists of candidate terms generated by TermoPL structured around the node term *strona* [party] refer almost exclusively to the parties to the proceedings before the respective courts, e.g. *strona postępowania* [party to the proceedings], *strona pozwana* [defendant], *strona powodowa* [complainant], or parties to legal agreements, e.g. *strona umowy* [party to the agreement] (only in the case of the national corpora) (see Table 9.8).

The data show that, overall, both EU and national judgments have a divergent distribution of *strona*-based complex terms, even though the total number of types is similar in both cases. CJ and SN judgments share three terms, *strona pozwana* [defendant], *druga strona* [the other party], and *strona skarżąca* [applicant], whereas GC judgments only share the last two. Only two complex terms with the head term *strona* [party], *druga strona* [the other party] and *strona skarżąca* [applicant], show signs of conceptual convergence at the supranational-national level, despite naturally having different referents. Other complex terms seem to be system-bound.

The collocational range established with the Collocates functionality of WS is not as extensive as in the case of *sąd*-based complex terms.

| | |
|---|---|
| CJ: | *argumentacja stron* [arguments of the parties] (248), *strona internetowa** [website] (107), *żądanie strony przeciwnej* [the other party's request] (84) [439] |
| GC: | *strona przegrywająca* [the unsuccessful party] (90), *strona wnosząca sprzeciw* [the opposing party] (14) [104] |
| SN_2011–2015: | *strona internetowa** [website] (96), *zgodny zamiar stron* [common intent of the parties] (55), *apelacji strony powodowej* [complainant's appeal] (43), *apelacji strony pozwanej* [defendant's appeal] (39), *strona postępowania* [party to the proceedings] (10) [243] |
| SN_1999: | *strona przeciwna* [the other party] (14) [14] |

The complex term *strona postępowania* [party to the proceedings] found in post-accession SN judgments is yet another term which denotes a concept shared by the two legal systems. One term found in the CJ corpus and the post-accession SN corpus evoked a concept not related to the parties to the proceedings, namely *strona internetowa* [website]; it occurs in both CJ and post-accession SN judgments. Out of the remaining complex terms, several are used to identify parties to the proceedings, such as *strona przegrywająca* [the unsuccessful party], *strona wnosząca sprzeciw* [the opposing party] (GC corpus), *strona postępowania* [party to the proceedings] (post-accession SN corpus), or *strona przeciwna* [the other party] (pre-accession SN corpus). The complex term *argumentacja stron* [arguments of the parties], which can be found in CJ judgments, is very important from the point of view of the genre structure:

(4) CJ (C-29/14): **Argumentacja stron**
*Komisja podnosi, że transpozycja do polskiego porządku prawnego wskazanych dyrektyw jest niekompletna, gdyż* [...].

**Table 9.8.** *Agentive and institutional complex terms with the head term strona [party]*

| Translated EU case law | | | | | | |
|---|---|---|---|---|---|---|
| **CJ** | | **CJ vs GC (%DIFF)** | **CJ vs SN_2011–2015 (%DIFF)** | **GC** | | **GC vs SN_2011–2015 (%DIFF)** |
| ***strona postępowania*** **[party to the proceedings]** | 103 | −48 % | - | ***druga strona**** **[the other party]** | 198 | +274 % |
| ***druga strona**** **[the other party]** | 94 | −48 % | +77 % | ***strona skarżąca**** **[applicant]** | **182** | +420 % |
| ***zainteresowana strona*** **[interested party]** | 59 | +59 % | - | ***zainteresowana strona*** **[interested party]** | 37 | - |
| ***strona skarżąca**** **[applicant]** | 53 | +61 % | +51 % | ***strona postępowania*** **[party to the proceedings]** | 33 | - |
| *strona przeciwna* [the other party] | 49 | - | - | | | |
| *strona pozwana** [defendant] | 43 | - | −93 % | | | |
| **Total (6 types) CJ vs GC overlapping types: 4 CJ vs SN_2011–2015 overlapping types: 3** | **401** | −11 % | **−71 %** | **Total (4 types) GC vs SN_2011–2015 overlapping types: 2** | **450** | **−67 %** |

(*continued on next page*)

**Table 9.8.** *Continued*

| Non-translated PL case law | | | | |
|---|---|---|---|---|
| **SN_2011–2015** | | **SN_2011–2015 vs SN_1999 (%DIFF)** | **SN_1999** | |
| *strona pozwana** [defendant] | 635 | +124 % | *strona powodowa* [complainant] | 369 |
| *strona powodowa* [complainant] | 549 | +49 % | *strona pozwana* [defendant] | 283 |
| *strona umowy* [party to the agreement] | 108 | +9 % | *strona umowy* [party to the agreement] | 99 |
| *druga strona** [the other party] | 53 | - | | |
| *strona skarżąca** [applicant] | 35 | - | | |
| **Total (5 types) SN_2011–2015 vs SN_1999 overlapping types: 3** | **1,380** | **−100 %** | **Total (3 types)** | **751** |

> [**Arguments of the parties**
> The Commission contends that the transposition of the directives at issue into Polish law is incomplete, in view of the fact that […].]

It is used by the Court to introduce the section of judgments recounting the arguments raised by the parties to the proceedings[190] (cf. Chapter 5):

**3. *Spółka* [company] (CJ: 2,229 NF; GC: 2,817 NF; SN_2011–2015: 1,813 NF; SN_1999: 1,330 NF)**

The node term *spółka* [company] produces two types of concepts related to the functioning of companies and enterprises and interpersonal relations:

1. organization (company) – an enterprise constituted by a written contract of a minimum of two natural or legal persons making a contribution, the goal of which is to make a profit,
2. joint action – joint activities of several people which aim to achieve a certain goal.

Complex terms with this node as a head term evoke almost exclusively the first concept. There are no 4-grams in the Eurolect corpora with this node; however, in the post-accession SN corpus, there are two bundle types with this node — *spółki z ograniczoną odpowiedzialnością, spółka z o.o.*

Complex terms built around the node term *spółka* [company] have the lowest number of types among terms belonging to the category of agentive and institutional node terms. In this category, the EU corpora contain only two types of terms, while the SN corpora only one. *Spółka zależna* [subsidiary] is a term which can be found in both EU corpora, whereas *spółka cywilna* [civil law partnership] can be found in both national corpora (see Table 9.9).

The term *spółka cywilna* [civil law partnership] has not been extracted from the EU corpora, which clearly shows that it refers to a concept bound to the national context. Strangely, the lists of complex terms generated with TermoPL did not contain any more types with the present node indicating other types of companies and partnerships allowed for under EU and Polish law, for instance, *spółka akcyjna* [joint stock company] or *spółka jawna* [general partnership].

Based on the list of complex terms extracted with TermoPL, it can be observed that none of the terms in EU and SN judgments overlap, suggesting little thematic convergence as regards references to various types of companies. In order to gain a more comprehensive view of terms with the node *spółka* [company], it was necessary to examine its collocational environment. The analysis has shown that the manual extraction of complex terms is helpful in supplementing the list of terminological units extracted from the corpora with TermoPL (see Table 9.9):

190 For more information on the topic of genre structure of CJEU and SN judgments, see Chapter 5.

**Table 9.9.** *Agentive and institutional complex terms structured around the node term spółka [company]*

| Translated EU case law | | | | | | |
|---|---|---|---|---|---|---|
| **CJ** | | **CJ vs GC (%DIFF)** | **CJ vs SN_2011–2015 (%DIFF)** | **GC** | | **GC vs SN_2011–2015 (%DIFF)** |
| ***spółka zależna* [subsidiary company]** | 205 | −71 % | - | ***spółka zależna* [subsidiary company]** | 708 | |
| *spółka kapitałowa* [capital company] | 55 | - | - | | | |
| **Total (2 types) CJ vs GC overlapping types: 1 CJ vs SN_2011–2015 overlapping types: 0** | **260** | **−63 %** | **+534 %** | **Total (1 type) GC vs SN_2011–2015 overlapping types: 0** | **708** | **+1627 %** |
| **Non-translated PL case law** | | | | | | |
| **SN_2011–2015** | | | **SN_2011–2015 vs SN_1999 (%DIFF)** | **SN_1999** | | |
| *spółka cywilna* [civil law partnership] | | 41 | −66 % | *spółka cywilna* [civil law partnership] | | 119 |
| **Total (2 types) SN_2011–2015 vs SN_1999 overlapping types: 1** | | **41** | **−65 %** | **Total (1 type)** | | **119** |

**CJ:** *spółka dominująca* [parent company] (57) [57]
**GC:** *spółka dominująca* [parent company] (180) [180]
**SN_2011–2015:** *zobowiązanie spółki* [obligation of a company] (88), *członek zarządu spółki* [member of the board of directors of a company] (85), *majątek spółki* [assets of a company] (69), *wspólnik spółki cywilnej* [partner of a civil law partnership] (43), *spółka akcyjna* [joint stock company] (28), *spółka jawna* [general partnership] (10) [323]
**SN_1999:** *pozwana spółka* [defendant company] (42), *powodowa spółka* [claimant company] (40), *spółka akcyjna* [joint stock company] (22) [104]

As for the overall distribution, collocates of the node *spółka* [company] and complex terms extracted with TermoPL are more frequent in the Eurolect, albeit SN judgments have a higher variety of types. Complex terms with this node show that company-related terms and underlying concepts are inextricably connected with the individual legal systems.

**4. *Państwo* [state] (CJ: 5,681 NF; GC: 1,604 NF; SN_2011–2015: 1,488 NF; SN_1999: 900 NF)**

All concepts evoked by the node *państwo* [state] are related to the functioning of individuals in society in general and the functioning of the state (WSJP entry – *państwo*). The relevant entries in the WSJP dictionary are as follows:

1. Poland – a politically organized large group of people, mostly of the same nationality, with an independent form of government, occupying a territory with strictly defined borders,
2. authority – all individuals and institutions representing and managing the state or an organization,
3. state – territory of a state or an organization.

The lists of refined 4-grams contain only several types containing the node *państwo* [state] in the CJ and the post-accession SN corpus — CJ: *w innym państwie członkowskim, na terytorium państwa członkowskiego*, SN_2011–2015: *na rzecz Skarbu Państwa*, which suggests that EU judgments frequently evoke the concepts authority and state-related concepts encompassing all or most Member States, whereas Polish judgments display a frequent usage of the first concept, that is Poland, which acts as a narrow designation limited to the territory of Poland, its citizens and political organization.

In the case of the last term in the category of agentive and institutional node terms, *państwo,* [state] which is used to create a range of complex terms (were extracted with TermoPL), there is no overlap between the EU corpora and the national corpora (see Table 9.10).

Overall, terms with the node *państwo* [state] as a head term have a varied distribution among the corpora, from among which the corpus of CJ judgments has the highest number of occurrences of such terms due to the large distribution of the complex term *państwo członkowskie* [Member State], the corpus of GC judgments has the lowest distribution, and the corpus of SN judgments has a moderate number of occurrences due to having only one term type, *Skarb Państwa* [State Treasury].

The concept of *Skarb Państwa* [State Treasury] refers to the representation of the Polish state acting in the field of civil law relations in which it is equal to private entities (Brzozowski *et al.* 2015: 17):

(5) SN (I CSK 77/12): […] ***Skarb Państwa*** *odpowiada za szkodę wyrządzoną niewydaniem aktu normatywnego, którego obowiązek wydania powstał po wejściu w życie Konstytucji Rzeczypospolitej Polskiej.*
[[…] **The State Treasury** is responsible for damage caused by failure to issue a normative act that was subject of an obligation which arose after the entry into force of the Constitution of the Republic of Poland.]

**Table 9.10.** *Agentive and institutional complex terms with the head term państwo [state]*

| Translated EU case law | | | | | | |
|---|---|---|---|---|---|---|
| **CJ** | | **CJ vs GC (%DIFF)** | **CJ vs SN_2011–2015 (%DIFF)** | **GC** | | **GC vs SN_2011–2015 (%DIFF)** |
| ***państwo członkowskie*** **[Member State]** | 3,981 | +462 % | - | ***państwo członkowskie*** **[Member State]** | 708 | - |
| ***państwo trzecie*** **[third country]** | 455 | +671 % | - | ***państwo trzecie*** **[third country]** | 59 | - |
| *państwo pochodzenia* [country of origin] | 33 | - | - | | | |
| **Total (3 types) CJ vs GC overlapping types: 2 CJ vs SN_2011–2015 overlapping types: 0** | **4,469** | **+483 %** | **+256 %** | **Total (2 types) GC vs SN_2011–2015 overlapping types: 0** | **767** | **−39 %** |
| **Non-translated PL case law** | | | | | | |
| **SN_2011–2015** | | | **SN_2011–2015/ SN_1999 (%DIFF)** | **SN_1999** | | |
| *Skarb Państwa* [State Treasury] | | 1,256 | +54 % | *Skarb Państwa* [State Treasury] | | 813 |
| **Total (1 type) SN_2011–2015 vs SN_1999 overlapping types: 0** | | **1,256** | **+54 %** | **Total (1 type)** | | **813** |

The Collocates functionality in WS led to the identification of a wider range of complex terms with *państwo* as a head term and their collocational environment than TermoPL (see Table 9.10).

**CJ:** *zainteresowane państwo członkowskie* [the Member State concerned] (35), *państwo członkowskie pochodzenia* [Member State of origin] (14) [49]
**GC:** *państwo niderlandzkie* [the Dutch State] (53), *zainteresowane państwo członkowskie* [the Member State concerned] (37), *państwo francuskie* [the French State] (12) [102]
**SN_2011–2015:** *własność Skarbu Państwa* [property of the State Treasury] (63), *budżet państwa* [budget of the state] (57), *odpowiedzialność Skarbu Państwa* [responsibility of the State Treasury] (53), *minister Skarbu Państwa* [Minister of the Treasury] (49), *prokuratoria generalna Skarbu Państwa* [State Treasury Solicitors' Office] (35), *odpowiedzialność odszkodowawcza Skarbu Państwa* [State Treasury's liability for damages] (20) [277]
**SN_1999:** *odpowiedzialność Skarbu Państwa* [responsibility of the State Treasury] (77), *jednostka organizacyjna Skarbu Państwa* [organisational unit of the State Treasury] (22) [99]

It should be noted that post-accession SN judgments have a higher number of types of complex terms built around *państwo* [state] than each of the EU corpora. In addition, all terms in the national corpora are related solely to the Polish state entity.

### 9.5.2 Node terms related to substantive law and case-law and their environment

Complex terms related to substantive law and case-law refer, among other things, to various concepts of substantive law, e.g. *prawo krajowe* [national law], *prawo autorskie* [copyright], *prawo cywilne* [civil law], case-law, e.g. *wyrok Trybunału* [Judgment of the Court], *wyrok Sądu Najwyższego* [judgment of the Supreme Court], and various (administrative) documents, e.g. *decyzja administracyjna* [administrative decision], *decyzja ramowa* [framework decision]. This category involves terms structured around four node terms: *wyrok* [judgment], *prawo* [law], *decyzja* [decision], and *wniosek* [application].

**1. *Wyrok* [judgment] (CJ: 4,348 NF; GC: 3,474 NF; SN_2011–2015: 5,869 NF; SN_1999: 8,634 NF)**
In judicial language, the node *wyrok* [judgment] evokes mainly one case-law-related concept. The WSJP dictionary states that the word *wyrok* is polysemous and enumerates several concepts related to the functioning of individuals in society and the human as a psychological being involved in assessment and evaluation procedures:

1. in court – a decision of a judge or a panel of judges constituting a decision in a criminal or civil trial,
2. an unquestionable opinion – an unquestionable and unfavorable opinion on some matter,
3. twist of fate – an event that occurs in life regardless of human will.

The fact that this node evokes primarily the first concept is reflected in the 4-grams extracted from the corpora: CJ/GC: *ww wyrok w sprawie, zob wyrok z dnia, podobnie wyrok z dnia, r wydaje następujący* wyrok, SN_2011–2015: *wyrok SN z dnia, r uchyla zaskarżony wyrok, wyrok w imieniu Rzeczypospolitej, Sąd Najwyższy w wyroku.*

Complex terms structured around the most salient node term in this category, *wyrok* [judgment], which were identified using only TermoPL, are markedly underrepresented in EU judgments relative to national judgments, particularly in CJ judgments, both in terms of the total number of types and tokens (see Table 9.11).

All of the complex terms refer to judgments passed by various types of courts, e.g. *wyrok Sądu* [judgment of the General Court] and *wyrok Sądu Rejonowego* [judgment of the District Court]. The corpora of EU judgments have only two types of complex terms with the node *wyrok* [judgment], whereas non-translated national judgments have a total of 11 types. In the EU corpora, the term *wyrok Trybunału* [Judgment of the Court] is present in both corpora, whereas in the pre- and post-accession SN corpora, there are five overlapping terms. The terms extracted with TermoPL show that none of the terms in EU judgments overlap with those from national judgments, which is indicative of the lack of conceptual fit between the supranational and the national contexts. Overall, the complex terms with the node as a head term convey highly specialized meanings which may not be readily accessible to a non-expert audience.

The very frequently occurring complex terms, such as *wyrok Trybunału* [Judgment of the Court] and *wyrok Sądu Najwyższego* [judgment of the Supreme Court], are used by the courts to refer to established case-law, effectively serving as intertextual references, as in:

(6) CJ (C-32/13): *Wniosku tego nie podaje w wątpliwość wspomniana przez sąd odsyłający okoliczność, że rzeczona renta wychowawcza posiada istotne cechy renty [...] (zob. analogicznie* ***wyrok Trybunału*** *z dnia 31 maja 2001 r. w sprawie C-43/99 Leclere i Deaconescu, Rec. S. I-4265, pkt 50).*
[The fact, noted by the referring court, that that pension for bringing up children contains essential elements of a pension [...], does not call that conclusion into question (see, by analogy, **Case** C-43/99 Leclere and Deaconescu [2001] ECR I-4265, paragraph 50).]

(7) SN (I CSK 29/12): *Wspomniane przytoczenie nie oznacza bowiem, że zawarty w nim przepis prawa jest objęty podstawą kasacyjną i podlega kontroli kasacyjnej (por.* ***wyrok Sądu Najwyższego*** *z dnia 5 listopada 2003 r., IV CSK 173/02, niepubl.).*
[The aforementioned citation does not mean that the legal provision contained therein provides grounds for cassation and is subject to cassation control (cf. **judgment of the Supreme Court** of 5 November 2003, IV CSK 173/02, unpublished).]

**Table 9.11.** *Complex terms related to substantive law and case-law structured around the term node wyrok [judgment]*

| **Translated EU case law** | | | | | | |
|---|---|---|---|---|---|---|
| **CJ** | | **CJ vs GC (%DIFF)** | **CJ vs SN_2011–2015 (%DIFF)** | **GC** | | **GC vs SN_2011–2015 (%DIFF)** |
| ***wyrok Trybunału*** **[Judgment of the Court]** | 217 | −62 % | - | *wyrok Sądu* [judgment of the General Court] | 769 | - |
| | | | | ***wyrok Trybunału*** **[Judgment of the Court]** | 572 | - |
| **Total (1 type)<br>CJ vs GC overlapping types: 1<br>CJ vs SN_2011–2015 overlapping types: 0** | **217** | **−84 %** | **−88 %** | **Total (2 types)<br>GC vs SN_2011–2015 overlapping types: 0** | **1,341** | **−27 %** |

| **Non-translated PL case law** | | | | |
|---|---|---|---|---|
| **SN_2011–2015** | | **SN_2011–2015 vs SN_1999 (%DIFF)** | **SN_1999** | |
| *wyrok Sądu Apelacyjnego* [judgment of the Court of Appeal] | 655 | −19 % | *wyrok Sądu Najwyższego* [annulment of the Supreme Court] | 1,643 |
| *wyrok Sądu Najwyższego* [annulment of the Supreme Court] | 606 | −63 % | *wyrok Sądu Apelacyjnego* [judgment of the Court of Appeal] | 809 |
| *wyrok Sądu Okręgowego* [District Court nnulment] | 346 | - | *wyrok Sądu Wojewódzkiego* [judgment of the Provincial Court] | 709 |
| *wyrok sądu pierwszej instancji* [judgment of the court of first instance] | 75 | −19 % | *wyrok Sądu Rejonowego* [judgment of the District Court] | 202 |

(*continued on next page*)

**Table 9.11.** *Continued*

| Non -translated PL case law | | | | |
|---|---|---|---|---|
| *wyrok Trybunału Konstytucyjnego* [annulment of the Constitutional Tribunal] | 73 | - | *wyrok sądu pierwszej instancji* [judgment of the sourt of first instance] | 93 |
| *wyrok Sądu Rejonowego* [judgment of the District Court] | 47 | –77 % | *wyrok sądu I instancji* [judgment of the court of I instance] | 63 |
| *wyrok zaoczny* [default annulment] | 33 | –37 % | *wyrok zaoczny* [default annulment] | 52 |
| | | | *wyrok rozwodowy* [divorce judgment] | 42 |
| | | | *wyrok sądu drugiej instancji* [judgment of the court of second instance] | 38 |
| **Total (7 types) SN_2011–2015 vs SN_1999 overlapping types: 5** | **1,835** | **–50 %** | **Total (9 types)** | **3,651** |

In CJ judgments, for instance, the complex term *wyrok Trybunału* [Judgment of the Court] serves as a metadiscursive marker identifying the type of judgment and the date on which it was passed (cf. Chapter 5):

(8) CJ (C-42/14): ***WYROK TRYBUNAŁU** (trzecia izba)*
*z dnia 16 kwietnia 2015 r.*
[**JUDGMENT OF THE COURT** (Third Chamber)
16 April 2015]

In national judgments, the same function is performed by the complex term *Wyrok w imieniu Rzeczypospolitej Polskiej* [Judgment in the name of the Republic of Poland].

(9) SN (I CSK 156/14): *Sygn. Akt I CSK 156/14*
***WYROK W IMIENIU RZECZYPOSPOLITEJ POLSKIEJ***
*Dnia 12 marca 2015 r.*
*Sąd Najwyższy w składzie:* [...].
[Ref. Act I CSK 156/14
**JUDGMENT IN THE NAME OF THE REPUBLIC OF POLAND**
March 12, 2015
The Supreme Court in a panel of: [...].]

The complex terms with the node as a head term and collocates of the node *wyrok* [judgment], identified with the Collocates functionality of WS, show the variety of uses of the node. These uses include referring to individual parts of judgments (e.g. *uzasadnienie wyroku* [justification of the judgment] and *sentencja wyroku* [operative part of the judgment]), or certain aspects of procedural law (e.g. *uchylenie zaskarżonego wyroku* [annulment of the contested decision]).

**CJ:** *zaskarżony wyrok* [annulment under appeal] (62), *wyrok w sprawach połączonych* [annulment in Joined Cases] (45) [107]
**GC:** *wyrok w sprawach połączonych* [annulment in Joined Cases] (125) [125]
**SN_2011–2015:** *Wyrok w imieniu Rzeczypospolitej Polskiej* [Judgment in the name of the Republic of Poland] (387), *uchylenie zaskarżonego wyroku** [annullment of the contested decision] (212), *uzasadnienie wyroku* [justification of the annulment] (83), *uchylenie wyroku* [annullment of a annulment] (55), *podstawa zaskarżonego wyroku* [basis of the contested annulment] (41), *sentencja wyroku* [operative part of the annulment] (35), *uzasadnienie wyroku Sądu Najwyższego* [justification of the Supreme Court annulment] (31), *wyrok reformatoryjny* [altering annulment] (10) [854]
**SN_1999:** *uchylenie zaskarżonego wyroku* [annulment of the contested decision] (295), *sentencja wyroku* [operative part of the judgment] (107), *uzasadnienie wyroku* [justification of the judgment] (87), *podstawa zaskarżonego wyroku* [basis of the contested judgment] (77), *wydanie zaskarżonego wyroku* [delivery of the contested judgment] (67), *podstawa wydania zaskarżonego wyroku* [basis of the delivery of the contested judgment]

(54), *wydanie wyroku* [delivery of the judgment] (50), *uchylenie wyroku* [annulment of the judgment] (44), *zmiana wyroku* [variation of the judgment] (42) [823]

As opposed to complex terms identified solely with TermoPL (see Table 9.11), application of the Collocates functionality led to the identification of a wider range of complex terms and collocates of the node *wyrok* [judgment]. In this case, SN judgments also exhibit a higher number of both types and tokens. There is no overlap between both EU corpora and the post-accession SN corpus, which further strengthens the impression of a very low degree of conceptual fit in the case of *wyrok*-based terms and their collocates.

**2. *Prawo* [law] (CJ: 4,084 NF; GC: 3,007 NF; SN_2011–2015: 4,642 NF; SN_1999: 4,189 NF)**

As evidenced by the WSJP dictionary definition, *prawo* [law] evokes a number of concepts. These are related generally to the functioning of an individual in society (principles of community life), their educational and scientific activities, and the products of human intellectual activities. The concepts most frequently evoked by this term in judicial language are:

1. general legal provisions – all provisions in force in a country or community, established by persons or institutions authorized to do so, referring to the principles of proper conduct, the violation of which is subject to punishment,
2. rule of conduct – the rule of conduct in force in some social group or community (principle of community life)

This is confirmed by a handful of 4–grams containing this node term — SN_2011–2015: *prawa materialnego tj art*, SN_1999: *zarzutu naruszenia prawa materialnego, spółdzielcze prawo do lokalu.* No 4–grams containing this term were extracted from the Eurolect corpora.

In general language, there are also other concepts evoked by these terms:

1. discipline of knowledge – a discipline of knowledge, the subject of which is the general provisions in force in a country or community, established by authorized persons or institutions, referring to the principles of proper conduct, the violation of which is subject to punishment,
2. field of study – a field of study at a university devoted to law as a discipline of knowledge,
3. law faculty – an administratively separate university unit in which law-related courses are taught,
4. Opportunity – a specific type of opportunity that someone is entitled to in accordance with applicable regulations or rules adopted in some community or results from the consequences of events,
5. scientific – natural regularity governing some processes or phenomena.

The second term node for *prawo* [law] is by far the most productive as regards the total number of types of complex terms generated with it as a head term from all node terms presented in this conceptual category. There is an abundance of complex terms built around this node term in both EU judgments (CJ – 17 types, GC – 14 types) and in the national corpora (17 and 13 types, respectively) (see Table 9.12).

On the whole, complex terms with the node *prawo* [law] are almost equally distributed in CJ and post-accession SN judgments; distribution in GC judgments is lower in comparison to post-accession SN judgments (see Table 9.12). In general, complex terms with the node *prawo* as a head term refer to various concepts of EU and domestic substantive law, e.g. *prawo podstawowe* [fundamental right], *prawo Unii* [European Union law], *prawo własności* [right of ownership], *prawo użytkowania wieczystego* [right of perpetual usufruct], as well as case-law and its interpretation, e.g. *orzecznictwo Europejskiego Trybunału Praw Człowieka* [case-law of the European Court of Human Rights], and *wykładnia prawa* [interpretation of the law]. There is a very low degree of overlap between the EU corpora and the national corpus. CJ and post-accession SN judgments share the following terms: *przepis prawa* [provision of law] and *prawo człowieka* [human right], while GC judgments and post-accession SN judgments share only the term *przepis prawa* [provision of law]. The highest degree of overlap was established in the case of both national corpora, which share a total of 7 complex terms: *prawo materialne* [substantive law], *przepis prawa* [provision of law], *prawo własności* [right of ownership], *prawo bankowe* [banking law], *prawo spółdzielcze* [co-operative law], *moc prawa* [binding law], and *prawo wieczystego użytkowania* [right of perpetual usufruct]. The fact that post-accession CJEU and SN judgments share only two types of complex terms, *przepis prawa* [provision of law] and *prawo człowieka* [human right], indicates, yet again, the low overall conceptual fit. Where the EU judgments refer to the EU legal system and the legal systems of the individual Member States, e.g. *prawo Unii* [European Union law], *prawo niemieckie* [German law] and *prawo francuskie* [French law], national judgments refer frequently to the individual branches of Polish law, e.g. *prawo cywilne* [civil law] and *prawo rzeczowe* [property law].

The complex terms with *prawo* as a head term indicate that the national court does not attach much importance to EU law by not referring to its provisions. EU courts, on the other hand, stress the divide between the EU and national law with frequent use of the metadiscursive terms *prawo Unii* [European Union law] and *prawo krajowe* [national law]. When adjudicating in individual cases, EU judges provide the exact legal context and state the provisions of related acts of primary and secondary EU law and national law, as in:

(10) CJ (C-34/10): *Ramy prawne*
*[...]*
***Prawo Unii***
*W preambule dyrektywy wskazano:*

**Table 9.12.** *Complex terms related to substantive law and case-law with the head term prawo [law]*

| Translated EU case law | | | | | | |
|---|---|---|---|---|---|---|
| CJ | | CJ vs GC (%DIFF) | CJ vs SN_2011–2015 (%DIFF) | GC | | GC vs SN_2011–2015 (%DIFF) |
| ***prawo Unii*** **[European Union law]** | 572 | +312 % | - | ***prawo podstawowe*** **[fundamental right]** | 169 | - |
| ***prawo krajowe*** **[national law]** | 342 | +660 % | - | ***prawo Unii*** **[European Union law]** | 139 | - |
| *prawo pobytu* [residence right] | 174 | - | - | *prawo własności* [right of ownership] | 120 | - |
| ***prawo podstawowe*** **[fundamental right]** | 111 | −34 % | - | ***pewność prawa*** **[legal certainty]** | 114 | - |
| ***prawo autorskie*** **[copyright]** | 70 | +67 % | - | *prawo konkurencji* [competition law] | 96 | - |
| *prawo niemieckie* [German law] | 70 | - | - | *zasada pewności prawa* [principle of legal certainty] | 63 | - |
| ***pewność prawa*** **[legal certainty]** | 68 | −40 % | - | *prawo głosu* [voting right] | 57 | - |
| ***przepis prawa**** **[provision of law]** | 43 | −12 % | −74 % | ***przepis prawa**** **[legal provision]** | 49 | −71 % |
| *prawo podstawowe Unii Europejskiej* [EU fundamental right] | 43 | - | - | ***prawo krajowe*** **[national law]** | 45 | - |

| | | | | | | |
|---|---|---|---|---|---|---|
| *prawo człowieka**<br>[human right] | 41 | - | −20 % | *nieograniczone prawo orzekania*<br>[unlimited jurisdiction] | 45 | - |
| *prawo międzynarodowe*<br>[international law] | 35 | - | - | ***prawo autorskie***<br>**[copyright]** | 42 | - |
| *wtórne prawo Unii Europejskiej*<br>[secondary law of the European Union] | 23 | - | - | *prawo dostępu*<br>[access right] | 37 | - |
| ***ogólna zasada prawa Unii***<br>**[general principle of Union law]** | 21 | −32 % | - | ***ogólna zasada prawa Unii***<br>**[general principle of Union law]** | 31 | - |
| *prawo powszechne*<br>[ordinary law] | 14 | - | - | *prawo weta*<br>[right of veto] | 16 | - |
| *prawo patentowe*<br>[patent law] | 12 | - | - | | | |
| *prawo francuskie*<br>[French law] | 12 | - | - | | | |
| *prawo austriackie*<br>[Austrian law] | 10 | - | - | | | |

(*continued on next page*)

**Table 9.12.** *Continued*

| | | | | | | |
|---|---|---|---|---|---|---|
| **Total (17 types)**<br>**CJ vs GC overlapping types: 7**<br>**CJ vs SN_2011–2015 overlapping types: 2** | **1,661** | +62 % | +2 % | **Total (14 types)**<br>**GC vs SN_2011–2015 overlapping types: 1** | **1,023** | –37 % |

| **Non–translated PL case law** | | | | |
|---|---|---|---|---|
| **SN_2011–2015** | | **SN_2011–2015 vs SN_1999 (%DIFF)** | **SN_1999** | |
| *prawo materialne*<br>[substantive law] | 425 | –65 % | *prawo materialne*<br>[substantive law] | 1225 |
| *przepis prawa**<br>[provision of law] | 167 | +45 % | *przepis prawa*<br>[provision of law] | 115 |
| *prawo własności*<br>[right of ownership] | 142 | +38 % | *prawo własności*<br>[right of ownership] | 103 |
| *prawo autorskie*<br>[copyright] | 98 | - | *prawo bankowe*<br>[banking law] | 103 |
| *prawo użytkowania wieczystego*<br>[right of perpetual usufruct] | 98 | - | *prawo lokalowe*<br>[housing law] | 71 |
| *prawo własności czasowej*<br>[right of temporary ownership] | 83 | - | *spółdzielcze prawo do lokalu*<br>[co-operative right to premises] | 69 |
| *wykładnia prawa*<br>[interpretation of the law] | 81 | - | *moc prawa*<br>[force of law] | 69 |
| *prawo bankowe*<br>[banking law] | 81 | –21 % | *prawo procesowe*<br>[procedural law] | 63 |

| | | | | |
|---|---|---|---|---|
| *prawo cywilne*<br>[civil law] | 73 | - | *prawo użytkowania*<br>[right of use] | 52 |
| *prawo prasowe*<br>[press law] | 63 | - | *prawo upadłościowe*<br>[bankruptcy law] | 48 |
| *prawo spółdzielcze*<br>[co-operative law] | 57 | +68 % | *prawo spółdzielcze*<br>[co-operative law] | 34 |
| *prawo rzeczowe*<br>[property law] | 57 | - | *własnościowe prawo do lokalu*<br>[co-operative ownership right to premises] | 30 |
| *moc prawa*<br>[binding law] | 53 | −23 % | *prawo wieczystego użytkowania*<br>[right of perpetual usufruct] | 24 |
| *prawo podmiotowe*<br>[individual right] | 51 | - | | |
| *prawo człowieka**<br>[human right] | 51 | - | | |
| *prawo wodne*<br>[law on water] | 22 | - | | |
| *prawo wieczystego użytkowania*<br>[right of perpetual usufruct] | 22 | −8 % | | |
| **Total (17 types)<br>SN_2011–2015 vs SN_1999<br>overlapping types: 7** | **1,624** | **−19 %** | **Total (13 types)** | **2,006** |

> *[...]*
> ***Prawo krajowe***
> *Paragraf 2 Patentgesetz (ustawy o patentach), w brzmieniu zmienionym w celu transpozycji art. 6 dyrektywy (BGBl. 2005 I, s. 2521, zwanej dalej "PatG"), ma następujące brzmienie:* [...].
> [Legal context
> [...]
> **European Union legislation**
> The preamble to the Directive states as follows:
> [...]
> **National law**
> Paragraph 2 of the Patentgesetz (Law on patents), as amended for the purposes of transposition of Article 6 of the Directive (BGBl. 2005 I, p. 2521; 'the PatG'), is worded as follows: [...].]

The collocates of the node term *prawo* [law] and other complex terms with that term as a head term, which were additionally extracted with WS, can be examined below.

**CJ:** *naruszenie prawa** [infringement of a right] (129), *przepis prawa krajowego* [provision of national law] (123), *przepis prawa Unii* [provision of Union law] (78), *Karta praw podstawowych Unii Europejskiej* [Charter of Fundamental Rights] (37), *ochrona praw człowieka* [protection of human rights] (23), *wyłączne prawo* [exclusive right] (14) [404]
**GC:** *naruszenie prawa** [infringement of a right] (153), *unieważnienie prawa* [annulment of a right] (49), *przepis prawa Unii* [provision of Union law] (37), *podział prawa własności* [division of ownership right] (35), *Karta praw podstawowych Unii Europejskiej* [Charter of Fundamental Rights] (24), *ochrona praw człowieka* [protection of human rights] (18), *nieograniczone prawo orzekania* [unlimited jurisdiction] (18), *orzecznictwo Europejskiego Trybunału Praw Człowieka* [case-law of the European Court of Human Rights] (14) [348]
**SN_2011–2015:** *naruszenie prawa** [violation of law] (159), *przepis prawa materialnego* [provision of substantive law] (65), *zarzut naruszenia prawa materialnego* [allegation of a violation of substantive law] (61), *przepis prawa podatkowego* [tax law provision] (31), *podstawa naruszenia prawa materialnego* [basis of a violation of substantive law] (28), *naruszenie przepisów prawa materialnego* [violation of the provisions of substantive law] (22) [366]
**SN_1999:** *zarzut naruszenia prawa materialnego* [allegation of a violation of substantive law] (220), *przepis prawa materialnego* [provision of substantive law] (145), naruszenie prawa [violation of law] (67), *podstawa aruszenie prawa materialnego* [basis of a violation of substantive law] (55), ocena *zasadności zarzutu naruszenia prawa materialnego* [assessment of the pertinence of the infringement of substantive law] (20), *ocean trafności zarzutu naruszenia prawa materialnego* [assessment of the accuracy of the infringement of substantive law] (14) [521]

Both EU and post-accession SN judgments have a similar range of types of complex terms built around the node *prawo* [law] and its collocates identified using the Collocates functionality in WS.

(11) CJ (C-72/12): *W tym względzie należy przypomnieć, że art. 10a tej dyrektywy pozostawia państwom członkowskim znaczny zakres swobody w celu ustalenia, co stanowi* ***naruszenie prawa*** [...].
[In that regard, it should be borne in mind that Article 10a of that directive leaves the Member States significant discretion to determine what constitutes **impairment of a right** [...].]

(12) SN (I CSK 126/12): ***Naruszenie prawa materialnego*** *polega na niezastosowaniu art. 415 k.c. przez uznanie, że pozwany nie był obowiązany do naprawienia szkody wyrządzonej powodowi* [...].
[The **violation of substantive law consists** in not applying Article 415 of the Polish Civil Code by recognizing that the defendant was not obliged to repair the damage incurred by the claimant [...].]

The excerpts show that the respective courts in both legal systems pay particular attention to violations of law, as evidenced by the frequent use of such complex terms as *naruszenie prawa* [infringement of a right] and *naruszenie prawa materialnego* [violation of substantive law].

**3. *Decyzja* [decision] (CJ: 2,623 NF; GC: 7,971 NF; SN_2011–2015: 1,943 NF; SN_1999: 491 NF)**

In general, the node term *decyzja* [decision] presents the concept of a decision made after reflection (WSJP – entry *decyzja*). This concept is related to the products of human intellectual activities. The WSJP dictionary definition fails to mention the concept of a judicial or administrative determination which follows consideration of the facts of a given case and the law (Garner 2009: 467). The 4-grams extracted from the corpora show that judicial language makes use primarily of the second concepts: CJ: *generalnego decyzję o rozstrzygnięciu*, GC: *stwierdzenia nieważności zaskarżonej decyzji, w zaskarżonej decyzji Komisja, zaskarżonej decyzji wynika że, zwaną dalej zaskarżoną decyzją.* No 4-grams containing this node term were extracted from the national corpora.

Complex terms containing the head term *decyzja* [decision] and extracted with TermoPL refer to written decisions adopted by either the EU or national institutions, e.g. *decyzja ramowa* [framework decision], *decyzja Komisji* [Commission decision], *decyzja podatkowa* [tax notice], and *decyzja administracyjna* [administrative decision]. Compared to post-accession SN judgments, EU judgments, CJ judgments in particular, are characterized by underrepresentation in terms of both the total number of types and their tokens (see Table 9.13).

**Table 9.13.** *Complex terms related to substantive law and case-law with the head term decyzja [decision]*

| Translated EU case law | | | | | | |
|---|---|---|---|---|---|---|
| **CJ** | | **CJ vs GC (%DIFF)** | **CJ vs SN_2011–2015 (%DIFF)** | **GC** | | **GC vs SN_2011–2015 (%DIFF)** |
| *decyzja ramowa*<br>[framework decision] | 129 | - | - | ***decyzja Komisji***<br>**[Commission Decision]** | 143 | - |
| ***decyzja Rady***<br>**[Council decision]** | 55 | −53 % | - | ***decyzja Rady***<br>**[Council decision]** | 116 | - |
| ***decyzja Komisji***<br>**[Commission Decision]** | 33 | −77 % | - | *decyzja wstępna*<br>[initial decision] | 39 | - |
| | | | | *decyzja podatkowa*<br>[tax notice] | 33 | - |
| | | | | *decyzja Izby Odwoławczej*<br>[decision of the Board of Appeal] | 31 | - |
| **Total (3 types)**<br>**CJ vs GC overlapping types: 2**<br>**CJ vs SN_2011–2015 overlapping types: 0** | **217** | **−40 %** | **−58 %** | **Total (5 types)**<br>**GC vs SN_2011–2015 overlapping types: 0** | **362** | **−29 %** |

| Non-translated PL case law | | | | |
|---|---|---|---|---|
| SN_2011–2015 | | SN_2011–2015 vs SN_1999 (%DIFF) | SN_1999 | |
| *decyzja administracyjna* [administrative decision] | 263 | +183 % | *decyzja administracyjna* [administrative decision] | 93 |
| *decyzja nadzorcza* [supervisory decision] | 122 | - | | |
| *nieważność decyzji* [invalidity of a decision] | 41 | - | | |
| *wadliwa decyzja administracyjna* [faulty administrative decision] | 41 | - | | |
| *ostateczna decyzja administracyjna* [final administrative decision] | 26 | - | | |
| *decyzja Samorządowego Kolegium Odwoławczego* [decision of the local government appeals board] | 18 | - | | |
| **Total (6 types) SN_2011–2015 vs SN_1999 overlapping types: 1** | **511** | **+449 %** | **Total (1 type)** | **93** |

As regards the degree of overlap between the EU corpora and the post-accession SN corpus, none of the complex terms appear in both EU and national judgments, suggesting no conceptual overlap. *Decyzja administracyjna* [administrative decision] is the only term which appears in both national corpora and refers to decisions adopted by administrative bodies as opposed to courts. The complex terms extracted from the Eurolect corpora, *decyzja Rady* [Council decision] and *decyzja Komisji* [Commission Decision], show that both CJEU courts refer quite frequently to either non-legislative or legislative acts of the Council and the Commission.

The collocational range of *decyzja* [decision] is broad in both EU corpora, in particular in GC judgments, and in the post-accession SN corpus. The Collocates functionality in WS did not identify any complex terms or collocates of the node in the pre-accession SN corpus (see Table 9.13).

**CJ:** ***zaskarżona decyzja* [contested decision]** (263), *sporna decyzja* [contested decision] (84), *stwierdzenie nieważności spornej decyzji* [annulment of the contested decision] (59), *wydanie decyzji** [adoption of a decision] (43), *podjęcie decyzji* [adoption of a decision] (35), ***stwierdzenie nieważności decyzji** [annulment of a decision]** (35) [519]
**GC:** *zaskarżona decyzja* [contested decision] (437), *stwierdzenie nieważności zaskarżonej decyzji* [annulment of a contested decision] (186), *wydanie zaskarżonej decyzji* [adoption of a contested decision] (122), *stwierdzenie nieważności decyzji** [annulment of a decision] (112), *nieważność zaskarżonej decyzji* [annulment of the contested decision] (63), *zmieniona wersja decyzji* [amended version of a decision] (61), *sentencja zaskarżonej decyzji* [operative part of the contested decision] (47), *uzasadnienie zaskarżonej decyzji* [justification of the contested decision] (35), *zmiana zaskarżonej decyzji* [amendment of the contested decision] (33), *treść zaskarżonej decyzji* [content of the contested decision] (31), *decyzja związków przedsiębiorstwo* [decisions of associations of undertakings] (27), *początkowa decyzja* [first decision] (12), *stwierdzenie częściowej nieważności decyzji* [partial annulment of the decision] (12), *stwierdzenie nieważności części zaskarżonej decyzji* [annulment of a part of the contested decision] (12), *ostateczna decyzja* [initial decision] (10), [1200]
**SN_2011–2015:** *wydanie decyzji** [adoption of a decision] (104), *stwierdzenie nieważności decyzji** [annulment of a decision] (47), *wydanie wadliwej decyzji* [adoption of a faulty decision] (24), *decyzja zatwierdzająca* [approval decision] (12), *decyzja stwierdzająca nieważność decyzji* [decision confirming the invalidity of the decision] (10) [197]
**SN_1999:** *none*

The above complex terms and collocates of the node term *decyzja* [decision] refer primarily to various issues of legal or administrative procedure connected with adopting or annulling decisions, e.g. *wydanie decyzji administracyjnej* [adoption of an administrative decision], *stwierdzenie nieważności decyzji* [annulment of a decision], *wadliwa decyzja administracyjna* [faulty administrative decision], or *praktyka decyzyjna* [practice in previous decisions]. Some complex terms are also used by the courts to indicate specific decisions – *zaskarżona decyzja* [contested decision]. There are only three types of complex terms extracted from the corpora with WS which overlap between the Eurolect and post-accession SN judgments – *zaskarżona decyzja* [contested decision], *stwierdzenie nieważności decyzji* [annulment of a decision], and *wydanie decyzji* [adoption of a decision]. Considering the total number of types of complex and phrasal terms and their collocates, the overall degree of conceptual fit as regards the present node term between the Eurolect and national judgments is quite low.

**4. *Wniosek* [application] (CJ: 1,770 NF; GC: 1,833 NF; SN_2011–2015: 1,636 NF; SN_1999: 1,225 NF)**

According to the WSJP dictionary, the node term *wniosek* [application] evokes two concepts, both of which are used in judicial language:

1. logic – reasoning result
2. application – an official request or proposal to consider and decide (cf. Garner 2009: 115).

There is only one type of 4–gram which has been extracted from the corpus of CJ judgments and which contains this node term: *wniosku o udzielenie azylu*. This bundle type refers to EU immigration policy. The refined lists of 4–grams extracted from the national corpora contain no bundles with this node term.

Based on the list of complex terms extracted with TermoPL, it can be concluded that the node term *wniosek* [application] is not as conducive to the formation of complex terms as the previously presented nodes belonging to the category of substantive law and case-law node terms. Complex terms with this node as a head term refer to evidence-related procedural applications, e.g. *wniosek dowodowy* [request for evidence], or to applications for cassation proceedings to be opened by the SN, *wniosek kasacyjny* [cassation] (see Table 9.14).

Overall, complex terms with the present node extracted from the lists of candidate terms generated by TermoPL are underrepresented in EU judgments. The term *wniosek dowodowy* [request for evidence] appears in both EU and pre- and post-accession SN judgments, suggesting a certain degree of conceptual overlap.

The use of the Collocates functionality allowed for determination of the collocational range of the node *wniosek* [application], which seems to display little conceptual fit between EU and national judgments:

**CJ:** *wniosek o wydanie orzeczenia w trybie prejudycjalnym* [reference for a preliminary ruling] (144), ***złożenie wniosku* [submission of an application]** (78), *wniosek o udzielenie azylu* [application for asylum] (14), *wniosek o przyznanie statusu uchodźcy* [application for refugee status] (10) [246]

**GC: *złożenie wniosku* [submission of an application]** (76), *wniosek potwierdzający* [confirmatory application] (41), *przedmiot wniosku* [subject-matter of an application] (33), *wniosek o stwierdzenie nieważności* [application for annulment] (29), *wniosek o*

**Table 9.14.** *Complex terms related to substantive law and case-law with the head term wniosek [application]*

| Translated EU case law | | | | | | |
|---|---|---|---|---|---|---|
| **CJ** | | **CJ vs GC (%DIFF)** | **CJ vs SN_2011–2015 (%DIFF)** | **GC** | | **GC vs SN_2011–2015 (%DIFF)** |
| --- | --- | --- | --- | *wniosek dowodowy** [request for evidence] | 43 | −59 % |
| **Total (0 types) CJ vs GC overlapping types: 0 CJ vs SN_2011–2015 overlapping types: 0** | --- | --- | --- | **Total (1 type) GC vs SN_2011–2015 overlapping types: 1** | **43** | **−59 %** |

| Non-translated PL case law | | | | |
|---|---|---|---|---|
| **SN_2011–2015** | | **SN_2011–2015 vs SN_1999 (%DIFF)** | **SN_1999** | |
| *wniosek dowodowy** [request for evidence] | 106 | +7 % | *wniosek dowodowy* [request for evidence] | 99 |
| | | | *wniosek kasacyjny* [cassation] | 38 |
| **Total (1 type) SN_2011–2015 vs SN_1999 overlapping types: 1** | **106** | **−23 %** | **Total (2 types)** | **137** |

*stwierdzenie częściowej nieważności* [application for partial annulment] (27), *wniosek o udzielenie zezwolenia* [application for annulment] (20), *wniosek o unieważnienie* [application for annulment] (12), *wniosek o zwolnienie z grzywny* [application for immunity from fines] (10) [248]

**SN_2011–2015:** *niezłożenie wniosku* [failure to submit the application] (136), *wniosek o ponowne rozpatrzenie sprawy* [request for re-examination] (26), *wniosek strony* [request of one of the parties] (16), *wniosek powódki* [claimant's application] (14), *wniosek użytkownika wieczystego* [perpetual user's application] (12), *wniosek powoda* [claimant's application] (12), *wniosek pozwanego* [request of the defendant] (10), *wniosek o przyznanie prawa własności czasowej* [application for the right of temporary ownership] (10), *wniosek o odszkodowanie* [application for damages] (10) [246]
**SN_1999:** *wniosek o uchylenie zaskarżonego wyroku* [application for the annulment of the contested decision] (34), *wniosek o ogłoszenie upadłości* [application to open insolvency proceedings] (12) [46]

Most of the above complex terms and collocates of the node refer to various types of applications, such as *wniosek o udzielenie azylu* [application for asylum], *wniosek o stwierdzenie częściowej nieważności* [application for partial annulment], *wniosek o przyznanie statusu uchodźcy* [application for refugee status], *wniosek o odszkodowanie* [application for damages], and issues of legal procedure connected with the submission or not of such applications, e.g. *niezłożenie wniosku* [failure to submit the application]. Several terms in the post-accession SN corpus indicate the party who submitted the application – *wniosek powódki* [claimant's application], *wniosek powoda* [claimant's application], and *wniosek pozwanego* [request of the defendant].

From the perspective of the European legal system, the most important type of specialized application is *wniosek o wydanie orzeczenia w trybie prejudycjalnym* [reference for a preliminary ruling]. Upon the submission of the reference for a preliminary ruling by a national court, the CJEU needs to interpret the EU law and determine its application in a given matter:

(13) CJ (C-5/11): ***Wniosek o wydanie orzeczenia w trybie prejudycjalnym*** *dotyczy wykładni art. 34 TFUE i 36 TFUE.*
[This **reference for a preliminary ruling** concerns the interpretation of Articles 34 TFEU and 36 TFEU.]

With the distribution of units forming the collocational range of the node term *wniosek* [application], the EU corpora, in particular CJ judgments, are marked by slight overrepresentation.

## 9.5.3 Legal procedure node terms and their environment

Legal procedure complex terms refer to various aspects of procedural law and types of proceedings before the EU and national courts, as well as administrative bodies, e.g. *postępowanie cywilne* [civil proceedings] and *postępowanie administracyjne* [administrative procedure]. This category contains the least node terms: *postępowanie* [proceedings] and *koszt* [cost].

**1. *Postępowanie* [proceedings] (CJ: 3,491 NF; GC: 3,088 NF; SN_2011–2015: 2,847 NF; SN_1999: 3,193 NF)**

The WSJP dictionary (entry – *postępowanie*) lists two concepts which the node *postępowanie* [proceedings] evokes. The first refers to the concept of a human as a psychological being and his or her character, temperament and skills, whereas the second refers to the functioning of individuals in society and aspects of legal or administrative procedure:

1. behavior – the way someone acts,
2. judicial proceedings – actions taken by justice or administration bodies.

Garner (2009: 1324) states that proceedings are, among other meanings, the regular and orderly progression of a lawsuit, including all acts and events between the time of commencement and the entry of judgment. The corpora of judgments contain 4-word bundles which are related exclusively to the second concept: CJ: *strony postępowania przed sądem, postępowanie przed sądem krajowym, uwzględniając pisemny etap postępowania, sporu w postępowaniu głównym, dla stron w postępowaniu*, GC: *regulaminu postępowania przed sądem, w toku postępowaniu administracyjnego, obciążenie skarżącej kosztami postępowania*, SN_2011–2015: *w postepowaniu przed sądem, tytułem zwrotu kosztów postępowania, orzeczenia o kosztach postępowania.*

Complex terms with the node term *postępowanie* [proceedings] as a head term refer mainly to various types of judicial procedure, e.g. *postępowanie dowodowe* [evidence proceedings] and *postępowanie apelacyjne* [appeal proceedings], and administrative proceedings, e.g. *postępowanie administracyjne* [administrative procedure] (see Table 9.15).

Complex terms with the node term *postępowanie* [proceedings] have a similar distribution in the GC corpus and the post-accession SN corpus. The CJ corpus and the pre-accession SN corpus have a two times higher distribution than the two remaining corpora. The CJ corpus exhibits a single aberration, namely the high distribution of the term *postępowanie główne* [main proceedings]. It has been observed that this is due to its inclusion in the phrase marking the generic structure of CJ judgments — *Postępowanie główne i pytania prejudycjalne* [The dispute in the main proceedings and the questions referred for a preliminary ruling] (cf. Chapter 5). As regards the degree of overlap between the corpora, *postępowanie administracyjne* [administrative procedure] is the only term shared by the CJ corpus and the post-accession SN corpus. The GC corpus and the post-accession SN corpus share a total of four terms — *postępowanie administracyjne* [administrative procedure], *postępowanie sądowe* [court proceedings], *postępowanie upadłościowe* [insolvency proceedings], and *postępowanie egzekucyjne* [enforcement procedure]. This is indicative of only a limited degree of conceptual fit between supranational and national judgments. The highest degree of overlap can be observed in the case of both national corpora, which share five *postępowanie*-based complex terms (see Table 9.15). Despite the fact that post-accession SN judgments contain four more types of complex terms than pre-accession SN judgments, it cannot be

**Table 9.15.** *Legal procedure complex terms with the head term postępowanie [proceedings] in the corpora*

| Translated EU case law | | | | | | |
|---|---|---|---|---|---|---|
| **CJ** | | **CJ vs GC (%DIFF)** | **CJ vs SN_2011–2015 (%DIFF)** | **GC** | | **GC vs SN_2011–2015 (%DIFF)** |
| ***postępowanie główne* [main proceedings]** | 945 | +2764 % | - | ***postępowanie administracyjne** [administrative procedure]** | 253 | +83 % |
| *postępowanie likwidacyjne* [winding-up proceedings] | 117 | - | - | *postępowanie sądowe** [court proceedings] | 118 | +162 % |
| ***postępowanie odwoławcze* [appeal proceedings]** | 59 | +90 % | - | *postępowanie upadłościowe** [insolvency proceedings] | 100 | +113 % |
| ***postępowanie administracyjne** [administrative procedure]** | 45 | −18 % | −67 % | *postępowanie układowe* [conciliation procedure] | 39 | - |
| *formalne postępowanie wyjaśniające* [formal investigation procedure] | 20 | - | - | *postępowanie egzekucyjne** [enforcement procedure] | 35 | −73 % |
| *postępowanie wpadkowe* [interlocutory procedure] | 10 | - | - | ***postępowanie główne* [main proceedings]** | 33 | - |
| | | | | ***postępowanie odwoławcze* [appeal proceedings]** | 31 | - |
| | | | | *postępowanie wyjaśniające* [investigation procedure] | 14 | - |
| **Total (6 types) CJ vs GC overlapping types: 3 CJ vs SN_2011–2015 overlapping types: 1** | **1,196** | **+92 %** | **+86 %** | **Total (8 types) GC vs SN_2011–2015 overlapping types: 4** | **623** | **−3 %** |

(*continued on next page*)

**Table 9.15.** *Continued*

| Non–translated PL case law | | | | |
|---|---|---|---|---|
| **SN_2011–2015** | | **SN_2011–2015/ SN_1999 (%DIFF)** | **SN_1999** | |
| *postępowanie administracyjne** [administrative procedure] | 138 | - | *postępowanie kasacyjne* [cassation proceedings] | 597 |
| *postępowanie egzekucyjne** [enforcement proceedings] | 130 | - | *postępowanie dowodowe* [evidence proceedings] | 252 |
| *postępowanie kasacyjne* [cassation proceedings] | 81 | −86 % | *postępowanie apelacyjne* [appeal proceedings] | 196 |
| *postępowanie dowodowe* [evidence proceedings] | 77 | −69 % | *postępowanie cywilne* [civil proceedings] | 129 |
| *postępowanie apelacyjne* [appeal proceedings] | 73 | −63 % | *postępowanie sądowe* [court proceedings] | 44 |
| *postępowanie upadłościowe** [insolvency proceedings] | 47 | - | | |
| *postępowanie sądowe** [court proceedings] | 45 | +2 % | | |
| *postępowanie cywilne* [civil proceedings] | 43 | −67 % | | |
| *postępowanie karne* [criminal proceedings] | 10 | - | | |
| **Total (9 types) SN_2011–2015 vs SN_1999 overlapping types: 5** | **644** | **−47 %** | **Total (5 types)** | **1,218** |

concluded that the EU has had any direct effect on the variety of types of domestic proceedings.

The collocational range of the node term *postępowanie* [proceedings] established with WS is as follows:

**CJ:** *język postępowania* [language of the case] (193), *koszty postępowania** [costs of proceedings] (172), *postępowanie ma charakter incydentalny* [the proceedings are incidental] (135), *pisemny etap postępowania* [written procedure] (113), *regulamin postępowania* [Rules of Procedure] (111), *przedmiot postępowania głównego* [subject-matter of the main proceedings] (88), *postępowanie przed sądem krajowym* [dispute in the main proceedings] (47), *formalne postępowanie* [formal procedure] (41), *przepis postępowania* [procedural provision] (35), *zasądzenie kosztów postępowania* [order for costs of the proceedings] (26), *postępowanie przed Trybunałem* [proceedings before the Court] (27), *postępowanie poprzedzające wniesienie skargi* [pre-litigation procedure] (21), *postępowanie przed Sądem* [main proceedings] (21) [1030]
**GC:** *koszty postępowania** [costs of proceedings] (337), *regulamin postępowania* [Rules of Procedure] (314), *język postępowania* [language of the case] (100), *przebieg postępowania* [proceedings] (88), *pisemny etap postępowania* [written procedure] (51), *wszczęcie postępowania* [opening of proceedings] (51), *ustny etap postępowania* [oral procedure] (37), *postępowanie w sprawie identyfikacji* [identification proceedings] (22), *postępowanie w sprawie sprzeciwu* [opposition proceedings] (20), *wyrok kończący postępowanie* [final procedure] (18) [1038]
**SN_2011–2015:** *koszty postępowania** [costs of court proceedings] (816), *wznowienie postępowania* [reopening of the procedure] (69), *nieważność postępowania* [invalidity of the proceedings] (57), *postępowanie przed sądem* [court proceedings] (14) [956]
**SN_1999:** *koszty postępowania kasacyjnego* [costs of cassation proceedings] (484), *naruszenie przepisów postępowania* [infringement of procedural law] (240), *Kodeks Postępowania Cywilnego* [Code of Civil Procedure] (117), *nieważność postępowania* [invalidity of the proceedings] (83), *zarzut naruszenia przepisów postępowania* [allegation of infringement of procedural provisions] (73), *zmiana Kodeksu Postępowania Cywilnego* [reform of the Code of Civil Procedure] (44), *podstawa naruszenia przepisów postępowania* [basis of the infringement of the procedural provisions] (42), *przeprowadzenie postępowania dowodowego* [conducting evidence proceedings] (34), *postępowanie przed sądem* [court proceedings] (18) [1135]

Complex terms and collocates of the node presented above provide a wide range of references to, for instance, the language of the case (*język postępowania* [language of the case]), court costs (*koszty postępowania* [costs of court proceedings] and *koszty postępowania kasacyjnego* [costs of cassation proceedings]) and stages of the proceedings (*wszczęcie postępowania* [opening of proceedings] and *wznowienie postępowania* [reopening of the procedure]). Post-accession SN judgments and the Eurolect corpora share only two types of complex terms: *koszty postępowania** [costs of court proceedings] and *postępowanie przed sądem* [court proceedings]. This further confirms the low degree of conceptual fit. Overall, complex terms with the node term *postępowanie* [proceedings] express more highly specialized concepts than the node by itself.

**2. *Koszt* [cost] (CJ: 1,249 NF; GC: 1,506 NF; SN_2011–2015: 1,789 NF; SN_1999: 1,774 NF)**

The second and last node term from the semantic field of legal procedure node terms evokes the concept of a certain amount of money spent on buying or paying for something (WSJP entry – *koszt*). The post-accession corpora contain several 4-grams with this node term: CJ: *kosztami zostaje obciążona na, należy rozstrzygnięcie o kosztach*, GC: *obciążenie skarżącej/Komisji kosztami postępowania*, SN_2011–2015: *tytułem zwrotu kosztów postępowania, orzekł o kosztach procesu, o kosztach postępowania kasacyjnego.*

Complex terms with the node *koszt* [cost] as a head term refer predominantly to the costs incurred by the parties as a result of the judicial proceedings before the EU courts and the SN, e.g. *koszty postępowania* [costs of the proceedings] and *koszt zastępstwa procesowego* [cost of lawyers' fees] (see Table 9.16).

The data show that complex terms with the node *koszty* [costs] are more varied in the national corpora, in which, in addition, there are three overlapping terms, *koszty postępowania kasacyjnego* [costs of cassation proceedings], *koszty procesu* [costs of proceedings], and *koszty postępowania apelacyjnego* [costs of appeal proceedings]. Both EU corpora share a single term with the post-accession SN corpus, *koszty postępowania* [costs of the proceedings], which is the only term individuating the limited conceptual fit of complex terms structured around the present node term. This complex term may be regarded as a genre-marker, owing to its presence in judgments from two separate legal systems:

(14) CJ (C-63/12):

*Z powyższych względów Trybunał (wielka izba) orzeka, co następuje:*
*1) [...]*
*2) Komisja Europejska zostaje obciążona* ***kosztami postępowania.***
[On those grounds, the Court (Grand Chamber) hereby:
1. Dismisses the action;
2. Orders the European Commission to pay **the costs**;]

(15) SN (I CSK 197/13):

*Sąd Najwyższy w składzie:*
*[...]*
*oddala skargę kasacyjną i nie obciąża powoda* ***kosztami postępowania*** *kasacyjnego*
[The Supreme Court in a panel of:
[...]
dismisses the cassation complaint and does not charge the claimant with the **costs of cassation proceedings**]

**Table 9.16.** *Legal procedure complex terms with the head term koszty [costs]*

| Translated EU case law | | | | | | |
|---|---|---|---|---|---|---|
| **CJ** | | **CJ vs GC (%DIFF)** | **CJ vs SN_2011–2015 (%DIFF)** | **GC** | | **GC vs SN_2011–2015 (%DIFF)** |
| ***koszty postępowania****<br>**[costs of the proceedings]** | 172 | –49 % | –79 % | ***koszty postępowania****<br>**[costs of proceedings]** | 337 | –59 % |
| **Total (1 type)<br>CJ/GC overlapping types: 1<br>CJ/SN_2011–2015 overlapping types: 1** | **172** | **–49 %** | **–90 %** | **Total (1 type)<br>GC/SN_2011–2015 overlapping types: 1** | **337** | **–80 %** |
| **Non-translated PL case law** | | | | | | |
| **SN_2011–2015** | | **SN_2011–2015 vs SN_1999 (%DIFF)** | | **SN_1999** | | |
| *koszty postępowania**<br>[costs of court proceedings] | 816 | | - | *koszty postępowania kasacyjnego*<br>[costs of cassation proceedings] | | 484 |
| *koszty postępowania kasacyjnego*<br>[costs of cassation proceedings] | 448 | | –7 % | *koszty procesu*<br>[costs of proceedings] | | 353 |
| *koszty procesu*<br>[costs of proceedings] | 262 | | –26 % | *koszty postępowania*<br>[costs of court proceedings] | | 137 |
| *koszty postępowania apelacyjnego*<br>[costs of appeal proceedings] | 81 | | +189 % | *koszty sądowe*<br>[judicial costs] | | 40 |
| *koszty zastępstwa procesowego*<br>[costs of lawyers' fees] | 49 | | - | *koszty postępowania apelacyjnego*<br>[costs of appeal proceedings] | | 28 |
| **Total (5 types)<br>SN_2011–2015 vs SN_1999 overlapping types: 3** | **1,656** | | **+59 %** | **Total (5 types)** | | **1,042** |

Overall, complex terms with the node term *koszt* [cost] which were extracted solely with TermoPL are underrepresented in translated EU judgments, as regards both the total number of types and tokens.

The collocational range of the node term *koszty* [costs] established with the Collocates functionality in WS shows a higher degree of convergence, in particular, between CJ and post-accession SN judgments.

**CJ:** *własne koszty* [own costs] (197), *pokrycie kosztów utrzymania* [coverage of maintenance costs] (21) [218]
**GC:** *koszty personelu* [labour costs] (45) [45]
**SN_2011–2015:** *koszty budowy* [construction costs] (163), *zasądzenie kosztów postępowania* [order for costs of the proceedings] (26) [189]
**SN_1999:** *zwrot kosztów* [recovery of costs]_(46), *zasądzenie kosztów procesu* [order for costs of the proceedings] (24), *koszty budowy* [construction costs] (12) [82]

There are several complex terms which refer to other types of costs incurred outside of the legal proceedings which are strictly connected with their subject-matter, e.g. *koszt budowy* [construction costs], *koszty personelu* [labor costs] and *pokrycie kosztów utrzymania* [coverage of maintenance costs], which further strengthens the impression of a low degree of conceptual overlap between supranational and national judgments.

## 9.6 Conclusions

The methodology applied in the present study enabled the identification of a wide range of law-related terms and the measurement of the approximate degree of terminological overlap between the CJEU and national corpora. The application of TermoPL, a tool facilitating automatized extraction of candidate simple and complex terms, has proven itself useful in automatically generating lists of candidate terms based on genre-restricted comparable corpora. It should be noted, however, that the lists of candidate terms generated by this tool required manual refinement, in order to eliminate wrongly extracted terms. Subsequently, the refined lists of simple and complex terms generated by TermoPL were used to analyze the distribution of the most frequently occurring terms in the corpora of CJ and GC judgments, as well as pre- and post-accession SN judgments. Based on the total number of types and tokens of simple and complex terms in the EU and SN corpora following the refinement stage and the analysis of the top 30 simple and top 15 complex terms, it was concluded that the terminological profiles of CJEU and SN judgments are indeed divergent. The analysis of the top 30 simple terms led to the identification of a small, manageable set of 10–node simple terms occurring simultaneously in both corpora of CJEU judgments and the corpus of post-accession SN judgments. These terms presented an interesting starting point for further manual analysis using the Collocates functionality in WS, which allowed for the verification of their collocational environment through the extraction of complex terms with the nodes acting as head terms and collocates of the nodes, thus amply

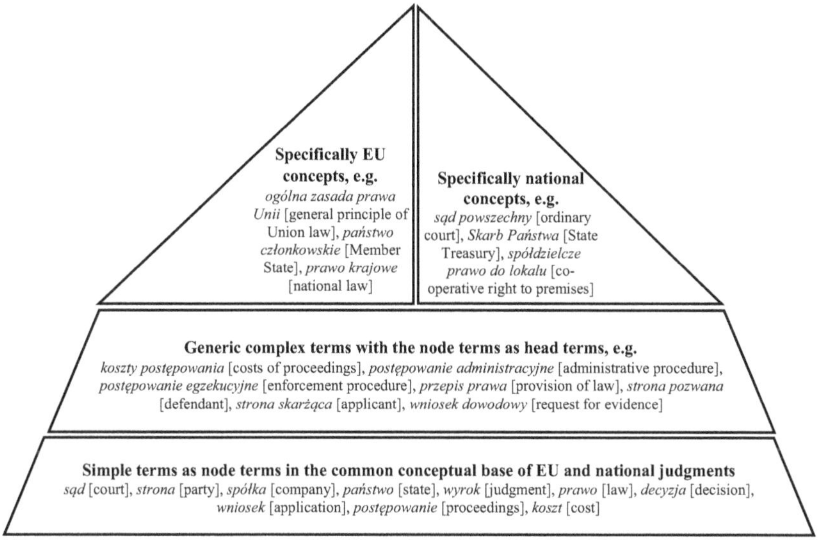


**Figure 9.1.** *Common conceptual base of supranational and national judgments and its further specialization at the level of complex terms*

supplementing the lists of terms previously identified with TermoPL. The procedure has shown that supranational and national judgments share a common conceptual base structured around the key (node) simple terms (see Figure 9.1).

The analysis of the most frequent simple and, in particular, complex terms proved that EU and national judgments differ in terms of the most frequently evoked law-related concepts as shown by the distributional divergences and low degree of overlap. The comparison of the degree of terminological overlap between both EU corpora and between the EU corpora and the corpus of post-accession SN judgments showed that supranational judgments have a considerably dissimilar conceptual spectrum compared to national judgments. The differences are indicative of the fact that supranational and national judgments are passed in two related but different legal systems, which emphasize different substantive and procedural aspects of the adjudication process. The differences can also be traced back to the historical development of both legal systems.

Nevertheless, there are certain simple terms which appear across all EU and national post-accession corpora, while being among the top 30 simple terms in each of them.[191] These are perceived to be crucial to the genre as a whole and were

191 The total number of simple terms which appear in both EU corpora and the post-accession SN corpus is 85 terms (see Section 9.3); however, due to space constraints, only the most salient terms were analyzed further.

labeled as node terms owing to the fact that they occupy central points in the three identified semantic fields forming the wider conceptual system (knowledge structure) of judicial language. In fact, these node terms act as points of access to concepts which allow for the activation of relevant background knowledge (cf. Biel 2008: 23). By belonging to both the national and supranational conceptual system, they are, in a way, bi-jural and not entirely system- and culture-bound (cf. Section 9.5):

(1) agents and institutions (*sąd* [court], *strona* [party], *spółka* [company], *państwo* [state]),
(2) substantive law and case-law (*wyrok* [judgment], *prawo* [law], *decyzja* [decision], *wniosek* [application]),
(3) legal procedure (*postępowanie* [proceedings], *koszt* [cost]).

These node terms may be regarded as expressing key concepts which form the conceptual foundations and "aboutness" of the genre of judgments (cf. Biel *et al.* 2018a: 261). These simple terms are very productive in that they are used as head terms to create a whole array of complex terms which generally have more specialized conceptual load compared to simple terms and typically involve either an adjective and a noun (or vice versa), or two nouns, depending on the length. The complex terms created with the node terms acting as head terms can be divided into three groups: generic complex terms which are shared by the supranational and the national legal system (which are in preponderance), specifically EU-related terms, and specifically national terms (see Figure 9.1). Complex terms belonging to all three categories express highly specialized concepts with a high degree of terminologicality, which may be inaccessible to a non-expert audience. This, in turn, may be the reason for the common perception of legal (and thus also judicial) texts as highly "technical." Terms expressing concepts strictly related to either the supranational or national context, in particular proper names of various types of courts, may also be the cause of translational difficulties, due to the incongruity of the respective legal systems.

The higher distribution of both simple and complex terms in national judgments might be suggestive of higher complexity when compared to EU judgments. As a consequence, this confirms the widely held view that content knowledge of law and legal language is a pre-requisite for the proper understanding of the subject matter of judgments; this, however, is not limited to national judgments, but also applies to supranational judgments, despite the smaller distribution of simple and complex terms. It should be borne in mind, however, that the applied tool, TermoPL, did not extract many terms which were later extracted from the corpora using WS and its Collocates functionality. Therefore, it may not be best suited to the extraction of terms from large-sized corpora.

Regarding the degree of Europeanization of national judgments, it cannot be maintained, based on the corpora used in this study, that the co-existence of the European legal order and the national legal system of Poland directly affected the terminological content of post-accession national judgments. Any differences in the distribution of the node terms, including the most frequent simple and complex terms, in the pre- and post-accession SN corpora can be more likely attributed to the evolution of Poland's political, legal and administrative structures. According to the data, national judgments, similar to pre-accession judgments, do not contain simple or complex terms which could be inextricably linked to the EU legal system. The quantitative discrepancy between the pre- and post-accession SN corpora, however, is not to be regarded as definite; it is highly probable that the upwards normalization of quantitative data inflated the results in the case of both simple and complex terms in the pre-accession SN corpus.

It may be concluded that the terminological profile is yet another feature indicating the divergent textual fit of translated EU judgments to non-translated national judgments. The analysis made it possible to establish the properties of terminological units found in EU and Polish judgments (cf. Biel 2014a: 39–42). The totality of legal terms found in one legal genre cannot be fully comprehended without the basic knowledge of the corresponding constitutive genre, in this case legislation, and its terminology. Therefore, terminological units cannot be clearly linked to a single genre, as the identified terms form vast interrelated conceptual systems spanning two legal systems which interact with one another – the national legal system of Poland and the supranational legal system of the European Union. Since the terminological content of judgments, as a reproductive legal text type, is largely drawn from the overarching genre, i.e. legislation (cf. Biel 2012: 227), further analyses into the nature of terminological units should focus on the relation of terms found in legislative acts and terms in adjudicative documents.

# Chapter 10. Latinisms

Latin has exercised a great deal of influence on many languages over the course of their development, including Polish (Comrie 2008: 16–21). The inclusion of original Latin words and phrases (also known as macaronicisms) in utterances and writings in vernacular Polish became particularly popular in the Renaissance and later became a characteristic feature of various terminological systems, mostly used by the well-educated. It is especially typical in the humanities and social sciences (Markowski 1999: 37).

The use of Latin terms, phrases and maxims[192] (a maxim is also described in Latin as a *paraemia*, *maxima*, or *regula*) constitutes another distinguishing feature of legal (and, as might be expected, judicial) language (cf. Matilla 2006: 4, 125–158). Due to their archaic nature, Latinisms may be perceived as a highly-specialized and impenetrable sub-field of legal terminology (cf. Chapter 9). They are particularly prevalent in the civil law tradition in Continental Europe, where they are of international character (cf. Matilla 2006: 152) and act as facilitators of understanding among lawyers from various legal traditions in EU Member States. Latinisms are used when it is necessary to aid communication across borders, which is why "new legal phenomena of an international character often acquire a Latin name" (Mattila 2006: 144). For instance, the new unified European law is sometimes termed *jus commune novum* – the new common law, and a company formed under EU legislation is designated as *Societas Europaea (SE)* (IATE ID: 791246),[193] that is a European company (Mattila 2006: 144 after Biel 2014: 267; Matilla 2008: 253–255).

Despite being of service in the communication of lawyers, the use of Latinisms in legislative acts is generally discouraged. The *Joint Practical Guide* of the European Parliament, the Council and the Commission for persons involved in the drafting of European Union legislation (European Union 2015), which is a platform of general drafting principles, recommends that: "Jargon, certain vogue words and certain Latin expressions used in a sense other than their generally accepted legal meaning should also be avoided" (European Union 2015: 18). Based on this, it may be assumed that Latinisms could contribute to misinterpretation, hence the recommendation for drafters to refrain from using untypical legal senses of Latin expressions. The question of using foreign words and phrases, and hence Latinisms, in non- and translated English texts has also been raised in the *English*

---

192 In the following, for the sake of brevity, I will refer to them as Latinisms. These are loan words, phrases or syntactical structures directly derived from or suggestive of Latin and adapted into another language, for instance, *nihil novi, qui pro quo, summa cum laude, tabula rasa* (Markowski 1999: 37).

193 Regulation (EC) No 2157/2001 of 8 October 2001 on the Statute for a European company (SE)

*Style Guide* (DGT 2020[194]), which contains a set of accepted linguistic conventions recommended for in-house use by translators and drafters. The recommendations are quite specific, as they pertain to, among other things, the use of *e.g.*, *et al.*, *ibid.*, and *i.e*, which, according to the guide, like all Latin abbreviations, should be written in roman (unitalicized) (DGT 2020: 45, 48–49). The guide also mentions that:

> Latin should be used sparingly as even common phrases are often misused or misunderstood. When faced with such phrases as a translator, check whether they have the same currency and meaning when used in English (DGT 2020: 48).

It is presumed that the same pertains to texts translated into Polish. However, the *Polish Style Guide* (DGT 2016: 66) mentions that foreign words and phrases, including Latinisms, should be written in italics.[195] In the context of the Polish legal system, § 8 Section 2(2) of the Ordinance of the President of the Council of Ministers of 29 February 2016 on Principles of Legislative Drafting Technique[196] suggests that legislative drafters should avoid using foreign language terms or loan words, unless they have no exact equivalent in Polish, which also applies to Latinisms. Since these guidelines concern a different genre, they do not apply directly to texts produced by the CJEU and national judges. The question of signaling the distinct nature of Latinisms is also raised in the general rules on editing Polish written texts meant for publication (Wolański 2008). According to these rules, authors of various types of texts in Polish should italicize "words, phrases or entire sentences which function as quotes from a foreign language, with the exception of commonly used words and expressions" (e.g. *postscriptum* [postscript], *incognito*) (Wolański 2008: 37).

Considering the popularity of Latinisms in the judicial discourse community, a large proportion in their texts may be unitalicized, which is also indicative of foreignization, though to a lesser extent. In turn, italicization of phrases such as *status quo* may mean that the usage of a given Latinism is not yet common (habitual), hence the emphasis on its foreign character through italicization. In general, the issue of the language users (judges) either stressing the foreign nature of Latinisms or (consciously or not) emphasizing their domesticated character concerns what Contact Linguistics views as linguistic assimilation and

---

194 https://ec.europa.eu/info/sites/info/files/styleguide_english_dgt_en.pdf (accessed: August 18, 2020)

195 As will be shown later in this Chapter, typographic conventions may affect the degree to which Latinisms are perceived as foreign.

196 Obwieszczenie Prezesa Rady Ministrów z dnia 29 lutego 2016 r. w sprawie ogłoszenia jednolitego tekstu rozporządzenia Prezesa Rady Ministrów w sprawie "Zasad techniki prawodawczej" Dz.U. Poz. 283 [Ordinance of the President of the Council of Ministers of 29 February 2016 on the publication of the consolidated text of the President of the Council of Ministers on "Principles of legislative technique" Dz.U. Item 283]

"insertional" codeswitching (codemixing), that is the alternation of languages in-between utterances or phrases (cf. Matras 2009: 101). Although it may be perceived as language corruption, judges are certainly motivated by situational and contextual interests when they use Latinisms[197] (cf. Poplack 1978; Poplack *et al.* 1988; Matras 2009: 101).

The easily perceptible permeation of judgments as a legal genre by Latinisms, such as *lucrum cessans*, *lex retro non agit*, *clara non sunt interpretanda*, which express basic legal rules and concepts (cf. Kacprzak *et al.* 2001: 6), may impact the processes of communication and translation. The use of Latin can cause misunderstandings, as it often happens that variants of Latin expressions translated directly from Latin have different meanings in different countries (Burr and Gallas 2004: 232 after Matilla 2006: 147). Šarčević warns against Latin equivalents (after Berteloot 1988), as they often acquire "national coloring" (Šarčević 1997: 263–264). She further notes that "instead of serving as a reliable source for alternative equivalents, the use of Latin phrases by lawyers generally makes the translator's task more difficult," in particular in EU translation where translators encounter Latinisms in texts written in different languages (Šarčević 1997: 263–264). Matilla observes that the translation technique of direct quotation, that is a direct transfer of Latinisms from the ST to the TT, may not be the most suitable solution, as they may not be included in dictionaries of legal Latin[198] in countries with different legal traditions and their meaning may differ from one legal system to another (Matilla 2008: 269). Matilla suggests that Latinisms should be translated in parentheses, with the help of legal Latin dictionaries written in the context of the legal culture where the ST has been produced, as a shorthand for the explanation given in the same sentence (Matilla 2008: 269). The exception may be made in the case of commonly known and used Latin units, such as *circa* (IATE ID: 1317321), *inter alia* (IATE ID: 788706), or *vice versa* (IATE ID: 788617). He also remarks that this translation technique is followed by the Finnish translation unit at the CJEU[199] (Matilla 2008: 269).

In general, the use of Latin may seem self-evident to legal professionals, such as judges and attorneys-at-law, who are acquainted with at least the basics of legal Latin and its roots in Roman law (Wołodkiewicz 2001b: 7–15; Kacprzak *et al.* 2001: 3–5). However, this is not the case for individuals with no background in law or Latin itself, who, for example, still want to fully comprehend the contents of judgments passed in cases in which they are parties to the proceedings.

This chapter aims to answer several research questions concerning the usage of Latin in Polish language versions of CJEU judgments and non-translated SN judgments, namely:

---

197 The discourse functions of Latinisms are described in Section 10.6.

198 For a more detailed discussion on legal Latin dictionaries in various countries (England, France, Germany, Spain, Portugal, Italy, Russia), see Matilla 2006: 157–158.

199 For information on how many Latin phrases and maxims are frequently used by Estonian and Finnish lawyers, see Ristikivi (2005: 201).

1. Are Latinisms part of the active vocabulary of CJEU and SN judges?
2. Do CJEU and SN judges use a common set of Latinisms?
3. Are Latinisms used in judgments primarily of a legal character or do they also include commonplace expressions and abbreviations, such as: *e.g.*, *i.e.*, *etc.*, *ca.* (cf. Ristikivi 2005: 201)?
4. Has the usage of Latinisms increased in national judicial writing of the post-accession period (2011–2015) compared to the pre-accession period (1999), and can such a development be attributed to the Europeanization of the language of Polish judges (under the assumption that the use of Latin is more widespread in EU than in national judgments)?

The answers to the research questions above will allow me to determine whether the usage of Latin is another major generic feature of EU and national judgments at the terminological level (cf. Chapter 3, Section 3.3).

## 10.1 Research material and methodology

Latinisms are studied using three unsampled post-accession corpora of judgments – two EU corpora of CJ and GC judgments, and a reference corpus of post-accession SN judgments (cf. Chapter 4). The fourth corpus, a corpus of SN judgments from 1999, is used to verify whether Polish judges' recourse to Latin has changed relative to the post-accession period of 2011–2015.

Prior to the distributional analysis of Latinisms, it was necessary to create an extensive search list of Latin terms, phrases and maxims. I intended to include not only those which are inextricably connected with the sphere of law and adjudication, but also those of general application which are used by lawyers in day-to-day matters to demonstrate erudition (cf. Zajadło 2020: 249). The following Polish, English and German works on Latin in legal language were consulted in order to create that list: Lieberwirth (1986), Emanuel (1999), Kacprzak *et al.* (2001), Wołodkiewicz (2001), Rezler (2003), Heimbach (2004), Stone (2005), Benke *et al.* (2009), Pieńkos (2010), Gałuskina and Sycz (2013), Brzozowski *et al.* (2015), Brzozowski *et al.* (2016), Szczygielski (2017), Burczak *et al.* (2018), Radwański and Olejniczak (2018), Radwański and Panowicz-Lipska (2019), and Zajadło (2020, chapters 3 and 7). Latinisms found in these works were later supplemented by Latin maxims and phrases available on the online portal Infor.pl,[200] which is addressed primarily to government officials, legal professionals and entrepreneurs, and the website of the Regional Prosecutor's Office in Zielona Góra.[201] The final search list contained a total of 4498 Latinisms[202] and was fed into WS to generate four lists

200 https://www.infor.pl/prawo/paremie-lacinskie (accessed: August 8, 2019)
201 http://www.zielona-gora.po.gov.pl/index.php?id=180 (accessed: August 8, 2019)
202 This list is available at the website of the Eurolect project https://eurolekt.ils.uw.edu.pl/publications-and-materials/additional-materials/ (accessed: August 8, 2019)

of concordances, one for each corpus. The lists obtained with the corpus software were saved as Excel spreadsheets to automatically segregate the data. All quantitative data presented in this chapter encompass both raw frequencies (RF)[203] of occurrence and frequencies normalized to one million words (NF) to enable more detailed comparisons between the corpora, as well as to provide an insight into the actual (RF) and approximate (NF) distribution of Latin expressions across the corpora.

The degree of overlap of Latinisms in the translation corpora and the non-translation corpora (see Section 10.5) was determined with an Excel formula – *=IF(OR(S2=S3;S3=S4);"X";"")* (the numbers stand for the numbers of rows in a column). If both an EU corpus and a national corpus were found to contain the same Latinisms (type) (upon an ordering of the results from both corpora in a single Excel chart and marking them in two different colors), the respective rows were automatically marked with an "X."

## 10.2 Distribution of Latinisms in the corpora

Quantitative data on the global distribution of Latinisms in the corpora of CJEU and national judgments are shown in Table 10.1. Overall, Latinisms are not excessively salient compared to standard terminological units (cf. Chapter 9). The three following sets of aggregate data on their distribution were calculated using three different frequency thresholds, in order to determine whether a high threshold value might negatively affect the outcome of the analysis by not allowing for the extraction of particularly idiosyncratic (uncommon) types of Latinisms:

(1) an RF of 1 occurrence or more in a corpus, which allows for the extraction of both very salient (frequent), typical (moderately frequent) and idiosyncratic (infrequent) types of Latinisms,
(2) an NF of 1 occurrence or more occurrences per million words (pmw), which omits all idiosyncratic types,[204]
(3) an NF of 5 or more occurrences pmw, which allows for the extraction of only the most salient (frequent) types of Latinisms (cf. Table 10.1).[205]

203 Latinisms are not as frequent as, for instance, binomials (see Chapter 8), and for this reason raw frequencies were also included in the presentation of quantitative data to portray the distributional characteristics of Latin borrowings more adequately.
204 In the case of the respective corpora 1 NF equals: 3 RF (CJ), 3 RF (GC), 4 RF (SN_2011–2015). In the SN_1999 corpus, 1 RF is equal to 2 NF, which means that there are no Latinisms with 1 NF.
205 In the case of the respective corpora 5 NF equals: 25 RF (CJ), 21 RF (GC), 31 RF (SN_2011–2015), 3 RF (SN_1999), and 1 NF equals: 3 RF (CJ), 3 RF (GC), 4 RF (SN_2011–2015), 0 RF (SN_1999). In the case of the SN_1999 corpus, the lowest noted NF value is 2.

The reason for not setting a higher frequency threshold, as in the case of the analysis of lexical bundles (cf. Chapter 7), is that a higher frequency (e.g. an NF of 10 occurrences pmw) would allow for the extraction of only a handful of Latinisms, which generally are not expected to be highly recurrent. Since my intention was to thoroughly establish what types of Latinisms are used by CJEU and SN judges, I decided to adopt the lowest possible frequency threshold, namely RF≥1.

The data show that Latinisms are strikingly underrepresented in translated EU judgments compared to the post-accession corpus of non-translated national judgments as regards both the total number of their types and tokens. This applies to data collected with all three thresholds. Considering the overall idiosyncratic nature of Latinisms, their sparse distribution in judgments and for the sake of clarity of presented data, it is probably most advantageous to first consider the data gathered using the NF≥1 threshold, since it cuts off all particularly idiosyncratic types of Latinisms (see Table 10.1). All types of Latinisms with only several occurrences in each of the corpora (i.e. with NF=0) are presented in an aggregate manner beneath Tables 10.2 and 10.3. Latinisms with an NF equal to or higher than 1 may be perceived as (moderately) typical and their usage as (more or less) habitual, depending on their overall distribution.

The data contained in Tables 10.2 and 10.3 present all types of Latinisms with a total NF≥1. For the purposes of the analysis, it is assumed that this frequency threshold allows for the extraction of all non-idiosyncratic (frequent and moderately frequent) types and their occurrences.

It is also possible to analyze the degree of idiosyncrasy of Latinisms with dispersion plots in WS. A dispersion value is "the degree to which a set of values are uniformly spread across texts" (Scott 2017). A Latinism with a moderate or high overall distribution may be perceived as salient or typical, but in fact it may be idiosyncratic in that it may appear only in several texts from the corpus. This idiosyncrasy may also be content-related, especially in the case of Latinisms expressing legal rules. For instance, in the CJ corpus, the Latinism *erga omnes* occurs 37 times; however, it is spread only across eight different texts (in two it occurs as many as 10 and 12 times); in the SN_2011–2015 corpus, the Latinism *essentialia negotii* occurs 32 times, 4 times in one text, twice in five texts, and once in 18 texts. These examples indicate that the use of Latinisms is rather idiosyncratic (in particular of those with very low RF, see below); however, this finding needs to be confirmed in a future analysis, which could, potentially, also take into consideration the formations of judges' chambers, in order to determine which judges tend to rely heavily on Latinisms. Since the goal of this Chapter was to provide an overview of the distribution of Latinisms in the corpora, I decided not to undertake a detailed analysis of the distribution of their different types in individual texts.

**Table 10.1.** *Distribution of Latin phrases and maxims in the corpora*

| | Translated EU case law | | | | | | | | |
|---|---|---|---|---|---|---|---|---|---|
| | CJ | | | | | GC | | | |
| | Total types | RF | NF | CJ vs GC (%DIFF) | CJ/SN_2011–2015 (%DIFF) | Total types | RF | NF | GC vs SN_2011–2015 (%DIFF) |
| (1) RF≥1 | **99** | **1,114** | **236** | **–9 %** | **–55 %** | **109** | **1,171** | **259** | **–50 %** |
| (2) NF≥1 | 60 | 1,063 | 225 | **–10 %** | **–55 %** | 58 | 1,103 | 249 | **–50 %** |
| (3) NF≥5 | 14 | 649 | 138 | **–23 %** | **–59 %** | 18 | 813 | 180 | **–46 %** |
| | Non-translated PL case law | | | | | | | | |
| | SN_2011–2015 | | | | | SN_1999 | | | |
| | Total types | RF | NF | | SN_2011–2015 vs SN_1999 (%DIFF) | Total types | RF | NF | |
| (1) RF≥1 | **241** | **3,595** | **519** | | **+273 %** | **51** | **139** | **278** | |
| (2) NF≥1 | 131 | 3,422 | 502 | | **+261 %** | 51 | 139 | 278 | |
| (3) NF≥5 | 25 | 2,273 | 333 | | **+292 %** | 13 | 85 | 168 | |

**Table 10.2.** *Latinisms in the EU corpora (idiosyncratic types with 0 NF are not shown)*[a]

| Translated EU case law | | | | | |
|---|---|---|---|---|---|
| **CJ** | **RF** | **NF** | **GC** | **RF** | **NF** |
| ne bis in idem | 80 | 17 | a fortiori | 96 | 21 |
| sui generis | 58 | 12 | non bis in idem | 86 | 19 |
| a priori | 51 | 11 | de facto | 67 | 15 |
| de facto | 53 | 11 | a priori | 58 | 13 |
| mutatis mutandis | 52 | 11 | in fine | 55 | 12 |
| pro rata temporis | 50 | 11 | ex ante | 54 | 12 |
| ratione temporis | 51 | 11 | sensu stricto | 45 | 10 |
| a fortiori | 46 | 10 | a posteriori | 43 | 10 |
| ex post | 45 | 10 | de minimis | 43 | 10 |
| a posteriori | 39 | 8 | prima facie | 43 | 10 |
| erga omnes | 37 | 8 | ex post | 37 | 8 |
| de minimis | 33 | 7 | etc. | 36 | 8 |
| ex ante | 28 | 6 | ne bis in idem | 34 | 8 |
| in fine | 26 | 6 | mutatis mutandis | 27 | 6 |
| lex concursus | 27 | 6 | ratione materiae | 24 | 5 |
| a contrario | 19 | 4 | ad hoc | 22 | 5 |
| lex specialis | 19 | 4 | in dubio pro reo | 22 | 5 |
| prima facie | 18 | 4 | a contrario | 21 | 5 |
| ratione materiae | 18 | 4 | curriculum vitae | 20 | 4 |
| in dubio pro reo | 16 | 3 | erga omnes | 19 | 4 |
| inter partes | 16 | 3 | sine qua non | 18 | 4 |
| quasi | 16 | 3 | vice versa | 18 | 4 |
| ad hoc | 15 | 3 | ratio legis | 17 | 4 |
| lex fori concursus | 15 | 3 | nullum crimen, nulla poena sine lege | 13 | 3 |
| sensu stricto | 15 | 3 | inter partes | 12 | 3 |
| in concreto | 14 | 3 | lex specialis | 10 | 2 |
| lex causae | 14 | 3 | sic | 10 | 2 |
| per analogiam | 14 | 3 | status quo | 10 | 2 |
| nulla poena sine lege | 13 | 3 | ex tunc | 9 | 2 |
| contra legem | 12 | 3 | probatio diabolica | 9 | 2 |

**Table 10.2.** *Continued*

| Translated EU case law | | | | | |
|---|---|---|---|---|---|
| sine qua non | 12 | 3 | lex specialis derogat legi generali | 9 | 2 |
| in vitro | 11 | 2 | in concreto | 8 | 2 |
| probatio diabolica | 11 | 2 | de iure | 7 | 2 |
| ratio legis | 11 | 2 | ab initio | 6 | 1 |
| ex tunc | 10 | 2 | ex aequo et bono | 6 | 1 |
| non bis in idem | 10 | 2 | ex post factum | 6 | 1 |
| lex specialis derogat legi generali | 8 | 2 | per se | 6 | 1 |
| a quo | 7 | 1 | alias | 5 | 1 |
| in abstracto | 7 | 1 | ex nunc | 5 | 1 |
| vacatio legis | 7 | 1 | nota bene | 5 | 1 |
| acquis communautaire | 6 | 1 | via | 5 | 1 |
| dies a quo | 6 | 1 | de jure | 4 | 1 |
| ex nunc | 6 | 1 | in abstracto | 4 | 1 |
| ius cogens | 6 | 1 | ius cogens | 4 | 1 |
| per se | 6 | 1 | in extenso | 4 | 1 |
| vice versa | 6 | 1 | modus operandi | 4 | 1 |
| de iure | 5 | 1 | non concedit venire contra factum proprium | 4 | 1 |
| etc. | 5 | 1 | alibi | 3 | 1 |
| in situ | 5 | 1 | condicio sine qua non | 3 | 1 |
| lex mitior | 5 | 1 | ex-ante | 3 | 1 |
| ratione personae | 5 | 1 | ex post facto | 3 | 1 |
| status quo | 5 | 1 | in vitro | 3 | 1 |
| ultra vires | 5 | 1 | ipso facto | 3 | 1 |
| contra factum proprium | 4 | 1 | ipso iure | 3 | 1 |
| de jure | 4 | 1 | quasi | 3 | 1 |
| nemo potest venire contra factum proprium | 4 | 1 | reformatio in peius | 3 | 1 |
| numerus clausus | 4 | 1 | sensu largo | 3 | 1 |
| obiter dictum | 4 | 1 | ultra vires | 3 | 1 |

(*continued on next page*)

**Table 10.2.** *Continued*

| Translated EU case law | | | | | |
|---|---|---|---|---|---|
| petitum | 4 | 1 | | | |
| pro forma | 4 | 1 | | | |
| inter alia | 3 | 1 | | | |
| ipso iure | 3 | 1 | | | |
| lex generalis | 3 | 1 | | | |
| statu quo ante | 3 | 1 | | | |
| **64 types** | **1,115** | **236** | **58 types** | **1,103** | **249** |

[a] Underlining is used to mark types of Latinisms used in both legal and general language. The use in general language has been confirmed by searching for the respective Latinisms in the balanced version of the National Corpus of Polish (NKJP) and verifying whether they appear in non-legal sources. Same applies to Table 10.3.

In addition, the data also show that a higher threshold would effectively leave out a high number of Latinisms, which are, in fact, also crucial to judicial language, all of which are presented below[206]:

**RF=3 (NF=0):**

**SN judgments_2011–2015**: *a posteriori; ad eventum; culpa in contrahendo; ex ante; favor contractus; extra commercium; iuris dispositivi; ius abutendi; ius disponendi; ius possidendi; in fraudem creditoris; lex concursus; lex contractus; lex posterior derogat priori; lis pendens; mala fides superveniens non nocet; pro rata; traditio longa manu.*

**RF=2 (NF=0):**

**CJ judgments**: *damnum emergens; del credere; ex parte; ex post facto; forum rei sitae; gratis; in limine litis; ipso facto; ius publicum privatorum pactis mutari non potest; locus standi; nemo tenetur se ipsum accusare; ratione loci; res iudicata.*

**GC judgments**: *amicus curiae; acquis communautaire; ceteris paribus; contra legem; de lege ferenda; ex hypothesi; in absentia; in limine; in vivo; iuris tantum; locus standi; nemini licet venire contra factum proprium; obiter dictum; per analogiam; post factum; pro forma; terra nullius.*

**SN judgments_2011–2015**: *accidentalia negotii; actio Pauliana; animus novandi; actus nullus; animus possidendi; causa finite; cessio in solutum; culpa lata; culpa lata dolo aeuiparatur; error contra ius in hypotesi; in fraudem legis; ius novorum; ius utendi;*

206 Latinisms found in the SN_1999 corpus occur at least twice pmw.

**Table 10.3.** *Latinisms in the SN corpora (idiosyncratic types with 0 NF are not shown)*

| Non-translated PL case law | | | | | |
|---|---|---|---|---|---|
| **SN_2011–2015** | **RF** | **NF** | **SN_1999** | **RF** | **NF** |
| in blanco | 453 | 66 | in fine | 20 | 40 |
| in fine | 325 | 48 | petitum | 12 | 24 |
| ex lege | 202 | 30 | in blanco | 8 | 16 |
| ex tunc | 157 | 23 | per facta concludentia | 8 | 16 |
| lucrum cessans | 106 | 16 | ex lege | 7 | 14 |
| conditio sine qua non | 92 | 13 | statio fisci | 5 | 10 |
| in solidum | 92 | 13 | vide | 5 | 10 |
| damnum emergens | 91 | 13 | de facto | 4 | 8 |
| de lege lata | 75 | 11 | in concreto | 4 | 8 |
| lex specialis | 68 | 10 | animus testandi | 3 | 6 |
| res iudicata | 60 | 9 | ex post | 3 | 6 |
| ratio legis | 57 | 8 | praesumptio iuris tantum | 3 | 6 |
| sine qua non | 50 | 7 | ratio legis | 3 | 6 |
| lex retro non agit | 47 | 7 | a limine | 2 | 4 |
| expressis verbis | 44 | 6 | ad solemnitatem | 2 | 4 |
| a contrario | 43 | 6 | culpa lata | 2 | 4 |
| in principio | 41 | 6 | damnum emergens | 2 | 4 |
| ad quem | 35 | 5 | del credere | 2 | 4 |
| de facto | 35 | 5 | ex nunc | 2 | 4 |
| imperium | 35 | 5 | ex tunc | 2 | 4 |
| ex contractu | 34 | 5 | expressis verbis | 2 | 4 |
| ex post | 33 | 5 | gravamen | 2 | 4 |
| ex nunc | 33 | 5 | ius cogens | 2 | 4 |
| petitum | 33 | 5 | lucrum cessans | 2 | 4 |
| essentialia negotii | 32 | 5 | mortis causa | 2 | 4 |
| per facta concludentia | 30 | 4 | negotium claudicans | 2 | 4 |
| superficies solo cedit | 30 | 4 | nota bene | 2 | 4 |
| erga omnes | 29 | 4 | pro forma | 2 | 4 |
| datio in solutum | 28 | 4 | verba legis | 2 | 4 |
| in casu | 27 | 4 | a priori | 1 | 2 |

(*continued on next page*)

**Table 10.3.** *Continued*

| | | | | | |
|---|---|---|---|---|---|
| a priori | 23 | 3 | actio Pauliana | 1 | 2 |
| prima facie | 23 | 3 | causa solvendi | 1 | 2 |
| per analogiam | 22 | 3 | communis opinio | 1 | 2 |
| verba legis | 21 | 3 | compensatio lucri cum damno | 1 | 2 |
| a limine | 20 | 3 | culpa in kontrahendo | 1 | 2 |
| dominium | 20 | 3 | culpa in contrahendo | 1 | 2 |
| gravamen | 20 | 3 | de lege lata | 1 | 2 |
| in concreto | 20 | 3 | error in iudicando | 1 | 2 |
| rebus sic stantibus | 20 | 3 | in casu | 1 | 2 |
| ad probationem | 18 | 3 | in dubio pro cive | 1 | 2 |
| condictio indebiti | 18 | 3 | in extenso | 1 | 2 |
| condictio ob rem | 18 | 3 | in merito | 1 | 2 |
| pactum de non cedendo | 17 | 2 | in principio | 1 | 2 |
| ad hoc | 16 | 2 | in solidum | 1 | 2 |
| cessio legis | 16 | 2 | inter vivos | 1 | 2 |
| nota bene | 16 | 2 | iuris cogentis | 1 | 2 |
| pro forma | 16 | 2 | pacta sunt servanda | 1 | 2 |
| quorum | 16 | 2 | quasi | 1 | 2 |
| sensu stricto | 16 | 2 | quorum | 1 | 2 |
| iuris cogentis | 16 | 2 | sensu stricto | 1 | 2 |
| vide | 16 | 2 | status quo | 1 | 2 |
| clara non sunt interpretanda | 15 | 2 | | | |
| ex delicto | 15 | 2 | | | |
| sui generis | 15 | 2 | | | |
| tempus regit actum | 15 | 2 | | | |
| contra proferentem | 14 | 2 | | | |
| condictio sine causa | 14 | 2 | | | |
| da mihi factum dabo tibi ius | 14 | 2 | | | |
| quoad usum | 14 | 2 | | | |
| a tempore facti | 13 | 2 | | | |
| compensatio lucri cum damno | 13 | 2 | | | |
| condictio causa finita | 13 | 2 | | | |
| a quo | 12 | 2 | | | |

**Table 10.3.** *Continued*

| | | | | | |
|---|---|---|---|---|---|
| corpus | 12 | 2 | | | |
| lex posterior generalis non derogat legi priori speciali | 12 | 2 | | | |
| pacta sunt servanda | 12 | 2 | | | |
| nemo plus iuris in alium transferre potest, quam ipse habet | 12 | 2 | | | |
| cessio | 10 | 1 | | | |
| da mihi factum, dabo tibi ius | 10 | 1 | | | |
| ipso iure | 10 | 1 | | | |
| meritii | 10 | 1 | | | |
| sensu largo | 10 | 1 | | | |
| venire contra factum proprium nemini licet | 10 | 1 | | | |
| de minimis | 9 | 1 | | | |
| lege non distinguente | 9 | 1 | | | |
| praesumptio iuris tantum | 9 | 1 | | | |
| quasi | 9 | 1 | | | |
| a fortiori | 8 | 1 | | | |
| a maiori ad minus | 8 | 1 | | | |
| ab initio | 8 | 1 | | | |
| da mihi factum ego dabo tibi ius | 8 | 1 | | | |
| de iure | 8 | 1 | | | |
| exceptiones non sunt extendendae | 8 | 1 | | | |
| ignorantia iuris nocet | 8 | 1 | | | |
| in dubio contra proferentem | 8 | 1 | | | |
| lex generalis | 8 | 1 | | | |
| negotium claudicans | 8 | 1 | | | |
| causa donandi | 7 | 1 | | | |
| in extenso | 7 | 1 | | | |
| lex specialis derogat legi generali | 7 | 1 | | | |

(*continued on next page*)

**Table 10.3.** *Continued*

| | | | | | |
|---|---|---|---|---|---|
| post factum | 7 | 1 | | | |
| sensu stricte | 7 | 1 | | | |
| stationes fisci | 7 | 1 | | | |
| animus rem sibi habendi | 6 | 1 | | | |
| causa petendi | 6 | 1 | | | |
| condictio causa data non secuta | 6 | 1 | | | |
| conditio iuris | 6 | 1 | | | |
| contra factum proprium | 6 | 1 | | | |
| contra legem | 6 | 1 | | | |
| de lege ferenda | 6 | 1 | | | |
| iura novit curia | 6 | 1 | | | |
| in abstracto | 6 | 1 | | | |
| a tempore scientiae | 5 | 1 | | | |
| actio in rem | 5 | 1 | | | |
| ad solemnitatem | 5 | 1 | | | |
| causa cavendi | 5 | 1 | | | |
| dolus eventualis | 5 | 1 | | | |
| etc. | 5 | 1 | | | |
| inter partes | 5 | 1 | | | |
| inter vivos | 5 | 1 | | | |
| ius retentionis | 5 | 1 | | | |
| ius utendi, ius fruendi, ius disponendi | 5 | 1 | | | |
| lex loci delicti commissi | 5 | 1 | | | |
| negotiorum gestor | 5 | 1 | | | |
| nemo plus iuris | 5 | 1 | | | |
| res iudicata ius facit inter partes | 5 | 1 | | | |
| animus detendi | 4 | 1 | | | |
| animus possidendi rem pro alieno, animus detendi | 4 | 1 | | | |
| causa solvendi | 4 | 1 | | | |
| condictio causa data non secuta | 4 | 1 | | | |

**Table 10.3.** *Continued*

| | | | | | |
|---|---|---|---|---|---|
| corpus mechanicum | 4 | 1 | | | |
| culpa levissima | 4 | 1 | | | |
| ergo | 4 | 1 | | | |
| ex officio | 4 | 1 | | | |
| falsus procurator | 4 | 1 | | | |
| ius in re aliena | 4 | 1 | | | |
| lex commissoria | 4 | 1 | | | |
| numerus clausus | 4 | 1 | | | |
| pactum in favorem tertii | 4 | 1 | | | |
| per se | 4 | 1 | | | |
| praesumptio iuris ac de iure | 4 | 1 | | | |
| **131 types** | **3,422** | **502** | **51 types** | **139** | **278** |

*lex fori; lex loci damni; lex posterior derogat legi priori; mutatis mutandis; ne bis in idem; negotiorum gestio; negotium mixtum cum donatione; nemo plus iuris in alium transfere potest;*[207] *quam ipse habet; op. cit.; per analogiam legis; restitutio; restitutio in integrum; status quo; venire contra factum proprium.*

**RF=1 (NF=0):**

**CJ judgments**: *a casu ad casum; ad interim; ad valorem; alias; ex officio; forum externum; i.e.; in camera; in casu; in personam; explicite; expressis verbis; in rem; in solidum; in vivo; jus imperii; lex lata; lucrum cessans; nulla poena sine lege certa; obiter dicta; pacta sunt servanda; par in parem non habet imperium; pari passu; pro rata; quo ante; reformatio in peius; sensu stricte; ultima ratio.*

**GC judgments**: *a maiore ad minus; a quo; actori incumbit onus probandi; addendum; affidavit; corrigenda; dies a quo; do ut des; expressis verbis; dolo agit, qui petit, quod statim redditurus; ex officio; ex parte; fraus omnia corrumpit; ibidem; idem; in casu; infra; inter alia; nemo tenetur se ipsum accusare; nulla poena sine lege; onus probandi; opinio iuris; post mortem; pro rata; quo ante; ratio decidendi; ratione loci; ratione personae; rebus sic stantibus; status quo ante; tabula rasa; tempus regit actum; ultra petita; veto.*

**SN judgments_2011–2015**: *acquis communautaire; a minori ad maius; actio in personam; actio in rem scripta; actio negatoria; actio popularis; ad acta; ad personam;*

207 An abbreviated form of the maxim *nemo plus iuris in alium transferre potest, quam ipse habet.*

*argumentum a fortiori; causa acquirendi; causa efficiens; cedenta ipso iure; codex iuris canonici; condicio iuris; contra proponentem; constitutum possessorium; culpa in custodiendo; culpa in eligendo; culpa levisima; dies ad quem; dies incertus an, incertus quando; ex definitione; dolus; dolus directus; eo ipso; error contra similem vel rationem legis; error facti in iudicando; error in procedendo; error iuris in iudicando; ex animo; ignotum per ignotum; in corpore; in dubio pro libertate; in favorem debitoris; iudex in re sua; iuris vinculum; ius cogentis; ius infinitum; lex fori processualis; minima non curat praetor; negotium mixtum; nemo iudex sine actore; non adimpleti contractus pacto; non facere; in favorem tertii, pactum de contrahendo; pactum de non petendo; pars pro toto; pretium affectionis; pro viribus patrimonii; questio facti; ratione valoris; res ipsa loquitur; res perit domino; sententia non existens; solo consensus; summum ius summa iniuria; superfluum; traditio corporalis; versus; vis armata; vis imperii; volenti non fit iniuria.*

Data in Tables 10.2 and 10.3 on the distribution of Latinisms with a frequency equal to or higher than 1 NF, that is ones viewed as non-idiosyncratic, make it possible to answer several research questions. Overall, the data show that Latinisms are a crucial part of the language of both EU and Polish judges, although there are a few very telling differences.

First of all, it can be observed that the Eurolect, that is both CJ and GC judgments, contain, on average, about half as many occurrences of Latinisms as post-accession SN judgments. The discrepancy concerns the total number of types in each of the corpora – EU judgments contain approximately 45–60 % fewer types of Latinisms. Consequently, they also contain fewer tokens of Latinisms – approximately 70 %. This finding clearly shows that Polish judges rely on Latin to a much greater extent than EU judges (see Figure 10.1).

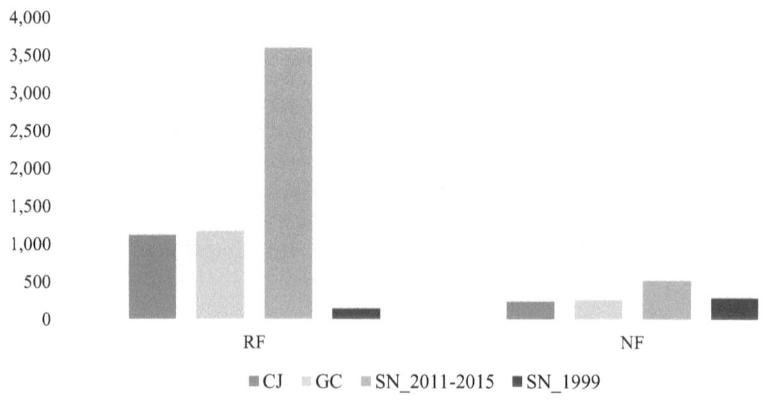


**Figure 10.1.** *Distribution of Latinisms in the corpora (RF≥1)*

However, this finding seems to be at odds with the assumption one might make as regards the assumed higher usefulness of Latin in EU judgments, in which Latinisms could potentially be conducive to communication among legal professionals from various national legal systems. Since CJEU judgments are passed at the supranational level, often concerning more than one Member State, one might assume that CJEU judges would need to express certain concepts in a succinct and understandable way to the whole audience of their judgments, which could possibly be achieved with Latin. However, it does not seem to be the case, as CJEU judges manage to get by without such heavy usage of Latin as Polish judges, despite the fact that they operate at the supranational level. It remains to be verified whether CJEU and Polish judges use Latin to aid their audience, e.g. as glosses by inserting the Latinisms in parentheses to serve as a shorthand for the explanation provided in the same sentence or whether, for instance, they apply Latinisms without any further explanation (see Section 10.5).

The next finding concerns the division of Latinisms into those which are exclusive to legal discourse, e.g. *sine qua non*, *lex specialis*, *inter partes*, and those which are common in not only legal language but also general Polish, e.g. *de facto*, *vide*, *nota bene*.[208] It appears that around 32 % of all types (19 types) of Latinisms in CJ judgments are also used commonly in general Polish. In the case of the corpus of GC judgements, this proportion is even higher – about 52 % of all types (29), which is indicative of inter-generic variation. About 18 % of all types of Latinisms (23 types) found in the post-accession corpus of SN judgments also appear in general Polish (cf. NKJP). However, in the pre-accession corpus of national judgments this proportion was higher, amounting to about 27 % of all types (14). Based on that, it can be established that the use of Latinisms in judgments is not limited to strictly legal ones, because a substantial, although not overly high, number of Latinisms is also used in general language. This, in turn, might mean that judgments contain certain Latinisms which should not pose particular problems to non-specialists, assuming, however, that individuals not versed in legal matters are well-read in general, as the knowledge and use of those commonplace Latinisms in society is still not customary.

Lastly, as regards the hypothesized Europeanization of national judgments, it cannot be established that post-accession judgments (2011–2015) have been affected by translated EU judgments, as the latter contain a lower number of types and tokens of Latinisms than the former. However, it should be noted that the number of texts included in the pre-accession corpus is quite low; therefore, it could be assumed that the data would be different if it included a substantially higher number of texts. In general, the data from the pre-accession national corpus

208 Riley (1995: 73–74) claims that legal Latin maxims, e.g. *volenti non fit injuria*, and Latin words and phrases, e.g. *ex parte*, *certoriari*, are a distinguishing feature of English legal language. The present findings show that Latinisms are also present in general language, in this case Polish.

show that, over time, the Polish Supreme Court started to rely on Latinisms more heavily. At this point, it may only be hypothesized whether this has to do with the display function of Latin or the fact that it enables the precise expression of legal concepts and principles (see Section 10.6).

Section 10.4 will examine the degree of overlap between both EU corpora and the two national corpora, in order to determine to what degree the tradition of the usage of Latinisms varies between EU and Polish national judicial culture. In addition, I will also inspect the context of use and degree of integration of a narrow range of Latinisms which are shared between the EU corpora and the national corpus. For want of space, the analysis will be limited to Latinisms which are key to the genre of judgments as a whole.

## 10.3 Overlap of Latinisms between the corpora

As it was to be expected, the degree of overlap of Latinisms is the highest within the Eurolect. At every threshold level, CJ and GC judgments were found to share more Latinisms than each of the EU corpora together with the corpus of post-accession SN judgments (see Table 10.4).

Moreover, it was observed that in the case of the first two threshold values, RF>1 and NF>1, CJ judgments share slightly more Latinisms with SN judgments than GC judgments; however, in the case of the third threshold, NF>5, this trend is reversed, as GC judgments contain one more Latinism shared with SN judgments than CJ judgments. Additionally, the inclusion of the pre-accession corpus of national judgments made it possible to evaluate the development of the usage

**Table 10.4.** *Overlap between the translation and non-translation corpora (types)*

| | **Translated EU case law** | | | **Non-translated PL case law** |
|---|---|---|---|---|
| | **CJ vs GC** | **CJ vs SN_2011–2015** | **GC vs SN_2011–2015** | **SN_1999 vs SN_2011–2015** |
| **(1) Total types (RF>1)** | **61 (out of: 99 vs 109)** | **50 (out of: 99 vs 241)** | **47 (out of: 109 vs 241)** | **41 (out of: 52 vs 241)** |
| **(2) Total types (NF>1)** | 37 (out of: 60 vs 58) | 33 (out of: 60 vs 131) | 29 (out of: 58 vs 131) | 37 (out of: 52 vs 131) |
| **(3) Total types (NF>5)** | 10 (out of: 14 vs 18) | 3 (out of: 14 vs 25) | 4 (out of: 18 vs 25) | 7 (out of: 13 vs 25) |

of Latinisms in the language of SN judges. In the case of the first two threshold values, approximately 79 % of all Latinisms appearing in the pre-accession corpus are shared with the post-accession national corpus, whereas in the case of the third threshold value, NF>5, that proportion equals 54 %. Taking into consideration the fact that the pre-accession corpus contains 92 % fewer tokens than the post-accession corpus, this finding is not very reliable, and subject to verification, although it does indicate that the reliance of Polish judges on Latin has increased in the post-accession period compared to 1999. The collection of Latinisms which were common to the SN prior to Poland's accession to the EU includes 34 Latinisms, namely: *a limine, a priori, actio Pauliana, culpa in contrahendo, culpa lata, damnum emergens, de facto, de lege lata, ex lege, ex nunc, ex post, ex tunc, gravamen, in blanco, in casu, in concreto, in extenso, in fine, in solidum, inter vivos, lex retro non agit, lucrum cessans, nota bene, pacta sunt servanda, per facta concludentia, praesumptio iuris tantum, pro forma, quasi, quorum, ratio legis, sensu stricto, status quo, verba legis, vide.* It is not certain, however, what is the immediate cause of the higher dependence on Latin by Polish judges. It does not seem that the accession of Poland to the EU resulted in Polish judges adopting a larger body of Latinisms. It may be that the discourse functions of Latin are so unique and convenient that national judges increasingly avail themselves of Latinisms.

Critical from the perspective of genre analysis is what types of Latinisms can be considered as key in judgments passed at both supranational and national level. The determination of the degree of overlap between the EU corpora and the national corpus made it possible to construct a repertoire of 25 such Latinisms, all of which have at least one occurrence (pmw) across the corpora and occur in the CJ, GC and SN corpora (see Table 10.5 and 10.6).[209]

Tables 10.5 and 10.6 present the same set of Latinisms;[210] however, Table 10.5 shows Latinisms ordered according to the aggregate normalized frequency of occurrence in both EU corpora, whereas Table 10.6 presents the same borrowings ordered according to their frequency of occurrence in the post-accession SN corpus. This set of 25 Latinisms shows that although overall EU judges employ a lower number of types of Latinisms than Polish judges, they seem to do so more consistently, at least considering the aggregate NF of types found in both EU corpora. However, this observation is nullified if we observe the NF values in each of the EU corpora separately. Considering the total normalized number of occurrences of

209 The context of use of core Latinisms key to the genre of judgments is presented later in this section.

210 Although Table 10.4 shows that the EU corpora share a different number of Latinisms with the national corpus, Tables 10.5 and 10.6 contain only 25 foreign imports classified as "key." This is due to the fact that only 25 Latinisms occur in both of the EU corpora as well as in the national corpus. This was done in order to correlate the Eurolect data with the data collected from national judgments based on excerpts containing the key Latinisms.

**Table 10.5.** *Latinisms shared by both EU corpora and the SN_2011–2015 corpus ordered according to the aggregate NF in both CJ and GC*

| Translated EU case law | | | | | | | | |
|---|---|---|---|---|---|---|---|---|
| **CJ and GC** | **RF CJ** | **NF CJ** | **CJ vs GC (%DIFF)** | **CJ vs SN_2011–2015 (%DIFF)** | **RF GC** | **NF GC** | **GC vs SN_2011–2015 (%DIFF)** | **Aggregate NF** |
| *a fortiori* | 46 | 10 | −52 % | −79 % | 96 | 21 | −56 % | 31 |
| *de facto* | 53 | 11 | −27 % | −52 % | 67 | 15 | −35 % | 26 |
| *a priori* | 51 | 11 | −15 % | +10 % | 58 | 13 | +30 % | 24 |
| *ex post* | 45 | 10 | +25 % | +25 % | 37 | 8 | 0 % | 18 |
| *in fine* | 26 | 6 | −50 % | −14 % | 55 | 12 | +71 % | 18 |
| *de minimis* | 33 | 7 | −30 % | 17 % | 43 | 10 | +67 % | 17 |
| *prima facie* | 18 | 4 | −60 % | −20 % | 43 | 10 | +100 % | 14 |
| *sensu stricto* | 15 | 3 | −70 % | −40 % | 45 | 10 | +100 % | 13 |
| *erga omnes* | 37 | 8 | +100 % | +60 % | 19 | 4 | −20 % | 12 |
| *a contrario* | 19 | 4 | −20 % | 0 % | 21 | 5 | +25 % | 9 |
| *etc.* | 5 | 1 | −88 % | −67 % | 36 | 8 | +167 % | 9 |
| *ad hoc* | 15 | 3 | −40 % | 0 % | 22 | 5 | +67 % | 8 |
| *sine qua non* | 12 | 3 | −25 % | 0 % | 18 | 4 | +33 % | 7 |
| *lex specialis* | 19 | 4 | +100 % | +100 % | 10 | 2 | 0 % | 6 |
| *inter partes* | 16 | 3 | 0 % | 50 % | 12 | 3 | +50 % | 6 |
| *quasi* | 16 | 3 | +200 % | +200 % | 3 | 1 | 0 % | 6 |
| *ratio legis* | 11 | 2 | −50 % | +100 % | 17 | 4 | +300 % | 6 |
| *in concreto* | 14 | 3 | +50 % | +200 % | 8 | 2 | +100 % | 5 |
| *ex tunc* | 10 | 2 | 0 % | +100 % | 9 | 2 | +100 % | 4 |
| *lex specialis derogat legi generali* | 8 | 2 | 0 % | +100 % | 9 | 2 | +100 % | 4 |
| *de iure* | 5 | 1 | −50 % | 0 % | 7 | 2 | +100 % | 3 |
| *ex nunc* | 6 | 1 | 0 % | 0 % | 5 | 1 | 0 % | 2 |
| *in abstracto* | 7 | 1 | 0 % | 0 % | 4 | 1 | 0 % | 2 |
| *per se* | 6 | 1 | 0 % | 0 % | 5 | 1 | 0 % | 2 |
| *ipso iure* | 3 | 1 | 0 % | 0 % | 3 | 1 | 0 % | 1 |
| **Total (25 types)** | **496** | **105** | **−29 %** | **−27 %** | **652** | **147** | **+2 %** | **253** |

**Table 10.6.** *Latinisms shared by the SN_2011–2015 corpus and both EU corpora ordered according to the NF in the SN_2011–2015 corpus*

| **Non-translated PL case law** | | |
|---|---|---|
| **SN_2011–2015** | **RF** | **NF** |
| *in fine* | 325 | 48 |
| *ex tunc* | 157 | 23 |
| *lex specialis* | 68 | 10 |
| *ratio legis* | 57 | 8 |
| *sine qua non* | 50 | 7 |
| *a contrario* | 43 | 6 |
| *de facto* | 35 | 5 |
| *ex post* | 33 | 5 |
| *ex nunc* | 33 | 5 |
| *erga omnes* | 29 | 4 |
| *a priori* | 23 | 3 |
| *in concreto* | 20 | 3 |
| *prima facie* | 23 | 3 |
| *sensu stricto* | 16 | 2 |
| *ad hoc* | 16 | 2 |
| *a fortiori* | 8 | 1 |
| *de minimis* | 9 | 1 |
| *etc.* | 5 | 1 |
| *inter partes* | 5 | 1 |
| *quasi* | 9 | 1 |
| *lex specialis derogat legi generali* | 7 | 1 |
| *de iure* | 8 | 1 |
| *ipso iure* | 10 | 1 |
| *in abstracto* | 6 | 1 |
| *per se* | 4 | 1 |
| **Total (25 types)** | **999** | **144** |

key Latinisms, it may be concluded that the profile of their usage in the GC corpus is the most convergent with that of national judgments, although there are noticeable differences in the distribution of individual types of Latin units, such as *in fine*, *a fortiori* or *ex tunc*.

Since it would be impractical to describe the context of use of all Latinisms occurring in the corpora, the following section intends to provide an account of only those which may be perceived as fundamental to the genre as a whole. The description is limited to providing the meaning of the Latinisms, excerpts from the corpora of CJ and SN judgments, and their collocational range.

## 10.4 Repertoire of key Latinisms in the genre of judgments

This section describes 25 Latin borrowings regarded as fundamental to the genre of judgments owing to their presence in both CJEU and SN judgments, and thus non-idiosyncratic nature. As already shown above, EU and national judges use a wide range of Latinisms. An understanding of key Latinisms used regularly by both EU and Polish judges might be of importance to translators and legal professionals. For instance, when a translator (or a lawyer-linguist) encounters the Latinism *a contrario*, they need to decide whether to copy it into the TT or to domesticate it in the TL (cf. Matilla 2008: 269). Considering their salience, these key Latinisms call for further explanation of their meaning, collocational range and discourse functions in translated EU judgments and non-translated Polish judgments.[211]

In the presentation of key Latinisms, I consulted the IATE termbase[212] as well as the following dictionaries[213]: (1) *Jowitt's Dictionary of English Law* (Jowitt *et al.* 2010[1977]), (2) *Oxford Dictionary of Law* (Martin 2003[1983]), (3) *Longman Dictionary of Law* (Curzon and Richards 2007[1979]), *Dictionary of Law* (Collin 2004[1986]), (4) *Black's Law Dictionary* (Garner 2009[1891]), (5) *Nolo's Plain-English Law Dictionary* (Hill and Hill 2009), (6) *Webster's New World Law Dictionary* (Ellis Wild 2006), (7) *Latin for Lawyers: The Language of the Law* (Emanuel 1999), (8) *Prawo rzymskie: słownik encyklopedyczny* [Roman Law: Encyclopedic Dictionary] (Kamiński and Wołodkiewicz 1986), and (9) *Słownik terminów, zwrotów i sentencji prawniczych: łacińskich oraz pochodzenia łacińskiego* [Dictionary of Latin Legal Terms, Phrases and Maxims] (Kuryłowicz 2012). This presentation is not meant to be exhaustive. The Latinisms are presented in alphabetical order.

---

211 Excerpts from CJ and SN judgments are unitalicized in order to show whether Latinisms occurring in them are italicized or unitalicized. Latinisms, or their equivalents, are bolded to make them easily noticeable.

212 IATE – European Union Terminology. https://iate.europa.eu/home (March 8, 2020)

213 Dictionaries 1 to 3 are of British origin, dictionaries 4 to 7 were published in the United States, while dictionaries 8 and 9 were published in Poland.

1) ***a contrario*** **(CJ: 19 RF, 4 NF; GC: 21 RF, 5 NF; SN: 43 RF, 6 NF)**
The first key Latinism is *a contrario* [conversely, on the contrary] (cf. Kuryłowicz 2012: 9), which is used by the judges as a means of providing arguments. It is based on the principle that if a legal norm[214] binds consequences only to the facts mentioned in it, these consequences do not entail other facts. The IATE definition states that an *a contrario argument* involves "arguing from an accepted conclusion to the rejection of its contrary" (IATE ID: 794326). Therefore, it is antonymous to an analogy and analogical reasoning. By presenting *a contrario* arguments judges are able to provide solutions not currently foreseen by the legal system (1) or to negate the interpretation of courts of lower instance (2):

| | | |
|---|---|---|
| (1) | CJ (C-135/11P): | *Z powyższego wynika* ***a contrario****, że instytucja, która nie uzyskała zgody danego państwa członkowskiego, nie jest uprawniona do ujawnienia dokumentu (...).*<br>[It follows, **conversely**, that an institution which does not have the agreement of the Member State concerned is not entitled to disclose the document (...).] |
| (2) | SN (I CSK 673/13): | Przepis ten – z uwagi na wycinkowy charakter regulacji – nie upoważniał do wniosków wywodzonych w drodze rozumowania ***a contrario***.<br>[This provision – due to the fragmentary nature of the regulation – did not authorize the conclusions drawn by **a contrario** reasoning.] |

What is peculiar is that the English-language version of the CJ judgment (case no. C-135/11P) does not contain the Latinism *a contrario*, but instead its English equivalent *conversely*. In both the Polish and English language versions of the above CJ judgment *a contrario* and *conversely* are not italicized, suggesting habitual and frequent usage in EU judgments. This pertains also to other CJ judgments, but not all. The phrase *a contrario* appears in the Eurolect with a lower frequency than in national judgments. In the second excerpt, on the other hand, *a contrario* is italicized, which emphasizes the foreign origin of the Latinism. It is also rarely used instead of a Polish word in national judgments, typically as an adverb, as in *(a contrario art. 12)*. The following collocates of *a contrario* are representative of its typical environment in CJ and SN judgments[215]:

**CJ:** *wynikać/wskazywać a contrario* [to follow/point out a contrario], *zob. a contrario wyrok* [see, a contrario, judgment], *wykładnia a contrario* [a contrario interpretation],

214 For more information on the distinction between legal provisions and legal norms in the Polish legal system, see Ziembiński (1960, in Polish), Grabowski (2009, in English).

215 For want of space, this section does not present excerpts and collocations of Latin phrases and maxims from the corpus of GC judgments. In general, the manner

**SN:** interpretować/wynikać a contrario [to interpret/follow a contrario], wnioskowanie/ wykładnia a contrario [a contrario inference/interpretation], (a contrario art. 12) [(a contrario Article 12)].

In both the CJ and SN corpus, a contrario is used primarily in verb phrases, only rarely being used as a post-modifier in noun phrases. It replaces equivalent Polish descriptions of this specific type of reasoning and tends to be used to indirectly assess the type of interpretation used by either the referring court (in the case of EU judgments) or court of the lower instance (in the case of SN judgments).

**2) *a fortiori* (CJ: 46 RF, 10 NF; GC: 96 RF, 21 NF; SN: 8 RF, 1 NF)**
The Latinism *a fortiori* means "even more so" (Garner 2009: 69) or "with even stronger reason" (Hill and Hill 2009: 17):

| | | |
|---|---|---|
| (3) | CJ (C-219/14): | *Ten sam wniosek narzuca się* ***a fortiori****, gdy urlop został wykorzystany nie w okresie, w którym został uzyskany i w którym pracownik pracował w niepełnym wymiarze czasu pracy, lecz w okresie późniejszym (...).*<br>[The same conclusion should be drawn ***a fortiori*** where the leave is not taken during the period in which it accrued, in which the worker worked part-time, but during a later period (...).] |
| (4) | SN (II CSK 605/12): | *Przyjął mianowicie, stosując metody wykładni* ***a fortiori****, że kontraktowa odpowiedzialność odszkodowawcza obejmuje nie tylko szkody wynikające z niewłaściwego wykonania umowy, (...).*<br>[It assumed, using methods of **a fortiori** reasoning, that contractual liability for damages includes not only damages resulting from improper performance of the contract, (...).] |

This phrase is used to state reasoning with regard to situations in which if one thing is demonstrably true and compelling, it can be inferred that another one is even more true (Emanuel 1999: 16). In logic, the inference that something must be true is made if it is encompassed within another thing that is obviously true and accurate; for instance, if a man is dead, then, *a fortiori*, he cannot commit any act (Emanuel 1999: 16), or if a 19-year-old is legally an adult, then a 20-year-old is also an adult (Ellis Wild 2006: 291). An *a fortiori argument* (Latin: *argumentum a fortiori*) is presented by following the logic that a point that is to be proved is followed by a stronger claim (see excerpt 4). In the CJ corpus, there are mainly verbal complements of this phrase, whereas in the SN corpus, this Latinism denotes ways of reasoning and interpretation as a noun complement:

how Latin units are used in GC judgments does not differ greatly from that of CJ judgments.

**CJ:** *mieć zastosowanie a fortiori* [to be applicable a fortiori], *wynikać a fortiori* [to result from sth a fortiori]
**SN:** *wnioskowanie/argumentacja/wykładnia a fortiori* [a fortiori reasoning/argumentation/interpretation]

*A fortiori* seems to be more integrated (habitual) in EU judgments due to it being unitalicized, although it is italicized in the English-language version of the judgment from which the excerpt was extracted.

**3) a priori (CJ: 51 RF, 11 NF; GC: 58 RF, 13 NF; SN: 23 RF, 3 NF)**
The next Latinism is *a priori,* which typically occurs in the following contexts:

| | | |
|---|---|---|
| (5) | CJ (C-308/11): | *Z powyższego wynika, że nie można* ***a priori*** *wykluczyć, iż substancja, której molekuły nie współdziałają z ludzkim składnikiem komórkowym, może stanowić produkt leczniczy (...).* [It follows that it is not **a priori** inconceivable that a substance the molecules of which do not interact with a human cellular constituent may constitute a medicinal product (...).] |
| (6) | SN (I CSK 796/10): | *Nie można zakładać* ***a priori****, że jedynym motywem wyboru dostawcy usługi jest cena, a rozsądny i dobrze poinformowany konsument zawsze wybierze towar lub usługę oferowaną w niższej cenie.* [It cannot be assumed **a priori** that the only motive for choosing a service provider is the price, and that a reasonable and well-informed consumer will always choose a good or service offered at a lower price.] |

*A priori* is a Latinism meaning "from the previous (i.e. from cause to effect)" (Martin 2003: 31). It is used to describe or relate to reasoning which is based on abstract ideas, predict the effects of particular causes, or (more loosely) make presumptions that are true in light of general principles or accepted truths (Emanuel 1999: 26), which may also be termed as deductive reasoning (Martin 2003: 31; Ellis Wild 2006: 29). *Black's Law Dictionary* provides another equivalent in the English language, namely "from what is before," which relates to arguing from the general or seemingly self-evident to the particular (Garner 2009: 118). It can also refer to ascertaining the truth by "proceeding from an assumption to its logical conclusion rather than by actual experience or observation" (Ellis Wild 2006: 29). For instance, an *a priori argument* is the result of reasoning based on ideas or assumptions, not on real examples. The opposite of *a priori* is *a posteriori* (Martin 2003: 31), which is not a core Latin borrowing (cf. Tables 10.5 and 10.6). In the corpora, there are several frequent collocates of *a priori*:

**CJ:** *nie można a priori wykluczyć/twierdzić* [it cannot be a priori ruled out/claimed]
**SN:** *nie można przyjmować/uznawać/wykluczyć/założyć a priori* [it cannot be assumed/accepted/ruled out/presumed a priori]

The collocates of *a priori* show that this Latinism is closely connected with the assessment of the courts as to which types of reasoning and their outcomes are acceptable.

**4) ad hoc (CJ: 15 RF, 3 NF; GC: 22 RF, 5 NF; SN: 16 RF, 2 NF)**
The Latinism *ad hoc* means "for a special purpose," "for a particular purpose," "for this particular case at hand" (Ellis Wild 2006: 291; Curzon and Richards 2007: 10; Jowitt 2010: 52; IATE ID: 952600). In the corpora, it is used as a pre- and post-modifier in noun phrases:

| | | |
|---|---|---|
| (7) | CJ (C-409/13): | *Taka poprawka oznaczałaby bowiem utrzymanie procesu przyznawania pomocy* ***ad hoc*** *przez Parlament i Radę w ramach zwykłej procedury ustawodawczej (...).*<br>[Such an amendment would have entailed keeping the process whereby MFA is granted, **on a case by case basis**, by the Parliament and the Council under the ordinary legislative procedure.] |
| (8) | SN (II CSK 872/14): | *Sąd mógł natomiast rozważyć (...) zasięgnięcie w sprawie opinii prof. dr hab. A. P., w określonych w postanowieniu dowodowym dziedzinach wiedzy specjalnej, jako tzw. biegłego* ***ad hoc****.*<br>[On the other hand, the court could have considered (...) to consult Professor dr hab. A. P., in the areas of special knowledge specified in the evidentiary ruling, as a so-called **ad hoc** expert.] |

According to the *English Style Guide* (DGT 2019: 45, 48–49[216]), Latinisms are not hyphenated when used adjectivally, e.g. *ad hoc meeting*, which holds true in the case of both Polish language versions for EU judgments and non-translated national judgments. *Ad hoc* is used to describe, among other things, types of decisions adapted only for a specific purpose (IATE ID: 952600) or on the spur of the moment (Emanuel 1999: 12), such as granting aid or designating experts who are to make their knowledge available to the court. These are the typical collocates of *ad hoc* in the corpora:

**CJ:** *pełnomocnik/decyzja/wnioski/pomoc ad hoc* [ad hoc agent/decision/conclusions/assistance]
**SN:** *biegły/wyrok Sądu Polubownego ad hoc* [ad hoc expert/arbitration award]

This Latinism has a slightly wider collocational range in CJ judgments.

**5) *de facto* (CJ: 53 RF, 11 NF; GC: 67 RF, 15 NF; SN: 35 RF, 5 NF)**
*De facto* means existing "in fact" or "in reality," either in accordance with law or not (Curzon and Richards 2007: 173; Garner 2009: 479). In other words, something

216 https://ec.europa.eu/info/sites/info/files/styleguide_polish_dgt_pl_0.pdf (accessed: August 18, 2020)

exists as a matter of fact rather than of right, that is *de iure* (or *de jure*). For instance, the government of a given country may recognize a foreign government *de facto* if it is actually in control of a country, even though it has no legal right to rule, effectively usurping authority (Martin 2003: 140). Other situations in which authority is claimed or exercised without legal right may involve a *de facto judge*, a *de facto board of directors*, etc. (Emanuel 1999: 81). It refers primarily to past or current actions, or events; however, it may also be used to refer to hypothetical situations and their legal effects, as in the excerpt from the CJ judgment:

| | | |
|---|---|---|
| (9) | CJ (C-157/12): | *Taka możliwość kontroli merytorycznej stanowiłaby* ***de facto*** *dodatkowy środek zaskarżenia przeciwko orzeczeniu, które w państwie członkowskim pochodzenia stało się prawomocne.*<br>[Such a possibility of review as to the substance would ***de facto*** constitute an additional means of redress against a judgment which has become final in the Member Sate of origin.] |
| (10) | SN (IV CSK 48/12): | *Wprawdzie w osobnych pismach, to jednak strony* ***de facto*** *złożyły zgodne oświadczenia woli co wyboru prawa materialnego polskiego, które powinno być stosowane w tym postępowaniu.*<br>[Although in separate letters, the parties **de facto** submitted consistent statements of will as to the choice of Polish substantive law, which should be applied in this proceeding.] |

This Latinism is not italicized in the Polish-language version of the CJ judgment, while Polish judges emphasize the foreign origin of this phrase by italicizing it.

**CJ:** *dotyczyć/powodować/umożliwiać/wykluczać de facto* [to concern/cause/enable/preclude de facto], *klauzula de facto zakazująca* [clause prohibiting de facto], *przedsiębiorstwo de facto kontrolowane przez państwo* [undertaking de facto controlled by the state]
**SN:** *występować de facto w roli* [to act de facto as], *podważać de facto skuteczność* [to de facto undermine the effectiveness of], *wykładnia de facto wyklucza* [interpretation de facto rules out]

The above shows that CJ judgments exhibit a wider collocational range.

**6)** ***de iure*** **(CJ: 5 RF, 1 NF; GC: 7 RF, 2 NF; SN: 8 RF, 1 NF)**
The use of the Latinism *de iure* is very similar to that of *de facto*. Contrary to the meaning of the phrase *de facto*, which refers to matters of fact, *de iure* refers to matters of law and legal status and means "by right," "by force of law," "by law," or "as a matter of law"; as an adjective it means "lawful," "legitimate" (Emanuel 1999: 84; Garner 2009: 490):

(11) CJ (C-477/13): *W większości państw członkowskich działalność w dziedzinie architektury prowadzona jest* ***de iure*** *bądź de facto przez osoby posiadające wyłącznie tytuł architekta lub dodatkowo także inny tytuł, (...).*
[In most Member States, activities in the field of architecture are pursued, **de jure** or de facto, by persons bearing the title of architect alone or accompanied by another title, (...).]

(12) SN (II CSK 872/14): *Z mocy art. 415 k.p.c. dla uwzględnienia wniosku restytucyjnego, na podstawie art. 410 § 2 k.c., istotne jest to, czy* ***de iure*** *doszło do spełnienia świadczenia (...).*
[Under Article 415 of the Code of Civil Procedure in order to take into account the restitution request, pursuant to Article 410(2) of the Code of Civil Procedure, it is important whether the performance has **de iure** been provided (...).]

*De iure* appears solely in verb phrases:

**CJ:** *przepisy, których przestrzeganie jest de iure obowiązkowe* [provisions, the observance of which is de iure compulsory]
**SN:** *spełnić świadczenie de iure* [to provide a service de iure], *być de iure sprawą gospodarczą* [to be de iure an economic matter]

In general, it should be observed that *de iure* is substantially less frequently used in the corpora compared to *de facto*, which is why it has fewer collocates. Another spelling variant of *de iure* is *de jure* (cf. Martin 2003: 142; Garner 2009: 490) – it occurs only in the EU corpora and is less frequent than *de iure*.

**7) *de minimis* (CJ: 33 RF, 7 NF; GC: 43 RF, 10 NF; SN: 9 RF, 1 NF)**
The literal English equivalent of *de minimis* is "trifling, minimal" (Garner 2009: 496). In general, this phrase is part of a Latin maxim *de minimis non curat lex* meaning "the law does not take account of trifles" (IATE ID: 1681803; Martin 2003: 143), which does not, however, appear in the corpora. Based on this maxim, the court cannot, for example, award damages for a trifling nuisance. In the EU context, the *de minimis rule* applies in competition law, for example (Martin 2003: 143).

(13) CJ (C-111/10): *Podobnie możliwe jest przyznanie pomocy* ***de minimis*** *dopuszczonej na mocy rozporządzenia nr 1535/2007.*
[Equally, recourse can be had to the ***de minimis*** aid authorised under Regulation No 1535/2007.]

(14) SN (IV CSK 585/13): *(...) organ podatkowy, na wniosek podatnika prowadzącego działalność gospodarczą może udzielić ulg w spłacie zobowiązań podatkowych określonych w art. 67a, m.in. tych, które stanowią pomoc* ***de minimis*** *(...).*

[(...) the tax authority, at the request of a taxpayer conducting business activity, may grant relief in payment of tax obligations specified in Article 67a, including those that constitute **de minimis** aid (...).]

*De minimis* appears most commonly with the noun *pomoc* [aid] as part of a complex term, *pomoc de minimis* [de minimis aid], which denotes a mechanism for small-scale state aid provided to businesses which is not intended to distort competition.[217] *De minimis aid* cannot exceed a certain fixed amount over a given period of time, and is therefore exempt from the requirement to notify the European Commission in advance (IATE ID: 2108019).

**CJ:** *pomoc/komunikat de minimis* [de minimis aid, de minimis notice]
**SN:** *pomoc/zasada de minimis* [de minimis aid/rule]

The collocates of *de minimis* show that the Latin phrase constitutes a part of multiword terms which appear mostly in the EU corpora.

**8) *erga omnes* (CJ: 37 RF, 8 NF; GC: 19 RF, 4 NF; SN: 29 RF, 4 NF)**
The Latin phrase *erga omnes* means "towards all" (Curzon and Richards 2007: 222). It denotes legal obligations and rights of universal validity. *Erga omnes* obligations are of particular importance in international law, as all states have a legal interest in their fulfilment because their subject matter is of significance to the international community as a whole. An example of an *erga omnes* obligation is an individual's right to self-determination (Martin 2003: 179).

| | | |
|---|---|---|
| (15) | CJ (C-335/09 P): | *Zgodnie z art. 4 wymienione produkty są objęte należnością celną przywozową* ***erga omnes****, jeżeli w nowych państwach członkowskich zostanie stwierdzone istnienie w dniu 1 maja 2004 r. nadmiernych zapasów.*<br>[Thus, in accordance with that Article 4, the products referred to are subjected to an ***erga omnes*** import duty where the inventoried stocks in the new Member States are shown to be in surplus on 1 May 2004.] |
| (16) | SN (V CSK 454/12): | *Ponadto Sąd również naruszył art. 134 (...), co zdaniem skarżącego wywołuje skutek* ***erga omnes*** *(...).*<br>[In addition, the Court also violated Article 134 (...), which, according to the applicant, has an **erga omnes** effect (...).] |

217 Commission Regulation (EU) No 1407/2013 of 18 December 2013 on the application of Articles 107 and 108 of the Treaty on the Functioning of the European Union to *de minimis* aid

*Erga omnes* is present mainly in noun phrases but also appears in verbal phrases:

**CJ:** *skutek/skutki erga omnes* [erga omnes effect(s)], *ze skutkiem erga omnes* [with erga omnes effect], *należności celne erga omnes* [customs duties erga omnes]
**SN:** *skuteczny/-e erga omnes* [effective erga omnes], *obowiązek o charakterze erga omnes* [erga omnes obligation], *skutek/skutki erga omnes* [(erga omnes effect(s)), *działać wobec wszystkich (erga omnes)* [to apply to all erga omnes], *ze skutkiem erga omnes* [with erga omnes effect], *wywoływać skutek erga omnes* [to have an erga omnes effect]

This Latinism is unitalicized in most SN judgments; however, it also occasionally appears in parentheses (cf. SN judgment case no. V CSK 305/11).

**9) *etc.* (CJ: 5 RF, 1 NF; GC: 36 RF, 8 NF; SN: 5 RF, 1 NF)**
*Etc.* is an abbreviation of the Latin phrase *et cetera,* which means "and so on" or "and so forth" (Emanuel 1999: 113; IATE ID: 784371) – its direct equivalent in Polish is *itd.*, which is an abbreviation of *i tak dalej* [and so on]. It is used solely in place of omitted things of the same kind:

| | | |
|---|---|---|
| (17) | CJ (C-117/07&C-121/07): | *Ponadto według spółek grupy Areva wspomniany sekretarz nie mógł sam ponosić ciężaru materialnego (monitorowanie, sporządzanie protokołów* ***etc.****) (…).* [Moreover, that secretary was not alone in bearing the material (monitoring, drafting of minutes, **etc**) (…)] |
| (18) | SN (IV CSK 312/14): | *Rzeczpospolita Polska zgodziła się, aby prawa własności w razie, gdy nie były jeszcze wpisane do ksiąg hipotecznych, na imię posiadających je osób prawnych (Biskupstw, Kapituł, Kongregacji, Zakonów, Seminariów, Beneficjów proboszczowskich,* ***etc.****) zostały do nich wpisane, (…).* [The Republic of Poland agreed that property rights in the event that they were not yet entered in the mortgage books, in the name of legal persons owning them (Bishops, Chapters, Congregations, Orders, Seminaries, Benefices, **etc.**) have been entered into them, (…).] |

This Latin abbreviation has no direct collocates. It is also common, as far as the use of Latinisms goes, in higher registers of general Polish (cf. NKJP).

**10) *ex nunc* (CJ: 6 RF, 1 NF; GC: 5 RF, 1 NF; SN: 33 RF, 5 NF)**
The Latin phrase *ex nunc* means "from now" and refers to the effects of legal actions by describing certain legal effects which are applicable solely from a given point in time and therefore do not affect past actions (Chauvin *et al.* 2017: 116–119):

| | | |
|---|---|---|
| (19) | CJ (C-174/12): | *Trybunał, (...), orzekł w pkt 50 tego wyroku, że dyrektywa ta nie stoi na przeszkodzie, aby orzeczenie o rozwiązaniu umowy wywołało skutki* ***ex nunc****.*<br>[(...) the Court held, in paragraph 50 of that judgment, that that directive did not preclude the termination of the contract being ordered to have ***ex nunc*** effects.] |
| (20) | SN (V CSK 633/13): | *[Sąd Apelacyjny] nie podzielił poglądu Sądu Okręgowego, że w zakresie niewykonanym odstąpienie od umowy miało skutek* ***ex nunc****.*<br>[[The Court of Appeals] did not share opinion of the District Court that in the scope not performed the withdrawal from the contract had **ex nunc** effect.] |

*Ex nunc* is domesticated in CJ judgments, whereas in national judgments its foreign nature is emphasized through italicization. In addition, the latter exhibit a slightly wider collocational range of this phrase:

**CJ:** *skutek ex nunc* [ex nunc effect], *ze skutkiem ex nunc* [with an ex nunc effect]
**SN:** *ex tunc czy ex nunc* [ex tunc or ex nunc], *skutek ex nunc* [ex nunc effect], *ze skutkiem ex nunc* [with an ex nunc effect]

*Ex nunc* typically collocates with the noun *skutek* [effect] which refers to legal effects of legal acts.

**11) *ex post* (CJ: 45 RF, 10 NF; GC: 37 RF, 8 NF; SN: 33 RF, 5 NF)**
The phrase *ex post* has a wide range of meanings – "based on or determined by actual results, rather than expectations" (IATE ID: 786621), "based on knowledge and fact; viewed after the fact" as well as "objective; retrospective" (cf. Garner 2009: 661). The meaning of *ex post* may be opposed to the meaning of the phrase *ex ante*, as in *(ex ante, nie ex post)* [*ex ante*, not *ex post*] (SN judgment case no. II CSK 9/14).

| | | |
|---|---|---|
| (21) | CJ (C-380/09 P): | *Jeżeli chodzi o środki* ***ex post****, (...), Sąd przeanalizował ich skuteczność za pomocą ustaleń faktycznych, co również nie podlega kontroli Trybunału na etapie odwołania.*<br>[As for the **ex post** measures (...), the General Court assessed their efficacy in findings of fact which, similarly, it is not for the Court of Justice to review in the context of an appeal.] |
| (22) | SN (II CSK 202/12): | *Rozważanie* ***ex post****, co można było uczynić, żeby zapobiec utracie przesyłki, przy braku jednoznacznie rażących uchybień pracowników powoda, nie może prowadzić do wyłączenia odpowiedzialności ubezpieczyciela.* |

> [**Ex post** consideration, which could have been taken to prevent the loss of the parcel, in the absence of explicit blatant faults of the plaintiff's employees, cannot lead to the exclusion of the insurer's liability.]

*Ex post* occurs in noun and verb phrases and has a similarly wide collocational range:

**CJ:** *kontrola/potwierdzenie/uzasadnienie/zakaz taryfikacji ex post* [ex post control/acceptance/justification/prohibition of tariffs]
**SN:** *zobowiązanie/przyjęcie ex post* [ex post obligation/assumption], *przeprowadzona ex post kontrola* [inspection conducted ex post], *(ex ante, nie ex post)* [ex ante, not ex post]

Another variant of *ex post* is *ex post facto* meaning "by a subsequent act" or "after the fact" and describes any legal act, such as a statute, that has retrospective effect (Emanuel 1999: 124; Martin 2003: 193). An *ex post facto law* is a law that retroactively changes the legal status of actions that were committed before the enactment of the law. An *ex post facto statute* has a retrospective effect (Curzon and Richards 2007: 238).

**12) *ex tunc* (CJ: 10 RF, 2 NF; GC: 9 RF, 2 NF; SN: 157 RF, 23 NF)**
The Latinism *ex tunc* means "from the beginning" and refers to the effects of legal actions by describing certain legal effects that can affect situations prior to a given point in time and therefore can affect past actions – its meaning stands in contrast to the phrase *ex nunc* (Chauvin *et al.* 2017: 116–119):

(23) CJ (C-41/11): *Jednakże ta strona skarżąca przyznała przed sądem krajowym, że stwierdzenie nieważności zarządzenia może być orzeczone bez skutku* ***ex tunc****, pod warunkiem że utrzymanie skutków zaskarżonego aktu byłoby ograniczone w czasie.*
[However, it accepted before the referring court that annulment could be ordered without **retroactive** effect provided that the maintenance of the effects of the contested measure was limited in time.]

(24) SN (I CSK 559/13): *W zależności od treści lub charakteru stosunku prawnego, który orzeczeniem sądu ma być ukształtowany, orzeczenie konstytutywne wywiera skutek od chwili jego uprawomocnienia się albo z mocą wsteczną (****ex tunc****).*
[Depending on the content or nature of the legal relationship that is to be shaped by a court decision, a constitutive decision takes effect as soon as it becomes final or retrospective (**ex tunc**).]

(25) SN (V CSK 389/12): *Wynika z nich obowiązek zwrotu wzajemnych świadczeń przy odstąpieniu od umowy wzajemnej, które wywołuje skutek* ***ex tunc****, (…).*
[They show the obligation to reimburse mutual benefits when withdrawing from a mutual agreement that has an **ex tunc** effect, (…).]

The collocates show that Polish judgments display a wider collocational range of this Latinism.

**CJ:** *ze skutkiem/bez skutku ex tunc* [with/without ex tunc effect], *skutek ex tunc* [ex tunc effect]
**SN:** *działanie ex tunc* [ex tunc action], *działać/wywierać skutki prawne ex tunc* [to act/have legal effects ex tunc], *oświadczenie skuteczne ex tunc* [declaration effective ex tunc], *ze skutkiem ex tunc* [with ex tunc effect], *skutek ex tunc* [ex tunc effect], *z mocą wsteczną (ex tunc)* [with retroactive effect (ex tunc)]

However, both in CJ and SN judgments, the most frequent collocate is the noun *skutek* [effect], which refers to legal effects of legal acts (cf. *ex nunc*).

**13) *in abstracto* (CJ: 7 RF, 1 NF; GC: 4 RF, 1 NF; SN: 6 RF, 1 NF)**
*In abstracto* means "in general" or "in abstract terms" (Zajadło 2020: 264). The courts use it to refer negatively to certain actions or issues performed or to be performed by various institutions, third parties or other courts:

(26) CJ (C-404/10P): *Komisja nie mogła uwolnić się od tego obowiązku przez przeprowadzenie analizy **in abstracto** tych dokumentów.*
[Thus, the Commission could not avoid that duty by means of an examination **in abstracto** of those documents.]

(27) SN (II CSK 708/12): *Kontrola postanowienia wzorca umowy nie odbywa się bowiem **in abstracto** i zawsze powinna uwzględniać także pozostałe postanowienia konkretnego wzorca umowy (art. $385^2$ i art. $385^3$ k.c.).*
[Controlling the provisions of the standard contract does not take place **in abstracto** and should always take into account the other provisions of the specific standard contract.]

(28) SN (IV CSK 496/11): *Nawet uzasadniony merytorycznie (**in abstracto**) wywód prawny co do wykładni (zastosowania) konkretnego przepisu prawa materialnego, nie jest usprawiedliwioną podstawą skargi kasacyjnej, gdy nie odnosi się do stanu faktycznego (ustaleń) będącego podstawą zaskarżonego wyroku.*
[Even substantively substantiated (**in abstracto**) legal reasoning as to the interpretation (application) of a specific provision of substantive law is not a justified basis for a cassation appeal, when it does not refer to the facts (findings) underlying the judgment under appeal.]

This Latinism appears only once in parenthesis in SN judgments, although it should be noted that it does not serve as a shorthand for the explanation provided in the same sentence in Polish, as it merely provides additional information (see excerpt 28). *In abstracto* primarily forms noun phrases with nouns such as: *analiza* [analysis] or *kontrola* [inspection], but it also forms verb phrases which refer mostly to the argumentation of either referring courts (EU context) or lower instance courts (national context).

**CJ:** *przewidywać/odmawiać mocy dowodowej in abstracto* [to predict/deny evidential value in abstracto], *analiza/odmowa in abstracto* [analysis/refusal in abstracto]
**SN:** *określać/urzeczywistniać/określać in abstracto* [to define/materialize/determine in abstracto], *kontrola in abstracto* [inspection in abstracto]

The collocational range of *in abstracto* is similar in both CJEU and SN judgments.

**14) *in concreto* (CJ: 14 RF, 3 NF; GC: 8 RF, 2 NF; SN: 20 RF, 3 NF)**
*In concreto* means "in reality," "in a given case" (Zajadło 2020: 264), and it is the antonym of *in abstracto*. It is used by both the CJ and the SN to state that certain issues should be assessed legally in factual terms, not hypothetically:

| | | |
|---|---|---|
| (29) | CJ (C-421/13): | *Ów odróżniający charakter oznaczenia należy oceniać* ***in concreto****, po pierwsze, w stosunku do towarów lub usług objętych zgłoszeniem (...).*<br>[The distinctive character of the sign must be assessed **in concreto** by reference to, first, the goods or services in question (...)] |
| (30) | SN (V CSK 312/14): | *Zastosowanie domniemania faktycznego zawsze należy ocenić* ***in concreto*** *przy uwzględnieniu wszystkich okoliczności danej sprawy.*<br>[The application of an actual presumption must always be assessed **in concreto**, taking into account all the circumstances of the case.] |

*In concreto* occurs in both verbal and nominal phrases:

**CJ:** *badanie in concreto* [in concreto study], oceniać/sprawdzać in concreto [to assess/verify in concreto], *wykazywać występowanie in concreto związku między* (...) [demonstrate in concreto the relationship between]
**SN:** *ocena in concreto* [in concreto assessment], *dokonanie in concreto oceny konsekwencji prawnych* [performance of an in concreto assessment of legal consequences], *podlegać ocenie/rozpatrywać in concreto* [to be assessed/considered in concreto], *in concreto oznaczać* [to in concreto indicate]

The collocational ranges of *in concreto* are similar in both CJ and SN judgments.

**15) *in fine* (CJ: 26 RF, 6 NF; GC: 55 RF, 12 NF; SN: 325 RF, 48 NF)**
*In fine* is a Latin phrase which stands for "in short" or "in summary," or "at the end of" (Garner 2009: 848; IATE ID: 876256). It may also serve the function of textual reference by conveying the meaning "at the end of," as in the following excerpts:

(31) CJ (C-456/13 P): *Wnoszące odwołanie uważają, że w pkt 58–60 zaskarżonego wyroku Sąd dokonał zawężającej wykładni art. 263 akapit czwarty* ***in fine*** *TFUE.*
[The appellants consider that, in paragraphs 58 to 60 of the judgment under appeal, the General Court gave a narrow interpretation of **the final limb of** the fourth paragraph of Article 263 TFEU.]

(32) SN (I CSK 1003/14): Poza tym, aby art. 118 ***in fine*** k.c. miał zastosowanie musi zachodzić związek pomiędzy prowadzoną przez przedsiębiorcę działalnością gospodarczą i dochodzonym roszczeniem majątkowym.
[Besides, in order for Article 118 **in fine** Civil Code to apply there must exist a relationship between the entrepreneur's business activity and the claimed property claim.]

This Latinism is used consistently in intertextual references to legal provisions. However, the English-language version of the CJ judgment (excerpt 31) does not contain the Latin phrase, using instead the phrase "the final limb of."

**CJ:** *art. 12 in fine dyrektywy/rozporządzenia/TFUE* [Article 12 in fine directive/regulation/ TFEU]
**SN:** *art. 12 in fine k.p.c./k.c./k.s.h.* [Article 12 in fine Code of Civil Procedure, Civil Code, Commercial Companies Code]

The excerpt from the Polish judgment (excerpt 32) shows that *in fine* is foreignized through italicization. With its help, EU judges indicate various directives, regulations, treaties, etc., in primary and secondary EU law, whereas Polish judges refer to codified statutes, such as the Polish Code of Civil Procedure.

**16) *ipso iure* (CJ: 3 RF, 1 NF; GC: 3 RF, 1 NF; SN: 10 RF, 1 NF)**
*Ipso iure* and its variant *ipso jure* mean "by the law itself" (Garner 2009: 905; IATE ID: 1393933). *Ipso jure* does not appear in any of the corpora. It is used to describe consequences that occur automatically by operation of legal norms:

(33) CJ (C-132/14&C-136/14): *Trybunał miał bowiem już sposobność wyjaśnić, że prawo wtórne ma co do zasady taki sam zakres stosowania jak same traktaty i stosuje się w tym zakresie* ***ipso iure*** *(...).*
[Indeed, the Court has already had occasion to state that secondary legislation applies **in principle** to the same area as the Treaties themselves and applies automatically in that area (...).]

(34) SN (IV CSK 272/14): *Dlatego, gdy postępowanie egzekucyjne zostaje umorzone* ***ipso iure*** *(...), że wszczynający to postępowanie wniosek nie wywiera żadnych skutków, jakie ustawa wiąże z jego złożeniem.*
[Therefore, when the enforcement proceedings are discontinued **ipso iure** (...) it should be assumed that the application initiating the proceedings has no effects whatsoever that the Act entails with its submission.]

The italicization of *ipso iure* in national judgments stresses its foreign origin. Surprisingly, the English-language version of the CJ excerpt does not contain this Latin phrase, but instead uses the phrase *in principle.*

**CJ:** *stosować/być skutecznym ipso iure* [to apply/to be effective ipso iure]
**SN:** *przysługiwać/powstawać/um*arzać ipso iure [to be entitled to sth/to occur/to redeem ipso iure]

*Ipso iure* has a slightly wider collocational range in the national corpus, as shown above.

**17) *inter partes* (CJ: 16 RF, 3 NF; GC: 12 RF, 3 NF; SN: 5 RF, 1 NF)**
The phrase *inter partes* means "between the parties" (Collin 2004: 160; Garner 2009: 893). It may refer to, among other things, the effectiveness of legal agreements (Emanuel 1999: 190) or judicial proceedings:

(35) CJ (C-402/11 P): *Sąd oddalił ten zarzut z uzasadnieniem, że wskazany przepis znajduje zastosowanie wyłącznie w postępowaniach* ***inter partes***, *(...).*
[The General Court rejected that plea on the ground that that provision is applicable only to ***inter partes*** proceedings (...).]

(36) SN (V CSK 414/10): *Te umowy wywoływały bowiem skutki tylko między ich stronami (****inter partes****), w związku z czym mogłyby stanowić podstawę ewentualnej odpowiedzialności kontraktowej jedynie między ich stronami, (...).*
[These agreements had effects only between their parties (**inter partes**), and could therefore give rise to possible contractual liability only between their parties, (...).]

The excerpt from the SN judgment (case V CSK 414/10) in which *inter partes* is used in parentheses as a gloss is indicative of a lower degree of integration than in the case of this phrase in the excerpt from the CJ judgment. *Inter partes* refers primarily to contract law, according to which contractual obligations are to be settled between the parties; however, it also refers to a type or stage of proceedings in CJ judgments:

**CJ:** *postępowanie/etap/skutek inter partes* [inter partes proceeding/stage/effect], *mieć charakter inter partes* [to have an inter partes character]
**SN:** *wywierać skutki inter partes* [to have inter partes effects], (*inter partes*) [inter partes]

This Latinism has the completely opposite meaning to the previously described phrase *erga omnes* meaning "towards all" (Martin 2003: 179).

**18) *lex specialis* (CJ: 19 RF, 4 NF; GC: 10 RF, 2 NF; SN: 68 RF, 10 NF)**
According to Jowitt's dictionary (2010: 1342), *lex specialis* refers to "a doctrine of statutory interpretation derived from the Latin maxim *lex specialis derogat legi generali*." The IATE termbase provides information that *lex specialis* denotes a law governing a specific subject matter (IATE ID: 1089217). A specific legal norm is opposed to *lex generalis*, a general norm (cf. Garner 2009: 993). *Leges specialis* (pl.) establish exceptions from the application of *leges generales* (pl.) (cf. Chauvin *et al.* 2017: 126–127).

| | | |
|---|---|---|
| (37) | CJ (C-412/11): | *Komisja twierdzi, że art. 29 dyrektywy 2001/14 nie stanowi* ***lex specialis*** *będącego odstępstwem od ogólnej zasady.*<br>[The Commission submits that Article 29 of Directive 2001/14 is not a ***lex specialis*** derogating from the general rule.] |
| (38) | SN (II CSK 491/11): | *Relacja powyższa odpowiada stosunkowi lex generalis –* ***lex specialis***. [The above relationship corresponds to that of lex generalis – **lex specialis**.] |
| (39) | SN (I CSK 397/13): | *(...) poprzez niewłaściwą wykładnię (...) polegającą na pominięciu okoliczności, że przepisy art. 40 ust. 1 i ust. 2 ustawy o Agencji, stanowią przepisy szczególne (****lex specialis****) wobec późniejszych przepisów (...).*<br>[(...) through incorrect (...) interpretation involving the omission of the fact that the provisions of Article 40(1) and (2) of the Act on the Agency, constitute special provisions (**lex specialis**) in relation to the later provisions (...).] |

Polish judges sometimes use *lex specialis* in parentheses, which foreignizes this Latinism, but at the same time serves as a shorthand (gloss) for the explanation provided in the same sentence. The following collocates of *lex specialis* illustrate its collocational range:

**CJ:** *mieć charakter/stanowić lex specialis* [to have lex specialis character/to constitute lex specialis], *zasada lex specialis* [lex specialis principle]

**SN:** *przepis lex specialis w stosunku do/względem przepisu* [provision lex specialis in relation to the provision], *relacja lex specialis – lex generalis* [lex specialis-lex generalis relation]

The collocational ranges in both CJ and SN judgments exhibit similar collocates of *lex specialis*, although in national judgments this Latinism tends to occur primarily in noun phrases with *przepis* [provision].

**19) *lex specialis derogat legi generali* (CJ: 8 RF, 2 NF; GC: 9 RF, 2 NF; SN: 7 RF, 1 NF)**

*Lex specialis derogat legi generali* is a rule which is applied in the case of a collision of legal norms – when two rules regulating the same subject matter are in conflict, priority is to be given to the more specific one (IATE ID: 3527988; cf. Jowitt 2010: 1342). This means that a more particular norm prevails over a general one, unless it is a lower-tier norm (cf. Chauvin *et al.* 2017: 147).

| | | |
|---|---|---|
| (40) | CJ (C-48/14): | *Wbrew zaś twierdzeniom Parlamentu zasada* ***lex specialis derogat legi generali*** *znajduje zastosowanie, nawet jeżeli lex generalis i lex specialis zostały wydane przez tę samą instytucję.*<br>[Contrary to the Parliament's claims, the principle of ***lex specialis derogat legi generali*** is applicable even if the lex generalis and the lex specialis emanate from the same institution.] |
| (41) | SN (I CSK 333/11): | *Powyższe wskazuje na podrzędny charakter normy wynikającej z art. 632 § 2 k.c., co uzasadnia posłużenie się regułą* ***lex specialis derogat legi generali****.*<br>[The above points to the subordinate nature of the norm resulting from Article 632 § 2 of the Civil Code, which justifies the use of the rule **lex specialis derogat legi generali**.] |

*Lex specialis derogat legi generali* is crucial for the efficiency of a legal system which might, despite best legislative efforts, contain contradictory norms. This Latin conflict-of-law rule (cf. Chauvin *et al.* 2017: 147–149) is applied by judges to remove contradictions from the legal system. In the language of Polish judgments, *lex specialis derogat legi generali* has a much wider collocational range:

**CJ:** *zasada lex specialis derogat legi generali* [principle lex specialis derogat legi generali]
**SN:** *reguła (wykładni)/zasada/analiza w kategoriach/relacja lex specialis derogat legi generali* [rule (of interpretation)/principle/analysis in terms of/relation lex specialis derogat legi generali

Overall, this Latin legal principle enables succinct expression of a fundamental legal concept (cf. Matilla 2006: 143).

**20) *per se* (CJ: 6 RF, 1 NF; GC: 5 RF, 1 NF; SN: 4 RF, 1 NF)**
*Per se* is another Latinism used habitually by judges which is also common in everyday language. It means "by itself," "taken alone" (Jowitt *et al.* 2010: 1690), or "inherently," "intrinsically" (Emanuel 1999: 284), as in the following excerpts:

| | | |
|---|---|---|
| (42) | CJ (C-29/14): | *Z tego względu zdaniem Rzeczypospolitej Polskiej – wbrew twierdzeniu Komisji – owe normy nie mogą zostać zrównane ze zwykłą praktyką administracyjną i uważane za pozbawione* ***per se*** *wszelkiego charakteru wiążącego.*<br>[Thus, contrary to what is claimed by the Commission, those rules could not be treated as amounting to a mere administrative practice and regarded as lacking, **in themselves**, all binding character.] |
| (43) | SN (I CSK 147/12): | *To sam ustawodawca przesądził o tym, że te (...) zachowania kwalifikowane są* ***per se*** *jako postacie czynu nieuczciwej konkurencji, (...).*<br>[The legislator themselves decided that the behaviors (...) are **per se** qualified as acts of unfair competition, (...).] |

*Per se* does not appear with any equivalents in Polish. The lack of italicization additionally contributes to a greater degree of domestication of this Latinism.

**CJ:** *być pozbawionym per se charakteru wiążącego* [to lack per se all binding character], *skutkować wyłączeniem per se stosowania art. 12* [to result in exclusion per se of the application of Article 12], *oceniać per se* [to assess per se]
**SN:** *per se implikować* [per se imply], *kwalifikować per se jako* [to qualify per se as]

Both CJ exhibit a broader collocational range of *per se*, which, however, occurs mostly in verb phrases both in CJ and SN judgments.

**21) *prima facie* (CJ: 18 RF, 4 NF; GC: 43 RF, 10 NF; SN: 23 RF, 3 NF)**
The meaning of *prima facie* is "at first sight" (Jowitt *et al.* 2010: 1786) or "on the face of things" (Martin 2003: 379; IATE ID: 793821). *Prima facie evidence* has two meanings – it may either relate to evidence that is sufficient to discharge any evidential burden of proof borne by a party and that may be sufficient to discharge the persuasive burden of proof if no evidence in rebuttal is presented, or evidence of a fact that is of sufficient weight to justify a reasonable inference of its existence but does not amount to conclusive evidence of that fact (Martin 2003: 379; cf. Jowitt *et al.* 2010: 1786).

(44) CJ (C-552/10 P): *Artykuł 8 rozporządzenia podstawowego, zatytułowany "Zobowiązania," stanowi w ust. 1, 7 i 9: (...) Każda zainteresowana strona albo państwo członkowskie może przedstawić informację zawierającą dostateczny dowód [dowody **prima facie**] naruszenia zobowiązania.*
[Article 8 of the basic regulation, entitled 'Undertakings,' provides in paragraphs 1, 7 and 9 thereof as follows: (...) Any interested party or Member State may submit information showing **prima facie** evidence of a breach of an undertaking.]

(45) SN (II CSK 816/14): *Za podstawę tych domniemań i dowodu **prima facie** mogą posłużyć różne okoliczności (...).*
[The basis for these presumptions and prima facie evidence may be served by various circumstances (...).]

The corpus of CJ judgments has a wider range of collocations involving this phrase:

**CJ:** *badanie/dowody/stwierdzenie/ustalenie prima facie* [prima facie study/evidence/statement/finding], *zbyt długi prima facie termin* [excessively long prima facie period]
**SN:** *dowód prima facie* [prima facie evidence], *prima facie nasuwa się wniosek* [prima facie conclusion can be drawn]

Considering its placement in the syntactic structure, *prima facie* seems to be highly integrated in both EU and national judgments; however, as shown in the excerpt from the SN judgment, Polish judges may also emphasize the foreign origin of this Latinism through italicization.

**22) *quasi* (CJ: 16 RF, 3 NF; GC: 3 RF, 1 NF; SN: 9 RF, 1 NF)**
*Quasi* is a Latin prefix with the meaning of "apparent," "having some resemblance to, but lacking some requisites" (Curzon and Richards 2007: 484), "as if" (cf. Garner 2009: 1363). *Quasi* (used either with or without the hyphen) is used before nouns to suggest that the thing signified by the combination of "quasi" with the noun does not strictly comply with the definition of the noun, but only shares its qualities (Jowitt *et al.* 2010: 1861). The resulting phrase conveys the sense of approximate but inexact similarity (Emanuel 1999: 316).

(46) CJ (C-546/12 P): *W pkt 137 zaskarżonego wyroku Sąd uzasadnił zaś zastosowanie przez zasad wywiedzionych w wyroku ILFO/ Wysoka Władza (...) do Izby Odwoławczej na tej podstawie, że izba ta jest organem **quasi**-sądowniczym.*
[In paragraph 137 of the judgment under appeal, the General Court justified the application by analogy of the principles established in the judgment in ILFO v High Authority (...) to the Board of Appeal on the ground that it is a **quasi**-judicial body.]

(47) SN (V CSK 67/13): *Uwzględniając przytoczone regulacje trzeba zgodzić się z poglądem wyrażanym w doktrynie, że samorządowe kolegia odwoławcze są organami **quasi** sądowymi, spełniają bowiem funkcje orzecznicze.*
[Taking into account the quoted regulations, one must agree with the view expressed in the doctrine that the self-government appeal colleges are **quasi**-judicial bodies, because they fulfill judicial functions.]

The corpora contain many words preceded by this prefix:

**CJ:** *postępowanie quasi-sądowe* [quasi-judicial proceeding], *akty/przepisy/uprawnienia quasi-ustawodawcze* [quasi-legislative acts/provisions/rights], *norma quasi-proceduralna* [quasi-procedural norm], *organ quasi-sądowy* [quasi-judicial body]
**SN:** *quasi-własność* [quasi-property], *świadczenia quasi-alimentacjne* [quasi-maintenance payments], *organ quasi-sądowy* [quasi-judicial body], *quasi-poręczenie* [quasi-guarantee]

Overall, *quasi* indicates a strong superficial analogy between, for instance, *judicial proceedings* proper and *quasi-judicial proceedings* which only partly relate to or involve the handing out of adjudicative acts (Garner 2009: 1364). This Latin prefix is italicized in SN judgments, which points to its foreign nature.

**23) *ratio legis* (CJ: 11 RF, 2 NF; GC: 17 RF, 4 NF; SN: 57 RF, 8 NF)**
The Latinism, *ratio legis*, means "the reason or purpose for making a law" (Garner 2009: 1376). It refers to the underlying principle or reasoning behind a given legal provision or statute (cf. Zajadło 2020: 277). *Ratio legis* may be a part of the maxim *ratio legis est anima legis*, which means that the reason for the law is the soul of the law, or, in other words, that it is necessary to understand why the law came into existence in order to properly understand it (Jowitt *et al.* 2010: 1893). The courts use this phrase to examine whether statutes or regulations have a rational basis and genuine purpose (Emanuel 1999: 322):

(48) CJ (C-174/12): *Takie nabycie przez spółkę jej własnych akcji wynika z obowiązku ustawowego, (…), a taki obowiązek nie ma żadnego związku z **ratio legis** tego artykułu.*
[Such an acquisition by the company of its own shares is a consequence of the legal obligation under (…), that obligation being wholly unrelated to the ***ratio legis*** of that article.]

(49) SN (V CSK 147/15): ***Ratio legis** takiego rozwiązania prawnego podyktowane zostało potrzebą ułatwienia sytuacji dowodowej (…) użytkownika wieczystego w postępowaniu sądowym.*
[The ratio legis of such a legal solution was dictated by the need to facilitate the evidentiary (…) situation of the perpetual usufructuary in court proceedings.]

The lack of italicization of *ratio legis* as part of nominal and verbal phrases means that this Latinism is highly integrated in both EU and national judgments:

**CJ:** *ratio legis uregulowań/artykułu 12/przepisu/zasady słuszności* [ratio legis of regulations/Article 12/provision/principle of fairness]
**SN:** *mając na uwadze/biorąc pod uwagę/z uwzględnieniem ratio legis* [taking into account/ with reference to ratio legis], *ratio legis przepisów/rozporządzenia/ustawy/wydziedziczenia* [ratio legis of provisions/regulation/act/disinheritance]

The above collocates of *ratio legis* show that it has a broader collocational range in SN judgments.

**24) *sensu stricto* (CJ: 15 RF, 3 NF; GC: 45 RF, 10 NF; SN: 16 RF, 2 NF)**
The phrase *sensu stricto* means "in the strict sense" (IATE ID: 890324). It is used to point out that the word or term preceding that phrase is used in the sense of the original author, that is literally and without exaggeration or approximation:

(50) CJ (C-388/09): *Tym samym, w sytuacji takiej jak rozpatrywana w postępowaniu przed sądem krajowym, to właśnie Republika Portugalska, (...), powinna, jako państwo członkowskie jego miejsca zamieszkania, zapewnić mu wypłatę świadczeń w razie choroby* ***sensu stricto*** *(...).*
[So in the situation at issue in the main proceedings it is for the Portuguese Republic (...) as his Member State of residence to ensure payment of sickness benefits **stricto sensu** (...).]

(51) SN (V CSK 9/12): *Zgoda na plan połączenia wyrażany w uchwale połączeniowej dotyczy planu połączenia* ***sensu stricto*** *(...).*
[The consent to the merger plan expressed in the merger resolution applies to the merger plan sensu stricto (...)]

The Polish judgment (see excerpt 51) shows the lack of determination on the part of Polish judges to foreignize this Latin phrase, as only its second constituent word is italicized; however, it may also be only a typographic error. These are the most common collocates of *sensu stricto*:

**CJ:** *świadczenia w razie choroby/gry losowe/analiza prawna sensu stricto* [sickness benefit/ gambling/legal analysis sensu stricto]
**SN:** *roszczenie/postępowanie rozpoznawcze/powództwo/choroba psychiczna sensu stricto* [claim/exploratory negotiations/action/mental illness sensu stricto]

There is also an inverted variant of *sensu stricto, stricto sensu*, which can be observed in the English-language version of the excerpt from the CJ judgment, or the spelling variant *sensu stricte*, which occurs 7 times in SN judgments and only once in a CJ judgment.

**25) *sine qua non* (CJ: 12 RF, 3 NF; GC: 18 RF, 4 NF; SN: 50 RF, 7 NF)**
*Sine qua non* is the last Latinism on the list of those key to the genre of judgments. It means "without which not" (Ellis Wild 2006: 240) or "without which it could not be" (Hill and Hill 2009: 393). It refers to an indispensable condition or something on which the existence of something else necessarily depends (Garner 2009: 1511), as in *conditio sine qua non* (IATE ID: 896292):

| | | |
|---|---|---|
| (52) | CJ (C-287/11 P): | *Pozwane w postępowaniu odwoławczym kwestionują natomiast antykonkurencyjny charakter tych zachowań, stanowiący warunek* ***sine qua non*** *stwierdzenia naruszenia art. 81 WE.*<br>[However, the respondents contested the anti-competitive nature of that conduct, which is a **prerequisite** for a finding of an infringement of Article 81 EC.] |
| (53) | SN (I CSK 344/13): | *Dla uznania szkód powstałych podczas "bitwy o halę" za pozostające normalnym związku przyczynowym z niewykonaniem umowy polegającym na niewydaniu obiektu w terminie, należałoby wykazać nie, że szkoda ta nie wystąpiłaby, gdyby pozwany nie zaniechał wydania hali powodowi (warunek* ***sine qua non****), lecz także, iż występujący związek przyczynowy ma charakter adekwatny, (...).*<br>[In order to recognize damage caused during the "battle for the hall" for remaining in a normal causal relationship with non-performance of the contract consisting in not issuing the object in time, it should be demonstrated not only that the damage would not occur if the respondent did not give up the court to the claimant (**sine qua non** condition) but also that the causal relationship has an adequate nature, (...).] |

It is present as a post-modifier in noun phrases, although example 53 shows that it is used in parentheses in the domestic judgment as a shorthand for the explanation provided in Polish within the same sentence.

**CJ:** *warunek/przesłanka sine qua non* [sine qua non condition/premise]
**SN:** *warunek/test/relacja (conditio) sine qua non* [sine qua non condition/test/relation (conditio)]

The most frequent collocate of *sine qua non* in both corpora is the noun *warunek* [condition], which is sometimes replaced by the Latin word *conditio.*

## 10.5 Degrees of textual integration and discourse functions of Latinisms

In the process of analyzing the distribution of Latinisms in the corpora of EU and national judgments and their immediate context through concordances, I established that Latinisms exhibit various degrees of textual integration indicating either habitual or non-habitual usage (codeswitching, cf. Matras 2009: 101–145), based on their degree of syntactic fixedness and typographic variation (italicization or lack thereof). As regards the frequency of occurrence of Latinisms, "the more frequently a Latin phrase occurs, the more integrated it may be considered" (Kurzon 1987: 234). Based solely on the frequency of occurrence criterion, the data show that Latinisms are generally more integrated in national judgments. However, they are a valuable part of both supranational and national judgments.

According to Kurzon (1987: 234–239), Latinisms in English legal and general texts may be grouped according to their levels of textual integration – they may occur as:

(1) an entire Latin sentence within a text (with or without an explanation or translation), e.g.:

A person who consents to run the risk of injury cannot maintain an action in tort against the person who causes that injury. *"Volenti non fit injuria"* ("Where there is consent there is no injury") (James 1979: 368 after Kurzon 1987: 235);

(2) a Latin term, phrase or maxim within a sentence, e.g:

*Volenti non fit injuria...* has been a respected legal maxim for centuries (Morris 1980: 24 after Kurzon 1987: 236).

This *"ultra vires"* doctrine [...] (Kurzon 1987: 237 after James 1979: 91);

(3) a Latin term, phrase or maxim enclosed in parentheses within a sentence, typically as a gloss for identifying and understanding a legal term or institution in the sentence (cf. Matilla 2006: 140), e.g.:

Any act which its agents do in excess of these powers ("ultra vires") will be effective to bind it (James 1979: 91 after Kurzon 1987: 236).

The analysis has shown that Latinisms in CJEU and SN judgments do not occur as separate sentences, but rather show a high degree of textual integration by acting in the syntactic structure mostly as standalone replacements of equivalent Polish terms or phrase-level paraphrases and reiterations (cf. Matras 2009: 106). Their usage does not require high proficiency in Latin, but rather high content knowledge of law and legal concepts and corresponding Latin equivalents; the insertion of Latinisms in judicial utterances does not correlate with (full) bilinguality (cf. Matras 2009: 112). The manner of using Latinisms is indicative of the habitual reliance of judges on Latinisms to either report on the arguments of third parties or convey their own arguments. Kurzon (1987) also observes that a Latin expression may function in an English sentence as a qualifier of a noun, which is also often the case in Polish, e.g. *wykładnia a fortiori* [a fortiori reasoning], *rozumowanie a contrario* [a contrario reasoning], *biegły ad hoc* [ad hoc expert], *skutek erga omnes* [erga omnes effect] (see Section 10.4), and also corresponds to the second level of textual integration. As regards the third level of textual integration, only SN judges tend to enclose Latinisms in parentheses as glosses (explanations) for information conveyed in Polish. This boosts, to a certain degree, the foreign character of such Latinisms. Furthermore, an important typographic feature concerning the usage of Latinisms in judgments is their use of or lack of italicization. The analysis shows that the foreign nature of Latin borrowings in SN judgments is often emphasized through italicization, while their domestication is stressed when they are unitalicized. However, this feature of Latinisms in judgments needs to be investigated in greater detail using a larger data set.

Latinisms serve three main discourse functions: (1) precise expression of legal concepts and principles, (2) a rhetorical function, and (3) a display function (Matilla 2006: 140–146). Probably the most important characteristic feature of Latinisms from the point of view of legal professionals is that they enable the precise and succinct expression of legal concepts and principles (Matilla 2006: 143). This is demonstrated in the corpora, as Latinisms are sometimes added by judges in parentheses next to the corresponding concepts to increase the information value of their utterances (cf. *ex tunc, inter partes, lex specialis*, Section 10.5). Latinisms may seem to be of particular importance in the language of CJEU judges, who need to guarantee comprehension at the EU supranational level of their national audience in Member States. Yet, as shown by the data, they do not rely on them heavily, at least when compared to Polish judges. Judging by their high distribution, Latinisms are very important in the language of SN judges (see Section 10.3). The rhetorical function of Latin quotations in the language of judges consists of raising the level of solemnity of judicial decisions (Matilla 2006: 140–141). Instead of using equivalent words with essentially the same meaning in their own language (or a foreign language if it is a procedural language in which the judges deliberate, cf. Derlén 2015), judges use expressions of Latin origin such as: *a contrario* [EN: conversely, PL: (wprost) przeciwnie], *de facto* [EN: in fact, PL: faktycznie], *de iure* [EN: based on the law, PL: według prawa], *ipso iure* [EN: by the operation of the law itself, PL: na mocy prawa], or *per se* [EN: on its own, PL: samo w sobie], etc. With regard its display function, Latin is universally held in high regard by legal professionals, as it is a symbol of the roots of the European legal tradition (Matilla 2006: 141; Dajczak *et al.* 2018: 605). The importance of the influence of the Roman legal tradition on today's Polish legal system is emphasized by the row of columns outside of the building of the Supreme Court of the Republic of Poland in Warsaw, which are decorated with 86 Latin maxims of universal and everlasting character[218] and their translations into Polish, and which are meant to reflect the ideology of the court (cf. Kacprzak *et al.* 2001: 14, 17–21). Some notable examples of Latin maxims from this collection include *summus ius, summa iniuria* [extreme law, extreme injury], which means that the law, when strictly interpreted, may be the greatest source of injustice, or *leges ab omnibus intellegi debent* [statutes should be comprehensible to everyone], which serves as a reminder to the legislative bodies who draft legal provisions.

## 10.6 Conclusions

The frequent recourse to Latin by EU and Polish judges is unquestionably indicative of the continued influence of the classical Roman legal tradition, and its further development in Antiquity and the Middle Ages (cf. Matilla 2006: 140, 2008: 235), on contemporary legal systems and judicial argumentation. Throughout the development of European legal systems, a number of Latin maxims were adapted to European codifications of, for instance, civil law – *superficies solo cedit* (Article 552 of the French Civil Code; § 946 of the German Civil Code; Article 191 of the Polish Civil Code), *nulli res sua servit* (Article 617 of the French Civil Code; § 889 of the German Civil Code; Article 247 of the Polish Civil Code) (Dajczak *et al.* 2018: 605). Many legal principles have also been recognized and repeated by the judicature; for instance, the Polish Supreme Court solidified the Latin principle *nemo plus iuris in alium transferre potest, quam ipse habet* [one cannot transfer to another more rights than they have] (cases V CSK 72/12, I CSK 74/13, II CSK 451/12) (Dajczak *et al.* 2018: 605), whereas, at the supranational level, the Court of Justice of the European Union has relied on Latin maxims on numerous occasions, such as the maxim *nulla poena sine lege* [no penalty without a law] (cases C-352/09P, C-194/14P). This shows that the common legal tradition of European countries serves as a basis for CJEU judges to further develop and unify EU law. Matilla rightly points out that legal authors in Poland, a post-communist country in Central and Eastern Europe, rely increasingly on Latinisms to stress the fact that they and their country belong to the common legal tradition of Europe (Matilla 2008: 256). This is why there are certain Latinisms in use in Poland which have a purely national character (Matilla 2008: 259), such as the maxim *lex retro non agit* [the law is not valid retroactively], although the legal principle itself is recognized and acted upon by other countries governed by law (cf. Wołodkiewicz 2001a).

Latinisms may be a source of problems for the audience of judgments not versed in law due to their archaic nature, as well as translators (or rather lawyer-linguists)

---

218 Approximately 15 of these Latin maxims only loosely refer to the sources of Roman law, meaning that they were coined in Antiquity or later (cf. Wołodkiewicz and Krzynówek 2001: 24; Matilla 2006: 141–142). For a detailed description of the Latin maxims on the columns of the Supreme Court of the Republic of Poland, see Kacprzak *et al.* 2001.

who need to decide whether to simplify the TT by using an equivalent expression in the target language, to simply use the same Latin expression, or to use it as a gloss in parentheses. This issue is demonstrated by the fact that English-language versions of judgments often do not contain the Latin expression, using equivalent English expressions instead (see Section 10.4). It should be noted, however, that these language versions are also the end products of a translation process in which lawyer-linguists may, for instance, domesticate foreign words and phrases present in French language originals (cf. Chapter 1), simply conforming them to TL expectancy norms. On the other hand, the data show that Latinisms are a crucial part of the language of both EU and Polish judges, with several important differences. The Eurolect, that is both CJ and GC judgments, contains, on average, about half as many occurrences of Latinisms as SN judgments passed in the post-accession period (2011–2015) – EU judgments contain ca. 50 % fewer types of Latinisms. This means that Polish judges rely on Latin to a much greater extent than EU judges. This finding seems to be at odds with the assumption regarding the expected higher usefulness of Latin in EU judgments; since CJEU judgments are passed at the supranational level, Latin was expected to be widely used as a tool for facilitating communication among lawyers from various national legal cultures. However, CJEU judges manage to communicate their decisions without such heavy reliance on Latinisms as Polish judges, despite the fact that they operate at the supranational level. Therefore, the hypothesis regarding the supposed Europeanization of Polish judgments should be negated. The strong dependence of Polish judges on Latinisms may be indicative of their continued willingness to repeatedly demonstrate their sense of belonging to the common legal tradition of Europe (cf. Matilla 2008: 256). This is indicated by the marked rise in the total number of types and tokens of Latinisms compared to the pre-accession period, in which Latinisms were not as prevalent. Nevertheless, this finding should be confirmed in future studies on a larger sample of pre-accession SN judgments.

The analysis has shown that both EU and Polish judges are determined to continue to rely on Latinisms, as they perform several important functions. First, Latinisms raise the perceived level of solemnity and gravity attached to the judgments by the *communis opinio*, while at the same time stressing the universal and lasting nature of the law and its practical applications, adjudication in this case, allowing for concise and precise expression of crucial legal concepts and principles. In addition, it has been observed that judges use Latinisms to succinctly signal their applied methods of argumentation and inference (for instance, *a maiori ad minus, a minori ad maius, a fortiori*), or to indicate various conflict-of-law rules (for instance, *lex posterior derogat legi priori, lex specialis derogat legi generali, lex posterior generalis non derogat legi priori speciali*). On the whole, they are well integrated in the language of judgments, both as regards their syntactic and typographic qualities. They appear mostly as Latin phrases or maxims within a sentence and may also be enclosed in parentheses within a sentence (primarily in SN judgments). Borrowings, such as *i.e., e.g., per se,* also tend to be used in general Polish, although their usage varies depending on the genre and functional varieties of Polish. The question of signaling the distinct nature of Latinisms with typographic methods cannot be settled definitively based on the small sample of contexts of Latinisms presented in Section 10.4. Although judges should generally italicize foreign imports which are not commonly used in general language (cf. Wolański 2008: 37), they are not consistent in indicating the foreign nature of Latinisms in this manner, even though most Latinisms are not used in general Polish, e.g. *ex nunc*, *ipso iure*.

It can be concluded, then, that the use of Latin certainly constitutes yet another major linguistic feature of the genre of judgments. In addition, were it completely free of Latinisms, judicial writing would certainly lack some of its existing character. It might be assumed, however, that the lack of archaic and obscure Latinisms which are not as frequent in general Polish could result in judgments being more reader-friendly. The discourse functions of Latinisms are certainly favorable for the discourse community of judges, as they may allow them to assert more power and dominance (cf. Van Dijk 2008: 50), thus privileging the authority of the judicial institutions, and, in turn, contributing to greater non-negotiability of judgments. However, their deliberate use may be perceived as obscuring the content value of judgments due to the introduction of undue complexity to the already complicated technolect. The reliance of judges on Latinisms may also be the direct result of their legal socialization, that is the process of developing beliefs about the law, legal institutions and learning about the role of a judge during legal studies and adapting one's own behavior by observing experienced peers (cf. Goldberg 1984). It remains to be verified whether the absence of Latinisms would positively affect the reception of judgments on the part of the non-legal audience without harming their communicative potential. At this point, it may be assumed that a greater degree of domestication on the part of lawyer-linguists when translating from French into Polish, by substituting Latinisms with equivalent words and phrases in Polish, could potentially benefit the non-legal audience of EU judgments.

Based on the data presented, it can hardly be concluded that Latin on its own could serve as a legal *lingua franca* fostering international communication within the EU, although Latinisms seem to create firm foundations for communication spanning the EU and Polish legal cultures in Europe. Latinisms are indeed of service to legal professionals, allowing them to succinctly express legal concepts, as proven by the set of key Latinisms found in both EU and national judgments (see Section 10.3, Tables 10.5 and 10.6). Apart from the issues signaled above, further research should also investigate whether Latinisms in judgments are derived from European and national legislation or whether they are used exclusively in the metalanguage of the law (that is in judicial writing) (cf. Matulewska and Wasielewska 2003: 16). Moreover, it would be advantageous to learn whether judges in other EU Member States also rely on Latin as heavily as Polish judges and whether this is the immediate result of their legal training and professional socialization. Lastly, what should also be investigated is the degree to which Polish lawyer-linguists domesticate Latinisms when translating from French and whether they do so consciously.

# Chapter 11. Synthesis and conclusions

This study is, to date, the first large-scale corpus analysis of intra-linguistic variation in Polish judicial language, and more specifically its translated and non-translated varieties. This chapter aims to discuss and synthesize the results in a broader context. It also discusses the limitations of the study, suggestions for further research (see Section 11.3) and its practical applications (see Section 11.4).

## 11.1 Divergence of translated EU judgments from non-translated Polish judgments, internal variation within the Eurolect, and judicial Polish against general Polish

This section summarizes the observations concerning the degree of textual fit between translated CJ and GC judgments and non-translated post-accession SN judgments at the micro (local) level (see Chapter 3, Section 3.3). It was hypothesized that the former exhibit a divergent textual fit from the latter, therefore confirming the existence of the judicial variety of the Polish Eurolect. The discussion is divided into three sections – the level of chosen lexico-grammatical features, the phraseological level and the terminological level. The following sections also examine the degree of internal variation within the Eurolect, as well as the fit of non-translated judicial Polish to general Polish (NKJP).

### 11.1.1 Pillar I – Divergence at the lexico-grammatical level: CJ and GC vs SN_2011–2015, CJ vs GC, SN_2011–2015 vs NKJP

Table 11.1 summarizes the distribution of Pillar I linguistic features in the micro-level operationalization of the relation of textual fit.

The first sign of a divergent textual fit of CJEU judgments at the global textual level is the longer average word length. Divergence is also indicated by longer average sentence length – CJ sentences are longer by 3.77 words and GC sentences by 4.2 words. As it has been noted, it remains to be verified to what degree the changes are perceptible by the addressees. The data in Table 11.1 confirm the divergence of translations from non-translations due to the considerable deviation from the TL conventions of post-accession SN judgments which are characteristic of the wider national judicial context. The divergence manifests itself through the marked overrepresentation of most linguistic features subjected to analysis. The profiling of the Eurolect involved two corpora, which may, to a certain degree, inhibit a direct comparison with the corpus of post-accession SN judgments. For this reason, the column **CJ and GC vs SN_2011–2015** presents aggregate

**Table 11.1.** *Pillar I – Divergence of translated CJEU judgments from non-translated SN_2011–2015 judgments at the level of chosen lexico-grammatical features*

| | Translated EU case law | | | | | | Non-translated PL case law | | |
|---|---|---|---|---|---|---|---|---|---|
| | **CJ** | **CJ vs GC (%DIFF)** | **CJ vs SN_2011–2015 (%DIFF)** | **GC** | **GC vs SN_2011–2015 (%DIFF)** | **CJ and GC vs SN_2011–2015 (%DIFF)** | **SN_2011–2015** | **SN_2011–2015 vs SN_1999 (%DIFF)** | **SN_1999** |
| **I. Global changes** | | | | | | | | | |
| 1. Word length | 5.92 | +1 % | +5 % | 5.87 | +4 % | +4.5 % | 5.65 | 0 % | 5,67 |
| 2. Sentence length | 27.43 | −2 % | +16 % | 27.86 | +18 % | +17 % | 23.66 | +10 % | 21,44 |
| **II. Phraseological framing with prepositions** | **170,694** | **−3 %** | **−1 %** | **175,530** | **+2 %** | **+1 %** | **172,320** | **+6 %** | **162,897** |
| 3. Simple prepositions | 129,170 | −1 % | −3 % | 130,917 | −2 % | −2,5 % | 133,744 | +5 % | 127,740 |
| 4. Compound and secondary prepositions (RF>1): | 41,524 | −7 % | +8 % | 44,613 | +16 % | +12 % | 38,576 | +10 % | 35,157 |
| 1) Time | 7,234 | −23 % | −40 % | 9,422 | −22 % | −31 % | 12,136 | +9 % | 11,091 |
| 2) Cause-effect, result, contravention and condition: | 5,273 | +2 % | −16 % | 5,174 | −17 % | −16.5 % | 6,270 | +29 % | 4,859 |
| a) cause-effect | 2,487 | 0 % | −26 % | 2,489 | −26 % | −26 % | 3,373 | +42 % | 2,368 |
| b) result | 845 | −15 % | −41 % | 993 | −31 % | −36 % | 1,429 | +9 % | 1,316 |
| c) contravention | 439 | −16 % | −32 % | 524 | −18 % | −25 % | 641 | −1 % | 650 |
| d) condition | 1,502 | +29 % | +82 % | 1,168 | +41 % | +61.5 % | 827 | +58 % | 525 |
| 3) Reference | 10,493 | −17 % | +102 % | 12,701 | +144 % | +123 % | 5,201 | +34 % | 3,868 |
| 4) Intra- and inter-textual reference | 7,246 | 0 % | +55 % | 7,244 | +55 % | +55 % | 4,678 | +13 % | 4,155 |

| | Translated EU case law | | | | | | Non-translated PL case law | | |
|---|---|---|---|---|---|---|---|---|---|
| | CJ | CJ vs GC (%DIFF) | CJ vs SN_2011–2015 (%DIFF) | GC | GC vs SN_2011–2015 (%DIFF) | CJ and GC vs SN_2011–2015 (%DIFF) | SN_2011–2015 | SN_2011–2015 vs SN_1999 (%DIFF) | SN_1999 |
| 5) Participation | 907 | −15 % | −59 % | 1,061 | −52 % | −55.5 % | 2,209 | +13 % | 1,960 |
| 6) Modality | 840 | −17 % | −41 % | 1,018 | −28 % | −34.5 % | 1,421 | −16 % | 1,682 |
| 7) Apposition | 1,412 | +43 % | +20 % | 988 | −16 % | +4 % | 1,179 | −46 % | 2,186 |
| 8) Manner and instrumental relations | 1,708 | +74 % | +45 % | 981 | −17 % | +28 % | 1,177 | +8 % | 1,094 |
| 9) Adversariality | 1,229 | −48 % | +37 % | 2,386 | +167 % | +102 % | 894 | −35 % | 1,376 |
| 10) Measure | 358 | −40 % | −55 % | 601 | −25 % | −40 % | 801 | +15 % | 699 |
| 11) Inclusivity/ exclusivity | 734 | +12 % | −5 % | 658 | −15 % | −10 % | 774 | +6 % | 731 |
| 12) Commutative relations | 904 | +647 % | +45 % | 121 | −81 % | −36 % | 624 | +110 % | 297 |
| 13) Purpose | 1,699 | +56 % | +365 % | 1,088 | +198 % | +281.5 % | 365 | +17 % | 311 |
| 14) Distribution | 433 | +4 % | +24 % | 415 | +19 % | +21.5 % | 350 | +46 % | 240 |
| 15) Comparison | 252 | −21 % | +17 % | 320 | +48 % | +32.5 % | 216 | −31 % | 312 |
| 16) Space relations | 622 | +240 % | +242 % | 183 | +1 % | +121.5 % | 182 | +54 % | 118 |
| 17) Partitive relations | 115 | −27 % | +105 % | 157 | +180 % | +142.5 % | 56 | −50 % | 111 |
| 18) Active relations | 65 | −32 % | +51 % | 95 | +121 % | +86 % | 43 | −36 % | 67 |
| **III. Structurization of judicial arguments** | **61,202** | **−4 %** | **+14 %** | **63,535** | **+19 %** | **+16.5 %** | **53,518** | **+3 %** | **52,074** |
| 5. Parataxis | 32,630 | +7 % | +8 % | 30,599 | +1 % | +4.5 % | 30,147 | +8 % | 27,915 |
| 1) Additive coordinating conjunctions | 24,944 | 0 % | 0 % | 25,049 | +1 % | +0.5 % | 24,833 | +8 % | 23,046 |

(*continued on next page*)

**Table 11.1.** *Continued*

| | Translated EU case law | | | | | | Non-translated PL case law | | |
|---|---|---|---|---|---|---|---|---|---|
| | CJ | CJ vs GC (%DIFF) | CJ vs SN_2011–2015 (%DIFF) | GC | GC vs SN_2011–2015 (%DIFF) | CJ and GC vs SN_2011–2015 (%DIFF) | SN_2011–2015 | SN_2011–2015 vs SN_1999 (%DIFF) | SN_1999 |
| 2) Alternative coordinating conjunctions | 6,254 | +69 % | +175 % | 3,697 | +63 % | +119 % | 2,272 | +30 % | 1,743 |
| 3) Adversative coordinating conjunctions | 1,097 | −19 % | −51 % | 1,353 | −39 % | −45 % | 2,231 | −13 % | 2,550 |
| 4) Inclusive coordinating conjunctions | 335 | −33 % | −59 % | 500 | −38 % | −48.5 % | 810 | +41 % | 575 |
| 6. Hypotaxis | **28,572** | **−13 %** | **+22 %** | **32,936** | **+41 %** | +31.5 % | **23,371** | **−3 %** | **24,159** |
| 1) Complementizers | 14,427 | −20 % | +18 % | 18,108 | +48 % | +33 % | 12,222 | −5 % | 12,933 |
| 2) Relative pronouns | 13,663 | −1 % | +28 % | 13,847 | +30 % | +29 % | 10,670 | −1 % | 10,745 |
| 3) Concessive subordinators | 481 | −51 % | +1 % | 981 | +105 % | +53 % | 479 | −1 % | 482 |
| **IV. Deixis** | **43,624** | **−1 %** | **+47 %** | **43,955** | **+48 %** | **+47.5 %** | **29,750** | **−10 %** | **33,057** |
| 7. Personal pronouns (3rd person sg./pl.) | 2,539 | −17 % | +116 % | 3,065 | +161 % | +138.5 % | 1,176 | −10 % | 1,308 |
| 8. Possessive pronouns | 8,219 | −17 % | +4 % | 9,945 | +26 % | +15 % | 7,912 | +4 % | 7,620 |
| 9. Demonstrative pronouns | 21,800 | +13 % | +34 % | 19,216 | +18 % | +26 % | 16,235 | −12 % | 18,440 |
| 10. Indefinite pronouns and quantifiers | 3,556 | −15 % | +120 % | 4,180 | +158 % | +139 % | 1,618 | −11 % | 1,815 |

| | | | | | | | | | |
|---|---|---|---|---|---|---|---|---|---|
| 11. Adjectival deictic expressions | 7,510 | −1 % | +167 % | 7,549 | +169 % | +168 % | 2,809 | −27 % | 3,874 |
| **V. Depersonalization** | **26,812** | **−1 %** | **+12 %** | **27,208** | **+14 %** | **+13 %** | **23,955** | **0 %** | **24,061** |
| 12. Auxiliary verbs *być* [to be] and *zostać* [to become] | 12,647 | +3 % | +13 % | 12,331 | +10 % | +11.5 % | 11,237 | −3 % | 11,607 |
| 13. Passive voice | 6,557 | +2 % | +45 % | 6,456 | +42 % | +43.5 % | 4,537 | +16 % | 3,902 |
| 14. The *się* impersonal pattern | 6,513 | −4 % | 0 % | 6,805 | +5 % | +2.5 % | 6,509 | −11 % | 7,309 |
| 15. The *-no/to* impersonal pattern | 1,095 | −32 % | −35 % | 1,616 | −3 % | −19 % | 1,672 | +35 % | 1,243 |
| **VI. Legal reasoning** | **18,566** | **−7 %** | **0 %** | **20,067** | **+8 %** | **+4 %** | **18,657** | **−12 %** | **21,098** |
| 16. Verdictive, exercitive (argumentative) and reporting verbs | 7,750 | −14 % | −27 % | 8,960 | −16 % | −22 % | 10,681 | −14 % | 12,417 |
| 1) Verdictive verbs | 386 | +127 % | −46 % | 170 | −76 % | −23 % | 721 | −26 % | 975 |
| 2) Exercitive (argumentative) verbs | 701 | +101 % | +9 % | 349 | −46 % | +63 % | 644 | +22 % | 529 |
| 3) Reporting verbs | 6,663 | −21 % | −28 % | 8,441 | −9 % | −19 % | 9,316 | −15 % | 10,913 |
| 17. Causal patterns | 4,161 | −26 % | −13 % | 5,648 | +18 % | +5 % | 4,803 | −17 % | 5,820 |
| 18. If-then conditionals and related patterns | 3,076 | +39 % | +40 % | 2,207 | +1 % | +21 % | 2,196 | +19 % | 1,844 |
| 19. Patterns of purpose | 3,579 | +10 % | +266 % | 3,252 | +233 % | +250 % | 977 | −4 % | 1,017 |
| **VII. Framing with adverbials and participles** | **29,114** | **−92 %** | **+70 %** | **36,242** | **+112 %** | **+91 %** | **17,086** | **−6 %** | **18,187** |

(*continued on next page*)

**Table 11.1.** *Continued*

| | Translated EU case law | | | | | | Non-translated PL case law | | |
|---|---|---|---|---|---|---|---|---|---|
| | CJ | CJ vs GC (%DIFF) | CJ vs SN_2011–2015 (%DIFF) | GC | GC vs SN_2011–2015 (%DIFF) | CJ and GC vs SN_2011–2015 (%DIFF) | SN_2011–2015 | SN_2011–2015 vs SN_1999 (%DIFF) | SN_1999 |
| 20. Adverbials | 11,715 | −17 % | +20 % | 14,057 | +44 % | +32 % | 9,729 | −3 % | 10,054 |
| 1) Addition | 3,823 | −16 % | −14 % | 4,572 | +3 % | −11 % | 4,460 | +1 % | 4,423 |
| 2) Exemplification and particularization | 4,065 | +7 % | +106 % | 3,790 | +92 % | +99 % | 1,973 | −10 % | 2,204 |
| 3) Enumeration | 1,221 | −49 % | +622 % | 2,371 | +1303 % | +962.5 % | 169 | +12 % | 151 |
| 4) Stance | 1,338 | −32 % | −18 % | 1,959 | +20 % | +2 % | 1,637 | −14 % | 1,895 |
| 5) Contrast and exclusion | 1,268 | −7 % | −15 % | 1,365 | −8 % | −11,5 % | 1,490 | +8 % | 1,381 |
| 21. Participles | 17,399 | −22 % | +136 % | 22,185 | +202 % | +169 % | 7,357 | −10 % | 8,133 |
| 1) Adjectival participles | 7,973 | −25 % | +166 % | 10,568 | +253 % | +209.5 % | 2,998 | −2 % | 3,070 |
| 2) Adverbial participles | 9,426 | −19 % | +116 % | 11,617 | +167 % | +141.5 % | 4,359 | −14 % | 5,063 |

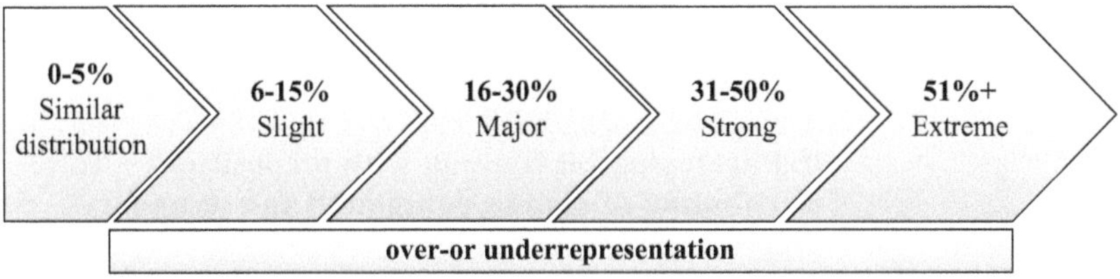


**Figure 11.1.** *Scale for the assessment of the degree of divergence*

percentage values on an over- and underrepresentation of individual linguistic features in the CJ and GC corpora. In this way, it will be possible to easily assess the degree of divergence of the judicial variety of the Eurolect as a whole from the language of Polish judges.

As previously mentioned, the overall textual fit may be described as considerably divergent. In order to assess the degree of fit according to the breakdown by the individual functional categories, it is necessary to devise an assessment scale. Its malleable values are only my own suggestion – they occupy a continuum, from a similar distribution to an extreme over- or underrepresentation. Its general purpose is to provide an overview of the degree of divergence (or convergence) within the individual lexico-grammatical categories. The values are presented in Figure 11.1.

According to the proposed scale for the assessment of the degree of divergence of translations from non-translations, there are five levels: similar distribution as well as slight, major, strong and extreme over- or underrepresentation. Their purpose is to facilitate the final discussion. It should be noted that the comparison of the distribution of phraseological (Pillar II) and terminological units (Pillar III) in non-translated post-accession SN judgments against general Polish (NKJP) has not been possible due to the shortcomings of the PELCRA search engine.

*Divergence at the level of chosen lexico-grammatical features: CJ and GC vs SN_2011–2015*

The degree of textual fit at the level of chosen lexico-grammatical features is assessed as **broadly divergent**. The aggregate data presented in Table 11.1 provide information on the internal and external variation as well as micro-diachronic language change. The over- and underrepresented features have been grouped according to the assessment scale for the degree of divergence.

Overall, taking advantage of the scale presented in Figure 11.1, the sub-genre of translated CJEU (that is both CJ and GC) judgments is characterized as follows:

1. 0–5 % = similar distribution

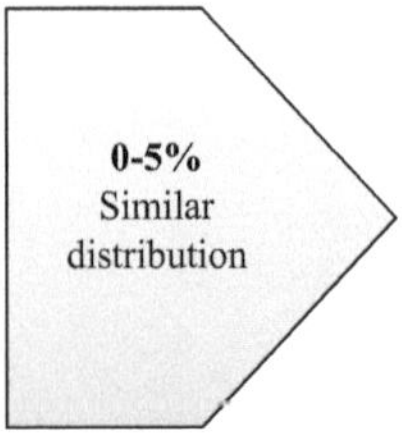


**I. Global changes:**
Average word length (+4.5 %)
**II. Phraseological framing with prepositions – Total distribution of simple, compound and secondary prepositions (+1 %)**
Simple prepositions (–2.5 %)
Compound and secondary prepositions conveying apposition relations (+4 %)
**III. Structurization of judicial arguments:**
Total distribution of all types of paratactic devices (+4.5 %)
Parataxis – additive coordinating conjunctions (+0.5 %)
**V. Depersonalization:**
The się impersonal pattern (+2.5 %)
**VI. Legal reasoning – total distribution of reasoning patterns (+4 %)**
Causal patterns (+5 %)
**VII. Qualification and cohesion:**
Stance adverbials (+2 %)

At the first level of the assessment scale, there are only two main categories which display a similar distribution: (1) total distribution of simple, compound and secondary prepositions which are indispensable to the phraseological framing, and (2) total distribution of reasoning patterns. Both of these functional categories can be regarded as crucial to judicial language and the presentation of argumentation. Patterns related to legal reasoning, including verdictive, argumentative and reporting verbs, despite having a similar distribution in both EU and national judgments, show major internal variation in the Eurolect. Apart from these two main categories, there are also several sub-categories which have a similar distribution in the Eurolect and national judgments, none of which have a decisive impact on the degree of divergence of the corresponding categories. Generally, a similar level of distribution of linguistic features is assumed not to signal any perceptible divergence understood as decreased naturalness.

2. 6–15 % = slight over- or underrepresentation

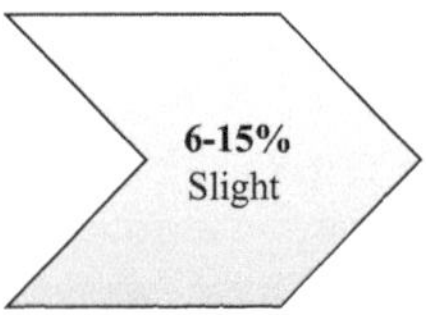


**II. Phraseological framing with prepositions:**
Compound and secondary prepositions (all types of relations) (+12 %)
Compound and secondary prepositions conveying inclusivity/exclusivity relations (–10 %)
**IV. Deixis:**
Possessive pronouns (+15 %)
**V. Depersonalization – all types of depersonalized patterns** (+13 %):

Auxiliary verbs być [to be] and zostać [to become] (+11.5 %)
**VII. Qualification and cohesion:**
Addition adverbials (−11 %)
Contrast and exclusion adverbials (−11.5 %)

A slight overrepresentation can be attributed only to two main functional categories – the total number of depersonalized patterns and the total number of compound and secondary prepositions expressing all types of relations. Apart from these two categories, there are also five sub-categories indicating either a slight over- or underrepresentation, none of which have a prevailing influence on the distributional characteristics of the overarching categories. As the name suggests, slightly over- or underrepresented linguistic features may only marginally contribute to a lower level of naturalness of translations.

3. 16–30 % = major over- or underrepresentation

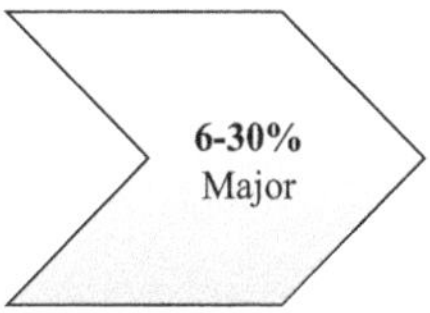


**I. Global changes:**
Sentence length (+17 %)
**II. Phraseological framing with prepositions:**
Compound and secondary prepositions conveying the following relations: cause-effect, result, contravention and condition – all 4 types (−16.5 %), cause-effect (−26 %), contravention (−25 %), manner and instrumental relations (+28 %), distribution (+21.5 %)
**III. Structurization of judicial arguments – all structuring patterns (+16,5 %):**
Hypotaxis – Relative pronouns (+29 %)
**IV. Deixis:**
Demonstrative pronouns (+26 %)
**V. Depersonalization:**
The *-no/to* impersonal pattern (−19 %)
**VI. Legal reasoning:**
Verdictive, exercitive (argumentative) and reporting verbs (−22 %)
Verdictive verbs (23 %)
Reporting verbs (19 %)
If-then conditionals and related patterns (+20.5 %)

In general, a major over- or underrepresentation of linguistic features may be assumed to be perceptible by the audience of judgments. However, it may also be the case that linguistic features over- or underrepresented to a major degree are only discernible in a quantitative study. The features over- or underrepresented to a major degree are expected to considerably impact the degree of naturalness of translations relative to non-translations, but not to a great degree. The categories of average sentence length and the total distribution of all structuring patterns are the main functional categories overrepresented to a major degree.

The remaining categories are only sub-categories of the main functional categories, the overall divergence of which cannot be classified as major. The category of average sentence length seems to be very conspicuous, in that the audience of EU judgments could potentially be aware of longer sentences, although this needs to be verified in further research. The same pertains to the other (sub-) categories from this group, as they may be expected to create the impression of decreased naturalness.

4. 31–50 % = strong over- or underrepresentation

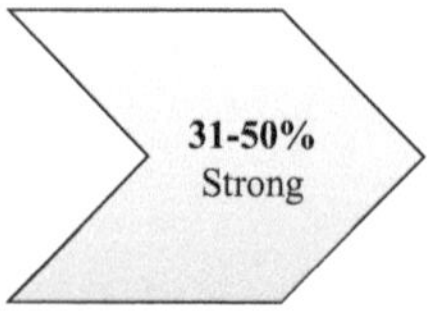


**II. Phraseological framing with prepositions:**
Compound and secondary prepositions conveying the following relations: time (–31 %), result (–36 %), modality (–34.5 %), measure (–40 %), commutative relations (–36 %), comparison (+32.5 %)
**III. Structurization of judicial arguments:**
Parataxis – Adversative coordinating conjunctions (–45 %)
Parataxis – Inclusive coordinating conjunctions (–48.5 %)
Hypotaxis (all types) (+31.5 %)
Hypotaxis – Complementizers (+33 %)
**IV. Deixis – all deictic devices (+47,5 %):**
**V. Depersonalization:**
Passive voice (+43,5 %)
**VII. Qualification and cohesion:**
Adverbials (all) (+32 %)

The only main functional category with a strong level of divergence is the category of all deictic devices. The remaining categories in this group are only functional sub-categories. A particularly high underrepresentation has been observed in the case of two sub-categories of paratactic devices and one functional category of compound and secondary prepositions. The remaining sub-categories are strongly overrepresented, most notably all types of hypotactic devices and passive voice markers. A strong over- or underrepresentation of the identified feature may be expected to be very salient.

5. 51 % or more = extreme over- or underrepresentation

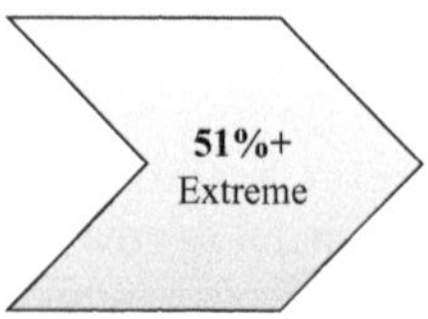


**II. Phraseological framing with prepositions:**
Compound and secondary prepositions conveying the following relations: condition (+61,5 %), reference (+123 %), intra- and inter-textual reference (+55 %), participation (–55,5 %), adversariality (+102 %), purpose (+281,5 %), space relations (+121,5 %), partitive relations (+142,5 %), active relations (+86 %)

**III. Structurization of judicial arguments:**
Parataxis – Alternative coordinating conjunctions (+119 %)
Hypotaxis – Concessive subordinators (+53 %)
**IV. Deixis:**
Personal pronouns (3rd person sg./pl.) (+138.5 %)
Indefinite pronouns and quantifiers (+139 %)
Adjectival deictic expressions (+168 %)
**VI. Legal reasoning:**
Exercitive (argumentative) verbs (+63 %)
Patterns of purpose (+250 %)
**VII. Qualification and cohesion – all type of patterns (+91 %):**
Exemplification and particularization adverbials (+99 %)
Enumeration adverbials (+962,5 %)
Participles – all types of participles (+169 %)
Adjectival participles (+209,5 %)
Adverbial participles (+141,5 %)

The last level in the assessment scale groups (sub-)categories which display an extreme over- or underrepresentation. Nearly all (sub-)categories in this group are extremely overrepresented in translations relative to non-translated national judgments, except for the functional category of compound and secondary prepositions expressing participation relations. The overrepresented (sub-)categories may be those which are particularly crucial from the perspective of the realization of genre goals in CJEU judgments. An exceptional level of overrepresentation can be attributed to all types of qualifying and cohesive patterns. All of the functional (sub-)categories in this group are regarded as affecting the divergence of translations to the greatest degree — the textual fit in these areas is regarded as diverging most from national judgments, which may be easily perceived (especially in the case of unnaturally overrepresented linguistic features) by the audience of the translations.

The functional categories listed above confirm unequivocally that the subgenres of CJEU judgments depart from the conventions of national, non-translated judgments. The Eurolect's general tendency is to overrepresent linguistic features. Out of the group of 21 main functional categories (see Table 11.1), only two show underrepresentation (a total distribution of simple prepositions — 2.5 % and performative, exercitive and reporting verbs —22 %). The differences are related mostly to the lexico-grammatical level as subjected to analysis. What is particularly interesting is that the linguistic features which can be most directly associated with the formulation of legal reasoning and argumentation are similarly distributed in both supranational and national judgments, with the exception of, for instance, the epistemic modal verb *należy* [(it/one) must/should be]; at the global level, these are: phraseological framing with prepositions, legal reasoning patterns and stance adverbials. This observation should be confirmed by further research. Overall, the **divergent textual fit of translated CJEU judgments** from non-translated SN judgments confirms the existence of a distinct judicial variety of the Polish Eurolect, which is molded by both the translation process and the contextual factors affecting the drafting of supranational judgments (cf. Sections 11.1.2, 11.1.3).

*Internal variation within the Eurolect: CJ vs GC*
In this study, the sub-corpora of CJ and GC judgments were used to measure the degree of internal variation in the Eurolect, in order to compare it to the degree of divergence of translated CJEU judgments from non-translated national judgments. As expected, the fit of both sub-genres of CJ and GC judgments is convergent, although there are certain salient differences, mostly at the level of the individual functional sub-categories. The degree of convergence is evaluated primarily using the proposed assessment scale (see Figure 11.1):

1. 0–5 % – similar distribution

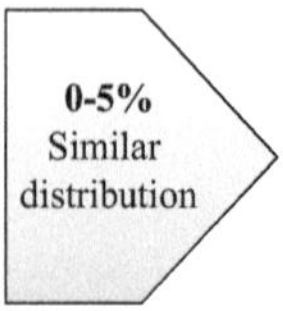


**I. Global changes:**
Average word length (+1 %)
Average sentence length (−2 %)
**II. Phraseological framing with prepositions – Total distribution of simple, compound and secondary prepositions (−3 %);**
Simple prepositions (−1 %)
Compound and secondary prepositions conveying the following relations: cause-effect, result, contravention and condition: (+2 %), cause-effect (0 %), intra- and inter-textual reference (0 %), distribution (+4 %)
**III. Structurization of judicial arguments – all structuring patterns (−4 %);**
Parataxis – Additive coordinating conjunctions (0 %)
Hypotaxis – Relative pronouns (−1 %)
**IV. Deixis – all deictic devices (−1 %):**
Adjectival deictic expressions (−1 %)
**V. Depersonalization – all types of depersonalized patterns (−1 %):**
Auxiliary verbs być [to be] and zostać [to become] (+3 %)
Passive voice (+2 %)
The się impersonal pattern (−4 %)

2. 6–15 % – slight over-/underrepresentation

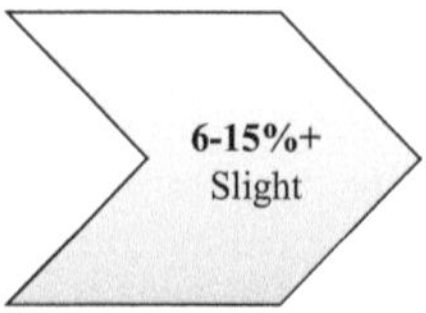


**II. Phraseological framing with prepositions:**
Compound and secondary prepositions: (−7 %)
Compound and secondary prepositions conveying the following relations: result (−15 %), participation (−15 %), inclusivity/exclusivity (+12 %)

**III. Structurization of judicial arguments:**
Parataxis (+7 %)
Hypotaxis (−13 %)
**IV. Deixis – pointing devices:**
Demonstrative pronouns (+13 %)
Indefinite pronouns and quantifiers (−15 %)
**VI. Legal reasoning – total distribution of reasoning patterns (−7 %):**
Performative, exercitive (argumentative) and reporting verbs (−14 %)
Patterns of purpose (+10 %)
**VII. Qualification and cohesion:**
Exemplification and particularization adverbials (+7 %)
Contrast and exclusion adverbials (−7 %)

3. 16–30 % — major over-/underrepresentation

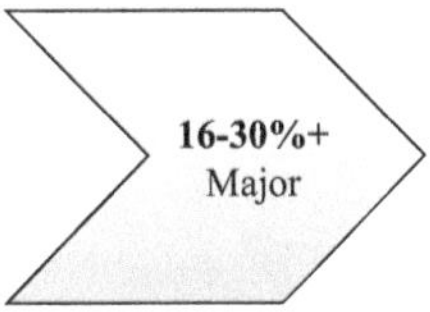


**II. Phraseological framing with prepositions:**
Compound and secondary prepositions conveying the following relations: time (−23 %), contravention (−16 %), condition (+29 %), reference (−17 %), modality (−17 %), comparison (−21 %), and partitive relations (−27 %)
**III. Structurization of judicial arguments:**
Parataxis – Adversative coordinating conjunctions (−19 %)
Hypotaxis: complementizers (−20 %)
**IV. Deixis:**
Personal pronouns (3rd person sg./pl.) (−17 %)
Possessive pronouns (−17 %)
**VI. Legal reasoning:**
Reporting verbs (−21 %)
Causal patterns (−26 %)
**VII. Qualification and cohesion:**
Adverbials (−17 %): addition (−16 %)
Participles (−22 %): adjectival participles (−25 %), adverbial participles (−19 %)

4. 31–50 % — strong over-/underrepresentation

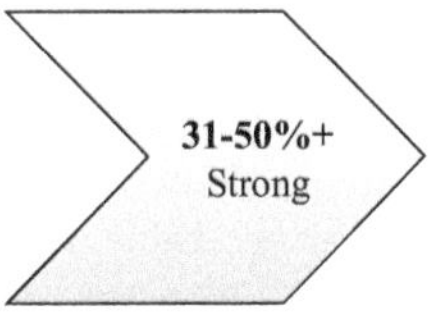


**II. Phraseological framing with prepositions:**
Compound and secondary prepositions conveying the following relations: apposition (+43 %), adversariality (−48 %), measure (−40 %), active relations (−32 %)
**III. Structurization of judicial arguments:**
Parataxis: inclusive coordinating conjunctions (−33 %)
**V. Depersonalization:**
The *-no/to* impersonal pattern (−32 %)

**VI. Legal reasoning:**
If-then conditionals and related patterns (+39 %)
**VII. Qualification and cohesion:**
Adverbials: enumeration (–49 %), stance (–32 %)

5. 51 % or more — extreme over-/underrepresentation

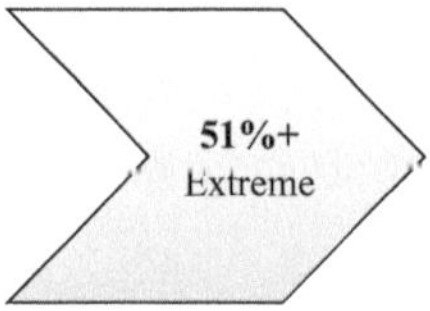


**II. Phraseological framing with prepositions:**
Compound and secondary prepositions conveying the following relations: manner and instrumental relations (+74 %), commutative relations (+647 %), purpose (+56 %), and space relations (+240 %)
**III. Structurization of judicial arguments:**
Parataxis: alternative coordinating conjunctions (+69 %)
Hypotaxis: concessive subordinators (–51 %)
**VI. Legal reasoning:**
Verdictive verbs (+127 %)
Exercitive (argumentative) verbs (+101 %)
**VII. Qualification and cohesion – all types of patterns (–92 %)**

The main reason for the assessment of the fit of translated CJ and GC judgments as fairly convergent is the similar distribution among five out of the seven main functional categories: global changes, phraseological framing with prepositions – total distribution of simple, compound and secondary prepositions, structurization of judicial arguments – all structuring patterns, deixis – all deictic devices, and depersonalization – all types of depersonalized patterns. The same pertains to the category legal reasoning – total distribution of reasoning patterns, as its markers are only slightly underrepresented in translated CJ judgments (by 7 %). The only peculiarity pertains to the extreme underrepresentation of all types of qualifying and cohesive patterns (by 92 %), although this functional category may not necessarily be directly associated with the goals of the two EU sub-genres. All of this indicates that the internal similarity of the two Eurolect sub-genres stands in stark contrast to the overall divergence of the Eurolect from non-translated national judgments (see above).

*Judicial Polish against general Polish: SN_2011–2015 vs NKJP*
The study data also comprise data from the balanced version of the NKJP corpus. Although the PELCRA search engine (as opposed to WS), which was used to search this corpus, did not facilitate more complicated queries, it made it possible to extract some data related to the comparison of non-translated judicial Polish and general Polish. This entails that the analysis is not exhaustive. Table 11.2 presents a comparison of the quantitative data from the SN_2011–2015 corpus and NKJP.

**Table 11.2.** *Pillar I – Non-translated judicial Polish against general Polish (NKJP)*

| | Non-translated PL case law | | General Polish |
|---|---|---|---|
| | SN_2011–2015 | SN_2011–2015 vs NKJP (%DIFF) | NKJP |
| I. GLOBAL CHANGES | | | |
| 1. Word length | 5,65 | N/A | N/A |
| 2. Sentence length | 23,66 | N/A | N/A |
| **II. PREPOSITIONS** | **172,320** | **+111 %** | **81,602** |
| 3. Simple prepositions | 133,744 | +93 % | 69,162 |
| 4. Compound and secondary prepositions (RF>1): | 38,576 | +210 % | 12,440 |
| 1) Time | 12,136 | +314 % | 2,928 |
| 2) Cause-effect, result, contravention and condition: | 6,270 | +268 % | 1,702 |
| a) cause-effect | 3,373 | +278 % | 892 |
| b) result | 1,429 | +550 % | 220 |
| c) contravention | 641 | +241 % | 188 |
| d) condition | 827 | +106 % | 402 |
| 3) Reference | 5,201 | +296 % | 1,312 |
| 4) Intra- and inter-textual reference | 4,678 | +758 % | 545 |
| 5) Participation | 2,209 | +481 % | 380 |
| 6) Modality | 1,421 | +140 % | 592 |
| 7) Apposition | 1,179 | +198 % | 396 |
| 8) Manner and instrumental relations | 1,177 | +104 % | 576 |
| 9) Adversariality | 894 | +102 % | 443 |
| 10) Measure | 801 | −6 % | 848 |
| 11) Inclusivity/exclusivity | 774 | −13 % | 891 |
| 12) Commutative relations | 624 | +134 % | 267 |
| 13) Purpose | 365 | +38 % | 265 |
| 14) Distribution | 350 | +169 % | 130 |
| 15) Comparison | 216 | +23 % | 175 |
| 16) Space relations | 182 | −65 % | 526 |
| 17) Partitive relations | 56 | −86 % | 388 |

*(continued on next page)*

**Table 11.2.** *Continued*

| | Non-translated PL case law | | General Polish |
|---|---|---|---|
| | SN_2011–2015 | SN_2011–2015 vs NKJP (%DIFF) | NKJP |
| 18) Active relations | 43 | −43 % | 76 |
| **III. STRUCTURIZATION OF JUDICIAL ARGUMENTS** | **53,518** | **+35 %** | **39,615** |
| 5. Parataxis | 30,147 | +53 % | 19,710 |
| 1) Additive coordinating conjunctions | 24,833 | +82 % | 13,661 |
| 2) Alternative coordinating conjunctions | 2,272 | +51 % | 1,503 |
| 3) Adversative coordinating conjunctions | 2,231 | −43 % | 3,917 |
| 4) Inclusive coordinating conjunctions | 810 | +29 % | 629 |
| 6. Hypotaxis | 23,371 | +17 % | 19,905 |
| 1) Complementizers | 12,222 | +54 % | 7,918 |
| 2) Relative pronouns | 10,670 | −4 % | 11,106 |
| 3) Concessive subordinators | 479 | −46 % | 881 |
| **IV. DEIXIS – POINTING DEVICES** | **29,750** | **+16 %** | **25,554** |
| 7. Personal pronouns (3rd person sg./pl.) | 1,176 | −23 % | 1,527 |
| 8. Possessive pronouns | 7,912 | +17 % | 6,751 |
| 9. Demonstrative pronouns | 16,235 | +28 % | 12,671 |
| 10. Indefinite pronouns and quantifiers | 1,618 | −59 % | 3,952 |
| 11. Adjectival deictic expressions | 2,809 | +330 % | 653 |
| **V. DEPERSONALIZATION** | **23,955** | **N/A** | **N/A** |
| 12. Auxiliary verbs *być* [to be] and *zostać* [to become] | 11,237 | −29 % | 15,821 |
| 13. Passive voice | 4,537 | N/A | N/A |
| 14. The *się* impersonal pattern | 6,509 | −32 % | 9,587 |
| 15. The *-no/to* impersonal pattern | 1,672 | N/A | N/A |
| **VI. LEGAL REASONING** | **18,657** | **N/A** | **N/A** |
| 16. Verdictive, exercitive (argumentative) and reporting verbs | 10,681 | N/A | N/A |
| 1) Verdictive verbs | 721 | N/A | N/A |
| 2) Exercitive (argumentative) verbs | 644 | N/A | N/A |
| 3) Reporting verbs | 9,316 | N/A | N/A |

Table 11.2. *Continued*

| | Non-translated PL case law | | General Polish |
|---|---|---|---|
| | SN_2011–2015 | SN_2011–2015 vs NKJP (%DIFF) | NKJP |
| 17. Causal patterns | 4,803 | +16 % | 4,135 |
| 18. If-then conditionals and related patterns | 2,196 | +19 % | 1,839 |
| 19. Patterns of purpose | 977 | −61 % | 2,489 |
| **VII. QUALIFICATION AND COHESION** | **17,086** | **+42 %** | **12,017** |
| 20. Adverbials | 9,729 | −5 % | 10,270 |
| 1) Addition | 4,460 | +13 % | 3,954 |
| 2) Exemplification and particularization | 1,973 | −3 % | 2,035 |
| 3) Enumeration | 169 | −25 % | 224 |
| 4) Stance | 1,637 | −31 % | 2,386 |
| 5) Contrast and exclusion | 1,490 | −11 % | 1,671 |
| 21. Participles | 7,357 | +321 % | 1,747 |
| 1) Adjectival participles | 2,998 | +290 % | 768 |
| 2) Adverbial participles | 4,359 | +345 % | 979 |

The data show that the key genre features of national judgments are as follows:

1. extreme overrepresentation of simple, compound and secondary prepositions,
2. strong overrepresentation of patterns structuring judicial argumentation,
3. major overrepresentation of deictic devices,
4. strong overrepresentation of qualifying and cohesive devices.

It was not possible to thoroughly verify the status of depersonalized constructions and patterns related to legal reasoning in non-translations due to the mentioned difficulties.

### 11.1.2 Pillar II – Divergence at the phraseological level: CJ and GC vs SN_2011–2015, CJ vs GC

Table 11.3 summarizes the data on the distribution of formulaic units investigated within Pillar II.

**Table 11.3.** *Pillar II – Divergence of translated CJEU judgments from non-translated SN_2011–2015 judgments at the phraseological level*

| | Translated EU case law | | | | | | Non-translated PL case law | | |
|---|---|---|---|---|---|---|---|---|---|
| | **CJ** | **CJ vs GC (%DIFF)** | **CJ vs SN_2011–2015 (%DIFF)** | **GC** | **GC vs SN_2011–2015 (%DIFF)** | **CJ and GC vs SN_2011–2015 (%DIFF)** | **SN_2011–2015** | **SN_2011–2015 vs SN_1999 (%DIFF)** | **SN_1999** |
| **I. Lexical bundles (total number of types and occurrences)** | | | | | | | | | |
| 2–grams – types | 1,826 | 0 % | +1 % | 1,828 | +2 % | +1.5 % | 1,800 | −12 % | 2,036 |
| 3–grams – types | 660 | +8 % | +7 % | 611 | −1 % | +6 % | 615 | −22 % | 784 |
| 4–grams – types | 318 | +54 % | +22 % | 207 | −21 % | +1 % | 261 | −26 % | 353 |
| 5–grams – types | 202 | +122 % | +52 % | 91 | −32 % | +20 % | 133 | −27 % | 183 |
| 6–grams – types | 151 | +268 % | +113 % | 41 | −42 % | +71 % | 71 | −34 % | 107 |
| 7–grams – types | 120 | +532 % | +161 % | 19 | −59 % | +102 % | 46 | −34 % | 70 |
| 8–grams – types | 100 | +900 % | +223 % | 10 | −68 % | +155 % | 31 | −23 % | 40 |
| 2–grams – occurrences | 242,915 | −3 % | −5 % | 251,397 | −2 % | −3.5 % | 255,857 | −14 % | 298,271 |
| 3–grams – occurrences | 73,507 | +8 % | −5 % | 68,330 | −12 % | −8.5 % | 77,275 | −25 % | 103,542 |
| 4–grams – occurrences | 30,550 | +60 % | +2 % | 19,153 | −36 % | −34 % | 30,082 | −34 % | 45,753 |
| 5–grams – occurrences | 17,407 | +162 % | +21 % | 6,655 | −54 % | −33 % | 14,354 | −45 % | 25,979 |
| 6–grams – occurrences | 12,462 | +351 % | +65 % | 2,765 | −63 % | +2 % | 7,535 | −52 % | 15,777 |
| 7–grams – occurrences | 9,196 | +651 % | +108 % | 1,225 | −72 % | +36 % | 4,415 | −52 % | 9,110 |
| 8–grams – occurrences | 7,327 | +1078 % | +157 % | 622 | −78 % | +79 % | 2,854 | −40 % | 4,788 |
| **2–8–grams – Total types** | **3,377** | **+20 %** | **+14 %** | **2,807** | **−5 %** | +9 % | **2,957** | **−17 %** | **3,573** |
| **2–8–grams – Total occurrences (NF)** | **393,364** | **+12 %** | **0 %** | **350,147** | **−11 %** | −11 % | **392,371** | **−22 %** | **503,219** |

| | | | | | | | | | |
|---|---|---|---|---|---|---|---|---|---|
| **II. Binomials** | | | | | | | | | |
| **Non-extended binomials** | **1,077** | **+9 %** | **+206 %** | **984** | **+180 %** | +193 % | 352 | **–68 %** | **1,108** |
| *i* [and] | **623** | –21 % | +90 % | **786** | +140 % | +115 % | **328** | –69 % | **1,056** |
| *lub* [or] | **455** | +130 % | +1796 % | **198** | +725 % | +1260.5 % | **24** | –54 % | **52** |
| **Extended binomials** | **1,046** | **+24 %** | **+122 %** | **843** | **–1 %** | +121 % | **855** | **–9 %** | **935** |
| *i* [and] | **837** | +92 % | +106 % | **437** | **–45 %** | +61 % | **788** | –5 % | **831** |
| *lub* [or] | **209** | –49 % | +312 % | **406** | **+506 %** | +409 % | **67** | –36 % | **104** |

*Divergence at the phraseological level – CJ and GC vs SN_2011–2015*
Table 11.3 shows that lexical bundles (n-grams) greatly contribute to the formulaic profiles of both the Eurolect and non-translated SN judgments. The data on the total number of types and occurrences of 2–8–grams are inconclusive; they lead to the conclusion that translations are both slightly less formulaic or slightly more formulaic than their non-translated national counterparts; the final outcome of the comparison depends on which factor (total number of types vs occurrences) is perceived as decisive. As regards Mauranen's hypothesis, according to which translations use more varied patterns, only CJ judgments have a broader range of bundle types than SN judgments (by 14 %), while GC judgments have about 5 % fewer bundle types. The findings did not decisively confirm Toury's law of growing standardization and Baker's normalization hypothesis – the total number of tokens of 2–8–grams in the CJ corpus is only slightly higher than in the corpus of non-translations, whereas in the GC corpus the total number of tokens is about 11 % lower than in national judgments.

The impact of binomials on the overall formulaic profiles is less than that of lexical bundles, which occur with an incommensurately higher frequency than the former in all the corpora. Non-extended and extended binomials are considerably more frequent in translations compared to non-translations – the degree of their overrepresentation relative to non-translations may be assessed as extreme.

The assessment scale in Figure 11.1 has been used to more precisely determine the degree of divergence of the formulaic profile of CJEU judgments from that of non-translated SN judgments:

1. 0–5 % – similar distribution

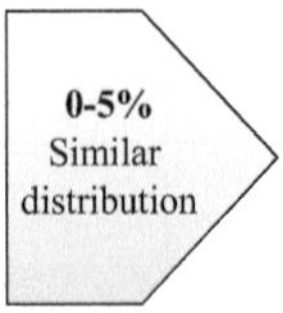


**Lexical bundles:**
2–grams – Total types (+1,5 %)
2–grams – Total occurrences (NF) (–3,5 %)
4–grams – Total types (+1 %)
6–grams – Total occurrences (NF) (+2 %)

2. 6–15 % – slight over-/underrepresentation

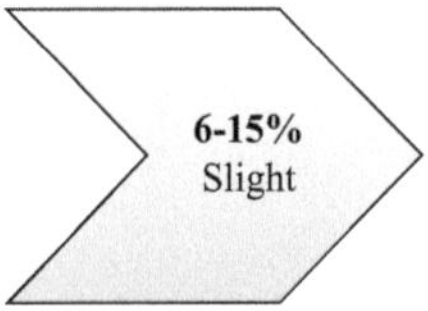


**Lexical bundles:**
3–grams – Total types (+6 %)
3–grams – Total occurrences (NF) (–8,5 %)
**2–8–grams – Total types (+9 %)**
**2–8–grams – Total occurrences (–11 %)**

3. 16–30 % – major over-/underrepresentation

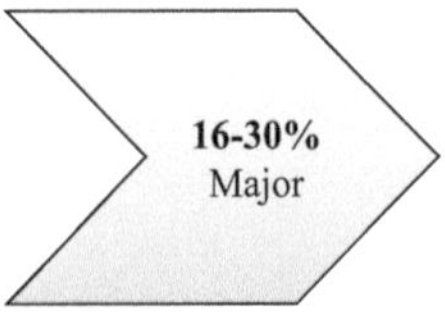


**Lexical bundles:**
5–grams – Total types (+20 %)

4. 31–50 % – strong over-/underrepresentation

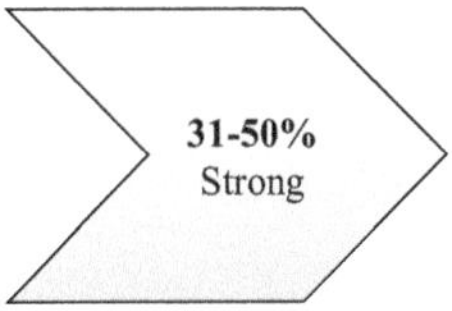


**Lexical bundles:**
4-grams – Total occurrences (NF) (– 34 %)
5-grams – Total occurrences (NF) (– 33 %)
7-grams – Total occurrences (NF) (+36 %)

5. 51 % or more – extreme over-/underrepresentation

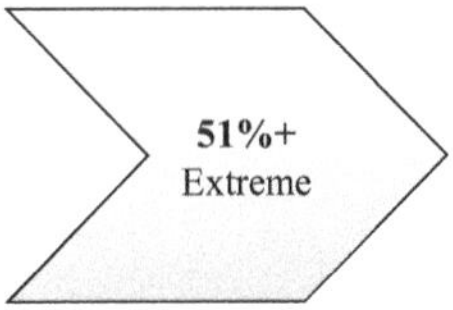


**Lexical bundles:**
6-grams – Total types (+71 %)
7-grams – Total types (+102 %)
8-grams – Total types (+155 %)
8-grams – Total occurrences (NF) (+79 %)

**Binomials:**
**Non-extended binomials (+193 %):**
*i* [and] (+115 %)
*lub* [or] (+1260.5 %)
**Extended binomials (+121 %):**
*i* [and] (+61 %)
*lub* [or] (+409 %)

Overall, the formulaic profile of translated CJEU judgments is assessed as divergent due to the considerable departures from TL conventions. More specifically, it has, in principle, more varied bundles (types) but fewer tokens. The only points of convergence are sporadic and limited to lexical bundles at the level of 2-grams (total number of types and occurrences), 4-grams (total number of types), and 6-grams (total number of occurrences).

## *Internal variation within the Eurolect at the phraseological level: CJ vs GC*

At the phraseological level, the analysis of lexical bundles and binomials has exposed a high degree of internal divergence within the Eurolect itself. This had not been expected, considering that both CJ and GC judgments are drafted at the supranational level, which could entail, following the outcome of the analysis of internal variation within Pillar I (see Section 11.1.1), that both sub-genres of translations should be convergent. Precise data on over- and underrepresentation are presented below:

1. 0–5 % – similar distribution

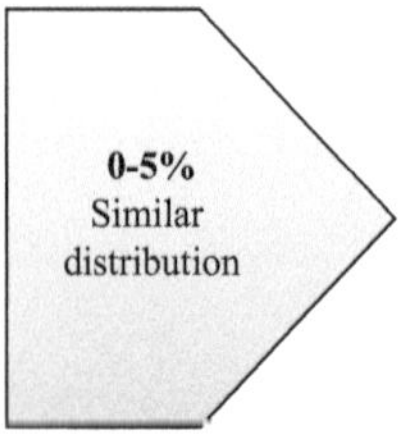


**I. Lexical bundles:**
2–grams – Total types (0 %)
2–grams – Total occurrences (NF) (–3 %)

2. 6–15 % – slight over-/underrepresentation

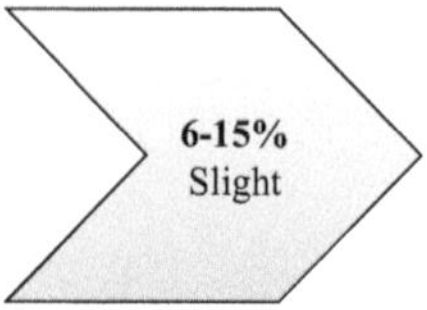


**I. Lexical bundles:**
3–grams – Total types (+8 %)
3–grams – Total occurrences (NF) (+8 %)
**2–8–grams – Total occurrences (+12 %)**

**II. Binomials:**
**Non-extended binomials (+9 %)**

3. 16–30 % – major over-/underrepresentation

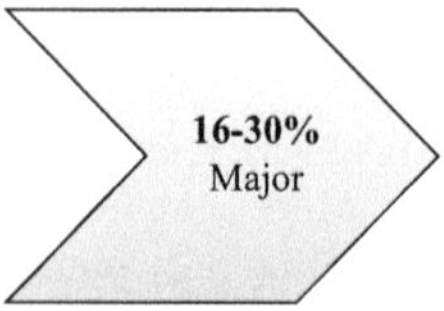


**I. Lexical bundles:**
**2–8–grams – Total types (+20 %)**

**II. Binomials:**
*i* [and] (–21 %)
**Extended binomials (+24 %)**

4. 31–50 % – strong over-/underrepresentation

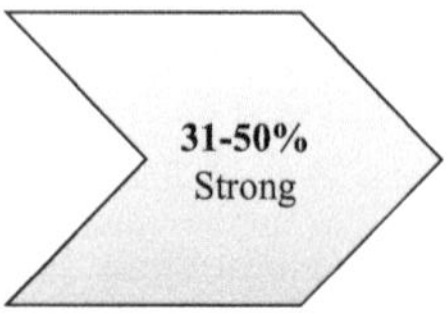


**II. Binomials:**
*lub* [or] (–49 %)

5. 51 % or more – extreme over-/underrepresentation

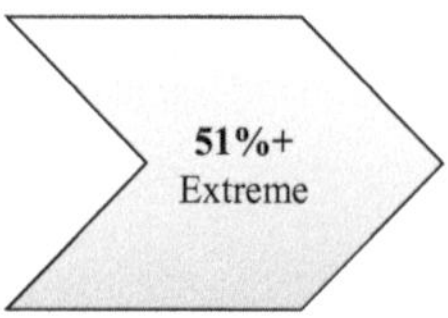


**I. Lexical bundles:**
4–grams – Total types (+54 %)
4–grams – Total occurrences (NF) (+60 %)
5–grams – Total types (+122 %)
5–grams – Total occurrences (NF) (+162 %)
6–grams – Total types (+268 %)
6–grams – Total occurrences (NF) (+351 %)
7–grams – Total types (+532 %)
7–grams – Total occurrences (NF) (+651 %)

8-grams – Total types (+900 %)
8-grams – Total occurrences (NF) (+1078 %)

**II. Binomials:**
*lub* [or] (+130 %)
*i* [and] (+92 %)

The data show that the formulaic profiles of CJ and GC judgments are highly divergent. This is mainly due to the extreme overrepresentation of 4–8-grams in CJ judgments. The only point of limited convergence is the similar distribution of 2-grams.

### 11.1.3 Pillar III – Divergence at the terminological level: CJ and GC vs SN_2011–2015, CJ vs GC

The analysis of the distributional characteristics of simple and complex terms has proven that EU and national judgments differ as to the most frequently evoked law-related concepts. This is so despite the fact that they share a common conceptual base which comprises node simple terms, which are used as head terms to create complex terms conveying more specialized concepts.

The terminological profile of translation, both at the level of simple and complex terms and Latinisms, diverges from the TL conventions of non-translated SN judgments (see Table 11.4).

*Divergence at the terminological level – CJ and GC vs SN_2011–2015*
Precise evaluation of the degree of divergence of translations from non-translations can be examined with the help of the assessment scale:

1. 0–5 % – similar distribution

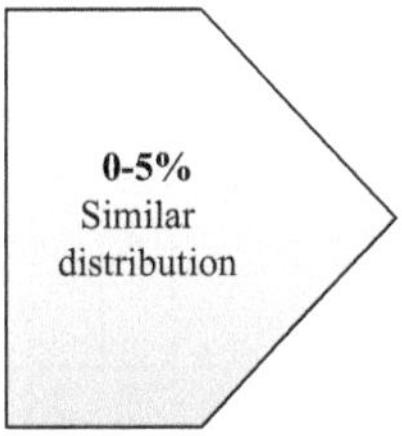


**I. Terminology:**
Legal procedure node terms (all) +1 %

2. 6–15 % – slight over-/underrepresentation

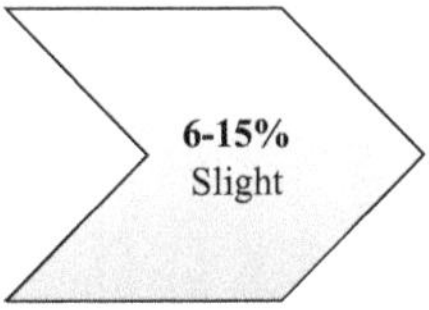


**I. Terminology – total number of simple and complex terms (after refinement) (–12,5 %):**
Complex terms (types) (–10,5 %)
Node terms related to substantive law and case-law (+7 %): *wniosek* [application] (+10 %)
Legal procedure node terms: *postępowanie* [proceedings] (+15,5 %)

**Table 11.4.** *Pillar III – Divergence of translated CJEU judgments from non-translated SN_2011–2015 judgments at the terminological level*

| | Translated EU case law | | | | | | Non-translated PL case law | | |
|---|---|---|---|---|---|---|---|---|---|
| | CJ | CJ vs GC | CJ vs SN_2011–2015 | GC | GC vs SN_2011–2015 | CJ and GC vs SN_2011–2015 | SN_2011–2015 | SN_2011–2015 vs SN_1999 | SN_1999 |
| **I. Terminology – total (after refinement)** | **712** | **+6 %** | **−10 %** | **671** | **−15 %** | −12.5 % | **792** | **+51 %** | **525** |
| Simple terms (types) | 164 | +15 % | −14 % | 142 | −26 % | −20 % | 191 | +35 % | 142 |
| Complex terms (types) | 548 | +4 % | -9 % | 529 | −12 % | −10.5 % | 601 | +57 % | 383 |
| **Agentive and institutional node terms** | **14,251** | **+38 %** | **−28 %** | **10,342** | **−48 %** | **−38 %** | **19,791** | **−23 %** | **25,755** |
| *sąd* [court] | 4,676 | +20 % | -64 % | 3,882 | -70 % | -67 % | 13,024 | -35 % | 19,974 |
| *strona* [party] | 1,665 | −18 % | -52 % | 2,039 | -41 % | -46.5 % | 3,466 | -2 % | 3,551 |
| *spółka* [company] | 2,229 | -21 % | +23 % | 2817 | +55 % | +39 % | 1,813 | +36 % | 1,330 |
| *państwo* [state] | 5,681 | +254 % | +282 % | 1,604 | +8 % | +145 % | 1,488 | +65 % | 900 |
| **Node terms related to substantive law and case–law** | **12,825** | **−21 %** | **-9 %** | **16,285** | **+16 %** | **+7 %** | **14,090** | **-3 %** | **14,539** |
| *wyrok* [judgment] | 4,348 | +25 % | -26 % | 3,474 | -41 % | -33.5 % | 5,869 | -32 % | 8,634 |
| *prawo* [law] | 4,084 | +36 % | −12 % | 3,007 | -35 % | -23.5 % | 4,642 | +11 % | 4,189 |
| *decyzja* [decision] | 2,623 | -67 % | +35 % | 7,971 | +310 % | +172.5 % | 1,943 | +296 % | 491 |

| | Translated EU case law | | | | | | Non-translated PL case law | | |
|---|---|---|---|---|---|---|---|---|---|
| | **CJ** | **CJ vs GC** | **CJ vs SN_2011–2015** | **GC** | **GC vs SN_2011–2015** | **CJ and GC vs SN_2011–2015** | **SN_2011–2015** | **SN_2011–2015 vs SN_1999** | **SN_1999** |
| *wniosek* [application] | 1,770 | −3 % | +8 % | 1,833 | +12 % | +10 % | 1,636 | +34 % | 1,225 |
| **Legal procedure node terms** | **4,740** | **+3 %** | **+2 %** | **4,594** | **−1 %** | **+1 %** | **4,636** | **−7 %** | **4,967** |
| *postępowanie* [proceedings] | 3,491 | +13 % | +23 % | 3,088 | +8 % | +15.5 % | 2,847 | −11 % | 3,193 |
| *koszt* [cost] | 1,249 | −17 % | −30 % | 1,506 | −16 % | −23 % | 1,789 | +1 % | 1,774 |
| **II. Latinisms** | | | | | | | | | |
| Total number of types (RF≥1) | **236** | **−9 %** | **−55 %** | **259** | **−50 %** | **−52.5 %** | **519** | **+273 %** | **278** |
| Total number of types (NF≥1) | 225 | **−10 %** | **−55 %** | 249 | **−50 %** | **−52.5 %** | 502 | **+261 %** | 278 |
| Total number of types (NF≥5) | 138 | **−23 %** | **−59 %** | 180 | **−46 %** | **−52.5 %** | 333 | **+292 %** | 168 |

3. 16–30 % – major over-/underrepresentation

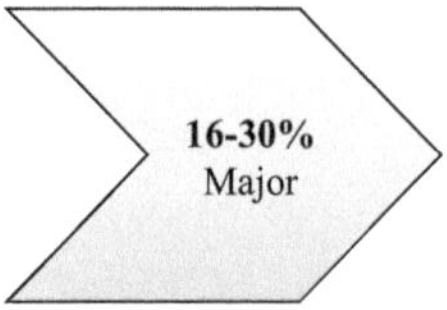


**I. Terminology:**
Simple terms (types) (–20 %)
Node terms related to substantive law and case-law: *prawo* [law] (–23,5 %)
Legal procedure node terms: *koszt* [cost] (–23 %)

4. 31–50 % – strong over-/underrepresentation

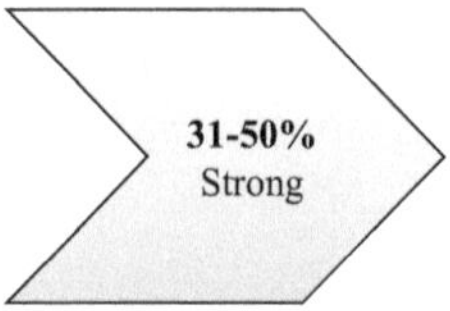


**I. Terminology:**
Agentive and institutional node terms (–38 %): *strona* [party] (–46,5 %), *spółka* [company] (+39 %)
Node terms related to substantive law and case-law: *wyrok* [judgment] (–33,5 %)

5. 51 % or more – extreme over-/underrepresentation

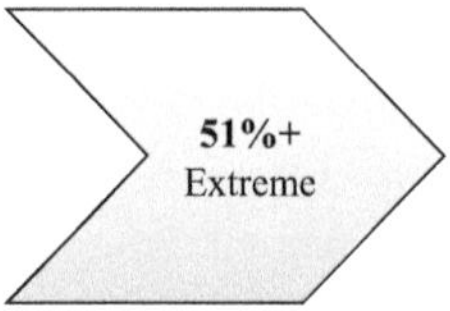


**I. Terminology:**
Agentive and institutional node terms: *sąd* [court] (–67 %), *państwo* [state] (+145 %)
Node terms related to substantive law and case-law: *decyzja* [decision] (+172,5 %)

**II. Latinisms:**
Total number of types (RF≥1) (–52.5 %)
Total number of types (NF≥1) (–52.5 %)
Total number of types (NF≥5) (–52.5 %)

At the level of simple and complex terms, the divergence of translations takes various forms from similar distribution to extreme overrepresentation, depending on the semantic category of terms. At the level of Latinisms, the divergence is one-dimensional – the distribution of Latinisms is characterized by extreme underrepresentation.

## *Internal variation within the Eurolect at the terminological level – CJ vs GC*

The terminological profile of CJ and GC judgments, that is the Eurolect, cannot be described as convergent due to the diverging patterns of use of simple and complex terms as well as Latinisms:

1. 0–5 % – similar distribution

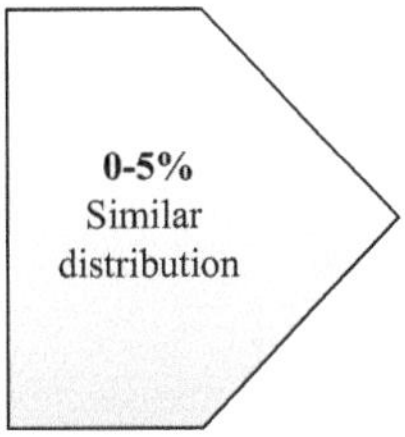


**I. Terminology:**
Complex terms (types) (+4 %)
Node terms related to substantive law and case–law: *wniosek* [application] (−3 %)
Legal procedure node terms (+3 %)

2. 6–15 % – slight over-/underrepresentation

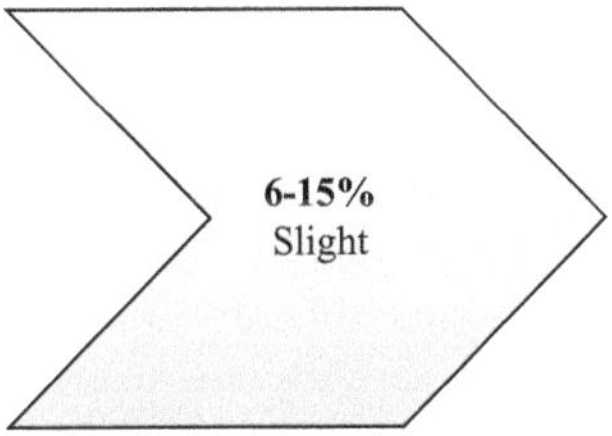


**I. Terminology:**
Simple terms (types) (+15 %)
Legal procedure node terms: *postępowanie* [proceedings] (+13 %)
**II. Latinisms:**
Total number of types (RF≥1) (−9 %)
Total number of types (NF≥1) (−10 %)

3. 16–30 % – major over-/underrepresentation

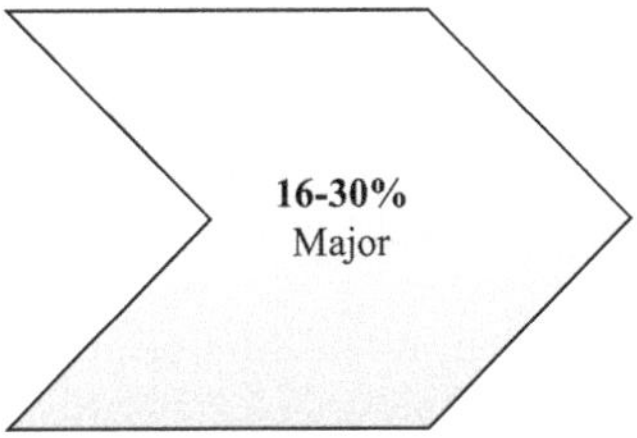


**I. Terminology:**
Agentive and institutional node terms: *sąd* [court] (+20 %), *strona* [party] (−18 %), *spółka* [company] (−21 %)
Node terms related to substantive law and case–law (−21 %): *wyrok* [judgment] (+25 %)
Legal procedure node terms: *koszt* [cost] (−17 %)
**II. Latinisms:**
Total number of types (NF≥5) (−23 %)

4. 31–50 % – strong over-/underrepresentation

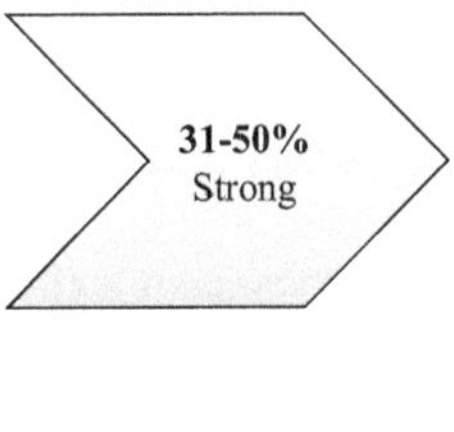


**I. Terminology:**
Agentive and institutional node terms (+38 %)
Node terms related to substantive law and case–law: *prawo* [law] (+36 %)

5. 51 % or more – extreme over-/underrepresentation

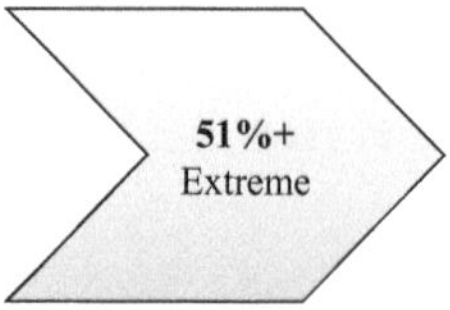


**I. Terminology:**
Agentive and institutional node terms: *państwo* [state] (+254 %)
Node terms related to substantive law and case-law: *decyzja* [decision] (–67 %)

Overall, within the Eurolect, the usage patterns of terminological units are divergent, with the over- or underrepresentation ranging from slight to extreme. Only a few categories related to the distribution of terms have similar distribution in CJ and GC judgments.

### 11.1.4 Possible causes of divergence and acceptability of translated language

Translations are a multidimensional phenomenon affected by a range of factors (cf. De Sutter and Lefer 2020). This renders studies into their nature difficult, requiring the adoption of multidimensional frameworks. Despite the fact that the present study adopted such a framework, focusing primarily on the analysis of the final translated texts, it was difficult, if not almost impossible, to pinpoint factors which directly contribute to the divergence of supranational translated judgments from non-translated national judgments. Although the study does provide information on the contextual factors affecting the process of drafting EU judgments and their translation, it does not investigate them thoroughly using sophisticated research methods (cf. Section 11.3). In order to be better able to identify factors contributing to the divergence of translated CJEU judgments from non-translations, it would be necessary to examine a wider range of factors in greater detail.

It is only natural that EU judgments exhibit a divergent linguistic (formulaic and terminological) profile from non-translations, as their (multilingual) context of production is different – this applies to the situational and communicative factors (cf. Chapter 5). The most obvious difference is that CJEU judgments are drafted at the supranational level, that is within the EU legal system. The different contexts of text production entail different institutional and professional norms as well as a different audience. The CJEU, taking into consideration its non-homogenous audience, needs to adapt its manner of deciding cases correspondingly to lay out arguments in a persuasive manner. The CJEU, while providing argumentation, often needs to rely not only on the relevant provisions of EU law, but also on the relevant provisions of national or international law, due to which its language may be shaped differently. The SN, as a national court, on the other hand, operates within a more culturally and linguistically homogenous community and relies almost exclusively on the provisions of national law.

It should be borne in mind that Polish language versions of CJEU judgments are the result of translation, which means that CJEU Polish is a variety of translationese subject to interferences and the effects of translation universals. Despite the fact that CJEU judgments are translated into Polish by native speakers, lawyer-linguists may have a tendency to translate in a manner more congruent with SL conventions rather than TL conventions. In addition, an over- and underrepresentation of certain linguistic patterns may be simply due to the macrostructural and text-structuring characteristics of the STs.

The divergence of translated CJEU judgments is not something that should be praised, as it may, to a certain degree, inhibit the reception of translations, mostly in the case of extreme over- or underrepresentation of linguistic features, but it is also not worthy of a reprimand. TL conventions should be taken into consideration when translating texts of any variety; however, this should not be done in a forced manner that could distort or skew the original meaning of the STs. An extreme degree of divergence could potentially have negative consequences, as certain members of the national audience, especially non-expert individuals, could become disaffected and sidelined, effectively becoming less tolerant of the foreign judgments.

To sum up, the two sub-genres of translated CJEU judgments alter, to a certain degree, the TL conventions of non-translated Polish by bending them to the needs of the supranational context. Despite the far-reaching divergence of translations, it cannot be concluded that the EU judicial variety of legal language colonizes the national judicial language, as the linguistic change in national judgments cannot be clearly linked to the influence of translations. For these reasons, the impact of the EU translationese cannot be unequivocally assessed as degrading the quality of the language of national judgments. Nevertheless, it seems safe to postulate that the EU Polish could potentially acquire more features typical of the TL conventions without running the risk of endangering the uniform interpretation and application of EU (case-)law.

## 11.2 The limited impact of translated EU judgments on national judgments (microdiachronic language change) – 1999 vs 2011–2015

This section outlines the microdiachronic language change that has been observed in non-translated post-accession SN judgments (2011–2015) compared to pre-accession SN judgments (1999). Its main purpose is to determine whether national judgments have evolved in a way that can be attributed to the influence of translated EU judgments. It was hypothesized that the inflow of translated EU case-law would, to a certain degree, impact the output of drafters of national judgments through exposure to translations in the period following Poland's accession to the EU.

The post-accession judgments do not exhibit any substantial changes in the generic macrostructure, which means that national judgments are *stable* at the macro level as opposed to the micro level. At the micro level, the changes are distribution-related – certain linguistic features are either overrepresented or underrepresented in post-accession SN judgments relative to pre-accession judgments. The most significant changes are those which can be traced back to major over- or underrepresentation of the most salient patterns in translations.

The choice of the years 1999 and 2011–2015 for the microdiachronic study of the potential Europeanization of national judicial language has been dictated by the framework of the Polish Eurolect project[219]: the former as a relatively early pre-accession date, while the latter is a post-accession time frame corresponding to the focus corpus. This design builds on that applied in Biel's study of Europeanization of Polish legislative texts (2014: 305). As regards the genre of judgments, it should be noted that drafters of national judgments are less exposed to EU texts compared to legislative drafters. While judges tend to use EU legislation and case-law as a point of reference, national drafters are required to transpose EU directives, effectively treating them as the conceptual and linguistic foundation of their work (Biel 2014a: 59; Biel and Doczekalska 2020b, *forthcoming*).

### 11.2.1 Pillar I – Microdiachronic change at the level of chosen lexico-grammatical features

Table 11.5 shows whether the increase or decrease in the distribution of certain lexico-grammatical, phraseological and terminological features coincides with their over- or underrepresentation in translated EU case-law. The quantitative data show the distribution of linguistic features in the post-accession judgments (SN_2011–2015) and the pre-accession judgments (SN_1999); the column with the heading SN_2011–2015 vs SN_1999 shows whether there has been an increase (+%) or a decrease (−%) in their usage. OR stands for overrepresentation of a given linguistic feature in the translated CJ and GC judgments compared to the pre-accession SN judgments, while UR, correspondingly, stands for underrepresentation. The sign "="[220] means a similar distribution in the SN_1999 corpus and the post-accession EU corpora.

There have been some pronounced changes at the global level of word and sentence length. In general, national judgments are starting to show a considerably longer sentence structure with the accompanying subtle reduction of word length. Although the finding concerning the word length hovers on the brink of statistical significance, the second discovery is noteworthy. It seems to confirm that the sentence structure of national judgments is becoming more complex, despite the slight decrease in the distribution of hypotactic markers. This may be attributed to the increase in the usage of coordinating conjunctions, compound and

219 https://eurolekt.ils.uw.edu.pl/ (accessed: August 18, 2020)

220 The same manner of presentation of data applies to the remaining tables in Section 11.2.

**Table 11.5.** *Pillar I – Microdiachronic change at the level of chosen lexico-grammatical features in non-translated national judgments: SN_1999 vs SN_2011–2015*

| | Non-translated PL case law | | | |
|---|---|---|---|---|
| | **SN_2011–2015** | **SN_2011–2015 vs SN_1999 (%DIFF)** | **Coincidence of increase/decrease with OR/UR in the translation corpora** | **SN_1999** |
| **I. GLOBAL CHANGES** | | | | |
| 1. Word length | 5.65 | Decrease: −0.35 % (OR) | NO | 5.67 |
| 2. Sentence length | 23.66 | Increase: +10 % (OR) | YES | 21.44 |
| **II. PREPOSITIONS** | 172,320 | INCREASE: +6 % (UR) | NO | 162,897 |
| 3. Simple prepositions | 133,744 | Increase: +5 % (UR) | NO | 127,740 |
| 4. Compound and secondary prepositions (RF>1): | 38,576 | Increase: +10 % (UR) | NO | 35,157 |
| 1) Time | 12,136 | Increase: +9 % (UR) | NO | 11,091 |
| 2) Cause-effect, result, contravention and condition: | 6,270 | Increase: +29 % (OR) | YES | 4,859 |
| a) cause-effect | 3,373 | Increase: +42 % (OR) | YES | 2,368 |
| b) result | 1,429 | Increase: +9 % (UR) | NO | 1,316 |
| c) contravention | 641 | Decrease: −1 % (UR) | YES | 650 |
| d) condition | 827 | Increase: +58 % (OR) | YES | 525 |
| 3) Reference | 5,201 | Increase: +34 % (OR) | YES | 3,868 |
| 4) Intra- and inter-textual reference | 4,678 | Increase: +13 % (OR) | YES | 4,155 |
| 5) Participation | 2,209 | Increase: +13 % (UR) | NO | 1,960 |
| 6) Modality | 1,421 | Decrease: −16 % (UR) | YES | 1,682 |
| 7) Apposition | 1,179 | Decrease: −46 % (UR) | YES | 2,186 |
| 8) Manner and instrumental relations | 1,177 | Increase: +8 % (OR) | YES | 1,094 |
| 9) Adversariality | 894 | Decrease: −35 % (OR) | NO | 1,376 |
| 10) Measure | 801 | Increase: +15 % (UR) | NO | 699 |
| 11) Inclusivity/exclusivity | 774 | Increase: +6 % (=) | NO | 731 |
| 12) Commutative relations | 624 | Increase: +110 % (OR) | YES | 297 |
| 13) Purpose | 365 | Increase: +17 % (OR) | YES | 311 |
| 14) Distribution | 350 | Increase: +46 % (OR) | YES | 240 |
| 15) Comparison | 216 | Decrease: −31 % (=) | NO | 312 |
| 16) Space relations | 182 | Increase: +54 % (OR) | YES | 118 |

(*continued on next page*)

**Table 11.5.** *Continued*

| | Non-translated PL case law | | | |
|---|---|---|---|---|
| | **SN_2011–2015** | **SN_2011–2015 vs SN_1999 (%DIFF)** | **Coincidence of increase/decrease with OR/UR in the translation corpora** | **SN_1999** |
| 17) Partitive relations | 56 | Decrease: −50 % (=) | NO | 111 |
| 18) Active relations | 43 | Decrease: −36 % (–) | NO | 67 |
| **III. STRUCTURIZATION OF JUDICIAL ARGUMENTS** | 53,518 | INCREASE: +3 % (UR) | NO | 52,074 |
| 5. Parataxis | 30,147 | Increase: +8 % (UR) | NO | 27,915 |
| 1) Additive coordinating conjunctions | 24,833 | Increase: +8 % (UR) | NO | 23,046 |
| 2. Alternative coordinating conjunctions | 2,272 | Increase: +30 % (UR) | NO | 1,743 |
| 3) Adversative coordinating conjunctions | 2,231 | Decrease: −13 % (OR) | NO | 2,550 |
| 4) Inclusive coordinating conjunctions | 810 | Increase: +41 % (OR) | YES | 575 |
| 6. Hypotaxis | 23,371 | Decrease: −3 % (UR) | YES | 24,159 |
| 1) Complementizers | 12,222 | Decrease: −5 % (UR) | YES | 12,933 |
| 2) Relative pronouns | 10,670 | Decrease: −1 % (UR) | YES | 10,745 |
| 3) Concessive subordinators | 23,371 | Decrease: −3 % (UR) | YES | 24,159 |
| **IV. DEIXIS – POINTING DEVICES** | 29,750 | DECREASE: −10 % (UR) | YES | 33,057 |
| 7. Personal pronouns (3rd person sg./pl.) | 1,176 | Decrease: −10 % (UR) | YES | 1,308 |
| 8. Possessive pronouns | 7,912 | Increase: +4 % (UR) | NO | 7,620 |
| 9. Demonstrative pronouns | 16,235 | Decrease: −12 % (UR) | YES | 18,440 |
| 10. Indefinite pronouns and quantifiers | 1,618 | Decrease: −11 % (UR) | YES | 1,815 |
| 11. Adjectival deictic expressions | 2,809 | Decrease: −27 % (UR) | YES | 3,874 |
| **V. DEPERSONALIZATION** | 34,537 | DECREASE: −5 % (UR) | YES | 36,304 |
| 12. Auxiliary verbs *być* [to be] and *zostać* [to become] | 11,237 | Decrease: −3 % (UR) | YES | 11,607 |
| 13. Passive voice | 4,537 | Increase: +16 % (UR) | NO | 3,902 |
| 14. The *się* impersonal pattern | 6,509 | Decrease: −11 % (OR) | NO | 7,309 |

**Table 11.5.** *Continued*

| | Non-translated PL case law | | | |
|---|---|---|---|---|
| | **SN_2011–2015** | **SN_2011–2015 vs SN_1999 (%DIFF)** | **Coincidence of increase/decrease with OR/UR in the translation corpora** | **SN_1999** |
| 15. The *-no/to* impersonal pattern | 1,672 | Increase: +35 % (=) | NO | 1,243 |
| **VI. LEGAL REASONING** | 7,976 | DECREASE: −8 % (UR) | YES | 8,681 |
| 16. Verdictive, exercitive (argumentative) and reporting verbs | 10,582 | Decrease: −14 % (OR) | NO | 12,243 |
| 17. Causal patterns | 4,803 | Decrease: −17 % (=) | NO | 5,820 |
| 18. If-then conditionals and related patterns | 2,196 | Increase: +19 % (UR) | NO | 1,844 |
| 19. Patterns of purpose | 977 | Decrease: −4 % (UR) | YES | 1,017 |
| **VII. QUALIFICATION AND COHESION** | 17,086 | DECREASE: −6 % (UR) | YES | 18,187 |
| 20. Adverbials | 9,729 | Decrease: −3 % (UR) | YES | 10,054 |
| 1) Addition | 4,460 | Increase: +1 % (=) | NO | 4,423 |
| 2) Exemplification and particularization | 1,973 | Decrease: −10 % (UR) | YES | 2,204 |
| 3) Enumeration | 169 | Increase: +12 % (UR) | NO | 151 |
| 4) Stance | 1,637 | Decrease: −14 % (=) | NO | 1,895 |
| 5) Contrast and exclusion | 1,490 | Increase: +8 % (=) | NO | 1,381 |
| 21. Participles | 7,357 | Decrease: −10 % (UR) | YES | 8,133 |
| 1) Adjectival participles | 2,998 | Decrease: −2 % (UR) | YES | 3,070 |
| 2) Adverbial participles | 4,359 | Decrease: −14 % (UR) | YES | 5,063 |

secondary prepositions, passive voice and *-no/to* impersonal patterns, as well as if-then conditionals.

In general, the data do not unequivocally confirm any direct relationship between the overrepresentation of given linguistic features in post-accession CJEU judgments and their increased distribution in post-accession SN judgments, or underrepresentation and decreased usage. From a more global perspective, it can be observed that the coincidence of an increase or a decrease with underrepresentation in the translation corpora has been confirmed only in the case of four functional categories – deixis (−10 %), depersonalization (−5 %), legal reasoning (−8 %), qualification and cohesion (−6 %). No coincidence has been observed in the case of the three remaining categories – prepositions (+6 %), structurization of judicial arguments (+3 %) and global changes. Based on these data alone, it might be assumed that national judgments are generally resistant to linguistic change in the microdiachronic perspective. However, this may be an overly simplified conclusion, as it is necessary to investigate the degree of coincidence (or its lack) at the level of the individual functional sub-categories. Within the main functional categories, some indicate clear coincidence, while others do not, which precludes more far-reaching conclusions.

From among the 21 categories within the seven overarching functional categories, 8 show increased distribution, while 13 note a decrease. Within these 21 categories, 9 sub-categories clearly coincide with either underrepresentation (decrease in post-accession SN judgments ranging from −3 % to −27 %); only one coincides with overrepresentation (10 % increase in post-accession SN judgments). In most cases, there is a coincidence if the over- or underrepresentation has about two times higher or lower distribution in translated CJEU judgments compared to pre-accession SN judgments, with the only exception being the increased sentence length, which is obviously unlikely to become about two times longer in such a short period. The sub-categories of the 21 categories with less salient features – reference compound and secondary prepositions, purpose prepositions, demonstrative pronouns, and, in particular, enumeration adverbials – show that exceptionally large over- or underrepresentation in translations does not necessarily translate into a strong and abrupt distribution increase or decrease. Nevertheless, the data reveal that drafters of national judgments may be prone to slight changes in the usage patterns of their own language through exposure to translated texts belonging to the same genre.

Closer examination of the 21 functional categories and their sub-categories shows that the average rate of increase in the usage of certain linguistic features is about 24 %. However, in the case of certain categories, such as compound and secondary prepositions expressing commutative relations (+110 %, mainly owing to *w imieniu* [on behalf of]), condition (+58 %, *w przypadku* [in the case of]), space relations (+54 %, mainly owing to *w obrębie* [within], *na terytorium* [in the territory of]), inclusive coordinating conjunctions (+41 %, mainly owing to *tj.* [i.e.-ABBRV]), the *-no/to* impersonal pattern (+35 %, mainly owing to *wskazano* [(one) indicated-IMPRS], *stwierdzono* [(one) found out-IMPRS]), the rate of change is noticeably higher than the average. On the other hand, the average rate of the decrease in the usage of certain patterns is about 15 %. A particularly high rate of change has been observed in the case of compound and secondary prepositions expressing partitive relations (−50 %, owing to *wśród* [among] and *spośród* [from]), active relations (−36 %, owing to *ze strony* [on the part of]), adjectival deictic expressions (−27 %, attributable to *wymieniony* [mentioned] and *ww.* [above-named-ABBRV]), and causal patterns (−17 %, owing to *bowiem* [since]). This shows that there exists a tendency when it comes to linguistic change in national judgments – increases in the usage of patterns seem to occur at a higher rate than their decreases.

Overall, the measured scale of microdiachronic change at the lexico-grammatical level measured within Pillar I confirms that national judgments are resistant to radical changes in the distributional patterns of the investigated functional categories. This means that the influence of translated EU case-law on national judgments is negligible and that the linguistic profile of non-translations remains stable, especially considering that any changes are related primarily to the distributional patterns and not to the introduction of foreign patterns. This was, to a certain degree, expected, since those involved in the drafting of judgments do not strictly rely on EU case-law as a reference as, for instance, the drafters of national legislative acts do. In a few areas, translations tend to be even more correct than non-translated texts, as shown by the lower reliance on the exclusion adverbial *za wyjątkiem* [except for (incorrect)], for instance. However, there is also one incorrect alternative coordinating conjunction which is used more frequently in translations – *i/lub* [and/or].

Taking into consideration the observations above, it should be remembered that certain linguistic changes cannot be attributed to the influence of CJEU judgments translated into Polish. It may very well be that certain changes are caused by, for instance, the national contextual parameters (spatio-temporal setting, scene, subject area, altering senders, communicative purposes, cf. Chapter 5).

### 11.2.2 Pillar II – Microdiachronic change at the phraseological level

The phraseological profile has been researched using (1) lexical bundles and (2) binomials. Table 11.6 shows whether the increase or decrease in the distribution of phraseological features in the form of lexical bundles and binomials may be coincident with their over- or underrepresentation in translated EU case-law.

The data show that the distribution of both lexical bundles and binomials has decreased over time in non-translated national judgments. There is not a single instance of an increase. This is surprising, since in the computerized era texts might be expected to show an opposite tendency, through a growing standardization and associated growth in formulaicity. On average, the rate at which the usage of different types of lexical bundles has decreased is about 31 %, while the rate in the case of non-extended and extended binomials is even higher, at −40 %. In the case of 2–/5–/6–word lexical bundles (both the total number of types of bundles and their occurrences), the decrease can be determined to coincide with underrepresentation in translations; coincidence can also be determined in the case of the total number of occurrences of 7– and 8–grams. No coincidence has been determined in the case of 3–4–grams, as well as the total number of types of 7–8–grams and the aggregate number of types and occurrences of 2–8–grams. In the case of binomials, coincidence can only be determined between the decrease in the usage of non-extended and extended binomials based around *i* [and], as well as the total number of occurrences of non-extended binomials based around *i* [and] and *lub* [or]. This shows that even though post-accession judgments seem to be less formulaic than pre-accession judgments, the totality of changes at

**Table 11.6.** *Pillar II – Microdiachronic change at the phraseological level in non-translated national judgments: SN_1999 vs SN_2011–2015*

| | Non-translated PL case law | | | |
|---|---|---|---|---|
| | **SN_2011–2015** | **SN_2011–2015 vs SN_1999 (%DIFF)** | **Coincidence of increase/ decrease with OR/UR in the translation corpora** | **SN_1999** |
| **I. Lexical bundles** | | | | |
| 2-grams – Total types | 1,800 | Decrease: −12 % (UR) | YES | 2,036 |
| 2-grams – Total occurrences (NF) | 255,857 | Decrease: −14 % (UR) | YES | 298,271 |
| 3-grams – Total types | 615 | Decrease: −22 % (OR) | NO | 784 |
| 3-grams – Total occurrences (NF) | 77,275 | Decrease: −25 % (OR) | NO | 103,542 |
| 4-grams – Total types | 261 | Decrease: −26 % (OR) | NO | 353 |
| 4-grams – Total occurrences (NF) | 30,082 | Decrease: −34 % (OR) | NO | 45,753 |
| 5-grams – Total types | 133 | Decrease: −27 % (UR) | YES | 183 |
| 5-grams – Total occurrences (NF) | 14,354 | Decrease: −45 % (UR) | YES | 25,979 |
| 6-grams – Total types | 71 | Decrease: −34 % (UR) | YES | 107 |
| 6-grams – Total occurrences (NF) | 7,536 | Decrease: −52 % (UR) | YES | 15,777 |
| 7-grams – Total types | 46 | Decrease: −34 % (=) | NO | 70 |
| 7-grams – Total occurrences (NF) | 4,415 | Decrease: −52 % (UR) | YES | 9,110 |
| 8-grams – Total types | 31 | Decrease: −23 % (OR) | NO | 40 |
| 8-grams – Total occurrences (NF) | 2,854 | Decrease: −40 % (UR) | YES | 4,788 |
| **2–8-grams – Total types** | 2,957 | Decrease: −17 % (OR) | NO | 3,573 |
| **2–8-grams – Total occurrences** | 392,371 | Decrease: −22 % (OR) | NO | 503,219 |
| **II. Binomials** | | | | |
| **Non-extended binomials** | 352 | Decrease: −68 % (UR) | YES | 1,108 |
| *i* [and] | 328 | Decrease: −69 % (UR) | YES | 1,056 |

**Table 11.6.** *Continued*

| | Non-translated PL case law | | | |
|---|---|---|---|---|
| | **SN_2011–2015** | **SN_2011–2015 vs SN_1999 (%DIFF)** | **Coincidence of increase/ decrease with OR/UR in the translation corpora** | **SN_1999** |
| *lub* [or] | 24 | Decrease: −54 % (OR) | NO | 52 |
| **Extended binomials** | 855 | Decrease: −9 % (=) | NO | 935 |
| *i* [and] | 788 | Decrease: −5 % (UR) | YES | 831 |
| *lub* [or] | 67 | Decrease: −36 % (OR) | NO | 104 |

various levels of formulaicity cannot be directly attributed to the influence of translations.

### 11.2.3 Pillar III – Microdiachronic change at the terminological level

The investigation into the terminological profile of judgments included: (1) analysis of the distribution of simple and complex terms and (2) analysis of the distribution of Latinisms. Table 11.7 shows whether the increase or decrease in the distribution of terminological features in the form of terminological units and Latinisms coincides with their over- or underrepresentation in translated EU case-law.

The distribution of terminological units in post-accession SN judgments has not evolved as uniformly as in the case of phraseological features. The average rate of change in the case of terminological units is about 48 %, while the rate in the case of Latinisms is about 275 %. There is a coincidence between the increased distribution of the types of both simple and complex terms identified following the refinement procedure. However, no coincidence has been observed between the increase in the usage of Latinisms and their underrepresentation in translations.

Although the overall usage of simple and complex terms as well as Latinisms has increased in post-accession judgments relative to pre-accession judgments, there are certain inconsistencies in the development of the distribution of the ten node terms and complex terms formed with them. The usage of node terms *sąd* [court], *strona* [party], *wyrok* [judgment], and *postępowanie* [proceedings] has decreased by about 20 %, on average; coincidence has been observed only in the case of the first three terms. In the case of the remaining node terms, *spółka* [company], *państwo* [state], *prawo* [law], *decyzja* [decision], *wniosek* [application], and *koszt* [cost], no coincidence has been detected between the increase of *prawo* [law] and *koszt* [cost]. Overall, the decreased distribution of node terms from all three categories

**Table 11.7.** *Pillar III – Microdiachronic change at the terminological level in non-translated SN judgments: SN_1999 vs SN_2011–2015*

| | **Non-translated PL case law** | | | |
|---|---|---|---|---|
| | **SN_2011–2015** | **SN_2011–2015 vs SN_1999 (%DIFF)** | **Coincidence of increase/ decrease with OR/UR in the translation corpora** | **SN_1999** |
| **I. Terminology – total (after refinement)** | 792 | Increase: +51 % (OR) | YES | 525 |
| Simple terms (types) | 191 | Increase: +35 % (OR) | YES | 142 |
| Complex terms (types) | 601 | Increase: +57 % (OR) | YES | 383 |
| **Agentive and institutional node terms** | | | | |
| *sąd* [court] | 13,024 | Decrease: −35 % (UR) | YES | 19,974 |
| *strona* [party] | 3,466 | Decrease: −2 % (UR) | YES | 3,551 |
| *spółka* [company] | 1,813 | Increase: +36 % (OR) | YES | 1,330 |
| *państwo* [state] | 1,488 | Increase: +65 % (OR) | YES | 900 |
| **Total – node terms** | 19,791 | Decrease: −23 % (UR) | YES | 25,755 |
| **Node terms related to substantive law and case-law** | | | | |
| *wyrok* [judgment] | 5,869 | Decrease: −32 % (UR) | YES | 8,634 |
| *prawo* [law] | 4,642 | Increase: +11 % (UR) | NO | 4,189 |
| *decyzja* [decision] | 1,943 | Increase: +296 % (OR) | YES | 491 |
| *wniosek* [application] | 1,636 | Increase: +34 % (OR) | YES | 1,225 |
| **Total – node terms** | 14,090 | Decrease: −3 % (=) | NO | 14,539 |
| **Legal procedure node terms** | | | | |
| *postępowanie* [proceedings] | 2,847 | Decrease: −11 % (OR) | NO | 3,193 |
| *koszt* [cost] | 1,789 | Increase: +1 % (UR) | NO | 1,774 |
| **Total – node terms** | 4,636 | Decrease: −7 % (UR) | YES | 4,967 |
| **Total – node terms (all three categories)** | 38,517 | Decrease: −15 % (OR) | NO | 45,261 |
| **II. Latinisms:** | | | | |
| 1) Total number of types (RF≥1) | 519 | Increase: +273 % (UR) | NO | 278 |
| 2) Total number of types (NF≥1) | 502 | Increase: +261 % (UR) | NO | 278 |
| 3) Total number of types (NF≥5) | 333 | Increase: +292 % (UR) | NO | 168 |

may coincide with their underrepresentation in translations. The present data also disprove the direct influence of translations on the terminological profile of judgments, as (1) there is no coincidence between the increased usage of Latinisms in post-accession SN judgments and their underrepresentation in translations and (2) there is no coincidence between the increase or decrease in the usage of certain node terms and their over- or underrepresentation in translated texts.

## 11.3 Limitations of the study and suggestions for further research

The data-driven, quantitative approach to the study of judicial language adopted in this study has proven adequate to determine the divergent degree of textual fit of translated EU judgments to non-translated national judgments. The structure of the genre-restricted JURIDIC corpus, made up of two CJEU sub-corpora and two national corpora, as well as the NKJP corpus representative of general Polish, enabled the collection of an extensive set of empirical comparative data. The quantitative data, in turn, were used to determine the degree of textual fit of translations to non-translated texts at the macro (global) and micro (local) level by measuring over- and underrepresentation of linguistic features and to identify the key genre (register) markers. The findings may act as reference for other synchronic and diachronic studies, such as studies on other specialized genres (cf. Biel 2016b), and in particular studies on legislative texts, which are perceived as a superordinate genre in relation to judgments. The data may be used, among other things to: (1) analyze in greater detail the internal variation of judicial Polish (including, for instance, orders and resolutions), (2) contrast the characteristics of the EU and Polish varieties of judicial language with judicial texts from other legal systems.

Despite the advantages of the approach adopted in this book, certain limitations could not be avoided. The chief limitation of this study, necessitated by its extensive scope, is that it has been conducted on a monolingual corpus of Polish-language judgments, which did not enable investigation into similar phenomena in other language versions of translated texts. This pertains in particular to French-language versions of CJEU judgments, which could, in further studies, be analyzed in light of the relation of equivalence to establish non-conformities between the STs and TTs and interferences brought about by the source language. In addition, the nature of the present study remains chiefly quantitative. Further research should incorporate methodological triangulation, including the methods of comparative law or Reception Studies.

As in all research methods, the corpus methodology has its disadvantages, which are mainly related to the design of corpora. In order to generate generalizable results, the corpora need to be representative, balanced, and comparable. These issues have already been discussed in Chapter 3. However, it should be noted that the large number of texts included in the corpora, that is all texts published in the given periods, made the whole endeavor time-consuming due to the sheer number of concordances that needed to be studied in some of the analyses. Therefore, further research should devise a method of collecting smaller samples of texts which could still produce results generalizable to the whole period under consideration. This, in turn, would necessitate the adoption of statistical significance tests (e.g. LL, BIC)[221] to allow for generalizations not limited to the period from which the texts were drawn; the employment of statistical regression modelling would also be of great use to this end. Another improvement could be achieved through more sophisticated software of corpus preparation and analysis, which is yet to be developed, although some interesting new features are available in Sketchengine. The use of methods for annotating the corpora with specialist software could potentially help in studying more complex lexical and grammatical phenomena. Additionally, advantage could also be taken of studying only the most crucial rhetorical moves in judgments containing judicial argumentation, which are the essence of judicial language, as opposed to the moves containing, for instance, the identification of cases, their history and the retrieval of relevant provisions (cf. Chapter 5). Further research should also involve the study of the equivalence relation (cf. Chapter 3, Section 3.3) using parallel corpora composed of STs and TTs to fully explain the interferences brought about by the translation process. This, however, would certainly be limited by the underdevelopment of relevant alignment, annotation and lemmatization software, which is not able to fully (that is in a fully automatic and error-free manner) account for the inflectional nature of Polish. As regards the analysis employing lexical bundles (see Chapter 7) in which I decided against setting different frequency thresholds despite the fact that the unsampled SN corpora differ in size from the unsampled EU corpora, future research should account for the fact that comparing corpora of different sizes as well as bundles of different length may require subtle adaptation of different methodological choices, especially those related to frequency thresholds.[222]

Since the study has not used annotated corpora, it was not possible to study all lexico-grammatical aspects of the textual fit within the first pillar. As regards the second and third pillar of the micro-level analysis, the study could also have operationalized the concepts of phraseological and terminological profile differently. Further research should focus on devising other methods concerning the study of these profiles. Lastly, further studies should focus to a greater extent on the context of production of translated texts, the translator profile, the translation process and the issue of reception of TTs. This would help to better gauge the expectancy norms of the target audience. These methods could involve, interviews and questionnaires, for example. Owing to the extensive nature of the present

221 More attention should also be paid to the normalization of quantitative data, as it has tremendous impact on the final results of any study using corpora, in particular on corpora of dissimilar sizes.

222 For more information on the Zipfian nature of the distribution of recurrent word sequences in corpora, see, for instance, Tullo and Hurford (2003), Bestgen (2019).

study, these aspects could not be studied in detail, although an attempt was made at uncovering the contextual aspects of the final translation products and comparable non-translated texts.

## 11.4 Practical applications of the study

The main objective of this study was to measure the degree of linguistic convergence or divergence at the macro level and, most importantly, the micro level between translated EU judgments and non-translated SN judgments. This led to the identification of linguistic features over- and underrepresented in Polish translations relative to non-translations, thus providing more insights into the nature of translated EU case-law and its influence on national judgments. The indirect aim of this study was to enable application of its findings in practice, namely in translator training and translation practice.

As regards translator training, the JURIDIC corpus, made up of comparable subcorpora of EU and national texts, could be applied in the teaching of translation, such as in corpus-based data-driven (discovery) learning (Granger 2003: 24–25; cf. Johns 1991; Bowker 1998; Zanettin 1998; Aston 1999; Bernardini 1997, 2016; Rodríguez-Inés and Gallego-Hernández 2016), to develop students' competences laid out by the EMT expert group (Toudic and Krause 2017) and, in particular, those translation competences which are related to the development and use of thematic and domain-specific knowledge relevant to translation needs (mastering systems of concepts, terminology and phraseology) (Scarpa and Orlando 2017: 26; Toudic and Krause 2017: 8). In general, comparable corpora comprising judicial texts may be used as a decision-making aid during the translation process, in order to increase the textual fit of trainees' translations by raising the awareness of TL conventions (terminological and phraseological nuances) (cf. Chesterman 1993: 9–10). This could contribute to reducing SL interference and strengthening the communicative potential of the translated language (Biel 2017a). The goal would be to sensitize novice translators to the phraseological characteristics typical of judicial language which can be placed along the plane of T-universals (cf. Chesterman 2010: 41–42) – over- or underrepresentation of TL-specific items, atypical lexical patterns (Chesterman 2010: 41–42) (cf. Chapter 3, Section 3.3). Comparable corpora may also be part of a hands-on experience based on studying professional translations, which are crucial for translation purposes, to develop critical thinking (Biel 2017a).

The second area of potential practical application of this study concerns translation practice, which could benefit from the development of resources, such as style guides tailored to the needs of practicing translators and lawyer-linguists. Their aim would be to sensitize translators to the phenomena connected with divergent textual fit and inadequate naturalness of translations. With their help, translators would be more conscious of linguistic features which, if over- or underused, may reduce the phraseological correspondence to non-translated comparable texts belonging to the same genre (more specifically, a different sub-genre). The application of resources, such as style guides, especially by external contractors co-operating with the Polish Language Unit at the CJEU, would allow for a greater degree of desirable (institutional) standardization in translations (cf. Biel 2014a: 37, 306–307). The empirical findings could also be potentially used to improve existing TQA and translation quality assurance models by incorporating the concept of textual fit. Lastly, the results could also serve to identify elements of the Polish language which could be prone to negative language change in the future and possible decline in the quality of language (cf. Bartoszewicz 2017).

# Bibliography


Aarts, Jan. 2002. "Does corpus linguistics exist? Some old and new issues." In *From the COLT's mouth... and others': Language Corpora Studies in Honour of Anna-Brita Stenström*, edited by Leiv Egil Breivik and Angela Hasselgren, 1–19. Amsterdam: Rodopi.

Alcaraz, Varó E. and Brian Hughes. 2002. *Legal Translation Explained.* Manchester: St. Jerome.

Altenberg, Bengt. 1993. "Recurrent word combinations in spoken English." In *Proceedings of the Fifth Nordic Association for English Studies Conference*, edited by Graham Caie, Kirsten Haastrup, Arnt Lykke Jakobsen, Jørgen Erik Nielsen, Jørgen Sevaldsen, Henrik Specht, and Arne Zettersten, 17–27. Reykjavik: University of Iceland.

Altenberg, Bengt. 1998. "On the Phraseology of Spoken English: The Evidence of Recurrent Word-Combinations." In *Phraseology: Theory, Analysis, and Applications*, edited by Anthony Paul Cowie, 101–122. Oxford: Oxford University Press.

Anthony, Laurence. 2014. AntConc. Tokyo: Waseda University.

Arnull, Anthony. 2018. "The Working Language of the CJEU: Time for a Change?" *European Law Review* 43: 904–919.

Asensio, Roberto Mayoral. 2007. "Specialised translation: A concept in need of revision." *Babel* 53(1): 48–55.

Aston, Guy. 1999. "Corpus use and learning to translate." *Textus* 12: 289–314.

Austin, John L. 1962. *How to do Things with Words.* Oxford: Oxford University Press.

Baaij, Cornelis J. W. (ed.) 2012. *The Role of Legal Translation in Legal Harmonization.* Alphen aan den Rijn: Kluwer Law International.

Baaij, Cornelis J. W. 2018. *Legal Integration and Language Diversity: Rethinking Translation in EU Lawmaking.* New York: Oxford University Press.

Bajčić, Martina. 2011. "Conceptualization of Legal Terms in Different Fields of Law: The Need for a Transparent Terminological Approach." *Research in Language* 9(1): 81–93.

Bajčić, Martina. 2017. *New Insights into the Semantics of Legal Concepts and the Legal Dictionary.* Amsterdam: John Benjamins Publishing Company.

Bajčić, Martina. 2018. "The Role of EU Legal English in Shaping EU Legal Culture." *International Journal of Language and Law* 7: 8–24.

Bajčić, Martina and Adrijana Martinović. 2018. "A Mutual Learning Exercise in Terminology and Multilingual Law." In *Language and Law*, edited by

Silvia Marino, Łucja Biel, Martina Bajčić, and Vilelmini Sosoni, 207–223. Cham: Springer.

Baker, Mona. 1993. "Corpus Linguistics and Translation Studies – Implications and Applications." In *Text and Technology: In Honour of John Sinclair*, edited by Mona Baker, Gill Francis, and Elena Tognini-Bonelli, 233–250. Amsterdam and Philadelphia: John Benjamins Publishing Company.

Baker, Mona. 1995. "Corpora in Translation Studies: An Overview and Some Suggestions for Future Research." *Target* 7(2): 223–243.

Baker, Mona. 1996. "Corpus-Based Translation Studies: The Challenges that Lie Ahead." In *Terminology, LSP, and Translation: Studies in Language Engineering in Honour of Juan C. Sager*, edited by Harold Somers, 175–186. Amsterdam and Philadelphia: John Benjamins Publishing Company.

Baker, Mona. 1999. "The Role of Corpora in Investigating the Linguistic Behaviour of Professional Translators." *International Journal of Corpus Linguistics* 4(2): 281–298.

Bańko, Mirosław. 2007. *Wykłady z polskiej fleksji*. Warszawa: Wydawnictwo Naukowe PWN.

Barbieri, Federica. 2018. "I don't want to and don't get me wrong." In *Applications of Pattern-driven Methods in Corpus Linguistics*, edited by Joanna Kopaczyk and Jukka Tyrkkö, 251–276. Amsterdam and Philadelphia: John Benjamins Publishing Company.

Bartoszewicz, Michał. 2017. *Język polski i jego ochrona prawna w porządku konstytucyjnym Rzeczypospolitej Polskiej*. Warszawa: Wydawnictwo Sejmowe.

Basaneže, Katja Dobrić. 2017. "Extended Binomial Expressions in the Language of Contracts." In *Phraseology in Legal and Institutional Settings. A Corpus-Based Interdisciplinary Perspective*, edited by Stanisław Goźdź-Roszkowski, Gianluca Pontrandolfo, 203–220. London: Routledge.

Basaneže, Katja Dobrić. 2018. "Binomials in EU Competition Law." In *Language and Law*, edited by Silvia Marino, Łucja Biel, Martina Bajčić, and Vilelmini Sosoni, 225–248. Cham: Springer.

Bazerman, Charles. 1994. "Systems of Genres and the Enactment of Social Intentions." In *Genre and the New Rhetoric*, edited by Aviva Freedman and Peter Medway, 79–101. London: Taylor and Francis.

Bąk, Piotr. 1984. *Gramatyka języka polskiego. Zarys popularny*. Warszawa: Wiedza Powszechna.

Bąk, Piotr. 2018. "Pleonazm jako reduplikacja semantyczna we współczesnym języku niemieckim." *Applied Linguistics Papers* 25(1): 9–24.

Benke, Nikolaus, Franz-Stefan Meissel, and Karl Luggauer. 2009. *Juristenlatein: 2800 lateinische Fachausdrücke und Redewendungen der Juristensprache*. Wien: Juridica-Verlag.

Bernardini, Silvia. 1997. "A 'trainee' translator's perspective on corpora." Paper presented at the conference Corpus Use and Learning to Translate (CULT) (Bertinoro, Italy, November 14–15, 1997).

Bernardini, Silvia. 2016. "Discovery Learning in the Language-for-Translation Classroom: Corpora as Learning Aids." *Cadernos de Tradução* 36: 14–35.

Berteloot, Pascale. 1988. "Babylone à Luxembourg, Jurilinguistique à la Cour de Justice." In *Vorträge, Reden und Berichte aus dem Europa Institut* 136, edited by Georg Ress and Michael R. Will, 1–32. Saarbrücken: Europa-Institut.

Bestgen, Yves. 2019. "Comparing lexical bundles across corpora of different sizes: The Zipfian problem." *Journal of Quantitative Linguistics* 27(3): 272–290.

Bhatia, Vijay K. 1987. "Language of the Law." *Language Teaching* 20(4): 227–234.

Bhatia, Vijay K. 1994. "Cognitive Structuring in Legislative Provisions." In *Language and the Law*, edited by John Gibbons, 136–155. London: Longman.

Bhatia, Vijay K. 2002. "Applied Genre Analysis: A Multi-Perspective model." *Iberica* 4: 3–19.

Bhatia, Vijay K. 2006. "Legal Genres." In *Encyclopedia of Language and Linguistics*, edited by Keith Brown, 1–7. Oxford: Elsevier.

Bhatia, Vijay K. 2013[1993]. *Analysing Genre – Language Use in Professional Settings*. London, New York: Longman.

Bhatia, Vijay K. 2014[2004]. *Worlds of Written Discourse: A Genre-Based View*. London: Continuum International.

Biber, Douglas. 1990. "Methodological Issues Regarding Corpus-Based Analyses of Linguistic Variation." *Literary and linguistic computing* 5(4): 257–269.

Biber, Douglas. 1991. *Variation across speech and writing*. Cambridge: Cambridge University Press.

Biber, Douglas. 1993. "Representativeness in Corpus Design." *Literary and Linguistic Computing* 8(4): 243–57.

Biber, Douglas. 1997. "Lexical Bundles in Spoken and Written Discourse: What the Grammar Books Don't Tell You." In *An Update on Grammar: How it is Learnt – How it is Taught (1996 Colloquium Proceedings)*, edited by S. B. Gerome, 4–8. Paris: TESOL France.

Biber, Douglas. 2006. *University Language: A corpus-based study of spoken and written registers*. Amsterdam and Philadelphia: John Benjamins Publishing Company.

Biber, Douglas. 2009a. "A Corpus-Driven Approach to Formulaic Language in English." *International Journal of Corpus Linguistics* 14(3): 275–311.

Biber, Douglas. 2009b. "Corpus-Based and Corpus-Driven Analyses of Language Variation and Use." In *The Oxford Handbook of Linguistic Analysis*, edited by Bernd Heine and Heiko Narrog, 159–191. Oxford: Oxford University Press.

Biber, Douglas. 2012. "Corpus-Based and Corpus-Driven Analyses of Language Variation and Use." In *The Oxford Handbook of Linguistic Analysis*, edited by Bernd Heine and Heiko Narrog, 159–191. New York: Oxford University Press.

Biber, Douglas, Stig Johansson, Geoffrey Leech, Susan Conrad, and Edward Finegan. 1999. *Longman Grammar of Spoken and Written English.* Harlow: Longman.

Biber, Douglas, Susan Conrad, and Viviana Cortes. 2003. "Lexical Bundles in Speech and Writing: An Initial Taxonomy." In *Corpus Linguistics by the Lune: A Festschrift for Geoffrey Leech*, edited by Andrew Wilson, Paul Rayson, and Tony McEnery, 71–92. Frankfurt am Main: Peter Lang.

Biber, Douglas, Susan Conrad, and Viviana Cortes. 2004. "If you look at...: Lexical Bundles in University Teaching and Textbooks." *Applied linguistics* 25(3): 371–405.

Biber, Douglas and Federica Barbieri. 2007. "Lexical Bundles in University Spoken and Written Registers." *English for Specific Purposes* 26(3): 263–286.

Biber, Douglas and James K. Jones. 2009. "Quantitative methods in corpus linguistics." In *Corpus Linguistics: An International Handbook*, edited by Anke Lüdeling and Merja Kytö, 1286–1304. Berlin: Walter de Gruyter.

Biber, Douglas and Susan Conrad. 2009. *Register, genre, and style.* Cambridge: Cambridge University Press.

Biel, Łucja. 2007. "Translation of Multilingual EU Legislation as a Sub-Genre of Legal Translation." In *Court Interpreting and Legal Translation in the Enlarged Europe*, edited by Danuta Kierzkowska, 144–163. Warszawa: Translegis.

Biel, Łucja. 2008. "Legal Terminology in Translation Practice: Dictionaries, Googling or Discussion Forums?" *SKASE Journal of Translation and Interpretation* 3(1): 22–38.

Biel, Łucja. 2010. "Corpus-Based Studies of Legal Language for Translation Purposes: Methodological and Practical Potential." In *Reconceptualizing LSP. Online proceedings of the XVII European LSP symposium 2009*, edited by Carmen Heine and Jan Engberg. Aarhus: Aarhus School of Business.

Biel, Łucja. 2012. "Areas of Similarity and Difference in Legal Phraseology: Collocations of Key Terms in UK and Polish Company Law." In *Phraseology and Discourse: Cross-Linguistic and Corpus-based Approaches*, edited by Antonio Pamies, Lucia Luque Nadal, and Jose Manuel Pazos Bretana, 225–233. Baltmannsweiler: Schneider Verlag Hohengehren GmbH.

Biel, Łucja. 2014a. *Lost in the Eurofog: The Textual Fit of Translated Law.* Frankfurt am Main: Peter Lang.

Biel, Łucja. 2014b. "Phraseology in Legal Translation: A Corpus-Based Analysis of Textual Mapping in EU Law." In *The Ashgate handbook of legal translation*, edited by Le Cheng, Anne Wagner, and King Kui Sin, 178–192. London: Routledge.

Biel, Łucja. 2015. "Phraseological Profiles of Legislative Genres: Complex Prepositions as a Special Case of Legal Phrasemes in EU Law and National Law." *Fachsprache* 37(3/4): 139–161.

Biel, Łucja. 2016a. "Mixed Corpus Design for Researching the Eurolect: A Genre-Based Comparable Parallel Corpus in the PL EUROLECT Project." In *Polskojęzyczne korpusy równoległe. Polish-language Parallel Corpora*, edited by Ewa Gruszczyńska and Agnieszka Leńko-Szymańska, 197–208. Warszawa: Instytut Lingwistyki Stosowanej.

Biel, Łucja. 2016b. "Wyrażenia przyimkowe w krajowych i unijnych aktach prawnych – analiza korpusowa funkcji przyimków w polskim języku prawnym." In *Język polskiego prawa: nowe wyzwania*, edited by Dorota Kondratczyk-Przybylska, Adam Niewiadomski, and Ewa Walewska, 9–35. Warszawa: Międzywydziałowe Koło Naukowe Kultury Języka Prawnego i Prawniczego LinguaIuris.

Biel, Łucja. 2017a. "Enhancing the communicative dimension of legal translation: comparable corpora in the research-informed classroom." *The Interpreter and Translator Trainer* 11(4): 316–336.

Biel, Łucja. 2017b. "Genre analysis and translation." In *The Routledge Handbook of Translation Studies and Linguistics*, edited by Kirsten Malmkjœr, 151–164. London and New York: Routledge.

Biel, Łucja. 2017c. "Lexical bundles in EU law: The impact of translation process on the patterning of legal language." In *Phraseology in Legal and Institutional Settings. A Corpus-Based Interdisciplinary Perspective*, edited by Stanislaw Goźdź-Roszkowski and Gianluca Pontrandolfo, 10–26. London and New York: Routledge.

Biel, Łucja. 2017d. "Researching Legal Translation: A Multi-Perspective and Mixed-Method Framework for Legal Translation." *Revista de Llengua i Dret (Journal of Language and Law)* 68: 76–88.

Biel, Łucja. 2018. "Observing Eurolects: The case of Polish." In *Observing Eurolects: Corpus analysis of linguistic variation in EU law*, edited by Laura Mori, 295–327. Amsterdam: John Benjamins Publishing Company.

Biel, Łucja. 2019. "Theoretical and methodological challenges in researching EU legal translation." In *Legal Translation: Current Issues and Challenges in Research, Methods and Applications*, edited by Marita Kristiansen and Ingrid Simonnæs, 25–39. Berlin: Frank and Timme.

Biel, Łucja. 2020. "Eurolects and EU Legal Translation." In *The Oxford Handbook of Translation and Social Practices*, edited by Meng Ji and Sara Laviosa. Oxford: Oxford University Press.

Biel, Łucja. 2020, *forthcoming*. "Legal Translation." In *Handbook of Translation*, edited by Kirstem Malmkjaer. Cambridge: Cambridge University Press.

Biel, Łucja and Justyna Giczela-Pastwa. 2016. "Metody korpusowe w analizie gatunków specjalistycznych: założenia, perspektywy i ograniczenia." In *Pod pretekstem słów: księga jubileuszowa dla Profesora Wojciecha Kubińskiego*, edited by Paula Gorszczyńska and Wioleta Karwacka, 140–168. Gdańsk: Części Proste.

Biel, Łucja, Agnieszka Biernacka, and Anna Jopek-Bosiacka. 2018a. "Collocations of Terms in EU Competition Law: A Corpus Analysis of EU English Collocations." In *Language and Law*, edited by Silvia Marino, Łucja Biel, Martina Bajčić, and Vilelmini Sosoni, 249–274. Cham: Springer.

Biel, Łucja, Dariusz Koźbiał, and Katarzyna Wasilewska. 2018b. "Zbitki wielowyrazowe w polskim eurolekcie – analiza gatunkowa formuliczności tłumaczeń. Badanie pilotażowe." In *Tom pamiątkowy in memoriam Prof. Anny Duszak*, Język w Interakcji Społecznej, edited by Urszula Okulska-Łukawska, Urszula Topczewska, and Anna Jopek-Bosiacka. Warszawa: Instytut Lingwistyki Stosowanej.

Biel, Łucja, Dariusz Koźbiał, and Katarzyna Wasilewska. 2019. "The formulaicity of translations across EU institutional genres: A corpus-driven analysis of lexical bundles in translated and non-translated language." Translation Spaces 8(1): 67–92.

Biel, Łucja and Vilelmini Sosoni. 2019. "EU Legal Culture and Translation in the Era of Globalisation. The Hybridisation of EU Terminology on the Example of Competition Law." In *Legal Linguistics Beyond the Borders: Language and Law in a World of Media, Globalisation and Social Conflicts. Relaunching the International Language and Law Association*, edited by Friedemann Vogel, 208–229. Berlin: Duncker & Humblot.

Biel, Łucja and Dariusz Koźbiał. 2020a, *forthcoming*. "How do translators handle (near-)synonymous legal terms? A mixed-genre parallel corpus study into the variation of EU English-Polish competition law terminology." *Estudios de Traducción.*

Biel, Łucja and Agnieszka Doczekalska. 2020b, *forthcoming*. "How do supranational terms transfer into national legal systems? A corpus-informed study of EU English terminology in consumer protection directives and UK, Irish and Maltese transposing acts." *Terminology.*

Bladowski, Bogdan. 2012. *Pisma sądowe w sprawach cywilnych.* Warszawa: Wolters Kluwer.

Bladowski, Bogdan. 2013. *Metodyka pracy sędziego cywilisty.* Warszawa: Wolters Kluwer.

Bobek, Michal. 2015. "The Court of Justice of the European Union." In *The Oxford Handbook of European Union Law*, edited by Anthony Arnull and Damian Chalmers, 153–177. Oxford: Oxford University Press.

Bocquet, Claude. 1994. *Pour une méthode de traduction juridique.* Prilly: Éditions CB.

Borchardt, Klaus-Dieter. 2017. *The ABC of EU Law.* Luxembourg: Publications Office of the European Union.

Borja, Albi A. 2013. "A Genre Analysis Approach to the Study of the Translation of Court Documents." *Linguistica Antverpiensia New Series* 12: 33–53.

Borja, Albi A., Isabel G. Izquierdo, and Vicent Montalt. 2009. "Research Methodology in Specialized Genres for Translation Purposes." *The Interpreter and Translator Trainer* 3(1): 57–77.

Bowker, Lynne. 1995. *A Multidimensional Approach to Classification in Terminology: Working within a Computational Framework.* PhD thesis. University of Ottawa.

Bowker, Lynne. 1998. "Using Specialized Monolingual Native-Language Corpora as a Translation Resource: A Pilot Study." *Meta: Translators' Journal* 43(4): 631–651.

Bralczyk, Jerzy. 1978. *O leksykalnych wyznacznikach prawdziwościowej oceny sądów.* Katowice: Uniwersytet Śląski.

Breeze, Ruth. 2013. "Lexical bundles across four legal genres." *International Journal of Corpus Linguistics* 18(2): 229–253.

Bronny, Piotr. 2009. *Trener prawniczy. Czytanie wyroków i orzeczeń. Kodeks Cywilny.* Warszawa: Wydawnictwo Naukowe PWN.

Brzozowski, Adam, Wojciech Kocot, and Elżbieta Skowrońska-Bocian. 2015. *Prawo cywilne, część ogólna.* Warszawa: Wolters Kluwer.

Brzozowski, Adam, Wojciech Kocot, and Wiesław Opalski. 2016. *Prawo rzeczowe: Zarys wykładu.* Warszawa: Wolters Kluwer.

Bukovčan, Dragica. 2009. "Binominal Expressions in the German and English Language of Criminal Law." In *Curriculum, Multilingualism and the Law,* edited by Lelija Sočanac, Christopher Goddard, and Ludger Kremer, 61–78. Zagreb: Nakladni zavod Globus.

Bunikowski, Dawid (ed.) 2016. *Historical and Philosophical Foundations of European Legal Culture.* Newcastle upon Tyne: Cambridge Scholars Publishing.

Burczak, Krzysztof, Antoni Dębiński, and Maciej Jońca. 2018. *Łacińskie sentencje i powiedzenia prawnicze.* Warszawa: C.H.Beck.

Burr, Isolde and Tito Gallas. 2004. "Zur Textproduktion im Gemeinschaftsrecht." In *Rechtssprache Europas. Reflexion der Praxis von Sprache und Mehrsprachigkeit im supranationalen Recht,* edited by Friedrich Müller and Isolde Burr, 195–242. Berlin: Duncker & Humblot.

Buttler, Danuta. 1971. "Źródła "redundancji" leksykalnej." In *Prace Filologiczne* 11, 249–263.

Cabré Castellví, María Teresa. 1999. *Terminology. Theory, Methods and Applications.* Amsterdam: John Benjamins Publishing Company.

Cabré Castellví, María Teresa. 2000. "Elements for a theory of terminology: Towards an alternative paradigm. Terminology." *International Journal of Theoretical and Applied Issues in Specialized Communication* 6(1): 35–57.

Cabré Castellví, María Teresa. 2003. "Theories of terminology: Their description, prescription and explanation." *Terminology* 9(2): 163–199.

Campo, Ángela. 2012. *The Reception of Eugen Wüster's Work and the Development of Terminology.* PhD thesis. Université de Montréal.

Cao, Deborah. 2009. "Legal Translation Studies." In *The Routledge Handbook of Translation Studies,* edited by Carmen Millán and Francesca Bartrina, 415–424. London and New York: Routledge.

Chalmers, Damian, Gareth Davies, and Giorgio Monti. 2010. *European Union Law: Cases and Materials.* New York: Cambridge University Press.

Chalmers, Damian, Gareth Davies, and Giorgio Monti. 2019[2010]. *European Union Law: Cases and Materials.* New York: Cambridge University Press.

Chauvin, Tatiana, Tomasz Stawecki, and Piotr Winczorek. 2017. *Wstęp do prawoznawstwa.* Warszawa: C.H.Beck.

Cheng, Le and King Kui Sin. 2008. "A court judgment as dialogue." In *Dialogue and rhetoric* 2, edited by Edda Weigand, 267–281. Amsterdam and Philadelphia: John Benjamins Publishing Company.

Cheng, Winnie and Le Cheng. 2014. "Epistemic modality in court judgments: A corpus-driven comparison of civil cases in Hong Kong and Scotland." *English for Specific Purposes* 33: 15–26.

Chesterman, Andrew. 1993. "From 'Is' to 'Ought': Laws, Norms and Strategies in Translation Studies." *Target* 5(1): 1–20.

Chesterman, Andrew. 2004. "Hypotheses about translation universals." In *Claims, Changes and Challenges in Translation Studies. Selected contributions from the EST Congress, Copenhagen 2001,* edited by Gyde Hansen, Kirsten Malmkjær, and Daniel Gile, 1–13. Amsterdam: John Benjamins Publishing Company.

Chesterman, Andrew. 2010. "Why study translation universals?" In *Kiasm. Acta Translatologica Helsingiensia (ATH) 1,* edited by Ritva Hartama-Heinonen and Pirjo Kukkonen, 38–48. Helsingfors: Helsingfors universitet, Nordica, svensk översättning.

Chromá, Marta. 2011. "Synonymy and Polysemy in Legal Terminology and Their Applications to Bilingual and Bijural Translation." *Research in language* 9(1): 31–50.

Comrie, Bernard. 2008. "Inflectional morphology and language contact, with special reference to mixed languages." In *Language contact and contact languages*, edited by Peter Siemund and Noemi Kintana, 15–32. Amsterdam: John Benjamins Publishing Company.

Corpas Pastor, Gloria, and Miriam Seghiri Domínguez. 2010. "Size matters: A quantitative approach to corpus representativeness." In *Lengua, traducción, recepción. En honor de Julio César Santoyo*, edited by Rosa Rabadán, Trinidad Guzmán, and Marisa Fernández, 111–145. León: Universidad de León Área de Publicaciones.

Cortes, Viviana. 2004. "Lexical bundles in published and student disciplinary writing: Examples from history and biology." *English for Specific Purposes* 23(4): 397–423.

Cortes, Viviana. 2008. "A comparative analysis of lexical bundles in academic history writing in English and Spanish." *Corpora* 3(1): 43–57.

Cortes, Viviana. 2013. "The purpose of this study is to: Connecting lexical bundles and moves in research article introductions." *Journal of English for Academic Purposes* 12(1): 33–43.

Cortes, Viviana. 2015. "Situating lexical bundles in the formulaic language spectrum: Origins and functional analysis development." In *Corpus-Based Research in Applied Linguistics: Studies in Honor of Doug Biber*, edited by Viviana Cortes and Eniko Csomay, 197–218. Amsterdam and Philadelphia: John Benjamins Publishing Company.

Coulthard, Malcolm and Alison Johnson. 2010. *The Routledge Handbook of Forensic Linguistics*. London and New York: Routledge.

Crystal, David. 2005. *The Stories of English*. London: Penguin.

Czachor, Małgorzata. 2019. "Dystrybucja polskich imiesłowów: styl funkcjonalny i długość zdania." *Polonica* 39: 219–242.

Daille, Béatrice. 2017. *Term Variation in Specialised Corpora*. Amsterdam and Philadelphia: John Benjamins Publishing Company.

Dajczak, Wojciech, Tomasz Giaro, and Franciszek Longchamps de Berier. 2018. *Prawo rzymskie. U podstaw prawa prywatnego* (3rd ed.). Warszawa: Wydawnictwo Naukowe PWN.

Danet, Brenda. 1980. "Language in the Legal Process." *Law & Society Review* 14(3): 445–564.

Danielewiczowa, Magdalena. 2002. *Wiedza i niewiedza. Studium polskich czasowników epistemicznych*. Warszawa: Katedra Lingwistyki Formalnej.

De Bessé, Bruno, Blaise Nkwenti-Azeh, and Juan C. Sager. 1997. "Glossary of terms used in terminology." *Terminology* 4(1): 117–156.

De Sutter, Gert and Marie-Aude Lefer. 2020. "On the need for a new research agenda for corpus-based translation studies: A multi-methodological, multifactorial and interdisciplinary approach." *Perspectives* 28(1): 1–23.

Derlén, Mattias. 2009. *Multilingual Interpretation of European Union law*. Alphen aan den Rijn: Kluwer Law International.

Derlén, Mattias. 2015. "A Single Text or a Single Meaning: Multilingual Interpretation of EU Legislation and CJEU Case Law in National Courts." In *Language and Culture in EU Law. Multidisciplinary Perspectives*, edited by Susan Šarčević, 53–72. Farnham: Ashgate.

Derlén, Mattias. 2019. "Multilingualism and the Dynamic Interpretation of European Union Law." In *Evolutionary Interpretation and International Law*, edited by Georges Abi-Saab, Kenneth Keith, Gabrielle Marceau, and Clément Marquet, 329–338. Oxford: Hart Publishing.

Doczekalska, Agnieszka. 2018. "Legal Languages in Contact: EU Legislative Drafting and Its Consequences for Judicial Interpretation." In *Language and Law*, edited by Silvia Marino, Łucja Biel, Martina Bajčić, and Vilelmini Sosoni, 163–178. Cham: Springer.

Dontcheva-Navratilova, Olga. 2009. *Analysing Genre: The Colony Text of UNESCO Resolutions*. Brno: Masaryk University.

Duszak, Anna. 1998. *Tekst, dyskurs, komunikacja międzykulturowa*. Warszawa: Wydawnictwo Naukowe PWN.

Earp, Brian and David Trafimow. 2015. "Replication, falsification, and the crisis of confidence in social psychology." *Frontiers in Psychology* 6.

Engberg, Jan. 2015. "Autonomous EU Concepts — Fact or Fiction?" In *Language and Culture in EU Law: Multidisciplinary Perspectives*, edited by Susan Šarčević, 169–182. London: Ashgate.

Faber, Pamela. 2009. "The Cognitive Shift in Terminology and Specialized Translation." *MonTi: Monografías de Traducción e Interpretación* 1: 107–134.

Faber, Pamela, Carlos Márquez Linares, and Miguel Vega Expósito. 2005. "Framing Terminology: A Process-Oriented Approach." *Meta: Translators' Journal* 50(4).

Faber, Pamela, Pilar León Araúz, Juan Antonio Prieto Velasco, and Arianne Reimerink. 2007. "Linking Images and Words: The Description of Specialized Concepts." *International Journal of Lexicography* 20(1): 39–65.

Faber, Pamela, Silvia Montero Martínez, María Rosa Castro Prieto, José Senso Ruiz, Juan Antonio Prieto Velasco, Pilar León Araúz, Carlos Márquez Linares, and Miguel Vega Expósito. 2006. "Process-oriented terminology management in the domain of Coastal Engineering." *Terminology* 12(2): 189–213.

Fairclough, Norman. 2003. *Analysing Discourse: Textual Analysis for Social Research*. London and New York: Routledge.

Fairclough, Norman. 2006. "Genres in Political Discourse." In *Encyclopedia of Language and Linguistics*, vol. 5 (2nd ed.), edited by Keith Brown, 32–38. Oxford: Elsevier.

Felber, Helmut. 2001. *Allgemeine Terminologielehre, Wissenslehre und Wissenstechnik. Theoretische Grundlagen und philosophischen Betrachtungen.* Wien: Termnet.

Felici, Annarita. 2010. "Translating EU law: legal issues and multiple dynamics." *Perspectives: Studies in Translatology* 18(2): 95–108.

Felici, Annarita. 2015. "Translating EU Legislation from a Lingua Franca: Advantages and Disadvantages." In *Language and Culture in EU Law: Multidisciplinary Perspectives*, edited by Susan Šarčević, 123–141. London: Ashgate.

Fischer, Márta. 2010. "Language (policy), translation and terminology in the European Union." In *Terminology in Everyday Life*, edited by Marcel Thelen and Frieda Steurs, 21–33.

Gablasova, Dana, Vaclav Brezina, and Tony McEnery. 2017. "Collocations in Corpus-Based Language Learning Research: Identifying, Comparing, and Interpreting the Evidence." *Language learning* 67: 155–179.

Gajda, Stanisław. 2001. "Gatunkowe wzorce wypowiedzi." In *Współczesny język polski*, edited by Jerzy Bartmiński, 255–268. Lublin: Wydawnictwo Uniwersytetu Marii Curie-Skłodowskiej.

Gałuskina, Ksenia and Joanna Sycz. 2013. "Latin maxims and phrases in the Polish, English and French legal systems – The comparative study." *Studies in Logic, Grammar and Rhetoric* 34(1): 9–26.

Gibbons, John P. 2006. *Language and the Law.* London and New York: Routledge.

Giltrow, Janet. 2001. "Meta-genre." In *The Rhetoric and Ideology of Genre: Strategies for Stability and Change*, edited by Richard M. Coe, Lorelei Lingard, and Tatiana Teslenko, 187–206. Cresskill: Hampton Press.

Goldberg, Susan. 1984. "Judicial Socialization: An Empirical Study." *Journal of Contemporary Law* 11(2): 423–451.

Goźdź-Roszkowski, Stanisław. 2006. "Recurrent word combinations in judicial argumentation. A corpus-based study." *Langue, Droit, Société/Language, Law, Society*, edited by Danuta Bartol, Anna Duszak, Hubert Izdebski, and Jean-Marie Pierrel, 139–152. Nancy: Presses universitaires de Nancy.

Goźdź-Roszkowski, Stanisław. 2011. *Patterns of Linguistic Variation in American Legal English: A Corpus-Based Study.* Frankfurt am Main: Peter Lang.

Goźdź-Roszkowski, Stanisław. 2013. "Exploring near-synonymous terms in legal language. A corpus-based, phraseological perspective." *Linguistica Antverpiensia, New Series–Themes in Translation Studies* 12. Antwerp: University Press.

Goźdź-Roszkowski, Stanisław. 2020. "Move Analysis of Legal Justifications in Constitutional Tribunal Judgments in Poland: What They Share and What They Do Not." *International Journal for the Semiotics of Law* 33(2): 381–401.

Goźdź-Roszkowski, Stanisław and Gianluca Pontrandolfo. 2013. "Evaluative patterns in judicial discourse: A corpus-based phraseological perspective on American and Italian criminal judgments." *International Journal of Law, Language and Discourse* 3(2): 9–69.

Goźdź-Roszkowski, Stanisław and Gianluca Pontrandolfo. 2015. "Legal phraseology today: Corpus-based applications across legal languages and genres." *Special Issue of Fachsprache* 3–4: 130–138.

Goźdź-Roszkowski, Stanisław and Gianluca Pontrandolfo (eds.). 2017. *Phraseology in Legal and Institutional Settings. A Corpus-Based Interdisciplinary Perspective*, 189–202. London: Routledge.

Grabar, Natalia and Marie-Aude Lefer. 2015. "A corpus-based analysis of English and French lexical bundles across genres." Paper presented at the conference Words, Words, Words-Lexis, Corpora and Contrastive Analysis workshop, ICAME36 conference (Trier, Germany, May 27–31, 2015).

Grabowski, Łukasz. 2013. "Register Variation Across English Pharmaceutical Texts: A Corpus-driven Study of Keywords, Lexical Bundles and Phrase Frames in Patient Information Leaflets and Summaries of Product Characteristics." *Procedia – Social and Behavioral Sciences* 95: 391–401.

Grabowski, Łukasz. 2014. "On Lexical Bundles in Polish Patient Information Leaflets: A Corpus-Driven Study." *Studies in Polish Linguistics* 9(1): 21–43.

Grabowski, Łukasz. 2015a. "Keywords and lexical bundles within English pharmaceutical discourse: A corpus-driven description." *English for Specific Purposes* 38: 23–33.

Grabowski, Łukasz. 2015b. "O frazeologii z perspektywy językoznawstwa korpusowego. Przegląd głównych nurtów badawczych ostatniego dwudziestolecia w Wielkiej Brytanii i USA." In *Problemy frazeologii europejskiej* 10: 23–48. Łask: Oficyna Wydawnicza LEKSEM.

Grabowski, Łukasz. 2015c. *Phraseology in English Pharmaceutical Discourse. A Corpus-Driven Study of Register Variation.* Opole: Uniwersytet Opolski.

Grabowski, Łukasz. 2018a. "Fine-tuning lexical bundles: A methodological reflection in the context of describing drug-drug interactions." In *Applications of Pattern-driven Methods in Corpus Linguistics*, edited by Joanna Kopaczyk and Jukka Tyrkkö, 57–80. Amsterdam and Philadelphia: John Benjamins Publishing Company.

Grabowski, Łukasz. 2018b. "On identification of bilingual lexical bundles for translation purposes: The case of an English-Polish comparable corpus of patient information leaflets." In *Multiword Units in Machine Translation and Translation Technology*, edited by Ruslan Mitkov, Johanna Monti, Gloria Corpas Pastor, and Violeta Seretan, 182–199.

Grabowski, Łukasz. 2018c. "Stance bundles in English-to-Polish translation: A corpus-informed study." *Russian Journal of Linguistics* 22(2): 404–422.

Grabowski, Paweł. 2009. "Enactment, provision, norm: reflections on the normativeness of provisions regulating the process of legislation." *Investigationes Linguisticae* 17: 129–140.

Granger, Sylviane. 2003. "The corpus approach: A common way forward for Contrastive Linguistics and Translation Studies." In *Corpus-Based Approaches to Contrastive Linguistics and Translation Studies*, edited by Jacques Lerot, Sylviane Granger, and Stephanie Petch-Tyson, 17–29. Amsterdam: Rodopi.

Granger, Sylviane. 2014. "A lexical bundle approach to comparing languages: Stems in English and French." *Languages in Contrast* 14(1): 58–72.

Granger, Sylviane and Magali Paquot. 2008. "Disentangling the phraseological web." In *Phraseology. An interdisciplinary perspective*, edited by Sylviane Granger and Fanny Meunier, 27–50. Amsterdam: John Benjamins Publishing Company.

Gray, Bethany and Douglas Biber. 2015. "Phraseology." In *The Cambridge Handbook of English Corpus Linguistics*, edited by Douglas Biber, 125–145. Cambridge: Cambridge University Press.

Gries, Stefan T. 2006. "Some Proposals Towards a More Rigorous Corpus Linguistics." *Zeitschrift für Anglistik und Amerikanistik* 54(2): 191–202.

Gries, Stefan T. 2009. "What is Corpus Linguistics?" In *Language and Linguistics Compass* 3: 1–17.

Grzegorczykowa, Renata. 2004[1998]. *Wykłady z polskiej składni.* Warszawa: Wydawnictwo Naukowe PWN.

Gustafsson, Marita. 1984. "The Syntactic Features of Binomial Expressions in Legal English." *Text-Interdisciplinary Journal for the Study of Discourse* 4(1–3): 123–141.

Handford, Michael. 2010. "What can a corpus tell us about specialist genres?" In *The Routledge handbook of corpus linguistics*, edited by Anne O'Keeffe, Michael McCarthy, 255–269. London: Routledge.

Hardie, Andrew and Tony McEnery. 2010. "On two traditions in corpus linguistics, and what they have in common." *International Journal of Corpus Linguistics* 15(3): 384–394.

Heimbach, Elizabeth. 2004. *Latin Everywhere, Everyday: A Latin Phrase Workbook.* Wauconda: Bolchazy-Carducci Publishers.

Hiltunen, Risto. 1990. *Chapters on Legal English: Aspects Past and Present of the Language of the Law.* Jyväskylä: Gummerus.

Horspool, Margot. 2006. "Over the Rainbow: Languages and Law in the Future of the European Union." *Futures* 38(2): 158–168.

Hu, Kaibao. 2016. *Introducing Corpus-based Translation Studies.* Berlin: Springer.

Husinec, Snježana. 2011. "The Importance of Content Knowledge for Successful Legal Language Acquisition." *Research in Language* 9(1): 125–133.

Hyland, Ken. 2004. "Graduates' gratitude: The generic structure of dissertation acknowledgements." *English for Specific Purposes* 23(3): 303–324.

Hyland, Ken. 2008. "As can be seen: Lexical bundles and disciplinary variation." *English for Specific Purposes* 27(1): 4–21.

ISO 1087–1:2000. 2000. *Terminology work – Vocabulary – Part 1: Theory and application*. Geneva: ISO.

ISO 1087:2019. 2019. *Terminology work and terminology science – Vocabulary*. Geneva: ISO.

Jablonkai, Reka. 2009. ""In the light of": a corpus-based analysis of lexical bundles in two EU-related registers." *WoPaLP* 3: 1–26.

Jablonkai, Reka. 2010. "English in the context of European integration: A corpus-driven analysis of lexical bundles in English EU documents." *English for Specific Purposes* 29(4): 253–267.

Jadacka, Hanna. 2002. *Poradnik językowy dla prawników*. Warszawa: Wydawnictwo Naukowe Semper.

Jadacka, Hanna. 2005. *Kultura języka polskiego. Fleksja, słowotwórstwo, składnia*. Warszawa: Wydawnictwo Naukowe PWN.

James, Philip S. 1979. *Introduction to English Law* (10th ed). London: Butterworths.

Johns, Tim. 1991. "From printout to handout: Grammar and vocabulary teaching in the context of data driven learning." In *Classroom concordancing. Special issue of ELR Journal* 4, edited by Tim Johns and Philip King, 27–45. Birmingham: University of Birmingham, Centre for English Language Studies.

Jopek-Bosiacka, Anna. 2006. *Przekład prawny i sądowy*. Warszawa: Wydawnictwo Naukowe PWN.

Jopek-Bosiacka, Anna. 2010. *Legal Communication: A Cross-Cultural Perspective*. Warszawa: Warsaw University Press.

Jopek-Bosiacka, Anna. 2011. "Defining Law Terms: A Cross-Cultural Perspective." *Research in Language* 9(1): 9–29.

Jopek-Bosiacka, Anna. 2019. *Teoretycznoprawne i logiczne uwarunkowania przekładu prawnego*. Warszawa: Wolters Kluwer.

Kacprzak, Agnieszka, Witold Wołodkiewicz and Jerzy Krzynówek. 2001. *Regulae iuris: łacińskie inskrypcje na kolumnach Sądu Najwyższego Rzyczypospolitej Polskiej*. Warszawa: C.H.Beck.

Kellerbauer, Manuel, Marcus Klamert, and Jonathan Tomkin (eds.). 2019. *The EU Treaties and the Charter of Fundamental Rights: Digital Pack. A Commentary*. Oxford: Oxford University Press.

Kenning, Marie-Madeleine. 2010. "What are parallel and comparable corpora and how can we use them." In *The Routledge Handbook of Corpus Linguistics*, edited by Anne O'Keeffe, Michael McCarthy, 487–500. London: Routledge.

Kierzkowska, Danuta. 2008. *Tłumaczenia prawnicze.* Warszawa: Tepis.

Kilgarriff, Adam, Vit Baisa, Jan Bušta, Miloš Jakubíček, Vojtěch Kovář, Jan Michelfeit, Pavel Rychlý, and Vit Suchomel. 2014. "The Sketch Engine: Ten years on." *Lexicography* 1(1): 7–36.

Kjær, Anne Lise. 1990. "Context-conditioned word combinations in legal language." *Journal of the International Institute of Terminology Research* 1(1–2): 21–32.

Kjær, Anne Lise. 2004. "A common legal language in Europe?" In *Epistemology and methodology of comparative law*, edited by Mark Van Hoecke, 377–398. Oxford and Portland: Hart Publishing.

Kjær, Anne Lise. 2007. "Legal Translation in the European Union: A Research Field in Need of a New Approach." In *Language and the Law: International Outlooks*, edited by Krzysztof Kredens and Stanisław Goźdź-Roszkowski, 69–95. Frankfurt am Main: Peter Lang.

Kjær, Anne-Lise. 2010. "Nonsense: The CILFIT Criteria Revisited: From the Perspective of Legal Linguistics." In *Europe. The New Legal Realism. Essays in Honour of Hjalte Rasmussen*, edited by Henning Koch, Jospeh H. H. Weiler, Karsten Hagel-Sørensen, and Ulrich Haltern, 217–396. Copenhagen: Djøf.

Klabbers, Jan. 2015. "Straddling the Fence." In *The Oxford Handbook of European Union Law*, edited by Anthony Arnull and Damian Chalmers, 52–74. Oxford: Oxford University Press.

Kłodawski, Maciej. 2012. "Pleonazmy i analityzmy – wyrażenia redundantne pragmatycznie w języku prawnym." In *Język współczesnego prawa*, edited by Adam Niewiadomski, Ewa Sztymelska, 121–132. Warszawa: Wydawnictwo Koła Naukowego "Lingua Iuris" Uniwersytetu Warszawskiego.

Kłodawski, Maciej. 2017. *Redundancja w tekście prawnym.* Toruń: Adam Marszałek.

Koester, Almut. 2010. "Building small specialized corpora." In *The Routledge Handbook of Corpus Linguistics*, edited by Anne O'Keeffe, Michael McCarthy, 94–107. London: Routledge.

Kopaczyk, Joanna. 2012a. "Applications of the Lexical Bundles Method in Historical Corpus Research." In *Corpus Data Across Languages and Disciplines*, edited by Piotr Pęzik, 83–95. Frankfurt am Main: Peter Lang.

Kopaczyk, Joanna. 2012b. "Long Lexical Bundles and Standardisation in Historical Legal Texts." *Studia Anglica Posnaniensia* 47(2–3): 3–25.

Kopaczyk, Joanna. 2017. "Terms and conditions: A comparative study of noun binomials in UK and Scottish legislation." In *Phraseology in Legal and Institutional Settings. A Corpus-Based Interdisciplinary Perspective*, edited by Stanisław Goźdź-Roszkowski and Gianluca Pontrandolfo, 160–185. London: Routledge.

Kopaczyk, Joanna and Hans Sauer (eds.). 2017a. *Binomials in the history of English: Fixed and flexible.* Cambridge: Cambridge University Press.

Kopaczyk, Joanna and Hans Sauer. 2017b. "Defining and Exploring Binomials." In *Binomials in the history of English: Fixed and flexible*, edited by Joanna Kopaczyk and Hans Sauer, 1–23. Cambridge: Cambridge University Press.

Koskinen, Kaisa. 2008. *Translating Institutions. An Ethnographic Study of EU Translation.* Manchester: St. Jerome.

Koźbiał, Dariusz. 2016. "Staże w instytucjach unijnych jako element kształcenia studentów i absolwentów specjalizacji tłumaczeniowych." *Lingua Legis* 24: 79–89.

Koźbiał, Dariusz. 2017. "Two-tiered approach to quality assurance in legal translation at the Court of Justice of the European Union." In *Quality aspects in institutional translation*, edited by Tomáš Svoboda, Łucja Biel, and Krzysztof Łoboda, 155–174.

Koźbiał, Dariusz. 2018a. "Phraseological Profile of Judgments: Complex Prepositions in EU Competition Law Judgments." In *Language and Law*, edited by Silvia Marino, Łucja Biel, Martina Bajčić, and Vilelmini Sosoni, 325–357. Cham: Springer.

Koźbiał, Dariusz. 2018b. "Przyimki w wyrokach unijnych i krajowych – analiza korpusowa dystrybucji i funkcji przyimków prostych, złożonych i wtórnych." *Comparative Legilinguistics* 35: 89–119.

Koźbiał, Dariusz. 2019. "Epistemic Modality: A Corpus-Based Analysis of Epistemic Markers in EU and Polish Judgments." *Comparative Legilinguistics* 41: 39–70.

Koźbiał, Dariusz. *forthcoming*. "Wykładniki modalności w wyrokach Trybunału Sprawiedliwości UE i Sądu Najwyższego RP – analiza korpusowa." *Studia Iuridica.*

Krummes, Cedrik, Sylvia Jaworska, and Astrid Ensslin. 2011. "The use of discourse-structuring sequences by advanced learners of German: Corpus-driven investigations." Paper presented at the conference Corpus Linguistics 2011 (Birmingham, UK, July 20–22, 2011).

Krzyżanowski, Michał and Ruth Wodak. 2010. "Hegemonic Multilingualism in/of the EU Institutions: An Inside-Outside Perspective on the European Language Policies and Practices." In *Mehrsprachigkeit aus der Perspektive zweier EU-Projekte: DYLAN Meets LINEE*, edited by Cornelia Hülmbauer, Eva Vetter, and Heike Böhringer, 115–135. Frankfurt am Main: Peter Lang.

Künnecke, Martina. 2013. "Translation in the EU: Language and Law in the EU's Judicial Labyrinth." *Maastricht Journal of European and Comparative Law* 20(2): 243–260.

Kurzon, Dennis. 1987. "Latin for Lawyers: Degrees of Textual Integration." *Applied Linguistics* 8: 233–240.

Kurzon, Dennis. 1989. "Language of the Law and Legal Language." In *Special Language: From Humans Thinking to Thinking Machines*, edited by Christer Lauren and Marianne Nordman, 283–290. Clevedon and Philadelphia: Multilingual Matters.

Kurzon, Dennis. 1997. " 'Legal Language': Varieties, Genres, Registers, Discourses." *International Journal of Applied Linguistics* 7(2): 119–139.

Łachacz, Olga and Rafał Mańko. 2013. "Multilingualism at the Court of Justice of the European Union: Theoretical and Practical Aspects." *Studies in Logic, Grammar and Rhetoric* 34(1): 75–92.

Łapa, Romana. 2006a. "Przyimki wtórne w tekstach prawnych." *Język Polski* 86: 358–366.

Łapa, Romana. 2006b. "W sprawie wydzielania relacji modalności wyrażanej przez przyimki wtórne." *Język Polski* LXXXVI(1): 7–10.

Łapa, Romana. 2013. "Konstrukcje z przyimkami w ustawach prawnych. Znaczenia gramatyczne." *Roczniki Humanistyczne LXI(6): Językoznawstwo*: 77–91.

Laviosa, Sara. 2002. *Corpus-based Translation Studies: Theory, Findings, Applications*. Amsterdam: Rodopi.

Lee, Changsoo. 2013. "Using lexical bundle analysis as discovery tool for corpus-based translation research." *Perspectives* 21(3): 378–395.

Lee, David Y. W. 2001. "Genres, Registers, Text Types, Domains, and Styles: Clarifying the Concepts and Navigating a Path through the BNC Jungle." *Language Learning and Technology* 5: 37–72.

Lee, David Y. W. 2008. "Corpora and Discourse Analysis: New Ways of Doing Old Things." In *Advances in Discourse Studies*, edited by Vijay K. Bhatia, John Flowerdew, and Rodney H. Jones, 86–99. London: Routledge.

Lee, David Y. W. 2010. "What corpora are available." In *The Routledge handbook of corpus linguistics*, edited by Anne O'Keeffe and Michael McCarthy, 107–121. London: Routledge.

Leech, Geoffrey. 1991. "The state of art in corpus linguistics" In *English Corpus Linguistics*, edited by Karin Aijmer and Bengt Altenberg, 8–29. London: Longman.

Leech, Geoffrey. 1992. "Corpora and theories of linguistic performance." In *Directions in Corpus Linguistics. Proceedings of Nobel Symposium* 82, edited by Jan Svartvik, 105–22. Berlin and New York: Mouton de Gruyter.

Leech, Geoffrey. 2007. "New resources, or just better old ones? The Holy Grail of representativeness." In *Corpus Linguistics and the Web*, edited by Marianne Hundt, Nadja Nesselhauf, and Carolin Biewer, 133–149. Amsterdam: Rodopi.

Lehto, Anu. 2018. "Lexical bundles in Early Modern and Present-day English Acts of Parliament." In *Applications of Pattern-driven Methods in Corpus Linguistics*, edited by Joanna Kopaczyk and Jukka Tyrkkö, 159–186. Amsterdam and Philadelphia: John Benjamins Publishing Company.

Lesz-Duk, Maria. 1993. "Wtórne przyimki lokatywne w języku polskim." *Poradnik Językowy* 7: 402–414.

Lesz-Duk, Maria. 2007. "Wtórne przyimki przyczynowe we współczesnym języku polskim." *Prace Naukowe Akademii im. Jana Długosza w Częstochowie. Filologia Polska. Językoznawstwo* 6: 67–73.

Lesz-Duk, Maria. 2011. *Przyimki wtórne w języku polskim. Stan współczesny i ewolucja.* Częstochowa: Wydawnictwo Akademii im. Jana Długosza.

Łętowska, Ewa, Ada Paprocka, and Iwona Rzucidło-Grochowska. 2015. "Podstawy uzasadniania w prawie konstytucyjnym i międzynarodowym." In *Uzasadnienia decyzji stosowania prawa*, edited by Iwona Rzucidło-Grochowska and Mateusz Grochowski, 15–42. Warszawa: Wolters Kluwer.

Lewandowska-Tomaszczyk, Barbara. 2005a. "Powstanie i rozwój językoznawstwa korpusowego." In *Podstawy językoznawstwa korpusowego*, edited by Barbara Lewandowska-Tomaszczyk, 7–26. Łódź: Wydawnictwo Uniwersytetu Łódzkiego.

Lewandowska-Tomaszczyk, Barbara. 2005b. "Analiza języka z zastosowaniem korpusu." In *Podstawy językoznawstwa korpusowego*, edited by Barbara Lewandowska-Tomaszczyk, 133–173. Łódź: Wydawnictwo Uniwersytetu Łódzkiego.

Lewandowska-Tomaszczyk, Barbara. 2012a. "Cognitive Corpus Studies: A New Qualitative and Quantitative Agenda for Contrasting Languages." *MFU Connexion: Journal of Humanities and Social Sciences* 1(1): 26–64.

Lewandowska-Tomaszczyk, Barbara. 2012b. "Explicit and tacit: An interplay of the quantitative and qualitative approaches to translation." In *Quantitative Methods in Corpus-Based Translation Studies*, edited by Michael P. Oakes and Meng Ji, 1–34. Amsterdam: John Benjamins Publishing Company.

Lewandowski, Sławomir, Hanna Machińska, Andrzej Malinowski, and Jacek Petzel. 2017. *Logika dla prawników.* Warszawa: Wolters Kluwer.

Lieberwirth, Rolf. 1986. *Latein im Recht.* Berlin: Staatsverlag der DDR.

Lüdeling, Anke and Merja Kyto. 2008. *Corpus Linguistics: An International Handbook, vol. 1.* Berlin and New York: Mouton deGruyter.

Lüdeling, Anke and Merja Kyto. 2009. *Corpus Linguistics: An International Handbook, vol. 2.* Berlin and New York: Mouton deGruyter.

Maley, Yon. 1985. "Judicial Discourse: The Case of the Legal Judgement." *Beitrage zur Phonetik und Linguistik* 48: 159–173.

Maley, Yon. 1994. "The language of the law." In *Language and the Law*, edited by John Peter Gibbons, 11–50. London: Longman.

Malinowski, Andrzej. 2006. *Polski język prawny. Wybrane zagadnienia.* Warszawa: LexisNexis.

Malinowski, Andrzej, Michał Pełka, and Radosław Brzeski. 2018. *Przewodnik do ćwiczeń z logiki dla prawników.* Warszawa: Wolters Kluwer.

Malkiel, Yakov. 1959. "Studies in Irreversible Binomials." *Lingua* 8: 113–160.

Malmkjær, Kirsten. 2011. "Translation Universals." In *The Oxford Handbook of Translation Studies,* edited by Kirsten Malmkjær and Kevin Windle, 83–93. Oxford: Oxford University Press.

Małocha-Krupa, Agnieszka. 2003. *Słowa w lustrze. Pleonazm – semantyka – pragmatyka.* Wrocław: Wydawnictwo Uniwersytetu Wrocławskiego.

Martín Martín, Pedro A. 2003. "Genre and discourse community." *Revista de filología inglesa* 25: 153–166.

Matras, Yaron. 2009. *Language Contact.* Cambridge: Cambridge University Press.

Mattila, Heikki E. S. 2006. *Comparative Legal Linguistics.* Aldershot: Ashgate Publishing.

Mattila, Heikki E. S. 2008. "European Integration and Legal Communication." In *Paradoxes of European Legal Integration,* edited by Hanne Petersen, Anne Lise Kjaer, Helle Krunke, and Mikael Rask Madsen, 253–276. Aldershot: Ashgate.

Matulewska, Aleksandra. 2007. "Judgments in Polish-English and English-Polish Translation." *Lingua Legis* 15: 23–32.

Matulewska, Aleksandra and Magdalena Wasielewska. 2003. "Latin Maxims and Expressions in English, Estonian and Polish Legal Language in the Aspect of Translation." *Investigationes Linguisticae* 10: 2–18.

Mauranen, Anna. 2006. "Translation Universals." In *Encyclopedia of Language and Linguistics,* vol. 13 (2nd ed.), edited by Keith Brown, 93–100. Oxford: Elsevier.

Mauranen, Anna. 2007. "Universal Tendencies in Translation." In *Incorporating Corpora. The Linguist and the Translator,* edited by Gunilla Anderman and Margaret Rogers, 32–48. Clevedon: Multilingual Matters.

Mauranen, Anna and Pekka Kujamäki (eds.). 2004. *Translation Universals. Do they exist?* Amsterdam and Philadelphia: John Benjamins Publishing Company.

Mazzi, Davide. 2007a. "The construction of argumentation in judicial texts: Combining a genre and a corpus based perspective." *Argumentation* 21: 21–38.

Mazzi, Davide. 2007b. *The Linguistic Study of Judicial Argumentation. Theoretical Perspectives, Analytical Insights.* Modena: Il fiorino.

Mazzi, Davide. 2010. ""This Argument Fails for Two Reasons…": A Linguistic Analysis of Judicial Evaluation Strategies in US Supreme Court Judgments." *International Journal for the Semiotics of Law* 23(4): 373–385.

Mazzi, Davide. 2017. ""By partially renouncing their sovereignty...": on the discourse function(s) of lexical bundles in EU-related Irish judicial discourse." In *Phraseology in Legal and Institutional Settings. A Corpus-Based Interdisciplinary Perspective*, edited by Stanisław Goźdź-Roszkowski and Gianluca Pontrandolfo, 189–202. London: Routledge.

McAuliffe, Karen. 2008. "Enlargement at the European Court of Justice: Law, Language and Translation." *European Law Journal* 14(6): 806–818.

McAuliffe, Karen. 2009. "Translation at the Court of Justice of the European Communities." In *Translation Issues in Language and Law*, edited by Frances Olsen, Alexander Lorz, and Dieter Stein, 99–115. New York: Palgrave Macmillan.

McAuliffe, Karen. 2010. "Language and the Institutional Dynamics of the Court of Justice of The European Communities: Lawyer-Linguists and the Production of a Multilingual Jurisprudence." In *How Globalizing Professions Deal with National Languages: Studies in Cultural Conflict and Cooperation*, edited by Michel R. Gueldry, 239–263. Lewiston, Queenstown, Lampeter: Edwin Mellen Press.

McAuliffe, Karen. 2011. "Hybrid Texts and Uniform Law? The Multilingual Case Law of the Court of Justice of the European Union." *International Journal for the Semiotics of Law* 24(1): 97–115.

McAuliffe, Karen. 2012. "Language and Law in the European Union: The Multilingual Jurisprudence of the ECJ." In *The Oxford Handbook of Language and Law*, edited by Peter M. Tiersma and Lawrence M. Solan, 200–216. Oxford: Oxford University Press.

McAuliffe, Karen. 2013a. "Precedent at the Court of Justice of the European Union: The Linguistic Aspect." *Law and Language: Current Legal Issues* 15: 483–493.

McAuliffe, Karen. 2013b. "The Limitations of a Multilingual Legal System." *International Journal for the Semiotics of Law* 26(4): 861–882.

McAuliffe, Karen. 2014. "Translating Ambiguity." *Journal of Comparative Legilinguistics* 9: 65.

McAuliffe, Karen. 2016. "Hidden Translators: The Invisibility of Translators and the Influence of Lawyer-Linguists on the Case Law of the Court of Justice of the European Union." *Language and Law* 3(1): 5–29.

McAuliffe, Karen and Aleksandar Trklja. 2018. "Superdiversity and the Relationship between Law, Language and Translation in a Supranational Legal Order." In *The Routledge Handbook of Language and Superdiversity*, edited by Angela Creese and Adrian Blackledge. Abingdon-on-Thames: Routledge.

McEnery, Tony and Andrew Wilson. 2001. *Corpus Linguistics: An Introduction.* Edinburgh: Edinburgh University Press.

McEnery, Tony and Costas Gabrielatos. 2006a. "English Corpus Linguistics." In *The Handbook of English Linguistics*, edited by Bas Aarts and April McMahon, 33–71. Oxford: Blackwell.

McEnery, Tony, Richard Xiao, and Yukio Tono. 2006b. *Corpus-Based Language Studies. An Advanced Resource Book*. London: Routledge.

McEnery, Tony and Andrew Hardie. 2012. *Corpus Linguistics: Method, Theory and Practice*. Cambridge: Cambridge University Press.

McVeigh, Joseph. 2018. "Join us for this: Lexical bundles and repetition in email marketing texts." In *Applications of Pattern-driven Methods in Corpus Linguistics*, edited by Joanna Kopaczyk and Jukka Tyrkkö, 213–250. Amsterdam and Philadelphia: John Benjamins Publishing Company.

Mellinkoff, David. 1963. *The Language of the Law*. Boston: Little Brown and Co.

Mikłaszewicz, Przemysław. 2015. "Uzasadnienia orzeczeń Trybunału Sprawiedliwości Unii Europejskiej." In *Uzasadnienia decyzji stosowania prawa*, edited by Iwona Rzucidło-Grochowska and Mateusz Grochowski, 170–199. Warszawa: Wolters Kluwer Polska.

Milewska, Beata. 2003a. *Przyimki wtórne we współczesnej polszczyźnie*. Gdańsk: Wydawnictwo Uniwersytetu Gdańskiego.

Mollin, Sandra. 2014. *The (Ir)reversibility of English Binomials: Corpus, constraints, developments*. Amsterdam: John Benjamins Publishing Company.

Morris, Clarence. 1980. *Morris on Torts*. Mineola: Foundation Press.

Myking, Johan. 2001. "Against Precriptivism? The 'Sociocritical' Challenge to Terminology." *IITF Journal* 12(1–2): 49–64.

Nesselhauf, Nadja. 2004. "What are collocations?" In *Phraseological Units: Basic Concepts and Their Application*, edited by David Allerton, Nadja Nesselhauf, and Paul Skandera, 1–21. Basel: Schwabe.

Nesselhauf, Nadja. 2005. *Collocations in a Learner Corpus*. Amsterdam: John Benjamins Publishing Company.

Newmark, Peter. 1981. *Approaches to Translation*. London and New York: Prentice Hall.

Nikitina, Jekaterina. 2018. *Legal style markers and their translation in written pleadings before the European Court of Human Rights*. PhD Thesis. University of Milan.

Norrick, Neal. 1988. "Binomial meaning in text." *Journal of English Linguistics* 21(1): 72–87.

Nowak, Tomasz. 2008. *Przyimki lokatywno-inkluzyjne we współczesnym języku polskim: w głębi, w obrębie, w środku, we wnętrzu*. Katowice: Wydawnictwo Uniwersytetu Śląskiego.

O'Keeffe, Anne and Michael McCarthy (eds.). 2010. *The Routledge Handbook of Corpus Linguistics*. London: Routledge.

Olohan, Maeve. 2004. *Introducing Corpora in Translation Studies.* London and New York: Routledge.

Palmer, Frank R. 2001. *Mood and Modality.* Cambridge: Cambridge University Press.

Paquot, Magali and Sylviane Granger. 2012. "Formulaic language in learner corpora." *Annual Review of Applied Linguistics* 32: 130–149.

Paunio, Elina. 2007. "The tower of Babel and the interpretation of EU law-implications for equality of languages and legal certainty." In *Private Law and the Many Cultures of Europe*, edited by Thomas Wilhelmsson, Elina Paunio, and Annika Pohjolainen, 385–402. Alphen aan den Rijn: Kluwer Law International.

Paunio, Elina. 2016. *Legal Certainty in Multilingual EU Law: Language, Discourse and Reasoning at the European Court of Justice.* London: Routledge.

Pearson, Jennifer. 1998. *Terms in Context*, vol. 1. Amsterdam and Philadelphia: John Benjamins Publishing Company.

Pecorari, Diane. 2009. "Formulaic Language in Biology: A Topic-specific Investigation." In *Academic Writing: At the Interface of Corpus and Discourse*, edited by Maggie Charles, Diane Pecorari, and Susan Hunston, 91–104. London: Continuum.

Peruzzo, Katia. 2019. *National law in supranational case-law: A linguistic analysis of European Court of Human Rights judgments in English.* Trieste: Edizioni Università di Trieste.

Pęzik, Piotr. 2012. "Wyszukiwarka PELCRA dla danych NKJP." In *Narodowy Korpus Języka Polskiego*, edited by Adam Przepiórkowski, Mirosław Bańko, Rafał L. Górski, and Barbara Lewandowska-Tomaszczyk, 253–279. Warszawa: Wydawnictwo Naukowe PWN.

Picht, Heribert, Jennifer Draskau. 1985. *Terminology: An Introduction*, vol. 2. Guildford: University of Surrey, Department of Linguistic and International Studies.

Pieńkos, Jerzy. 1999. *Podstawy juryslingwistyki. Język w prawie – prawo w języku.* Warszawa: Oficyna Prawnicza Muza SA.

Pieńkos, Jerzy. 2010. *Praecepta Iuris. Paremie, sentencje, wyrażenia łacińskie w układzie systematycznym i alfabetycznym.* Warszawa: Polskie Wydawnictwo Prawnicze Iuris.

Pietrzkowski, Henryk. 2007. *Zarys metodyki pracy sędziego w sprawach cywilnych.* Warszawa: C.H.Beck.

Pontrandolfo, Gianluca. 2013. *La fraseología en las sentencias penales: un estudio contrastivo español-italiano-inglés basado en corpus.* PhD thesis. University of Trieste.

Pontrandolfo, Gianluca. 2019. "Corpus Methods in Legal Translation Studies." In *Research in legal translation and interpreting: crossing methodological boundaries*, edited by Łucja Biel, Jan Engberg, Rosario Martín Ruano, and Vilelmini Sosoni, 13–28. London: Routledge.

Pontrandolfo, Gianluca and Stanisław Goźdź-Roszkowski. 2014. "Exploring the Local Grammar of Evaluation: The Case of Adjectival Patterns in American and Italian Judicial Discourse." *Research in language* 12(1): 71–91.

Poplack, Shana. 1978. "Syntactic structure and social function of code-switching." In *Latino Language and Communicative Behavior*, edited by Richard P. Durán, 169–184. Norwood: Ablex Publishing Corporation.

Poplack, Shana, David Sankoff, and Christopher Miller. 1988. "The social correlates and linguistic processes of lexical borrowing and assimilation." *Linguistics* 26(1): 47–104.

Prieto Ramos, Fernando. 2014. "International and Supranational Law in Translation: From Multilingual Lawmaking to Adjudication." *The Translator* 20(3): 313–331.

Prieto Ramos, Fernando and Diego Guzmán. 2018. "Legal Terminology Consistency and Adequacy as Quality Indicators in Institutional Translation: A Mixed-Method Comparative Study." In *Institutional Translation for International Governance: Enhancing Quality in Multilingual Legal Communication*, edited by Fernando Prieto Ramos, 81–101. London: Bloomsbury.

Prieto Ramos, Fernando, Giorgina Cerutti Benitez, and Diego Guzman. 2019. "Building representative multi-genre corpora for legal and institutional translation research: The LETRINT approach to text categorization and stratified sampling." *Translation Spaces* 8(1): 93–116.

Przepiórkowski, Adam, Mirosław Bańko, Rafał L. Górski, and Barbara Lewandowska-Tomaszczyk (eds.). 2012. *Narodowy Korpus Języka Polskiego.* Warszawa: Wydawnictwo Naukowe PWN.

Radwański, Zbigniew and Adam Olejniczak. 2018. *Zobowiązania. Część ogólna.* Warszawa: C.H.Beck.

Radwański, Zbigniew and Janina Panowicz-Lipska. 2019. *Zobowiązania. Część szczegółowa.* Warszawa: C.H.Beck.

Rasmussen, Kirsten Wølch and Jan Engberg. 1999. "Genre Analysis of Legal Discourse." *HERMES-Journal of Language and Communication in Business* (22): 113–132.

Rezler, Jan. 2003. *Język łaciński dla prawników.* Warszawa: Wydawnictwo Naukowe PWN.

Rieger, Burghard B. 1979. "Repräsentativität: von der Unangemessenheit eines Begriffs zur Kennzeichnung eines Problems linguistischer Korpusbildung." In *Empirische Textwissenschaft: Ausbau und Auswertung von Text-Corpora*, edited by Henning Bergenholtz and Burkhard Schaeder, 52–70. Königstein: Scriptor.

Riley, Alison. 1996. "The Meaning of Words in English Legal Texts: Mastering the Vocabulary of the Law – a Legal Task." *The Law Teacher* 30(1): 68–83.

Ristikivi, Merike. 2005. "Latin: The Common Legal Language of Europe?" *Juridica International* 10: 199–202.

Robertson, Colin. 2015. "EU Multilingual Law: Interfaces of Law, Language and Culture." In *Language and Culture in EU Law. Multidisciplinary Perspectives*, edited by Susan Šarčević, 33–52. Farnham: Ashgate.

Robertson, Colin. 2016. *Multilingual Law. A Framework for Analysis and Understanding*. London: Routledge.

Robinson, William. 2014. "Translating Legislation: The European Union Experience." *The Theory and Practice of Legislation* 2: 185–210.

Rodríguez-Inés, Patricia and Daniel Gallego-Hernández. 2016. "Corpus Use and Learning to Translate, almost 20 years on." *Cadernos de Tradução* 36: 9–13.

Römer, Ute. 2010. "Establishing the phraseological profile of a text type: The construction of meaning in academic book reviews." *English Text Construction* 3(1): 95–119.

Rzucidło, Iwona. 2011. "Funkcje uzasadnienia sądowego." *Studenckie Zeszyty Naukowe* 21: 52–58.

Rzucidło, Iwona. 2020. *Uzasadnienie orzeczenia sądowego. Ujęcie teoretyczne a poglądy orzecznictwa*. Warszawa: Wolters Kluwer.

Rzucidło-Grochowska, Iwona. 2013. "Uzasadnienie orzeczenia sądowego w świetle jednolitości orzecznictwa. Zarys problematyki." In *Jednolitość orzecznictwa. Standard – instrumenty – praktyka*, edited by Mateusz Grochowski, Michał Raczkowski, and Sławomir Żółtek, 62–72. Warszawa: Biuro Studiów i Analiz Sądu Najwyższego.

Rzucidło-Grochowska, Iwona. 2015. ""Część historyczna" uzasadnienia orzeczenia sądowego." In *Uzasadnienia decyzji stosowania prawa*, edited by Iwona Rzucidło-Grochowska and Mateusz Grochowski, 170–199. Warszawa: Wolters Kluwer Polska.

Rzucidło-Grochowska, Iwona. 2017. "Strategie i techniki formułowania uzasadnień orzeczeń sądowych." *Ruch prawniczy, ekonomiczny i socjologiczny* 79(2): 59–72. Poznań: Uniwersytet im. Adama Mickiewicza w Poznaniu.

Rzucidło-Grochowska, Iwona. 2019. "Argumentacja interpretacyjna w orzeczeniach TSUE." In *Wykładnia prawa Unii Europejskiej. System Prawa Unii Europejskiej. Tom 3*, edited by Leszek Leszczyński, 467–482. Warszawa: C.H.Beck.

Sageder, Dagmar. 2010. "Terminology Today: A Science, an Art or a Practice? Some Aspects on Terminology and its Development." *Brno Studies in English* 36(1): 123–134.

Sager, Juan C. 1990. *A Practical Course in Terminology Processing*. Amsterdam and Philadelphia: John Benjamins Publishing Company.

Sager, Juan C., David Dungworth, and Peter F. McDonald. 1980. *English Special Languages: Principles and Practice in Science and Technology.* Wiesbaden: Brandstetter Verlag.

Saldanha, Gabriela and Sharon O'Brien. 2014. *Research Methodologies in Translation Studies.* London and New York: Routledge.

Salmi-Tolonen, Tarja. 1994. "The Linguistic Manifestations of Primary and Secondary Functions of Law in the National and Supranational Contexts." *International Journal for the Semiotics of Law* 7(19): 13–39.

Salmi-Tolonen, Tarja. 2005. "Persuasion in judicial argumentation: The Opinions of the Advocates General at the European Court of Justice." In *Persuasion Across Genres: A linguistic approach*, edited by Helena Halmari and Tuija Virtanen, 59–101. Amsterdam: John Benjamins Publishing Company.

Šarčević, Susan. 1989. "Conceptual Dictionaries for Translation in the Field of Law." *International Journal of Lexicography* 2(4): 277–293.

Šarčević, Susan. 1997. *New Approach to Legal Translation.* The Hague: Kluwer Law International.

Šarčević, Susan. 2007. "Making Multilingualism Work in the Enlarged Europe Union." In *Language and the Law: International Outlooks*, edited by Krzysztof Kredens and Stanisław Goźdź-Roszkowski, 35–54. Frankfurt am Main: Peter Lang.

Šarčević, Susan. 2010. "Creating a Pan-European Legal Language." In: *Legal Discourse across Languages and Cultures*, edited by Christopher Williams and Maurizio Gotti, 23–50. Frankfurt am Main: Peter Lang.

Šarčević, Susan. 2013. "Multilingual Lawmaking and Legal (Un)Certainty in the European Union." In *Legal Discourse across Languages and Cultures*, edited by Christopher Williams and Maurizio Gotti, 1–29. Frankfurt am Main: Peter Lang.

Šarčević, Susan and Colin Robertson. 2013. "The Work of Lawyer-Linguists in the EU Institutions." In *Legal Translation in Context: Professional Issues and Prospects*, edited by Anabel Borja Albi and Fernando Prieto Ramos, 181–202. Bern: Peter Lang.

Scarpa, Federica and Daniele Orlando. 2017. "What it takes to do it right: An integrative EMT-based model for legal translation competence." *The Journal of Specialised Translation* 27: 21–42.

Schmidt, Susanne K. 2018. *The European Court of Justice and the Policy Process: The Shadow of Case Law.* New York: Oxford University Press.

Schmitt, Norbert. 2004. *Formulaic Sequences: Acquisition, processing and use.* Amsterdam: John Benjamins Publishing Company.

Scott, Michael. 2010. "Problems in investigating keyness, or clearing the undergrowth and marking out trails..." In *Keyness in Texts*, edited by Marina

Bondi and Mike Scott, 43–57. Amsterdam: John Benjamins Publishing Company.

Scott, Michael. 2017. WordSmith Tools version 7. Stroud: Lexical Analysis Software.

Searle, John R. 1969. *Speech Acts: An Essay in the Philosophy of Language.* Cambridge: Cambridge University Press.

Searle, John R. 1976. "A classification of illocutionary acts." *Language in Society* 5(1): 1–23.

Shelov, Sergej. D. 1982. "The Linguistic Nature of the Term" *Nauchno-Tekhnicheskaya Informatsiya* 16(9): 1–6.

Sinclair, John. 1991. *Corpus, Concordance, Collocation.* Oxford: Oxford University Press.

Sinclair, John. 2005. "Corpus and Text — Basic Principles." In *Developing Linguistic Corpora: A Guide to Good Practice*, edited by Martin Wynne, 1–16. Oxford: Oxbow Books.

Stefaniak, Karolina. 2017. "Terminology work in the European Commission: Ensuring high-quality translation in a multilingual environment." In *Quality aspects in institutional translation*, edited by Tomáš Svoboda, Łucja Biel, and Krzysztof Łoboda, 109–121. Berlin: Language Science Press.

Stone, Jon R. 2005. *The Routledge Dictionary of Latin Quotations: The Illiterati's Guide to Latin Maxims, Mottoes, Proverbs, and Sayings.* New York: Routledge.

Strębska-Liszewska, Katarzyna. 2017. "Epistemic modality in the rulings of the American Supreme Court and Polish Sąd Najwyższy: A corpus-based analysis of judicial discourse." PhD thesis. University of Silesia.

Stubbs, Michael. 1993. "British Traditions in Text Analysis: From Firth to Sinclair." In *Text and Technology: In honour of John Sinclair*, edited by Mona Baker, Gill Francis, and Elena Tognini-Bonelli, 1–36. Amsterdam: John Benjamins Publishing Company.

Stubbs, Michael. 1996. *Text and Corpus Analysis: Computer–assisted Studies of Language and Culture.* Oxford: Blackwell.

Stubbs, Michael. 2004. "Language Corpora." In *Handbook of Applied Linguistics*, edited by Alan Davies and Catherine Elder, 106–132. Oxford: Blackwell.

Swales, John M. 1981. *Aspects of Article Introductions.* Language Studies Unit: Aston University in Birmingham.

Swales, John M. 1990. *Genre Analysis. English in Academic and Research Settings.* Cambridge: Cambridge University Press.

Swales, John M. 2004. *Research Genres: Explorations and Applications.* Cambridge: Cambridge University Press.

Szczyrbak, Magdalena. 2014. *The Realization of Concession in the Discourse of Judges – A Genre Perspective.* Kraków: Jagiellonian University Press.

Taylor, Charlotte. 2008. "What is corpus linguistics? What the data says." *ICAME Journal* 32: 179–200.

Taylor, Charlotte and Anna Marchi (eds.). 2018. *Corpus Approaches to Discourse: A Critical Review.* London: Routledge.

Temmerman, Rita. 2018. "European Union multilingual primary term creation and the impact of its neologisms on national adaptations." *Parallèles* 30(1): 8–20.

Thelen, Marcel. 2002. "Relations Between Terms: A Cognitive Approach. The Interaction between Terminology, Lexicology, Translation Studies and Translation Practice." *Linguistica Antverpiensia* 1: 193–209.

Thompson, Geoff and Susan Hunston. 2006. *System and Corpus: Exploring Connections.* London: Equinox.

Tiersma, Peter M. 1999. *Legal Language.* Chicago and London: University of Chicago Press.

Tirkkonen-Condit, Sonja. 2002. "Translationese – A myth or an empirical fact? A study into the linguistic identifiability of translated language." *Target* 14(2): 207–220.

Tirkkonen-Condit, Sonja. 2004. "Unique items - Over- or under-represented in translated language?" In *Translation Universals: Do they exist?*, edited by Anna Mauranen and Pekka Kujamäki, 177–184. Amsterdam: John Benjamins Publishing Company.

Tognini-Bonelli, Elena. 2001. *Corpus Linguistics at Work.* Amsterdam: John Benjamins Publishing Company.

Tománková, Veronika. 2016. "Lexical bundles in legal texts corpora – Selection, classification and pedagogical implications." *Discourse and Interaction* 9(2): 75–94.

Toury, Gideon. 1995. *Descriptive Translation Studies and Beyond.* Amsterdam: John Benjamins Publishing Company.

Tridimas, Takis. 2015. "The ECJ and the National Courts: Dialogue, Cooperation, and Instability." In *The Oxford Handbook of European Union Law*, edited by Anthony Arnull and Damian Chalmers, 403–430. Oxford: Oxford University Press.

Trklja, Aleksandar and Karen McAuliffe. 2019. "Formulaic metadiscursive signalling devices in judgments of the Court of Justice of the European Union: A new corpus-based model for studying discourse relations of texts." *International Journal of Speech Language and the Law* 26(1): 21–55.

Trosborg, Anna. 1997. *Rhetorical Strategies in Legal Language: Discourse Analysis of Statutes and Contracts.* Tübingen: Stollfuß Medien.

Tullo, Catriona and James Hurford. 2003. "Modelling Zipfian distributions in language." In *Proceedings of language evolution and computation workshop/course at ESSLLI*, edited by Simon Kirby, 62–75. Vienna.

Tymoczko, Maria. 1998. "Computerized Corpora and the Future of Translation Studies." *Meta: Translators' Journal* 43(4): 652–660.

Van Dijk, Teun A. 2008. *Discourse and Power.* New York: Palgrave Macmillan.

Van Leeuwen, Theo. 2007. "Legitimation in Discourse and Communication." *Discourse and Communication* 1(1): 191–112.

Vannier, Guillaume. 2001. *Argumentation et Droit. Introduction à la Nouvelle Rhétorique de Perelman.* Paris: PUF.

Vázquez-Orta, Ignacio. 2010. "A Genre-Based View of Judgments of Appellate Courts in the Common Law System: Intersubjective Positioning, Intertextuality and Interdiscursivity in the Reasoning of Judges." In *Legal Discourse across Languages and Cultures,* edited by Maurizio Gotti and Christopher John Williams, 263–284. Bern: Peter Lang.

Visconti, Jacqueline. 2009. "Speech Acts in Legal Language: Introduction." *Journal of pragmatics* 3(41): 393–400.

Wasilewska, Katarzyna. 2018. "Frekwencja oraz funkcje przyimków złożonych i wtórnych w sprawozdaniach administracyjnych." *LingVaria* 25: 273–291.

Wodak, Ruth. 2003. "Populist Discourses. The Rhetoric of Exclusion in Written Genres." *Document Design* 4(2): 132–148.

Wolański, Adam. 2008. *Edycja tekstów. Praktyczny poradnik.* Warszawa: Wydawnictwo Naukowe PWN.

Wołodkiewicz, Witold. 2001a. "Lex retro non agit." In *Łacińskie paremie w europejskiej kulturze prawnej i orzecznictwie sądów polskich,* edited by Witold Wołodkiewicz and Jerzy Krzynówek, 153–192. Warszawa: Liber.

Wołodkiewicz, Witold. 2001b. "Łacińskie paremie prawne w orzecznictwie sądów polskich." In *Łacińskie paremie w europejskiej kulturze prawnej i orzecznictwie sądów polskich,* edited by Witold Wołodkiewicz and Jerzy Krzynówek, 7–30. Warszawa: Liber.

Wołodkiewicz, Witold and Jerzy Krzynówek (eds.). 2001. *Łacińskie paremie w europejskiej kulturze prawnej i orzecznictwie sądów polskich.* Warszawa: Liber.

Wołodkiewicz, Witold and Maria Zabłocka. 2014. *Prawo rzymskie. Instytucje.* Warszawa: C.H.Beck.

Wray, Alison. 2005. *Formulaic language and the lexicon.* Cambridge: Cambridge University Press.

Wray, Alison. 2009. "Identifying formulaic language: Persistent challenges and new opportunities." In *Formulaic Language: Distribution and Historical Change,* edited by Roberta Corrigan, Edith A. Moravcsik, Hamid Ouali, and Kathleen M. Wheatley, 27–52. Amsterdam and Philadelphia: John Benjamins Publishing Company.

Wray, Alison and Michael Perkins. 2000. "The functions of formulaic language: An integrated model." *Language & Communication* 20(1): 1–28.

Wright, Susan. 2016. "The Language of the Law in Multilingual contexts—Unpicking the English of the EU Courts' Judgments." *Statute Law Review* 37(2): 156–163.

Wright, Susan. 2018. "The Impact of Multilingualism on the Judgments of the EU Court of Justice," In *Institutional Translation for International Governance. Enhancing Quality in Multilingual Legal Communication*, edited by Fernando Prieto Ramos, 141–155, London: Bloomsbury.

Wróblewski, Bronisław. 1948. *Język prawny i prawniczy*. Kraków: Polska Akademia Umiejętności.

Wüster, Eugen. 1974. "Die allgemeine Terminologielehre — ein Grenzgebiet zwischen Sprachwissenschaft, Logik, Ontologie, Informatik und den Sachwissenschaften." *Linguistics* 119: 61–106.

Wüster, Eugen. 1979. *Einführung in die allgemeine Terminologielehre und terminologische Lexikographie*. Vienna: Springer.

Wynne, Martin (ed.). 2005. *Developing Linguistic Corpora: A Guide to Good Practice*. Oxford: Oxbow Books.

Yule, George. 1996. *Pragmatics*. Oxford: Oxford University Press.

Zajadło, Jerzy (ed.). 2020. *Łacińska terminologia prawnicza*. Warszawa: Wolters Kluwer.

Zanettin, Federico. 1998. "Bilingual Comparable Corpora and the Training of Translators." *Meta: Translators' Journal* 43(4): 616–630.

Zanettin, Federico. 2011. "Translation and corpus design." *SYNAPS – A Journal of Professional Communication* 26: 14–23.

Zanettin, Federico. 2012. *Translation-Driven Corpora. Corpus Resources for Descriptive and Applied Translation Studies*. Manchester: St. Jerome.

Zawidzka-Łojek, Anna and Adam Łazowski. 2018. *Podręcznik prawa Unii Europejskiej: instytucje i porządek prawny, prawo materialne*. Warszawa: Instytut Wydawniczy EuroPrawo.

Zieliński, Maciej. 1999. "Języki prawne i prawnicze." *Polszczyzna 2000. Orędzie o stanie języka na przełomie tysiącleci*, edited by Walery Pisarek, 50–74. Kraków: Uniwersytet Jagielloński. Ośrodek Badań Prasoznawczych.

Ziembiński, Zygmunt. 1960. "Przepis prawny a norma prawna." *Ruch Prawniczy, Ekonomiczny i Socjologiczny* 1: 105–122.

Ziembiński, Zygmunt. 1974. "Le langage du droit et le langage juridique. Les criteres de leur discernement." *Archives de philosophie du droit* 19: 25–31.

**Internet resources**

ANNEX – Specific features of the translation service of the Court of Justice and contributions to inter-institutional cooperation http://www.europarl.europa.eu/meetdocs/2009_2014/documents/budg/dv/2010_coj_02_annexe_/2010_coj_02_annexe_en.pdf (February 16, 2020).

Annual Report 2018 – The Year in Review https://curia.europa.eu/jcms/upload/docs/application/pdf/2019–05/rapport_gestion_2018_en.pdf (March 5, 2020).

AntPConc. https://www.laurenceanthony.net/software/antpconc/ (February 19, 2020).

CBOS. 2018. O nieufności i zaufaniu – Komunikat z badań 35 https://www.cbos.pl/SPISKOM.POL/2018/K_035_18.PDF (December 31, 2019).

CJEU – General Presentation http://curia.europa.eu/jcms/jcms/Jo2_6999/en/ (February 16, 2020).

CJEU – Language arrangements at the Court of Justice of the European Union. https://curia.europa.eu/jcms/jcms/Jo2_10739/regime-linguistique-de-la-cour-de-justice-du-tribunal-de-premiere-instance-et-du-tribunal-de-la-fonction-publique (February 16, 2020).

Commission Regulation (EU) No 1407/2013 of 18 December 2013 on the application of Articles 107 and 108 of the Treaty on the Functioning of the European Union to de minimis aid https://eur-lex.europa.eu/legal-content/EN/TXT/?uri=CELEX%3A32013R1407 (March 8, 2020).

Consolidated Version of the Statute of the Court of Justice of the European Union https://curia.europa.eu/jcms/upload/docs/application/pdf/2016–08/tra-doc-en-div-c-0000–2016–201606984–05_00.pdf (December 31, 2019).

Departament Języka Polskiego, Dyrekcja Generalna ds. Tłumaczeń Pisemnych, Komisja Europejska [DGT] 2019. VADEMECUM TŁUMACZA – Wskazówki redakcyjne dla tłumaczy https://ec.europa.eu/info/sites/info/files/styleguide_polish_dgt_pl_0.pdf (March 8, 2020).

Directorate-General for Translation [DGT], European Commission. 2012. Quantifying Quality Costs and the Cost of Poor Quality in Translation Quality Efforts and the Consequences of Poor Quality in the European Commission's Directorate-General for Translation. Luxembourg: Publications Office of the European Union. https://op.europa.eu/en/publication-detail/-/publication/d7c7f89c-3235–4b54–bab9–810802ef4b1b (March 24, 2020).

Directorate-General for Communication [DGC] 2016. Major changes in European public opinion regarding the European Union. Exploratory study https://www.europarl.europa.eu/at-your-service/files/be-heard/eurobarometer/2016/major-changes-in-european-public-opinion-2016/report/en-report-exploratory-study-201611.pdf (December 31, 2019).

Directorate-General for Translation [DGT], European Commission. 2020. *English Style Guide – A handbook for authors and translators in the European Commission* https://ec.europa.eu/info/sites/info/files/styleguide_english_dgt_en.pdf (March 8, 2020).

Directorate-General for Multilingualism https://curia.europa.eu/jcms/jcms/Jo2_10742/ (February 16, 2020).

Directorates for Legal Translation https://curia.europa.eu/jcms/jcms/Jo2_10744/ (February 16, 2020).

Division of competences within the European Union https://eur-lex.europa.eu/legal-content/EN/TXT/?uri=LEGISSUM%3Aai0020 (December 31, 2019).

Effect size metric (%DIFF) http://ucrel.lancs.ac.uk/ll/DIFF_FAQ.pdf (January 26, 2020)

EU languages https://europa.eu/european-union/about-eu/eu-languages_en (February 16, 2020).

EUR-Lex – Case-law from the CJEU https://eur-lex.europa.eu/collection/eu-law/eu-case-law.html (December 31, 2019).

European Union. 2015. Joint Practical Guide of the European Parliament, the Council and the Commission for persons involved in the drafting of European Union legislation https://eur-lex.europa.eu/content/techleg/KB0213228ENN.pdf (August 12, 2018).

How to become a lawyer-linguist at the Court of Justice? https://curia.europa.eu/jcms/jcms/Jo2_10740/recrutement-comment-devenir-juriste-linguiste-a-la-cour-de-justice (February 16, 2020).

IATE – European Union Terminology https://iate.europa.eu/home (March 8, 2020)

InfoCuria – Case-law http://curia.europa.eu/juris/recherche.jsf?language=en (February 20, 2020).

INFOR – List of Latin maxims https://www.infor.pl/prawo/paremie-lacinskie/ (April 9, 2019).

Judgment of the Court of 6 October 1982. Srl CILFIT and Lanificio di Gavardo SpA v Ministry of Health. Reference for a preliminary ruling: Corte suprema di Cassazione – Italy. Obligation to request a preliminary ruling. Case 283/81 http://curia.europa.eu/juris/showPdf.jsf?text=&docid=91672&pageIndex=0&doclang=EN&mode=lst&dir=&occ=first&part=1&cid=7715925 (March 24, 2020).

Konstytucja Rzeczypospolitej Polskiej z dnia 2 kwietnia 1997 r. (Dz.U. 1997 Nr 78, poz. 483) https://www.sejm.gov.pl/prawo/konst/angielski/kon1.htm (December 31, 2019).

LF Aligner https://sourceforge.net/projects/aligner/ (February 19, 2020).

List of Latin maxims and expressions at the website of the Regional Prosecutor's Office in Zielona Góra http://www.zielona-gora.po.gov.pl/index.php?id=180 (April 9, 2019).

Literary Exploration Machine (LEM) https://ws.clarin-pl.eu/lem.shtml (February 19, 2020).

Log-likelihood and effect size calculator http://ucrel.lancs.ac.uk/llwizard.htm (May 15, 2020).

Migration of CuriaTerm into IATE https://cdt.europa.eu/en/news/migration-curiaterm-iate (March 26, 2020).

Obwieszczenie Prezesa Rady Ministrów z dnia 29 lutego 2016 r. w sprawie ogłoszenia jednolitego tekstu rozporządzenia Prezesa Rady Ministrów w sprawie "Zasad techniki prawodawczej" (Dz.U. Nr 100, poz. 908) http://prawo.sejm.gov.pl/isap.nsf/download.xsp/WDU20160000283/O/D20160283.pdf (March 24, 2020).

On-line database of the Polish Supreme Court. http://www.sn.pl/orzecznictwo/SitePages/Baza_orzeczen.aspx (December 31, 2019).

PELCRA search engine http://www.nkjp.uni.lodz.pl (April 26, 2020).

Polish Language Department. Directorate-General for Translation (DGT), European Commission. DGT 2016. Vademecum Tłumacza. Wskazówki redakcyjne dla tłumaczy https://ec.europa.eu/translation/polish/guidelines/documents/styleguide_polish_dgt_pl.pdf (March 14, 2020).

Projects and Terminological Coordination Unit. CJEU https://curia.europa.eu/jcms/jcms/p1_641406/en (March 24, 2020).

Rules of Procedure of the General Court https://eur-lex.europa.eu/legal-content/EN/TXT/?uri=CELEX%3A32015Q0423%2801%29 (February 16, 2020).

Sketchengine https://www.sketchengine.eu (February 19, 2020).

Sources of European Union law http://eur-lex.europa.eu/legal-content/EN/TXT/?uri=URISERV%3Al14534 (December 31, 2019).

The Court in figures https://curia.europa.eu/jcms/jcms/P_80908/en/ (February 16, 2020).

Toudic, Daniel and Alexandra Krause. 2017. European Master's in Translation: Competence Framework 2017 https://ec.europa.eu/info/sites/info/files/emt_competence_fwk_2017_en_web.pdf (May 2, 2020).

Treaty on the Functioning of the European Union https://eur-lex.europa.eu/legal-content/EN/TXT/?uri=celex%3A12012E%2FTXT (December 31, 2019).

UCREL Semantic Analysis System http://ucrel.lancs.ac.uk/usas (March 29, 2020).

Ustawa z dnia 17 listopada 1964 r. – Kodeks postępowania cywilnego (Dz.U. 1964 Nr 43, poz. 296) http://prawo.sejm.gov.pl/isap.nsf/download.xsp/WDU19640430296/U/D19640296Lj.pdf (December 31, 2019).

Ustawa z dnia 8 grudnia 2017 r. o Sądzie Najwyższym (Dz.U. 2018 poz. 5) http://prawo.sejm.gov.pl/isap.nsf/download.xsp/WDU20180000005/T/D20180005L.pdf (December 31, 2019).

Wolter Kluwer's LEX database https://borg.wolterskluwer.pl (August 18, 2020).

Wordsmith Tools https://www.lexically.net/wordsmith/downloads/ (February 19, 2020).

Working as an English-language lawyer linguist at the Court of Justice of the European Union https://curia.europa.eu/jcms/upload/docs/application/pdf/2009–03/brochure_en.pdf (March 29, 2020).

TermoPL 3.1.2 user manual – Institute of Computer Science Polish Academy of Sciences http://zil.ipipan.waw.pl/TermoPL?action=AttachFile&do=view&target=TermoPL-user-manual.pdf (March 24, 2020).

TermoPL http://ws.clarin-pl.eu/termopl.shtml# (February 19, 2020).

**Dictionaries**

Collin, Peter Hodgson. 2004. *Dictionary of Law*. London: Bloomsbury Publishing.

Curzon, Leslie B. and Paul Richards. 2007[1979]. *The Longman Dictionary of Law* (7th ed.). London: Pearson Education.

Doroszewski, Witold (ed.). 1958–1969. *Słownik języka polskiego* [SJPD]. Warszawa: Wiedza Powszechna.

Ellis Wild, Susan. 2006. *Webster's New World Law Dictionary*. Hoboken: Wiley Publishing.

Emanuel, Lazar. 1999. *Latin for Lawyers: The Language of the Law*. Boston: Emanuel Publishing Corporation.

Garner, Bryan A., Jeff Newman, and Tiger Jackson. 2009. *Black's Law Dictionary* (9th ed.). St. Paul: West Publishing Company.

Hill, Gerard N. and Kathleen Hill. 2009. *Nolo's Plain-English Law Dictionary*. Berkeley: Nolo.

Jowitt, William Allen, Clifford Walsh, and John M. Burke. 2010[1977]. *Jowitt's Dictionary of English Law*. London: Sweet & Maxwell.

Kamiński, Janusz, Władysław Rozwadowski, and Witold Wołodkiewicz. 1986. *Prawo rzymskie: słownik encyklopedyczny*. Warszawa: Wiedza Powszechna.

Kuryłowicz, Marek. 2012. *Słownik terminów, zwrotów i sentencji prawniczych łacińskich oraz pochodzenia łacińskiego*. Warszawa: LEX.

Markowski, Andrzej (ed.). 1999. *Nowy słownik poprawnej polszczyzny PWN*. Wydawnictwo Naukowe PWN.

Martin, Elizabeth A. (ed.). 2003[1983]. *Oxford Dictionary of Law*. Oxford: Oxford University Press.

Milewska, Beata. 2003b. *Słownik polskich przyimków wtórnych*. Gdańsk: Wydawnictwo Uniwersytetu Gdańskiego.

Żmigrodzki, Piotr. 2007. *Wielki słownik języka polskiego PAN* [WSJP] http://www.wsjp.pl (May 10, 2020).

# Index


**A**

authentic version 39, 68

**B**

balance 28, 43, 77, 86–88, 364

**binomials** 27, 73, 90, 205, 208, 249, 363–418, 433, 499, 561–565, 577–579, 586, 599, 600, 603, 605
- extended binomials 364, 366, 372, 389–393, 396, 398, 402, 407, 408, 411, 417, 418, 561–564, 577, 579
- functional typology of binomials 411
- non-extended binomials 366, 372–376, 381, 382, 385, 388, 389, 390, 392, 396, 407, 408, 411, 417, 418, 561–564, 577, 578
- multinomials 73, 367–370, 372, 381, 389, 408–411, 417, 418

**C**

comparability 28, 77, 86, 88, 90, 93, 209, 275, 284, 292, 368

**concept** 421–423, 425, 427, 428, 430, 431, 457, 458, 461, 463, 465, 477, 484, 488, 532, 584
- common conceptual base 29, 421, 429, 432, 433, 435, 437, 445, 491, 565
- conceptual systems 421, 426, 428–430, 440, 493
- generic concepts 428
- legal concepts 40, 421, 422, 424–428, 431, 441, 448, 512, 532, 538, 539, 541, 542, 585
- EU concepts 429–430, 491, 594
- national concepts 427–430, 435, 491, 492

convergence 69, 71, 137, 283, 284, 292, 296, 302–307, 309, 359, 388, 427, 458, 461, 490, 549, 554, 563, 656, 583

**corpus** 27–610
- corpus design 77–79, 87, 369, 433, 587, 589, 613
- Corpus Linguistics 28, 61–63, 66, 277, 278, 282, 356, 432, 585–588, 591, 596–602, 604, 605, 611
- corpus methodology 28, 57, 64, 581
- corpus-based approach 278, 426, 432, 588, 597
- corpus-based data-driven (discovery) learning 583
- corpus-driven approach 28, 62, 63, 67, 278, 587
- monolingual comparable corpus 27, 67, 78, 79
- reference corpus 71, 72, 78, 79, 83, 86, 141, 145, 283, 286, 368, 369, 433, 498

**Court of Justice of the European Union (CJEU)** 27, 28, 33–45, 47, 48, 51–53, 55, 56, 59, 61, 67–70, 72, 73, 77–80, 82–84, 86–89, 93–100, 103, 106, 107, 109, 110, 122, 125, 127, 132, 134, 146, 147, 150,154, 156, 202, 205, 208, 209, 212, 213, 216, 218, 219, 221, 229, 230, 235, 236, 238, 241, 243, 249, 250, 254, 255, 258, 260, 261, 264, 269, 284, 287, 352, 357, 359, 363, 365–368, 372, 374–376, 381, 384, 388, 417, 418, 421–424, 427–429, 432, 433, 452, 453, 461, 471, 480, 483, 490, 496–500, 511, 516, 528, 538–541, 543, 544, 549, 553, 554, 560, 562,

563, 566, 570, 571, 575, 576, 577, 581, 584, 585, 590, 564, 600, 601, 604, 611, 614–616
- Court French 39
- Court of Justice (CJ) 27, 35, 37, 39, 42, 47, 71, 72, 77–83, 87, 94, 95, 97, 100, 103–108, 110, 112–115, 119, 120, 123–127, 129, 138–142, 145–148, 151, 154–156, 158, 164, 165, 167, 168, 171, 172, 174–176, 178, 181–206, 208–210, 212–214, 216–218, 220–229, 231, 232, 234–244, 246, 248, 250–252, 254–256, 258–266, 268, 269, 285, 286, 288, 290, 292–295, 297, 299, 301–305, 307, 308, 313–317, 320–351, 353–358, 360, 367, 369, 370, 373, 374, 376–378, 381, 382, 388, 390–392, 394–396, 398, 407–410, 412–414, 416, 417, 433–438, 441, 442, 445, 446, 450–459, 461–467, 469–472, 474, 476–478, 480–485, 487–490, 498–502, 504, 509–514, 516–537, 541, 543–549, 554, 556, 559, 560, 562, 563, 565–568, 570, 572
- General Court (GC) 27, 35, 37, 39, 42, 47, 71, 72, 77–83, 87, 94, 95, 97, 100, 103–108, 110, 112–115, 119, 120, 123–127, 129, 138–142, 145–148, 151, 154–156, 158, 164, 165, 167, 168, 171, 172, 174–176, 178, 181–206, 208–210, 212–214, 216–218, 220–229, 231, 232, 234–244, 246, 248, 250–252, 254–256, 258–266, 268, 269, 285, 286, 288, 290, 292–295, 297, 299, 301–305, 307, 308, 313–317, 320–351, 353–358, 360, 367, 369, 370, 373, 374, 376–378, 381, 382, 388, 390–392, 394–396, 398, 407–410, 412–414, 416, 417, 433–438, 441, 442, 445, 446, 450–459, 461–467, 469–472, 474, 476–478, 480–485, 487–490, 498–502, 504, 509–514, 516–537, 541, 543–549, 554, 556, 559, 560, 562, 563, 565–568, 570, 572

**D**

Deixis 73, 146, 149, 180, 212, 337, 546, 550–556, 558, 574, 575
**Discourse** 27–29, 47–53, 58, 59, 61, 63, 65–67, 70, 72, 78, 87, 93–99, 103–107, 148–150, 164–165, 170, 187, 202, 203, 229, 250, 273, 274, 276–279, 281–284, 296, 298, 310–316, 324, 326, 330, 332, 333, 337, 339, 345, 352, 359, 365, 367, 372, 411, 412, 416–418, 421, 429, 431, 496, 497, 511, 513, 516, 538, 539, 542, 587, 588, 594–597, 600–604, 606, 607, 609–612
- discourse community 48–53, 67, 107, 421, 496, 542, 603
**divergence** 69, 71, 137, 209, 437, 543, 544, 549–550, 552–554, 556, 559, 560, 562, 563, 565, 566, 568, 570, 571, 583
- scale for the assessment of the degree of divergence 549
**depersonalization** 149, 218, 219, 224, 261, 547, 550–552, 554–556, 558, 574, 575
- auxiliary verbs 147, 149, 218–220, 222, 547, 551, 554, 558, 574
- *-no/to* impersonal pattern 149, 226, 227, 547, 551, 555, 558, 575, 576
- passive voice 73,, 147, 149, 219, 221, 222, 547, 552, 554, 558, 574, 575
- *się* impersonal pattern 149, 219, 224, 550, 554, 558, 574
drafting 37, 38, 42, 45, 107, 130, 430, 495, 496, 524, 554, 570, 577, 594, 615

**E**

enlargement of the EU 40, 604
epistemic modality 235, 254, 255, 357, 592, 600, 610

– certainty-uncertainty continuum 255
Eurolect 25, 27, 28, 56, 61, 67, 70, 71, 78, 79, 84, 87, 88, 90, 100, 137, 138, 141, 174, 187, 191, 194, 202, 205, 208, 212, 221, 223–224, 234, 235, 238, 240, 243, 250, 254, 255, 258, 261, 264, 283, 285–287, 292, 296, 300, 302, 303, 307–309, 313, 320, 324, 326, 332, 337, 339, 341, 343, 345, 348, 350, 359, 369, 374, 388, 390, 418, 433–435, 437, 438, 440, 451, 461, 462, 470, 480, 481, 487, 498, 510, 512, 513, 517, 541, 543, 549, 550, 554, 556, 562, 563, 568, 570, 572, 589
Europeanization 71, 78, 84, 87, 440, 445, 492, 498, 511, 541, 572
expectancy norms 27, 67, 69, 541, 582

F
formulaicity 27, 29, 70, 73, 271, 273, 276, 283–285, 287, 292, 296, 298, 313, 359, 360, 367, 388, 577, 579, 590
**framing with adverbials and participles** 149, 249, 547
– adverbials 73, 148, 149, 249–251, 254–256, 258–260, 547, 548, 550–553, 555, 556, 559, 575, 576
– participles 73, 148, 149, 249, 260–266, 268, 269, 547, 548, 553, 555, 559, 575

G
**genre** 27–29, 33, 38, 47–59, 61, 62, 64–68, 70–74, 77–80, 83, 86–89, 90, 93, 98–100, 105–107, 134, 137, 138, 141, 145, 146, 149, 154, 155, 164–166, 170, 209, 216, 219, 238, 241, 249, 250, 273–278, 281, 283–285, 287, 295, 309, 310, 313, 316, 326, 332, 337, 352, 359, 361, 363, 367, 368, 372, 375, 388, 411, 417, 418, 430, 432–435, 441, 445, 448, 449, 451, 458, 461, 488, 490–493, 496, 497, 512, 513, 516, 537, 541, 543, 549, 553, 554, 556, 559, 563, 571, 572, 576, 581, 583, 586–591, 594–597, 601, 603, 607, 609, 610, 612
– genre analysis 28, 29, 47, 49, 57, 58, 67, 93, 98, 411, 513, 587, 589, 591, 607, 610
– genre-register approach 28, 47, 56, 57, 99
– primary genre 56, 55, 70, 72, 137
– secondary genre 56, 66, 137
– sub-genre 27, 28, 33, 47, 48, 55, 56, 68, 70–72, 77–80, 83, 88, 89, 93, 99, 100, 105, 107, 134, 137, 146, 216, 241, 295, 309, 363, 432, 449, 549, 554, 556, 563, 571, 583, 588

H
hypotaxis 73, 149, 209, 546, 551–556, 558, 574

I
interdiscursivity 49, 65, 98, 612
interference 45, 283, 571, 581–583
**intertextual relations** 68
– (textual) fit 27–29, 45, 49, 52, 61, 64, 66–71, 73, 74, 77, 78, 87, 93, 99, 137, 269, 277, 295, 300, 357, 360, 433, 493, 543, 549, 553, 581–584, 588
– concordance (equivalence) 67, 68, 87, 150, 154, 165, 184, 191, 198, 205, 241, 255, 261, 276, 310, 312, 360, 361, 368, 407, 418, 425, 499, 538, 582, 610
– continuity 45, 68, 69, 425
intertextuality 49, 98, 612

K

**keywords** 141, 145–148, 154, 209, 212, 213, 224, 234, 235, 246, 249, 250, 260–263, 596
- keywords overrepresented in translations 146–148
- keywords underrepresented in translations 147, 148

L

**language** 27–617
- judicial language 28, 29, 64, 65, 71, 77, 80, 86, 137, 149, 154, 164, 187, 191, 194, 198, 205, 208, 209, 212, 213, 216, 218, 219, 224, 226, 229, 230, 238, 240, 241, 243, 246, 249, 250, 254, 255, 258, 260, 261, 269, 287, 310, 313, 326, 357, 363, 374, 407, 411, 417, 425, 457, 465, 470, 477, 481, 492, 495, 504, 543, 550, 571, 572, 581–583
- language division 38–44
- language of the case 36–40, 45, 68, 80, 108, 487
- language of the law 48, 53–55, 516, 542, 587, 597, 601, 602, 605, 613, 617
- legal language 27, 28, 47, 48, 53–55, 66, 72, 73, 77, 88, 90, 145, 230, 277, 278, 282, 283, 328, 363, 366, 421, 424, 425, 427, 451, 492, 498, 511, 571, 588, 589, 594–597, 599, 601, 603, 608, 609, 611, 612
- microdiachronic language change 71, 571–573, 576–580
- official language 34, 36, 38–43, 45, 128, 430
- pivot language 38, 40, 41, 44
- pivot translation system 40, 41, 43–45
- working language 34, 36, 38–40, 585

Latinisms 28, 29, 73, 74, 426, 495–500, 502, 504, 505, 510–516, 520, 524, 538–542, 565, 567–569, 579–581

**law** 27–617
- supranational law 53, 607
- national law 27, 35, 42, 53, 67, 96, 104, 105, 112, 113, 115, 119, 120, 123, 282, 283, 296, 360, 427, 430, 447, 465, 471–473, 476, 491, 523, 570, 589, 594, 606, 607

lawyer-linguists 33, 38–45, 67, 95, 126, 205, 208, 238, 243, 254, 258, 260, 360, 374, 375, 389, 408, 418, 421, 422, 540–542, 583, 604, 609

**legal reasoning and argumentation** 146, 149, 229, 339, 350, 527, 547, 550, 551, 553, 555, 556, 558, 559, 575
- causal patterns 73, 149, 236, 246, 547, 550, 555, 559, 575, 576
- exercitive verbs 234, 236
- if-then conditionals and related patterns 149, 240, 242, 547, 551, 556, 559, 575
- patterns of purpose 73, 149, 246–248, 547, 553, 555, 559, 575
- reporting verbs 121, 131, 132, 147, 149, 224, 229–232, 234–236, 547, 550, 551, 553, 555, 558, 575
- verdictive verbs 127, 231, 234, 547, 551, 556, 558

legislative acts 66, 68–70, 72, 98, 155, 209, 249, 277, 284, 285, 316, 364, 365, 367, 424, 429, 480, 493, 495, 535, 577

**lexical bundles** 27, 29, 72, 73, 90, 249, 273–287, 292, 295, 296, 300, 309–314, 316, 320, 326, 330, 339, 352, 353, 355, 357, 359, 360, 367, 368, 388, 411, 418, 434, 449, 500, 560, 562–564, 577, 578, 582, 587–591, 593, 596, 598, 599, 601, 604, 605, 611

- bundles 27, 29, 72, 73, 90, 249, 273–287, 292, 295, 296, 300, 309–317, 320, 322, 324, 326, 328, 330, 332, 339, 352, 353, 355, 357, 359, 360, 367, 368, 388, 411, 418, 434, 449, 500, 560, 562–564, 577, 578, 582, 587–591, 593, 596, 598, 599, 601, 604, 605, 611
- discourse functions of lexical 29, 281, 310, 311
- n-grams 73, 273, 285, 292, 295, 296, 300, 302, 303, 306, 310, 320, 357, 359, 435, 562
- referential bundles 279, 281, 282, 310–317, 320, 322, 324, 328, 330, 359
- stance bundles 273, 276, 279–282, 310, 311, 313–316, 328, 352, 355, 357, 359, 596
- text-oriented bundles 276, 279, 280, 324, 330, 332

lexico-grammatical patterns 29, 69, 70, 89

N

naturalness 27, 28, 68, 69, 71, 99, 295, 360, 550–552, 583

normalization 28, 72, 77, 78, 89, 90, 138, 283, 284, 328, 360, 368, 445, 493, 562, 582

P

parataxis 73, 149, 205, 545, 550, 552–556, 558, 574

**phraseology** 273, 274, 277–279, 357, 583, 585, 586, 588, 589, 596, 597, 599, 604
- frequency-based (distributional) approach to phraseology 273, 274

**prepositions** 57, 73, 90, 140, 147–151, 153–203, 236, 246, 258, 434, 544, 550–557, 559, 573, 575, 576, 589, 600
- compound and secondary prepositions 73, 149, 150, 154–156, 164–167, 170, 171, 174, 175, 180, 181, 183, 185–199, 202, 203, 258, 544, 550–557, 559, 573, 576
- discourse functions of prepositions 148–150, 164–166, 187, 202, 203
- simple prepositions 148–151, 154, 155, 164, 202, 544, 550, 553, 554, 557, 573

policy of multilingualism 27, 33–35, 37, 41, 44, 53, 67

R

recurrence 65, 275, 285, 418

refinement 295–297, 299–309, 312, 313, 332, 434–437, 490, 565, 566, 579, 580

register 28, 47, 48, 50, 52, 56, 57, 59, 61, 72, 77, 78, 99, 100, 124, 137, 274, 275, 277, 279, 285, 326, 524, 581, 587, 588, 596, 598, 601

representativeness 28, 65, 77, 86–88, 93, 587, 593, 601

request for a preliminary ruling 41, 101, 320, 326

S

semantic fields 364, 365, 432, 435, 441, 448–451, 492

**statistics** 80, 137–139, 423
- statistical significance 90, 145, 572, 582
- statistical measures 77, 80, 89, 90, 368
- structural analysis 56, 93
- macrostructure 99
- move analysis 57, 59, 72, 93, 103, 107, 127, 595

style 27, 36, 37, 39, 47, 48, 50, 56, 58, 219, 250, 367, 381, 392, 396, 417, 418, 496, 520, 583, 584, 588, 601, 605

Supreme Court of the Republic of Poland (SN) 27, 35, 37, 39, 42, 47, 71, 72, 77–83, 87, 94, 95, 97, 100, 103–108, 110, 112–115, 119, 120, 123–127, 129, 138–142, 145–148, 151, 154–156, 158, 164, 165, 167, 168, 171, 172, 174–176, 178, 181–206, 208–210, 212–214, 216–218, 220–229, 231, 232, 234–244, 246, 248, 250–252, 254–256, 258–266, 268, 269, 285, 286, 288, 290, 292–295, 297, 299, 301–305, 307, 308, 313–317, 320–351, 353–358, 360, 367, 369, 370, 373, 374, 376–378, 381, 382, 388, 390–392, 394–396, 398, 407–410, 412–414, 416, 417, 433–438, 441, 442, 445, 446, 450–459, 461–467, 469–472, 474, 476–478, 480–485, 487–490, 498–502, 504, 509–514, 516–537, 541, 543–549, 554, 556, 559, 560, 562, 563, 565–568, 570, 572–576, 578–583

**Synonymy** 364, 365, 375, 381, 388, 389, 407, 418, 428, 592
- near-synonymy 364, 365, 375, 381, 388, 389, 407, 418, 428, 592

T

**terminology** 28, 38, 39, 52, 55, 58, 61, 65, 69, 70, 73, 89, 98, 278, 322, 328, 421–493, 495, 516, 565, 566, 568–570, 580, 583, 585, 586, 588, 590–595, 598, 599, 605–608, 610, 611, 615

terminological database 38, 422–424
- terminology work 73, 422, 424, 426, 591, 598, 610

**terms** 28, 29, 73, 430 432–459, 461–467, 469–472, 476–478, 480–485, 487–493, 565–570, 579–581, 590
- complex terms 28, 29, 73, 432–449, 451–459, 461–467, 469–472, 476–478, 480–485, 487–493, 565, 566, 568, 569, 579, 580
- national terms 430, 492, 590
- node terms 434, 435, 441, 445, 449–452, 461, 463, 465, 471, 481, 483, 485, 488, 491–493, 565–570, 579–581
- simple terms 432–443, 445, 448, 449, 451, 490–492, 565, 566, 568, 569, 580
- supranational terms 430, 590

**textual fit** 27–29, 45, 49, 52, 61, 64, 66–71, 73, 74, 77, 78, 87, 93, 99, 137, 269, 277, 295, 300, 357, 360, 433, 493, 543, 549, 553, 581–584, 588
- convergent textual fit 71
- divergent textual fit 27, 71, 493, 543, 553, 583

**threshold** 64, 273, 275, 284–288, 290, 293, 296, 359, 361, 369, 499, 500, 582
- distribution threshold 273, 284, 286, 287, 359
- frequency of occurrence 57, 71, 137, 141, 150, 154, 185, 317, 326, 333, 353, 359, 369, 372, 388, 390, 450, 451, 513, 538
- frequency threshold 64, 273, 275, 285, 286–288, 290, 293, 296, 359, 361, 369, 499, 500, 582

**translation** 27–617
- Legal Translation Studies (LTS) 33, 39, 64–66, 592, 606
- translation process 28, 33, 37–39, 41, 42, 44, 46, 49, 61, 66, 67, 70, 146, 202, 273, 541, 554, 582, 583, 589
- translation product 66, 72, 583
- Translation Studies (TS) 27, 47, 48, 55, 61, 62, 77, 276, 586, 589,

592, 593, 595, 597, 601–603, 606, 609, 611, 612, 613
– translation universals 63, 69, 70, 73, 571, 592, 603, 611
translationese 72, 570, 571, 611
type-token ratio 78

**V**
vanishing sources 39
**variation** 69–71, 105, 191, 194, 212, 221, 234, 240, 250, 255, 261, 292, 313, 376, 435, 451, 543, 549, 550, 554, 563, 568, 581
– external variation 71, 549
– internal variation 71, 105, 191, 194, 212, 221, 234, 240, 250, 255, 261, 292, 313, 376, 435, 451, 543, 550, 554, 563, 568, 581
– intra-linguistic variation 72, 543

**W**
wordlist 72, 141, 145, 241

**Studies in Language, Culture and Society**

Edited by Łucja Biel, Andrzej Kątny and Piotr Ruszkiewicz

The editors of this series invite books addressing the nexus between language, culture and society. Contrastive studies are welcome in particular, whether of a synchronic or diachronic orientation. Various perspectives on language / communication are of interest: grammatical, pragmatic, sociolinguistic, discursive and semiotic. A wide range of theoretical and methodological positions is accepted: cognitive / anthropological / corpus linguistics, as well as pragmatics, interactional sociolinguistics, (specialized) genre analysis, and critical discourse studies.

The cutting edge of the series is to publish innovative research elucidating the processes of *inter-* and *intra*-language variation and change, and - at the same time - relating them to flows *in* and *across* cognate categories of culture, community and society.

The series publishes monographs and edited volumes reporting on data-driven research that carries a potential for application in translation studies, language teaching, multilingual (multicultural) education, and interdisciplinary critical discourse studies.

The languages of publication are English and German, yet book proposals in other major languages will also be considered, if centrally contributive to the main aim of the series.

Vol. 1 Ewa Kucelman: Self-based Anaphora in Early Modern English. 2013.

Vol. 2 Łucja Biel: Lost in the Eurofog: The Textual Fit of Translated Law. 2014.

Vol. 3 Marek Kuźniak / Agnieszka Libura / Michał Szawerna (eds.): From Conceptual Metaphor Theory to Cognitive Ethnolinguistics. Patterns of Imagery in Language. 2014.

Vol. 4 Grzegorz Kowalski: Claim-making and Claim-challenging in English and Polish Linguistic Discourses. 2015.

Vol. 5 Małgorzata Tryuk: On Ethics and Interpreters. 2015.

Vol. 6 Anna Duszak / Grzegorz Kowalski (eds.): Academic (Inter)genres: between Texts, Contexts and Identities. 2015.

Vol. 7 Alicja Witalisz: English Loan Translations in Polish. Word-formation Patterns, Lexicalization, Idiomaticity and Institutionalization. 2015.

Vol. 8 Agnieszka Kampka / Katarzyna Molek-Kozakowska (eds.): Rhetoric, Knowledge and the Public Sphere. 2016.

Vol. 9 Maria Załęska / Urszula Okulska (eds.): Rhetoric, Discourse and Knowledge. 2016.

Vol. 10 Łucja Biel: Lost in the Eurofog: The Textual Fit of Translated Law. Second Revised Edition. 2017.

Vol. 11 Karolina Broś / Grzegorz Kowalski (eds.): Discourse Studies - Ways and Crossroads. Insights into Cultural, Diachronic and Genre Issues in the Discipline. 2017.

Vol. 12 Iga Lehman: Authorial Presence in English Academic Texts. A Comparative Study of Student Writing across Cultures and Disciplines. 2018.

Vol. 13 Katarzyna Stachowiak: Phonology Matters in Interpreting. 2018.

Vol. 14 Agnieszka Biernacka: Interpreter-Mediated Interactions of the Courtroom. A Naturally Occurring Data Based Study. 2019.

Vol. 15 Małgorzata Gaszyńska-Magiera: Traces of the Foreign. Prose in Poland in 1945-2005 from the Perspective of Intercultural Communication. 2019.

Vol. 16 Dariusz Koźbiał: The Language of EU and Polish Judges: Investigating Textual Fit Through Corpus Methods. 2020.

www.peterlang.com

www.ingramcontent.com/pod-product-compliance
Ingram Content Group UK Ltd.
Pitfield, Milton Keynes, MK11 3LW, UK
UKHW041824100926
8556IPUK00002B/5

9 783631 822265